I0576188

Writings from the Sand, Volume 1

Writings from the Sand, Volume 1
Collected Works of Isabelle Eberhardt

Ecrits Sur Le Sable, Tome I

ISABELLE EBERHARDT

Edited and with an introduction by
Marie-Odile Delacour and Jean-René Huleu
Preface by Edmonde Charles-Roux
Translated by Melissa Marcus

University of Nebraska Press · Lincoln and London

English translation © 2012 by the Board of Regents of the
University of Nebraska. *Ecrits Sur Le Sable, Tome I*
by Isabelle Eberhardt © by Les Editions Grasset and
Fasquelle, 1988. All rights reserved. Manufactured in the
United States of America. ∞

Cet ouvrage publié dans le cadre du programme d'aide
à la publication bénéficie du soutien du Ministère des
Affaires Etrangères et du Service Culturel de l'Ambassade
de France représenté aux Etats-Unis. This work received
support from the French Ministry of Foreign Affairs and
the Cultural Service of the French Embassy in the United
States through their publishing assistance program.

Publication of this book was assisted
by a grant from the National Endowment
for the Arts.

NATIONAL
ENDOWMENT
FOR THE ARTS   "A Great Nation Deserves Great Art"

Library of Congress Cataloging-in-Publication Data

Eberhardt, Isabelle, 1877–1904.
[Ecrits sur le sable. English]
Writings from the sand : collected works of Isabelle Eber-
hardt / edited and with an introduction by Marie-Odile
Delacour and Jean-René Huleu ; preface by Edmonde
Charles-Roux ; translated by Melissa Marcus.
p. cm.   Includes bibliographical references.
ISBN 978-0-8032-1611-2 (v. 1 : pbk. : alk. paper)
I. Delacour, Marie-Odile. II. Huleu, Jean-René. III. Mar-
cus, Melissa. IV. Title.
PQ2237.E13A23 2012   848'.809—dc23   2011040430

Set in Arno Pro by Shirley Thornton.
Designed by A. Shahan.

Contents

vii *Contents*

Foreword

MARIE-ODILE DELACOUR AND JEAN-RENÉ HULEU

The text of this edition has been reestablished, for the most part, according to the manuscripts from the Isabelle Eberhardt collection. Where no manuscript is available, we have referred to publications made during the lifetime of the author.

A few words crossed out by Victor Barrucand have been rendered illegible; others are missing, notably in the previously unpublished editions of *Sud oranais* (*Oranese South*). When the text allows, we restore them between parentheses, otherwise we indicate them with ellipsis points in brackets. Where the mud from the deluge has altered the manuscript too much, we publish the fragments rewritten by Barrucand and put them in italics.

We have kept Isabelle Eberhardt's spelling of Arabic words, which she sometimes transcribes in different ways. The words in italics whose meanings are not given in the text itself are grouped together in a glossary at the end of the volume.

Notes by the author, and sometimes those of previous editors, can be found at the bottom of the page.[1]

In order to facilitate reading, it seemed useful to us to clarify in notes, periodically between texts, a few biographical or bibliographical landmarks, and then to add the main variations or complementary texts at the end.

The appendix contains "Choses du Sud oranais" ("Things from the Oranese South"), reports and newspaper articles published by *La Dépêche algérienne* in 1904.

---

1. Translator's note: Notes by Isabelle Eberhardt, by previous editors, or by the translator are indicated as such. Notes that are not preceded by any attribution are those added by the editors of this volume.

Preface

Eighty Years Later . . .

EDMONDE CHARLES-ROUX

Isabelle lived poorly without ever stopping her writing—her correspondence testifies to this—or her dreaming that she would one day be welcomed into the literary world. And yet she was refused literary notoriety. She succeeded only in having herself published in a few Parisian journals, often with small circulation and of mediocre quality. Published two years after her death, her work gave rise to as much violence in the reviews as excessive praise, as soon as it appeared, to say nothing of the debates . . . They raged for a quarter of a century. Very strangely, Isabelle Eberhardt's celebrity started when, for other writers already settled in a lifetime of success, oblivion began. And it is a purgatory whose duration no one can foresee.

As soon as Isabelle disappeared, a new life opened for her, the posthumous life of her writings which, in the image of their author, would never fail to move or to make people indignant. Needless to say, it is this power of provocation, which she possessed to the highest degree, that I appreciate most in her. This provocation is there beneath any phrase that seems harmless at first sight; it flows from word to word with the badly contained violence of dangerous water due to its untamed quality. Could Isabelle die other than from drowning, carried away in her house by the furor of a *oued* in flood? "Everything about her was extraordinary," wrote Lesley Blanch in the best portrait of Isabelle that has been written. And Blanch added, *"Her death was strangest of all, for she was drowned in the desert."*[1]

---

1. From Lesley Blanch, "Portrait of a Legend," in *The Wilder Shores of Love* (London: John Murray, 1954).

Thus Isabelle's writings appeared in 1906. They appeared corrected, reworked, truncated, censored, with titles each more cursed than the others, always imposed by her worshippers.

To reestablish the work in its true form, decipher the manuscripts, suppress the doubtful versions and the additions—beneath the black erasure marks, to find again the original phrase which Barrucand the proofreader, carried away by admiration, judged to be of the sort that would imperil the reputation of his protégée—this was the task at which Marie-Odile Delacour and Jean-René Huleu worked very hard and with great success. Above all, what appears in their work is all the passion they brought to it, which was necessary in order to succeed. All their integrity was also needed. What a contrast between the versions that we knew—Isabelle's short narratives deriving from the "thing seen," of her travel notes, of her travel diaries—and the new form of these given to us today! And what a jolt! Certain people are going to be quite shaken up. They believed that they knew the original work of a woman vagabond, a mystical adventuress, a *reporter* of Islam, to repeat what Morand said of Cendrars when he qualified him as "God's reporter." And yet, what these well-informed amateurs, what these enthusiasts admired about Isabelle Eberhardt was nothing but a pale adaptation. To finally read the truth . . . a surprise anticipated for fully eighty years . . . It was time to stop delaying.

As for those who are going to read Isabelle Eberhardt for the first time, those who are just discovering these *Ecrits sur le sable* (*Writings from the Sand*), how could they know that if this new edition had not been undertaken, Isabelle would still and always be for them an unknown person? For everything of hers that was published between 1906 and 1944 cannot be found, and few libraries possess the totality of her work. How much fruitless pilfering I have done and how many raids for nothing in faraway bookstores! This will no longer happen today.

We must also consider a point that seems of secondary importance, but it is not. For this we are also indebted to Marie-Odile Delacour and Jean-René Huleu. For they endeavored to publish Isabelle Eberhardt's works in their chronological order. This became indispensable in order to establish at the same time the relationship of Isabelle's writings with the powerful scenes of her life, and to be able to measure the difference between what, in her work, is a product of experience and what is born from an imaginary universe.

With the publication of *Writings from the Sand*, Eberhardtian erudition is going to be utterly renewed. We are certain that this new edition will be appreciated by researchers. In particular, I am thinking of the North African students with whom I shared many hours of studious friendship and brotherly cheerfulness in the vast room of the Archives de l'outre-mer (Archives of the Overseas Territories in Aix-en-Provence). Their always-awakened curiosity when Isabelle's name is pronounced is finally, in *Writings from the Sand*, going to find the authenticity for which they clamor. What time will not be wasted, what hesitations will they be spared! It is also from this perspective that we must reiterate the degree to which Marie-Odile Delacour and Jean-René Huleu have done such useful work.

Introduction

MARIE-ODILE DELACOUR AND JEAN-RENÉ HULEU

It seems to me that I am going to embark on a very long voyage
toward unknown regions and that I will not return from them . . .

GUSTAVE FLAUBERT, *Letter to Tourgueniev*

Woman, illegitimate child, daughter of an exiled woman, Isabelle Eberhardt nevertheless takes revenge on the curses that overwhelmed her.
One day in May 1897, pushed by an irrepressible force, she boards a boat
in Marseille and heads for the Algerian coast. At the age of twenty she
has already long turned her back on civil proprieties, but in search of
herself she will have to defy other limits.

This first departure marks the beginning of a wandering that only
death will interrupt seven years later. As much by challenge as by inclination, she transforms herself. In the clothing and name of an Arabic
traveler, Mahmoud Saadi, she seeks to exhaust her destiny. To live all, to
know all: places of ill repute and sanctuaries. She wanders from brothels
to mosques, from the dregs of society in colonial towns to nomad camps
of the Sahara. She will alternately be an adventuress, a vagabond, a dis-
ciple of a Muslim brotherhood, a marabout, a war reporter, an inspired
mystic . . .

On the road, Isabelle Eberhardt will write hundreds of pages of notes,
of narratives, of short stories and an unfinished novel, revealing herself as one of those rare writers whose life lives up to the demands of
her work. To describe, to express what is radically foreign to you—the
East,[1] specifically Islam—and to live it so as to finally extract its first

1. Translator's note: The terms in French for East and West are "Orient" and "Occident."
In the colonial context, "Orient" designated North Africa and the Middle East, in addition
to what we call the Orient today: Japan, China, etc.

true depiction, is a task requiring an absolute approach always free from exoticism, vaster than the approach of a travel writer. The severance of departure is already a goal in itself as much as the attraction of arriving somewhere else and searching for a homeland.

She leaves in hopes of never returning. A Russian born in Geneva, a rebel resisting discipline, she wants to break with a century, a civilization, and certainly with a family that does not respond to her thirst for the absolute. The family romance, particularly turbulent and tragic, undoubtedly counts for a lot in the simultaneous and indissociable choices of elsewhere and literature.

Already, the story of her birth is a novel in itself. It seems that Isabelle Eberhardt never left the fiction that she muddles with delight: the register of births, marriages, and deaths of the district of Geneva does not mention the name of the father of "Isabelle Wilhelmine Marie, born February 17, 1877, daughter of Eberhardt, Nathalie Charlotte Dorothée originating from Moscow . . ." Did she know who her father was? Did she invent one while disowning her parent? In recently revealed private correspondence, she goes as far as claiming that she was born of a rape. A mystery never cleared up.

But it would be too simple to reduce her vocation as a wandering writer to the quest for her paternity. This would be denying the force of her imagination, which fed on the appeal of the unknown and led her down the road that merges with the thread of her writing.

Isabelle Eberhardt could have become a revolutionary like her anarchist friend Vera. At the age of twenty, she could have married Khoudja ben Abdallah, her first lover, or the following year, Rechid Ahmed, a young and seductive Turkish diplomat whom she met in Geneva. Instead, she chooses writing, which naturally directs her toward departure. She commits to literature; it is vital and becomes a requirement of freedom—to live freely, without ties, like a vagabond but also like a writer who is free to invent a world.

She takes this liberty entirely, impulsively, without waiting to assess its consequences. The need to wander leads her toward an imprecise goal: "I left, as always, without a fixed plan; I decided to go to the Algerian Sahara in order to wander there as long as possible . . ." A changeable itinerary: a stay in Bône, a return to Geneva, then Tunis before the southern routes, cavalcades through the desert all the way to El Oued, jewel of the Eastern Great Erg. Her *drifting*, a manner of lazy but provocative protest at the end of this colonial century, exposes her to every danger. The woman who "startled notaries and mandarins of all sorts" will be successively accused, exiled, and slandered, then tolerated, used, and celebrated after her death.

When her strongest emotional tie breaks, with the death of her mother in November 1897, Isabelle Eberhardt can let herself be completely carried away by her drifting, magnetized by the mythic South—the East—which feeds her literary vocation.

This drifting means refusing the West, escaping from it without violence, in the same way as the writer Pierre Loti had tried to do before her, but with more ambiguity. In the same way, more recently, as certain initiators of the hippie movement have done. Projected into the space of her desire, an East whose archaism further increases her estrangement, an unchanging desert vaster than the Russian steppes of her origins, she finds a country that, for the first time, gives back an image of her that is not split. And thus it seems to her to seize the truth. "I believe there are predestined hours, very mysteriously privileged moments, when certain lands, certain places, reveal to us their soul, when we instantly— through sudden intuition—understand the true, unique, and indelible vision. Thus my first vision of Eloued . . . ," she writes in one of her short stories, "Au pays des sables."

Desert, the landscape where she looks at herself, is where she at last becomes integrated into the scene she is describing. Thus, her inclination for cross-dressing, the "transvestism" that made her sign her first writings with a man's name, Nicolas Podolinsky, will be entirely reinvested in her desire for integration. In El Oued she truly becomes Mahmoud Saadi, the young Muslim man of letters traveling in order to educate himself. And paradoxically this is where, for the first time, she is herself: Isabelle Eberhardt. It is not a question of substitution but rather an accepted and expressed intensification of her identity.

To be part of the scene allows her not only to project her dreams but to exist there intensely: "The gunpowder will speak and the horses will gallop in the Teksebet plain. The horseman—dressed in *gandouras* and white burnooses, a tall white turban with a veil, wearing at his neck the black prayer beads of the Qadriya, his right hand wrapped with a red handkerchief in order to better hold the reins—this will be Mahmoud Saadi, adoptive son of the great *cheikh* Haoussine . . ." Moments of total exultation, of rare happiness in the accomplishment of desire, a tumultuous cavalcade but also feverish texts, a letter to her brother Augustine, accomplice of her tormented adolescence, and a short story, "Fantasia"—thus Isabelle Eberhardt measures the space of the earth that she had promised to herself, the homeland, the land of fathers. In order to conquer the right to live there, she escapes the saber of a fanatic, manages to thwart a deportation order, overcomes the slanders of the colonists, resists malarial fevers. The force of her drifting permits this "intensified" being to go through a thousand perils almost unscathed, as much in her life as in her work.

Eighty years later her work returns to us. Like its author, it could have disappeared on October 21, 1904, in the flood of the Oued Sefra, but the manuscripts are miraculously found intact in the mud, beneath the ruins of her house.

Her writings have not escaped the "covetousness of vultures who feast on posthumous works," as was extravagantly said at the time. Certain texts, narratives, or stories had been published during her life, mainly in the Algiers press. They were reunited and edited in bookstores with the unpublished material found in Aïn Sefra. They were saved from being scattered, but altered by corrections, the additions or the omissions of the first editors, and even plagiarized by a literary hack yearning for inspiration.[2] However, through these vicissitudes, the work was preserved from the greatest of dangers—oblivion—probably thanks to the permanence of the inspirational theme—the confrontation between East and West—but also because it constitutes a unique testimony about colonization; or yet again perhaps because it remains a seductive invitation to travel.

The intensity and the quality of Isabelle Eberhardt's drifting, in harmony with space and time, give her work its true dimension: she is

2. Paul Vigne d'Octon, *Mektoub* (Figuière, 1913).

calm and contemplative in Tunis before the departure for the South, fascinated in El Oued at the moment of its discovery, melodramatic in Marseille during the exile, lyrical at the heart of the Sahara, combatant in the colonial cities of the north, exalted behind the walls of a Muslim sanctuary . . . and for this reason, one can think that there is not a better biography of Isabelle Eberhardt than her work itself.

Starting in 1899—after the attempt at *Rêves azurés* (*Azure Dreams*), which she tried to write with her brother Augustine, but of which there are no traces, and after her introductory publications, notably in the *Athénée*—each coherent ensemble of her text marks an intense moment in her existence.

Heures de Tunis (*Tunis Hours*). Mourning her mother. The apprenticeship of solitude and emancipation from the fatality that had beaten down the lineage of women from which she issued. Isabelle Eberhardt will not have a daughter like her mother and her grandmother; how could she, in choosing to be Mahmoud?

Au pays des sables (*In the Land of Desert Sands*) and *Sahel tunisien* (*Tunisian Sahel*). The "revelation of El Oued" and the confirmation of her vocation: "to write about a totally unpublished country" and "perhaps to find notoriety in literature."

The beginning of the *Journaliers* (*Daily Journals*). "Yasmina," "Le Major," the first Algerian short stories. The so hoped for return to El Oued one year later in 1900. The desire for integration and the encounter with love beneath the features of a beautiful spahi, Slimène Ehnni, but also suspicion—who can understand at the time the authenticity of Isabelle Eberhardt's approach—and the double rejection, the Behima assassination attempt and the deportation pronounced by the colonial administration.

The continuation of the *Journaliers*, the notebooks from El Oued, *Printemps au desert* (*Spring in the Desert*), first draft of *Trimardeur*. Exile, for this daughter of an exile, in Marseille in 1901. On her own, her fatalistic nature seems stimulated by difficulties. She invents for herself the destiny of a marabout, imagines herself designated by Allah: martyrdom in the service of the Muslim cause. But she especially draws from her memories a new force of inspiration and writing, and she contemplates her first novel.

Retour au sud (*Return to the South*), the continuation of Algerian stories. Back to Algiers in the spring of 1902, Isabelle Eberhardt, French by her marriage with Slimène Ehnni, the spahi from El Oued, finds a friend, Victor Barrucand, defender of equal rights between the indigenous and the colonists. A platform for protest in his newspaper *Akhbar*, a cause aligning with the revolt of the *fellah* of the Mitidja. She responds with literature to the slanders made by the "ultras"; some of her stories thus become indictments.

Sud oranais, first part. The *bled el baroud*. A war reporter at the Algerian-Moroccan border in 1903, she develops an admiration for General Lyautey's personality that leads her to defend the "protectorate" thesis. But being an aesthete easily moved by rootless people, she is finally affected even more by the lives of the legionnaires, of *goumiers*, and of rebel tribes.

Sud oranais, second part. After action, contemplation. Return in 1904 to the Oranese South, where, at the end of the trip, she succumbs to the bewitchment of a desert religious citadel: Kenadsa. Her writings are sometimes enriched by a dreamlike dimension with mystical underpinnings.

Quite naturally, we have respected this chronological order of inspiration in order to construct the first volume of notes and stories. The same chronology will be found in the second volume, a fictional reflection of Isabelle Eberhardt's biography through her stories and her novel *Trimardeur*.

Among the texts dug out of the mud in Aïn Sefra, the last ones, written in Kenadsa, are strangely premonitory. They evoke dreams of ecstatic annihilation in the "paradise of waters." Is Isabelle Eberhardt exhausted from having drawn too long from the sources of life, from having so often braved danger? When the oued floods and she perishes, she is only twenty-seven years old, but so many trials have accumulated . . .

Sick and weakened by fever, she had to interrupt her long drift toward the South. However, in autumn 1904 she was still planning to leave for the oases of the Touat, to winter and write in Timimoun, to tell the stories of women's lives—big-hearted prostitutes, canteen women acting as sisters of charity, those who follow the military convoys in the conquest of the Sahara. This subject, so often treated since then in literature and in cinema, could perhaps have been for Isabelle Eberhardt the novel of her maturity.

What remains is an ensemble of texts, a work from her youth whose evocative power contrasts remarkably with the insipidness of the majority of works by Orientalist authors of the epoch and announces the talent of a true writer. What had the masters of the nineteenth century written by the age of twenty-seven? Flaubert was barely finishing the first *Education sentimentale* (*Sentimental Education*), which he judged unworthy of publication . . .

Isabelle Eberhardt never knew literary notoriety in her lifetime. At the most, Parisian salons were beginning to evoke the mystery of her elegant Arab horseman's silhouette. It was only after her death that the public was truly moved by the force and originality of her destiny—an emotion that led to the publication of her work and ultimately to her success. Posthumous work was published starting in 1906 without the author having left precise instructions.

Her editors, her adulators, contribute, with more or less happiness, to her success, though it was made ambiguous by the excess of praise and flights of lyricism of mediocre poets who had come to declaim on her tomb at the foot of the Saharan dunes.

The first person to reunite her texts is Victor Barrucand, who reassembles all the stories already published in the Algerian press along with those he had taken from the hands of Lyautey, who had searched the ruins of her house in Aïn Sefra for the manuscripts. The defender, the close friend, the editor believes he is authorized to structure the edition according to an entirely personal strategy. He splits *Sud oranais*—which Isabelle Eberhardt had copied into one notebook—into two parts. He will make of it two books—*Dans l'ombre chaude de l'Islam* (*In Islam's Warm Shadow*) and *Notes de route* (*Notes from the Road*)—and adds to them, without great logic, other texts.

Carried away by the legitimacy of his role as legatee, he cosigns the first of these works. Undoubtedly, he keeps a certain nostalgia from his close relationship with Isabelle Eberhardt—he might have been her lover for some time—and from their collaboration. Should that have authorized him to mix his writing with hers? Taking as pretext the deterioration of the manuscript of the second part of *Sud oranais*, he introduces, as he makes clear, "a little bit of fiction." In reality he is censoring the words, the sentences, the situations that evoke too much freedom of morals. Sometimes he weighs down the sober style of his dead collaborator with embellishments from his own flamboyant writing. Under the pretext of flexibility, he adds aesthetic and moralistic reflections of his own invention, thus replacing the author in a pleonastic manner in her text where she is always present through the acuity of her gaze. He sprinkles the stories with picturesque elements where nothing should be exotic, and this is perhaps the worst of betrayals.

For the footnotes of history, let us make clear that at the end of the general outcry raised by this posthumous collaboration, Barrucand has to resign himself to limiting his interventions to corrections of detail. On checking, the texts published starting in 1908—*Notes de route, Pages d'Islam*, and *Trimardeur*—are faithful to the manuscripts with very few exceptions.

However, at this period of colonization, it is not the least of Victor Barrucand's merits to have defended and popularized Isabelle Eberhardt's work by publishing it in Paris with Eugène Fasquelle. A journalist in complete support of the "progressive" arguments of the radical government, Barrucand leads this fight all the way to his death in Algiers in 1934. Many men of letters, taking a firm line and forcing voice and style, ardently dispute his exclusive right to his subject. The arguments around Isabelle Eberhardt's character sometimes become violent. Each person embellishes his own version and many people interfere: those who knew her, such as the colonial administrator and writer Robert Randau and his colleague, Judge Marival; the painter Maxime Noire; Jean Rodes, chronicler for the *Matin*; Ali Abdul Wahab, a Tunisian friend from her youth . . . and those who dreamed of her, such as the poetess Lucie Delarue-Mardrus; the militant feminist Séverine; the plagiarizer Vigne d'Octon, to name only a few.

Then comes the dispenser of justice. Starting in the 1920s, René-Louis Doyon—vigorous character, editor and director of the journal *La Connaissance*, and Andre Malraux's first mentor—publishes manuscripts that had remained unpublished but were recuperated unexpectedly in 1913 by Chloë Bulliod, one of Isabelle Eberhardt's admirers. *Mes journaliers* (*My Journals*, 1923) and *Au pays des sables* (1944) are wrongly presented by Doyon as the first authentic writings. Claiming himself as a biographer, he proves himself to be as sectarian as his predecessors. He wishes to dismantle the idol in order to find the woman; he forges a new legend.

In order to restore the work coherently, we had to try to grasp the coherence and the incoherence of the author. To follow her footsteps and her writings since her departure from Geneva requires many detours; we undertook this long voyage in order to accurately rediscover this seeker of the absolute. First, we explored the bookshelves of secondhand booksellers in order to gather first-edition volumes that for a long time could not be found in bookstores. Then we consulted archives and newspapers and journals of the period and particularly those that she had contributed to: *Athénée, Les Nouvelles d'Alger, La Dépêche Algérienne, Akhbar, Le Petit Journal, La Revue Blanche*, among others. Then, taking her writings as a guide, crossing a country eighty years later, meeting people so similar to those whose souls she had known how to reveal, we have strived to understand how they have changed and how they have remained the same.

When we found, in this South that she loved so much, the landscapes, the faces, the scenes that Isabelle Eberhardt described, we understood the truth of this individual better than we had after reading the innumerable texts published about her since her death. It remained for us to discover, to study the correspondence, the unknown notes from the majority of her biographies in order to try to outwit the traps of Isabelle's legend. Then it became possible to reestablish the truth of the work by comparing it, for the first time, with the saved manuscripts and the texts that had appeared during the lifetime of the author.

Indifferently speaking about herself in the masculine or the feminine, Isabelle Eberhardt wrote as she lived: simply, but guided by the flow of her emotions, openly, without tricks. With nonchalance, but set into motion by her passion. Shortly before her death, she was entering the phase of literary maturity when one begins to know how to recompose reality into fiction. Certain passages from her novel *Trimardeur* provide the proof of this.

Inspiration comes to her on the road. She briefly notes landscapes or encounters, a few features, landmarks, in her marble-covered school notebooks or, failing that, on hotel letterhead, on the back of a bill, and even on the back of a paper ballot. Later, sometimes even much later, she takes inspiration from her notes and her memories to write narratives and stories, which she often rewrites in successive versions and which she then recopies, without deletions, in black or violet ink in her tall, determined writing.

The manuscripts from the Isabelle Eberhardt collection, kept in the Archives d'outre-mer in Aix-en-Provence, have allowed us to return to the original text and to correct the first publications. One finds, still spattered by red mud from the deluge, the two parts of *Sud oranais*, several unfinished versions of the novel *Trimardeur*, the majority of the El Oued notebooks, those of *Sahel tunisien*, other notebooks, a few stories and very many fragments and variations, hitherto unpublished materials, and *Rakhil* and *El Moukadira*—drafts of an abandoned novel. These manuscripts, gathered and sometimes annotated for Barrucand's edition, were conserved by his family until 1956, then given to the archives of the governor-general of Algeria before being transferred to Aix-en-Provence.

Thus it was possible for us to reestablish words, sentences, titles, paragraphs, indeed entire narratives suppressed by Barrucand. We also removed his additions and reintroduced a few variations, beginnings of stories, and controversial texts, until then left out, to put together this collection of notes and stories, the first of two volumes of the complete works of Isabelle Eberhardt.

We tried to create an edition, to make authentic texts available for the first time, with neither alterations nor corrections, with both errors and strokes of inspiration. For us, this is the best way to pay homage to the individual and to the writer who has "delighted us" for so long.

This first publication of the complete works should further permit other works about Isabelle Eberhardt—dissertations, theses, critical studies—to be carried out.

At the beginning of the volume, the reader will find a text written at the end of 1902, which seemed to us to stand out as a good foreword. Isabelle Eberhardt praises "vagabonding," a title she chose to collect her first narratives.

The woman who left at the age of twenty without the desire to return finally accomplished her wish: "Under what sky and in what earth will I rest on the day predetermined by my destiny? Mystery . . . and yet, I would like my remains to be placed in the red earth of white Annaba's cemetery, where She sleeps . . . or perhaps anywhere in the desert's burned sand, far from the profane banality of the invading West . . ."

In the middle of the Sahara, the flow of the deluge put an end to her drifting, but something of the irrepressible force that drove Isabelle Eberhardt returns to us now, with her work.

Chronological Landmarks

1872   Nathalie de Moerder, born Eberhardt, wife of General de
       Moerder, after leaving St. Petersburg, lives in Switzerland
       with the private tutor of her four children, Alexander Trophi-
       mowsky, defrocked priest of Armenian origin. She gives birth
       to a fifth child, Augustine de Moerder, most likely the son of
       General de Moerder.

1877   *February 17:* Isabelle Eberhardt is born at the Maison des
       Grottes, in Geneva. The birth certificate does not mention the
       father.

1894   Augustine de Moerder, Isabelle's half-brother, abruptly leaves
       Geneva and enlists in the Foreign Legion in Sidi-Bel-Abbès.

1897   *Starting in May:* Isabelle Eberhardt and her mother stay in
       Bône (Annaba) on the Algerian coast.
       November 28: Nathalie de Moerder dies and is buried according
       to Muslim rites in the indigenous cemetery in Bône.
       December: Isabelle Eberhardt is forced to return to Geneva
       with her guardian Alexander Trophimowsky. She stays there
       one and a half years.

1898   *July:* Isabelle Eberhardt is engaged to marry Rechid Ahmed,
       Turkish diplomat. Isabelle Eberhardt does not follow up when
       Rechid Ahmed is posted in La Haye.

1899   *May 15:* Alexander Trophimowsky dies in Geneva from throat
       cancer. Isabelle Eberhardt spends time in Tunisia.
       July 8: Isabelle Eberhardt departs from Tunis for southern Con-
       stantine and first discovers the Sahara and the city of El Oued
       in the Souf.
       September 2: Returns to Tunis.
       September, October: Travels in the Tunisian Sahel.
       November: Stays in Marseille.

1900 *January:* Travels in Sardinia.

From February to July: Makes numerous trips back and forth between Paris and Geneva.

August 3: Arrives in El Oued, where she will stay until the end of the year. She meets Slimène Ehnni, noncommissioned officer with the spahis, a Muslim of French nationality, with whom she decides to spend her life. She is initiated into the brotherhood of the Qadriya and becomes the friend and confidant of the religious leader Sidi Lachmi ben Brahim.

1901 *January:* Slimène Ehnni is transferred to Batna because of his love affair with Isabelle Eberhardt.

January 29: In an assassination attempt in Behima, near El Oued, Isabelle Eberhardt is wounded with a saber on her left arm and on her head by Abdallah ben Mohammed, a member of the brotherhood of the Tidjaniya, who said he was inspired by Allah. She is hospitalized in El Oued until February 25.

February 25: Isabelle Eberhardt departs for Batna, where she is under police surveillance.

May 9: Believing herself to be in the grip of an expulsion order, Isabelle Eberhardt takes the boat from Bône to Marseille.

June 18: At the trial of Abdallah ben Mohammed in Constantine, Isabelle Eberhardt asks the court for leniency. He is condemned to hard labor. Immediately after the verdict, she is expelled from Algeria by the general government. She returns to Marseille and goes to her brother Augustine's house.

August 24: Slimène Ehnni is given permission to change regiment.

August 28: He joins Isabelle Eberhardt in Marseille.

October 17: Isabelle Eberhardt and Slimène Ehnni are married in a civil wedding in the Marseille City Hall.

1902 *January 15:* French because of her marriage, Isabelle Eberhardt can return to Algerian soil. She stays in Bône with Slimène's family. The couple settles in Algiers on rue de la Marine (Marine Street), then on rue du Soudan (Sudan Street) in the Casbah.

Spring: Isabelle Eberhardt first meets Victor Barrucand.

June, July: Isabelle Eberhardt travels to Bou Saada and to the *zaouïya* of El Hamel, where she meets with Lella Zeyneb, marabout of the brotherhood of the Rahmaniya.

July 7: The couple settles in Ténès where Slimène Ehnni is named *khodja*. They take numerous trips between Ténès and Algiers. The weekly *Akhbar* reappears and Isabelle Eberhardt becomes a regular contributor.

1903 *January:* Isabelle Eberhardt takes her second trip to Bou Saada and El Hamel and has her second meeting with Lella Zeyneb.

April, May, June: A campaign of slander is waged against Isabelle Eberhardt and her close relations, related to the electoral politics of prominent persons of Ténès. Slimène Ehnni resigns; he is named khodja in Sétif. Isabelle Eberhardt settles in Algiers.

September: She goes as a war reporter to the Oranese South, following the battles of El Moungar and the siege of Taghit.

October: Isabelle Eberhardt meets with Lyautey in Aïn Sefra. And after reporting in Beni Ounif on the situation at the Algerian-Moroccan border, she returns to Algiers at the end of the winter.

1904 Isabelle Eberhardt takes a trip to Oudjda (Morocco).

May: She stays for the second time in the Oranese South. Lyautey's troops occupy Bechar. Isabelle Eberhardt spends the summer in the Moroccan zaouïya of Kenadsa.

September: Sick, she returns to Aïn Sefra.

October 21: Isabelle Eberhardt dies in the Aïn Sefra flood.

1907 *April 14:* Slimène Ehnni dies.

1920 Augustine de Moerder commits suicide in Marseille.

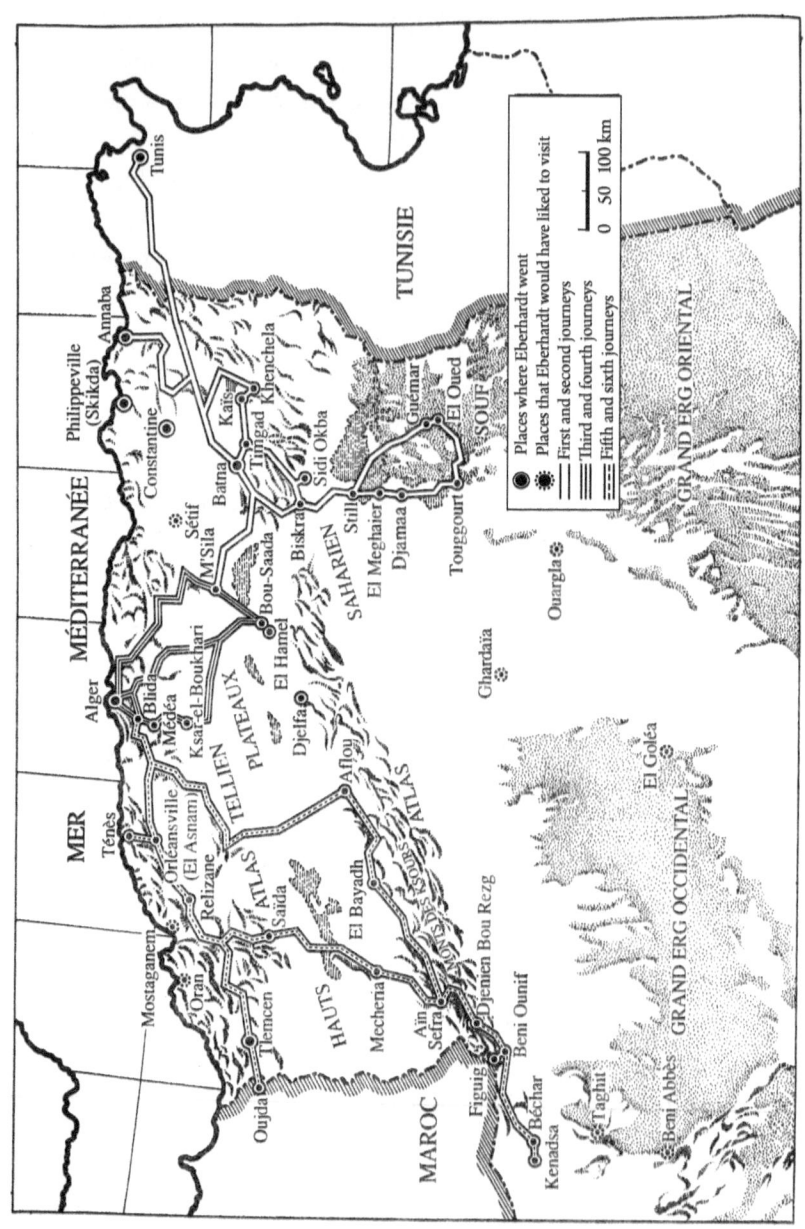

Isabelle Eberhardt's itineraries

Wanderings

A right that very few intellectuals think about claiming is the right to wander, to *vagabond*.

And yet, vagabonding is liberation, and life on the open road is liberty.

To one day courageously break all the fetters with which modern life and our weakness of heart have burdened our mere deeds under the pretext of liberty, to arm oneself with the symbolic staff and beggar's satchel, *to leave!*

For whomever knows the value, and too, the delectable taste of solitary liberty (for one is free only when alone), the act of leaving is the most courageous and the most beautiful.

An egotistical happiness, perhaps. But it is happiness for the one who knows how to savor it.

To be alone, to have *few needs*, to be unknown, everywhere a foreigner and at home, and to walk grandly and solitarily in conquest of the world.

Is not the sturdy vagabond, sitting beside the road, contemplating the wide and open horizon before him, the absolute master of lands, waters, and even the skies?

What lord of the manor can rival him in power and opulence?

His fiefdom has no limits and his empire no law.

No servitude demeans his bearing, no labor bends his spine to the earth, the earth that he possesses and which gives itself to him in its entirety, in goodness and in beauty.

In our modern society the nomad, the vagabond, is the pariah, "with no known address or residence."

By adding these few words to the name of some irregular,[1] those who make and enforce the laws believe they condemn him forever.

To have a home, a family, property, or a public function, a definite means of livelihood, to be, finally, a dependable cog in the social machine, all these things seem necessary, almost indispensable to the immense majority of men, even to intellectuals, even to those who believe themselves to be the most emancipated.

However, all of that is nothing but a different form of slavery into which we are forced by contact with our fellow creatures, especially regular and continual contact.

I have always listened with admiration, but without envy, to the tales of good folk who have lived twenty or thirty years in the same neighborhood, even in the same house, and who have never left their birthplace.

Not to feel the agonizing need to know and to see what is over there, beyond the mysterious blue wall of the horizon . . . Not to feel the depressing weight of monotonous surroundings . . . To look at the white road leading to far-off places without feeling the pressing need to give oneself over to it, to follow it, obediently, through mountains and valleys; all this fearful need for immobility resembles the unconscious resignation of the beast stupefied by servitude, who stretches out his neck for the harness.

Every property has its limits. Every power is constrained by laws; but the vagabond possesses the entire vast earth, whose limits are the imaginary horizon, and his empire is intangible, for he delights in and governs it through mind and spirit.

---

1. Translator's note: In both French (*irrégulier*) and English ("irregular"), an irregular is a soldier not belonging to the regular army organization, but recruited for a special purpose; hence, my translation: "irregular." However, given the tenor of this introductory text, Eberhardt seems to be clearly referring to any nonconformist, vagabond, or outsider who does not follow the established norms of society.

Tunis Hours

For two months during the summer of 1899, I pursued my dream of an antique Orient, mournful and resplendent, in the ancient whitewashed neighborhoods of Tunis, full of shadows and silence.

I was living alone with Khadidja, my old Moorish servant, and my black dog, in a very immense and very old Turkish house in one of the most isolated corners of Bab-Menara, almost at the top of the hill . . .

This house was a labyrinth, mysteriously laid out, complicated by hallways and rooms situated on different levels, decorated with colorful earthenware tiles from times past, and delicately sculptured lacelike plaster running along the vaulted ceilings of painted and gilded wood.

There, in the cool half-light, in the silence disturbed only by the melancholy chant of the muezzin, the days flowed by, deliciously languid, in sweet but not tiresome monotony.

During the suffocating hours of the afternoon rest, in my vast bedroom paneled with green-and-pink tile, Khadidja, huddled in a corner, slid the black beads of her rosary one by one with a rapid murmur from her faded lips. Daedalus, stretched out on the floor in a lionlike pose, his slender muzzle set on his powerful paws, attentively followed the slow flight of occasional flies . . . And I, stretched out on my low bed, abandoned myself to the voluptuousness of endless dreaming . . .

It was a period of rest, like a beneficial pause between two adventurous and almost-agonizing periods. And too, the impressions left by my life there are sweet, melancholy, and a little vague . . .

Behind my residence, separated from the street by inhabited Arab houses, fiercely closed off to the outside world, was a small old neighborhood, no longer inhabited, and with no way out, all in ruins . . . Sections of walls, vaulted ceilings, small courtyards, dark bedrooms, still-standing balconies—all of it invaded by Virginia creepers, ivy, and a population of flowers and encroaching grasses growing on the walls, a strange city, uninhabited for years. No one seemed to worry about these houses, whose inhabitants must have all died or left, never to return . . .

Yet in the mystical silence of moonlit nights, the closest of these ruined habitations came alive in a strange manner.

Through the wrought-iron grill of one of my windows, I could cast my eyes into the small interior courtyard. The high walls and two rooms of this single-story house had remained standing. In the middle, a fountain with a stone basin, badly chipped but still full of clear water, coming from I don't know where, almost disappearing under the exuberant vegetation that had grown there.

There were enormous jasmine bushes studded with white flowers, mixed with the pliant foliage of vines, and rose bushes sowed the white tile with purple petals . . . On balmy nights, a warm fragrance arose from this corner of shade and oblivion.

And every month, when the moon arrived to illuminate the sleepy ruins, I was able to attend, half concealed behind a thin curtain, a performance that soon became familiar to me, and which I awaited during the languorous days, but which remained an enigma to me . . . Besides, perhaps all the charm of this memory resides, for me, in the element of mystery . . . Without my ever knowing from whence he came, nor from whence he entered the small courtyard, a young Moor, dressed in delicately colored faded silk clothing, and draped in a light, snowy-white burnoose that made him look like an apparition, sat there on a stone.

He was perfectly beautiful and had the pale matte complexion of Arab city dwellers, along with their slightly nonchalant air of distinction.

But his face was marked by a profound sadness.

He would sit there, always in the same place; and lost in the infinite blue night, he would sing melodies born long ago under the Andalusian sky, smoothly flowing cantilena. Slowly, sweetly, his voice would rise into the silence, like a plaint or an incantation . . .

He seemed especially to prefer this song, the sweetest and saddest of all:

Enduring sadness grips my soul, as the night grips and erases things. Pain grips my heart and fills it with anguish, as the tomb grips bodies and annihilates them. There is no cure for my sadness, except for death with no return . . . but if my soul awakens for another life, be it even in Eden, my sadness will be reborn there.

What was this incurable sadness, the power of which he sang? The remarkable singer never said.

But his voice was pure and modulated, and never before had any voice revealed as fully to me the secret and indefinable charm of that Arab music from another time, which has enchanted many other sad souls before me.

Sometimes the young Moor brought along the small murmuring flute played by Bedouin shepherds and camel herders, the light reed which seemed to retain in its melodies something of the crystalline murmur of the brooks from which it was born.

For a long time, in the silence of late hours, when everything sleeps in Muslim Tunis, intoxicated by sweet smells, the stranger thus let flow melancholy and sighs. Then he would leave as he had come, without a sound, always with his ghostly air, returning to the shadows of the two small rooms, which must have connected to the other ruins.

Khadidja, a former slave, had lived for forty years in the most illustrious Tunisian families and had rocked several generations of young men on her lap. One evening, I called her and showed her the nocturnal musician. The superstitious old woman shook her head:

"I don't know him . . . and yet I know all the young men of the city's great families . . ."

Then, in a low voice, she added, trembling:

"Anyway, God knows whether he's really a living person. Is he maybe just the shadow of one of the former inhabitants, and is this music just a dream, a spell?"

Knowing the character of this race, for whom all questions about its private life, its comings and goings, are an insult, I never dared call out to the unknown man, the stranger, for fear of making him flee his refuge forever . . .

Yet, one evening I waited a long time for him in vain. He never returned. But the sound of his voice and the soft whispering of his flute often take me back during the moonlight hours. And sometimes I feel an indefinable anguish at the thought that I will never know who he was and why he came there.

Way up high, near the now commonplace casbah and the barracks,[1] is a charming place imbued with a very distinct and Eastern sadness. This place is Bab-el-Gorjani.

First, on a plot of land slightly elevated above the street and separated from it only by an old gray wall is an ancient cemetery, no longer used for burial, where the tombs disappear under the tangle of dried grasses and rose bushes in the century-old shadow of fig trees and black cypresses.

In Tunisia, access to Islamic mosques and cemeteries is, according to law, restricted to Muslims.

Thus, because the graves there are very old and no onlookers pass by, no one troubles the forgotten dead of Bab-el-Gorjani, where only the call of the muezzin and that of the Zouaves' bugles can be heard from among all the sounds of Tunis, which spreads out in a gentle slope until it reaches the still mirror of its lake.

I have always liked to wander under the cover of the egalitarian clothing of the Bedouins in Muslim cemeteries, where everything is peaceful and abandoned, where none of what makes Europe's cemeteries gloomy spoils the majesty of the place. And every evening, I took off on foot toward Bab-el-Gorjani.

At the divine hour of the *magh'reb*, when the sun is about to disap-

1. Translator's note: Any number of words may be used to translate from the French phrase, used by Eberhardt, *la casbah banalisée*: "vulgarized," "hackneyed," "picture postcard," "now boring," "vulgar commonplaces of the casbah." By the time Eberhardt had written this piece, the casbah and its inhabitants (in particular, women) had been photographed and reproduced by the thousands in the form of picture postcards for European consumption, starting in the late nineteenth century. Indeed, in her piece "Le portrait de l'Ouled-Naïl" (in *Oeuvres complètes II, Ecrits sur le sable*), she begins by mentioning the "curious eyes of foreigners" who see the picture of Achoura ben Saïd "in all photographers' shop windows." So often have the women dancers of the Ouled Naïl been stereotyped in pictures that place them in an exotic Oriental backdrop, that it is assumed that Achoura is also one of them. Instead, Eberhardt writes the real story of her life, in an attempt to change the stereotype of the exotic Arab woman.

pear on the horizon, the gray tombs take on the most splendid colors, and the slanting rays of the ending day slide in pink streaks onto this noble corner of indifference and of permanent oblivion . . .

Farther on, one passes under the gateway that gives its name to this neighborhood, and one finds oneself on a dusty road that, to the west, descends into the narrow valley of Bardo and, toward the east, leads to the large cemetery at the *marabout* of Sidi-Bel-Hassène, which towers over Lake El Bahira.

This road passes over the summit of the low hill of Tunis, abrupt and deserted on this side . . .

The sun is very low. The Djebel-Zaghouan becomes iridescent with pale colors and seems to melt into the limitless fire of the sky.

The enormous disk, devoid of rays, descends slowly, surrounded by a filmy violet-purple haze.

Far below, in the vast plain, the Chott Sedjoumi stretches out, dried up by the summer heat; and its even surface, a purplish brown where only a few salty crusts thrust forth white spots, deceptively takes on the character of a living ocean with the depth of an abyss.

At the foot of the hill, on the banks of the *chott*, fragrant eucalyptus trees have been planted in order to combat the miasmas from the stagnant saltpeter-filled waters. And these multiple rows of trees, with their very pale blue leaves, create a silver crown set in the accursed plain, where nothing grows, where nothing lives.

There, I remembered certain ancient impressions, gathered in the region of the great Saharan chotts, a country of visions.

The last faint light of the day throws long, bloody streaks onto the deserted chott, onto the now entirely blue eucalyptus trees, onto the reddish rocks and the gray wall. Then, suddenly all goes dark, as if the horizon's doors had again closed, and everything is engulfed in a bluish haze that creeps up toward the wall and the city.

As has been said time and again, all the changing beauty of this African earth lies in the prodigious play of light on monotonous sites and empty horizons.

Undoubtedly, it was this play of light, these delicious iridescent sunrises, and these evenings of purple and gold that inspired the Arab poets of bygone days to write their stories and songs.

Every day, an old blind man dressed in rags comes and sits in the gateway of Bab-el-Gorjani. In the eternal night of his blindness, he endlessly repeats his litany of misery, imploring the few believers passing by in the name of Sidi-Bel-Hassène-Chadli, the great Tunisian marabout.

Often, faced with these old blind and decrepit beggars of Islam, I have stopped and wondered if there were still souls and thoughts behind their emaciated masks, behind the lifeless mirrors of their lightless eyes ... A strange existence of indifference and mournful silence, so far from men who nevertheless live and move all around them!

Also, there, at nightfall, anonymous and sordid creatures in rags, Jewesses from Hara or Sicilians from "Sicilia serira" (little Sicily), wander in dangerous and seedy neighborhoods near the port.

The barracks draw them there. Beggars, and occasionally prostitutes, they come at suppertime, then wander along the walls and in the black corners, waiting for the soldiers to come out ...

Nevertheless, Bab-el-Gorjani remains one of the most deserted and the most deliciously peaceful corners of Tunis ...

One hot August night, when the heaviness of a storm floated in the air and I couldn't sleep, I had gone out and wandered, dreaming, in the labyrinth of the Arab streets, where life finishes with the day.

A little before sunrise, I ended up in the El Morkad neighborhood, where with the carelessness of the Arab race, a few abandoned small streets in ruin remain only two steps away from Souk el-Hadjemine, where during the day all humanity crawls and circulates.

Tired of wandering thus without a destination, I sat down on a pile of debris and awaited the daylight.

The darker predawn light enveloped the surroundings; but toward the east, the flat terraces of the houses began to stand out in black against the barely distinct gray-green horizon.

Nearby, the El Morkad mosque and its square minaret seemed as deserted as the surrounding ruins ...

All of a sudden a wooden shutter opened up above my head and clacked violently against the wall . . . A ray of reddish light slid the length of the wall and bloodied the pavement . . . The muezzin was getting up.

At once, as if still in a dream, slowly, in a very sad and soft melody, he began his call to prayer.

His young voice, perfectly modulated, seemed to descend from very high, to float in the silence of the sleepy town.

"God is great! *Allahou Akbar!*" proclaimed the muezzin, opening the four small windows of the minaret one after another.

From far away, other voices responded, while in a neighboring garden, birds were awakening and starting their own prayer of thanksgiving to the Source of all lives and all light.

"Prayer is better than sleep!"

The dream voice, slowly becoming stronger, cried out this last phrase very loudly, imperiously . . . Then, one by one, the four wooden shutters closed up again, with the same dry clack.

Everything fell back into shadow and silence, and a fresh breeze from the high sea passed over the city.

Slowly, unhurriedly, the slender canoe glides through the canal's purer and saltier water, between the low reddish banks separating it from the lake. We're approaching the high sea, which in the distance closes the horizon with a dark line.

We continue in the evening's pink radiance and the calm water, in the soft water of the sleeping lake. The canoe doesn't rock.

To the right, on its ocher and red hill dotted with white tombs and very dark green gardens, the bright marabout of Sidi-Bel-Hassène rises up; and farther ahead, drowned in purplish haze, stands the old and very massive crenellated fort.

The dark-blue twin summits of the great mountain of Bou-Karnine rise up, made hazy by the evening's arrival.

Then, very far away, Rhades's small white houses reflected in the living waters of the truly open sea.

And to the left, the august hill where Carthage once stood was outlined against the burning sky . . .

I look dreamily at this tongue of earth, this spur advancing toward the open sea, where, in times past, one of the most darkly prestigious pages of History unfolded . . . This corner of the earth for which so much blood was spilled.

The white monasteries, trying to evoke the memories of Byzantine Carthage, of the bastard Carthage of centuries of decadence, disappear in the western radiance, and the Punic hill seems deserted and bare.

And now all the splendid images of the past burst forth from this red flame and repopulate the sad hill . . . The palaces of the judges, the temples of dark divinities, the splendor and the pomp of the Barbarians, all this egotistical and ferocious Phoenician civilization that came from Asia in order to expand and to further magnify itself on Africa's harsh and ardent earth.

But then all of a sudden, when the sun has hardly disappeared on the horizon, the muezzins' solemn voices reach me from the faraway mosques. And all of the Carthage of my dream, woven of the ideal and of reflections of light, fades, goes out, with glimmers of the dying night's apotheosis.

Note

"Heures de Tunis" was published for the first time in July 1902 in number 28 of *La Revue Blanche* (whose table of contents features Apollinaire's signature); then published again with a few corrections by Victor Barrucand in *Akhbar* in April 1905; and then appeared in *Dans l'ombre chaude de l'Islam* (Fasquelle, 1906).

A variation that we reproduce below appeared in 1926 in *Akhbar*, under the title "Aperçu des manuscrits russes" ("Survey of Russian Manuscripts"), with this introduction by Victor Barrucand: "Among the essays that our collaborator Isabelle Eberhardt left us the task of looking at again and publishing, figured two notebooks written in Russian, the first entitled 'Sahara,' the second 'Vagabonds.'

"These are memories of El Oued and of Tunis presented with nonchalance. Mrs. Bentami, wife of the doctor and of Russian origin, has kindly given us the word for word translation. The Tunisian pages start thus . . ."

Russian Manuscripts

It has already been a month since I've begun leading a voluntarily cloistered and solitary life in a beautiful house in the most peaceful neighborhood of Tunis.

My days go by carefree. Peaceful and silent.

I have with me an old Moorish woman, seventy-five, the good Khadidja, deaf and stooped, and my faithful spaniel Daedalus, who followed
me when I left my now destroyed familial nest. Neither Khadidja nor
Daedalus troubles my dreamy states of mind.

I can stay for hours on my Arab bed, during the long days, following
the flight of my thoughts. My bedroom is a square room whose floor
and walls are adorned with a mosaic of earthenware tiles with magnificent Arab designs. In the middle of the ceiling is a sort of golden cupola
with incised plasterwork, sculpted and detailed like Eastern lace. Three
windows with louvered shutters, always closed, ventilate this vast room
and filter a mysterious half-light. The room looks onto a narrow but very
clean street from which no noise arises: no stores, no cafés.

Old moss-covered arches thrust forth like a bridge onto the small
street as if to hold up my house and the one across the way. Here the
constructions are delicate, but they can last for centuries.

The Saharan water carrier passes by rarely, his "burduque" on his
shoulder. One listens to the water splashing at the fountain, a few words
with the southern accent, then the steps move away and one hears nothing more. On this side of my house is a small passageway, Sidi Muached,
even more embedded in deadly silence.

Khadidja sat down on the carpet; she prays, her eyes closed, as she
tells the beads of her wooden rosary.

The Muslim rosary is made of one hundred beads. On each bead, a
quality of God is affirmed: the Only One, the Wise, the Omniscient,

the Generous, the Creator, the Judge, the Master of Worlds, and this ninety-nine times over; and on the one hundredth bead, which is the largest, one finally says: Allah!

Sometimes Khadidja's dry hand moves toward a container of perfumed cakes. She takes one and throws it under a small pot; then out of the fire rises a blue, light smoke that soon disappears in the air, leaving behind it a penetrating odor.

Daedalus is stretched out next to my bed; he seems to be sleeping, but is following the flies' flight with a weary eye. At noon and at four o'clock, the silence is troubled by a voice shouting out an unusual chant, at first very softly, then spreading a solemn melancholy. Then the voice rises up as if it were flying toward the void.

It is the old Moroccan *moueddhen-mufti* from the Sid-el-Baghdadi mosque, calling the faithful to prayer. And other far-off voices answer him, testifying to God's oneness, a principle of Islam.

This idea at first took hold of the Prophet's great and patient soul; it is the very essence of his revelation. And this is why it is repeated so often in the Koran that God is Unique and that there is no God but God.

But the great cry becomes less frequent, grows longer, and then finally dies out.

This life and this calmness, sometimes interrupted by the mysterious chant, plunge me into a sweet melancholy. I abandon myself entirely to my soul's repose, found at last.

Note

The following notes, unedited for the most part and which recount, in telegraphic style, Isabelle Eberhardt's first major voyage toward the South, partly contradict the contemplative atmosphere of "Heures de Tunis."

We will see that, in the summer of 1899, Eberhardt wore herself out through ceaseless crossings, as if she were hesitating to definitively break relations with Europe.

Notes from June 4 (Geneva) to August 3, 1899

Left Geneva June 4, 1899, at six thirty in the evening. Arrived Marseille the fifth at five thirty in the morning. Bauveau Hotel. The sixth, errands and Russian consulate. The seventh, spent in Toulon. Afternoon in Saint Mandrier with sailors from Inspection Office and from *L'Amiral-Duperré*. Night, Gabier Hotel, 7 rue d'Alger. The eighth, return to Marseille. The ninth and tenth in Marseille. Samuel's arrival. The tenth, in morning, Augustine and Thérèse's arrival.

The twelfth, departure for Tunis on board the *Saint Augustine*. The thirteenth at sea. The fourteenth, arrival in Tunis at eight fifteen in the morning. Spent day with Aly. Night, Sallès Pension, 10 rue d'Italie. The twentieth, evening, navy concert with Aly, Augustine, Abd-el-Aziz, Rachid, and Bourguiba. Night, Sallès Pension with Rachid. The twenty-third, another night with R., Zaouch house, 14 rue Bou Khris. The twenty-fifth, Augustine's departure for Marseille. Trip (night) to Rhadès with Si Moh.

Night, July 7, departure with Si Mohammed for La Goulette. Returned at two thirty in the morning. The eighth, eight in the morning, departure for Algeria. Lunch in Beja. Trajan Bridge. Dinner in Guelma. Arrived in Khroub at eleven fifteen in the evening. Spent night near train station. Hotel Victoria. Morning of ninth, errand in village. Left ten o'clock. Arrival in Batna at two thirty. Continental Hotel. Two days later (the eleventh) left at three o'clock in the morning by mule with Salah for Timgad. Took wrong road. Arrived in Timgad at ten thirty in the morning. Lunch and afternoon rest under Arch of Trajan. Altercation and quarrel with ruins inspector Vatin. Left again, four in the afternoon on Kenchela road. Returned galloping under bright moonlight all the way to the Negro village.

The twelfth, in the evening, with Salah and spahi Mahmoud ben Massine, spent all evening in Negro village. Dinner with Aly Franck, Café des Tirailleurs. Coffee with Aïcha bent Ahmed. Returned twelve thirty at night. Viewed the Joyeux nocturnal works at the artesian wells. Livestock market, then Constantine's arch.

The thirteenth, two thirty, left for Biskra. Arrived six thirty. Eight thirty, left by horse with guide Salah ben Mohammed for Sidi Okba. Arrived about midnight. Spent remainder of night in cheikh's courtyard on mats. Lunch in cheikh's garden. Trip to old Sidi Okba mosque. Interview at café with Caz [. . .] and Arab schoolteacher. Left again at about seven o'clock, returned ten o'clock. Horse fell on hotel veranda. The same day in the evening, with Salah and the spahi brigadier from Touggourt, Smaïn ben Hattab, at Hadj Aly's café across from Royal Hotel. Flute players and Ouled Naïl singers. Smoked *kif* until about midnight.[1]

Morning of the fifteenth, visit with Lieutenant Colonel Fridel at the Arab Bureau, then at his house. Lunch at his house. At dinner, Oasis Hotel, Captain de Susbielle proposes that I join him in his convoy in order to go to Touggourt. I accept. Long evening at Mohammed Chéoui Café, old Biskra, with Brigadier Smaïn. Exposes de Susbielle's bad intentions and his cruelty toward Muslims.

The sixteenth, received money from Augustine (four hundred francs). At dinner, Susbielle comes to get me in order to leave. Refusal under pretext that I'm waiting for money. He begs me to hurry and tells me that he'll wait for me in Chegga, second stopping place on the road to Touggourt.

The eighteenth, nine thirty in the evening, left with Salah and Bou Saadi Chlely ben Amar for Touggourt. Spent night until two o'clock at Chéoui Café in old Biskra with son of a marabout and spahis. Departure at two. The nineteenth at nine o'clock arrived in Bordj Saada, afternoon rest. After three o'clock played cards with Chéouiya caravan. Camped near *bordj*. French lesson for their cheikh. At *maghreb*, left again quickly at two thirty in the morning. Arrived in Chegga about three forty-five.

1. Translator's note: *Kif*, from the Arabic word meaning "ease" or "state of beatitude," refers to hashish powder mixed with tobacco, smoked in North Africa.

Joyeux coming from Guemar without officers to complain to general in Batna. Drank coffee with them.

Left again the twentieth, five forty-five. Arrived in Bir Sthil about eleven o'clock. Good water. Quarrel with guard. Fever. Intense thirst. Didn't find anything to eat (lived on bread since evening of eighteenth). Left again at nine in the evening.

Met at telegraph office, at nine o'clock, south of Sthil, Chaamba caravans going from Barika to Ouargla. Cheikh Abd el Kader ben Aly, model of good grace, proposed to take me to Ouargla with his caravan without remuneration.

At about one in the morning, almost died with my horse in a *sebkha* (dried up salt lake), to the west of the route.

At three in the morning, dismounted and lent my horse to a Chéoui worker who was on foot with us, in order not to be alone. Followed on foot the Société française plantations of the Oued Rir'. Arrival in El Merayer at five o'clock. Got drunk at the inn with Salah. Scandal in the village with Ouled Naïl girl. Evening, got more drunk with the two hunters from Africa of the Vimois and Chassard calligraphy office.

Left at nine o'clock. Took wrong road. Joined up again with the Chaamba at about midnight. Met nomads, man and woman going, conducted by Abou Fay, armed Negro, to the *djemâa* past Ourlana to get divorced. Traveled together.

Arrival on the twenty-second, about two o'clock, at the spring known as Aïn Sefra. Rested with the divorcing couple. Left, going by El Berd, at five in the morning. Joined up again with the Chaamba about seven o'clock. At nine o'clock, rested at the first fountain in the Ourlana oasis.

Went up to the bordj. Found de Susbielle's order not to let me stay in the bordj more than twenty-four hours. Story of shorting measures of cut barley and beating of a cheikh (or *caïd*?) with a riding crop. Day-long thirst and fever, under the protection of the troop.

Left at *moghreb*. Spent nearly an hour searching with matches for the only good spring in Ourlana, on the road to Maggar. Found it. Watered horse and sick mules with my tin. Changed *guerba* water. On the road, altercation with the cheikh from Ourlana.

About midnight, met the commandant of the Touggourt circle going on leave by cart. At about two in the morning, rested because of malaise, all three dizzy and vomiting. Slept on sand in the middle of the desert.

Search for animals when we awoke. The man from Bou Saada tries to light a cigarette with a pistol shot. Lakhdar, bread and water carrier, left behind with his mule.

The twenty-third, from two to four o'clock, crossing of the western end of the Chott Mérouan. Arrived (Salah and me) in El Maggar at four o'clock. Drank coffee in the Arab post house. Went to look for Chlely. Found him.

Left El Maggar at about six o'clock. Arrived in Touggourt about eleven o'clock. Slept all day long. Evening in bordello with women singers and Brigadier Smaïn. Afternoon rest at Mohammed ben Zahar's.

About four o'clock, the *khalifa* Abd el Aziz and the *deïra* Slimène came and got me to go to de Susbielle's house. Nearly two-hour-long interview, at first violent, then more courteous on the part of the captain. Icy and polite refusal to let me go to Ouargla, that is to say, to give my guides permission to accompany me.

Until ten o'clock in the evening, here I am looking for Chaamba in order to depart with them, leaving my guides in Touggourt.

Found Taïb, the Chéoui, who tells me that Cheikh Abd el Kader sent his greetings and that he had left for the *asr*, at about four o'clock.

On the twenty-fifth, returned to the Arab Bureau; asked for permission for guides in the Souf. Received.

Spent twenty-sixth, twenty-seventh, twenty-eighth in Touggourt. On the twenty-eighth, went by horse to Temassine. The twenty-ninth, about four in the afternoon, left for El Oued. Intense fever. Fell down in dune near the Mthil *guemira*. Traveled with Negro mailman Amrou. On the thirty-first, left again at two in the morning with postman Bel Kheir. Arrived about nine thirty in the morning in Ferdjenn. Found Brigadier Osman and spahi Mohamed ben Tahar. Spent all day with a fever.

August 1, two in the morning, left with *Soufi* guide Habib. Arrived in Moïet el Caïd about nine in the morning. Rested, then left after the moghreb.

Arrived about seven in the morning in Bir Ourmès. Spent all day in cheikh's garden. Guides quarrel and battle with the cheikh's sons. Spent night in front of the bordj.

The third, five in the morning, left. At four in the afternoon, short stop in Ksar Kouïnine to drink. Moghreb in the great dune.

Arrived in El Oued at seven o'clock. Encountered Muslim funeral.

In the Land of Desert Sands

There are exceptional times, very mysteriously privileged moments, when certain lands reveal to us, through sudden insight, their *soul*, perhaps even their very *essence*, moments when we develop an accurate and unique vision, and which months of patient study wouldn't know how to complete, or even modify. However, during these furtive instants, the *details* necessarily escape us and we are only able to perceive the totality of things . . . A peculiar state of our soul, or a special aspect of places, seized in passing and always *unconsciously*?

I don't know . . .

Thus, my *first* arrival in El Oued, two years ago, was for me a complete, definitive revelation of this harsh and splendid country that is the Souf, of its peculiar beauty, of its immense sadness, too.

After a rest in the shady gardens of the Ourmès oasis, my soul filled with anxious, irrational anticipation from my vision surpassing in splendor all that I had seen up until then, I once again took the eastern route with my small Bedouin convoy, a steep path which sometimes snakes through a fleeting succession of dunes, sometimes climbing dangerously onto the sharp ridges, at unbelievable heights.

After having slowly crossed the small abandoned towns squeezed around El Oued (Kouïnine, Taksebt, and Gara) as if in a dream—we reached the steep, shifting crest of the high dune known as Si Ammar ben Ahsène, after a dead man who had been killed and buried there long ago.

It was the chosen hour, that marvelous hour in the land of Africa when the great fiery sun is about to disappear at last, leaving the earth to rest in the blue shadow of the night.

From the top of this dune, one discovers the entire valley of El Oued, which the sleepy waves of the huge ocean of gray sand seem to engulf.

Laid out in terraces on the southern slope of a dune, El Oued, the strange town with innumerable small cupolas, slowly changed hue.

At the top of the hill, the white minaret of Sidi Salem rose up, already iridescent, already completely pink in the western light.

Shadows of things lengthened disproportionately, were contorted, and became pale on the ground that had become alive all around us; not a voice was to be heard.

All of the towns in the land of desert sands, built of light-colored plaster, have a wild, ruined, and crumbling look.

And very nearby, tombs upon tombs, an entirely separate city, that of the dead adjoining that of the living. The long, low dunes of Sidi-Messaour, towering over the city toward the southeast, now seemed like so many flows of incandescent metal, from glowing hearths, of an incredibly intense purplish-red color.

On the small round domes, on sections of walls in ruin, on the white tombs, on the disheveled crowns of huge date trees, the glimmering of the fire climbed, elevating the gray town into a blazing apotheosis.

The sea maze of the giant dunes of the other deserted route that leads to Touggourt, from where we had come via Taïbett-Guéblia, stood out, iridescent, drowned in the reflections of silvery fawn hues against the dark purple of the setting sun.

Never before, in any country on earth, had I seen the evening put on all its finery in such magical splendor!

In El Oued there is no dark forest of date palms encircling the city such as those in the oases of the rocky or salty regions . . .

The gray city lost in the gray desert, participating fully in its blazing and in its paleness, like it and in it, pink and golden on enchanted mornings, white and blinding during the blazing noon, purple and violet during radiant evenings . . . and gray, gray as the sand from which it was born, under the pale skies of winter!

White mists floating lightly in the blazing of the deep zenith, now left for other horizons, purple and fringed with gold, like the remnants of an imperial coat scattered by the capricious blowing of the breeze.

And still, during all these metamorphoses, during all this extravagant spectacle of things, not a being, not a sound.

The narrow alleyways, with their abandoned houses, opened up, deserted, onto the immensity of the vaguely perceptible cemeteries on fire, without walls, limitless.

Yet the purple tint of the sky, seemingly reflected in the chaos of the dunes, became darker and darker, more and more fantastic.

The huge disk of the sun, red and rayless, finished sinking behind the low dunes on the western horizon, in the direction of Allendaoui and Araïr.

All of a sudden, long processions of women emerged, emanating from all the lifeless alleys, veiled in the old style in blue and red rags and carrying large terracotta jugs on their heads or on one shoulder . . . with the same statuesque gesture that the women of the predestined race of Shem must have had when they fetched water at the wells of Cannaan thousands of years before.

In the limitless ocean of red light flooding the town and cemeteries, they resembled ghosts floating along the ground, women draped in dark cloth with Hellenic folds, moving silently toward the deep gardens hidden in the fiery dunes.

Very far away, a small reed flute began crying its infinite sadness, and its high plaintive song, modulating yet lingering and broken as a sob, was the only sound that animated, just a little, this city of dreams.

But now the sun disappeared, and almost immediately the flaming of the dunes around the cupolas began to slowly turn the dark violet color of the sea, and these deep shadows seemed to emerge from the darkened earth, climbing, extinguishing the lights, illuminating the summits one after another.

The small enchanted flute fell silent . . .

Suddenly, from all the numerous mosques, another voice rises, solemn and slow:

"*Allahou Akbar! Allahou Akbar! God is great!*" proclaims the muezzin to the four winds of the sky.

Oh! How they resound strangely, these thousand-year-old calls of Islam, as if distorted and darkened by the most wild and raucous voices, by the drawling accent of the desert muezzins!

From all the dunes and all the seemingly deserted small hidden valleys, a whole populace, silent and serious, dressed uniformly in white, descends toward the zaouïya and the mosques.

Here, far from the large cities of the Tell, there are none of these hideous creatures, bastard products of degeneracy and of a mixed race formed by the prowlers, the traveling merchants, the porters, and the filthy and ignoble people of the Ouled-el-Blassa.

Here, the bitter and silent Sahara with its eternal melancholy, its terrors and enchantments has jealously conserved the dreamy and fanatic race that came long ago from the distant deserts of its Asiatic homeland.

And they are very tall and beautiful in this way, the nomads with their biblical attitudes and clothing, who go pray to the one God, and whose healthy, simple souls are never touched by doubt.

And they are very much at home there in the empty grandeur of their unlimited horizon, where the splendid sovereign light reigns and lives . . .

The last violet light has gone out on the white minaret of Sidi Salem, on the crest of the dunes of Treffia, Allendaoui, and Debila. Now everything is uniformly blue, almost diaphanous, and the low rounded cupolas blend in with the rounded summits of the dunes, gradually, as if the city had suddenly spread all the way to the distant limits of the horizon.

The night sky finishes descending onto the sleepy earth . . . The women, in their clothing from days of old, have returned to the small ruined streets, and the great heavy silence, interrupted for a very short moment by a few human murmurs, descends once again on El Oued . . .

The immense Sahara seems to begin again its melancholy dream, its eternal dream.

Two years later, I would have the privilege of watching each day for months on end the sweet joys of the auroras and the apotheoses of the evenings, none of which are ever the same . . . Each reflection returning every night on some section of a wall, each shadow lengthening in the same place and at the same hour, each dome of the city and each stone in the cemeteries—all the most humble details of this chosen country, profoundly loved, became familiar to me and now remain present in my exile as nostalgic memories.

But never again did the land of desert sands reveal itself to me as deeply, as mysteriously, as on that first evening, already far off in the passing of the days.

Such hours, such exhilaration, felt only once, by exceptional luck, will never be found again . . .

Note

Au pays des sables appeared for the first time as a small volume with a circulation of 138 copies, edited by Chloë Bulliod (Bône [Annaba]: Imprimerie Thomas, at the end of 1914).

It was republished on April 8, 1915, in *Akhbar*; in 1944 by René-Louis Doyon, with Sorlot; and in 1986 in *Yasmina, et autres nouvelles algériennes* (*Yasmina, and Other Algerian Tales*) by Editions Liana Levi.

At the time of this first voyage, Eberhardt stays in El Oued only three days, but her decision is made: she will return to live there, which is what she does one year later. In the meantime, she begins once again her incessant trips back and forth and continues writing her notes.

Notes from August 6 to September 9, 1899

The sixth, seven o'clock in the evening, left, with Lieutenant Toulat and Major Mauriez, for Guémar. Convoy of Brigadier Belkacem ben Hadj Amar. Spahis, Belkacem ben Ahmed, Chaambi (etc.), nine camels, one méhari.

Spent night in the bled. The seventh, diffa and a rest in Guémar. Night in bordj, evening at Ouled Naïl performance at cheikh's house. Visit with cadi morning of the eighth.

The ninth, five-thirty in the evening, departure, major for El Oued and we for the North. Spent night in bled the tenth. Left three thirty, arrived about ten in the morning in Bir Bou Chama. Brigadier Belkacem lost his horse to sunstroke. A rest in Bir Bou Chama. Left again at the moghreb, arrived around midnight in Sif El Kenerdi. Spent night in bled.

The eleventh, left three thirty in the morning. Arrived about noon in Stah-Meraya. Took a rest. Left at moghreb. Wandered far from the convoy, which left first. Lieutenant, Soufi guide, and me. Found the convoy again in the bled at about two in the morning. Left again at four o'clock. Ten o'clock, rest at the moghreb in M'guebrah.

In Bir Bou Chama, entered the Chott Melghir. No potable water until Stah-Meraya. Turbid and putrid water. The Arabs in the bordj go to Guémar (seventy-five kilometers) to get their water. In M'guebrah, left Chott Melghir, bordj, and very well-kept garden.

Long prior to departing M'guebrah, in the absence of lieutenant and Brigadier Belkacem, battle in the bordj. Had a lot of trouble calming the spahis who wanted to massacre the bordj's inhabitants.

Since Sif and Menedi, violent fever. Between M'guebrah, left about eight o'clock, and Chegga, fit of delirium and driftings. Arrived in Chegga [. . .] in the morning, August 13.

Spent all day and night sick. Left at noon, me in the ammunition wagon of the equipment train. Left the train soldiers about three o'clock. Slept in bled near Djefaïr. Left again morning (sunrise). We arrived seven o'clock in Bordj Saada. Took a rest. Sent Hama Srir to Biskra to get some ice. Spent the night. The sixteenth, spent all day in Bordj Saada. Hama Srir back about noon. Left Bordj Saada the sixteenth at midnight. Arrived in Biskra August 17 five in the morning. The eighteenth, convoy's departure for El Oued. Adieu to diffa at the cadi's house.

The nineteenth, five o'clock departure for Batna with the lieutenant. Arrived ten in the morning. Dinner at Continental Hotel with Letord. The twenty-first, lieutenant's departure for Constantine. The twenty-second, left for Djebel Aurès at three in the morning with Taïeb ben Mohammed and deïra Hossine.

Night in the Oued-Hamla the twenty-third. A rest with forester Hammoud in Oued Azrag. Night at Hammoud's. The twenty-fourth, took a rest in Ouled Ahdi, at foot of the *djebel*. The twenty-fifth, entry into Ouled Soltan territory. The second, climbed Djebel-Zouggoun.

Night in cedar forest. The twenty-seventh, descent into Barika. No rest. Returned to Kenchela in the evening. Night in *fondouck*. Return to Batna. The twenty-eighth, ten at night, found Augustine's telegram. The twenty-ninth, left by train at ten o'clock. Arrived in Bône at ten thirty. Spent night at Orient Hotel. Visit to Muslim cemetery at midnight with driver Aly. Found Ahmed again the thirtieth. Visit to Sidi Brahim and Ras el Hamra. Evening arrival of Augustine and Hélène at seven thirty. Spent day in Bône September 1. Walk with Sidi Lakhdar in Oued Dhed. Trip with Ahmed and Dédale to *koubba* Miremondo (?).

September 2, nine-thirty train. Arrival in Tunis eleven thirty at night. Night in Paris Hotel. Morning of the third, eight o'clock, at Aly's, reconciled. Evening, trip to La Goulette.

The seventh, noon departure for Marseille aboard the *Eugène-Pereire* with Ahmed. Arrival the eighth at eight o'clock in the evening. The ninth, left again for Sousse at noon, *Général-Chanzy*.

An Autumn in the Tunisian Sahel

I had just gone through one of those moral crises that leave the soul exhausted as if turned in on itself, for a long time incapable of perceiving pleasant impressions, sensitive only to pain . . .

And yet, of all the voyages that I have made, that in the Tunisian Sahel was probably the calmest.

I was hardly settled into the Sousse train when I felt a remarkable sensation of sudden relief . . . And it was with the great joy of departing that I left Tunis.

The train leaves slowly, lazily stopping again and again in pretty and verdant stations. Maxula-Rhadès first, still close by, with its small white houses on the shore pounded by the waves from the open sea, whereas toward the northeast the calm mirror of the lake shines. Then the holiday resort of rich Muslims: Hammam-el-Lif.

Farther on, the rails move into the countryside, getting farther from the coast.

Here I joyfully find once more the familiar features of Bedouin lands: reddish hills, fields left all golden with stubble by Arab harvesters, gray pastures with their herds and nomad herders . . . Here and there, the immobile and strange silhouette of a camel . . . Sometimes, on a small iron bridge, the train crosses some unknown oued dried out by the summer and invaded by oleanders studded with flowers.

But after Bir-bou-Rekba, the track once again approaches the ocean, calm and violet, which we can see very high up in the implacable noon sky. On both sides, there are intensely green prairies and small olive groves, stripped of the summer's dusty shroud by autumn's first rains.

The lower coast is carved into graceful coves, into lacy tender green headlands set against the still, lilac sky of the Hammamet gulf. Here and there, a small fishing village nestled on a headland or at the bottom of a cove—all milky white under a coat of immaculate whitewash and topped by a small minaret—is reflected in the deep water.

Peaceful and sweet aspects of an ageless country enjoying eternal calmness and prosperity . . . and where it would be difficult to determine where one is on the globe, if at each level crossing one didn't notice the Bedouins, immobile on the bony horses and enfolded in their heavy *sefseri*, which in Tunisia replace, for the people, the Algerians' burnoose . . . Dry, tanned faces, often beardless, a classic example of a conspicuously Berber race . . . Indifferent eyes, somber for the most part.

Since Bou-Ficha, we've entered the immense olive groves that cover the Tunisian Sahel.

In the hot silent night, after Menzel-Dar-bel-Ouar, an aromatic but also heavy and nauseating odor begins to drift toward us from the sleepy countryside: we're approaching Sousse's numerous olive oil presses.

I was going there knowing no one, without a goal, without haste, moreover, without a fixed itinerary . . . My soul was calm and open to all the beloved sensations felt upon arriving in a new country.

Sousse, an Arab town, winding and charming, set in tiers on a high hill, still enclosed by a crenellated and snowy-white Saracen wall. On the slope of the hill, beyond the ramparts, immense cemeteries are surrounded by hedges of Barbary fig, burned and yellowed by the sun. Higher still are the red roofs and long, low buildings of the infantrymen's camp.

Sousse is pretty. In times past, it was called El-Djohra, "the pearl." Now it is called Souça, "the silk worm."

From Sousse to Monastir, the road descends toward the sea and runs alongside gardens and dilapidated Italian houses. Then it enters a deserted and dismal countryside made up of infertile fields cut into small, salty, and completely white sebkha.

For the first time, this desolate region appeared to me under a low sky full of clouds . . . and it spread out, bluish and sinister at nightfall one autumn . . .

But soon the gardens begin again, and we pass between forests of olive trees sheltering drinking troughs where the little Bedouin girls bring their herds and their unruly horses every night.

However, Monastir remains a unique city with a peculiar charm and sadness.

Set back a little from the sea, like all Arab cities of the lower coasts, built on a salty piece of land covered with saltpeter, Monastir resembles the melancholy Saharan oases with its grayish one-story houses and its unpaved roads, and it would be at home on the edge of some chott in the strange Oued Rir'...

But the coast is lined with breakwaters, and one hears the sea roaring incessantly around the raised promontory of the Kahlia separating the old city from the small modern port . . . It seems that I still hear it, after years, this eternal murmur, this deep, sweet moan, so much did its music charm me then during my solitary nocturnal outings and my long reveries by the shore.

The Monastirians no longer resemble the effeminate citizens of Tunis and Sousse, who are graceful, polished, and affable but have nothing left of the fierce majesty of the true Arab race, born to dream and to do battle.

Like Sousse, Monastir occupies the bottom of a large bay with rounded and gracious contours open to the Orient.

From Monastir to Kasr-Hellel, the road again follows the coast through harvested fields and olive groves.

In the morning, when the sun is emerging from the high purple sea, at the hour when all becomes iridescent and golden, one sees a population of fishermen descend into the shallow water, fully dressed, and go far off toward the middle of the bay, with baskets, nets, and very primitive fishing tools.

The indistinct, very often calm horizon is populated with an infinite number of small Roman sails, pink or purple in the reflection of the setting sun; these are the small fishing boats and tartans returning sometimes from very far away, from Sfax or Zarzis.

Kasr-Hellel . . . a village shrouded by whitewash between the blue sea and the dark woods of olive trees. Above the flat terraces and small domes, a white minaret stands out; and just next door, a large, solitary date tree, one of a kind, leans over in melancholy fashion . . . Every evening, the white houses of Kasr-Hellel turn purple and seem to be on fire, whereas the palm tree and the minaret appear to be haloed by red gold, very high up in the fiery sky.

Behind a rounded headland, the small fishing village Seyada forms a cluster across from the Kouriatine Islands, whose lighthouse shines on the horizon at night, with the immobile red light of Monastir and the turning lighthouse from Sousse, very far away, hardly visible, and only during those hours when the sea is very calm.

Seyada is lost in the middle of olive trees, cut across by cactus hedges bristling with spines, impenetrable except by jackals and Bedouin prowlers.

The girls of Seyada are renowned in all the Sahel for their beauty, and the young men from Moknine enjoy saying of their likeable neighbors, "He who once breathes in the salty sea air of Seyada, and the heady perfume of its girls, will forget his native soil."

Set in a fertile valley, Moknine is rather far from the sea. It's a small coquettish city of commerce, very Arab. There again, I rediscover the whitewashed corners, walls in ruin, sandy rocks, and heavy silences, which remind me of the beloved oases of the Saharan homeland.

In these cities of the Tunisian interior, the country people and the commoners don't wear the majestic burnoose, a ragged yet patrician toga, in which the poorest Algerian drapes himself.

The poor and the Bedouin wrap themselves in the white or black sefseri, a long piece of wool, one section of which they usually throw back onto their small turban; and by moonlight this drape gives them, in the solitary streets and the public squares, a fantastic look of ghosts still rolled in the *kefenn* of the tomb . . . The Bedouin and poor city women, here as elsewhere, put on the same dark blue or red veils, wear the same complicated and heavy structure of black hair, of braided wool, jewelry and silk handkerchiefs, the same loose belt, knotted very low, almost on their hips.

I spent some of my diffuse, delicious, and Oriental hours in Moknine—dream hours, in ancient surroundings, to the sound of instruments and songs from times past . . .

All of these villages of the Sahel are adorably pretty, as white as pearls in the dark velvety setting of the olive trees . . . Everything in them is pleasing, even their sonorous names: Ouardénine (the two roses), Souïssa (little Sousse), Menzel-bir-Taïeb (the village with the good well), Oued-Saya, Djemmal, Sidi-el-Hani, El-Djemm, Beni-Hassène . . .

The beauty of the countryside is unique on the fierce and splendid earth of Africa: everything here is soft and luminous, and even the melancholy of the horizons is neither menacing nor desolate, like everywhere else. The air of the Sahel is vivifying and pure, its sky is incomparably clear.

Beyond Moknine, the earth rises up and a wild, strange country begins, where the olive forests are sometimes cut across by large, desolate plateaus. This is Amira territory.

The inhabitants, farmers or shepherds, are feared in all the country, for they are reputed to be pillagers and fighters.

⁂

It was there, down on the eastern coast of Tunisia, in the deep olive groves of the Sahel, in autumn.

In male clothing and a borrowed personality, I was camping at that time in the *douar* of the Monastir *caïdat* in the company of Si Elarhby, khalifa.[1] The young man never suspected that I was a woman. He called me his brother Mahmoud, and for two months I shared his wandering life and his work.

We were busy, very reluctantly levying overdue payment of the *medjba*, the poll tax paid by Muslim males in Tunisia.

Everywhere among the gloomy, unruly, and poor tribes, the welcome was hostile. The spahis' red burnooses and the deïras' blue burnooses alone impressed the starving hordes . . . Si Larbi's good heart felt a pang of anguish, and we were ashamed of what we were doing—he out of duty, and I out of curiosity—like being ashamed of a bad deed.

---

1. Translator's note: A caïdat refers to an area under the caïd's jurisdiction.

However, I did spend some charming hours there . . . Certain names in this country evoke in me innumerable memories.

Leaving Moknine, separated from the olive groves by *hendi*—Barbary fig hedges—the road takes off, dusty and straight, and the olive trees seem to follow it endlessly, undulating and silvery at the top, like ocean waves.

A crude little mosque, its early yellow color a reminder of the buildings in the South made of *toub*, a few houses in the same ocher color, some debris, a few tombs scattered here and there: this is Sid'Enn'eidja, the first hamlet in Amira.

In front of the mosque, a small courtyard invaded by wild grasses, and in the back, a sort of arched recess, next to which a fig tree spreads its large velvety leaves. And that's where the well is, deep and icy.

We set ourselves up on a mat. In order to proceed more quickly, Si Larbi asks me to help him: I will be the clerk.

The spahis and the deïra introduce the cheikh—a tall old man with the profile of an eagle and tawny eyes—and all the old men of the tribe accompanied by their tall, thin sons in their ragged sefseri. What a strange bunch of faces, burned by the sun and the wind, with savagely energetic expressions, their gaze somber and closed!

The cheikh provides long, complicated explanations in a whining tone. Around him, great shouts break out every moment with the sudden vehemence of this violent race that moves from silence and dreaming to tumult. All of them affirm their misery.

I call them off from a list, one by one.

"Mohammed ben Mohammed ben Dou'!"

"*An'am.*" ("Present.")

"How much do you owe?"

"Forty francs."

"Why don't you pay?"

"*Je suis rouge-nu Sidi.*" (Tunisian idiom meaning *fakir*, poor.)[2]

"You have neither a house nor a garden—nothing?"

2. Translator's note: *Je suis rouge-nu* literally means, "I am red naked," and indicates a state of poverty.

With a gesture of noble resignation, the Bedouin raises his hand.

"*Elhal-hal Allah!*" ("Fortune belongs to God!")

"Move to the left."

And most often, the man moves away, resigned, and sits down, his head lowered; eventually the spahis chain them: tomorrow one of the red horsemen will take them to Moknine, and from there to the Monastir prison, where they will work like slaves until they've paid up . . .

Those who admit to owning something—a poor small cottage, a hamlet, a few sheep—are left free, but the khalifa has the deïra seize this poor piece of property in order to sell it . . . And our hearts bleed painfully when women in tears bring the last goat, the last ewe, on which they lavish farewell caresses.

Then, dragging along with us a troop of mournful and resigned men in chains, on foot between our horses, we go farther . . .

Chrahel, which the literate call Ichrahil.

A few houses scattered between olive trees more lush than anywhere else . . . We set up our low, long nomad tent made of goat hair.

The spahis and the deïra bustle about in their brightly colored clothing, light the fire, go and commandeer the diffa, the welcoming supper offered unwillingly, alas!

At sunset Si Larbi, the spahi Ahmed, and I wander off into the village.

We find a young woman alone gathering Barbary figs.

Ahmed steps forward and says to her:

"Give us some figs, kitten! Take out the thorns so that we won't poke ourselves, oh beautiful one!" The Bedouin is very beautiful and very stern.

With her big black eyes, she gives us a hostile closed look.

"May God's curse be on you! You've come to take our belongings!"

And she violently empties her straw basket of figs at our feet and leaves.

With a feline smile, the red horseman reaches out his hand to grab her, but we stop him.

"Isn't it bad enough we arrest poor old people? Let's not add touching the women!" says the khalifa.

"Oh! Sidi, I wasn't trying to hurt her!"

And yet these men dressed in bright colors come from this same people whose misery they know, having shared it. But the spahi is no longer a Bedouin; and because he is a soldier, he truly believes himself superior to his tribal brothers.

We spend another quarter hour chatting with an incredibly small black fellow whom we met along the road, who makes us burst out laughing with surprise at his repartees and his simian intelligence.

Then, after supper, stretched out lazily on our rugs, we listen to the young men's choir of Chrahel.

The Sahel people are eminently musical, and the shepherds of these regions still compose in our times perfectly rhythmical songs, equally beautiful in their words and chanting.

Oh mother, mother, my friend! Since they carried you to the cemetery, nothing in this world smiles on me any longer . . . Sadness lives in my heart, and the tears flow from my eyes, now but bitter streams.

I listen again:

I covered my head with my burnoose, and I cried because of Djenetta. I told her, "Don't come with me because I might die next to you. And on that day, if you cry, people will say: So and so was the lover of so and so, or yet again . . . The one she loved has gone. He swore eternal love to her, but during the year he forgot her. And shame would be on you . . .

It is very close to midnight when we return to our tents.

❧ ☙

The night before, we had arrived in Zouazra, the territory of the tribe of the same name, and we had put up our large goat hair tent near Cheikh Si Amor's *gourbi*.

Zouazra is situated in the middle of a green plateau and surrounded by the olive gardens that give the Tunisian Sahel its opulent appearance.

Toward our left, about sixty meters away, the olive trees began. Across, to our right, the African plain stretched out; as soon as it is not at all cultivated, it reverts to its character of infinite sadness . . .

The night had been bad. The wind had blown like a tempest, furiously shaking our tent. It had rained; the frightened horses had neighed and struggled, trying to free their ankles from the long rope stretched along the ground.

The agitated dogs had wandered around in the douar, whining pitifully. The guards posted around our encampment confirmed that they'd seen suspicious shadows lurking around the edges of the gardens . . .

Wrapped in our thick *ihram*, we had suffered from the cold and damp. At dawn, we had gotten up chilled to the bone in very bad moods.

Si Elarby's servant, Ahmed, had ordered the people of the tribe to make a big fire in front of our tents. The damp wood lit badly, and the wind blew clouds of acrid smoke into our faces.

I moved a little ways from the tent and went wandering toward the side of the plain.

The clouds had broken up, and a peaceful and clear dawn was breaking. On the western horizon, the powerful olive tree branches stood out black against the rosy background of the clear sky. Toward the west, the stars paled in the still-deep shadows. The great autumnal peace of this country evoked sad and sweet memories, the same impressions, felt in times past, in the same season in Bône at a completely different point on this Barbary coast—my country of choice, which I love with all its sorrows and in all its moods.

I went back toward the tent.

The triumphant and dazzling sun had come up.

In the middle of the douar, women were busying themselves around a large fire preparing our first meal.

The sick khalifa had lain down in front of our tent and was smoking, lazily letting himself be warmed again by the sun.

The three *makhzen* horsemen, the servant, and the mule handlers had begun playing cards.

I felt the delicious sensation of liberty, peace, and well-being, which for me always accompanies waking up in the middle of familiar scenes of nomadic life.

While we were impatiently waiting for the meal, we saw a young Bedouin horseman arrive quite suddenly, mounted on a white horse with neither saddle nor bridle. The man, his ihram blown back by the wind, was clinging to the long mane of the excited animal, was kicking its sides with his naked feet and crying out mournfully a sort of monotonous and continuous lamentation.

When he was closer, we realized that he was crying out:

"My brother is dead! My brother is dead!"

Instead of explaining to us what he wanted, he let himself fall to the ground at the hooves of his horse, where he rolled, twisting his hands together and continuing to cry out to us that his brother was dead . . .

Amira

During the night, a stormy wind chased away the swirls of rain, soaking the vast clay plain where we were camping, the barren fields, and
the thick olive groves cut into here and there by hedges of Barbary fig.

Our poor nomad tents, wet and heavy, seem like huge frightened
beasts flattened onto the red earth.

The colorless, sad autumn dawn breaks on this completely changed
African countryside, as if deformed by the cold mists floating on the
horizon.

Chilled to the bone and feeling morose, we sit quietly around a large,
pale, smoky fire and wait for the coffee that will give us back a bit of
strength and warmth.

It is one of those slow gray hours when the soul seems to fold in on
itself and feels, with painful and mournful intensity, the ultimate futil-
ity of human effort.

By random chance in my wanderer's life, I've been camping for two
months among the unruly tribes of these highlands of Amira, which
look down on the fertile prairies and the shady woods of the smiling
Sahel.

Having promised to a newspaper an account of my travel experiences in this country, I joined a small caravan charged by the Tunisian
authorities to make brief inquiries and to gather the Arab taxes, always
in arrears.

There is the small khalifa of the caïd of Monastir—a Moor from Tunis
who is thin, slightly built, very self-effacing, relatively just, not at all
cruel, and moreover not too greedy—and two elderly Arab notaries,
set in their ways, very sweet, very caring and smiling. Then, Ahmed,
the spahi brigadier from Oran, a singular mix of youthful grace, of often
wild violence, of nonchalance, and of profound reflection, much more

than his social status would suggest . . . Finally, Bedouins in red or blue burnooses, who are the spahis and the deïra of the makhzen.

For two months, I have been a spectator of what these people do, people whom I've only known since I've been wandering with them, living their life, who know nothing about me . . . For them, I am Si Mahmoud Saâdi, the little Turk who escaped from French secondary school . . .

And my notebook has remained so empty, in spite of some remorse, some vague desire to write . . . Once again the Bedouin life—easy, free, soothing—has taken me in order to intoxicate and subdue me. Write . . . Why?

While I'm dreaming, almost bored, about all these things in my current life, all of a sudden someone comes and gets us to go over there to the end of the plain in order to calm down a tribe who wants to go massacre someone else in another tribe in order to avenge the death of one of its own . . .

We have to abandon everything, leaving the campsite guarded by a deïra who will take care of transportation for this evening, and depart with the cheikh's envoy.

A frenzied race through thickets over the soft and slippery earth. We jump over ditches and Barbary fig hedges on horses who no longer want to obey, so unnerved are they by the wind and the rain.

But here already is the douar of the Hadjedj—about a hundred gourbi and low tents on a rounded hill, a site that is frightfully barren, not a tree, not a blade of grass . . .

An unusual commotion reigns in the douar, and from very far away we hear an angry clamor.

In between the tents, men in black or earthen-colored haïks blown about by the wind are carrying on, violently arguing in groups, while others, kneeling, polish and load old flint rifles, sharpen wooden-handled sabers, daggers, and scythes. In the middle of the douar, the women, wrapped in blue or red veils, are mourning around a black haïk, all sticky with blood, covering a corpse.

The men shout out death threats; and as in the times of ancestral migrations, they are preparing to go massacre and pillage the Zerrath-

Zarzour tribe, camped toward the west, beyond a ravine about one kilometer wide and deep as an abyss.

The young cheikh Aly, with magnificent energy and emotion, comes to meet us, a rifle in hand, and explains to us what is happening.

"This morning, a boy named Aly ben Hafidh, from the Zerrath-Zarzour tribe, came here with his brother Mohammed to sell two ewes to my khodja here. They met one of our tribe, Hamza ben Barek, whose family they've had problems with for a long time. All three were up there on that small hill outside of the douar. They got into a quarrel, and Aly ben Hafidh hit Hamza with a club, smashing his skull . . . Here's the corpse. The whole tribe and shepherds from the Melloul tribe saw the crime. But Aly and his brother fled into the ravine. In order to exact vengeance, now our family members want to go massacre the Zerrath-Zarzour tribe."

While the cheikh is talking to us, the men come closer and a great silence reigns over the douar, troubled only by the women's lamentations. The nomads stand and listen, their eyes menacing and firm, holding their weapons . . . The cheikh has hardly finished his words when the wild clamor bursts out again.

The gestures and cries are extraordinarily violent, and the angular faces of the skinny Hadjedj become frightening. Once again Cheikh Aly jumps toward them with exhortations and threats . . . I hear a tall old man with the profile of a bird of prey who answers him almost disdainfully:

"You're young, you don't know! It's the price of blood."

And suddenly the nomads break up, running, trying to reach the ravine.

But then the spahis and the deïra leave in all directions, also yelling loudly; they're happy, the nomads dressed as soldiers, happy to gallop, yell, and pursue, as if at war, these armed men who at any moment can turn on them and become menacing because they outnumber them . . . They're carried away by this manhunt, and their faces shine with the joy of unruly children, running free.

The tumultuous scene, under the low gray sky, in the furious wind, is wild and magnificent.

Finally the tribe is contained, pushed back into the douar, and kept under guard. Two or three of the most frenzied men are caught and chained. Now the search must begin, and two spahis leave to go look for the assassin.

This Aly ben Hafidh who is brought to us, panting, in a rage, his face covered in sweat and mud, his hands bound behind his back, is very young. He is pale, but the look from beneath his long reddish eyes is wild. His brother, a large skinny Bedouin with the dark face of a bandit, looks like a wild animal caught in a trap, ready to bound away . . .

However, he has not killed. It's Aly, the little nomad with golden eyes and a beardless face.

Aly ben Hafidh replies in monosyllables to the usual questions about his identity.

"Why did you kill Hamza ben Barek?" asks the khalifa.

Then the accused seems to gather himself together for a desperate defense. He hangs his head and looks at the ground:

"Between him and me, God's Prophet is the witness!"

Henceforth, as if in a dream, contradicting all common sense, against all evidence, he repeats his sentence, his pathetic sentence of childish denial, a sentence both frightened and obstinate.

He committed his crime on the open summit of the hill; about fifty people saw him. He fled and hid in a ravine with his brother. His declarations contradict those of his brother, who was interrogated in his absence . . . What does it matter? To all entreaties, threats, and prayer, he answers, in a lifeless voice, his eyes obstinately staring at the ground:

"Between him and me, God's Prophet is the witness!"

For three days we stay with the Hadjedj. Three days of discussion, yelling, threats, continuous alerts . . . Finally, when order and peace seem to be reestablished, we head off again on the road for Moknine, the capital of Amira.

The good weather is back. It's almost hot, and bushes of slender grass are sprouting all over out of the red clay, enriched by the rains.

It is still morning, the clear hour when the countryside stretches out, completely blue, under the seemingly enlarged infinitely pure and pale pink sky.

Our small caravan moves forward slowly, in spite of the enthusiasm of the joyful horses; we're dragging along with us a silent and mournful troop of twenty-five or thirty prisoners, arrested here and there among the tribes. Resigned, with neither a gesture nor a word of revolt, they walk, chained together two by two at the wrist and the ankle. They seem indifferent.

Aly, the only killer, has his arms tied behind his back, and his feet are shackled. He walks separately from the group between the spahis' horses. His impenetrable attitude doesn't change; and when, from afar, the Bedouins from his tribe manage to yell a few words of adieu to him, he answers again in a firm voice, as if it were true:

"Between him and me, God's Prophet is the witness!"

Calmed down now, the Hadjedj silently watch him go by, almost without hate, for he is in the hands of a human justice that the nomads, like all simple men, fear instinctively and dislike, for this justice is foreign to their ways and their ideas. For them, Aly is no longer the enemy whom they have the right to kill for the price of blood: he is a prisoner, that is to say, an object of pity, almost a victim of that feared and hated phantom: Authority. Now the hatred and revenge of the Hadjedj would rather more likely fall on the entire Zerrath-Zarzour tribe than on Aly, if they had the power to harm him.

All of a sudden, a group of women emerges from out of a ravine hidden by Barbary fig trees and hurtles toward us, moaning and lamenting. The oldest, led by a very beautiful little girl with burning black eyes, is blind. Her white hair falls on her mummy-like forehead. She weeps.

Still guided by the little girl, the old woman hangs onto the khalifa's stirrup and begs him:

"Sidi, Sidi, for the peace of your mother's soul, have pity on my only son, my Aly! Have pity, Sidi!"

Our convoy has stopped, and all the men look serious. We feel pangs of anguish in the face of the old blind woman in rags whom we are powerless to console.

The khalifa, almost in tears, stammers promises that he won't be able to keep, and Aly's mother pours forth her blessings. Then she falls on her son's chest and moans as if over a corpse.

Looking very pale, the little Bedouin trembles from head to foot.

"Your father is in bed in the gourbi," says the old woman, "and he is sick, very sick. His hour has undoubtedly come. He wants you to admit if you've killed so that God will have pity on us and on you and so that the Ouzara will not be completely without pity . . ."[1]

Then, all of a sudden, Aly begins crying convulsively, and his young face becomes completely childlike. He whispers very low:

"Forgive me, Muslims! I have killed a fellow creature."

Among the horsemen and Bedouins who had approached him, joyful words are repeated:

"He confessed! He confessed!"

It's like a watershed moment, and Aly immediately becomes for all these people an object of more profound pity, almost of concern. Brigadier Ahmed, a very harsh man, nevertheless leans toward Aly and undoes his hands.

"Kiss the old woman," he says.

Then there are farewells interrupted by sobs, cries, and the women's moans. After that the weeping group moves away, but for a long time still we hear the old mother tearing at her face with mournful cries.

The brigadier allows the Zerrath-Zarzour to approach Aly, bid him farewell, and give him a few copper coins for his food in prison . . . Among those who give alms to the prisoner, I recognize two or three old people of the Hadjedj, from among the same people who, the night before, tried to massacre Aly and his relatives.

"Here, we give this to you in the path of God!" they say. Then they move away, looking serious, almost solemn.

Soon the brigadier has to push everyone away, for the Ouled-Zerrath-Zarzour crowd is dense and the situation could become dangerous . . . So once again we take the road to Moknine, through olive trees where the dew drops make us shiver.

1. Eberhardt's note: The Ouzara Tribunal refers to the Muslim criminal court in Tunis. The crime of willful murder carries with it death by hanging.

Note

Written from September to October 1899 in Monastir, this collection of texts comes from a notebook entitled "An Autumn in the Tunisian Sahel." Barrucand slightly modified it in *Notes de route* (Fasquelle, 1908), then in *Akhbar* (April 25, 1915).

Eberhardt wrote other notes on this trip: "Souvenirs du Sahel tunisien" ("Memories of the Tunisian Sahel"), an article that went unpublished until April 15, 1915 (*Akhbar*), and a text without a title (more directly polemical and thus rare in her writing) of which we found the first two pages.

Memories of the Tunisian Sahel

The Tunisian Sahel is an immense, elevated, and fertile plateau with abundant springs and wells, much healthier than the rest of Tunisia and enjoying, especially next to the sea, a cooler climate. However, in all the Sahel there is but one river, a meager African stream named Oued Zeroud, which has its source in the elevated area of Tebessa in Algeria, crosses the entire width of Tunisia, and shoots into She-Dog Lake near Sousse.

The main cities are Hammamet, which gave its name to the gulf that bathes the Sahelian coast; Kairouan, a holy city in the history of the Muslim Conquest where magnificent rugs are made; Sousse; Monastir; Moknine; El Djem; and Sfax.

All of these latter cities are inhabited by farmers and producers of olive oils. The oils from Sousse, and especially Monastir, are very much sought after.

In Sousse and Monastir there are still large indigenous tuna fisheries.

Here and there in the Sahel, in the middle of the plain, are hills topped by plateaus. Seen from these heights, the country presents itself as an uninterrupted forest of magnificent and powerful olive trees, divided into gardens by hedges of Barbary fig trees.

Even in the summer, the Sahel's air is limpid and pure. Great northern and eastern winds come, dissipating the heat somewhat.

In Kalaâ-Srira, the last station before Sousse, the tracks—which to this point had climbed to the heights of the Sahel—descend abruptly at a steep angle toward Sousse, constructed like cities of the Orient on the slope of a hill in the middle of deep olive groves.

As soon as I approach the train station situated almost outside of the city, a strong odor of macerated olives reaches me, an aromatic and sickly smell that eventually fatigues and nauseates.

As I do everywhere in Muslim country, I arrive wearing the Arab costume, the opulent costume of Tunisian city dwellers.

No one in Sousse knows my true personality, not even the only friend that I have here, the lieutenant of the indigenous infantrymen, Abd el Halim Elrarby.

Lieutenant Elrarby, although a child of the people, is an educated and distinguished man known in all the regency for his energetic and even violent personality.

A few years ago, Elrarby, then a sergeant (all the indigenous officers come from the ranks), killed an individual—armed with a revolver and backed up by half a dozen other brigands—who was attacking him, stabbing him straight through the heart . . . Thus Elrarby withstood and repulsed this attack in a *café chantant* in Tunis.[1] After four months of being held in custody—the sergeant had acted in legitimate self-defense—the charges were dismissed . . . This adventure earned him respect and fear, not only on the part of the Muslims, but also on the part of the French.

He is not liked by the European leaders, who—knowing him to be *a whipping boy*, as they say in the regiment—have to deal with him.

Abd el Halim is waiting for me there on the train platform.

"Welcome, Sidi Mahmoud," he says to me; and according to Muslim custom, we embrace . . . How far he is from realizing I'm a woman!

I'm staying in the Sahel hotel situated in the European part of the city, built between the old Moorish walls and the sandy beach . . .

After a rapidly consumed communal dinner in the dining room full of French officers, with whom Abd el Halim exchanges only the usual cold salutation, we go up to the third floor.

My room looks out onto a vast tiled terrace, from where one can see the ocean on one side, and on the other, the immaculate walls of the indigenous city rising up like an amphitheater . . .

In Arab fashion, we put a blanket and pillows on the floor and stretch out.

Abd el Halim is quiet by nature. We smoke and we give ourselves over to sweet Arab dreaming, close to a slightly melancholy half slumber.

---

1. Translator's note: *Café chantant* ("singing café") refers to one of the nineteenth-century cafés in Tunis that presented original Tunisian songs and Arab musical masterpieces.

At first, we're plunged into shadow . . . We see only the city lights. Toward the southeast, far off among the stars, the Monastir fixed-beacon lighthouse appears, situated on the headland facing Sousse; then, even farther, toward the east, that of the Koudiati Islands.

But over there to the east, toward the high sea, a faint light starts to peek through, a sort of pale and discreet dawn . . .

It is the full moon that soon appears as if emerging from the waters.

Then the barely furrowed surface of the sea first takes on silvery reflections, then rose, an incredible golden rose color. Against the background of the black abyss, it oscillates, vibrates, like a delicate animated metallic web, slowly moved by a powerful breath.

The moon rises, rises, inundating the sky and the sea with opaline glimmers.

The stars pale and seem to go out.

And then the white phantom of Sousse bursts forth from the shadow, bluish, almost translucent . . .

Its minarets, its towers, and its crenellated walls seem like white arabesques outlined in bluish white on the still-dark western sky.

In the distance, military bugles shout out the clear and vibrant note of the roll call . . .

Then everything falls silent once more.

"I don't know," Abd el Halim says to me, "where my soul takes flight to at such moments. I don't know what I irresistibly aspire to, what my heart sighs for . . . I would like to be far away in unknown countries."

I, too, would like to escape to those faraway regions of the charming and mysterious unknown, sensed by the dreamy soul of this son of a nomadic race, a race of shepherds and improvisational rhapsodists.

I, too, would like to leave the earth's monotonous and sad life during these blessed hours when Nature reveals to us its most intoxicating splendors.

Abd el Halim received instruction in French. He was in a secondary school; he has read European books . . . But the harsh life of the camps that takes him far from the tainted milieu of the big coastal cities has saved him from the premature decay to which all Europeanized Muslims seem condemned.

He has kept the poetic and dreamy frame of mind, the taste for the supernatural and the mysterious, which characterizes the true Arab soul.

His company will be precious to me if I stay here for a long time . . . which, moreover, is quite unlikely.

"Tomorrow," he says to me, "come and eat with me in the infantry-men's camp there all the way up beyond the Muslim cemeteries. You'll see how I live!"

For the Arab, however poor he may be, hospitality is not a religious duty grudgingly fulfilled—it is a faith, an honor—and the arrival of a guest is always considered to be a happy event.

We take leave of one another at midnight.

As always, in a new city, a flow of thoughts, memories, and visions overcomes me, and sleep only comes very late, toward dawn, when the muezzin from the closest mosque has long ago finished his call to prayer.

In the course of my peregrinations in Tunisia, I have noticed once again how truly hollow are the beautiful ringing phrases with which politics decks itself and excuses all its self-interested, egotistical intrigues.

In fact, don't we read clichés such as these each day? "The civilizing and pacifying work of France in Africa," "Civilization's benefits offered to the indigenous peoples of our colonies," etc., etc.

Incontestably, it is in such a manner that all of upright France assures itself of its mission in the countries it has conquered or protected, which, in fact, constitute the very same thing.

But alas, the majority of those whom the mother country sends far off, to be the instruments of the fruitful work of which she dreams, do not understand it in this way.

In Tunisia, in particular, the protectorate is nothing but a euphe-mism—one born, moreover, of absolute necessity—concealing a com-plete annexation.

Unfortunately, such is the power of a word sometimes that Tunisians have seriously suffered from the phantom of the bey's extant authority; all the civil servants unfaithful to their mission answer the reproaches made by public opinion:

"It's not we, it's the bey. We can do nothing without him."

Thus the bey Aly, an old man who has completely lapsed into senility, serves as a screen for men lacking conscience.

Aided by singular good fortune, I have been able to see how overdue taxes are collected and how judicial inquiries are made. Well, I declare that both are practiced in the most revolting and barbaric manner, and not occasionally but rather constantly, openly, and publicly, by the majority of French civil servants and the military charged with monitoring the indigenous civil servants.

Moreover, today in all the Tunisian caïdats, the vice-governors, or khalifa, are chosen from among the young men graduating from French schools, and they serve as a moral intermediary between the civil auditors, the officers of the Arab bureaus, and the caïd.

Thus, it isn't the still-repressed vestiges of the infamous Muslim "barbarity" that I intend to recount further on, but rather the results of orders, advice, and examples given from above by men who understand remarkably well their pacifying mission.

In Tunisia, far from the large centers, as in so many southern Algerian localities, the reign of the truncheon is at its peak.

The tribal cheikhs, subordinate to the caïd and their khalifas, are always chosen from among the richest, and therefore the most apt at furnishing opulent presents. In this manner, moreover, they compensate themselves by ferociously exploiting their citizens.

They are the ones who draw up the lists of taxpayers and inform the authorities of crimes and offenses committed in their tribes. There again, the most insolent favoritism and self-indulgence reign.

I have seen entire tribes of one of the Sahel caïdats unanimously complain about their cheikh, to whom they had paid the personal tax, the medjba (about twenty-two francs per male inhabitant fasting during the month of Ramadan), from which only the citizens of Tunis and Sousse are exempt.

Notes from Winter 1899 and Spring 1900

Left Marseille November 19, 1899, at nine forty-five. Express train. Arrived Paris the twentieth, Sunday, at nine thirty. Went by Louna's the twentieth, twenty-first, twenty-second, twenty-third, twenty-fourth, Thursday. Friday the twenty-fifth, Aly's arrival.

December 4, changed lodging: 71 Cardinal-Lemoine. The fourteenth, Bourguiba's arrival. Spent the night at Dacia Hotel. The fifteenth, night with A. and A. at my place. The sixteenth, definitive quarrel with Aly. Spent night at Darcourt Hotel, Saint Michel Boulevard. Evening of the seventeenth, left by express.

Arrived eighteenth in Marseille at three in the afternoon, spent following eleven days at Bauveau Hotel. Left at six in the morning the twenty-ninth for Gênes. We arrived the thirtieth, eleven o'clock in the morning. Spent day at Hotel Franca. Evening, left on board *Persia* for Livourne. Arrived thirty-first in morning.

Left at midnight. Arrived in Cagliari January 1, 1900. Albergo A. Moni until the seventh. Changed lodging fourteenth via Barcellona [*sic*], to Madame Vicenza.

The twenty-ninth of January, problems with passports. The thirtieth, visits to the French and Russian consulates (piazzetta Martini d'Italia).

May 1900. Monday the twenty-first, 11:08 express (French time), left Marseille, arrived Geneva Tuesday the twenty-second at noon. Went to Vernier cemetery. Went to Avauchets Wednesday. Friday the twenty-fifth, night (Véra, Anna, N. Martimian) in Coligny, returned one o'clock.

Monday twenty-eighth, train, seven-twenty departure. Tuesday twenty-ninth, five in the morning, arrival. Sunday, June 3, left Marseille by train (express 11:08), arrived Geneva Monday the fourth, noon.

Sunday, June 10, 1900, spent at Bois castle. Returned train eleven fifteen.

Onward to the Blue Horizons

Before me on the wall is a map of Bône that Khoudja sent to me in Cagliari, and on this map is a point that I noted, a point that awakens in me a poignant memory.

Native cemetery. Those two such simple words, pinned on this ordinary road map, have already given to me several times an internal shiver, which, for me, is one of the essential conditions of moral hygiene. And during these blessed instants, I see, rising before me, the beloved ghost of this Anèba (Bône) that made me dream for two years, down there, in the land of exile.

Thus, the great soul that I felt surging within me several times is certainly in a mysterious state of incubation; and if I wish, I can make it gloriously blossom one day.

Praise be to the suffering of the heart! Praise be to death, which nourishes souls plunged into mourning! Praise be to the silent tomb that is not only the door of eternity for those leaving but also the door for the chosen souls who know how to look into these mysterious depths! Praise be to sadness and melancholy, these divine sources of inspiration!

Begone, cowardly despair and guilty indifference! Begone, oblivion!

By what aberration have the consoling silhouettes of the two funerary hills of Annaba and Vernier been, able sometimes to erase themselves from my memory, become all but nonexistent? Why?

No, begone, the trial and error of my sickly adolescence! Begone, this sensual and crude spirit that is not part of me, that comes to me out of disorder and that is my ruin.

If one day the Geneva clouds dissipate, the horizon then perceived will be resplendent like those of bygone days, down there, at the first awakenings of my intelligence when I admired the melancholy setting suns beyond the high silhouette of the morose Jura while I attempted to discern the great mystery of my future.

Come to me, memories; I will not chase you away. Come awaken in me the sacred flame that one day must consume all my soul's impurities, and cause it to burst forth strong and beautiful, ready for eternity. Inchoate and remarkable dreams, dreams that resist interpretation, you are my entire reason for being in this world . . .

MARCH 29, 1900, SIX THIRTY IN THE EVENING

My soul is certainly in a state of waiting; the painful sensations of the present hour will not last; I will awaken from the dark reality of my current Parisian life!

Maybe in a month I'll leave for there, for the great unknowable desert, in order to seek out new sensations and materials that will expedite the work I would like to accomplish.

But my entire moral education needs to be reconfigured. I should take my inspiration from the great moving ideas of the past, and from the Islamic faith, which is the soul's peace.

At the end of everything, there is certainly silence and the tomb. But everything I strive for will serve to soften the episodes of this inexplicable drama called life, which one surely has to play.

MAY 2, 1900

Ten o'clock in the morning.

For days and weeks, the sun has been beaming and the sky has been blue. Paris has outfitted itself in radiant colors. Everything is beaming and everything seems to be celebrating. And I too have come out of the state of limbo where I had been wandering since my return from Cagliari. My soul is progressing. Little by little, slowly still, it is detaching itself from the earthly miasma that seemed to have drowned it. My soul is slowly but surely rising toward the spheres of the ideal, which it will one day reach.

Same day, midnight.

I've just returned here, to this room where I will sleep for the last time. It's my last evening in Paris. Ah! This Paris that I have begun to love profoundly, where I have suffered and hoped so much. God only knows if I will ever see it again, and if I return here, when that will be and what I will bring back and what I will find here again! I still feel the mark of the great unknown weighing on me . . .

MARSEILLE, MAY 7, 1900

I arrived here and by no means reexperienced the evil, menacing atmosphere that had so painfully weighed on my soul, during my last stay in Marseille, upon my return from Cagliari.

Felt in Mâcon, I believe, an intense sensation of times past, of the last years at the Villa Neuve in the springtime. The train was parking at the entrance to the station, where a great silence reigned. In front of me, to the right of the track, there were groves of lilacs just shy of blooming; the notes of the nightingale's last song of the night fell one by one. That was all. A flash of lightning, a passing dream, inconsequential; and yet such sensations can shake the very core of one's hidden and mysterious depths.

In a few days I will be in Bône; I will see again the tomb of the woman who, three long years ago, disembarked with me to this Barbary Coast. Everything in Africa seemed like a chimera to me then.

May the shadow that I weep for inspire in me the necessary strength, patience, and energy to see to the end the heavy duties that my former life has settled on me!

During these days, the anniversaries of April 1898 and May 1899, my saddened spirit also returns to the two gravesites that remain in the land of exile, the sole vestiges of the suffering, the miseries, and the hopes of times past, because the poor dear dwelling place will be sold to strangers in a few days, to indifferent profaning people . . . I cast my memory back to these two gravesites, which undoubtedly I will never see again, doubtless invaded by weeds this year with the return of spring, drunken with eternal life and indestructible fertility . . .

Under what sky and in what earth will I rest on the day predetermined by my destiny? Mystery ... and yet I would like my remains to be placed in the red earth of white Annaba's cemetery, where She sleeps ... or perhaps anywhere in the desert's burnt sand, far from the profane banality of the invading West ...

What childishly sad preoccupations, and how immature, how naive, in the face of death's great charm!

ELOUED, SEPTEMBER 1900

I remember my July departure from Marseille. It was evening. The day's light was lowering under the thick boughs of the silent boulevard's tall plane trees ...

Standing at the window under the cage of the noisy canary, whose song slowly faded with the approach of evening, I was observing without seeing.

Everything was finished, wrapped, tied up. There was nothing left but my cot, set up for the last night in the sitting room.

I didn't really believe in this departure for the South of Algeria. So many unforeseen circumstances had already delayed it! I had asked myself anxiously so many times whether this project that had become so dear to me was not perhaps destined to remain a simple yet forever-unachievable dream!

It wasn't long ago that I was anxiously putting that very question to myself ... And lo and behold, now that everything was ready and nothing more could hold me back, now a great sadness was invading my heart, overtaking it little by little, slowly, like the descent of the summer's balmy sunset.

Yet I was only a stranger passing through this city, in my brother's house, where for months I had made just abrupt and brief appearances, only to be immediately carried far away by the fortunes of my wandering life ...

That night my sleep was disturbed by strange, vague, and menacing visions ...

When I awoke, there was nothing more, it was over, and I arose with that sort of nervous energy peculiar to me on days of momentous departures ...

Something strange . . . the last months of my life in Europe, darker and more tormented, seemed to me to have already receded into an unfocused distance . . . The beloved silhouettes from over there were drawing closer . . .

I board the Eugène-Pereire thinking of the voyage I made last year on this vessel . . . but under very different circumstances. In the place of the anguish suffered then—I was struggling in sheer darkness—a deep melancholy peace has come, a numbing of the many painful sensations . . .

On the quay, amid all the noise and the jostling crowd, one silhouette alone catches my eye: in his proper black clothes, my brother, clearly dedicated to a calm and sedentary life, has come once again to see me off. I am leaving for the unknown. He is staying.

And separated already by the ship's railings, we look at each other, pondering the strangeness of our destinies, and also, alas! of the inanity of all human volition, of all the beautiful azure dreams we created together in times past, in the land of exile where we both opened our eyes to the bitter reality of being . . .

The hoarse, thudding rasp of the siren, guttural and harrowing, responds to the final ring of the bell . . .

The quay seems to slowly move away. Then a large eddy forms in the blue-green water, and our speed increases.

Soon, amid the congestion on the quay, the dear silhouette becomes nothing more than a black spot, and that soon disappears when the ship tacks in order to take the African route via the southern channel. Once again I am alone, and I am on my way . . .

Leaning on my elbows on the ship's rail on the afterdeck, I contemplate the magical scene of Marseille.

In the foreground, the Joliette port, where the powerful silhouettes of red and black transatlantic liners, innumerable barges, and small boats seem to doze among other companies' ships.

The morose, tall black houses on the quays, as symmetrical as army barracks, look mournful.

Then the city, shaped like an amphitheater, cut toward the middle by the gap of the old port and the Canebière.

At first, Marseille appears to me as a delicate range of grays with varied nuances: the grayness of a vaguely smoky sky; the bluish gray of the far-off mountains; grayish-pink roofs and yellow houses; the gray of Endoume's boulders, chalky gray; and the flaming gray of the steep hill of Notre-Dame-de-la-Garde; then all the way at the bottom, the lilac-and-silver gray of the forts. Over these shades of gray, the tough, dry plants on the rocks cast greenish-brown spots of color. Only the avenues' plane trees and the cathedral's golden cupola stand out in lively clear strokes against this gray transparency . . . And way up high, as if hovering above the smoke and clouds, gleams the golden Virgin . . .

Gradually, we turn to the left, and Marseille takes on a uniformly golden hue, so incredible . . . Marseille, the city of departures, of adieus and nostalgias, is incomparable today, drowned in an ocean of light, crowned with molten gold.

An hour later we pass the last chalky boulders, pallid and white, beaten eternally by the waves coming from the high sea . . . then it's over, everything crumbles at the horizon, everything disappears.

But I remain leaning on the bridge, dreaming with resigned melancholy, of the unfathomable mystery of unknown tomorrows and of the obscure ends of things without actual duration that surround and govern our destinies, yet more ephemeral and furtive . . .

Then, since some souls are only attached to the earth by virtue of exile, and since nostalgia is—for them—the dawn of a deeply felt love of places they've left behind, of a love even deeper because the hope of return is less, I sense that I am starting to love this city, especially its ports, and that its silhouette, such as it appeared to me today, will always surge forth among the cherished visions that haunt my wanderer's dreams, the reveries of a loner.

The breeze has abated, and a great silence has fallen upon the sea, while on the western horizon, in the far distance amid the sea's indistinctness, the chimerical shipwreck of the sun takes place in the purplish-gray vapors of summer evenings.

The sea has turned a dark, severe violet . . . After a few moments of a diffuse glow, imprecise and hesitant, the dark and soft night falls very quickly.

I go downstairs for the inescapable drudgery of the table d'hôte. A whole table full of proper people on couches and Voltaire chairs in an out-of-balance sitting room. Not a kind face, not an energetic, truly intelligent, or passionate look among them ... The gray banality of a group of civil servants and society women, busy with empty chattering ... I feel alone and foreign among these people who know nothing of me and of whom I know nothing at all, and who obviously feel and think differently than I do. Besides, my Muslim fez isolates me even further from their society ... they all look at me as if I were some curious beast ...

As soon as I can, I go back up to the bridge, and I go to the front of the boat. A cool breeze has sprung up, deterring the other passengers; I can stretch out on a bench ...

During these cool and silent hours of summer nights on the sea, I always feel a singular impression of well-being and calm. I stay stretched out on the gently swaying bridge, contemplating the ship's two lanterns and, high up, the infinite falling stars. I feel alone, free, detached from the world, and I am happy.

I fall asleep peacefully.

At about two in the morning, the rolling of the ship becomes more noticeable, and I wake up. I get up, and to my right in the darkness, I see lights breaking through: those are the lighthouses of the Balearic Islands, and there's Majorca's revolving light ... we skirt the islands, and the sea is choppy.

Seeing these lights signaling lands I will probably never know, I feel a sensation of vague mystery ... Then very softly I fall asleep again ...

Reminiscences

Along with Eloued's stars, you still tremble in my heart, alluring and moist eyes of the great ship carrying me away to African soil . . .

I had once again found Marseille's life for a few weeks. I had very often come to this grand city of departures. Some contrary destiny had always seemed to pursue me there, and to prevent me from seeing it the way I like to see cities I pass through—dreaming, slow, and all alone—the length of quay walls and squares, dressed in borrowed clothing chosen according to places and circumstances.

In proper young European women's clothing I would have never seen anything—the world would have been closed to me—for life in the outside world seems to have been made for men and not women. However, I like to submerge myself in the flow of everyday life, to feel the crowd's waves wash over me, to suffuse myself with the essence of the common folk. Only by these means do I possess a town, know something about it that the tourist will never understand, in spite of all its guides' explanations.

I had always had to run, in a fever, through these bustling streets, my mind elsewhere, busy with uninteresting things; then immediately leaving in my wake an unknown Marseille, almost chimerical, I would embark for other ports, other countries: I went looking for silence and oblivion in the slumbering cities of the Barbary Coast, or the laughing dream of a face in Italy's perfect cities, and dead time in this strange Sardinia . . .

This time, by propitious chance, I've returned free, my soul almost at peace, my mind almost idle, and I was finally able to penetrate Marseille, feel the sensation, the very special excitement of its complex exoticism, the odors of tar, of sea water, and oranges.

In the month of July 1900, I left again for Algeria. I can see myself at sea, and this impression of space added itself to that of the desert, which overcomes me so voluptuously on these first exhausting hot evenings of the rediscovered Sahara. Thus I still exist at a distance in the woman I was yesterday.

The summer sun will slowly disappear over there, in the middle of the sea, into the peaceful waters. The white rocks have turned pink, and *Le Vierge de la Garde* suddenly shines with an almost-supernatural burst of light on her arid hill.[1]

Marseilles, the city of adieus, is incomparable on these evenings drowned in golden liqueur. Elusive serpents of fire glimmer and glide in the trembling water; a lukewarm wind softly caresses the houses, the boats, and the water, while on the horizon, in the indistinct flaming of the high sea, the shipwreck of the sun plays out like a drama.

The rusty cry of the capstans hauling in anchors awakens weighty memories in me; the ship's flanks have shuddered . . . It is my turn now to lean on the railing and dream with resigned melancholy of the unfathomable mystery of tomorrow, and of endings—about these fleeting things that surround and govern destinies. Just as exile attaches certain souls to their native land with a love more profound the less the hope of return, so I feel that I'm beginning to love this last European city, especially its port. And thus its dear silhouette etches itself with a tender stroke among my wanderer's and loner's visions . . .

But there on the horizon, the ocean has darkened. The sun has disappeared, and the sunset's fire finally extinguishes itself in violet shadows. Pale white caps appear and run on the dark ridge of the hollowed-out waves. Long undulations begin rolling on the still-calm surface of the sea: the weather will be bad . . .

The ship has left. Marseille has disappeared on the horizon, with its rocks and white islands. Roll, old ship; carry me away!

1. Translator's note: *La Vierge de la Garde* refers to the statue of the Virgin that stands over the city of Marseille on the hill named La Garde, a military outpost since the time of the Romans. The basilica was constructed in the nineteenth century and is a place of pilgrimage. The statue of the Virgin (9.70 meters tall) can be seen from numerous points in the city.

I remembered these words said by an old sailor in both a resigned and sententious tone: "Only the crazy and the poor go to sea . . ."

Those he called the poor are certainly true sailors, subjected to perpetual danger and the harshest of lives. As for "crazy people," they are all dreamers and restless souls, all lovers of the chimera, all those who—like us—"embark in order to leave," the emigrants and the hopeful.

Beyond every sea, there is a continent; at the end of each voyage, there is a port or a shipwreck . . .

Imperceptibly, gently, hope leads us to the grave. But what does it matter! The great sun will come up again tomorrow, the sea will put on its most sparkling colors, and the ports will always gleam.

Note

The beginning of these notes, written in a primary school notebook during a stay in Paris, refers to the Arab cemetery in Bône where Eberhardt's mother was buried. The Vernier cemetery in Switzerland shelters the body of Alexander Trophimowsky, officially Isabelle Eberhardt's tutor and her mother's companion. The tomb of Isabelle's brother, Vladimir, who died in 1899, is also found there.

Entitled "Toward the Blue Horizons" by the author and published in 1908 by Barrucand in *Notes de route*, this collection evokes a period in Eberhardt's life described in more detail in *Les journaliers*.

The following texts relate to the second trip to El Oued. They had been scattered in *Notes de route* and *Dans l'ombre chaude de l'Islam*.

For a better understanding, it should be noted that during this first stay in the Souf, on January 29, 1901, Eberhardt was the victim of an attack in Behima committed by a certain Abdallah ben Mohammed, who declared that he had acted on divine order.

❧ ☙

The Souf gardens are vast craters dug by hand between the dunes that vary in depth according to the depth of the subterranean water level. They are found along the Debila road; on the Zgorem, Guemar, and Touggourt roads; and around Teksebat and Kouïnine, which hug the ground. Others, specifically toward the South, occur in veritable abysses, accessible only by little serpentine paths. There are also very deep ones to the northwest of the city, near Sidi Abdallah and Gara.

The architecture of these excavated gardens is rather curious. They have an accessible slope on one side, and there are wells with frames built of palm tree trunks with a pole resting on a fulcrum and a counterweight. On one end is a big stone attached to a rope; and on the other, a leather *oumara*, a sort of flat basket suspended at the end of a rope. Around the wells, one can see vegetable gardens, young palm trees, and ground cover. The tallest trees are across from the wells toward nearly perpendicular walls whose tops are spiked with *djerid* in order to prevent the sand from coming in.

A country that resembles no other: in the summer at night, the traveler's ear is struck by an immense, plaintive, and sweet voice rising from the innumerable craters—it is the *Souafa* workers removing sand from the gardens, patiently carrying the heavy sand in baskets on their shoulders . . . This ant's work is done each night; and the next day, the Souf's eternal wind comes and annihilates the nocturnal labor. In the great silence of mild evenings, this plaintive song in minor notes brings with it a strange shiver of sadness, almost anxiety . . .

Over there, very far away, beyond the blue sea, beyond the fertile Tell, the morose Aurès, and the large chotts that must dry out, is the burned earth, the ardent and shining Souf earth, where the devouring flame of Faith burns, where at each step rises a mosque, a *koubba*, or a tomb said to be the site of saintly miracles, where the only religious sound is the Muslim *eddhen*, repeated five times, where one prays and believes . . . There is Salah ben Feliba's lively house and all its familiar scenery, immutable in this sublimely fanatic country. There are men in red burnooses who come home in the mist to gray dwellings with cupolas, or who assemble on mats in Belkassem Bebachi's café. There are blessed zaouïyas and their venerated leaders . . .

❧ ☙

Eloued: a completely Arab city built on the slope of a tall sand dune, with houses made entirely of plaster, by the Souafa (the inhabitants of the Souf). From this, the city takes on an Oriental aspect made of an ideal white.

The French buildings stand out clearly: the Arab Bureau, the barracks, the post office, the school, the customs office.

There are two caïdats in Eloued: that of the Achèche and that of the Messaaba.

The important Muslim constructions are the cadi's *mahakma*; the Azèzla, Ouled-Khalifa, Messaaba-Gharby, Sidi Selem, and Ouled-Ahmed mosques; and the mosque at the zaouïya of Sidi Abd-el-Kader.

None of Eloued's winding streets are paved. The market is a large square with two buildings, vaulted and domed, one for grains and the other for meat.

In the Eloued market, one sees Souafa from all of the tribes: Chaamba and even Touareg and Sudanese.

The Eloued market is held on Friday; and starting Thursday evening, the roads fill up with camels, donkeys, and pedestrians.

The main roads are, to the north, the road to the Tunisian Djerid via Behima and Debila; to the northwest, the Biskra road via Guémar; to the west, the Touggourt road via Kouïnine and that of Touggourt via Taïbeth-Guéblia, from which the Ouargla road also branches off through the desert; to the south, the Berressof and Ghadamès road via Amiche; and to the east, the road to Tunisia via the village of Tréfaoui.

Eloued is surrounded by numerous villages that make up the region called Oued-Souf.

I lived in this region for months. I came twice in the middle of summer, I spent winter there, and I almost died there. Wounded by a saber in the village of Behima, I stayed there while I was cared for at the military hospital . . . I could say something about that.

First of all, for me, Eloued was a revelation of visual beauty and profound mystery, taking possession of my wandering and restless being by an aspect of the earth that I'd never suspected. I stayed there only a little while, but I came back the following year, at the same period, irresistibly attracted by my memory of it.

I believe there are predestined hours, very mysteriously privileged moments, when certain lands, certain places, reveal to us their soul, when we instantly—through sudden intuition—understand the true, unique, and indelible vision.

Thus my first vision of Eloued was for me a complete and definitive revelation of this harsh and splendid country that is the Souf, of its strange beauty and its immense sadness, too. It was in August 1899, on a hot, calm evening . . .

Fantasia

Of all the strange memories, of all the evocative impressions left with me by my stay in Eloued—a gray city with a thousand low cupolas, a seemingly archaic, ageless country—the most profound, the most singular, is the unique spectacle that I was privileged to witness one clear winter morning of this magical winter down there, sunny and clear as spring.

The whole country had been celebrating for several days already: the great and venerated marabout, Sidi Mohammed Lachmi, was returning from his voyage to the distant, almost-chimerical country of France. It was an occasion to dress in brilliant costumes, to let a few fiery horses gallop in the wind and smoke, and especially to let the gunpowder speak.

Brightened by pink, infinite, shifting transparencies, the sun was coming up. Dawn is the chosen hour, the bewitching hour among all hours in the desert. The air is light and pure; a fresh breeze murmurs quietly in the palm trees' thick tough foliage at the bottom of strange gardens. No word can convey the unique enchantment of these instants in the great desert's peace.

We had come the previous evening to the Ourmès bordj—fourteen kilometers from Eloued on the Touggourt road—in order to meet the notable individual.

After a night spent with a small circle of close friends, listening to the marabout's fiery and powerful words embellished with images, I went out into the courtyard where our horses were waiting, already unnerved by the unusual noise of the past day and by the crowd, which had grown with newcomers all night long.

There were several hundred men sitting or lying on the sand, draped in their majestic white holiday burnooses . . . Energetic manly heads,

tanned faces beautifully framed by the snowy white of the veils draping down from their turbans; women enfolded in dark-blue and red
fabrics in the ancient style, decorated with strange gold jewelry from
distant Sudan and from which the first iridescent glimmers of the day
emitted sparks of fire.

Looking serious, making the habitual gestures of nomad life, all the
faithful were preparing their humble morning coffee around the fires.

All of them wore around their necks the long prayer beads of the
khouan of Sidi Abd-el-Kader of Baghdad.

Excited by a black mare with flaming eyes born under the burning sky
of far-off In-Salah, the stallions were stamping the ground, trembling,
and neighing, as they gracefully bent their powerful necks under their
heavy free-flowing manes.

Outside, the strange silhouettes of three giant *méhari* stood out
against the purple sky, placid and indifferent like giants from another
age, disdainful of all this trifling humanity bustling around them.

Finally, at an imperious gesture from one of the *mokaddem*, the courtyard emptied out and the doors closed; the hour of departure had come.

The marabout—dressed in the austere green silk robe, the green turban, and the long white veils befitting the Prophet's descendants—
appeared at the door. Gigantic in stature, he stopped for a moment,
and slowly, with gravity, the indefinable deep gaze of his large black
eyes shifted to the eastern horizon. The zeal of the faithful lent him an
air of calmness and impenetrability—no visible emotion was betrayed
on the regular features of his face, superb in its virile beauty and energy.

In the midst of the hubbub—servants' cries and the neighing of
impatient horses—we quickly mounted our horses. The double doors
opened; and with a furious leap, we were outside.

In front of us, four black musicians, from the territory of the Nefza-
oua in Tunisia and dressed in intensely colored silks, began playing
a strange and wild melody on their shrill flutes, accompanied by the
muffled beating of an enormous drum. A voice as vast as the ocean itself
rose from the crowd:

"Salutations, Son of the Prophet!"

The clamor was frenetically repeated again and again, and the tambourines, held at arm's length above the heads in the crowd, beat a crazy rhythm. At first, the frightened horses pulled back, reared up, and foamed at the mouth, and then rushed forward.

Still impassive, mounted on a white stallion from the Djerid, the marabout, his eyes lowered in silence, seemed busy only wordlessly restraining his mount, without a sudden movement on his furious beast.

Finally, a sort of procession formed, undulating and white, dominated only by the tall figure of the green-clad marabout.

We moved slowly toward the east as if to meet the rising sun, still hidden by the enormous dunes surrounding Eloued.

When we emerged from the windy paths still drowned in blue shadows and reached the hills, the red glimmer of the day magnified the white procession.

The silent and barren dunes seemed to give birth to crowds. Entire tribes hurtled down the hills, burst forth from the gardens . . .

All of a sudden a large empty circular space formed in front of us; and with a staccato and wild chant—an old war chant from long ago— twelve young men dressed in the most brilliantly colored Tunis silks burst forth into the arena armed with long inlaid rifles and blunderbusses. Simulating an attack, they rushed toward us with hoarse cries, simultaneously firing their arms into the sand near the frightened horses that were trying to buck away.

Then the horses rush forth, insane, pawing with their front feet above the crowd . . . Their eyes bulging, their mouths dripping with foam, they still want to pull back . . . But, urged on by sharp spurs, they race, rush toward the serpentine and shifting crowd, which parts and lets them pass.

And thus, wherever there is a slightly flat or open space, the wild scene starts again.

One would think one had returned to History's past, to eras when war was joy and splendor, something that impassioned souls and dominated them. All that was warlike, antiquated in these silent nomads' souls, was reawakened. This procession could have marched against the backdrop of unchanging dunes thousands of years earlier, for there was nothing modern about it.

The acrid, intoxicating odor of burned gunpowder followed us, inebriating men and beasts even more than the wild music and shouts.

But at the horizon, on the ridge of a high dune, a white procession soon appeared, seemingly encircled by a halo of gold in the eastern radiance. Preceded by three very old green, yellow, and red banners embroidered with faded inscriptions and decorated with shining copper bells, with the same tambourines raised above turbaned heads, this other enormous and yet dense crowd advanced. There were neither cries nor music. Only the very muted sound of the tambourines' counterpoint rhythm accompanied a unique, powerful chant emerging from a thousand lungs.

"Hail to thee and peace be with you, O Prophet of God! Hail to thee and peace be with you, O saints among God's creatures! Hail to thee, Djilani, Emir of the Saints, Master of Baghdad, whose name shines forth in the West and the East!"

Near the banners, on a tall immaculate mare, the brother of the marabout—himself a venerated saint—Sidi Mohammed Eliman moves forward. He is enormous and blond, a Celtic or Germanic blond, his white face lit up by the gently pensive gaze of his large blue eyes—strange eyes under the white burnoose and turban of Ismail's race, burned by the hottest suns over thousands of years.

The two troops meet again and merge. And still, from all the dunes surge forth countless white forms of men and blue patches of women.

I turn around: I see behind us a tumultuous sea of turbans and veils rolling as far as the eye can see on this road I had come to so many times in search of silence and solitude. And frenetic groups still surge forth, making the gunpowder speak and the horses race.

Now we seem to carry with us a cloud of smoke above our heads like a ragged grayish veil.

And the deep soft chant—sad, too, like all of those from the desert—grows louder and rises up toward the sky's pale azure.

Finally, we hurtle into an immense open plain dotted with tombs.

In front of us, the three mehara joined by others walk through the crowd impassively, without a shiver or any trace of fear. Their riders, faces half-veiled, also seem to be dreamers, perched on the strangely shaped Touareg saddle. The iron bells on the large old beasts ring at each step; and their long, strange, thick-lipped heads with big soft eyes sway slowly at the end of their flexible, outstretched necks.

But we, horses and riders, have sensed the open space before us, and so, leaving the three marabout and the old men to walk slowly in the shadow of the banners blowing in the wind, we take off, at last releasing the reins pulled so tight that they were about to snap. And there is furious galloping amid the admiring crowd; then we make more and more dramatic circles and curves at breathtaking speed on the vast plain.

All the suppressed wildness of the horses, all the fear too, is finally unleashed, and they flee, flee as if they would never stop again. The drunkenness of all these wild and sincere souls is contagious, and like the other riders, I too end up carried away by the insane race.

We rush past the gray town bursting with the faithful, and it is now over the immense plain and through the cemeteries that we once again flee. It seems as if a supernatural force gives life to our horses: tirelessly they keep rushing irresistibly forward, toward the faraway horizon, dripping with sweat, white with foam.

The plain is now no more than a multicolored ocean; the ever-increasing crowd has invaded it, and the three banners now float above thousands and thousands of Believers.

And the man for whom the love and veneration of this crowd swells continues to walk slowly, silently, impassive and pensive.

Around the zaouïya's large mosque topped with a high dome, the El-Beyada plain is deserted, infinite, inundated with subtle blue light.

Farther on, behind the houses, an immense nomad camp has been set up, a city born in one day, suddenly populating El-Beyada's desolate solitudes with black tents. This is the route toward all the interior's mysterious regions: Ber-es-Sof, Ghadamès, Black Sudan.

The deafening rhythmic beat of the tambourines continues over there; the enchanted songs and sounds of the little Bedouin reed flutes rise from over there, modulated and soft . . .

A great heavy silence weighs on the ruins of the mosque here, on the tombs and the tawny sand.

Down below, in a small barren valley scattered with oddly shaped gray stones and anonymous, unmarked, and abandoned tombs, a strange jagged wall rises up, standing out in black against the infinite blue of the night . . . In this enclosure without a bush, without a flower, contributing to the eternal sterility of the sand, small stones rise up, indicating the presence of burial places. Among them is a small tombstone, all milky white, onto which the lunar night shines.

A tall dark form emerges through the pointed arch of the mosque. It slowly glides through the illuminated space, then descends toward the funerary valley. Then it enters the enclosure and stays there, immobile, its head bent forward in mute contemplation of the small white tombstone.

And meanwhile down below in the great ephemeral city, under the black tents, a whole faithful people sing his glory, and that of his ancestors, who sowed the seeds of renewed faith throughout the boundless nation of Islam.

But the tall pensive marabout, who has remained there, came alone in the night to dream and perhaps to reexperience everlasting regrets as he contemplates the tomb of his firstborn, who disappeared into mystery's abyss, his eyes having barely opened on the radiant horizon of his prestigious country.

Notebooks

Sick for a while now, suffering from intolerable pain in all my limbs and from an absolute lack of appetite, I sometimes wonder if I should stay here. This idea doesn't frighten me . . . In any case, I don't desire any change in my existence.

I've become attached to this country, though it be one of the most desolate and most violent. If I should ever leave this gray city with its innumerable little archways and cupolas, lost in the gray immensity of barren dunes, I will carry with me the intense nostalgia for a lost corner of the earth where I pondered and suffered so much, and where, too, I finally encountered the simple, naive, and deep affection that alone lights up my sad life with a ray of sun at this moment.

I've been here too long and the country is too compelling, too simple in its menacingly monotonous lines, for this feeling of attachment to be a passing and aesthetic illusion. Certainly, no, never has any other site on earth bewitched me, charmed me as much as the moving solitude of the great dried-up ocean that leads from the rocky plains of Guémar and the cursed shallows of the Chott Mel'riri to the waterless deserts of Sinaoun and Ghadamès.

Often when the sun sets, leaning on the dilapidated parapet of my crude terrace; waiting for the hour when the neighboring muezzin announces that the sun has disappeared on the horizon and the fast is broken; or contemplating the tawny-, bloody-, or violet-colored dunes, or those livid under the low, black, more and more–glacial winter sky, I feel a great sadness invade me, a sort of dark anguish: one could say that at this hour, when my spirit suddenly awakens, I feel more than ever the deep isolation of this city inscribed in the insurmountable—it seems to me—behind the dunes, six days from the railway and Europe's life . . . And it seems to me then, under the great violet night, that the enormous dunes move closer and rise up like monstrous animals, that they hem in the city and my dwelling place, the last in the Ouled-Ahmed neighborhood, even more, in order to guard us more jealously, and forever.

At times, I begin chewing on Loti's words: "The poor man, he loved his Senegal!"

Yes, I love my Sahara, and with an obscure, mysterious, deep, inexplicable love, but a very real and indestructible one.

Now it even seems to me that I will no longer be able to live far from these southern countries.

However, I would need the strength to leave, to pull myself from this encirclement . . . But where can I find this reactive force so contrary to my nature?

❊ ❊

MARSEILLE, MAY 16, 1901

Evening sensations during Ramadan in Eloued. Leaning on the dilapidated parapet of my crude terrace, I was contemplating the undulating horizon of the vast, dried-up, and unmoving ocean stretching all the way to the waterless solitudes of Sinaoun and Rhamadès from the rocky plains of El M'guébra; and under the crepuscular sky—sometimes soaked with blood, or mauve or pink, sometimes dark and drowned in sulfurous glimmers—the big monotonous dunes seemed to be moving in, tightening around the gray town with its innumerable cupolas, the peaceful Ouled-Ahmed neighborhood, and Salah ben Feliba's closed and silent dwelling place, as if to seize us and very mysteriously keep us forever . . . O fanatic and burning earth of the Souf! Why didn't you keep us, we who loved you so much, who still love you, and who are incessantly haunted by your nostalgic and troubling memory?

In the southeastern neighborhood of Eloued, at the end of a cul-de-sac opening onto Ouled-Ahmed Street, which leads to the cemetery of the same name, there was a vast terraced house, the only one in the city of cupolas. A rickety old door with loose planks defended the entryway. This permanently closed door bore witness to the desire of the inhabitants to remain sequestered far away from the world and its bustle. This quite-ancient house, built of limestone, reinforced by yellowish-gray plaster like all the Souf's dwellings, had a vast interior courtyard where the pale sand of the surrounding desert reappeared.

The most tranquil at first, and then the most strange, the most melancholically troubled days of my stormy existence went by there, in this dwelling, formerly owned by Salah ben Feliba (brother of the former caïd of the Messaaba) but now passed into the hands of an old Chaambi living near Elakbab.

At first they were the hours of tranquility of *Chaabane* and Ramadan: days spent on simple household tasks or on trips to the blessed, great zaouïya on my poor faithful Souf;[1] nights of love and absolute security in one another's arms, according to Slimane's so exact expression; enchanted, calm, pink dawns after nights of Ramadan prayers; ardent or pale twilights during which, from the top of my terrace, I watched the sun disappear behind the elevated crests of the enormous dunes of the Oued Allenda and Taïbet-Gueblia road, where I had gone and lost myself one morning . . .

I was waiting, first, for the gray cupola of the market and then the dazzling white minaret of Sidi Salem to fade, for the pink radiance of the setting sun to go out on the mosque's western facade . . . Then from very far away, from the Ouled-Khelifa mosque, then from that of Azèzba, the prolonged and wild moaning of the moueddhen rose up: "God is the greatest!" he said, and every burdened breast heaved a sigh of relief . . . The market square immediately emptied and became silent and deserted.

Downstairs in a wide-open bedroom, sitting across from each other, cigarettes in hand, Slimane and Abdelkader were silently waiting for this moment, the wooden-crate table between them . . . And I often amused myself by discouraging them, crying out to them that Sidi Salem was still all red. Slimane was spewing curses against the Ouled-Ahmed moueddhen-Mozabite, who he said unnecessarily prolonged the fast. Abdelkader joked with me, as usual, calling me "Si Mahfoudh." Khelifa and Aly waited with their pipes in hand, one with kif and the other with

1. Translator's note: Eberhardt named her horse Souf, after the region in southern Algeria.

ar'ar; and Tahar was pouring the soup into the dish so we wouldn't have to wait.

And I was melancholically prolonging my fast, fascinated by the unique sight of Eloued, at first purple, then pink, then mauve, then finally—after the rapid extinction of the western fire—uniformly gray . . .

At other times outside the fast, going outdoors at the hour of the sunset in order to wait for "the man in the red jacket," I would sit down on the boundary marker near the spahi Laffati's door all the way at the end of the vast rectangle separating the neighborhood and the city's Arab Bureau, across from the great empty expanse of the desert, starting at the low dune with the lime ovens and continuing past the cone-shaped dunes on the road to Allenda. There, in the horizon's incomparable blaze, grayish silhouettes would appear on the dune with the lime ovens, deforming, stretching to gigantic proportions, outlined against the purple sky . . .

Then, from the eternally guarded door, in front of which the little blue infantryman strolled with his fixed bayonet, emerged the completely red shadow, which I was never able to see appear without a certain rush, a shiver in my heart that was simultaneously gentle, a bit voluptuous, and strangely sad . . . Why? I will never know.

I was sitting there on that stone one evening, already at dark, when suddenly, close by, strange little Hania (Dahmane's daughter) burst forth out of the shadow with her pearly and ambiguous laugh—a laugh all her own—and the sensual sadness of her eyes. Wrapped in her dark-blue and red *Soufia* rags, she was carrying wood to Ahmed ben Salem's house.

It is also from Salah ben Feliba's peaceful home that I left, melancholy, after the crazy night of January 28, spent in furious caresses on both sides—the last night that I was destined to spend under my own roof. I knew then that I was already exiled, but felt very calm, leaving for sinister Behima, whose fatal silhouette has remained engraved in my memory such as it appeared to me from the top of the last dunes. At the end of an immense desolate plain scattered with tombstones (similar to that of Tarzout) and gray walls, and towering over everything—an immense and solitary palm grove . . . All of this stood out against the gray sooty horizon of that winter afternoon when the violent *chehili* (sirocco) raged, filling up the dunes with haze and stirring up the moving sand.

Impressions of malaise in the Souf in autumn: Far from the gardens deep in their craters, far from the "sehan" on the road to Debila. Nothing on this earth could accentuate time's flight and the change in seasons. Autumn, winter, spring, summer—everything merges and goes by uniformly on the dead solitude of the dunes, eternally the same through the heavy silence of the centuries.

Never does a human voice disturb that silence with its moaning or its song; yet very similar to a moan—the great sea-like voice of the rustling chehili rolling its meager gray waves or that hardly perceptible voice of the *bahri*, cool but futile, for nothing could return life to the waterless solitudes.

The sky, more white-hot, more transparent, more azure; the whiter light of the sun; the milder black shadows; and in the air, a special lightness—these are the only signs by which one can recognize that autumn has arrived, that the gloomy days of despondency are over, and that life will soon be reborn in the gardens.

The tough esparto grass grows again in the labyrinth of the dunes except on the lugubrious road to Allenda and that to Bar-es-Sof, and the spindly sedum wilts . . . Flowers . . . nowhere. In the gardens, the bahri that has returned shakes the dust from the palm trees, which once again don their bright green color; the carrots, the *felfel* (peppers), the *nana* (mint), and other ephemeral grasses display an unheard-of luxurious green, whereas the last leaves of the russet-colored pomegranate trees, fig trees, and those of the rare grapevines fall; and cucumbers, melons, and watermelons reappear . . . Birds also appear, rapid swallows who've migrated here. The earlier, quicker nightfall makes evenings more melancholy, the sunsets occur on more tender horizons, and the mornings—the blessed hour of the desert, the hour when one feels light, light and happy to be alive—are fresher and begin later . . .

But the Souf's rigid appearance remains irrevocably the same. Only a few details and the light have changed. But the stormy horizon, the indefinable color of the sands, the silence and the solitude, all of that will never change . . . An impression of vague malaise and of greater sadness when one reflects that elsewhere nature—ready to fall asleep—is adorning herself with her last splendors, whereas here she seems to only gather her thoughts . . .

What can one say, what can one sing about the desert's sunsets? Where can one find sufficient words to portray their splendor, express their charm, melancholy, and mystery? In my previous "daily journals," I noted quite imperfectly several of these sublime moments . . .

How many times, especially during the waiting periods of Ramadan, have my astonished eyes contemplated this spectacle without name! How many times, while the tyrannical star was disappearing behind the dunes, did my heart not bleed voluptuously, deliciously, sadly . . .

I remember the evening when I had ridden out on my fiery Souf, bareback, to get a saddle from Abdelkader Belahlali's deïra in the Messaaba, west of town along the road to exile, in the direction of Touggourt and Biskra; and there, dazzled, I witnessed crowning moments of unusual splendor.

Another time, coming back from my long trip in search of Sidi Elhussine on the road to Bar-es-Sof, I had stopped on the ridge of the dune that towers over the Ouled Touati—overcome by religious admiration—in order to look at the peaceful hamlet, the house in ruin, or unfinished, one story high with an unusual ogival gallery, that stood alone on this road leading to the great unknown, to all the troubling, compelling mystery of the Sahara and distant Sudan. The low houses covered with a series of little cupolas, the *zeriba* made of dried djerid! . . . A few silhouettes of camels lying down, with their resigned and dreamy manner, their backs topped with the pack saddle of wooden slats; a big gray dromedary, standing, immobile, one foot held up and shackled according to custom; a few women in blue tatters—almost black—of Hellenic shape, returning to their dwelling bent under the weight of heavy guerba, or jars resembling the amphorae in which the women of the predestined race of Sem drew water from the fountains of Canaan thousands of years before . . . All of that in pink, iridescent, pearly glimmers level with the white ground of the immense plain of the Ouled-Touati...

One evening after a short walk and a stop in the shade of the low palm trees of Chott Debila, Souf had suddenly balked, refusing to allow himself to be mounted and requiring me to lead him all the way to the Eloued slaughterhouse in order to leap onto him from a low archway.

I had returned alone, bearing to the right from Douei Rouha, the miraculous Kadry village, and I had taken the dangerous winding and narrow paths along the sharp crests that breathtakingly tower above the gardens.

At the hour when the eddhen and the *mogh'reb* had just died out and when the devout were beginning to pray in snowy-colored groups, I passed in front of the little Ouled-Kelifa mosque, or the Messaaba R'arby mosque (I never knew exactly their respective position, and they are adjacent to each other). Everything around me was radiant with purple and gold, and my heart, blinded by the transitory nature of being, plunged into darkness and was peaceful...

And so it was on many other evenings until this one—filled with anxiety, speeding along in haste at the long stride of Dahmane's horse, I crossed the Ouled-Ahmed, the Ouled-Touati, the El-Beyada on my way to ask for help from Sidi Eliman...I still see the large zaouïya in ruin, the oldest in the Souf, rising up on its low hill, with two symmetric koubba, all lighted at an angle by lilac glimmer, barely the lightest of pinks. An enchanted evening of strange calm, a respite from the anguish of these days preceding exile...

And still this mogh'reb before leaving, when—my heart gripped by anxiety bordering on fear—I was waiting for Slimane on the dune that towers, to the west, over the lugubrious Christian and Jewish cemeteries, and to the east, the peaceful necropolis of the Ouled-Ahmed...The *misbah* of holy and fateful Friday nights were lit up, yellow, pale flames in the immense conflagration of the hour; and the faithful Aly was wandering among the tombstones, not knowing what to do with Slimane's burnooses...

The desert's last sunset was also our last adieu to the Sahara...Alone, we were about to enter the shade of old Biskra's palm groves when I begged Slimane to stop and turn back. Behind us, the Sahara's immensity still stretched out, quite darkened. The sun's disk, red and devoid of rays, was descending toward the desert's almost-black line in the middle of an ocean of purple. "This is our country," I said, and added, "In châ Allah! We'll return soon never to leave it again." "Amin" he said, as depressed and saddened as I to leave this land, the only one where we would have liked to die.

Since then, I have never again seen the magic of the mogh'reb in the Desert. Will I ever see it again? . . .

Winter skies, gray or black, above the livid dunes where dead sands flow, participating only in the capricious life of the winds!

Hazy mornings, saline perfumes of damp sand, the peacefulness of things, and the rebirth of beings . . . During my days of internment and captivity, I was lingering there. With a friendly eye, I watched from the top of the doctor's terrace my faithful Souf—already no more than a beast to me, foreign to my life—whom I was about to leave.

To the right across the courtyard where Souf was eating his evening barley alongside the doctor's horse—the wall of the henhouse spiked with broken glass; the new well being drilled by the prisoners guarded by a deïra; the big rectangular gray school building, the secondary school; then, as they say down there, the dunes . . .

Across the way, the neighborhood courtyard's vast square . . . The seconded servicemen, the infantrymen, the French brigadier's bedroom, the square where I waited so many times for the return of Slimane, whom I saw when he left the house of the caïd of the Messaabba; then under the stables' archways, horses of various colored coats, in front of which a few red burnooses wandered . . . I knew that the single silhouette among these familiar ones that my eyes used to always seek out would never pass by again . . . The wall of the Arab Bureau, the disciplinary premises with the sinister cell where I knew Abdallah ben Mohammed to be, the police station where Slimane and I had smoked kif with the *turcos* during one distressing evening, the door to the bench where the guards sat down . . . then my hospital, the long building with the slightly sloped roof, across from the "room of the stiffs," the laundry and the wash room . . . right in the middle of the inclined courtyard, the large, squat supply office, then the drinking trough and the wash house. There, graceful captive gazelles wandered, abruptly leaping back in response to the soldiers' taunts . . .

Here also are the familiar profiles: Lieutenant Lemaître yelling about contraband, using Arabic words in front of the disciplinary offices; Lieutenant Guillo, laced up tight in his corset, walking the length of the hospital on his way home; Sergeant Othman, a fat brute, beating the detachment's poor little *sloughi* dog; the French corporal with the face of a Marseille butcher, alongside the heavy Isoard; then the crazy infantryman, his long blue silhouette under a cape, wandering silently, his Sidi Ammar prayer beads in hand; finally the spahis riding bareback on their return from the drinking trough, and their usual parading that the marabout Slimane, as they said, will never again carry out with them . . .

There they all are: the Brigadier Saïd, a man of faith and duty, stooped a bit as if bent under the light yoke of Eloued discipline; the old pest and job seeker Slami, busy playing the brigadier; the traitor Embarek, with his blond beauty and his crazy manner; the imbecile informer Saïd Zemouli, without a doubt invoking at this moment, like at all others, his Bent Elhahid; Mansour the drunkard, with his joking manner; Ben Chaabane, prying and servile; Zardy, calm and gentle; Aly Chaambi, with the equivocal manner of a beautiful girl, his eyes painted with khol; the old coward Nasr ben Ayéchi; the brute Hannochi, stooped, his arms dangling; big Saouli; arrogant Sadock, married at Ben Dif Allah's house; the assassin Tahar ben Meurad, with a gentle, good-natured manner; Amor, the tailor, a handsome boy with a white complexion; heavy Saoudi of the Ouled Darradj; the ignoble valet Slimane Bou-Khlif, with a lush's nose and the eyes of a thief; and the unnatural Laffati, with his Hindu nabob's beard, an insolent manner; the benevolent spouse of Chaamba; and finally, the drunkard and womanizer Dahmane ben Borni, alone as always, going off on his own, the rebel of the detachment, with a bandit's fierce, withdrawn look . . . There they all are.

Here is Khelifa, too, slow under his vast and countless layered burnooses and gandoura, his pipe and his piece of rag filled with kif in the *tabourcha* of his burnoose, leading Souf by the reins. His head is lowered; he is shaking his short mane and prancing happily, knowing well that after water comes the barley treat.

All of this passes before me under a darkening sky as evening approaches and the West lights up with a sulfurous glimmer. And then an immense sadness hovers over Cham's earth as the winter night descends and the pure voices of the muezzin proclaim the call to God to protect the creatures whom he created, from evil, from nightfall's evil spell, from those who blow on rope knots (who cast spells), from the hypocrisy of the traitorous flatterer, from perfidious men.

Sinister winter down there, for it robs this country of its glory and splendor: the triumphant light, with its abundant, reinvigorating sun . . .

Jostled for nearly three hours on a stretcher over the dunes under a gray winter sky, I finally see at first the high arched doorway of the neighborhood go by above my head. I perceive the sentinel—an impassive tanned face, his pointed bayonet flashing—the curious faces of the guards, then another lower archway to the right; and an odor of phenol grabs me by the throat.

At first, it's physical torture, stupid and lugubrious, where all one's animal nature revolts and cries; overcome by the fear of surgical butchery, I am lying down, my teeth chattering, on the operating table in the small well-lit room.

I see that room again: The gray wooden door fitted with an open window; to the left, a shelf with a few books and the indispensable Drapeau Almanac. Along the wall, steaming pans containing swabs and bandages, the temperature chart, the thermometer; then the table covered with jars and big enameled basins where barbaric instruments soak; tweezers, surgical scalpels, curettes, scissors, needles, an entire workshop of suffering. The bluish flame of the alcohol lamp, like an ironically vacillating shooting star. In the corner, a high window looking onto the vaulted gallery and the supply office, which seemed faraway from the false perspective of this courtyard's elusive proportions. And here in the middle, the table where I'm lying on a mattress. Under my left side, a black oilcloth leading to the bucket of water streaked with blood.

Then the medicine chest, a sort of chest of drawers in gray wood. The walls merge with the archway, thus giving the room the heavy feeling of a dungeon or an underground room. They are painted a pale color, while the base is black with red markings. The floor is paved in gray.

There, moving around me, the doctor in a gray cardigan, with his good young face and his pince-nez for nearsightedness; Corporal Rivière, his kepi pushed back, with his double-pronged ruddy Jesus beard; the little corporal Guillaumin, a beardless kid—all of them in short sleeves rolled up on neat white arms, wearing big bibbed aprons. Finally, wearing white, a red belt, and a flat *chechiya*, Ramdane the infantryman—a young mountain man with a calm, frank face who rarely laughs, very touchy, easily taking offense at the teasing jokes made about religion by the "*toubib*."

My mind foggy, my limbs broken, I'm put back on the stretcher and transported into the neighboring room, and there they lay me down on a high, narrow bed where I find no room for my bruised body and my horribly painful arm.

The torrid summer heat is not there for the purpose of completing the illusion of agony, but "the smell of death" is; and the deadly gloom of feverish nights engenders murky visions, shapeless terrors, unspeakable anguish, intense despair—it incites insane pleas for liberating death.

Thoughts of isolation, abandonment, and mournful sadness, especially since February 9 . . .

The long, narrow, vaulted room—painted yellow with a gray bottom, separated by a red-brown line and gray tiles—was across from the laundry room. The heavy door's sign read: "Isolation Ward."

Two beds separated by the three-legged night table. The headboards of the beds are topped by a small shelf holding an herbal tea pot, a pewter cup, and a white spittoon. On the night table, Slimène's little candleholder, tobacco, kif, the eternal glasses of wine, and unfinished coffee accumulate. Across from my bed, stuck to the wall with four triangles of bug paper, the inscription, in beautiful script: "El Oued Annex—Military Hospital—Health Service Regulations."

This sheet, the work of some sergeant from long ago or of our Gauguin himself, ended with this column: "Disciplinary Measures Inflicted on Civilian Patients."

To the left of the window, covered by a brown troop blanket, is the oil night-light whose pale pinkish glow illuminates my horrible nights. Above, the polished copper "class suitcase" . . . Later, as a favor, a cane chair for visitors.

In this room, in spite of the suffering and anguish of the upcoming separation, we had two different nights, a few moments of drunkenness for which the good doctor later harshly reproached me, ranting and raving, threatening, disarmed in the end, citing love's omnipotence, love that dominates everything and drives what happens to everything, tyrannical and beguiling love.

After a very short time, this "hospice" became as familiar to me as a real home. Unending conversations with the doctor, at first at my hospital bed, then at his home; the impoverished state of this white room, contrasting with the deceptive luxury of the Guillots' sitting room next door.

Now gay, now annoyed and caustic, observant and thoughtful, a soul searcher, nonplussed by me, brotherly, often admiring and aggressive, especially in regard to religion, Doctor Taste very quickly became my friend, even more intimately so, simpler too, than Domerg who was calmer, more down-to-earth. Taste, who was passionate above all, often poured out his soul to me, telling me all about his mistresses and his ideas, his adventures and his dreams; especially curious about the sensual world, a seeker of rare sensations and foreign experiences, he probed my past and especially the recent past, sensing rightly that—of all that I could know—there could only be truth and sincerity in what I could have learned, casually, from the only person I've ever loved and who has loved me; for love's miracle—I was going to say love's sacrament—only comes about when love is shared and not one-sided, as it were.

Taste was trying to get to know Slimène's emotional and sensual personality in order to better guess mine, having begun by completely misinterpreting the former because of prejudices based on caste, rank, and especially race: the Frenchman imagined the Arab to be only instinctive, animallike, seeing in love only the brutal act without anything uplifting or refining, the officer necessarily imagining the noncommissioned officer to be the type—and this he still believes, with a lot of leniency—who moves from being the sentimental musketeer spewing the questionable rosewater of pompous declarations (the Abdelaziz type) to the brutality of animal fulfillments. His interest in the case and his sincere admiration for me grew from the very day when he knew about Slimène things that Slimène himself is almost unaware of: namely, the uniqueness of his completely exceptional nature, in both a good sense and bad.

My life at the hospital—in spite of the bitterness of the separation from Rouha Khala and the harsh battle for my defense against the prevailing covetousness—often so brutal as to cause me a weighty malaise, or useless to the point of distressing me, was one of the most tolerable among the last periods of my life in Africa.

And of this hospice—refuge from pain, lost in the far-off oasis—I keep a good and tender memory. I liked it, and often since then, especially during the black days of Batna, I have missed it, that place the military refers to as a "place for people to die," cemetery lobby, stiff factory . . . often, so be it! But often, also, it is a blessed refuge for the abandoned, the exiled, the ill-fated, the poor, and the homeless soldier without a family—and this more often, I believe . . .

EL OUED, FEBRUARY 1901

After the first days of fever and vague anguish without cause, following horrible nights—thundering, sleepless nights—I am quickly starting to come alive again.

Still weak, I can get up and go out, sit down for a few hours under the low portico that runs the length of the hospital toward the south, and there in the quite-hot sun, I feel a pleasant sensation of renewal.

However, this vast courtyard of the casbah, where the hospital is located, with all the other military buildings, is gray and sad.

Nothing will ever turn green again in this countryside of stone and sand. Everything here is immutable, and only the more burning and golden light of the sun tells us that spring is returning.

No more sirocco; no more gray and heavy clouds. The air is pure and light; the breeze is already almost warm.

I've become accustomed to this monotonous life in this unchanging framework, and to these figures who come and go around me, always the same.

At dawn, close by under the portico of the soldiers' barracks, the reveille sounds—at first hoarse, like a sleepy voice, then clear and imperious.

The big door immediately creaks open. The comings and goings start. With us, it is the male nurses in Arab *babouches* who get up.[2]

After a moment, someone knocks on my door, only half-shut; the rules, displayed on the wall, forbid locking oneself in for the night. It's Goutorbe, a tall, blond, and silent boy, bringing the beaker of coffee, always asking the same question:

"Well, madame, how's it going today?"

I still get up with great difficulty and despite the advice of the good doctor, who yells a lot and rants and raves, but who always ends up letting me do as I please.

My head is spinning a bit, my legs are wobbly; but this sort of drunkenness is sweet, and my mind seems exalted, more easily able to receive joyful impressions of these hours of convalescence.

This morning I went out; and putting my elbows on the outer walls, I looked at Eloued through the battlements . . .

No words are able to express the bitter sadness of this impression: it seemed to me that I was looking at any landscape, for example that of an unknown city, any city, seen from a ship's bridge during a brief call at a port. The profound link that attached me to the *ksar*, to this Souf that I wanted to make into my country, this almost-painful link seemed to me broken forever. I am nothing more than a foreigner here . . .

In all likelihood, I will leave with the convoy on the twenty-fifth, and it will be finished . . . maybe finished forever.

And in order to flee this mournful sadness, I moved away from the crenellated edge so as to no longer see anything other than the "neighborhood" with its special life, always the same.

For the time being, we have here a tall, skinny Kabyle with a bony profile and hollow eyes that blaze. The doctor says that this Omar is crazy . . . The Arabs say he's become a marabout.

2. Translator's note: *Babouches* are leather slippers, without a heel or sides, used as shoes or slippers.

All day long he wanders in the courtyard, his head lowered, his prayer beads in hand. He speaks to no one, doesn't respond to questions.

When Omar happens to meet me during our walks, he takes my hand without a word, and we walk like that, slowly, in the heavy sand . . . From time to time the infantryman talks to me when we are far away from intruders. His ideas are disjointed, but he doesn't ramble too much. He is very gentle, and I've become accustomed to him.

"Si Mahmoud, you have to pray; when you leave, you have to go to a zaouïya and pray . . ."

Springtime in the Desert

I have only caught sight of a few glimmers of spring in the Souf, con-fined as I am to the "gray neighborhood" where the hospital is located among the barracks, the stables, and the officers' lodgings . . . there, everything is sand and stone, and nothing will ever turn green again . . .

However, prior to the sandstorms of the last few days, the air had become balmier, and a great languor had spread all through the coun-try on hot sunny afternoons when I had the opportunity to go out on horseback to the surrounding areas. I also saw the deep gardens of the Souf again, veritable abysses between the undulating dunes, beautiful with a unique beauty, a splendor that I had not seen until that evening when I had first had tea at Sidi Lachmi's with the doctor and when we had pushed on as far as Elakbab, knowing all the while that the enor-mous redheaded cheikh, the blue-eyed colossus, was in the djerid.

So we had returned by way of the eastern gardens, falling back on El Beyada near the dunes.

But the place where I really recognized the strange Saharan spring in all its sweet melancholy was on the road in the solitudes separating Eloued from Biskra.

On this road, after the small, fanatic, and dark town of Guemar, the citadel of the Khouan Tidjanyia, there was nothing—not a hamlet, not a douar, not a nomad tent—nothing but solitary bordj with strange names: Bir bou Chahma, Sif el Ménédi, Stah el Hamraïa, El Mguebra (the cemetery), and the guemira, little pyramids of piled-up stones, gray lighthouses scattered in the gray immensity.

At about seven o'clock I left the friendly shadow of the Sidi Mohamed Houssine *zaouïa*, and I soon rejoined the convoy with which I was sup-posed to travel—an Arab Bureau supply convoy, made up of the service camels that arrive every fifteen days. First there was the *bach amar* (the head of the convoy) Sassi, a silent and obstinate man; Lakhdar, drunkard and poet who charmed us with his songs; and then two old men exiled in Chellala, and a curious band, two pseudodervishes whom someone sent to Biskra in order to get rid of them, as they make it their profession to beg throughout Algeria, faking insanity and passing themselves off as mute. An old woman with her son . . . and those on fatigue duty—camel drivers from the Ouled-Ahmed-Achèche tribe.

At first, up to Sif el Ménédi, the undulating plain was cut by dunes sown with innumerable dark-green bushes with small red branches, twisted, contorted as if clenched in eternal pain . . . thorny jujube trees, tufts of pale-green and gold *drinn*, silvery *chich* spreading their aroma on enchanted pink mornings.

In Sif el Ménédi, a bit below the bordj, a lush garden enclosed by toub like those in the Oued Rir'.

Silvery canopies of the date trees; the leafless tangle of the fig trees; pomegranate trees and vines covered with pale buds; nana, basil and fragrant mint plants—the lush vegetation . . . lower down, peppers, delicate grasses leaning over the soft murmur of the magnesian *seguia*. At night, the multiple voices, soft and melancholic, of innumerable miniscule toads rise from all these clear streams.

There, sitting in a corner of the courtyard on still-chilly evenings, we warm ourselves around the fire, wrapped in our burnooses. In these remarkable surroundings, I think with delicious melancholy about all the strange aspects of my life . . . And I listen to the plaintive songs of the camel drivers and the deïra, my eyes half-closed. As always on the road in the desert, I feel a great calm come over my soul. I regret nothing, I desire nothing, I am happy.

It is there, after long months, that I first saw bare soil and delicate wild grass, things equally unknown in the Souf.

Farther on, the road descends into the ruddy, clayey shallows, interrupted by still-dry, dark-brown sebkha, and winds around small cone-shaped hillocks tinted bluish.

We then enter the region of the great chott, one of the strangest on earth.

At first we follow a somewhat rocky and solid path between the treacherous depths hiding under an apparently dry crust, unfathomable abysses of mud.

Right and left, we look out over two bluish seas of an almost-milky-white color toward the imperceptible horizon under the pale sky with which they seem to blend. And there are also countless archipelagos of clay and multicolored stones, perpendicular and stratified projections amid the immobile crystal of the salty waters.

Not a single living being, not a tree, not a bush, nothing. We notice two little pyramids built of dry rock. There in the past, two tribes came and settled an ancient quarrel, guns in hand. The powder spoke; there were deaths . . .

Seen from up high in the evening, after the maghreb, this kind of desert produces the effect of a somewhat stormy high sea at the same hour. It has the same dark-blue shade and the same clear high horizon . . . Soon the bordj appears, a gray building with a mournful appearance on the crest of a gray dune.

Some pious Muslim hand must have erected those stones to serve as a monument to the deceased. More than thirty years have passed since this obscure episode of nomadic life, and the miniscule pyramids remain there, perpetuating the memory of these dead whose names no one knows any longer.

The true Bou-Djeloud starts here, a maze of deep canals, of small islands, potholes, salt flats and saltpeter . . . a leprous region where all of the earth's secret chemistry stretches out under the immense sun.

Toward the left to the west is the hazy, imprecise horizon of the flooded Chott Merouan, extending to the low oases of the Oued Rir'. Toward the east is the great Melriri, which stretches to join up with the sebkha and the chott of the Tunisian Djerid.

A great strange sadness reigns over this remarkable region "where God's blessing was withdrawn," perhaps a vestige of a forgotten Dead Sea, where bitter salt, sterile clay, saltpeter, and iodine now reign . . .

Sad ephemeral lakes devoid of fish, birds, and boats; sand islands without vegetation; an absolute desert, more dismal than the most desiccated dunes!

Elsewhere, life can be generated by man—the soil is fertile. Here, death is irreversible; and except for winter flooding, nothing marks the succession of the days.

And yet they have their splendor and magic, the rock salt valleys, these transparent lakes where mirages occur, where imaginary cities, palm tree groves, and dream mosques are reflected, where countless herds—merely white vapors overheated by the sun—come to quench their thirst! Country of illusions, of reflections, visions, and ghosts, country of the unreal and of mystery, of still-intact memories of the planet's oceanic origins, or slow crumbling wounds, scourges, premature gangrenes already exploding on the earth's face . . . Who knows?

Stah-el-Hamraïa, the most charming of the bordj, perched on the top of an arid hill towering over the immensity of the chotts, seems like a sentinel guarding the solitudes.

At the foot of the hill, a small flooded garden without a fence, a few solitary palm trees, a few scrawny and barren fig trees, and deciduous trees that must be aspens or some species of sickly eucalyptus . . . On the ground, in the water—tall, coarse, and dark grasses, like drowned heads of hair . . .

Then the road, after having crossed the zone of ruddy clay, enters the scrub, scattered with sharp stones. There, spring is at its height. Everything is turning green and becoming green again; everything seems full of life and youth [. . .]

The large dark-needled Saharan bushes have shed their winter dust and seem dressed in velvet. The jujube trees, shriveled as if huddled on themselves and looking miserable, are covered with little round tender green leaves, an almost-golden color; the broom shrubs are all studded with white flowers, like little ingenuous perfumed slippers; grasses swollen with sap are standing upright; tufts of drinn, rigid and brilliant bundles, are green and have already blossomed; here and there, an asphodel stretches its tall stalk upward and its little pale bells; a violet iris and humble little blue flowers are hiding in the friendly shade of the bushes . . .

From all this greenery, from all of yesterday's budding riches, spread out for a few days under the sky that will soon be leaden and stop smiling for months and months, rises an intoxicating medley of perfume, a languid hot scent.

An infinite number of migrating birds flit about and sing in the celebratory desert. The larks rise up toward the nascent day, cry out tenderly as they beat their wings, then drop back into the bushes as if swooning.

And on all this ephemeral joy, the mysterious sadness of the desert casts its eternal shadow all about.

The caravan advances in disorderly fashion.

The camels are grazing. The *halessa*, the workmen, big tanned Souafa from the Ouled-Ahmed-Achèche tribe, sing interminable laments as if in a dream. Lost in this celebration of renewal, they long for their barren dunes and their gray city with a thousand low cupolas. Two giant mehari from the deïra of Lakhdar and Nasser solemnly wander with their Tuareg saddles and their long woolen tassels, making the little bells jingle at each step. Rezki, the little infantryman "who has finished his time" and who is journeying back to his native mountains of the Djurdura, sings to himself gracious cantilenas that none of us understand.

In the morning, at dawn, we leave the Chegga bordj, built in the middle of a swamp, whose saltpeter and iodine are slowly causing the walls to crumble.

We are no longer in the immaculate Oued Souf, a land of harsh and splendid sands, but rather in the salty Oued Rir', the hostile and deadly lands—the Oued Rir', with its own beauty and its special enchantments, its elements of a magic spell.

Since yesterday from the El-Mguébra bordj, we've been able to see the giant jagged outline of the ever-bluer Aurès over there on the horizon, and lower in the plain the slender black lines of the last oases: Biskra-Laouta, Beni-Mora, Sidi-Okba.

The environs of Biskra are without charm—desolate, sterile, and gray—where there is already a real road instead of the charming unpredictability of the Saharan trails. It is not any more the desert than Biskra is today the queen of oases. Demeaned, sullied queen, a token oasis planned for the amusement of the lazy, for whom the soul, the Sahara's deep mystical soul, will forever be closed and hostile.

It's the last evening, alas! We arrive alone under the powdery shadows of Old Biskra.

Ended, the long rides against the backdrop of the sands. Ended, the reveries tasted in the shadow of the saintly zaouïya; ended, too, are the joyous desert awakenings! For one last time we turn our horses' heads toward the south, and silently, with the eyes of exiles, we look at the dark Sahara below which the sun's great bloody disk descends.

Bewitching country, unique country, where there is silence, where peace reigns through the monotonous centuries. Country of dream and mirage, where modern Europe's sterile agitations don't reach at all.

In the distance, the sun has finished setting, and only a red glow remains. Then the desert—with its high, clear horizon and its undulations blue as an abyss—becomes like the stormy high sea at sunset in clear weather. And since this last evening of spring, I have not again seen the splendid and mournful Sahara.

Oh! The sweet numbing of the senses and the conscience in the monotonous life in the countries of the sun! Oh! The sweet sensation of letting oneself live, of no longer thinking, of no longer taking action, of no longer forcing oneself to do anything, of no longer regretting, of no longer desiring anything but the indefinite duration of what is! Oh! The blessed annihilation of the self in this contemplative life of the desert!... However, sometimes there remain troubled hours when the spirit and the conscience, I don't know why, wake up from their long drowsiness and torture us.

How many times have I not felt a pang of anguish when thinking about my writing and intellectual vocation, my former love of study and books, my intellectual curiosities of long ago ... Hours of remorse, anguish, and mourning. But these feelings have almost no effect on my will, which remains inert and doesn't act at all ... Then the surrounding peace and silence recapture us, and once again the contemplative life— the sweetest but also the most sterile of all—resumes for us again. "In sorrow thou shalt bring forth children," it was said to the first woman; and equal obligation undoubtedly weighed on the destinies of the first Prometheus of thought, the first Heracles of art. A secret voice must have said to him, "When your spirit is no longer tortured, when your heart no longer suffers, when your conscience no longer subjects you to severe interrogations, you will no longer create ..."

My hand remains inert, and my lips silent. Yet I understand universal fatality well: it is the delicious and agonizing burning to love that makes the bird sing in springtime, and the immortal masterpieces of thought originate in human suffering . . .

Before arriving at M'guébra, walking along next to Souf, I saw toward my right, to the north, thick strangely shaped clouds the color of gray-blue steel accumulating on the horizon.

"Hey," I said to the infantryman, "don't those look like mountains? . . ." But there are no mountains in the desert, except for sand dunes!

Farther on, between M'guébra and Chegga, we saw the wind break up these thick clouds, and the Aurès suddenly appeared to us, bluish and winding, outlined against a pale sky. I hadn't been mistaken . . . But I, too, had lost the notion of mountains, also lost that of the earth, in the immensity of the white sand dunes, delicate and light as dust . . .

Felt a strange sensation in finding again the real earth . . .

In Batna, vague but delicious impression at first, seeing large trees again, greenery, fields, and prairies . . . then, soon, unfathomable sadness and intense nostalgia for sand and palm groves.

Never will the thick and weighty shadow of the forests equal the delicate splendor and the nimble grace of the fine shadows of palm trees bent like a dome over the white sand! Never will the moon's rays play as magnificently between the oak trees' or beech trees' rough trunks as they play between the slender trunks—delicate spiral columns—of soaring date palms! Never will the murmur of soft leaves equal that of the silvery djerid, metallic and musical! Never will the abundant streams' water intoxicate an oppressed bosom like that of the fresh wells in the night, after a scorching day! Never will any garden equal in grace and splendor the Souf's deep *rhitan*, where the palm trees selected from different sizes gather—from miniature palm trees and young subjects with immense curved leaves, to venerable giants, often leaning over the surrounding green family . . . Never will the richest orchards give a hint of these gardens in August when the heavy clusters array themselves, according to species, some in all nuances of yellow, others in bright pink, in crimson, in velvety purple, under the canopy—dusty above, an ardent silvery green below—of the flexible djerid . . .

Left Batna, Monday, May 6 at four in the morning.

Calm morning, moonlight, very quiet in the streets. Went all the way down to the Sétif gate with Slimane, Labbadi, and Khelifa . . . In the avenue leading to the train station, made short stop with Slimane. Turned around one last time in order to see the dear red silhouette already almost lost in the shadows.

The countryside from Batna to El-Guerrah is sad and poor. Beyond there, the colors and hues are rich beyond belief: poppies spattered like spots of blood in the dark green of fields of grass, red gladiolas, anemones, cornflowers, then splashes of gold from the rapeseed . . . It's similar to my field over there on the Lambèse road, at the fourth kilometer, where I used to come on clear April mornings with my poor, faithful Souf . . . Where is Batna, the city of bitterness and exile that I miss today thinking of my poor friend with a good and faithful heart who stayed there? Where is Souf? Where is Khelifa? Where are all those poor things brought back from Eloued, pious reminders of our house down there . . . ?

Arrived in Bône at three o'clock. Intense impression of days from times long past at Khoudja's in the narrow blue courtyards, where mamma also came to sit so many times.

Reminders of times past, during my whole stay, except for the last day. Dreamy impression left by this city, of which I never again saw anything except for this Arab dwelling and the silhouette of departure.

Interrupted these sad notes with a brusque surge of all the despair caused by my separation from Ouiha . . . How to live without him, God knows for how long—exiled without lodgings, I who had become used to having a home of my own, however modest it was.

Days full of boredom and oppression in Bône. Struggling with the anguish of having left Slimane and against a persistent feeling of the unreality surrounding me. Departure in feverish haste on the Berry, under the name of Pierre Mouchet. Spent the days of the seventh, eighth, and ninth in Bône. Boarded the ninth at three o'clock. Left about six o'clock. Looked at the outline of the city so familiar in times past, now forever foreign, and the quay and the ramparts and L'Edough and Saint Augustine and the sacred green hill with its dark funerary cypresses.

This last return to Bône resembled a dream, so furtive and short did it seem, agitated and tormented, especially.

First moment, sitting on my bundle of clothes near the winch in my miserable sailor's getup; deep sadness, heartbreak at leaving the blessed African earth, and leaving Ouiha, and being so poor, so alone, and so abandoned on earth.

Dreamed of scenery from times past, when I chose to wear sailor's suits, dreamed of days of prosperity.

Started to doze on a thought, calmed already by the habit of suffering ... "Eden-Purée" the soldiers wrote on the door of the Kef-Eddor bordj ... One can find pleasure in joking about one's misery. Violent storm, rain, wandered on the bridge with my wet bundle, finally found refuge under the forward bridge with Neapolitans and the old Japanese man in the black *kachebia*.[1] A good enough night. Slept until Friday about four in the afternoon. The storm is beginning. Remained lying down in the water near the old, hideously sick Neapolitan. Fit of seasickness. Settled down behind the anchor winch on a pile of rigging. Horrible night. Took on huge amounts of water up front, splattering on me. Half delirium all night, serious fears of misfortune. The great voice of fear, the wind's and the sea's furious voices screamed all night, terrible. From this night's desperately lucid reasoning, a shiver stayed with me:

It is Death's voice, and it is Death raging against the little shaken and tortured thing, tossed about like a feather on the ill-tempered vastness of the sea.

Surprising care taken in making sentences, searching for words, as if for writing during these hours of anguish and physical suffering: seasickness, stomach and side cramps, freezing cold, fatigue, backache from getting stiff on the wet, hard riggings ...

1. A *kachebia* (or the more common spelling *kachabia*) is a man's wool winter overgarment, worn mostly by peasants in southern Tunisia. It is shin length and has long sleeves and a hood with a tassel.

Arrived on a clear afternoon. Disembarked on the pier, quietly climbed onto the tramway, and left from the Magdeleine on foot with my bundles, with difficulty, out of breath, no strength left.

Fear at not finding news from Slimane. I had such an anguished awakening during the night that I almost woke up Augustine. All morning without a single moment of rest until the arrival of Ouiha's dispatch: he is alive and he remembers me. That gives me courage to undergo this new trial, the cruelest of all: separation.

Here, I am happy—not for me—but to find, if not substantial comfort, at least the security of a kind of well-being . . .

The lively impressions of my November 1899 stay returned. Just a moment ago, I heard Marseille's heavy suspension bells: memory of sunny days when we were arriving, Popowa and I, in this city that I love with an odd kind of love, and that I don't like living in . . . Visit at the Chateau d'If, visit in Saint Victor, a wedding morning . . .

Clear autumn Provence days, already so distant!

But who will give back to me my eternally sunny bled and our white zaouïya and the calm houses with vaulted ceilings and the infinite horizons of sand and "Rouïha kahla" and the good faithful servants and Souf, my humble and faithful companion, and Belissa, the malicious one, and my rabbits, my hens, my pigeons and all the humble daily routine of our peaceful existence down there? Who will give the poor exile back her roof; who will give the orphan back her family . . . ?

Everything is there, but we are no longer there, in our arid country where mystical Faith alone flourishes, to be admired and loved . . .

A bit nearer—yet how far away from me, alas!—is an ordinary little city, completely French, in a sad valley in the shade of the great Chaouïya Mountains, where one sees only barracks, hospital, prison, and other administrative and military buildings, where one meets only spahis, Zouaves, *tringlots*, and artillerymen.[2] In this city, adjacent to the camp, there is an old one-story house. In front, in a warren of rooms inhabited by spahis and their wives, right near the staircase where one

2. Translator's note: *Tringlot* or *trainglot* is French army slang for the soldiers posted on trains transporting provisions and munitions.

hears nothing but the jangling of sabers and spurs, there are two miserable rooms looking out onto the neighboring rooftops and the city's rampart.

In this house, almost two months of my life went by, two months that seemed longer than two years to me . . .

And in this city there is a being whom I cherish . . .

And yet these African scenes seem very unreal; they seem to have been only fruitless daydreams, fugitive visions; and Slimane's personality itself doesn't seem very real to me, either.

As for other countries of the earth where my stormy and troubled past has taken place, those don't seem to me to have ever existed outside of my imagination! . . . From the bridge of the *Berry*, looking at the sacred hill of Bône's cemetery, in spite of a violent effort of my will, I didn't succeed at all in giving myself the real and poignant sensation that mamma had really been there, asleep in the tomb, for four years . . . And it seemed to me that I had never lived in Bône, and that this city was as foreign and indifferent to me as any other!

Often, since I left Slimane, I've felt an agonizing desire to cover the distance separating us, the absolute, intimate need to have him near me, him and nothing but him, and the irremediable despair of being exiled, of not being able to run to him, a grim and painful thirst to hear his voice, to see his eyes meet mine, to feel his presence, to feel again this sensation of absolute security that we share.

How long will exile last?

What would the sad and wild song be like, the great free song of the wandering camel driver in the desert, behind his slow camels on a theater stage or in a salon?

In Stah-el-Hamraïa, in the large, stark room of the bordj, half reclining on a *tellis* in the evening, I listened to the deïra Lakdar, one of the Khallassa, and Brahim singing the free and wild songs of the Sahara for the crowd assembled around them.

Tapping irregularly on an old tin crate, Lakhdar, drunk as usual, sang passionately . . . And this song had all the great poetic melancholy of wandering desert life.

I also remember those whom I listened to, sitting with the camel drivers in the corner of the Bir-bou-Chahma bordj courtyard near the fire where supper was cooking outdoors. The night was dark, and the voices rang strangely in the courtyard of this bordj, the most isolated and the saddest of all on this deserted route.

There, with intimate voluptuous pleasure, I thought about the engaging strangeness of my situation and about the happiness of being a vagabond and a wanderer, one of my happiest feelings, most strongly felt.

Alas! No home, not even the one that belongs to me, my humble pauper's home, could replace my Sahara, my vague and undulating horizon, my sweet dawns breaking on the infinite grayness and my sunsets soaking the little strangely named crumbling cities with blood, my poor unforgettable Souf, the humble companion of my solitary rides in the dear country whose name I gave to him, my Saharan garb, my liberty, and my dreams!

Made this remark about *Netotchka Neswanova*, that Dostoyevsky, that unparalleled painter of suffering, that novelist of morbid souls, loved to, and knew more than anyone how to portray childlike souls, especially those of unhappy children, in his eternal compassion for suffering. Of all the characters in his novels, there is not one who is not living, true, movingly and sometimes frighteningly true. With him, not one of these pale, conventional characters that proliferate in words by other authors reputed to be masters.

Nothing could equal in splendor and mystery moonlit nights in the desert of sand.

The chaos of the dunes, the tombs, the houses and gardens—everything is blurred and blends together. The desert, a snowy white, fills with ghosts, with reflections sometimes pink, sometimes bluish, with silvery glowing . . . No clear and precise contour, no fixed and distinct form: everything glows, everything scintillates infinitely, but everything is indistinct.

The dunes seem like vapors gathering at the horizon. The closest slopes disappear in the infinite clearness from above. Men dressed in white walk like apparitions, barely distinguishable, like vapor.

Often noticed the supernatural aspect taken on in the moonlight by a little section of remaining wall in the corner of the ruin situated behind the "neighborhood," above the infantrymen's garden. In spite of myself, it always seemed from far away to be a human silhouette standing there on my path, and it has happened that I've trembled at seeing it.

A distant memory now, already a year old, of a first night in the Bir Azzély garden above the Christian cemetery.

Reclining on the moonlit slope of the dune, in the deep crater, we were watching the mystery of the garden, where the moon's silvery rays were playing in the shadow of the palm trees between the slender trunks on the white sand.

And the other garden, in the caïdat of the Achèche, where we cried like children, accurately predicting, alas, with sudden and mutual intuition, all the misfortunes that would befall us a few months later . . . Oh unplumbed mystery of human premonition, of these vague presentiments, without any material and reasonable foundation, which never trick us, however! . . .

Moonlit nights, limpid and mystical, spent racing along the deserted roads of the Souf!

That night also, in the big rundown courtyard of the Elakbab zaouïya, while awaiting Sidi Mohammed Eliman, I was leaning against the mosque's little window, where, under the gray vaulted ceilings in the mysterious glow of a few candles, the khouan were reciting the *dikr* after the mogh'reb prayer . . .

I remember, too, the profound, infinite peace that had entered my soul that evening, while I was crossing the holy villages of Elbeyada and Elakbab, inundated with the last rays of the sunset . . . And yet, in what anguish, under what cruel circumstances I had come there! But do all these material things, all these ephemeral miseries, touch the souls of the initiated? One can, during certain blessed hours, make an abstraction of all the painful circumstances and give oneself to other impressions: those that we carry in us and those that come to us from the Unknown, through the sublime prism of the vast Universe!

How miserable are those who—made irremediably filthy by daily base material things—squander the brief hours of life in useless and inept recriminations against everyone and against everything, and who remain blind in the face of the ineffable beauty of things and in the face of the sad splendor of painful humanity.

Happy is he for whom everything does not capriciously end stupidly and cruelly, for whom all of earth's treasures are familiar, and for whom everything does not finish stupidly in the gloom of the grave!

There are disgraced beings who envisage the world in the most somber of colors, who see nothing of inexhaustible Beauty, which is the essence itself of the Universe and of Life.

It is the most disinherited of the disinherited of this world, an exiled woman without a home and without a country, an orphan stripped of everything, who is writing these lines. They are sincere and true.

Often during those vanished hours in a time of prosperity, I found life boring and ugly. But since I've possessed nothing more than my wakened spirit, since pain has drenched my soul, I feel with absolute sincerity the ineffable mystery suffusing all things . . .

The Bedouin shepherd, illiterate and unconscious, who praises God in the face of splendid desert horizons when the sun rises and who still praises him when facing death is much superior to the pseudointellectual who accumulates sentence upon sentence in order to denigrate a world whose meaning he does not understand and to insult Pain, this beautiful, this sublime and healing beneficial educator of souls . . .

Formerly, when I materially "lacked nothing," but when I was lacking everything intellectually and morally, I became dark and stupidly spewed curses against the Life that I didn't know. It is only now, in the heart of the destitution of which I am proud, that I affirm it is beautiful and worth living.

Three things can open our eyes to the exploding dawn of truth: Pain, Faith, Love—all of love.

Return to the South

Bou-Saâda

Fleeing Algiers's banality, its noise and its crowds, I wanted to see the South again, the country of healing silence, to relive—if only for a moment—the free life down there that I've missed for so long in the hostile atmosphere of large cities, bogged down in "civilization."

And very quickly, almost furtively, I went as far as Bou-Saâda, drowsy on the banks of its tranquil oued, embedded in the greenness of its gardens.

It was a short, rapid succession of visions, like veils suddenly lifted and then just as quickly falling back down on corners of very different countries.

First, under a black sky made hazy by the sirocco, the silhouette of Bordj-bou-Arreridj, with its old reddish citadel, a little town lost in the plain's immensity, already stripped by the harvesters.

On a hot bench, in a shop invaded by flies, a short rest lasting barely one hour.

The merchant is a Soufi from the Zegoum tribe. Both of us saddened—each in our own way—we talk about the radiant country, down there, very far away under the celebrated sun.

Then we have to leave immediately in a rickety cart covered by planks, harnessed with two scrawny old nags, and driven by the man named Bou-Guettar, a coachman who resembles a brigand.

The heat is overwhelming; a swarm of flies follows us; the cart gives epileptic jolts . . . however, that's always much better than the "mail coach."

My traveling companion and guide is Si Abou Bekr, a man about forty years old, thin and sickly looking, with a tanned and ascetic face, and a withdrawn, sad, almost-dark look. This man, authorized representative of the venerated *maraboute* of Bou-Saâda, and who manages immense riches, wears gandoura and burnooses, but worn-out and of great simplicity. He lives like a poor man but enjoys great serenity of mind.

Both of us sitting in the back of the cart, our feet dangling in empty space, we talk in a carefree way about things of the South, touching upon faith and Islamic jurisprudence.

Si Abou Bekr knows perfectly well who I am: he knows my story, and after having examined my case attentively, he approves of the way I live . . .

However, I cannot contain my joy at seeing the sky clear and the countryside change progressively as we advance toward the South . . . The country becomes harsher and more deserted. We catch a glimpse of a few rare toub hamlets, perched on the slopes of arid hills. Halfway there, on the bank of the Oued M'sila, there is a stopover; and the square-shaped bordj, with its big carriage entrance—built above the flowing murmuring river between a maze of oleanders and reeds—lends this stop in Medjez the deceptive feel of a Saharan caravansary.

I am taken for a Kabyle because of my complexion, and one of the inhabitants of Medjez insists on speaking to me in this language, affirming to me that he saw me in Tizi-Ouzou, where I've never been . . . I let him talk while waiting to leave, and a few little incidents of this type make me laugh with rediscovered cheerfulness.

We leave again, and we try to sleep, I perched on a crate and Si Abou Bekr rolled into a ball in the corner of the cart . . . Vague sleep, troubled at each instant, formless dreams, mixed with bits of reality, becoming strange.

Finally, before dawn, we arrive in M'sila. On foot, we follow a long alley of blackberry bushes, and we arrive at a big square, crisscrossed with little streams where toads are singing. At the end of it are buildings made of toub; and in front of a Moorish café, city dwellers are sleeping on mats, fleeing the heat of their houses.

After exchanging some salaams with people whom I don't know and who, in my half sleep, seem like ghosts to me, we too stretch out on our own mats.

I still hear, as if from afar, the imperious voice of a man who is actually very close by, on the threshold of the café, awakening the sleepers:

"Prayer is worth more than sleep!" White forms move, stretch, and get up. Tin cans ring against the fountain copings. Then everything sinks into the oblivion of an oppressive sleep.

◅❧▻

Noon. With their straight monotonous lines, the grayish walls of toub cut into the sky's incandescent paleness.

In the dusty little streets, near the ageless, peeling, cracked walls, in the short blue shadows, men in soiled burnooses sleep jumbled with the black goats. Only the flies swarm on the dried-out refuse, on the sweaty faces, on the tawny-colored rags.

Everything sleeps and pants in the crushing heat. In its white stone bed the oued flows with a tiny clear murmur, and in the distance the flaming green Boudjemline gardens stretch out voluptuously.

On the iron bridge, the hideous gray bridge, an old blind beggar crouches, slowly shaking his sonorous *bendir*; and in the immense surrounding sleep, these mute sounds punctuate the lamentation of the old man, for whom time no longer exists:

"In the name of Sidi Abdelkader Djilani, Master of Baghdad and lord of the heavens, give alms, oh Muslims!"

The blind man repeats his litany over and over, which no one hears, to which no one responds . . .

In a recess made of crude walls, two men stretched out on a mat seem to confer mysteriously . . .

Without a doubt some serious question regarding the South's complicated politics, or possibly even a plot . . . but no. One of them, quite simply, a thin *taleb* with a black beard, hooded in white, is explaining the origin of dreams to his companion.

"The soul," he says, "is what animates the body. The creator sometimes takes it out, either momentarily, as during sleep, or definitely, as in death. The soul is a luminous substance that emits rays as soon as it is delivered from the chains of the flesh. Then according to whether these rays fall in the visible world, on earth, or whether they head for the beyond, the sleeper sees the cities, the countries, the trees, the flowers, the men, the prophets, and the armies that inhabit the earth . . . In the beyond, he sometimes perceives fragments of the unknown in death . . . Then the rays go out, and the soul returns to its dark carnal prison . . ."

And in M'sila's sleepy exhaustion, the two sophists with their mysterious airs continue to slowly enumerate their dogmas from long ago, in the midst of the earth and sun's changing backdrop . . .

After sunset. In a smoky room falling into ruins of old, worn-out toub, under the roof's black joists—five tree trunks barely squared off with an ax, still showing the robust veins of the South's slender trees, are grouped together in a strange family. A dim smoking lamp illuminates three hooded men who are beating their cracked bendir and swaying in rhythm as they slowly chant the litanies of Sidi Abdelkader, the great saint of Baghdad . . . And the lamp's red glow slowly casts their distorted shadows onto the rough walls where little furtive yellow scorpions and gray tarantulas sometimes run.

All around, draped bodies are piled up, twisted into languid positions; eagle-like profiles lean toward the singers; long shadowy-black or red-gold eyes half close . . .

Two delicious little suntanned girls, dressed in bright green dresses with silver hook-and-eye fasteners, and silk scarves embroidered with gold on their black hair, listen, attentive and serious, standing in the middle of the Moorish café, Tebberr and Oum-Henni, Poudre-d'Or and Mère-de-la-Paix, the café owner's two little girls.[1]

In a shady narrow street, a door opens onto a dimly lit courtyard. Crouching along the wall, in light-colored dresses, adorned like idols, streaming with gold coins, they maintain the studied immobility of statues, their eyes vague in the cigarette smoke . . . Sometimes a burnoose goes by, threads its way through, disappears in the courtyard, a white burnoose from M'sili, the blue burnoose of a deïra . . . Then one of the idols gets up with a jangling of her jewels and follows the visitor into the warm shadows of a poor cell.

And thus M'sila falls asleep, saintly and prostituted, drowsy and pas-

---

1. Translator's note: *Poudre-d'Or* means "gold powder," and *Mère-de-la-Paix* means "mother of peace."

sionate, in the night's heavy heat. The *benadir*, the old religious cantilenas, and the ringing of the Ouled-Naïl's bracelets, slowly rock her.

M'sila is as charming as a Saharan ksar. The oued of the same name cuts it in two, flowing to the bottom of the wide and deep ravine. Over pebbles, an iron bridge connects the two M'sila.

We're in the new M'sila, of recent construction, where the streets are wide, where there are no corners of shadow and mystery, and where everything—even convenience—is sacrificed to the *roumi* preference for straight lines.

On the other bank is the old city, piled up, chaotic, with all its houses in blackish toub and its nameless streets, misaligned and without cobblestones, deliciously full of surprises and yet all similar.

The sirocco blows all day long; the burning, devouring wind has not left us since the blazing Gehenna of Portes-de-Fer. The background scenery is ablaze and deformed, and the dust rises in gray whirlwinds that fly away on the roads. Roused by the heat, the flies buzz furiously and bite.

Only the mosque, situated on the bank of the oued, whose windows open onto the water, still retains some coolness; and that's where we take refuge all day long.

Toward evening, the wind abruptly changes direction; and while Si Abou Bekr leaves to search for mounts and to make a few visits, I go sit alone on the elevated bank of the oued.

The sky is now almost completely pure, and the air has cooled down. The sun sets in a light haze, still vaguely yellow, above the great barren plain that is the entrance to Hodna from the west.

Across from me, outlined in a warm brown color against the translucent lilac color of the horizon, the old M'sila rises up, surrounded by very green and dense gardens, whereas behind me the new city's houses stand out almost golden against the rosy golden hue of the setting sun.

Women draped in red or blue cloth come down into the bottom of the oued carrying goatskins or heavy amphorae of porous earth . . . Walking barefoot in the gravel and sand, they glide like apparitions, adding a special note to the peaceful charm and sweet melancholy of this countryside.

There again, added to the very real intoxication of this place and this hour, comes the intoxication of memory's evocations of other places, of regions, compared to which those I am crossing seem to be only a pale reflection. The M'sillia do not have the strange grace and mysterious attraction of the girls who go at dusk in search of the cool well water in the Souf's enchanted gardens . . .

Ah! If only Africa's summer sunsets lasted indefinitely, and if only the despotic stupidity of men enamored with banality did not trouble the poet's dreams! But the horses are there in front of the mosque, and we must leave. I'm given a beautiful white mare, saddled in red *filali*, and we descend into the bed of the oued. Naked and tanned little boys are there bathing stallions, and their passionate beasts dilate their nostrils and rear up, greeting my trembling mare with a resonant neighing.

Across the way, in the velvety green of gardens where the tops of a few disheveled date trees rise up, some small and strangely shaped koubba built of toub lie hidden.

One of them resembles a Chinese pagoda, with its stacked roofs and strange point, and I like seeing there the remains of a native pre-Islamic art, very wild and very strangely troubling.

A taleb, mounted on a well-behaved mule carrying our baggage, accompanies us. We leave the oued and have a last glance at M'sila before entering the great plain.

This Hodna plain resembles the desert, which, in the evening's penumbra, seems infinite . . . The far-off mountains, an iridescent blue, fade and melt into the paleness of the sky, and the open space seems limitless.

The horses sense this calm and free vastness . . . They would like to launch themselves into it and become intoxicated with breathtaking races.

The plain is dotted with small, low, pale-green bushes the dusty color of the soil. A few small dried-out ravines; not an undulation, not a hill. It is grand, monotonous and soothing . . .

We gently move forward at a walk, and night falls. Balminess like a caress passes through the unbreathed air, unsullied by any blemish.

Once again, I find there that impression of absolute silence that I loved so much, of immense peace that nothing ever comes to disturb.

It is completely dark when we see a black wall rising up before us: it is the Si-el-Raâb bordj, owned by the *habous* of the zaouïya of the Bou-Saâda Rahmania; its dense gardens form a chaotic, giant black mass.

After a quick supper, we stretch out on a blanket in the courtyard, for it is hot and scorpions haunt the houses made of toub. The garden and the bordj along with the horses and the mules grazing in the country-side are in the care of a few knowledgeable *tolba*, who live there alone on the plain as recluses, and who use their free time to read old books and pray, like monks.

It's the second night spent without sleep, and our eyes close . . . But fleas—the curse of the douar—swoop down on us . . . The tolbas, who are used to them, sleep deeply. Fatigue ends up overwhelming my companion, and he falls asleep. Then, left alone, I get up and stretch outside on the dry hot earth.

There I wait for the moon to rise—the hour of departure—while dreaming in the darkness under the breathtaking falling stars . . . I hear my heart being reborn to life; and with happiness, I feel the vitality of my youth, which I often forget in my anguish . . .

Finally, when the quarter moon's deformed pallid disk rises above the plain, which appears dotted with hovels in ruins and planted with little gardens as thick as groves, I return to awaken Si Abou Bekr and the tolba, who are sleeping deeply in the cool of the morning.

We leave again. On our mounts, we sleep as if numbed. In the deep silence, from time to time, one of the horses snorts or takes a false step.

Then the tolba start singing one of the slow songs from the South, which helps when crossing large monotonous spaces:

"A-ya-â-â-ya-â-â! . . . I called out and no one answered . . . A-ya-â-ya-â-ya-â-â! . . . I begged and no one gave me alms . . ."

Then the dream voice is once again silent, and in silence we continue our ghostly walk.

But we enter a region where the horses, who are frightened, advance reluctantly. There are an endless number of completely round bushes— black below and silvery above—which from afar resemble reclining men or ghosts. For fear of falling, we have to wake up completely.

The day rises. A delicious coolness flows to us from the hazy blue distance, and the long night gives way to this renewal of youth and gaiety, which this first hour of the day always brings in the vast and deserted regions of the South . . .

We pass in front of about twenty sleeping houses made of toub, where only ferocious dogs remain awake, greeting us with their raucous and guttural barking . . . This is the village of Saïda: not a tree, not a blade of grass.

Afterward, we return to the silvery-colored scrub from which rises the strange, melancholy moan, like a call without an echo, of the kérouan, the ground-dwelling desert bird that prefers to come out at night to sing.

It's fully daylight when we arrive at the western bay of the Hodna: a yellowish-brown sebkha stretching out, uniform, level, without a bump, without any grass. Then the tolba dismount from their horses in order to pray the *fedjr*, a dawn prayer.

After nearly a year, I have become unaccustomed to the hardness of Arab saddles and stirrups, and I feel exhausted, my legs limp and painful.

Si Ali, the taleb who had been accompanying us, leaves and returns to M'sila. Si Abou Bekr climbs onto his she-mule, and we disappear into the sebkha.

The sun rises, red, already blazing. The heat begins almost immediately.

Baniou—a grayish-white military bordj on the heights. A row of poplars leads to the well whose warm water is murky and revolting. Surrounding it, a few constructions made of toub. Below, there is sand, real sand, a bit reddish, it's true, but dry and delicate. Here and there, tamarisk bushes' roots, choked with sand, form mounds, like those of all Saharan trees. We rest in the shade of one, in order to greedily drink liquid mud and a horrible cup of coffee full of flies.

It is getting hotter and hotter, and we leave again.

Two hours go by, and we arrive in Bir-Khali. There are houses made of toub, abandoned in the summer; and there is a well of very pure and almost-cool water. We drink with rage . . . I don't know what other term to use.

Afterward, there are the leaden midday hours, on the barren and sun-baked plain. But we have across from us the rest of the mountains that enclose the horizon and, between two elevated peaks, Bou-Saâda on its low hill. One can see clearly the *kasbah* overlooking the city and the black of the gardens.

And the South's eternal illusion begins again: The city seems close to us, and yet we keep moving forward without the distance seeming to diminish. And this vision of a bewitched city fleeing on the horizon becomes agonizing in the long run. The heat is scorching. Our lips dry out and split. The sirocco burns us.

We pass a camel driver who gives us water; then, very quickly, the man and his great slow beast lose their shape and melt with hardly perceptible undulation into the plains' indistinct contours.

Bou Saâda, a gracious vision that appeared to me, crowned by the sun, gilded and set into the living emerald of its gardens!

By a long and circuitous route, the Oued Bou-Saâda flows over white pebbles at the foot of the city. To the left, overflowing the walls of yellow toub, the bushy gardens are like a virgin forest crowned by the date trees' royal plumage. On the right, emerging from a belt of fig trees, oleanders, and pomegranate trees, tall earthen houses laid out in a pleasant and very Saharan disorder.

Walking in the water, toward which our thirsty beasts lean, we followed the bottom of the oued all the way to a very cool fountain bursting out of rock at the foot of the city: Aïn Bessem, "the smiling fountain." There we drink again.

Bou-Saâda is also divided into two cities, separated by a deep ravine and joined again by a bridge.

In one of them are European buildings—the Arab Bureau, the Justice of the Peace. In the other, the old mass of molded earth that is the true Bou-Saâda.

The twin city is hemmed in by tall reddish hills, dominated by the mountains, the strange mountains of this southern chain, stratified and topped with steep terraces, a few of which are overhanging.

The people of Bou-Saâda resemble the people of the Sahara, deeply attached to ancient customs and practices from times past . . . this people who, the more one distances oneself from large cosmopolitan and corrupt cities, the more they seem to climb farther up the ladder of old lost centuries.

Tanned faces under the white turban or the veil attached with a beige camel hair cord, male or ascetic faces, wild and sunken eyes glowing with a dark flame under the canopy of the *guelmouna* [the cape of the burnoose], rosaries at their neck, countenances from another age, almost from another world.

The women's outfit is more difficult to wear: muslins draped like a Greek tunic, belted very low, voluminous hairstyle—all of this is becoming only on tall and svelte women, especially very lithe ones. And you don't see them in the streets, only poor old pathetic worn-out mummies instead.

We have our beds prepared—mats and rugs—under the arches of a big house that is dependent on the zaouïya and located in a remote corner of the new city, near the Justice of the Peace, separated by a deep hollow where there is a very beautiful garden, a chaos of powerful greenery.

Across from us, a scrawny plantation of mimosas and misshapen blackberry bushes, the whole thing sadly enclosed by an artificial bramble thicket. How pitiful these symmetrically aligned gardens, without the unexpected and without charm, seem next to splendid Arab gardens planted haphazardly according to fancy, very close to nature and rich like her!

Unlike the ignorant and poetic fellah, morose disciplinarians, the poor ragged prisoners and their guardians do not know how to entwine the light-colored vine with the dark foliage of fig trees, how to cast the light pink of oleanders amid powerful palm trees and the incarnadine red of the pomegranate into the impenetrable shadow of apple trees.

Time passes and as soon as it is dawn, we leave again for the zaouïya over there, following the appealing Djelfa and desert route.

After running along the Oued Bou-Saâda, the path passes between the mountains, which are turning blue in the dawn's clear light.

Summer has dried out the meadows and the scrub. Everything is again taking on the neutral but infinitely varied shades of the earth. Red brick, sienna earth, yellow ocher, greenish ocher—hardly perceptible, harmless, ashy hues, the prodigious range of grays, pale pinks, pallid whites. This neutrality of shades, their lack of precision, gives great charm to the play of light that one cannot find anywhere else and that is the miracle of these harsh regions.

At the Zaouïya

Once again, we approach the oued, both banks of which are planted with gardens, always of the same green, almost unbelievable because it is so cool and delightful.

There are a few toub houses in a sort of very uniform zone: it is another of the tolba retreats, dependent, like their gardens, on the El-Hamel zaouïya.

El-Hamel, a poetic name meaning "the Lost," which suits this wild and grandiose place very well, is lost, in fact, in a valley enclosed on one side and open on the other, toward the oued, on a vast, azure horizon.

And the zaouïya appears to us on the hill: two large main bodies of the building, one very white and European looking and the other made of very light-colored toub with only a few narrow openings.

Below, a town of earthen houses, then the Chorfa tribe's village, and a picturesque mass of crumbling houses, like all these toub constructions.

Even farther down, a sea of greenery topped by date trees, like a splendid canopy.

All of this stands out very, very delicately against the hill's indefinable shades of color, in the mountain's pure air. This place has a particular aspect, very much its own, due neither to the Sahara nor to the ordinary countryside of the High Plateau.

I fall asleep immediately on a rug in a little bedroom made of toub, very poor and very simple, which is the dwelling place of Si Abou Bekr, while a joyful coming and going bids us welcome.

Upon awakening, I again find there these calm, secret, and polite conversations that make the long hours of endlessly similar days go by, in all those places where, still intact, the great Islamic lack of concern has not been touched by corrupting European bustle.

Here, in this lost place where the setting is grandiose and simple, the noise of our fierce and useless battles comes and dies in the great immutable silence, and everyday affairs, always more or less the same, are merely incidents.

In order to live with these withdrawn and sensitive men, one must have penetrated their ideas, have made them one's own, have purified them by making them return to their antique source ... Then life is easy and very gently soothing in this world of burnooses and turbans, forever hidden from the observations of a tourist, however attentive and intelligent she might be.

Speak little, listen much, do not open up—these are the rules to follow in order to please in the Arab milieus of the South, and in order to feel at ease there ...

After crossing several halls and vast dark courtyards, we enter a large interior courtyard enclosed by very high and very old walls made of brownish toub. In there, a young fig tree grows, and in a few years, it will shade this place where a great silence reigns. In this courtyard, we saw a sort of bed, a large polished slab posed on four stone supports: this is where Sidi Mohammed Belkassem, the deceased marabout, lay.

◄◄ ►►

In a corner, near to the door of the interior apartments, on a sort of stone set of steps, sits a woman wearing the costume of Bou Saâda, white and very simple. Her face, tanned by the sun—for she travels a lot in the region—is wrinkled. She is approaching about fifty years old. In the black pupils of her soft eyes, the flame of intelligence burns as if veiled by great sadness. Everything, in her voice, in her manners, and in her welcoming of the pilgrims, denotes the greatest simplicity. It is Lèlla Zeyneb, the daughter and heiress of Sidi Mohammed Belkassem.

The marabout, lacking a male heir, designated his only child, whom he had instructed in Arabic like the best of the tolba, to succeed him after his death. He prepared his daughter for a very different role from that generally allotted an Arab woman, and today it is she who directs the zaouïya and the khouan, affiliated members of the brotherhood.

The zaouïya are not, as asserted by certain authors who know them only by name, "schools of fanaticism." Besides the Islamic instruction, the zaouïya distribute the benefits of their charity to thousands of poor people, orphans, widows, and disabled, who, without them, would be homeless and without aid. More than any other, Lèlla Zeyneb's zaouïya is a refuge for the disinherited who flock there from all over. Lèlla Zeyneb, afflicted with a painful throat ailment, fights courageously against all the enemies whom certain jealousies create for her, and she continues her work of devotion and self-denial.

My case, my way of life, and my story keenly interest the maraboute. When she has heard all, she approves of me and assures me of her friendship forever. However, all of a sudden she becomes sad, and I see tears in her eyes.

"My daughter . . . I have given all my life to create good on God's path . . . And men do not recognize the good that I am doing them. Many hate me and are jealous of me. And yet, I have renounced all: I have never married, I have no family, no joy . . ."

I feel myself becoming sad in the face of this unjust pain, likely hidden for years and which comes out only in the presence of another woman whose destiny is also very removed from the ordinary.

From time to time, a hoarse cough shakes Lèlla Zeyneb's chest . . . I sense that she is very sick, alas! She who watches over the large family pressing around her, and who is rich in misfortunes. And what will become of the beneficent zaouïya, the day, without a doubt in the near future, when Lèlla Zeyneb will die?

This figure of a woman, living in celibacy and playing an important religious role, is unique, perhaps, in the Muslim West, and certainly would deserve to be studied better than I have been able to do during a too-brief stop at the zaouïya . . .

I spend the night alone in a vast room with a vaulted ceiling. The mountain wind shakes the window shutters violently. It cries and moans in the valley and among the tombs of the nearby cemetery.

A dream voice, melancholy and infinitely gentle, awakens me in the early morning.

"God is one and helpful . . . He has not at all been created and has not created . . . God has no equal!" the voice chants slowly, slowly.

I get up, thinking sadly that it is the last day, and I approach the window: downstairs an old man walks, reciting the verses of the Book to a melody of long ago.

I said goodbye to Lèlla Zeyneb, and I left the El-Hamel zaouïya . . .

In Bou-Saâda I get into a nondescript rattletrap packed with Jews going to Aumale across 130 kilometers of jolts and ruts.

At first there are red sands, sparse tamarisks, a vast and empty horizon that resembles the Sahara, from which I am distancing myself once again.

The first stops still have familiar and appreciated features: abandoned bordj, palm trees grouped in the shallows; then everything changes. We head up again toward the High Plateaus, and the countryside becomes severe and sad, a sadness that I don't like. It's over . . .

This seven-day dream has vanished after so many others, and I'm almost to the point of wondering whether it is really true, if all this rapid fairytale world is not a dream, if this Bou-Saâda and this zaouïya, and this maraboute in white veils, if all of this does not stem from my nostalgic imagination.

How greatly would I miss Bou-Saâda, its incomparable light, its warm and picturesque bustle.

Shortly afterward I left for boring Ténès, where I lived for long months near Tell fellah. There I could attentively study the relationships between the natives and the colonists . . . The Arab peasant has the patience of the muzhik. The colonist is most often a courageous man who doesn't understand his neighbor.

I often went to Algiers to write. One rainy day, I met Abou Bekr underneath the arches.

"Won't you come anymore to see us down there? . . . the trees are beginning to blossom . . . the maraboute speaks often of you . . ."

And two days later, I am once again en route for Bou-Saâda, light and joyful, in spite of the season's cold weather, as if I were going to gather flowers in the garden.

Note

Published in part in *Les Nouvelles d'Alger* (*The News from Algiers*), these notes from a trip in July 1902 have been edited in full in *Notes de route.*

After an exile of eight months in Marseille, under an order of expulsion from the general government, Eberhardt returned to Algeria in 1902.

In Ténès, a coastal city to the west of Algiers, she composes "Nouvelles algériennes" ("Algerian Stories"), which appear regularly in *Akhbar*, for which she has become a privileged contributor. In the autumn of 1903, she will again travel the southern route.

Oranese South,

PART I

The last days of summer dropped away monotonously, one by one. Algiers slept under the oppression of a cloudless sky. The streets, where passersby were rare, seemed wider, and swarms of blue flies buzzed in the meager shade offered by the houses. The Mustapha hills were hazy with fine dust, and the milky whiteness of the upper city faded out. There, however, in the narrow, strangled streets, life continued, ardent, drunk with light and color, with fruit and cloth stalls, and the pensive song of the captive nightingales in front of the Moorish cafés.

A heavy tedium weighed on Algiers, and I abandoned myself to a vague drowsy state without joy or sadness and that without desires also could have brought with it the sweetness of annihilation.

All of a sudden the El-Moungar fighting began, and with it, the possibility of seeing again the harsh southern regions: I was going into the Sud-Oranais as a reporter . . . The dream of so many months was going to come true, and so abruptly.

The long train ride, through all of Algeria's West and Southwest, was charming.

In the first joyful emotion of going away, I had a few hours of rest and daydreaming.

There are thus, at certain periods of life, moments when nothing extraordinary takes place, but which one never forgets later on, for they are of inexpressible sweetness.

It was in Perrégaux where one must wait for the train from Arzew that goes down toward the South.

Perrégaux is nothing but a Spanish market town, set in the middle of an immense fertile plain with large green gardens. However, this very poor corner of the Algerian Tell seemed smiling, almost beautiful to me.

The clear day was drawing to a close over the calm of the countryside. A tall hill blocked the horizon, which was lighting up bit by bit. At the top was a little chapel of Sidi Abdelkader of Baghdad, which seemed all pink, between a few silhouettes of gray olive trees. There in the dried-out grass, crude stones were hidden: the Muslim cemetery, a place of calm melancholy, with nothing gloomy about it.

In the evening, I would go stretch out on a mat in front of a Moorish café. Next door, above the carriage entrance of a Spanish inn, one could read in large awkward characters: *Defendido entrar gitanos*, "No Gypsies Allowed."

Across the way, a barren wall stood out against the pink opal color of the sunset. Squatting on the ground, Arab nomads were dreaming. In the hot air, familiar scents trailed behind Bedouin-country scents of summer evenings: thuja or juniper smoke, goatskin smells, tar, the odor of sweaty tanned skins. And I was tasting the deep voluptuousness of the wandering life, the joy of being alone—unknown beneath my Muslim burnoose and turban—and the joy of peacefully watching the day finish in red glimmers on the simplicity of things, in this village where nothing held me and that I was to leave at nightfall.

Afterward, there were once again long hours at the train car window, through more deserts and harsher regions as the slow little train descended toward the South.

Villages and market towns went by in the lunar night, rapid and furtive like visions.

Toward the middle of the night, there it was: sad Saïda, where so many human wrecks come searching for oblivion under the Foreign Legion's anonymous greatcoat. Then the rugged climb of the high plateaus on the winding road. The train's two engines got out of breath, hiccupped like short-winded beasts.

At the top, at the entryway onto the immense barren plain, twin marabouts seemed to be on guard.

Halts in open country for villages unseen or distant douar: Aïn-el-Hadjar, Bou-Rached, Tafaroua . . .

The day finally lit up in a green and red sky on the small white dunes of Khreider.

And thus, indefinitely, it was always the serious monotony, the sadness and also the great poignant charm of the southern plain, with its rare clumps of tough esparto grass and its creeping gray shrubs on the blood-red soil. Barely distinct diaphanous chains of mountains retreated in the distance.

The sun came up, and we arrived across from the sturdy crest of the Djebel-Antar advancing into the vagueness of flat horizons. At the foot of this high blue wall was Mechéria, a few pink roofs, a few slender yellowed trees, then, immediately afterward, nothing more, once again the steppe's emptiness where the iridescent glimmers of the morning played together.

After Khreider, the forsaken train stations had changed in appearance: they were now high small fortresses flanked with gray watchtowers closed by heavy iron doors.

Mountains finally burst forth from the warm azure of the distances: the Djebel-Mektar, the Mir-el-Djebel, and the Sfissifa Mountains. Beyond, toward the West, lay Morocco.

Big reddish dunes stormed Mektar like breaking waves. A belt of bluish greenery hemmed in the redoubt's tall brick buildings.

Toward the right, a few Saharan houses made of toub squeezed one against another, clumps of black fig trees, a few date tree silhouettes, a few white marabouts. Finally, there was Aïn Sefra, which I was only to pass through in order to continue on to Beni-Ounif-de-Figuig.

Reflections of War

Aïn-Sefra, not long ago a poor garrison fallen into a deep sleep and the routine of military life in times of peace.[1]

Today, with the troubles in the South and the torment rumbling once again through Morocco in ferment, Aïn-Sefra seems to be awakening, taking on once again elements from long ago in Bou-Amama's heroic times. More numerous and noisier troops, the arrivals and the departures, the waiting, sometimes the anguish, a highly unusual motion fills up the narrow sandy alleys.

Mixing in the sun, *goumiers* mounted on small skinny horses, all muscle; *mokhazni* in long black burnooses embroidered at the chest in red, their belts bristling with cartridges; blue infantrymen; spahis in red coats . . . Finally, legionnaires, these blond men from the North, tanned, weathered by the colonies' distant suns.

In the cantinas and the Moorish cafés full of a joyous racket, the most unexpected contrasts clash. Here the saucy verses from twopenny songs—the recent repetitive songs—mix with the crooned sentimentalities of German or Italian ballads. And next door the old African *rhaïta* cries and yells out its strange triplets, accompanying slow threnodies interrupted, by way of a refrain, by long desolate cries.

In the same intoxication of music and noise, the two neighboring worlds, the European world and the Arab world, rub shoulders and mix, without ever merging.

To all these ineffaceable dissonances, the Foreign Legion comes and

1. Victor Barrucand's note: Aïn Sefra, dual scenery of a French village in the pale Tell greenery—silvery poplars, sickly yellowed plantain trees—and of a *ksour* made of gray toub with uneven and deserted streets. At the foot of very blue and very high mountains, the jagged crests of tawny dunes, the soft undulations of red sand, and the invasion of stormy grass.

adds even more far-off notes. And with all this racket and all these men, in the hour's temporariness and uncertainty, Aïn-Sefra is beautiful . . .

⋘ ⋙

I go up to the hospital in the redoubt overlooking the city.

Big red, brick buildings surrounded by galleries with archways. The El-Moungar wounded wander in the shade, with bandages made of very white cloth, in the idleness of their convalescence.

Two or three Frenchmen among these foreigners . . . the rest, Germans or Italians: rough impudent faces, pleasant smiles.

Sort of proud to be "interviewed"—a word they were taught—they are, however, intimidated. Then in a very military way, they end up having me speak to their head, Corporal Zolli.

Young, tall, and thin, comfortably wearing the hospital's gray outfit, he speaks accurate, sometimes even elegant French. Used to it, he doesn't become flustered.

Clearly, vividly, he recounts the imprudent halt, without any precaution, in the valley between El-Moungar and Zafrani, the fatal lack of concern of the unfortunate Captain Vauchez, who said, laughing, that he would go in his shirtsleeves to Tafilalet, and that was a few days before his death . . . However, the corporal vouches for the beautiful, calm gallantry of the captain who, mortally wounded, found the will to write a few words in pencil to send a warning to Captain de Susbielle in Taghit.

Through the corporal's story also passes the melancholy silhouette of the Danish officer, Lieutenant Selkauhausen, who had come to serve in the Foreign Legion, with his rank, in order to educate himself, and who died down there in this unknown corner of the southern Oranais.

"It appears that the lieutenant was engaged to be married in his own country," adds the corporal. "Regardless, his death is very sad!"

Zolli knows how to relive the torments of that day of fierce unequal battle, far from all help. He is modest, not exaggerating his own role, admitting to the wound on his right hand that from the beginning prevented him from shooting.

A former soldier under General Menotti Garibaldi in Macedonia, Zolli likes war: he always arranges to be where there is fighting.

Sometimes the coarser men get bolder, risk a word, some simple and poignant memory or some joke about their own misfortune.

"We were damned thirsty that day," said one of them who doesn't seem to remember anything else. "And since there wasn't water, we knocked back many liters of pure wine in the evening when it was done. That bowled us over and made us a little drunk."

Very nice, these poor devils who suffered and almost died over issues that are not theirs, and which leave them profoundly indifferent.

On the ground floor is a little room filled with sick infantrymen.

There, lying down out of boredom, Mouley Idriss, a tall, tanned, muscled lean mokhazni, with the regular and energetic features of a nomad.

This mokhazni was wounded by a *djich* a few days before El-Moungar. At first very primitive and very withdrawn, Mouley Idriss ends up, however, reassured and smiling. He expresses what all the Arabs of the Southwest think. For them, it is a question neither of war with Morocco nor particularly of a holy war. The area has always been *bled-el-baroud* (a country of gunpowder), and the tribes of the ill-defined border have always conducted raids on one another. Mouley Idriss designates the enemy by a telling name: *el khian*, the thieves, the bandits.

Quite simply, he considers the current military operations to be counterraids and reprisals against the *djiouch*.

This explains clearly why the so-precious indigenous auxiliaries—mokhazni, goumiers, mail-raiders, *sokhar*, most of whom are recruited from among the country's nomads—feel no repugnance at all in combating the pillagers and give the example of valor, endurance, and devotion beyond all praise.

Mouley Idriss, without insisting on what he had to suffer from the enemy, vigorously condemns the acts of those he calls "road cutters" and vultures.

In the end, he must not sincerely desire all of this outcome: he is a nomad, thus a man of gunpowder, and he likes to fight.

Mouley Idriss belongs to *mokhzen* Sidi Mouley Ould Mohammed's *agha* of the Amour of Aïn-Sefra, one of the most sympathetic toward and devoted to the French cause among the indigenous personalities of the Southwest.

While I chat with Mouley Idriss, the infantrymen, his companions, surround us.

Half-undressed with their old hospital gowns that look so bad on them, and shaved around their heads, the infantrymen are funny. They play pranks and burst into laughter, a contrast to their robust square shapes and their masculine faces.

All this suffering little world waits impatiently for the day when, even poorly healed, they'll be allowed to leave: the Arabs consider the hospital to be a deadly place, like prison.

Eight o'clock in the evening, a great feeling of suffocation over Aïn-Sefra, in the dark of closed shops, cafés locking up, like on long evenings of epic drunkenness, when the Legion performs. No civilian passersby, a heavy silence, almost the impression of a city in danger.

The shopkeepers, the *mercantis*, as the Arabs call them, assemble in closed rooms around the green field of deserted billiard tables. They have serious, worried looks. There are long complaints, the eternal exaggeration about things, the inordinate magnification caused by fear. They talk about strategy; they find the garrison ridiculously insufficient; they calculate the risk of awakening the next morning with the railroad and the telegraph cut. They announce a *harka*, a large band of pillagers, coming from near Sfissifa. They even go so far as to evaluate the distance between the village and redoubt, a safe refuge . . .

Near panic in Aïn-Sefra this evening. And all because a patrol was attacked twenty kilometers from here in Teniet-Merbah and because a mokhazni was killed . . . In addition, a djich was seen near the Mékalis train station.

In a Mozabite shop where I've come for a little light and gaiety, a spahi enters, a handsome boy with a sweet and expressive face.

He seems worried.

"Adieu," he says, "pardon me if I have wronged any of you."

"But where are you going?"

"Eh! Didn't I take an oath? He who joins puts his neck in the noose; afterward he will do what he is ordered to do, without thinking any longer about his tent or his friends. For me, it's not of being killed that I'm afraid. You only die once. It's walking alone in the night without a human being to talk to . . . I'm being sent with a letter for Beni-Yaho."

And all the assistants embrace the spahi, while thinking of the makhzen trooper killed in the morning.

And it is the only really sad and poignant note in all this alarmed city's atmosphere—the departure of this poor soldier who himself is truly risking his life out in the threatening darkness and silence of the countryside.

Everything goes well, however; and the slow night hours flow by without the slightest alert, without the least echo of a gunshot.

The day rises, radiant, vanquishing the ghosts evoked the night before.

Someone announces to me that the spahi Abdelkader was not attacked. And everything in the village calms down; its monotonous life returns to normal.

Mograr-Foukani

Today, I'm going down toward Hadjerath-M'guil in order to see the other El-Moungar wounded who have stayed there.

A little after sunrise, the train enters a unique region of gripping strangeness.

No more sand or esparto grass, nothing more than stone, an immense chaos of broken, rolled, jagged stones, torn out of the ground as if by a horrifying cataclysm.

Sharp edges overlap one another or are superimposed like monstrous lace pulled across the boulders on the clay hills. Trenches, narrow and deep as corridors, overhung by enormous blocks poised in a dangerous balance, ready to detach themselves and smash the passing train.

It's like a gigantic lava flow spewed forth by the dark peaks enclosing the horizon, and having invaded the valley so as to cool off there and congeal around more-ancient, harder masses, then forming a coarse, blistered crust, a whole city's carcass destroyed by the sky's fire.

And what an unheard-of range of colors among this debris! What fiery reflections! Dark pinks from barely extinguished cinders, rusty yellows and ocher greens, manganese violets and dark crimsons on cold clays, with grayish-blue protruding veins and mournful reddish glows on the sheer cliffs!

On all these stone surfaces, an even shade of soot black still retains something like the traces of the fire and primeval smoke.

Somber and splendid scenery of a petrified blaze, lunar landscape of indescribable desolateness, and tragic grandeur under a smiling sky in the morning's clear light . . .

All of a sudden, at the end of a trench, after a train station, a very unexpected vision of fertility and life: the charming Mograr-Foukani ksar, with its little palm grove in the humid bed of the oued.

About thirty tall Berber houses made of toub, pale and fawn colored, squeezed one against another, stretch across dark alleys and group their uneven terraces in gracious disorder.

At the top of the walls, under the roof beams made of date palm trunks, a crude decoration made of dried-earth bricks placed sideways to form pointed festoons.

In the palm grove, very green shimmering ripples of small barley fields under the murmuring family of blue palm trees, between low walls where flowering pomegranate trees lean.

The rising sun's oblique rays slip between the chiseled trunks, lighting, at the end of the palm leaves, short steel-like glimmers, playing with each other on the golden earth, on the blood-red fruits of the tomatoes and peppers.

An outspread oasis at the break of day, in the midst of this volcanic torment, enclosed in a narrow fissure in the dead lava.

Above the road, on a rock, a little girl dressed in purple wool, bathed in blond light, watches the train go by.

She is beautiful and cheerful, with the simple grace of her movements, naive joy lighting up her little round face, her amber complexion, and the caress of her large reddish-brown eyes.

Another little girl appears; and playfully, flirtatiously, in order to show off, they tickle each other, laughing.

But suddenly we return to the phantasmagoria of stone, to full, dark, and silent mineral life.

Hadjerath-M'guil

A train station, isolated dungeon among the jagged rocks.

Fifteen hundred meters away, a redoubt made of toub towering over a few wooden hovels on the slope of a rock at the base of the last foothills of the Djebel Beni-Smir.

A oued invaded by esparto grass and oleanders, a few scattered palm trees. Beyond the redoubt, at the edge of the oued, two small French tombs.

One already three years old, the other very recent where a few pitiful wreaths have finally finished fading: that of the spahis' brigadier Marschall, killed a month earlier in the Chaa-beth-Hamra Pass, in the Beni-Smir, in pursuit of a djich.

These two soldiers' tombs with their forsaken black crosses seem abandoned and infinitely sad, very out of place in the great harsh desert scenery.

At the train station, where I happen to disembark without even knowing the direction of the redoubt where I'm going, I find a very brown Bedouin, the beautiful Arab type from the High Plateaus, unloading a saddle and harness from the train. In spite of his white veils, I easily recognize him as a soldier, a spahi in civilian clothing or a mokhazni.

I speak to him because he inspires confidence in me. I tell him a story in order to explain my identity and my presence there, and we immediately become comrades, with the good simple sociability of Muslims.

Taïeb ould Slimane of the Rzaïna tribe from Saïda has just left the spahis and is going to join up with the makhzen of Taghit. This very day, he is going to Oued-Dermel to buy his mount.

"If you want, come with me; we'll have coffee with my former comrades in the redoubt. You can take care of your business there, and then we'll go spend the night in Oued-Dermel, if you're capable of walking. Tomorrow we'll be given horses and return here for the train going south."

The man is right, and I accept.

We leave, first on the path of the train, then on a furrowed path.

A comic scene occurs at the redoubt.

The head of the outpost, a captain from the Legion, looks at me, stupefied. He doesn't understand at all the link between my woman journalist's card and the very young Arab man holding it out to him. We end up, however, explaining ourselves.

It's impossible to interview the legionnaires without authorization from their superiors. All in all, that doesn't upset me, and I go join Taïeb and the spahis once again.

They're below a long group of huts made of planks and adobe, with straw mattresses arranged on the ground. The horsemen in cotton clothing and red belts joyfully surround the freed man; and since he has brought me, they celebrate my presence, too.

They quickly spread out quilts and make us sit down. Then, after the long polite Arab formalities, the repeated good wishes, they urge us to drink four or five quarts of coffee, a clear and odorless juice that resembles the hospital's licorice tisane.

However, we don't dare refuse it, all this coffee so heartily offered . . . And anyway, we've already drunk much worse!

We don't stay very long, in spite of the spahis' wish to keep us there overnight.

Taïeb has an idea: he wants to go look for a certain Tidjani from Bou-Semrhoun, a train station worker who owns a mule.

Behind the redoubt, under a ragged tent, we find Tidjani's wife, her skin withered and leathery from the sun, but who must have once been beautiful.

She still knows how to drape herself gracefully in her red woolen rags.

Taïeb, who firmly believes in the reality of Si Mahmoud le Constantinois,[1] winks his eye at me as he smiles, leaving behind his beautiful solemnity of a few minutes ago.

1. Translator's note: Si Mahmoud from Constantine is one of Isabelle Eberhardt's adopted names.

"Hassouna is from Djebel-Amour, the country of beautiful girls."

Taïeb leans his elbows on an old wool pillow in order to have a better look at the Bedouin woman to whom he says in a purposely tender voice:

"Do you remember, two years ago in Duveyrier?"

Hassouna energetically denies anything but also has a confused laugh that contradicts her words.

"What in Duveyrier? You're crazy and you're lying. Between you and me there is nothing but good . . ."

"Of course! Is there a good comparable to that one? Speak, speak, like a lying bird who lays and then flies off while abandoning its eggs! If I don't know you, then who does?"

"My father who begot me!"

"Not as well as I do, who possessed you when you were young and fresh!"

They continue their brutal coquetries in this fashion but without obscenities. I firmly believe that if I were not there, Taïeb would push things further, in spite of Hassouna's incipient decrepitude.

She serves us coffee, looking beyond Taïeb, who makes the expressive gesture of embracing her and crushing her in his arms.

Tidjani arrives. He doesn't seem at all surprised to find us under the tent with his wife.

This Tidjani is a ragged man in old European castoffs and a *chechia*.

He is, however, one of the unknown heroes of the Chaabeth-Hamra battle where Brigadier Marschall died.

Tidjani, a mere civilian—and that by choice—borrowed a rifle from a Jew and left on foot, running with the spahis on horseback in pursuit of the djich.

While her husband goes to get his mule, the now subdued hetaera questions us in a friendly manner and talks about herself.

She lives where the gunpowder speaks every day, and yet she retains the most surprising carefreeness. She laughs about the djiouch holed up nearby in the Beni-Smir bush.

She says, jokingly, that among the Ouled-Abdallah pillagers there are handsome and proud boys, and that she would gladly welcome them were she not afraid of her husband's knife.

She says all that with a thousand provocative gestures for Taïeb. Sometimes, however, there is something like a shadow of nostalgia that passes over her aged face when she speaks of the hills of her native Djebel-Amour.

What a strange apparition this decrepit daughter of pain is, in this setting of stone and dust, in these troubled days!

◄◄ ►►

We leave, taking turns riding Tidjani's lame mule.

The fine man gives us a long speech to prove to us that his beast is good anyway.

Without listening to him, carefree Taïeb sings of the beautiful tattooed Amouriat women, and the long rides on arid trails, the war of skirmishes, and Destiny's omnipotence.

As for me, I watch the lines of the countryside grow wider, become regular and more harmonious, as we leave the maze of stones that crosses the railroad almost from Aïn-Sefra.

The wall of the Beni-Smir mountains grows fainter toward the west and the valley opens up. Red sand, hardly undulating, with the gray heads of hair of drinn, the southern grass, tougher and sadder still than the esparto grass of the High Plateaus.

On the sand's surface a recent wind has left tiny ripples, light waves that give this desert site a sort of marine character.

At the foot of the rounded peak of the Djebel-Tefchtelt, we find the douar of the Oued-Dermel makhzen: about twenty striped black-and-gray low nomad tents, flattened to the ground as if crouching in fear.

The mokhazni, recruited from among the Amour, are camped there with women and children in order to survey the train line and the surrounding mountains where the pillagers are holed up.

Between the tents, the small fettered horses melancholically eat armfuls of drinn.

A few black goats play with the little children and the dogs that leap bristling and ferocious with blood-red eyes as we approach.

A great feeling of solitude and sadness reigns in this encampment of Muslim soldiers.

The douar's cheikh, Abdelkader-Ould-Ramdane, still young, with an intelligent and closed face, receives us solemnly.

The good mokhazni offer us their hospitality under a big tent whose walls are covered with red woolen haïk. They serve us Moroccan mint tea and some galettes and butter. They recount the continual alerts, the attacks, the pursuits into the mountain, and the prowlers' tricks as if these were very ordinary things.

Here again, no idea at all of war in the real sense of the word, of a race against race battle or one of religion against religion.

The mokhazni speak only of brigands and pillagers. They are, with their slow ways of all nomads, very simple and very primitive people, herders and camel drivers continuing their usual existence while changing hardly a thing, under the black burnoose of the Aïn-Sefra makhzen.

Taïeb characterizes them with a somewhat disdainful French word, and very spahi: "They're not too bright."

Under the tent, it's hot where the men are piled up, half reclining, leaning on their neighbor's knees or shoulder in a brotherly way.

In the other half of the tent, behind the curtains with their sumptuous glimmers of purple wool, the rustling and whisperings of women keenly intrigue my companion. However, he forces himself to remain impassive and take no notice of anything that reveals the women's proximity.

We leave the tent's suffocating darkness, and Taïeb very regretfully follows us. We go lie down on a sandy hillock above the dried-up oued, which, for the mokhazni, represents the *hadada*, Morocco's contested border.

A light breeze runs over the fine sand, hardly rustling in the drinn and the thorny jujube trees curled in on themselves, bristly, unapproachable, like underwater plants.

A great silence weighs on this lost country, on this douar, and on our little group. Around me, about ten mokhazni are half reclining, their profiles simple and vigorous, almost all with beautifully pure features.

The sun goes down toward the golden mountain ridges, and pink glimmers brush the sand and light up the pappi with fire beneath the harsh vegetation. One more hour of rest, like a halt in my life, a vaguely melancholy hour of unconcern and dream, troubled neither by regrets nor by desires.

The day is going to fade out. Then, suddenly bursting out from behind a bush, a ragged Bedouin moves toward the chief of the makhzen, Abdelkader-Ould-Ramdane, to whom he speaks in a low voice. The chief gets up, his face anxious.

"Get up! . . . And the rest of you, go immediately drive all the animals into the middle of the douar. A half hour from here there's a djich from Ouled-Abdallah."

A djich! At first that seems not very serious to me. Besides, will the pillagers dare to attack the douar where there are about twenty rifles?

However, the mokhazni obey. Grumbling a little, they leave to go gather up the horses, mules, and goats grazing around the douar; all the sheep are to the north of Aïn-Sefra, safe.

Eight o'clock. The moon has not yet risen. We're in the tent leaning on our elbows on the rugs. The darkness is impenetrable: Abdelkader left us scarcely enough time to swallow a little barley couscous and a few glasses of tea, then had all the lights put out. The chief also placed sentinels on the ground in the four corners of the douar. The mokhazni lifted up the tent panel on the desert side, and they lay down, their loaded rifles within reach.

They search the night with their lynx eyes.

Now it seems more serious.

Then a long vigil begins. We speak in low voices; we hide in order to smoke. The silence is heavy, hardly troubled by the muffled and monotonous song of a woman rocking her little one next door in the women's side of the tent.

All of a sudden the dogs begin a muted growl. The mokhazni tremble and cease chatting and joking. The dogs become more agitated. Soon there's a commotion. They leap, furiously barking, onto the sides of the tent, where they run, covering us with dust.

"You hear," Taïeb says to me, "the dogs are barking in all directions: it's them, and they're surrounding us now. Ah! Si Mahmoud, if you and I at least had rifles!"

The sensation that I feel is not fear; but this whole commotion, all of the dogs' racket, with these people who hold a grudge against us, who are there in the night very close by and whom we don't see—all of that produces in me a strange impression of a slightly murky dream. However, I feel a childish desire for the attack to occur, for something to finally happen.

This situation lasts for more than two hours.

"Let them come, finally, or go to the devil!"

One of the mokhazni jokes: "Do us a favor and go tell them to leave!"

We all end up joking, laughing about this rather boring adventure, about these people who neither want to attack us nor leave.

"There must not be large numbers of them, and then, since there's no light in the douar, nor any animals outside, they know we've been warned," says Abdelkader, still solemn.

For almost anything, were it not for the chief's fear, the mokhazni would mock and swear at the invisible djich.

However, little by little, things calm down, the dogs remain silent, and we fall asleep.

In the middle of the night, another alert; once again the dogs tumble over our heads, baying. The mokhazni swear loudly: we won't be able to sleep in peace!

We stay up; we wait. Nothing. Silence falls once again on the douar with a predawn freshness. We fall asleep again, this time into a deep and exhausted sleep.

It's dawn, the most radiant hour of all in the desert. I awaken to the solemn murmur of the mokhazni praying outside, bathed in the iridescent glow of the rising day.

We go out and mount our horses to return to Hadjerath.

Around the douar, two hundred meters away at the most, the mokhazni find the djich's tracks: about twenty men on foot.

We leave again, going back up toward the jagged boulders of Hadjerath-M'guil.

Ghost Town

Once again the little train resumes its slow pace through the solitude. The train stations go by interspersed with long stops.

Djenien-bou-Rezg, the burning plain, a large reddish redoubt, a few forsaken hovels.

Now it is Duveyrier, the Arab's Zoubia, in a semicircle made of tawny-colored hills and black rocks.

Not long ago, the Saharan railroad stopped there, and the recent village, completely European, had sprung up. The low houses, coated with grayish earth, multiplied with the songs of those exiled from the Legion; canteens and refreshment stalls opened, huts made of wooden planks and the bases of old oil cans; a bold duenna had even brought a few nondescript courtesans, wrecks from the slums of Saïda and Sidi-bel-Abbès.

Long lines of camels came and knelt down in the sandy streets before going to take fresh supplies to forgotten posts in the South.

Duveyrier was the source of the river of abundance flowing toward the Sahara—apparent prosperity reigned there for several months. People began to get rich there, emigrating a little bit from everywhere toward the lure of easy trade, yet often even toward troubles.

During certain transactions, people whispered very quietly the name that has filled the echoes of Southern Oran for twenty-five years, the old, almost-legendary name that sounds more strangely troubling in this place where it carries reality: Bou Amama.

Then, one day, the small persistent path—the two iron rails that extend, gleaming and forlorn, through the desert—passed by Duveyrier in order to go stop even farther, across from fascinating Figuig. From one day to the next, another city burst forth, hurried like the Sahara's grasses under winter's first rains. And Duveyrier's ephemeral life disappeared, absorbed by the newcomer Beni-Ounif-de-Figuig.

Today, in the morning's pink light, Duveyrier gives a singular impression of untimely abandonment: houses with completely new walls, no roofs, with the black spheres of gaping doors and windows. The bazaar merchants took away all they could—beams, planks, casements, tiles—in their hurried exodus. The watering holes, closed or gutted, are already falling into ruin or sinking back into the sand. It seems like a calamity, fire or flood, has swooped down on this village of yesteryear and has returned it to the eternal silence of the desert.

And this corner of abandoned country, with its debris, is poignantly sad.

The little garrison alone still gives a semblance of life to Duveyrier. The lengths of the streets are dotted with the bright poppy-red hue of a spahi's burnoose or cornflower hue of the infantrymen's outfit.

At the train station, everyone comes to see the train go by, a melancholy distraction, . . . and to see life leaving for elsewhere.

In Duveyrier, a surprise, a reflection of the troubled months flowing by: a squad of armed infantrymen mounts the train, in the event of attack.

And once again, in spite of that, as in Aïn-Sefra, as in Oued-Dermel, no real sensation of danger in the sunny plain's great calm and smile.

Beni-Ounif

The Zousfana, an iron bridge painted in gray, very ugly and out of place in the scenery of the esparto grass, reeds, and oleanders.

The oued rolls its murky and reddish water over the white pebbles, with the thin pure trickle of some neighboring spring in the middle of the current.

The Zousfana—which with its tributary, the Guir, forms the Oued Saoura at Igli—never runs dry. In the middle of the summer, its banks turn green around the little bordj guarded by infantrymen, and the hovels serving as a train station.

The air here is humid and warm with a white mist that obscures the distance.

After here, to the left, is the great Djenan-ed-Dar plain. A red horizon with the clear silhouette of Djebel-Sidi-Moumène, a square, geometric terrace rising toward the south very far away. We enter the dusty valley of Beni-Ounif, formed out of dry hills that open toward the west onto an incandescent horizon.

How different it is—this country of dust and stone—from the beloved regions of the Southwest, from the great immaculate Erg, from the Souf's pure and iridescent dunes, and from the immense chotts, and from the mysterious palm groves of the salty Oued-Rir'h.

To the right is Figuig, in the semicircle of high mountains with harmonious lines . . . We still see only palm groves: against a neutral background of an indefinable color, yet glowing, the black flecks of date palms.

Finally, here is Beni-Ounif, the little train station, with the poignant melancholy of the tracks that stop abruptly across from the vast expanse.

Toward the right is the low redoubt, all white and in ruins.

And beyond, across from the powerful green flow of the Zenaga pass, with sober and clear lines of dark violet framing the invading palm trees, is Beni-Ounif's old ksar on a gentle slope, a charming tumble of pale-gold and glowing fawn-colored ruins, in the dark velvet of the palm grove.

❧ ❧

Here and there in the middle of the ruins, a few still-standing alleys, inhabited, covered—like almost all the ksar's streets—with palm beams: dark, fresh avenues with earthen benches cut out of the wall's thickness where the never-ending discussions of the Berber djemaâ are held.

All of a sudden there are shafts of sunlight cutting into the blue and tawny shadows of the covered passages.

Elsewhere among the ruins, gutted houses showing the remains of humble Arab households: pieces of pottery shards, rags still fading in the sun, traces of black smoke on the light-colored walls.

Life is withdrawing from the old ksar so it can move to the new village: utilitarian, noisy, and ugly.

Toward the south, the houses descend to the bottom of the dried-up oued, to the capriciously crumbled banks. There, it is the damp realm of gardens crisscrossed by little earthen walls, so as to block the heat of the sun.

Here and there, *feggaguir*, underground springs, tapped and redirected toward a maze of often still-functioning subterranean corridors under the gardens and streets—a whole city full of endless shadow and mystery, from where the laughter and voices of women bathing burst forth on burning summer days. This is where they get their waxen pallor and the languor of their gestures.

Up high, toward the west, a gaping hole in the middle of the ruins. A goat path crosses it, leading to the nearly intact rampart found here. Only the ridge is slowly crumbling away into strange jagged outlines.

A small suspicious door, narrow, so low that one must bend double to go through it, opens onto the large cemetery without walls and devoid of sadness, where the feeling of death vanishes in the scenery's empty monotony.

Beyond a few groves, between a few spindly date palm tufts, the koubba of Sidi Slimane.

The hours go by monotonously in the dying ksar. Only the ramparts' dull ocher color and the fragment of sky silhouetted by the door change, going from the iridescent mauve of morning to the incandescent blue of midday, to the crimson red of sunsets splashed with gold, and to the sea-like transparencies of moonlit nights.

In the evening, the little door seems to open onto a blazing furnace whose burning reflection reaches all the way to the bottom of the ruins.

In the ksar, as in the village—as all over the Beni-Ounif valley—is the never-ending reddish lime dust that beclouds and stains everything, that flutters about oppressively in the blazing air on the days of *adjedj*.

Rare are the passersby.

Sometimes a fellah pushes a donkey along before him, disappearing beneath a load of palm leaves that brush the walls with a metallic rustle. The man walks with a vacant gaze, a stick on his shoulders, standing very tall with a hieratic gesture like one sees in the figures on Egyptian bas-reliefs. He sings an old threnody softly to himself; he exchanges a few distracted salaams with the immobile white ghosts along the walls. An old woman appears, bent under the weight of a water skin. Sitting or half reclining on the earthen benches, the *ksourians*—white Berbers— or the *Kharatines*—autochthonous blacks—speak slowly, intoxicating themselves on shade and prolonged immobility.

The Zoua, Arabs who have strongly crossbred with the Berbers, drape their scrawny bodies in thick white wool: the influx of impoverished ksourian blood through the centuries and the indolent life, always in the shade, have caused their Arab blood to degenerate, and they no longer have either the beautiful presence nor the supple robustness of nomads. A few of them are beautiful, however, but of a pale, effeminate beauty, as must have been seen in the young men on the streets of Carthage. They are artisans and scribes and not men of war.

However, the Zoua are distinguishable from the fellah of pure Berber race. Among themselves they speak Arabic, and they keep to themselves, very proud of their origins as marabouts. They all claim the lineage of Sidi Tadj, descendant of Sidi Slimane Bou-Semakha, and of the Sidi Cheikh. Thus, they are Bou-Amama's relatives.

The Zoua who remained in Beni-Ounif, after the exodus of their people who followed Bou-Amama, live off what their gardens produce and also off the *ziara*—offerings to Sidi Slimane—which they share among themselves.

Today, their leader is the caretaker of the koubba—a certain Ben Cheikh—a man about forty years old, poorly dressed, with mild and ingratiating manners. However, his tanned and emaciated mask-like expression, combined with his evasive eyes, exudes shrewdness and will.

Below the Zoua and the white Berber fellah are the Kharatine, the truly indigenous people of the Sahara, of almost pure black blood. Tall, with long lanky limbs and elongated angular faces, they resemble all the black tribes scattered throughout the Sahara.

They speak *Chel'ha*, a Berber idiom resembling somewhat the M'zab *Zenatia*.

Other blacks, slaves, who came from Touat or Gourara, even from the Sudan, speak other idioms of Negro origin, known under the generic name of *kouria*.

When the Zoua had left Beni-Ounif after the French occupation, the Kharatine remained masters of the country. This explains—besides certain political reasons—why it is one of them, Bou-Scheta, who was named caïd, to the great dismay of the Zoua.

All the whites, even the Berber ksourians, look down on the Kharatine, not long ago still their slaves. Despite being Muslims, the Kharatine had no more voice in the djemaâ than did the Jews.

The caïd Bou-Scheta is rather comical in appearance. Very tall, with long arms, clumsy manners, lacking in dignity, Bou-Scheta wears nothing but his beautiful red burnoose and wears a serious mien only on celebration days in order to present himself to the French leaders.

The Zoua openly make fun of the caïd, calling him "El Khartani" or "Elabd" (the Negro, the slave).

Good-natured Bou-Scheta, with his large yellow-toothed smile and his monkey-like gestures, pretends he sees nothing, keeping his fear of the marabouts to himself.

Little Fathma

The children, only lively note, only gay note in the necropolis-like silence, the ksar's sad nostalgia.

The littlest ones are especially funny, mostly black, naked under skimpy shirts, a long lock of wooly hair mixed with tiny white shells or amulets atop their shaved heads.

They have already learned to beg for coins from the passing officers. They jump around them; they stamp their feet; they work furiously away at them with the charm and caresses of little cats, then ferociously fight each other for the copper coins tossed their way; they roll about, eating the dust.

The leader is little Fathma.

She could be eleven years old. Her prepubescent body, supple as a cat's, disappears under green wool rags, fastened over her frail chest with a gorgeous hook-and-eye clasp of embossed silver, decorated with deep-red coral in an unusual shape.

Little Fathma is of mixed race. Her round face and velvety cheeks, of a warm copper color, are at once insolent and gentle, with caressing eyes and quite voluptuous lips. In a few years, Fathma will be very beautiful and very shameless.

Leading the turbulent flock of little amber-colored or black children, she gallops through the ruins, breaking out in her clear crazed nymph's laughter. She appears all of a sudden, precariously perched on the edge of a crumbled terrace or on the top of a shaky wall. She implores, she simpers, she smiles.

One day I saw her, as a way of saying thank you, take the hand of a *roumi*—an officer—between her tiny warm hands, and say with a troubling seriousness, "I love you very much, ya *sidi*!" The man smiled and attributed the caress to an appeal for more coins. Then little Fathma pouted sadly with a scolding shake of her head. "No, no, it's not that. I love you like this, for God!" Which signified, in Arabic, that her sudden tenderness had no ulterior motive.

Strange little creature, like the charming but disappointing and fugitive soul of the reddish-colored ruins.

Sidi Slimane

Today I felt a sensation of intense movement backward in time toward previous centuries. On a feverishly hot morning, I went to visit the tomb of Sidi Slimane Bou-Semakha.

Wise politics, respecting Muslim sensitivities, have protected the inviolability of the koubba to the present time: never has any Christian, not even the officers, entered there.

I, as a Muslim, am allowed there, for Sidi Slimane is the great healer of the sick.

It is with Ben Cheikh, the leader of the Zoua, that I go to the great marabout's tomb.

After a long paved corridor, we turn right and take off our shoes.

It's a domed chapel.

The tomb is in the middle of a small, completely white room, mysteriously lit from above. It is made of a wooden pyramid shape and draped with green and red silk.

Like everything in this place, these cloths exude the great charm of dilapidation, with their faded colors further softened by the blue half-light.

A railing made of carved wood, so old that it crumbles at a touch, surrounds the tomb, enclosing it even further. Heavy rosaries of scented wood with beads as large as small apples hang at the feet and head of the saint.

By some strange whim, a very tall and very old European clock has been placed there; its wooden box is daubed with primitive cinnabar, indigo blue, and gold flowers.

By what chance, after what vicissitudes and what peregrinations did this clock end up here, in this Figuig sanctuary? A piece of wreckage from some Barbary Coast, plundered from the coasts of Italy or Spain, sent as an offering on the backs of beasts through Morocco?

The movement of the hands has stopped on some forgotten midday or midnight, and nothing troubles the pious silence any longer . . .

Small candles made of pure wax and earthenware dishes full of benzoin make the air heavy under the low dome.

A very old person, all white and completely stooped under long immaculate veils, receives the ziara, the offering; and he accompanies us with blessings murmured in a faint voice, as if from far away.

We leave, and the great outdoor light dazzles me in the barren plain, dotted only with immaculate tombs.

VARIATION

One very hot and very clear October morning, visit to the koubba of Sidi Slimane Bou-Semakha. Intense impression of suddenly going back toward previous centuries of faith and immobility.

Wise politics have respected, to the present time, the inviolability of the sanctuary in order not to offend the local and especially neighboring sensibilities (Figuig): no Christian has ever entered there. The French officers, at the time of the occupation, contented themselves with receiving the ksourians' submission in the koubba's exterior corridor.

I go with Ben-Cheikh to the *makam* of the great southwestern saint.

Past the paved corridors, we turn right and take off our shoes. The makam, the tomb, is in the middle of a completely white small room, mysteriously lit from above. The tomb is made up of a wooden pyramid shape, draped with red and green silk.

Like everything in this place, these old fabrics from times past have a dilapidated charm, with their faded colors softened by the bluish half-light. A carved wooden railing, so old that it crumbles under my fingernail, surrounds the makam. By some strange fantasy, a very tall and very antique European clock has been placed there; its wooden case is daubed with naive flowers in cinnabar, indigo, and gold.

By what unforeseen chance, after what singular vicissitudes, did this clock end up here, in the middle of the desert, at the gates of Figuig? Doubtless, wreckage from some far-off pillaging on the Andalusian coast, handed on as an offering after a long peregrination through Morocco . . .

The movement of the hands stopped long ago and no longer troubles the pious silence. Small, pure-wax candles and earthenware dishes filled with benzoin make the air heavy under the low dome.

A very old mokaddem, stooped under his immaculate woolen veils, receives the ziara, accompanying us with a few blessings murmured in a faint voice . . . We leave and are dazzled by the great golden light on the barren plain, dotted with small gray raised stones: tomb upon innumerable tomb.

Toward the village's south and southwest, a high rocky hill marks the horizon. At the foot of this ocher-colored wall, a charming spot: at the bottom of the oued's desiccated bed, a group of date trees and oleanders around a well.

Toub bricks have been made and the hill has been excavated where the quarry opens like pink wounds with red chalk scree. Moroccan workers in ragged European clothes and low turbans work as they sing, under the supervision of an old tanned weather-beaten Spaniard with a coarse face made wild by an unkempt gnome's beard.

Toward the Oued Ben-Zireg and Oued Béchar, nothing more, the barren plain, the *hamada* paved with black stones, cut by small jagged ridges. At nightfall, high mountains whose colors change and the little palm grove of Mélia hidden at the entrance of a deep gorge: yet another djiouch hideaway and, it is said, not a very safe place despite seeming very peaceful and quite deserted when seen from afar, across the mournful, splendid, and grand landscape of the plain and hill.

From this side, the capricious light alters the perspective in a peculiar way, bringing closer or making distant the undulating landscape. One morning, a long procession of camels that were grazing far away at the foot of the hills seemed to me to get larger, to be distorted all of a sudden, to become gigantic . . . then little by little, as the sun was shifting, they became very small again, hardly visible in the incandescent haze.

Sunday in the Village

The sky is overcast; the sirocco is breathing its hot breath, its fatal and burning caress onto the morbid sweatiness of irritated bodies.

The racket and yells are starting in the Moorish cafés: at Returning from Béchar, at the Southern Star, at the Soldier's Mother, at the Figuig Oasis.

The Legion brings to its saloons a deep undercurrent of desperation and regret unleashed by the persistent and terrible drunkenness of the northern peoples. Open doors unleash waves of red light onto the sandy dark streets. There is a confused conglomeration of blue greatcoats at the wooden counters. The absinthe is flowing and the sirocco is blowing.

Things are starting to heat up, and it is now but a Babel of songs—slow Germanic or Batavian dialects; Italian babbling; hoarse, jerky syllables of Spanish dialects.

Then, all of a sudden, for no apparent reason, there are outpourings that at first sight seem funny, but in the end are sad enough to make one cry, because they rise from the depths of human pain in all these disinherited refugees living the harsh existence of southern soldiers.

Among the drunken men, hugging and kissing begins, ending in disputes, punches, and sometimes blood.

Outside, a patrol passes by solemnly, rifle on shoulder, waiting for the predictable fights and the inevitable falls.

A short pale German plays the accordion in a dining hall, while others dance.

The Moorish cafés, empty white rooms with the *oudjak* in the corner and stacks of pearly porcelain cups on the shelves, the varied fiery light of small multicolored tea glasses, and the pale suns of copper trays.

Here is the faded dark blue of the infantrymen, with the purple flowering of chechia, the scarlet crowd of Spaniards wearing tall white turbans with tawny-colored or black cords. There are also the blue burnooses of the makhzen, with their cartridge belts where the lamp's red rays create copper flashes, and the Bedouin's white or earth-colored burnooses.

The infantrymen are the noisiest; crying out joyfully, they play cards or dominos.

People sing.

Half reclining against a tall infantryman's shoulder, a very young mokhazni with a delicate impassive face, and undoubtedly a bit drunk, blows with all his might into a rhaïta whose furious lament pierces and dominates all the noises.

A bearded infantryman gets up, borrows two red silk scarves from his comrades, and dances the dance of the girls from Djebel-Amour in the midst of laughter, imitating the lascivious swaying walk and the artificial quivering of a dancer's flesh.

Then, born of a need for movement in their drunkenness, the soldiers play and fight, furiously rolling on the mats and benches like children.

Nine o'clock. In the redoubt, the trumpet calls out the melancholy signal to extinguish the fires, hastily done here, in order to avoid mishaps.

Drunken men litter the streets; the cries and the songs finish, and in the suffocating darkness rise only groans and complaints caused by the rage and pain of a months-long unsatisfied lust of the males calling out in vain for embraces and caresses, for women's flesh.

VARIATION

At the Soldier's Mother, a short pale German plays the accordion and others dance . . . They're excited and sweating; they start undressing, randomly throwing their clothes around. Then they overturn the benches; they break and tip over everything. Then the owner, a former canteen woman, shows up, a raw-boned and hip-swaying mare, with a pale bony muzzle with yellow hair on a pointed skull. With an iron fist, swearing louder than the privates, she throws out the unruliest ones . . .

At the Southern Star, there's a group of officers who don't dare get drunk and carouse in public, but nonetheless are in the grips of boredom and the "blues" . . . They sequester themselves there to drink slowly, for hours, while listening to an old Spanish woman with a hard ruddy mask-like face crooning a sentimental love song, "La Paloma."

In the Moorish cafés, there is the indistinct blue of the infantrymen, with the flowering of red chechias and the scarlet slump of the Spaniards' burnooses. With great outbursts and formidable explosions of laughter, they play cards . . . They sing.

Half reclining against the shoulder of a tall tanned infantryman with a delicate and impassive face, a very young mokhazni—perhaps a bit drunk—blows with all his might into a rhaïta whose boisterous moan pierces and dominates all the noise. An infantryman gets up to borrow two red cotton scarves with a crude leafy design in canary yellow, and amid laughter, dances the Ouled-Naïl's dance, that of the girls of his region, imitating their lascivious swaying walk and the artful quivering of their flesh.

Then out of a need to clench live flesh with their eager hands, the soldiers—drunk on smoke and Moroccan tea—fight and roll around furiously on the mats and benches with loud cries.

Nine o'clock. Drunkards litter the streets. The cries and the songs are going quiet; rising alone in the shadow and heat, just the groan and the furious complaint, all the rage, the months-long unsatisfied rut of males calling in vain for a woman's embraces and caresses.

The Marabouts

Evening in the ksar of Beni-Ounif.

A stark room of very old gray toub, a sort of den with irregular walls, a low ceiling of blackened palm stalks, all buckled.

A cell's timeworn barrenness. Nothing marks the flow of time in this Muslim corner of immobility and unconcern, among these people who indifferently watch the decay of things, who never rebuild ruins.

Stuck on the rough ground, a thin yellow wax candle weakly lights the room. The evening wind penetrates the cracks in the wall, and the red flame quivers, casting large black shadows on the dull walls. At the back of the room, holes of darkness dissolve into formless objects.

In the wall, almost just above the ground, a small square window opens onto sleepy palm groves, onto the sky's dying redness, onto the plain's immense silence.

We're in a circle, half reclining on a threadbare mat and an old tattered rug.

In the middle, small glasses in soft colors on a pewter tray, adorned with crude golden flowers, a metal tea pot, a conical sugar loaf, all the old tea paraphernalia of Moroccan hospitality, perfumed with sweet, heavy, intoxicating, peppery mint: the beverage of slow talks and low voices, interspersed with dreams.

Crouched against one of the rough earthen pillars, Ben-Aïssa, the marabout storyteller, pale, cheerfully ugly in his grubby veils, seriously prepares the tea, his elbows at his knees, only his naked arms moving in his body's weary nonchalance.

My head rests on my folded burnooses. I look at the host, certainly the best among the dark Zoua of Bou-Amama, the simplest and the most astute, a sort of welcoming, laughing derouich . . . Next to him, sluggishly stretched out in a position of feline grace, my sometime travel companion, the former spahi Taïeb Rzaïni, wrapped in a thin burnoose made of new wool with long soft folds. A faint smile with very white teeth lights up the dark bronze of this Bedouin face—worn, angular— and the shadow of big harsh eyes.

The candle's uncertain light strangely carves out the thin bird-of-prey profile of the big mokhazni Abd-el-Hakem, his angular and robust body disappearing under the heavy drapery of his blue burnoose: a silent man, that one, very coarse and very disoriented in the "service" of the French makhzen.

Behind them, a few immobile silhouettes from Figuig, white wool framing waxy faces. All the way to the back, with an ebony mask, Tahar the *Khartani*, Ben-Aïssa's half-brother.

All are quiet, listening attentively to the host speaking in his remarkable, rapid staccato voice, sometimes inflected by a complaint or a childish caress. "Si Mahmoud, have you seen the stone there, outside, leaning against the wall of the house? This stone has a story. Long ago, during the lifetime of our blessed master Sidi Abdelkader Mohammed, Figuig's patron—may God let us profit from his virtues—terrible quarrels broke out endlessly between Figuig's different ksour, over the water from the seguia and the feggaguir. Each ksar, even each contingent, wanted to channel the waters and thus doom the neighbors' gardens to drought and death.

"For a long time, Sidi Abdelkader Mohammed urged the ksourians to act equitably, to share the water given to them in abundance by the Dispenser of All Goods in a brotherly manner. He spoke to them for a long time, and his speech had the sweetness and amber perfume of honey. But the impious are deaf, and the eyes of the stubborn don't open, even to the dazzling sun. The blood kept flowing, and the fratricidal hands picked up the sword more often than the mattock. One day, after a great massacre among the Hammamine, the saintly man of God grew weary. He reached the limits of his anger, and he cursed the impious in these terms: 'Be cursed, ksour of Figuig, who harbor impiety, who shelter discord and cruelty! Cursed be you, you and your earth, yea even unto the stones of your mountains.' Then three sacred stones loosened themselves from the ground and were swept away by the saint's curse. One of the stones took refuge in Sidi Slimane's koubba, where it can still be seen. The second remained on the believers' path, to instruct them and exhort them to exercise leniency. It is the one near to which our ancestors—may God grant them his mercy—built this house, which is very old. The third stone . . ."

"Si Ben Aïssa, how old is your residence?"

Ben Aïssa makes a vague gesture: "God alone knows, for only he counts interchangeable years that flow over creatures and things as they pass by."

Taïeb has been very busy for a moment, preparing kif in the bottom of a couscous dish made of Ouzzan wood; he cuts the cannabis branches and leaves into tiny pieces with his long Moroccan knife; then he rubs the pieces between his two hands, turns them into dust, and mixes them with pulverized Moorish tobacco.

A very small iron pipe on a long reed tube circulates from one person to another.

Little by little, everything quiets down. A heavy silence—where there is nothing of the erotic dreams attributed, in Europe, to kif smokers, weighs on the old crumbling house—on the room filled with shadows and blue smoke. The hour is late. The little candle drips and goes out. We fall asleep in the sweet tranquility of a vague dream floating in limbo.

Oh voluptuousness of chance abodes, where, carefree, alone, unknown to anybody, one hallucinates! Shadow, friend of temporary ports, of long stops on the free vagabond's road bathed in sunlight! Infinite sweetness of excessively refined and subtle dreams, in abysses of silence, in Islam's countries.

Mériéma

A low, impenetrable, white-hot sky, a dull rayless sun that nonetheless burns. On the dust covering everything, on the white or gray facades of the houses, a mournful blinding reflection that seems to emanate from an interior inferno. On the angular peaks of the arid hills, dark flames are smoldering, and reddish-brown haze is piling up behind Figuig's mountains.

Nothing sparkles, nothing lives in all this blaze. Sometimes only a breath of dryness comes—one doesn't know from which far-off furnace—and stirs up little whirlwinds of dust that flee, rapidly, toward the east and dissipate in the valley.

At the train station, between the black train cars and the torn-open fences, people wait for the train, the Europeans overwhelmed, the Arabs with weary gestures.

Resigned horses and mules stretch their necks toward the ground, their heads hanging, their nostrils bloody.

And on all of that, an inexpressible and weighty silence is felt. This silence is neither rest nor delight: it is morbid languidness to the point of anguish.

This was one of my first impressions of Beni-Ounif . . . No guide, no foreign vision coming between my senses and things, no pointless explanation, as I wandered, all alone, in this corner of the country that was new to me.

At the village's exit, toward the train station, an elevated section of wall the color of fiery-gray molten metal. Farther on, beyond the blue rails ending in a red trench, nothing but the plain scattered with black stones, more dust, a burning infinite barrenness. At the very base of the wall, a thin shaft of tawny-colored, transparent shadow with no coolness.

There I saw Mériéma, crouched in front of a small pile of scrap and debris of all kinds. A naked, misshapen, demeaned body, empty, hanging breasts, black sagging flesh soiled by garbage and dirt. A boy's frizzy shaven head, a thin wrinkled face, a broad thick mouth opening onto large yellow teeth, and protruding eyes, the poor eyes of a sick animal: a sadly simian face of suffering, fear, and distraction.

Her head was nodding strangely as she rummaged through the pile of rags and sweepings with her long bony fingers.

And she spoke to an audience, without stopping, in an incomprehensible barbaric-sounding idiom that I later found out is *Kouri*, a vague black Sudanese or Saharan language.

I spoke to her in Arabic. Her babbling continued, rising into a sort of irritated wail.

I held my hand out to her. She then pulled on each of the knuckles of my fingers without stopping her verbiage. Nightmarish grimaces convulsed her face.

A male inhabitant of Figuig who was looking at her said:

"You know, this woman is not from here. She was a slave of the Muslims, in Méchéria; she was married; she had a son named Mahmoud. Here is what destiny is: This Mériéma was pious, calm, sensible. Among women, she enjoyed a reputation of virtue. Then, one day, God took her son away from her. She then went mad, and she fled, alone and naked. She stopped speaking Arabic and took up her ancestors' language once more from very far away, far beyond Touat. She traveled up and down the roads and villages, like this, living off the charity of believers. A few times she was taken to the ksar Oudarhir, in Figuig, where some pious Muslims took care of her. But she always returns to Beni-Ounif. She lodges under a pile of boards. However, the children torment and tease her there. Sunday nights, when the legionnaires and infantrymen are drunk, they forget that she is a poor innocent woman, and they rape her, in spite of her moans and screams . . . A drunken man resembles a wild animal . . . God protect us from a destiny like that of this creature!"

A morning of light. The sirocco has calmed on the plain, where, during heavy days, it scattered red ashes.

At dawn, a light wind from the north shook the dust off the date palms turning green in the valley around the ocher ksar.

The day rises in clear green light. The infantrymen pass by on their way to the bottom of the oued where a few palm trees and oleanders grow in the seams of reddish-colored toub.

Wearing heavy white cotton clothing—with their brass instruments upon which the rising sun ignites gold sparks—and the more severe paraphernalia of the Arab *nouba*, the musicians are going to practice, and wake the dead valley's echoes until nine o'clock with the exploding notes of bugles, the plaintive, tinny notes of the rhaïta, and the muffled pounding of drums.

They cross the village, and the glory of the morning hour puts a smile on their brown faces with white teeth, and a caress on their naked and muscular necks.

With a precise mechanical gesture, all their arms simultaneously raise the brass instruments; and an alert music, carefree and cheerful, explodes.

All of a sudden, bursting out of a shadowy hole, like a black jack-in-the-box, Mériéma appears. She has decked herself out in a ragged gandoura and an old woman's straw hat with faded blue ribbons.

In front of the group of laughing infantrymen, she dances and leaps with the little cries of a nervous monkey. Little by little, speeding up her movements, with a frenetic swaying of her hips, she rips off her gandoura and continues to dance naked, with only her hat held on by a cord.

All the way to the clay quarries, Mériéma accompanies the music of the infantrymen who come in the joy of the cloudless morning.

A day of calm in the silent desert, in the village. A light white mist clouds the sky crossed by the flights of migrating birds. Mériéma is sitting at the bottom of the oued, among the black slabs of stone, underneath the sharp foliage of the blue date palms.

She has decorated bushes with multicolored rags gathered in the streets, as if for some odd ceremony of a fetishistic cult. With her long, thin, gnarled arms raised above her head, she taps rhythmically on an old can that she uses for a drum.

She sings an unintelligible threnody in a monotonous tune and a shrill falsetto voice.

Acrid smoke rises in gray spirals from a small fire made of camel drop-pings that the crazy woman has lit in front of the trees.

However, the soil is spreading the sickly smell of a charnel house, bones are lying around, a big pool of blood is turning iridescent and putrefies . . . this place serves as a slaughterhouse.

But Mériéma doesn't see the horrible carnage, the sordid pigs that come and turn over the bloody debris with their greedy snouts and lick the coagulated blood. She doesn't smell the horrible odor of death. She prays, chants, cries, cut off forever from the communion of beings, plunged into the gloomy solitude of her confused soul.

I met Mériéma for the last time one evening when I was leaving. It was very late; the waning moon was rising, pale, as if furtive, on the blue plain. And Mériéma was dancing alone on a low dune, completely naked and completely black.

Lizards

Against the crumbling walls that time has made golden and cut into strange jagged outlines, little by little the wind accumulates sand.

At the bottom, where the humidity lasts underground, the inhabitants of the ksour have planted date palms with dense foliage, bursting out of the ground and curving into arches.

It's the beginning of autumn, and tiny grasses are sprouting under the palm trees. The air has a slightly salty freshness in the shadow of the old walls. In the sun that is still hot, caressing breaths go by.

This corner of the Ounif palm grove has been abandoned by the fellah. No noise reaches it; one can sense a beneficial silence, something like a slow movement toward hoped-for nonexistence.

I've been lying on the sand for instants or for hours; I no longer know for how long. The least movement would trouble the harmony of my tenuous, fleeting sensations.

Near to me, Loupiot, my black dog, a strange griffon born and baptized in a barracks, shares my immobility. Sitting down, he poses like a caryatid in order to watch out for vague moving forms somewhere in the distance.

The oblique sun turns and glides on a section of wall where the rainwater has carved out tiny blackish-colored fissures.

Then, on the striated toub, the lizards come to enjoy themselves. They're opposite me, and for a long time they captivate my attention.

There are little tiny ones, as thin as needles and ashen gray, who, rapid and flexible, play at chasing each other, making quick circles of pale shadow on the wall's surface.

Other fatter bluish ones flatten out and puff up, inflating their coarse bellies. The most beautiful ones bloom into rare colors like long venomous flowers. There are a lot of very fat ones colored a pure emerald green, their bodies all covered with little golden pustules similar to dragonfly eyes. On their flat heads, purple eyes make a complicated design.

These ones are entirely absorbed by the heat's voluptuousness, stretched out and lazy, their tails soft and hanging. Drowsy and happy, they stand still in this way yet without falling. Sometimes their mouths open as if to sensually yawn. They seem full of disdain for the childish agitation of the little gray lizards who continue their circular race, as if dizzy.

All of a sudden the dog notices them.

He gets up and approaches slowly and prudently, without any noise. He stretches out his hairy muzzle with a puzzled look and with his ears perked up. He sits down in front of the wall and, surprised, studies the lizards' game.

But the sun is sinking toward the horizon and is projecting the dog's deformed shadow onto the family of peaceful beasts.

Then the frightened and rapid lizards flee, disappearing into the fissures in the old wall, into the shadowy holes where they were living.

The wall remains naked and golden in the evening's paler sun . . .

Agony

The convoy from Béchar left at about noon, carrying beams and planks.

Maamar-ould-Djilali's gray she-camel Messaouda, weakened by long marches, didn't go far: across from Melias's small palm grove, her long feet suddenly trembled and sagged, she kneeled down with a hoarse moan, and then she keeled over onto her side.

Maamar knew that his camel was dying; and he called upon God, for a great sadness had seized his Bedouin heart.

The convoy stopped. With shouts and curses, they made other camels kneel down, and they redistributed the dying beast's load. They took everything off her, including her triangular-shaped packsaddle and the rags protecting her hairless hump. For an instant Maamar, dismayed, his arms dangling by his side, his eagle's head bowed, studied his camel. Then, with a sigh, he picked up his stick and set off again, pushing his two other camels ahead of him with a short whistle and a guttural "*ah!*"

The day was ending in glory on the dreary valley enclosed between severe mountains and small, dry, arid, grassless hills the dull color of reddish-brown smoke.

Fiery reflections flowed over the boulders, which took on the shades of dimly glowing embers.

The camel, collapsed on the scorching ground, was still alive, resigned.

However, a long spasm suddenly shook her body, from her outstretched feet all the way to her small head with its long yellow teeth, with her big, soft, and pain-filled crying eyes.

And these heavy, slow real tears were poignantly and disconcertingly sad on the face of this primitive beast, suddenly brought so strangely closer to our humanity by the anguish of death.

Afterward there was an immense convulsion. Her feet twitched and tucked under themselves as if to withdraw.

Then her long supple neck stretched out and jerked backward in a gesture of supreme abandon.

Her eyes became glassy and went out. Her coat stained, her limbs rigid, Messaouda, the gray she-camel, was dead.

For three days, the convoy from Béchar had been passing through the Mélias valley.

Noon. The sun was beating straight down onto the black slabs. The dead camel's carcass gaped open.

On her long neck, among exposed vertebrae, on her small head, shreds of silky hair remained, soiled by coagulated blood. On her ribs, a thin layer of skin remained stretched, with transparent red membranes.

In the course of their nocturnal battles, the jackals and hyenas have opened up Messaouda's belly, tearing out the entrails and viscera that they then angrily fought over with funereal snarling.

In the sun, legions of burying beetles—black and tinged with the splendid sapphire and emerald colors of putrefaction—launched an attack on the rotting carcass.

Scrap by scrap they ate her, thus hastening the work of her destruction.

With the innermost depths of their mortal flesh and the dark fear of things related to death, the horses pricked up their nervous ears and moved abruptly away from Messaouda's remains, abandoned at the edge of Béchar's deserted road like the hull of a small boat washed up on the shore.

VARIATION

When horses go by, they prick up their nervous ears and snort, with a dark fear of things related to death, which make them shudder, as if they felt its breath penetrating to the depths of their mortal flesh . . .

And trembling, they move away from the gray female camel, abandoned at the edge of the deserted path, like the hull of a small boat washed up on the shore . . .

Market

The Beni-Ounif market takes place every morning.

In front of the low dugouts of the Arab Bureau, about twenty inhabitants of the ksour and Figuig—dressed in earth-colored wool—squat in front of wide heaps. Heavy wool burnooses with long fringes around the hood, filali skins, baskets of eggs, piles of onions and turnips, kid skins filled with butter or tar, clusters of golden dates, bundles of wool dyed red, green, violet: that's all.

Spahis, mohkazni, orderlies, and Spaniards crowd around and barter. Still frightened and withdrawn, the people from the West reply in monosyllables, their heads bowed fiercely.

The lure of profit, however, is beginning to attract them, and little by little they are becoming accustomed to the unusual calm and security.

"The onion market," say the spahis derisively. They are children of the Tell or the High Plateaus, and full of the disdain and hereditary hatred of the Algerians for the people of the West.

To the side, under narrow ragged flea-ridden tents, Kenadsa Jews are making jewelry.

Dressed in green or dirty-white gandoura, wearing a small black turban on their long red hair, the latter have the pale and swollen faces of recluses, invaded by unhealthy fat. Squatting, they work at their little forges in the fetid odor of their rags and the bitter smoke of molten metal. Their bony fingers shape heavy rings, large hook fasteners for women, or little balls made of silver for perfuming tea.

They're given louis d'or and silver duros that they melt and transform into jewelry.

And there, too, for so many exiles, endless haggling fills the emptiness of the hours.

This embryonic market, one of the proofs of peace for the country, is also one of Ounif's rare leisure activities; people come here to avoid the South's spleen, its melancholy.

Djenan-ed-dar

In the petrified scenery of Beni-Ounif, there are heavy evenings, funereal evenings, when the sirocco sows gray cinders on things, when black depression invades souls and folds them in on themselves in mournful anguish.

No calm and no voluptuous annihilation of being, in this countryside devoid of softness, full of hard uneven lines and faded colors.

On those evenings, in order to look for the familiar and loved aspects of the soothing desert, I flee toward Djenan-ed-Dar, close by, a little fistful of human dust, a timid attempt at life lost in the emptiness and sterility of the immense, free, tranquil plain.

To the south of Ounif, the low chain of the Gara stretches out, culminating in a very pink rounded outcrop, hollowed out by the large wounds of quarries.

And there at the bend, everything suddenly changes. It is limitless space, with soft imprecise lines, unimposing to the eye, fleeing toward light's unknowns.

A monotonous harmony of things, scorching red soil, a changing fiery horizon.

The only vegetation, looking mineral-like itself, is the silvery *degaâ*, which soldiers have nicknamed the "cauliflower" for its innumerous bumps, the strange plant of the hamada, a tight round bunch of little hard pointed stars, held in the ground by a single weak woody stalk.

And nothing else, hardly a few tufts of esparto grass. Toward the east, as vague as a mass of bluish clouds, a chain of mountains and the Zousfana dunes, spotted with the scattered date palms' blackness.

To the south, nothing more, the empty, glorious, blazing horizon . . . Very far away, barely perceptible, the rectilinear silhouette of Djebel-Sidi-Moumène, fading in the sky's mournful radiance.

Djenan-ed-Dar, a gray, severe citadel, completely new and completely alone on a low hillock.

To the right, a camping area where ephemeral towns, swarms of white tents, bloom and follow one another in almost-constant renewal.

Infantrymen, legionnaires, come camp there while waiting to be deployed to the posts in the Southwest. Little temporary lives take shape there; little habits begin. Then, the next day, everything is over with, swept away and very quickly forgotten.

Still farther away, in a slightly fertile depression, a few clumps of very tall and very slender date palms with multiple trunks shelter the clay hovels of the officers' circles.

A corner of freshness and oblivion where the hours of waiting flow by slowly in front of the opal color of nostalgic drinks . . .

Yet another bare field dotted with stones, then the low cracked and crumbling walls of the old redoubt where spahis and legionnaires still lodge.

To the right, what used to serve as the Arab Bureau when Djenan-ed-Dar was the center of the region—four or five little shacks of earth and planks in a courtyard opening onto the desert.

That's where I'm going to stretch out on a ground cloth or a comforter, for the peaceful sleep of carefree nights.

A spahi and two mokhazni guard this street and keep order in the skeletal hamlet. Behind the old redoubt are a street, two rows of rickety shacks, canteen shops, a Moorish café, a butcher shop—all of this starts in the sand and immediately ends in empty space. That's all. It's nothing really, compared to quite prosperous Beni-Ounif, in full feverish activity.

And yet Djenan-ed-Dar has more character and more originality. It's very much the military village born of the exigencies of war, and it will disappear with the latter.

And then, in Djenan-ed-Dar, a sensation of distance and isolation is beginning to be felt in the scenery's immobility, which the railroad's presence is erasing in Beni-Ounif, embryo of a new Biskra.

A few Spanish or Jewish bazaar merchants live off the Arabs' or foreigners' scanty coins. At the back of their hovels made of old materials that have already served elsewhere, in other temporary villages, the "pioneers of civilization" pour elixirs of oblivion for those struck down by spleen.

Sitting in front of the door of her black gourbi, an ageless, thin Spanish woman with an angular mouth and a stiff black mane of hair waits with weary passivity for the soldiers who throw themselves onto her doleful body during evenings of malaise, evenings of wild rutting.

As soon as a man goes in, the woman quickly double-locks the door. Outside, violent quarrels explode—sometimes battles even—when the hardheaded men of the Legion clash with the infantrymen. All of them cry out their desire brutally, shamelessly; and in their eyes, this pathetic, still-female-looking rag has grace, appeal, almost beauty in their state of distress.

After several hours of slow strolling in Djenan, after some long stops on the mats of the Moorish café, I go back to the Arab Bureau's ruins.

There, by candlelight, the three Arabs and I prepare a cheerful meal of peppery sauce. Then, drinking coffee out of old tin beakers, I listen to the silent night descend on the desert.

The mokhazni, very primitive, and the very dreamy children of the Géryville steppes are quiet. The spahi, a cheerful man from Tlemcen, sings long languorous laments or recounts his country's legends.

Slowly, gently, I fall asleep in the calmness of the shack whose door doesn't shut, in the unguarded courtyard, opened wide onto the darkness of the bled.

Douar of the Makhzen

Like Oued-Dermel, like Aïn-Sefra, like all the region's posts, Beni-Ounif has its douar of the makhzen, its striped tents raised on the earth's dusty barrenness.

It appears to be very calm and sleepy, this isolated douar toward the southwest of the ksar, at the edge of the garden. And yet it conceals intrigues, outlines of novels, indeed even dramas.

Amour of the Aïn-Sefra circle, Hamyan of Méchéria, Trafi of Géryville, many of the mokhazni are married and drag along with them *smalah* of women and children, whom the needs of service make them abandon for months.

Volunteer cavalrymen without enlistment uniforms and undergoing no military training, the mokhazni remain the most culturally rooted of all the Muslim soldiers recruited in Algeria by France, retaining their traditional morals underneath their blue burnooses.

They also remain very attached to the Muslim faith, unlike the majority of infantrymen and many spahis.

Five times each day, one sees them withdraw into the desert to pray; they are solemn and indifferent to everything surrounding them. With their noble gestures, they are thus very beautiful at this hour when they become themselves again.

However, when in contact with the regular military personnel—the spahis and the infantrymen—many mokhazni take on the flippant, more rebellious mood of the indigenous private. Without any moral profit, they free themselves from some of the patriarchal observances, from the great reserve of the nomads' language. And too, they end up in the long run viewing their tents almost as accidental lodgings.

And besides, in their difficult existence full of constant alerts, fatigue, and tomorrow's uncertainty, love's intrigues—already so enjoyed in their native douar—take on an even greater savor and charm.

Inevitably, morals are relaxed; what was done back home under the seal of secrecy, in the darkness of night when love closely rubs shoulders with the tomb, is now done almost openly in the makhzen douar.

Every evening the beautiful tattooed women with tanned complexions and fierce looks under their beautiful rags of purple or dark-blue wool take off in groups for the oued's feggaguir.

They chatter and laugh among themselves and are solemn and silent only when some Muslim male goes by.

The cavalrymen in red or blue burnooses, leading their small lively horses to the drinking trough, go as close to the voluptuous fountains as possible. Not a word is exchanged between them and the Bedouin women. And yet offers, confessions, refusals, promises are exchanged through small discreet gestures.

The man, very serious, runs his hand through his beard, meaning, "May one shave my beard, take from me the visible attribute of my virility, if I don't succeed in possessing you!"

The woman answers with a smile in her eyes, with a shake of her head, a mere provocative gesture. Then, furtively, distrustful even of her companions, she lightly moves her hand.

That's enough; the promise has been made. It'll cost a few old clothes in bright colors, or a few pieces of white cloth purchased in the Mozabite's shop—not much.

Then, later on, passion will seize the two lovers, maybe Arab passion—tormented, jealous—which often takes on the appearance of craziness, throwing men out of their apparent usual impassiveness.

Thus, at the same time that it is an encampment of tireless and valiant soldiers, the makzhen douar is also a small city of ephemeral and dangerous loves. For here, shots are easily fired, and it is so easy to blame them on some djich . . . The bled has no echoes.

The unmarried mokhazni sleep under the stars in the courtyard of the temporary Arab Bureau.

The guards themselves doze rolled up in their burnooses, with the absolute lack of concern so characteristic of people from the South, forever accustomed to feeling danger nearby in the night's shadows.

And it is these isolated mokhazni who haunt most audaciously the douar's outskirts and who poach the most frequently in the domain of their married comrades, of whom they are jealous and whom they look down on somewhat, for being such unhappy husbands.

A large convoy of camels and the cavalrymen's goum are camping in the valley near the palm groves, having arrived on a gray autumn day.

There are a few white tents belonging to officers or caïd in the middle of the chaotic pile of things, among the shackled and neighing horses and the camels kneeling down with muted complaints.

Piles of *haraïr*, carpet scraps, blankets, smoky cooking pots, hairy water skins suspended by a tripod of sticks, the flash of a brand new dish in the jumble of warm and dark Bedouin rags where red and scorched black stand out . . . All of that is accumulated and mixed together in wild and magnificent disorder.

Men circulate, recognize each other, settle in.

Goumiers in white burnooses, their belts bristling with cartridges, sokhar (escorts), real desert men, skinny and weather beaten, robust under their frayed and gritty cotton shirts, cinched at the waist with a crude leather belt or a rope, their feet in *naala* (sandals), completely covered with old scars, their heads simply veiled with a cloth and sometimes with small braids of hair hanging alongside their cheeks . . . They are men who have remained much as they must have been at the time of the patriarchs and the prophets at the dawn of the world . . .

The *bach-hammar*, the heads of groups of sixteen sokhar, gallop on their skinny horses and yell out orders.

Within a few hours these arrivals of goum and convoys change the appearance of the gray valley, which seems to serve as a temporary base for an entire migrating populace.

They are very archaic and very impressive, these displays of old things that have remained unchanged throughout the centuries, these loads of people with the clothing and gestures of long ago, having come there for a few days and who will tie up their things again some following morning and again set off, taking their beautiful and poor nomadic baggage far away.

The winter day rises on the black hamada. At the horizon, above the Zousfana dunes, a sulfurous glimmer dims the thick, heavy gray clouds. The misty mountains and hills stand out as indistinct neutral-colored silhouettes against the opaque sky. The frozen palm grove with its disheveled date palm tops fills with pale dust, and the old houses made of toub, standing in the middle of the ruins, emerge—yellowish—as if dirtied by the valley's murky shadow beyond the big isolated cemeteries.

The desert has stripped itself of its costume of light, and an immense mourning veil hovers over it.

In the camps, around the horses covered in silk rags and around the camels, goumiers and sokhar are waking up. A murmur rises from the pile of damp burnooses rolled onto the hard ground.

Awakening upon being bumped into, the sullen camels begin complaining. Silently and unenthusiastically, the nomads get up and light the fires. In the cold humidity, the djerid smoke cheerlessly.

The icy wind abruptly sweeps through the camps; it lifts whirlwinds of dust and smoke, snapping the stretched cloth of the goum leader's tent decorated with a tricolor pennant.

The French lieutenant's silhouette passes by. Placid, his eyes sad, his hands shoved into the pockets of his blue heavy cotton pants, he smokes his pipe while distractedly inspecting men and animals.

He also feels weighing on him the malaise of this morning of beginning again, after months and months of this difficult job of "camel leader," as he calls it, always en route, always alone, with, as his only consolation, this melancholy pipe where the monotonous hours of his life are consumed in light smoke . . .

The nomads prepare coffee in their pewter mess tins; and then, under the screaming wind, they get up slowly, lazily, as they shake off the dirt weighing down their burnooses.

They attend to the camp's minor affairs.

The goumiers and the sokhar throw armfuls of esparto grass in front of their animals. The officer's gray horse is given a cursory grooming. A few men, sitting in the smoke of the fires, start repairing their harnesses or their burnooses. Others go up to the village for the never-ending bargaining with the Jews and for the long drinking sessions of Moroccan tea in the crude rooms of the Moorish cafés.

Camels snort and bite their haraïr. A horse comes untethered and gallops furiously through the camps. Two men argue over an armful of esparto grass . . . And that's all, like every day in boredom's long hours, hours of waiting.

For a long time the nomads have forgotten the solitude of their traditional existence on the High Plateaus, with no other worry than the herds and the eternal quarrels between tribal factions who sometimes empty a few echoless rifle shots.

They have been marching in this manner through the desert for a long time, with the columns and convoys, in the continual insecurity of lands crisscrossed by starving bands, kept like packs of jackals lying in wait in the inaccessible mountain gorges.

Now winter is going to come, the dark icy winter, the nights without shelter near heatless fires. And with the great resignation of their race, they've become used to this life, because like everything here below, it comes from God.

In these chance neighborhoods, friendships based on food and bedding are born among the nomads, are the result of soldiers' rapid yet fleeting kinships declared one day at first sight.

Small groups of men tether their horses together or push their camels toward the same corner of the camp, eat from the same big wooden bowl, and share the simple interests in their life: the purchase of food stuffs; the care of their animals, their only fortune; and sometimes, too, the clandestine forays into the homes of the beautiful, lusted-after women of the douar of the makhzen, indeed even to the Amouriat of Figuig, the skinny dissident prostitutes of Zenaga and Oudarhir.

It's the evening, the hour of songs, long monotonous chants, naive and poignant improvisations about things concerning war and love, exile and death, in the style of ancient rhapsodists.

The leaders announce to us a far-off expedition:
My heart warns me;
It announces imminent death to me.
Who will see me die? Who will pray for me?
Who will make alms at my tomb in memory of me?
Oh! Who knows what God's destiny reserves for me?
My white gazelle will forget me.

Another will mount my gentle mare . . .
Oh my heart, hush! Don't weep, my eye!
These tears don't help.
No one will attain that which has not been written,
And what is written, no one will avoid . . .
Calm yourself, my soul, until God has pity,
And if you are not able to calm yourself,
There is death . . .

The singers modulate their elegies, accompanied by the soft *djouak*, the little Bedouin flute, with its mysterious whisperings also interrupted sometimes by the wild cries and shrill sounds of the rhaïta.

After a twilight the color of murky blood, under the darkening vault of the clouds, night fell, heavy and opaque.

The numerous fires are lit, fires made of dry djerid with tall joyous flames rising straight up into the darkness, fires made of camel droppings, little braziers with a dull reddish glow.

A breeze blows; the glimmers vacillate, pulling vague strange forms from the shadows, like ghostly groups and attitudes.

An angular, black silhouette of a camel is deformed and becomes almost frightening. The shadow of a white horse shakes its long mane.

Around a large bright fire stand a group of Bedouins in white, the soft panels of their burnooses waving like giant wings. Others, sitting in a circle, busy themselves preparing the meal. Among the sharp profiles of these men of prey, there are some faces with very simple pure lines, where a less mixed Asiatic blood has kept the ancient Arab beauty.

Attitudes of repose and abandon, indistinct groupings of recumbent bodies . . . Then, all of a sudden, with no apparent cause, restlessness, magnificent gestures under violently lit up cloth.

In the fever of their arrival, the nomads keep watch for a long time.

But above, on the plateau of the redoubt, the bugles' drawling notes mark the extinguishing of the fires . . . Little by little the braziers' flames subside and go out. Night thickens over the camps; the nomads roll themselves up in their rags and stretch, their rifle or their club under their hand, with their shoe serving as a pillow.

Near the last fire, a young man wearing two little braids of black hair falling the length of his powerfully angled cheeks stirs the cinders with the end of his stick, still singing almost in the background.

VARIATION

Two mokhazni from the Géryville circle, very young children from the broad horizon of the esparto grass steppe sitting across from each other, begin singing a plaintive cantilena whose refrain is a long sad cry that finishes in a sort of desolate groan.

At first they seem to doze, their eyes closed and their voices like the murmuring of flowing water:

"Yesterday, I moaned and I cried all day long: I missed my tent, I missed my gazelle. Today the sun looked at me, and sadness moved away from my heart."

The voices rise imperceptibly, strengthen, and become more rapid:

My heart, be quiet,
and don't weep, my eye!
Tears serve nothing.
No one can attain what has not been written.
And what is written,
no one can avoid.
Ours is the country of gunpowder,
and our graves are marked in the sand.
Calm yourself, my soul,
be quiet until your wound has healed,
and if it does not heal,
console yourself,
there is death . . .

Then from the circle of mokhazni, another voice rises, even more unpolished and hoarser, singing a desolate complaint of the Muslim soldier's fate:

God has abandoned me, for I am a sinner.
I've left my tribe and my tent;
I've put on the blue burnoose;
I've taken a rifle as my wife.
The leaders are announcing to us
an imminent departure.
My heart warns me:
it announces imminent death to us.
Tomorrow the hour will sound;
the angel of death will approach.
Will it be a ragged Guilil
or a pitiless Filali whose bullet will annihilate me?
This is one of God's secrets.
And who will pray the prayer of the dead for me?
Who will cry at my tomb?
I will die, and no one will take pity on me.

The voices, more and more numerous, rise up into the quiet night, and the pipes murmur ethereal sadness.

Yesterday, I cried all day:
I missed my tent,
I missed my gazelle.
Today the sun rose, and I smiled.
There are some who went to Tafilalet, to Béchar,
Others who were present, who fought
In the days of Timmimoun and El-Moungar.
God protected them.
Others never left their tents,
And they died . . .
Life is in God's hands,

And there is but one death, conceal no thought in your heart.
Our country is the country of gunpowder,
Our graves are marked in the sand,
And the grave is open, oh son of Mimoun! . . .

◀❧ ❧▶

Last beautiful days when the desert seems to gather its thoughts before the horror of the sand's torments.

The pale sky grows misty with milky condensation. No wind; sometimes there is hardly still a mild breeze. In Beni-Ounif there is a feverish coming and going, an unusual activity; the great Beni-Abbès convoy, which also resupplies the distant Saharan oases, is setting off tomorrow.

For the Géryville goumiers, the marching orders have been given; they are leaving for Béchar. The nomad city is going to scatter into the hamada and the sand solitudes.

Crouched in circles in small groups in the village's streets among the piles of stones and rubble, the blue mokhazni, the red spahis, and the tawny-colored nomads tumultuously divide up the supplies and money; before separating, shared, temporary, finished lives are settled up.

Toward the Zousfana, dawn rises out of the clear night. In the middle of the chaotic and black pile of the camps, a few red flames come alive again in last night's braziers. Then an immense and monotonous whisper rises from the already-troubled sleep of men and beasts. The nomads are praying: with voices raised, they are invoking the Lord at the break of day.

The light, at first hesitant, almost furtive, reaches the zenith, and the big shining stars pale and go out.

Only the morning star, the Bordj-en-Behar, twinkles—a lamp of joy and hope lit in the day's smiling nativity.

Still very low to the east, a few light cloud clusters are set ablaze, swimming in oceanic transparencies of green gold.

And there is a streaming of opaline light on the street where life seems light and good at this first hour.

The camps immediately fill with confused noises and shouts.

With discontented moans, the camels reluctantly get up in order to go back up to the village, where, for hours, they will be parked between the train station and the redoubt among piles of completely filled bags, planks, tin trunks, and crates bearing distant addresses: Taghit, Igli, Beni-Abbès, In-Salah, Adrar . . .

At the redoubt, the bugle bursts out hoarse notes at first, then the brilliant and imperious notes of reveille.

In front of the still-sleeping hovels of the Arab Bureau, a few blue or red burnooses pass through the green or black rags of the Jews of Kenadsa who've come from the South to sell their forged metal jewelry.

Finally, after several hours of work, the camels, nearly two thousand of them, are massed together among the loads waiting to be taken.

They're standing, and the slanting sun slips into the countless jumble of big immobile camel feet onto curious, attentive, and undulating heads, onto humped backs and mangy gray, drab-white, brown, or reddish flanks . . .

A few funny little young camels with long soft heads, a strangely childish expression of naïveté, with the grace of young downy birds, press against their mothers, their already-hairy lower lip searching for a pointed nipple.

Now the sokhar make their beasts kneel down with little taps of a stick above their knees.

The loading begins.

Then there is an indescribable racket, quarrels breaking out around each animal, with furious shouts, guttural exclamations, insults and frenzied gestures, as if all of it were going to end up in a massacre.

God is called to witness; the Prophet is called to witness a badly attached piece of string made of palm tree fibers, a bag fastener. And this goes on without any concern for time and with increasing noise.

The equipment train's squealing *arabas* and the horsemen setting off at a gallop go by, spreading disorder and fear among the camels, who abruptly stand up again, throwing off their half-amassed loads, and run away, followed by the sokhar's curses.

The bach-hammar, on their horses as soon as it's morning, staff in hand, harass and hurry their men, angrily shouting out orders, threatening and striking them.

From very far away, the nomads call out to each other and speak to each other in loud drawn-out cries.

Oh! The gullets of these people from the South! What bronze are they made of that they don't break or bleed from all these deep cries, all these calls that ring out like trumpets?

A few camels revolt, stamp their feet in place, or escape clumsily on three feet, the fourth one folded under.

Horses rear up, neighing to the passing mares. All of a sudden the wind comes up and makes the rags snap like swollen sails. Whirlwinds of dust fill the camps, burning eyes and drying out lungs.

The military uniforms, the red or blue burnooses, throw a few cheerful splashes of color onto this swell of dark or earthy colors.

The hour passes, and the leaders, losing their heads, run around to hasten the departure and yell, too. But their French voices are too weak to pierce the Bedouin cries and shouts, and they are lost in the racket that increases with the last moment's fever.

And dominating this rising tumult are the hoarse and wild voices, the continual immense moan of the camels, filling the plain all the way to the eternal silence of far-off lands.

However, with security and the railroads, this great vision of primitive life, whose unforgettable splendor we will soon no longer see, is going to end.

Bypassing the redoubt's corner, a goum is the first to leave at a trot toward the west with his tricolor pennants above the drab white of the burnooses and the dusty horses' coats: it's the Trafi of Géryville who are to accompany the little Béchar convoy.

Another goum from the Amour of Aïn-Sefra gets ahead of the big Beni-Ounif convoy by taking the southern route.

The escort's infantrymen, in chechia and scarlet belts against the white canvas of their battle dress uniforms, set off and march with the sound of a large herd's trampling hooves. The sun glints in white flashes off the steel of the rifles.

The camels, standing, become quiet, as if meditative, then descend into the valley going toward Djenan-ed-Dar. For an hour, they spread out in an unending line undulating through the plain. At the reddening horizon where glowing mists float, the convoy vanishes.

Toward the west, very far away, a few vague mountains with strange hardly distinct forms: truncated cones, jagged ridges or terraces . . . All around, an infinite plain, burned, red, its earth cracked, with the innumerable seedlings of green esparto grass, tufts toward the bottom, becoming disheveled like gray fluff toward the tops of the dried out stalks: a panther skin's dark flecking spread out under the warm limpidity of an autumn sky.

Light breezes pass over the plain and caress it. The cavalrymen pass in review on dry horses, all full of bones and tendons, their bristly body hair gray and their eyes glowing. The black burnooses and the heavy and earthy wool haïk make them look impressive.

They have thin faces, dark lines, harsh features with the tawny glimmer of an eagle's eyes. A beautiful bearing, broad gestures, dignified attitudes. One would almost take them for marabouts, without the rifle worn across their bodies or raised with the butt leaning on their knee. Convoy bach-hammar, they are sometimes also men of war, brave by tradition and out of a profound indifference for death.

Far behind them, spread out in the esparto grass, nomads approach, with a band of tawny-colored small ropes around their foreheads over a thin veil, a staff across their shoulders, their thin weather-beaten chests thrown out, crisscrossed by thick muscles in the half opening of their dust-colored rags; in front of them, they push their big slow animals, without loads, with only the small triangular pack saddle.

The long supple necks stretch out; the thick-lipped muzzles graze on a few thick gray bushes hidden between the black rocks and tufts of esparto grass.

The camels stop. Then because that lasts too long, the sokhar let out a hoarse cry, a guttural *ah!* from the bottom of their brass throats, and a brief whistle. The undulating necks slowly lift back up, and the heads with elements of both snake and sheep—the strange disdainful heads with soft eyes—regain their normal motion. Their long yellow teeth chew with the continual sound of a mill.

The troop goes by. The men, being smaller, disappear first into the infinite waves of esparto grass. Then the camels' shapes deform, become round, and merge with the ground's hazy undulations.

Thus they come from all the douar of the High Plateaus, descending toward the south, slowly crossing the smiling solitudes, which they alone, shepherds and wanderers, know and love with the unconscious love of gazelles and wild birds.

These are the last beautiful days before the sand's torments. The pale sky is covered by a milky haze. No wind, sometimes there is hardly still a mild breeze.

In Beni-Ounif, in the valley near the ksar, a sudden appearance of noisy life.

Nomads arrive every day with long processions of camels, in order to camp next to the goumiers.

The sokhar encampments are cruder and more confused, and more colorful, too.

There is a chaotic pile of things: the haraïr, long narrow bags made of gray and black wool connected to the sides of the camels' pack saddles; carpet scraps; frayed blankets among smoky pots; hairy water skins hung from a tripod; the flash of a new pewter mess tin in the heap of dark, warm-colored Bedouin rags dominated by red and blackish brown; everything accumulates and mingles around the fires burning palm fronds or droppings, among the recumbent camels chewing, whereas others seem to dream, towering over everything with their tall angular silhouettes.

Camaraderie based on bedding and food, born along the long route, continues; other companionships are born; others are broken in terrible fights . . . Then blood sometimes flows.

And these sokhar and migrating camels keep coming, as they have since the beginning of time.

At the redoubt, the bugle calls out hoarse notes at first, then the bursting and pressing notes of reveille.

In front of the still-sleepy hovels of the Arab Bureau, a few blue or red burnooses pass through the green or black rags of the Jewish nomads from Kenadsa who have come from the South to sell silver and gold jewelry.

There is also unusual movement among the goumiers: the Aïn-Sefra Amour are leaving in a column toward the west, to Bechar. The Géryville Trafi are descending toward Taghit and Beni-Abbès in order to protect a convoy. The names of El-Moungar and Zafrani still evoke death's shiver.

And here, finally, after several hours of work and yelling, all the camels, nearly two thousand of them, are massed among the loads waiting to be taken.

They are standing, and the slanted sun slips into the innumerable jumble of big immobile feet, onto undulating, curious, attentive heads, and onto the tawny, gray, drab-white, brown, or red backs and sides.

A few priceless young camels, with long soft and naive heads, with the grace of large dark downy birds, press against their mothers, looking for a pointed nipple with their already-hairy lower lip.

Now the sokhar make the animals kneel down with little taps of their staffs above the knee. They start loading. Then there is an indescribable tumult, quarrels exploding around each camel, with furious yelling, gesturing, as if it must end in a massacre. God and the Prophet are called to witness a *schritt*, a badly attached date fiber string, a bag fastener.

All of this continues without any worry about the passing time.

The more it continues, the louder the noise gets.

Squealing arabas, horsemen off to a gallop, go by, creating disorder and fear among the camels, who get up, throw off their half-piled loads, and flee, followed by the sokhar's curses.

The *bach-hamar*, on their horses as soon as it's morning, harass and hurry their men, yelling out orders, threatening, even sometimes hitting.

The Bedouins call out and speak to each other, managing to understand one another from very far away.

Oh! These southern gullets, out of what bronze are they made that they don't break and bleed from all these deep cries, these calls that sound out like the notes of a trumpet?

A few camels revolt, run away, trample in place; horses rear up.

The rising wind makes the rags snap like swollen sails in the raised dust.

Military uniforms, scarlet or blue burnooses, create gay splashes of color on this swell of dark or earthy colors.

French voices, too weak, try to pierce the Bedouins' cries and are lost.

And it is the hoarse and wild voice, the continual immense moan of the camels that dominates all this noise, which rises, filling the plain all the way to the eternal silence of far-off lands.

However, it is going to end, this great vision of primitive life whose splendor we will soon no longer see, with the arrival of security and the railroad.

The escort's infantrymen, in chechia and scarlet belts against the white cloth of their battle dress, move off and march with the loud trampling sound of a herd. The sun makes white flashes glint off the steel of their rifles.

A goum goes off toward the west, behind the redoubt, with its tricolor pennants against the drab white of the burnooses.

Everything is loaded; it's over.

The camels slowly descend again into the valley, which they cross, leaving for Djenan-ed-Dar.

For an hour, they spread out in an endless undulating line through the plain where the dust is gilded by the sun.

Then, at the horizon where glowing mists hang in the air, the convoy disappears, vanishes.

The Bible

At dusk on Sunday, drunkenness was on the rise in Djenan-ed-Dar, and alcohol rolled its sad craziness and its songs of exile through the canteens and the streets of sand.

There was, however, a peaceful corner where I went to isolate myself during the hours when I no longer felt the painful need to wander among the groups and plunge myself into Gehenna outright...

It was behind the only Moorish café, on a wobbly old bench propped up by a petroleum can.

There was no more noise there, no longer anything. A little barren valley, a low dune, and beyond—the fiery sunset of the day's end.

From the smoky room came monotonous Arab chants, a pipe's slow moans, a rhaïta's lamentations, lost in the silence.

You felt good there, stretching out and dreaming, experiencing the delicious expansion of your being.

One time, I found a legionnaire sitting on my bench. A Germanic blond face under the South's strong suntan, a thoughtful, almost-sad look.

After a moment, our conversation began, at first in short sentences.

In order to reply to the legionnaire's surprise at hearing an Arab speak to him in his own language, I made up some story as best I could. He then began evoking far-off recollections, making a whole epic of a ruined life, of vagabonding through the world, go by me with a certain unconscious artistry, which made me sympathize with him.

Born in Düsseldorf, he had been seized as a law student at age twenty by an unconquerable urge for travels and adventure. He'd enlisted. He'd been sent to China under Marshal Waldersee's orders.

One day on the way back, he'd deserted, out of disgust for the barracks. One after another, he'd been an acrobat in Chinese ports, a scribe in a consulate, then a sailor. Finally, five years after leaving his native town, he'd ended up in Algiers with no money, and he'd enlisted in the Legion.

Auguste Seemann relived, without regret, the years that had gone by. It was true that his life was ruined, but after all, what did it matter? He had not been bored, he'd seen the world, and he now knew men and things.

The deserter and I quickly became friends; and almost every time I came to Djenan-ed-Dar, he hurried to join me at the Moorish café, which he preferred to the tumultuous canteens, for he didn't drink.

One evening, Seemann said to me:

"The misfortune here is that there's nothing to read, not even a newspaper. We're becoming mindless from living like animals. It'd be nice, at this time of day, to read here together while drinking coffee."

He seemed to hesitate.

"I do have a book . . . But you see, you're not a Christian, and you undoubtedly wouldn't want . . ."

I spoke to him about the close relationship between Islam and ancient Judaism, of their fierce monotheism. Then, full of joy, he ran to his primitive room in the old redoubt made of crumbling toub.

When he returned, he piously unfolded a very old scarf made of yellow cashmere.

The black morocco leather binding was decorated with a cross angled against a golden dawn, a large sun rising behind a dark indistinct horizon.

German names and quite ancient dates, written in beautiful Gothic letters on the book's yellowed flyleaf, brought back memories from long ago. Between the worn-out thin leaves, common flowers were fading; pansies, eglantines, dead violets, falling to dust, once gathered on far-off prairies.

"It's the Bible that the pastor from back home gave to my mother on the day of her marriage. It's all I've kept of hers and from the dear house back there . . ."

For a moment the legionnaire's voice seemed to tremble a bit. Then, opening the book to Lamentations and the great Isaiah's prophecies of destruction, he read seriously, almost chanting.

On the empty desert, plunged into pink transparencies, the evening was lighting up.

From one horizon to the other, a swell of purple flame rolled through the green and gold sky.

The soldier's slow voice separately articulated the verses, and his northern tongue sounded strange at this hour and in this scenery. The little black book, a touching talisman brought from the northern mists where centuries of exile had altered and dimmed its splendor, slowly became again Israel's book, imagined on the very same earth as that of the radiant ancient Judea.

At the Home of Bou-Amama's Cousin

Friendly smiles on rested faces and slow serious gestures under white veils. Silence and contemplation in vast courtyards where men glide noiselessly like ghosts. Whispered prayers, attitudes of ecstasy . . . Immobility of things throughout the centuries . . .

At first sight, one discerns nothing else in the old zaouïya of the West, the only impregnable places in the torment brewing around and among the ruins of a crumbling world.

And yet, behind this facade of haughty indifference, in this distancing from things of this century, there is something else: mysterious intrigues that, in Morocco, often end in bloodshed, age-old hatred, absolute devotion side by side with scholarly betrayals, violently terrible passions lying dormant in men's hearts, fomenting wars and massacre.

But in order to notice all these hidden things, one must be admitted into the zaouïya, live there, earn trust; for on the outside, everything is white and appeased.

In Bou-Amama's former zaouïya, in Hammam-Foukani, after a hot day shot through by blasts of a thunderstorm, there is now a heavy calm evening with distinct oppression in the silence.

The sun goes down without the usual clear iridescence, without the delicate color tones, in a violent fire, without transition from the horizon's bloody red to the zenith's sulfurous green where a few thick fleshy pink-colored clouds float.

The neighboring palm grove sinks hurriedly into a dark-blue shadow, almost black already, while a few red-gold flames still run across the disheveled tops of the date trees.

Beyond the low walls of the courtyard, the vast plain behind Figuig stretches all the way to the abrupt Djebel-Grouz. Sandy, hardly undulating, it burns with a colorless fire like an immense brazier covered with poorly extinguished embers.

To the right and below, in the middle of a rocky arid valley, rises the koubba of Sidi-Abdelkader-Mohammed, patron of Figuig. Its large white cupola takes on shades of overheated copper, and reflections of molten metal flow on its walls.

Across the way, very far away, are ksour under the blazing jagged outlines of the mountains, and a scarcely visible black line: El-Ardja's palm trees.

Closer by is the Dar-el-Beïda,[1] the Moroccan makhzen's barracks, which glow red in the plain's already-dimming light.

Toward the left, to the west, the robust wall of the darkened Grouz and Djebel-Mélias's oblique silhouette on fire. Grand scenery where a fairy-tale world of lights plays.

Night is falling.

The moghreb eddhen rises in slow notes from the tall white minarets of Elmaïz and Oudarhir. Rapid great blue shadows emerge from hollows in the ground and move toward the summits, which—bit by bit—are extinguished, drowned in ocean-like transparencies.

Then, furtively skirting Oudarhir's walls, about ten haggard men burst forth, unexpected and worrisome, emaciated and dressed in nondescript rags. They're armed with Mauser rifles and push a few skinny sheep ahead of them . . . Near me, one of the zaouïya's servants, serious and with a cajoling and dark look, finishes praying.

"Si Mohammed," I say to him, "who are these people?"

"Oh, no one, just shepherds from Mélias."

"But they're wearing the Beni-Guil veiled turbans."

"No, they're our Arabs. They dress like the Beni-Guil because they've stayed for a long time in the Chott Tigri."

But Si Mohammed abruptly leaves me and disappears around the corner of a hallway. As the darkness grows, these shepherds who resemble pillagers enter Hammam-Foukani's covered streets. After a moment, I hear bleating in the zaouïya's courtyard.

Si Mohammed, who returns shuffling in his old worn-out leather shoes, explains:

1. Eberhardt's note: *Dar-el-Beïda*, the white house.

"These poor people come here, suffering from the war, to sell their sheep and beg for the blessing of the cheikh and his ancestors—may God grant them his mercy!—they have no other refuge but this house . . ."

A long room with barren walls, the ground covered with thick-napped woolen carpets, and scattered around, long yellow and green cushions with brocaded gold flowers.

In a tall candlestick, a single candle lights the room. The diffuse light flows in purple and green waves onto the rugs, creating violet and bronze reflections according to the wool's pure warm shades.

In a corner, a mauve spark lights up on the protruding curve of a Moroccan kettle made of red copper sitting on a tall tripod. On the ground, a small tray shines like a pale moon. Adamantine waters flow from a white crystal pitcher next to the multicolored gems of the small tea glasses . . .

Si Mohammed ben Menouar, cousin and brother-in-law of Bou-Amama, the zaouïya's current master, is half reclining on the rug. His robust and supple body is draped with a burnoose of garnet-colored cloth, and a haïk made of delicate wool frames his thin brown face, of a pronounced ksourian type with a black beard where a few white hairs are starting to show.

A mask-like expression of intelligence, cunning, and sharpness, with a look alternately affable, almost tender, or suddenly hard, with a smile devoid of softness, often ironic. His numerous and lively gestures are without the serious amplitude and the imposing reserve of the other marabouts of the South.

Si Ahmed likes to joke and laugh. When he is with Europeans, he tries to imitate their light mocking tone. Si Ahmed shows the French favorable feelings and proves his devotion . . .

At this hour, at home, he seems preoccupied. He talks to me for a long time about the Mélias palm grove and people of Foukani, without my asking him questions. He insists in a way that he usually doesn't, he who moves so easily away from a subject that he doesn't care to talk about.

Across from us is Ben Cheikh, guardian of Sidi Slimane, with whom I came.

He looks sickly, and frankly ascetic with an extraordinary intensity of life in his evasive eyes.

He speaks freely in front of the man replacing the exiled master. He also is important, for he is Bou-Amama's most devoted servant in Beni-Ounif.

He tells me that some of the faithful left that morning to go on a pilgrimage to the marabout, there to his nomadic zaouïya, which is now at the foot of Djebel-Teldj,[2] a five- or six-day walk to the northwest of Figuig. With a deep sigh, Ben Cheikh laments the destiny holding him back; he would so much like to see the master again. Then, perhaps for the hundredth time since I've known him, he says to me with an engaging smile, "Si Mahmoud, you should go see Sidi Bou-Amama. With the protection of Sidi Ahmed and me, you have nothing to fear. You'll go to his zaouïya like you come here. As for Sidi Bou-Amama, he'll receive you with open arms, as if you were his son . . . You should do that, Si Mahmoud. Afterward, upon your return, you could say to the French, 'I saw Bou-Amama; he did me no harm. He received me like he receives all Algerian Muslims. He is not France's enemy, and between them there is nothing other than a misunderstanding . . .'"

I listen and respond evasively: "*In châh Allah*—God willing—I'll go!" And maybe someday I'll go . . .

Silence falls again. Si Ahmed vaguely smiles. Ben Cheikh seems immersed in the fanatic regrets of a servant. The light vacillates and crosses the white walls in large deformed shadows.

I watch these two men whose polished and welcoming veneer hides abysses, these men with closed souls, and whose wills are stubbornly directed toward one goal alone: to serve Bou-Amama.

And I prefer them thus, having become themselves again, serious and silent, more in harmony with the calmness of the hour and the place . . .

The door is open on the large covered gallery surrounding the first floor. Across the way, a heavy square pillar made of toub emerges from the shadows beneath the candle's reddish light. A white form stoops on the ground. One cannot distinguish the face of the black male servant

2. Eberhardt's note: *Djebel-Teldj*, the mountain of snow.

under the heavy immobile mass of the heavy veils. People speak in low voices in the courtyard. The slave's naked feet make light rustling sounds. Heavy oppression weighs on the sleeping oasis and on this house.

The hour advances in the oppressive night.

Si Ahmed retires to his apartments, forgetting next to me, as if by chance, his revolver in a green velvet holster.

Ben Cheikh rolls himself up in his old burnoose, and I stretch out near the still-open door.

At first, vague things float through my mind, visions that I've caught a glimpse of here. Then they become more precise: those shepherds armed with rifles who came here so furtively at nightfall—who are they? Yet here there's nothing to fear . . .

One can sleep in perfect security.

But sleep doesn't come.

It's hot, and feverish smells hang in the air. I get up and go downstairs noiselessly. On the dark patio, men sleep. I find another half-open door.

There, under the stars' dim light, the Mélias shepherds are asleep, their rifles beneath their heads, their cartridge belts cinched tightly against their hollow abdomens, on top of their ragged *djellaba*.

At rest, their faces are emaciated and show signs of suffering and toughness: their cheeks look hollow and their sunken eyes are shut with fatigue.

In a corner, a whitish soft mass undulates periodically; it's the sheep.

I go back in and lie down upstairs under the gallery. After a moment, two servants who were sleeping downstairs wake up. They speak in muted voices:

"Will the Beni-Guil leave tomorrow morning?"

"Sidi said they'd leave at dawn."

Then they continue in Berber, and I only vaguely understand. They talk about the pasha from Oudarhir and about Sidi Bou-Amama.

The men I took for shepherds are in reality dissident Beni-Guil, the remains of some djich that disbanded due to death and hunger; they've come from very far away, maybe, with these sheep acquired by God knows what means.

They've come with news from the West, maybe from Djebel-Teldj, and to get fresh supplies.

But finally sleep—very calm and sweet—overcomes me, at this fresher hour of midnight.

When the dawn is mauve colored, in the joy of awakening, the zaouïya's courtyard is empty: the Beni-Guil have disappeared with the last shadows.

Trades from the Past

A dark alley leading to an open-air square where reflections of gold colors flow along the pale walls: the djemaâ of Elmaïz.

A few cramped shops that one enters by means of narrow doors, resembling the mouths of silos. And there, generations of ksourians turn pale over minor jobs and small monotonous trades.

Wrapped in white wool, a few of them bow their white foreheads over unreadable Arabic scrawls, their large black eyes squinting. These are scribes, men of law or public writers.

Others run their agile fingers over supple red filali. They create vividly colored silk, absorbing the bloody color of the leather with pale blue settings, the golden yellow colors with glowing greens or warm violets.

Their labor resembles a game, so rapid and easy are their movements, limited to their wrists only against the immobility of their leaning bodies and their crossed legs.

Sometimes a rider's saddlebag hung on a nail creates a bright splash of color on the pallor of a bare wall.

Under a very ancient portico with heavy square pillars, an old man is sitting on a mat. The old Berber is calm and smiling, dressed in white veils.

Every day, starting at dawn, he comes and sits there for a long time. There are several earthenware jars filled with water placed in front of him. Inside each one floats a copper funnel with a hole in the bottom, slowly filling.

Long ago the ingenious ksourians calculated the time necessary for irrigating each part of the palm grove, and they invented this curious funnel system of which each one corresponds to a given part: as much time is needed for the funnel to fill as for each part to receive the water necessary for its fertility.

In order to avoid the endless, often bloody quarrels, the djemaâ appointed a calm and wise old man to direct the waters; he spends his life keeping watch over these archaic contraptions beneath the ruins of the old portico . . .

Across from him is a wall made of toub, with arabesques made overseas; and at the foot of this wall, on dirt benches, the members of the djemaâ come and discuss the ksar's affairs.

In the past they decided about matters relating to peace and war; they judged men's mistakes and sometimes condemned them to death.

For years and years, the *cheikh-el-ma*[1] has been attending, unmoving, the most-tumultuous, never-ending discussions. Smiling, he vaguely watches his jars; and on the wall across from him—above the as yet young heads growing overwrought and restless—the play of the sun and the reflection of the sky.

1. Eberhardt's note: *Cheikh-el-ma*, the old man of the waters.

Legionnaires

A day of farewells on the crowded train station platform. An old officer said to me, with a melancholy look at the busy legionnaires passing
over and over before us:

"A bunch of ex-convicts, of stateless men . . . what do I know! This is
how the Legion is generally judged. We certainly do have a lot of human
wrecks, of life's shipwrecked men, you know! And it's true that the
legionnaires drink heavily and their drunkenness is often terrible. But
what the devil! That's not all there is, and the men don't only have faults.
Oh! Besides that, if only their difficult life were known, always in the
bled, where everything is lacking and where they die, especially where
there is no audience to encourage and admire you! Here, for example,
we're coming back from Ben-Zireg, where we built and defended the
outpost, and where, for months, we haven't had a single day of peace,
where we lost some people . . . Well, you should damn well know that
we were sent there to rest. And now, hardly back on our feet, we're going
to Tonkin . . . Voilà!"

And the old officer made a vague gesture, an Arab gesture that
seemed to say *Mektoub*! May it be what is written . . .

A few days previously, I had seen them return, these legionnaires from
the Ben-Zireg detachment. It was on the low dune behind Beni-Ounif,
where one overlooks the western road, on a clear winter Saharan afternoon, in a pallor, a saddened languidness of things.

At first, a few scattered camels, a few bach-hamar, some spahis burst
out of the rocky valley.

Then came the legionnaires, parched and weather-beaten, hollow-
eyed, feverish, their greatcoats faded and worn, with their old, dust-
covered, worn-out equipment.

The officers leaned over their saddles to shake the hands of their comrades who'd come out to greet them.

And they, too, showed in their eyes the intense joy at seeing this corner of Beni-Ounif again, as if they had returned to a dream capital city after months of exile.

They were beautiful thus, with their sorry old clothes, in the calm day's glory, these legionnaires who had become wild—buried in dismal *hamada* . . . so totally unlike the braggart soldiers prancing about or moving about uselessly on the streets of friendly cities . . .

In the horizon's mournful menace and splendor, on this soothing and deadly earth where their life is bitter and joyless, the soldiers take on another appearance.

Figuig

The Figuig valley opened like a large pale calyx in the sun.

I was sitting on the parapet of a high crumbling tower constructed of golden earth, so old and so fragile that it seemed ready to disintegrate into dust. The tower was mirrored in the dark water of a pond at the edge of the El-Oudaghir gardens. Situated very high up, it dominated the whole valley.

Alone in the splendor of the nascent day, I dreamed as I watched Figuig, the queen of oases, which had never appeared so beautiful to me, perhaps because I was going to leave the following day.

In the distance toward the south, above the mountains of Taghla and Melias, the red desert rose far up into the sky, adjacent to the horizon in a clear dark line, like the high sea.

The powerful break of the Zenaga Pass opened like the bed of a river where the black wave of date palms flowed between the intense indigo blue of Djebel-Taarla and the obliquely lit pink of Djebel-Zenaga.

To the right, the Jewess Pass, arid and rocky between the barren hillsides, and the Moudjabedine Pass, where mirages play during the oppressive heat of summer midday.

The flat and sterile entrance of the valley glittered under the sun. Closer, just beneath my feet, the palm grove of Zenaga rolled its immense swell, undulated, battering the Djorf, the high gray cliff that separates the two terraces of Figuig.

The thick heads of the date palms took on the colors of pale-blue velvet where silvery reflections glided. Toward the right, the old ksar of Zenaga was like a splash of tawny gold, even more blazing in all its delicate pallor. Over the mountain and the valley, the morning sun spread waves of azure light, alive and infinitely clear. At the foot of the tower, standing with his back against the crude wall, an old blind man held out his hand silently toward the path where the believers were walking.

He was very tall and very beautiful, his face emaciated, with hollow eyes expressing the impassiveness of dark bronze. His bony body was magnificently draped in his earth-colored rags.

Farther away, two Berber women stopped on the sunny road, and the light played in the heavy folds of their clean purple wool coverings sweeping in the dust.

Above a wall, the small soft head of a young dromedary swayed back and forth with a plaintive hoarse cry and a strange grimace showing long yellow teeth.

A fragment of toub broke off the top of the tower and fell into the stagnant water of the pond, where large silver circles spread out, then died at its moist edges.

I went back down toward Zenaga on the Djorf path, where horses slip and tremble as they walk alongside the valley's abyss. As I went lower, the wall of murmuring date palms rose up, hiding, little by little, the clarity of far-off lands.

Down below, under the blue shadow of the palm grove, the water of a seguia was flowing over moss. The gardens of the ksar spread out the luxury of their teal greens, their lustrous bronze greens. The sun, filtering through the high palms hardly moved by the wind, scattered golden specks onto the red sand and onto the white pebbles. Nearby, delicious paths full of shadow and freshness opened between the garden walls of light-colored toub.

Under the curved arches of the palms, fig trees leaned toward the light, their leaves gilded by autumn, mixed in with russet vine leaves next to those pomegranate and peach trees still red like faded flowers.

Charming half-light softened the lines and colors in this maze of uninhabited little lanes, so quiet that one could hear the wild turtle-doves cooing softly in the nearby trees.

Sometimes, at an abrupt turn in the path, there was a large bluish pond, an immobile mirror where the leaning date palms were reflected, their trunks invaded by parasitic grasses.

And everywhere the unbroken murmur, the profuse song of the seguias' flowing water, bursting out of a wall, disappearing all of a sudden underground with a fresh waterfall sound, only to reappear two steps later under the gentle lace of green ferns.

The sun was slowly rising, as if in triumph, on the peace and joy of the delicious oasis.

Beyond the palm grove, I entered the eternal shade of the covered streets of Zenaga, where white forms passed by in silence as if furtively hugging the walls.

Doors suspiciously opened just a crack; and in the irregularly shaped squares, blue light coming from openings hollowed out above.

In all this mistrust, all this silence, one could sometimes hear the muffled drone of an old African hand mill through the thickness of blind walls, and the monotonous chanting in the Berber tongue of some invisible woman of the ksar.

I left slowly, dreaming with sadness that, without a doubt, in a few years, the ferocious lucre, the stupidity, and the alcohol that have polluted Biskra will come and destroy the remaining charm of this old Saharan hideout.

Such as it has been jealously preserved throughout the centuries, in its far-off place, the Figuig oasis seemed to me a perfectly beautiful pearl.

On the dusty trail, in the scorching barrenness of the valley, the inhabitants of Figuig approach on horseback, escorting donkeys loaded with sacks of barley and wheat grown by black Kharatine slaves.

The Berbers, very white and very calm under their woolen veils, moved slowly forward, slackening their reins onto the necks of their peaceful mounts.

With a vague look, their large black eyes wandered far off onto the mountains of their country, where the pink fairy-tale light of the morning was dying out.

They passed in front of my friend in his blue burnoose and me and distractedly called out the greeting of peace that is like the watchword of Islam, the sign of solidarity and brotherhood between all Muslims, from the far reaches of China to the shores of the Atlantic, from the shores of the Bosporus to the sandbars of Senegal.

Watching these men walk in the valley, I understood more intimately than ever the soul of Islam, and I felt it vibrate within me. In the splendid harshness of the setting, the resignation, the very vague dream, I tasted the deep insouciance about things concerning life and death.

And I also understood why the blind beggar was so noble and so calm, his hand stretched out toward the passersby he did not see in the eternal night of his blindness, and why, instead of bustling and toiling with the sweat of their brow, the Arabs doze in the monotonous course of calm days, stretched out in the shade of old crumbling walls that no one rebuilds, on this naked earth, so sweet to them . . .

At the Cherifien Amel's Home

A visit with Abdesselam, *amel* of Figuig. Under the blazing sun, beyond the wasteland dotted with tombs [...].

[...] crenellated white wall: the ksar of Oudarhir, (coming under the governor) Moroccan.

(Beyond the) walls, about twenty nomad tents [...] prostitutes.

(In the interior) of a big courtyard where the wind sweeps up small dust clouds, a half-dozen soldiers sleep on the ground in front of their stacked rifles.

They're tall, robust, wearing the red chechiya on their lively northern Moroccan heads.

Across the way, another newer and whiter wall [...]

To the right, a small bare room used as a soldiers' post, with a vaulted ceiling where the amel receives the commoners and metes out justice.

We're shown into the interior courtyard, where young fig trees throw their green shadows onto the milky-colored walls and *riad*,[1] the large arched portico [...] where rugs are spread out.

This is where we're received.

The amel Si Abdesselam greets us, along with his secretary and interpreter.

He's a man of about fifty, robust, with an expressive, tanned face and beautiful eyes that are alternately tender or piercing, intelligent and deep.

He welcomes us with perfect good grace and slow gestures from underneath the soft folds of his djellaba made of fine black woolen cloth.

A friend of Mohammed el Guebbas, Si Abdesselam was vested with the almost-illusory authority of the sultan's amel in Figuig, when the

---

1. Translator's note: A *riad* is a traditional Moroccan urban home with an interior garden or patio.

French, settled in Djenan-ed-Dar and later in Beni-Ounif, were at the door of the oasis.

The pasha, as they say here, only truly governs the ksar of Oudarhir.

The other ksour only verbally recognize his authority; and barring the neighboring French Commissariat of Figuig in Beni-Ounif [. . .], they would immediately revolt.

Si Abdesselam has lived in England and knows how to speak English. He (understands) French without speaking it.

(For conversations) that are European, he has an interpreter, an individual (with correct manners), a bit pretentious, ingratiating [. . .], who speaks at length about Paris to my French colleagues.

Like everything Moroccan, the small surrounding courtyard has a mysterious and dignified atmosphere . . .

Among the officers, there is one who seems the most important.

[. . .] (tall) and very thin with bony limbs under a djellaba [. . .] is a somber and harsh face with eyes [. . .], framed by a few long waves of gray hair under a red chechiya folded down the middle.

This officer would make a very good executioner, and I imagine him lopping off heads [. . .] with his large golden-handled *koumia*.[2]

He contents himself, however, with serving the tea, pastries, and dates . . .

We talk in measured and courteous terms about current events; we glorify the sultan, curse the Pretender,[3] and heap insults on Bou-Amama . . .

Long heavy silences interrupt this excessively official and formal meeting, which weighs on me even more as my colleagues, out of habit, begin to take notes under the immediately suspicious eyes of the Moroccans.

More polite remarks, then the session ends. We take off again. The amel accompanies us all the way to the door of his palace. The interpreter, all the way to the ksar.

2. Eberhardt's note: *Koumia*, a Moroccan cutlass with a curved blade.

3. Translator's note: Bou-Hamara, "the Pretender," successfully usurped the throne of Morocco and ruled ruthlessly for a time by claiming to be Mouley Mohammad, brother of Sultan Mouley Abdelaziz.

All in all, I take away, from this white and sleepy casbah, a poignant impression of irreparable decay, of the end of [...] rotten and crumbling *mogh'rib* ...

[...] it feels so good in the great sun of the South, in the (immense) [...] with its eternal aspects, after the languor and [...] the refuge of a finished nation ...

Lovers' Corner

The mokhazni Abdelkader and I ask permission of [. . .] to go spend the day in Zenaga . . .

After lunch with a notable, we go (celebrate) with the courtesans . . .

We walk along streets open to the sky, deserted streets where (sand) from the plain flows. Finally, we stop at the foot of a crumbling wall in front of a low rickety door.

Abdelkader quickly removes his blue burnoose; if anyone were to see this badge of the French makhzen, no one would ever open the door to us, for the djemaâ forbids all prostitutes to receive soldiers from Beni-Ounif, or else they will be beaten. The avowed reason for this measure is the fear of scuffles with the Moroccan makhzen, but in fact, it is the profound hatred of the Moroccans for the *m'zanat.*[1]

We knock.

After a moment we perceive the two gummy eyes of an old woman observing us through a crack. Abdelkader grows impatient; it's not an artist's curiosity that brings him there . . .

Other eyes, very big and black, appear in the half-light.

"Who are you?"

"We're Trafi . . . open up, daughters of sin, or we'll break down the door."

"What do you want?" It's a young singsong voice that through the (crack begins the negotiations).

Abdelkader shakes the door by pounding with his fists.

"What [. . .]! We're in the burning sun! Open up!"

[. . .] seeing that we've decided not (to leave) [. . .] agrees to open.

(With the door closed) Abdelkader spreads out his blue burnoose (in front of the) frightened women.

1. Eberhardt's note: *M'zanat*, corrupted, perverted, traitorous—name given by the Moroccans to Algerian Muslims, whom they profoundly detest.

"Tomorrow you'll receive a beating, but today you can thank God that we didn't break down the door."

There are three young women and a hideous old hag with flabby skin who moans and curses us.

The courtyard is large, half full of debris, with low walls falling into ruin into which are crammed two long rooms, as black as dens, with low doors.

A nomad tent is pitched in the middle of the courtyard. There, old rugs; beautiful scarlet, green, and yellow rags; smoky earthenware utensils; a gorgeous tray made of engraved copper; and a tambourine are piled up.

Four men are sitting along the wall. One of them is sewing a shirt, holding the cloth with his right big toe. The three others are dreaming, with their eyes half closed, like happy cats. There are no Moorish cafés in Figuig, and the brothels serve as a meeting place for nomads, except for leaders and old men.

Those whom we find with our hostesses are sokhar, Ouled Bou-Oua-nane, a fraction of the Douï Ménia, who welcome us [...].

We settle onto scratchy rugs. (I openly play) my role as the son of an important family.[2] I (allow myself) to be fussed over by the slightly timid women.

[...] *mlahfa* lemon yellow, Reguia, the oldest, drapes (her body), thin but supple. She has a small face [...] with fleshy lips, with large red eyes that [...]

[...] round, with more ample shapes, better formed, a strange truly Egyptian beauty with her oval face, with [...], with curved lips, her face illuminated by long shadowy eyes [...].

Serious, with feline movements; and when she walks, her full hips undulate with perfect grace under the long folds of her purple veils.

When resting, loaded with heavy jewels, she resembles a remote idol.

Her name is Marhnia, and she was born in the Angad plain near Oud-jda. Moroccan soldiers brought her to Figuig and left her there.

The third one, Khedidja, almost a child, a mulatto, with wonderful enameled teeth under large red lips.

2. Translator's note: Eberhardt's description is more colorful and contextualized: "the son of a great tent."

Marhnia prepares the tea and performs the dwelling's honors. Relieved, I see that in spite of the rag piles and the courtyard's disorder, these Zenaga hetaera are less dirty and less flea ridden than their poorer sisters lodging under the tents of Oudarhir . . . They are also more likeable, less beggarly.

Like all Arab prostitutes, when they haven't been contaminated by contact with soldiers, these three women behave well, without obscenity in their gestures and language.

They are, however, gay, lavishing us sometimes with very reserved (caresses) and sometimes childlike coquetries and allusions [. . .], but very veiled.

(The camel drivers), attracted by the tea, come join us [. . .] Abdelkader, after long hesitation, (slipped away with Reguia), not without excusing himself to me, very [. . .]

(I stretch out) on the rug and watch the childish games (of the nomads) with Marhnia and Khedidja.

They jostle and pinch each other, wrestling with loud bursts of laughter and piercing shrieks.

(With their) belts bristling with cartridges and their soiled burnooses and their tattered veils framing their beautiful vivacious heads, the Ouled Bou-Ouanane resemble bandits.

(Their firearms) are there on the rug within reach. They've certainly pulled off more than one audacious coup in their lives . . .

And now, here, they're playing like laughing, carefree children, and they're singing.

They seem completely trustworthy and good-natured, and one could travel with them throughout Morocco without suspicion . . . This is definitely the nomad personality, the great lack of concern, the extreme mobility of spirit, the instability of passions, sometimes childish, sometimes deep, but never very long lasting.

Were the slightest incident to occur here in their pleasure sanctuary, the smallest quarrel, these men who seem so inoffensive would leap up and reach for their rifles again. They would suddenly become threatening, prepared to kill.

Marhnia, with her little chirping Moroccan woman's accent, speaks with me about Oudjda, which she would very much like to see again. Yet she suffered there with the makhzen soldiers and the young debauched men from the schools.

She recounts her life there in a hovel in the casbah, caught in the middle of often bloody quarrels and brawls, passing [...] from one man to another, tugged at and pushed about like some poor thing [...] as well as she could through the turmoil.

(Now), in Figuig's calmness and relative security, (she) is bored and yearns for this terrible (Moroccan) life (where stories) of love end in blood.

[...] the Douï Ménia begin recounting the [...] the helping hands, the razzia, the disputes, [...] the murders, and the loves in the desert [...] ksour of the Oued Ghir.

(All) of these stories of gunpowder are marked by complete (contempt) for human life, even their own, a kind of absolute heedlessness of nomads used to living [...], without thinking about tomorrow.

Or instead, they then (laugh) about risqué jokes, jokes from the past, repeated a thousand times, peddled through all of the Southwest's encampments.

The women laugh as they modestly cover half their faces with sections of their veils . . .

The hours flow by slowly, peacefully, in this Arab lovers' corner in the heart of silent Zenaga.

The sun goes down on the horizon, and a large blue shadow invades the courtyard.

It is the hour of the asr, the afternoon prayer. The camel drivers get up and step to the back of the courtyard. Marhnia also leaves us and disappears behind a section of wall with an earthenware vase full of water.

When she returns, her face, arms, and bare feet are damp, and clear drops are still flowing on her golden bronze skin.

Very serious and far from what she was a few moments before, the carefree friend of camel drivers and Moroccan soldiers turns toward the *guebla*[3] and prays in a low voice, bowing low [...] in the dust with a resonant jingling of (her bracelets).

3. Eberhardt's note: In the direction of Mecca.

Beni Israël

Dark covered corridors interrupted, here and there, at junctions open to the sky through which a blue-green light of day falls as if into a well. Sometimes, on an ocher-colored wall, there is the cheerful note of an oblique ray of sun amid the disquieting darkness: these are Zenaga's streets.

Abrupt turns, lower and blacker, corridors that horses will not pass through and where we must creep one after another.

Uncertain white ghosts go by noiselessly. Others, on white earthen benches dug into the walls' thickness, maintain poses like statues.

Everything in Figuig is hushed, sleeping. No disturbance, no yelling in these corridors with the cool freshness as sonorous as a cloister's, where horses' hooves awaken multiple and distant echoes.

A narrower little street that descends toward a crowded crossroad between high rough walls with protruding angles. There is no opening to the outside light, nothing but an eternal night where the Beni Israël live, bent under the Muslim yoke, denied, like the black Kharatine, the right to participate in the ksour's djemaâ, condemned to obey and to say nothing, in return for which they are not molested or persecuted in the least.

In the Muslim neighborhoods, extreme cleanliness, vigilantly cared-for houses, walls, no ruins, not a pile of garbage or rubble: this is the first impression, the first surprise upon entering the ksour.

Here, on the contrary, is a lingering odor of debris, an unheard-of cramming together of human lives, or courtyards as large as dungeons.

Outside in the palm grove, the blue date trees were bathed in the blond light, and rays of gold played on the peaceful water of large blue-green pools.

In the somber *mellah*, in the heavy darkness, the stench made us choke.

In order to find the door lined with the old bottoms of oil cans, we had to light a match.

Finally, someone slowly and suspiciously opened the door for us. We were in an irregularly shaped narrow courtyard the size of a room, surrounded by a large covered gallery on the upper two floors that led to low-ceilinged bedrooms.

Gray daylight, the false light of a dungeon, fell on the garbage-strewn ground soaked with viscous water.

A horde of red-haired children in dirty gandoura swarmed. When we entered, they fled and hid themselves behind the very shiny pillars blackened with grease.

The acrid smoke from dried palm leaves rose into the air and crept the length of soot-colored walls. In the corner were piles of garbage, rags, shapeless old-fashioned things, undisturbed for years.

The women sitting by the fire turned to see us. They wore the mlahfa of Bedouin women but in dirty white cotton, very roomy, dragging, and belted very low.

On their foreheads, half covering the black headbands, a tightly pulled dark silk scarf held up small silver chains that joined the heavy gold rings worn in their ears. Even more than the Muslim women of the ksour, these women were listless, weakened, and as pale as wax. Yet a few of them were beautiful, with round faces, very black big eyes, and heavy eyelids.

Only the moving sparkle of the jewelry gave a little life and cheer to these disturbing death masks.

The most beautiful one, her magnificent eyes reddened by tears, her face voluptuous and bitter, isolated herself in a corner, looking fierce.

She gave us a black look.

Near her, an old mummy of a woman, a blind grandmother, lamented aloud as she twisted hands numbed by the cold.

Haïm the jeweler left his small forge and tiny instruments in order to welcome us. He apologized for the state of his home, which misfortune had just struck: The night before, Esthira, Haïm's wife, was going to the home of relatives in the ksar of Oudarhir. They came upon nomad shepherds who approached them and went so far in their effrontery as to uncover Esthira's face. They were about to rape her when some horsemen maghzen from the pasha of Oudarhir passed by. The nomads fled. Shame and sorrow now still cast a shadow on the house.

Esthira was the beautiful weeping woman.

As Haïm moved away in order to make us coffee, my companion, the mokhazni, began to laugh:

"Among my people when such a thing happens, the man finds the guilty one and kills him. These people settle for whimpering like mice whose tails have been stepped on. Besides, the Jewish woman is beautiful, and the shepherds were right. She's really stupid if she truly resisted: look at how ugly her Jew is!"

Haïm, who was tall, had arms and legs full of yellow fat under his grease-stained gandoura, and a larger neckerchief with blue dots was placed under his small black turban and knotted under his chin, in the style of old women. This dress was undoubtedly forced on the Jews of Figuig in times past, out of Muslim disdain.

Haïm spread out his works before us. *Bzaïm*, hook-and-eye fasteners in the shape of leaves or stars, heavy carved rings, brooches with small silver bells, gold earrings decorated with the dull blood color of garnets and the milky iridescence of opals. All of this was piled pell-mell on the shimmering background color of a scrap of silk cloth.

The noise had hushed when we came in. Even the children whispered shyly. One could only hear, as if falling from far above—because it came from a neighboring courtyard—the nasal and monotone voice of a rabbi reciting prayers in the sacred ancient tongue of Israel. And this Jewish house, this antiquated voice, all of this gave me an impression of a particularly closed, old, unchanging world in the midst of all the secular inertia of Figuig.

The sirocco had come up, full of sand and dust, under the incandescent and tarnished sky.

The members of the djemaâ of Zenaga were in session on the benches of an intersection, with a dull light flowing in between two walls to their right.

Slowing down beneath the smothering sirocco, they gave in to the somnolent torpor of things.

Haïm stopped at the entrance to the intersection and took off his worn-out old shoes. Then, bent all the way to the ground, he kissed the edge of each burnoose worn by the impassive inhabitants of the ksar.

Haïm had come there to demand justice regarding the shepherds who had gravely offended his wife . . . But he had almost no hope. However, crouched down close to the ground, he told his story.

When he had finished, a tall, very stooped old man, his eyes still fiery under thick white eyebrows, made a vague gesture.

"What can we do about it? If the man who gravely offended your wife were one of ours, we would punish him, for those acts are unworthy of a Muslim. As for some nomads . . . you yourself are guilty of letting a woman travel alone through the ksour . . . no, Jew, we can do nothing about it!"

Haïm timidly tried to insist. Then the old man frowned and said harshly:

"We have spoken, Jew! Get out!"

Haïm got up and left, walking backward and bowing very low. He had to give in, for he whose arm is not strong, who doesn't know how to hold a rifle, can only humble himself and shut up in the country of gunpowder.

Starting at dawn, the urchins of Israel, redheaded and half naked, leave for the gardens, where the shade of the moist feggaguir opens, carpeted with ferns and light mosses.

Taking infinite precautions, they descend noiselessly to the underground seguia and kneel in the blackish mud for hours in order to watch for colorless fish and blind, lightly silver-colored fish in the diffuse light and the green water.

The urchins catch the rapid creatures with their hands. At the slight rippling of the water, the fish flee into the darkness of the impassable tunnels.

Toward noon, if the fishing has been fruitful, cries stream forth from the subterranean passages toward the cheerfulness of the gardens swooning under the sun's caress.

Waving their bunches of sticky fish held by the gills, the little Jews run joyfully toward the mellah's small dark streets, where their pale-faced mothers wait for them.

The Djich

The Ouled Daoud, a fraction of the dissident Amouria, numbered no more than about ten. They'd been holding the mountains for months, starving and looking out for some emaciated herds to raid.

Their ragged clothing had taken on the reddish color of the soil. Unkempt beards made their angular faces, burned by the sun and the wind, look shaggy. Old cartridge pouches made of red filali, worn over their fringed *abeya* and their tawny burnooses, squeezed their hollow abdomens. They were miserable and fierce, as distrustful as desert animals, hunted by hunger, and pursued.

After the Taghit affair, the southern route had become too dangerous for them, and they had gone back up north, prowling around the douar and encampments, bursting forth everywhere there was gunpowder.

Squeezed into the dry gorges and thickets of the Beni-Smi, they had suffered horribly from hunger.

One day, luck had returned, and they'd stolen a few sheep and camels near Ich. Then they'd come down again toward Figuig. At nightfall, on the side of the deserted valley, they were following the high walls of the ksar of Andarh'ir [sic, Oudarhir], made of tawny-colored toub. Their black eyes opened greedily on the fertile gardens, the big closed and mute earthen houses, and a kind of joy revived their vulture-like eyes.

Tall and round, with small arrow slits carved into them, the earthen guard towers flanking the walls stood out in dark gold against the evening's last red colors, against the immobile foliage of the black date palms. At the foot of the ramparts, in about twenty low gray tents, the Amouria camp—a place of sordid poverty and prostitution—lay hidden. Small smoky braziers cast the fires' light onto the tents and the walls, sometimes showing black silhouettes of women wearing ragged clothing draped about their bodies in the growing shadow.

The scrawny djich came and collapsed near the tents like a flock of birds, exchanging joyful salaams with the girls of their race and with a few skinny nomads stretched out by the fire.

Dry djerid thrown onto the ashes suddenly ignited a very tall and very clear flame that shot straight up into the calm air. Like giants, the distorted shadows of men and things danced against a dark background of dust. Voices and cheerful cries rose out of the joy of return and the hour's temporary security.

Thin women with tattooed faces came and went, welcoming the prowlers, recognizing them and asking them for news of their comrades. And since most of them were dead and had their bones scattered in the mountain without proper burial, the women called for divine mercy for the deceased.

The Amouria gorged themselves greedily on peppered couscous, in which they bit into sand, and on lean meats. Then they ceremoniously prepared the tea themselves, a task reserved for the men.

Their tired bodies were comfortably strewn on old carpets. However, all of them kept their rifles nearby, out of habit and also because the makhzen of the pasha of Oudarh'ir, a friend of the Christians, was close.

The brazier's flames cast their blood-colored light across the dried-out faces with the profile of a gyrfalcon. Only the whites of his eyes and the dull sheen of his teeth were visible on a tall, black Khartani man who passed among them.

They exchanged news of the bled, repeating stories of pillaging, exalting the valor of some, cursing the desertion of others. In all these speeches, one name was often piously repeated, evoking the memory of the master, the venerated cheikh: Bou-Amama. And Bou-Amama's name was mentioned again and again. There were Ouled-Daoud and very tanned little boys from the Amouria named Bou-Amama.

In the women's camp, a lot of tea was drunk that evening. Then a rhythmic and monotonous chant arose. At regular intervals, the voice rose incredibly in the clear tones of an oboe . . . then it faded in a desolate moan.

The road cutters said:[1]

1. Translator's note: *Coupeurs de route* literally means "road cutters," which refers to fighters cutting off routes via sabotage.

Yesterday, all day long, I cried, I moaned;
the sun rose and I smiled.
Our country is the country of gunpowder,
and our tombs are marked in the sand."

And the small reed *djouaks* softly accompanied the ethereal sadness, the bandits' death song, with their murmuring.

The night's mute hours advanced; the fires grew dim. Then, slowly, stretching their muscular catlike bodies, the Amouria arose and followed the women into the warm shadows of the tents for passionate embraces after war's long chastity. Silver jewelry clicked for an instant. A vague, discreet, and voluptuous murmur floated above the tents, over the wild fate of the nomads. There was plaintive bleating from awakened ewes whose sleep had been disrupted and a few hoarse barks from anxious dogs in the vicinity of all these strangers.

Then all these noises were hushed, and a great silence reigned in the prostitutes' camp and over Figuig, which had fallen asleep in the damp shadows of its palm groves, where large bluish ponds lay dormant.

The day rose pink and lilac on the valley's harmonious lines. The jagged summit of the tall sheer mountains lit up with red glimmers, and metallic reflections slid over the gardens' blue velvet colors. In the morning's joy, the tawny-colored ksour were all ablaze in gold.

Men with remarkable and serious faces, dressed in navy-blue djellaba and armed with rifles, emerged from the walls of Oudarh'ir. A tall thin Moroccan, dressed in a white djelleba and wearing on his head a red chechia folded in the middle over strange curls of graying hair, walked at the head of the group. His pale face was ugly, and his eyes were evasive.

The Amouria sprang up, grabbing their rifles. The officer of the pasha's makhzen came forward: "Peace be with you! Who are you, and why have you come here?"

"We are Amouria, and we've come from the north to ask for *aman* and hospitality from the people of Figuig."

The pasha had promised not to receive dissidents or pillagers: "Get out!"

Their heads bowed, their eyes fierce, the Amouria listened. There were only ten of them. If the gunpowder spoke, it would mean their death.

So without a word, they gathered their grubby, ragged clothing, and they left by the valley, toward the west, for other plundering.

The women and the pasha's makhzen followed them with their eyes as they grew more distant in the pink clarity of the day, rising calmly and smiling.

Ramadan Evenings

It is the first day of the long and difficult Muslim fast.

This day of abstinence seems unending, without even the consolation of a cigarette.

Since morning, people have been wandering, wrapped up and shivering in their burnooses, their daily routines now in disarray. Others slump at the foot of walls in fierce or sullen attitudes. Quarrels break out due to edginess caused by the oppressive hours. Finally the sun goes down.

Then groups form in the street for the suddenly joyful and impatient waiting period of the last moments.

All eyes turn toward the west, toward valleys of black stone and the jagged mountains of Morocco, where the sun is going down, dipping little by little into a world of copper-colored vapors.

The people of the South are beautiful in their severe clothing, standing in the blood-colored mist that seems to rise from the red earth, their enormous shadows stretching out over the slowly trampled dust.

Outside, too, people wait around the fires among the reclining camels in the nomads' camp. Douï-Ménia and Ouled-Djerir from Oued Guir—only yesterday mere dissidents and pillagers—today take on the air of peaceful camel herders, in order to come and restock at the markets following the terrible famine of the last few months.

Around them the other Bedouins laughingly tell old stories of their impiety.

In former times the Douï-Ménia were returning from war. It was during the fast, and they were suffering from hunger, for the days of walking in the desert were long. Their hearts felt anguished because they had five more days of walking in the bled. They met an Arab walking all alone, his staff on his shoulder. Out of boredom, they shouted out to him and asked him his name. "My name is Ramadan," answered the poor soul. Then the Douï-Ménia seized him and said the following:

"So you're Ramadan, the one who makes us suffer from hunger and thirst every year!"

Then they killed the poor wretch; they broke their fast and returned to their tribe. There they made fun of those who were still fasting: "You don't need to fast any longer. We met Ramadan on the road, and we killed him."

"Yes," says another, "the Douï-Ménia killed Ramadan . . . but there are still people fasting . . . only they arrange things much better than we do: they collect a group of thirty people, and each one fasts for one day. Then they believe that the fast has received its due, since you must fast for thirty days . . ."

In spite of all these jokes, the former bandits seem indifferent and drape themselves silently in their magnificent rags.

In the Moorish cafés, the waiters, with multicolored *fouta* around their waists serving as aprons, place full cups in front of the Muslims rolling their cigarettes.

These are the last moments of waiting, the most feverish. On pale, drawn faces, the shadow of boredom is disappearing.

Laughter and jokes rise up. I'm treated mockingly as a *Meniaï* because, having seen the Douï-Ménia start eating, I'd had the naïveté to propose breaking the fast.

Now the evening fades out into violet night, and things take on bluish tints, dark and cold.

Then, from very far away, from the ruins of the ksar, from the end of the valley, a slow, melancholy voice rises up; it is the muezzin announcing the magh'reb prayer and the breaking of the fast.

An immense sigh of relief bursts forth from all lungs. Everyone praises God out loud. With slow gestures, pious men go outside to the pathway as always, in order to pray seriously and without haste, instead of throwing themselves onto the tobacco and coffee.

These first hours of the evening during Ramadan have their charm. An uncommon atmosphere of brotherly intimacy reigns in the Moorish cafés.

And in a corner, I silently begin to recall visions of other past Ramadans, from already a few years ago, in different corners of the chosen earth . . . There are the discreetly sensual landscapes of Tunis, the fever of troubled Algiers, then the splendid and fanatic country of the Oued-Souf, the small domed cities scattered across the blazing Erg.

VARIATION

It's the first day of the long and difficult Muslim fast, and the complete abstinence, without even the consolation of a cigarette, confuses and disorganizes the seemingly endless hours.

Since morning, huddled silhouettes in burnooses wander in the village streets or collapse onto the sand, to deal with the slow boredom.

Then, as the sun goes down in the calm and clarity of autumn, the great wait begins.

The day's heavy drowsiness dissipates. Muslims form groups in front of the Moorish cafés, their faces turned toward the west, toward the Moroccan valleys where the magical evening is fading.

Disproportionately long shadows stretch out. It is the hour of the great daily fire, the hour, too, that rekindles hearts and evokes hope.

Outside, among their kneeling camels, the skinny Douï-Ménia, yesterday still dissidents and pillagers, today peaceful-looking traders, also wait, disdainful of the jokes made about them, deserved because of their reputation as bad Muslims.

Around them, in the groups' idleness and impatience, people laughingly tell old tales about their impiety.

And the nomads from the hamada drape themselves in their rags with the pride and defiance of those who know they are still feared.

As soon as the twilight's redness has gone out, the Douï-Ménia are the first to hurriedly break the fast.

Sitting in the midst of their morose indifference, I too was awaiting the hour of the maghreb.

Evening Gatherings

The night is cold and clear. The Ramadan moon is full. Torrents of blue-green light flow over the village, where the brutal red flames of lanterns burn in front of the cantinas.

Here in the courtyard of the Arab Bureau, between the crumbling hovels, the hobbled horses are dozing.

Sometimes a stallion awakens and neighs, his nostrils dilated, reaching toward the corner where the peaceful mares are chewing their dry hay.

The mokhazni are having a great celebration tonight.

About fifty of them come and sit on the sand in a circle. In the middle, stuck into the sole of an overturned shoe, a flickering candle lights up the masculine energy and the childlike cheerfulness of the faces.

It feels good to stretch out on the ground, in the clear night, under the caress of a large *kheïdous*, the burnoose made of black camel hair worn by the people from the West. It feels good, silent and still, to listen for hours to the nomads' songs, their loud desolate cries about love and death, accompanied by the silvery, watery sound of the reed djouak.

Two mokhazni from the Géryville circle, children of the esparto grass steppes, sit across from each other so they can sing a doleful cantilena whose refrain is a long sad cry in a minor key.

At first they seem to doze with their eyes half closed, and their voices are like the wind's murmuring.

> Little dove, oh little dove!
> You have burned me, you have killed me,
> You have sickened my heart,
> And I will not recover . . .
> Little dove, oh little dove!

My heart is dead, and I have buried it in the desert;
The day that I buried it, no one was present.
No one mocked me.
I was alone, my burnoose covered my head, and I wept.
Oh my God, my God, how much did I weep!

Little dove, oh little dove!
You have sickened my heart; you have killed me.
I ache, and there is no cure
For a wounded heart,
Except for resignation and the tomb's rest.

Little dove, oh little dove!
In one night you have killed me.
Near dawn I found myself wounded.
And I will not heal . . .

Then from the mokhazni circle, another even more unpolished and hoarse voice arises, that of my friend Abdelkader ben Chohra:[1]

Friend, weep for me, weep for the exiled one!
When I left my douar, Embarka went outside . . .
As a sign of mourning, she covered her head with dust.
Yet each person follows his destiny, and I left,
And I took the route to the South . . .

Forty days, forty nights, I wept
Until my heart had dried out,
And it became harder than rocks.
In front of the most beautiful woman of all the beauties of the earth,
My heart would not speak.

1. Eberhardt's note: A few days later, Abdelkader ben Chohra was killed by a bullet in the Oued Zousfana.

Ah! When the heart is dead,
Nothing can cause its rebirth,
Except for the gazelle's gaze,
For it is like desert rain . . .
I will see Embarka again, or I will die.

More voices rise into the peaceful night, and the enchanted pipes distill unspeakable sadness.

The illiterate nomads and the coarse soldiers from the country of gunpowder improvise more and more songs for a long, long time.

Toward midnight, I close my eyes as the cold wind rises.

It feels good to fall asleep in this way, beneath the stars, knowing that one will leave the next day and without a doubt never return, that all that is will not last . . . while the Bedouins sing, the djouak cry, while thought disappears, going out like a useless flame.

Last Visions

Things took on familiar aspects as my eyes became accustomed to them. The stone valley; the feverish village; the small barren room where I was camped out and where there were always baggage, burnooses, rifles, shapeless piles of rags; the spahis and the mokhazni—all these things that had framed my existence for three months were starting to be dear to me.

During the daily wait in Ramadan for the liberating evening, I was leaning on the small outer wall of the old Arab Bureau. I was watching the sun's red disk sink—lifeless and without rays—into an ocean of purplish vapors, above the already-darkened earth.

And perhaps for the first time, I felt that this corner of land, so deprived, had, in the long run, captured a bit of my heart and that later I would miss it after so many others to which I will never return.

Today, everything sinks into the black rain, into the horror-stricken, as a known country is brutally changed, plunged into darkness all at once. The train leaves amid violent wind gusts.

And suddenly I feel all the bitterness of abrupt departures, of the destruction of small ephemeral things. After the charm and intoxication of the nomadic life come regrets and feelings of loss.

The train goes back up toward the North slowly, as if regretfully; under the gray sky the country seems threatening to me, transformed as if in a nightmare. The hazy sand horizons rise very high into the murky sky, and the colorless light of the dying day distorts faraway places.

Hadjerath-M'guil, Mograr, all the wondrous chaos of black shining rock becomes today an indefinable shade of ash. The wild gorges, the defiles crowded with rocks struck by lightning, everything is invaded by a soot-colored haze. An icy wind blows like a tempest through the loose doors of the old train car, making the dusty curtains flutter. Abysmal sadness, almost desolation, descends into my soul. I wrap myself up in my burnoose; I try to fall asleep, in order to see nothing, in order to no longer think.

A dismal awakening on the quay of the Aïn-Sefra train station, swept by icy winds from Mektar, which is covered in snow all the way to its dune, in a strange contrast. Gloomy streetlamps sway in the night, hoarse voices curse, stooped silhouettes flee in haste.

VARIATION

There again, as in so many other corners of the African Muslim earth, I was going to leave a little bit of myself; I would take away vivid regrets and a lasting nostalgia.

I almost began to blame nomadic life. I thought of the sadness of abrupt departures, the destruction of small ephemeral things, of life's small backdrops to which one becomes accustomed, which one already loves without even noticing until the inevitable end.

Harsh and splendid land of the Oranese South, fierce and wild, without softness and almost no smile, old earth of plunder and gunpowder, where men are as coarse and hard as the arid soil!

During this last evening, there stirred in the depths of my soul the eternal question, will I ever see all of this again?

The spahis and mokhazni were slowly returning, in small groups, for the first meal after the day's fast.

I contented myself with lighting up a cigarette, and I stayed there watching the fine simple comrades walk past me, companions of my walks and evening gatherings from days gone by.

All of a sudden my vague sadness became darker and more heartrending: which ones among those filing past me were destined to fall soon under Moroccan bullets and to sleep their last sleep on this scorched earth, far from their native steppes? Most of them were young, full of laughter and of simple, marvelous lightheartedness. They went by singing, and some of them came up to me:

"Si Mahmoud," they said, "stay with us. We've gotten used to you; we're your brothers now. And we'll miss you if you leave, because you're a fine boy, because you've eaten bread and salt and ridden with us."

They knew, from so many European indiscretions, that Si Mahmoud was a woman. But with beautiful Arab discretion, they told themselves that it wasn't their business and that it would have been improper to allude to it; and they continued to treat me as they had during the first days—as a literate and slightly superior comrade.

The spahis and the mokhazni passed by.

I left.

Them, too, like the beautiful ksar made of golden toub, like the sad gray village, like the arid valley, like Figuig and Djenan—I felt like I loved them now, and I missed them.

Night fell, black, deep, and sonorous as an abyss.

A great silence hung over the village, where the cantinas' lanterns alone gleamed red like the lifeless eyes of wild animals lurking in the darkness.

Sometimes a gust of wind passed through the darkness with a long howl—an infinitely sad moan.

I was lying down in the alcove near a large room barely lit by a single candle, where five or six Moroccan *assa* were sitting in a circle on a mat, their shotguns on their knees. They smoked kif and sang with their heads thrown back and their eyes closed as if in ecstasy. In the courtyard anxious horses snorted and stirred. I couldn't sleep. Indistinct visions haunted me.

Toward morning the candle went out in the guardroom. The weary Moroccans became quiet. The horses dozed off. A delicate steady rain fell with an immense murmur on the sad sleep of things.

The drab day broke, drowned in an opaque mist with heavy greenish clouds resembling strips of rotting flesh.

The ksar seemed to be made of dirty waterlogged mud, and the palm grove swelled like a raging sea, under the wind's furious shaking.

In this darkening of things, the treeless village had the sinister ugliness of a prison, without a speck of green. I left Beni-Ounif drowned in black water, changed, almost frightening.

Slowly, as if with regret, the train went back up the misty plains and the chaos of Hadjerath-Mguil's and Mograr's black boulders.

And sad enough to cry, I wrapped myself in my Moroccan burnoose, and I lay down, closing my eyes in order to see nothing, so as to take from there only a sunny vision.

Aïn-Sefra under icy moonlight. The high mountains rose up and were covered with snow all the way to their foot. In the night's blue-green glimmer, they looked soft with wooly round contours.

And like monstrous waves, the huge tawny dunes frozen in place attacked the mountain in their eternal anger.

It was a strange vision, those desert dunes that I had seen blazing under the early autumn sun, and which now were standing out against the completely white very northern mountains . . .

Aïn-Sefra, with its gardens full of bare trees and the spindly skeletons of its young poplars, was dozing in the calm night, huddled against the cold.

Aïn Sefra's Market

Beginning Sunday night, on all trails, across all the dunes, the nomads arrive on horseback, by mule, on foot, urging along small patient donkeys and tall slow camels who stretch out their supple necks and their greedy lower lips toward tufts of green esparto grass. "Amour" and "Beni-Guil," all these perpetually migrating people are gathering in Aïn-Sefra for the big Monday morning market.

The market plays a major role in the life of the Arab, especially the nomadic Arab.

It is where people meet and gather, where one gets news, and especially where one earns a little money.

Beginning at dawn, on a wasteland between the village and the cavalry barracks, the crowd gathers with great noise that will grow louder all the way until noon.

Camels kneel down with muffled groans; horses tethered to the boulevard's spindly acacias snort and neigh at the passing mares. Men exert themselves and cry out.

Above all this commotion are the plaintive bleating of the sheep tied to one another by the neck and the mooing of small oxen and black cows hardly larger than calves.

On the ground, southern merchandise accumulates in glorious disorder: fleece smelling violently of suint, spongy gray pieces of raw salt; goatskins filled with soured milk, butter, or thuja tar; baskets woven with esparto grass; bright-colored blankets and haïk; brand-new, still-stiff burnooses; horseshoes; earthenware jars; wool cords; saddles; etc.

The nomads circulate amid all the chaos of these things for sale; ragged and glorious "Amour," "Beni-Guil" in tatters, their belts, as reddish colored as the ground, bristling with cartridges.

Women also mix with these groups, most often old women who are worn down, dried out, their faces tattooed and weather-beaten by long summers, walking confidently with male gestures. Rarely one sees a somewhat young face, beautiful azure eyes and white teeth partly hidden under a long veil embroidered with flowers.

Since the Beni-Guil obtained the aman and started coming to the border markets, they've been recovering from the frightening misery they went through last year while holding the mountain. The bandits have withdrawn their hooked claws. They are circulating in the village, already less ragged looking, if not less fierce at first.

They pass by, watching the m'zanat indifferently, almost disdainfully. They enter stores in a group, suspiciously. The interminable bargaining begins there. The nomads discuss for hours as they consult each other about minor purchases.

In the Moorish cafés, they socialize in groups of three or four to drink their tea with a piece of dry bread. What heads they have under the large turban covered with a canopy-shaped veil! What bird-of-prey profiles, their noses shaped like ferocious beaks and their eyes shining!

At the market, fights erupt over the slightest challenge, and one can guess what it must be like in the Moroccan *bled-es-siba*, far from any surveillance. There, in the even more tumultuous markets, gunpowder speaks, cadavers roll amid the merchandise, and blood flows on the beaten earth. Here, the Beni-Guil are satisfied with wild gestures, threats, and epic insults: "Wait, son of an infidel, son begot of sin! Here, we're out of shape, we've become like women by dint of eating white bread and drinking running water! Wait until we're beyond Fortassa and we've drunk from the *redir*.[1] Then you'll see if we're males . . ."

Against the earth's red backdrop, neutral colors dominate, the ocher of clothing, the dull reds and grays of the camels, the shining black of the cows and female goats, the gray dew of the sheep's piled-up fleece.

This is a portrait of nomad existence—harsh and full of life—that has remained as it must have been long ago in its so very distant prehistoric era.

---

1. Eberhardt's note: *Redir*, a natural reservoir where rainwater gathers. For the nomads, white bread and running water are luxuries that weaken.

Return

Under the winter sun, Aïn-Sefra would resemble a sad northern village, with its pale houses and leafless trees . . . But there is the African note of the reddish dunes and the military buildings with their arcades made of blood-red bricks and the great emptiness of the sand desert.

The air is limpid and cool, and in the clear sky, light caravans of wooly clouds pass by, walking their bluish shadows across the gilded plain.

I'm going to get back to the province of Algiers via the long route of the High Plateaus.

The mournful sadness of departure I felt in Beni-Ounif has disappeared. Today my sensations are slow and calm. I go without haste toward the ksar at the foot of the dunes. There are still a few Saharan features there: the tall date trees that don't change through the seasons, the white koubba, unchanging throughout the centuries in the dust and barrenness of this setting.

The holy koubba surround the ksar and watch over it like sentinels of dreams and silence: Sidi Bou-Thil, the patron of Aïn-Sefra; Sidi Abdelkader-Djilani, emir of Islam's saints; Sidi Sahali, protector of camel herders and nomads . . .

Today is the *Fedhila* of the month of Ramadan, the Arab version of the third Thursday of Lent, which doesn't suspend the fast and which is celebrated only by songs and visits to holy sites.

In the koubba's shadow, the pure voices of invisible girls chant antiquated litanies, accompanied by muffled tambourines. These clear voices take off and seem to dissipate in the infinite silence, which they do not disturb.

In the distance, on the Mékalis road, reddish-brown camels approach slowly, grazing on the bitter tasting *btom* that grows along the rocky trails. They come down through Aïn-Sefra toward Beni-Ounif to join one of the large convoys of the far South. I watch them go by, and I am tempted once again to go back down, with the carefree camel herders, toward the beloved horizons and to never return, instead of returning to the boredom of captivity in the city . . .

Tiout, a small smiling ksar in the green shrine of an oasis at the end of a valley full of sand and esparto grass.

Narrow paths, bordered by earthen walls under the eternal shadow of date palms, cross the charming disorder of gardens that are becoming green once again. Then, in the darkness of an alley of the ksar, the entrance to a white and silent residence with large sunny courtyards; the house of the agha of the Amour, Sidi Mouley, descendant of the great saint Sidi Ahmed ben Youssef of Miliana.

The agha is not at home, and it is Sidi Mohammed, his son, who receives me. The young man resembles a large wilted flower, with his very beautiful face as pale as wax and his big heavy black eyes, half opened as if tired.

He is gracious and shy, yet already possessing all the seriousness of someone of his social rank, and a slightly haughty reserve that he very quickly drops, becoming smiley and almost cheerful.

When night has fallen, I go to the *dar-diaf* to see the mokhazni and the spahis with whom I came and who are leaving to patrol the mountain.

In order to arrive at the dar-diaf, one must pass through a maze of black entangled streets. Here and there a weak stream of light abruptly leaks through a fissure in a wall or a closed door, soaking the dull toub of the street bloody-red. When this happens, these lanes devoid of passersby take on the depths and the distances of subterranean passages where indistinct shadows flicker.

In the courtyard of the dar-diaf, a scene from nomadic life, the scene that I will now see every evening for days and days in different settings.

The soldiers from the West are on mats, half reclining around a *medjmar*, an Arab brazier made of terra cotta, and a tea tray.

In the shadowy blue light behind them, the horses lazily chew drinn and snort.

The mokhazni sing, as they always do in the evening. They must be thinking of the beautiful, tanned, Amouriat women, scattered in the distance under tents, for they intone languorous love songs—sad ones, however, with the sadness of the abyss:

Blue starling flying away to my country,
Tell my gazelle, tell my friend
She must send someone to buy nine cubits of white cloth . . .
Tell her to sew her lover's clothing.
Ah! To sew it while singing,
Her friend's white clothing . . .
He will not put it on until after his body is washed
In much pure water,

When his eyes will have closed . . .
Tell her that her friend greets her and says adieu.
One day, overcome by madness and anger
He left his tent;
He bought a gray horse and he left.
He put on the blue burnoose,
He girded his gandoura with a cartridge holder made of red filali,
He threw a rifle onto his shoulder,
And he left for the border, for the country of gunpowder . . .

Blue starling, tell my friend
That her lover says adieu,
Beg of her to sew his shroud,
For he will die alone and far away . . .
The jackals will eat his flesh and lick his bones.

And the mokhazni sing their desolate lament without sadness or apprehension . . . However, the naive improviser maybe speaks the truth, and among them are some who will sleep in the deserted bled . . . But is there not Mektoub? And what good does it do to worry about what is written?

I go back to the agha's. In the large white room, tanned men in black burnooses converse cheerfully. In the corner near the chimney, where twisted and hard desert logs burn, rifles lean against the wall and cartridge belts are hanging.

Bags made of black and gray wool and heavy carpets from Djebel-Amour are piled on the ground. The leaders of the goum of Trafi from

Géryville tribe are heading back from the South after four months of fatigue and danger. They are also my future traveling companions all the way to Géryville. They recount their troubles down there in the desolate hamada; they also speak of the return to their tribes, and joy softens their harsh faces still blackened by the South's blazing sun.

The evening finishes in long weary silence, and I will go to bed dreaming about the next day, about this long trip on horseback, which consoles me somewhat for having to leave the South.

A great heavy silence weighs on the ksar. Somewhere, very far away in the goumier camp, a Bedouin pipe cries softly. I listen to it as if in a dream, for a long, long time.

The pipe becomes quiet, and everything falls into sleep. I fall asleep, dreaming vaguely about the joy of at least being free and feeling peaceful in the vast empty steppes, in preparation for the return to Algiers, which I would have so much wished to delay indefinitely yet again.

Note

The first part of *Sud oranais* finishes here. The last text, entitled "Retour" ("Return"), is not found at the end of the manuscript from Aïn Sefra but instead corresponds to notes written by the author on loose sheets of paper during the same time period. It was published during Isabelle Eberhardt's life and in the *Akhbar* dated June 5, 1905.

We have added two texts to the end of this first part: "Hauts Plateaux" ("High Plateaus") and "Oudjda." The first was inspired by the return trip to Algiers. The second recounts a brief trip to Morocco made shortly afterward. The first part of *Sud oranais* was originally published in *Akhbar* as Eberhardt's voyage proceeded. She undertook a second edition, enriched with new scenes, and then recopied the whole thing into a notebook that was found after the Aïn Sefra flood. This is the version that is reproduced here. It is also the one that Barrucand used to constitute most of the *Notes de route*—with the exceptions of "Chez l'amel chérifien" ("At the Cherifien Amel's Home") and "Coin d'amour" ("Lovers' Corner"), which were deleted for "diplomatic" reasons and out of consideration for moral standards, and "Le Djich" ("The Djich") and "Marché d'Aïn Sefra" ("Aïn Sefra Market"), which were published in other collections.

High Plateaus

It is morning, a pale, luminous winter morning whose sun caresses fig and barren pomegranate trees of the courtyard, and ignites white flames on the sharp palm fronds tossing slightly in the cold breeze.

The caïd of the Akkerma and his goum have already left before dawn. I will only see them again in the evening at our stopover.

Wrapped in large burnooses made of black goat hair, the old goumier, Mohammed Naïmi, and I mount our horses. We make our way silently, first across the gardens, then immediately into the uncultivated and deserted valley where the esparto grass rolls in grayish waves.

This early morning departure, while fasting, is not pleasant, and my mind turns in on itself in vague lifeless reverie. Yet the horses become excited in the cool air and snort joyfully.

Without eating, particularly without smoking, the day is going to be long in the monotony of the unending valley.

On both sides, layered mountains of a hazy, pale blue close the horizon. To the northwest, very far away, another mountain—rectilinear and powerful—rises bit by bit. And I think, with more bitter nostalgia, of the very similar silhouette of Djebel-Moumène, down there on the red horizon at Djenan-ed-Dar.

In the morning's whitish haze, the sun rises and the valley of esparto grass becomes more agreeable. The malaise caused by the first hours of fasting fades out little by little. I find consolation by saying to myself that I still have at least twenty days left of nomadic life.

On the Géryville road we only meet a few young shepherds crouching near esparto grass tufts, which they light on fire in order to warm themselves. Then we dismount, for our feet are becoming numb in our red filali boots, and our hands are so stiff that we can no longer hold the reins.

Mohammed Naïmi notices that I seem sad; and with the great affability of the nomads, he begins telling me stories to cheer me up.

The old goumier's stories are very simple and often very poignant: departing the native country with the Trafi horsemen, regrets and farewells, women and children crying, then days and days on the road in the hamada's monotony, sometimes pursuing the elusive djiouch, sometimes to scout out the route for, and escort, the slow convoys of camels. But Naïmi stretches voluptuously underneath his heavy burnoose and says with a smile full of very white teeth:

"Praise God! All of that is over, and tomorrow or the day after tomorrow, everyone will be back in their tents."

What he is clearly implying is the difficult celibacy for months on end and the solitude, far from the beautiful Bedouin women with their tattooed foreheads. Yet Naïmi is nearly fifty, and his beard is going gray.

I encourage him a bit, and he begins telling me about the amorous prowess of his youth, in appropriate and suggestive terms, but with a revived flame in his long bird-of-prey eyes. These nomad loves are no ordinary loves, and are really made to flavor the coarse nomad existence with a few romantic notes that later leave their imprint on the whole moral physiognomy of the Bedouins, on their character and attitudes.

What does it matter that the great wild poetry of their lives is unconscious!

The sun goes down on the horizon, and we arrive at a narrow gorge between two high mountains where the esparto grass is denser; the prickly underbrush allows fewer wild olive trees to grow. We descend again. Djebel-Breisath is to the right of the Géryville road.

In the middle of a clearing on a small plateau sloped toward the oued, there are about ten beautiful tents with red and black stripes topped with red woolen balls; this is the encampment of one of the fractions of the maraboutic Ouled-Sidi-Mohammed-el-Medjdoub.

Our goum's horses are tethered around the tents, and the people of the douar light large fires in order to prepare the diffa for Si Larbi ould hadj Ali, the caïd of the Akkerma.

My dog, Loupiot, who followed my baggage carried on a she-mule, rushes forward to greet me with joyful sounds.

It is a good moment, this arrival at the encampment during Ramadan, a sensation of "home" found once again under a foreign tent, which I will tomorrow leave forever, but where I feel so good this evening stretched out on thick haraïr.

The brave caïd sits imposingly among men tanned and quite ragged after four months in the South. Sitting in a half circle, chins on knees, the marabouts listen attentively to the stories and the news from the West told to them by the caïd.

All the Arabs from southern Oran are passionately interested in the affairs of the border and Morocco.

Among these Trafi and these Amour, of whom Bou-Amama was the leader twenty years ago, there is no longer any desire to follow the old bandit's fortune. Today they are the most courageous among the Muslim soldiers fighting for France down there.

We stay up late, waiting for the hour of the second meal; and a loud murmur rises from the encampment into the black night.

Nowadays the talk is of livestock, sheep, camels, esparto grass, and markets. And there are shepherds' conversations that I will hear repeated at every stopping place all the way to Géryville, all the way to Aflou, and all the way to Boghari . . .

Finally, long after midnight, everything quiets down, and I fall asleep despite the cold piercing through burnoose and blankets, and despite Loupiot's feline stretching as he lies curled against my chest.

We enter the plain at sunrise.

At first we follow a rocky path in unnatural terrain that becomes iridescent with purplish hues.

A high impenetrable gray wall rises up across from us: a zone of thick fog where the sun, rising on the other side, designs pale rainbows and large semicircles that seem like archways beneath which we must pass.

The fog is icy cold, and a silvery mist soon covers our burnooses, the horses' hair, and the goumiers' beards.

We try to warm ourselves by trotting for about a half hour, but the cold keeps increasing, and we descend into a small amphitheater formed by black hillocks where the esparto grass is very thick. Tall columns of gray smoke soon rise into the fog, and bright flames flow on the damp sand. The good heat gives us courage and brings back some cheer to our small troop whose awakening was morose.

A mokhazni and a few goumiers join us again. The mokhazni Ahmed approaches from Taghit all alone on his mouse-gray mare, in order to go see his parents, who are camping somewhere near Brézizina, toward the South.

An hour later, after the fog has lifted, we catch up to the slow camels belonging to the Trafi sokhar, who are carrying the luggage and about ten cases of cartridges that the goum must convey to the Géryville Arab Bureau.

It's noon, and now the sun is shining, hot and scorching as in the spring.

As we head back toward the North, the terrain becomes redder and rockier, and long undulations cross the plain, carving out large oueds, still dry. To the right, all the way at the far end, a small, very white ksar appears, with gardens full of bare trees.

Not a single date palm. It is Chellala Guéblia.

On a hill to the left, next to the road, one of the large koubba belonging to Sidi Abdelkader Djilani of Baghdad. A masonry square between high bare walls and an egg-shaped, very elongated cupola, all of it an ancient white color made slightly gold by the sun.

We arrive at the foot of a mountain whose geometric contours we had noticed since Tiout and which resembles Djebel-Sidi-Moumène.

In a small depression in the very red soil, a pretty ksar made of dark tawny-colored toub, and beautiful palm tree gardens: Chellala Dahraouïa, where we're going to spend the night.

The ksar is built on very uneven terrain, cut into by deep ravines. We pass through partly covered streets, the strange ksar-style streets full of shadow and mystery. On a narrow path, we skirt a large chasm, at the bottom of which are gardens and an old koubba whose whitewashed surface has flaked off and whose crude cupola matches the trail's height. Tombs—small upright gray stones—surround it.

We arrive at the house of caïd Hadj Ahmed. He is a jovial and welcoming old man who receives me in the guest room, a long whitewashed room with a European bed in one corner and rugs from Djebel-Amour stacked on the floor.

In order to wait for the magh'reb we go out onto a bare hillside above the ksar, and there we bask for a long time in the sun on the warm earth, in the company of the cadi, the caïd, and a few men of letters, among whom is a beautiful brown-haired young man who sings in a soft voice. He is the son of the caïd of Bou-Semghoun, a southwestern ksar in the region.

In Chellala the people of the ksar still speak *Chel'a*, and it is there that I hear, for the last time, this old, strange, and incomprehensible Berber idiom that still darkens all the sought-after mystery of indigenous life in Figuig: farther on we will return to purely Arab country.

When the sun sets, there is still the feeling of the rediscovered South.

As we're returning to the ksar, along the road leading to the wells, we meet a procession of women in long red or white veils arriving in the golden evening with amphorae and goatskins dripping wet on their shoulders.

Long violet shadows wend their way on the pink ground beginning at the women's feet . . .

All nomad life is summarized in this question that the caïd Larbi asks his colleague from Chellala, as he's departing:

"Could you tell me where my family is now camped?"

The caïd Hadj Ahmed makes a gesture, which to me seems very vague: he stretches out his right hand toward the northeast. That's enough; the caïd of Akkerma has understood, and he will find his family wandering more than one hundred kilometers away from where he had left them at the beginning of autumn . . .

Doueïs, a valley between rocky, bare hills and mountains whose names the caïd explains for me: Djebel-Bessebaa, Ousseïra, Mezrou, Tazina, where many fountains flow.

At the bottom of the valley is the gulley of a oued, as red as a long bleeding wound, and redir (ponds of a sort) that are starting to fill.

It's three o'clock when we approach the caïd's encampment. There are two or three rifle shots in the air, and the women's silvery ululations linger in the mountain's echoes.

The whole tribe runs out to greet the leader—a simple, rugged, and harmless man—and the brothers returning from the bled-el-baroud (land of gunpowder).

I must spend all day tomorrow here, and then I'll leave the brave Trafi in order to get back to Géryville.

After the magh'reb meal, I go wander alone in the esparto grass with Loupiot.

I would like the intoxication of my sadness to dissipate, because I understand that even were I to return there one day, I would not find any trace of what I'd left.

The whole evening and the night are spent in the guest tent where there are easily thirty of us piled in, the result of which is that we don't feel the terrible predawn cold very much.

In the morning, at about ten o'clock, I said adieu to the caïd Larbi and to all of the people of Akkerma. It was a fraternal and almost-moving adieu. Then I again took the route for Géryville, alone with a tall, clumsy, wild lad named Abdesselam, who started out with several hours of stubborn silence.

It is warm under a clear sky.

After ravines and crevices, we cross a large, completely Saharan-looking plain.

We have a stretch of ninety-five kilometers before we reach Géryville, and on this road is nothing, not a douar except for a miserable and half-ruined dar-diaf guarded by a few Bedouins of maraboutic lineage, who look more like prowlers: the Ouled-El-Hadj-ben-Amar.

The dar-diaf is very far away, at least sixty kilometers from Si Larbi's encampment; and we trot almost all day long in order to arrive there before nightfall.

Abdesselam slowly consents to chat, but I notice his incurable stupidity, and I prefer to listen to a monotonous and doleful chant with which my guide's full voice answers the echoes of the bled.

He lets me know that he has never been to Géryville and, furthermore, that he has never set foot in a French village. And he asks me the most preposterous questions to which I respond vaguely, my mind being elsewhere.

I miss the intelligent and interesting companion, Mohammed Naïmi, of my first day of travel.

The sun goes down. It is the magh'reb, and I have the consolation of being able to finally light a cigarette.

But there is still no trace of the dar-diaf and the Ouled-El-Hadj-ben-Amar.

The route threads straight through into the deserted plain, leading to the horizon and a chain of long low hills where a few wild olive trees have grown.

"Maybe this dar-diaf is over there at the foot of the hill?"

"God knows . . ."

Nothing else can be gotten out of the lout, and I content myself with taking off at a fast trot.

Night is going to fall, and we enter into a gorge where the route descends and where the evening's purple shadows are already making things hazy.

Here, finally, is the lopsided and crumbling dar-diaf in swampy terrain cut through by cool seguia. We let the two courageous mares drink, and then we look for the guardians.

They're camping in a sort of fissure in the mountain under sloped and flea-ridden tents, and they themselves look very poorly with their scrawny rapacious faces.

Long negotiations concerning the price of the diffa and the barley. Finally we have a bit of bad coffee and black couscous without meat, and we rest under the tents. The women's curious eyes watch us through a tear in the interior curtain.

Abdesselam wants to sleep there, and the "marabouts" would like to keep us.

But this place and these people weigh on me. I prefer the icy moonless night's silence, and I don't allow myself to be swayed. We get back on our horses, and we take off quickly to join up with the road again.

The darkness is impenetrable and a cold wind rises. Abdesselam grumbles a bit and then, seeing that I'm not listening to him, falls silent. Finally we find a fountain and a watering trough at the foot of a tall hill invaded by esparto grass. We go up to it, and we make a fire in order to warm ourselves and for light as we eat a bit of galette, the second meal of Ramadan night . . .

We arrived in Géryville. Other stopovers followed.

Going through Aflou in the Djebel-Amour, I gathered a few subjects for stories, and I was vividly struck by the strong and industrious character of the beautiful population of this region where the art of rug making has been conserved. In Aflou, people spoke a lot about the South and the war. The echoes of gunfire were amplified in these mountains, reported and commented on by the goumiers returning from a harsh campaign whose difficult marches and dangerous days have never been set down.

The siege of Taghit, recited by an Arab poet, gripped the audience of a Moorish café. You would have thought you were hearing a chant from the Crusades, as chanted verses explained how the horsemen of the harka from Tafilalet had come to get themselves killed by parading below the redoubt's gun slits and challenging Captain de Susbielle to single combat . . .

Oudjda

Throughout the years spent wandering, the sated eye becomes used to the most brilliant colors, the strangest backgrounds. It ends up discovering the earth's disappointing monotony and the similarity of beings— and it is one of the most profound disillusionments in life.

There are, however, parts of countries that have kept their character: those alone can return to the weariest souls the shiver of excitement believed to be forever lost.

Oudjda is among these forgotten corners, like boulders in the full torrent of the leveling forces of the century.

The impression is even more violent in that one arrives there through scenery whose beauty has been known for a long time, but with nothing to foretell the vision of Oudjda.

At first there is a brief vista of hazy Tlemcen drowned in rain, buried in its very green and cheerful gardens, with its high gray walls, its small streets and shops, its antiquated and yellow-brown colors, with the minaret of Sidi-Bou-Médine etched in black against the tearful horizon.

Then, as one departs under a weak ray of sun, furtive as a smile amid tears, the great silhouette of ruined, struck-down Mansourah, persistent in its endurance, stands still proud on the threshold of annihilation in the African spring's raging surge of plant life.

Beyond the bush and the peaceful hills, beyond muddy and insurgent Tafna, Lella Marhnia, a small military town with wide straight streets bordered by vast *fondouk* where the agitated wave of a Morocco in fermentation comes and pounds and foams in bitter commerce.

Behind Marhnia is the immense plain of Angad enclosed in its large amphitheater of mountains.

There is nothing more there than sadness and monotony, with the gray skeletons of leafless jujube trees and the long red wounds of deep oued furrowing the damp grass.

On the unpredictable path, gaping carcasses display the terror of their ripped out entrails under the caress of the pale sun covered slightly by light white vapors.

A belt of dense olive groves, fertile gardens, and small green velvety barley fields with the crimson blossoming of a peach tree sometimes at the corner of a dirt wall: a peaceful countryside resembling the Tunisian Sahel.

But all of a sudden the olive trees open up. A high rampart colored a lackluster white rises up, inaccessible, ferocious, pierced with a powerful arched door. This is Oudjda.

Sitting or half reclining on the ground, *asker*, the sultan's soldiers in scarlet jackets and chechia, guard the door. Indifferent, their eyes far away, these men watch us go by and respond distractedly to our salaam.

When the sun has gone down, at the moment when the *moueddhen* unleash the drawn-out notes of their call, Oudjda's doors, squeaking on their old iron hinges, will close. The keys will be carried into the kasbah to the amel's house, where they will stay until dawn. From sundown to sunrise Oudjda will thus be isolated from the rest of the earth, and no human being will be able to enter or leave it.

As soon as we have gone under the arch, an odor chokes us, a violent and motley odor made of the stench of rot, musk, decaying carcasses, and macerated olives.

And it is amid mud and putrefaction that we enter, among stagnant puddles adorned with greenish efflorescence where excrement, dead beasts, squalid debris, and rags stagnate.

Instead of the silence and contemplation of other Islamic cities, here is a compact, noisy, swarming multitude, struggling and wallowing in the sludge of the streets. It seems that a feverish wind has passed over Oudjda. The people—whom one expected to see walking slowly and seriously—seem to be in a hurry.

They jostle and squeeze each other. For what urgent business, to go where, since it is evening and the doors will be inexorably closed?

At first a few miserable small streets, a first square bordered by once-white houses now crumbling, displaying wide black peeling walls, showing deep cracks like wounds. Shops open on the earth's black mire, narrow cavities where merchandise and food are piled: black shiny olives, brown dates pressed into tanned animal skins, jars of greenish oil, sugar loaves wrapped in blue paper.

On the somewhat dry pathways, the crowd bunches up against the length of the walls polished and soiled by the continual rubbing of hands.

What a mix of races, types, and clothing! Citizens of Fez or Oudjda in djellabas made of delicate cloth, their faces white and impassive, looking cunning and proud . . . Nomads in soiled rags, wearing turbans and hoods, prayer beads at their necks, regular and hard profiles, yet more familiar and kinder . . . Pathetic women dressed in rags, rolled in old haïk made of dirty wool, dragging their worn-out old shoes in the mud . . .

Running between the pedestrians, fleeing like bands of mice under the horses' hooves, hordes of shameless beggar children, polite, however, with sweet little faces and long caressing eyes . . . Finally there are soldiers and prowlers, one hardly distinct from the other, faces of famine and pillage, the Gueballa from the center of the country, still robust after long months of atrocious misery, with bony faces, pointed teeth, and shining eyes. Some of them are wearing the red vest of the makhzen on top of indescribable rags.

All of these are speaking, fighting, laughing, singing, and joking all at the same time . . . For in this city of putrefaction and of misery, cheerfulness reigns, and there are bursts of laughter and songs at this last hour of the day.

And very strangely this cheerfulness underscores the sinister impression of the arrival and the dread inspired by these beings, exasperated and rushed to their limit, returning to savage animality.

Gibes and dirty jokes fly back and forth between the women, the children, and the soldiers. These men who are dying of hunger still dream of the pleasures painted in glowing colors before their greedy eyes on the long route, which from Taza has brought them back to this

Gehenna where so many of their own have died of hunger and illness in the wave of rising filth.

The two Beni-Ouassine horsemen from the border and I cross the entire city to go to a sure and calm refuge: the zaouïya of Sidi-Abdelkader of Baghdad.

And all of a sudden as the sun is setting, purple in its ocean of greenish gold, Oudjda; in faraway neighborhoods where the starving multitude no longer swarms, Oudjda raises its veils of mourning and terror; Oudjda smiles, white and pink; Oudjda, squeezed between Saracen walls with elegant crenellations and whispering olive trees. Everything is quiet except for the only human noise: the moueddhen calling the believers to the twilight prayer.

On the crumbling arches, where grass has grown, softly cooing wood pigeons smooth their iridescent plumage.

Here I suddenly find again the great peace, the immobility and the serious serenity of cities of Islam, so very unexpected after the nightmarish arrival.

The dark night has fallen under the sky filling up with clouds.

With a black slave from the zaouïya, a giant with a hoarse voice, I once again cross Oudjda on horseback in order to go visit the small French mission responsible for instructing the Moroccan gunners.

And then the city of hallucinations appears to me in a new way, gloomier and more eerie.

The coming and going continues in the shadows where lanterns of red, green, and blue glass cast long phosphorescent trails on the fetid pools from which bubbles arise, bursting.

The passersby wave their lanterns at the ends of poles in order not to sink in.

A square, one of the markets, is irregularly shaped and cut through by stinking ditches and piles of refuse. Piled in a corner are two or three dog cadavers, which the living dogs come and sniff only to then flee, terrorized, their tails between their legs, howling ghastly howls . . .

Under the miserable light of the lanterns, they sell vegetables, oranges, olives, lemons, dates, old clothes, kif; only bread cannot be found at this late hour, the bread for which the starving soldiers yearn. And the deformed, miserable, and threatening beings become more numerous, emerging from corners of darkness only to return there immediately, leaving one with the anxiety of a glimpsed sinister profile that is then lost, but which one feels somewhere, following very nearby.

My horse slips and trembles. He is afraid of all these lights and this entire racket. He rears up and we must move away in order not to crush the pedestrians and the gang of kids howling under our feet.

And it is there in the night that you feel the hunger, the furious hunger gnawing at the soldiers, the vagabonds, and those who have taken refuge here since the war.

A groaning monotonous clamor rises from all the squares, from all the small streets:

"In the path of God, bread! For Sidi Abdelkader Djilani, bread!"

And in the darkness beyond the market, one voice dominates the others—an innocent blind man's voice hammers out infinitely the same prayer in a monotone and halting voice:

"Who will favor me with bread for Sidi Yahia!"

And this name of Sidi Yahia, Oudjda's patron, returns as a refrain, rings with a harshness of expression that ends up rendering the beggar's supplication hostile.

Finally we find the kasbah, an enclosed house like all of those of Oudjda. There, abandoned by their students since the bread shortage, two officers and a French sergeant with two noncommissioned officers and the indigenous Algerian infantrymen remain alone, exiled, reduced to inaction in the dismal sadness of this corner of Oudjda. They remain at their soldiers' post, resigned to the incertitude and the uselessness of their presence—these poor courageous people who tomorrow perhaps will be the victims of Moroccan quarrels and pillaging.

In an antique bedroom I stretch out on the carpet and fall asleep. As if in a dream, half asleep, I at first hear an indistinct voice rising up from Oudjda's anguished silence, now finally calmed down. The voice rises, rises, ascending into the clearer sonorities of an oboe, ending in a soft dying moan, in a sigh: it is the Aïssaouah praying and chanting their dikr in the modest serenity of the night, hiding the rotting of things and the decay of human beings.

And there again, as at sunset, an impression of immense peace, of immobility, an intense impression of old Islam: indifferent in the face of death, unconcerned about ruins, pursuing through these centuries of war and blood its great serene dream of eternity.

Today has risen clear and radiant on the small rose garden hidden within the eroded mission's courtyard, in the shade of a silvery giant aspen, and the kasbah's old ramparts eroded by moss.

Return to the market, still on horseback for fear of walking in the liquid mud of soot and pus.

Oudjda breathes: four thousand starving and threatening men from the Taza army came out at dawn, almost all of them recruited from among the fearsome Gueballa. The *mahalla* has left,[1] straight in front of it, looking for the promised bread, and does not return . . . Woe to those who will meet this scraggly horde on the deserted routes!

However, still today, men run around auctioning useless rifles and their blood-colored jackets. They sell these things with a sort of determination, for whatever price, with insults and mockery for the powerless and lying makhzen. Their hatred explodes openly.

The more one advances, the more the streets become narrow, and the more the crowd compresses. Here in the air, in the overheated mud, a carcass is swelling. A horseshoe, a greedy dog's claw tears from it shreds of dead flesh, leaving seepages of blackish blood and pus.

And the city people, the clean and distinguished *khador*,[2] overwhelmed for months by the horde of *berrania*, no longer even try to clean their city: they pass in front of the refuse and turn away from it in disgust.

One also sees in the streets, cut through at each step by arches and successive enclosures, extraordinary swindling, blind men, lepers, cripples, and idiots . . .

Sensations of a dangerous back alley, of hovels and unsavory areas, a mix of revulsion, terror, and pity, all combine in me and oppress me.

1. Translator's note: Here, *Mahalla* refers to the group looking for pasture, food, water, work.
2. Translator's note: *Khador* refers to the locals.

Muscular men, almost all dressed in the old red castoffs of the makhzen, run through the city bumping into people. Attached to their necks by a long chain are a bowl and a small bell, all in yellow copper, which hang and jangle. On their backs they carry a full water skin: these are the *guerbadjia*, the water merchants who, with their unusual noise, add yet another note of disorientation.

All of a sudden, among the secondhand dealers, a tall handsome tanned soldier in a scarlet jacket raises in his outstretched arms, by the scruff of its neck, a howling bristly dog. In a loud voice, imitating the sellers, he yells out mockingly:

"Five pennies for the dog, my dear! He's a good guardian; this one never lies!"

And everyone understands the insulting allusion to the cheating makhzen. There is a thunderous burst of laughter, whereas the rescued beast barks furiously as he flees.

In the zaouïya, large light courtyards, long clean and white rooms, silence and contemplation.

Around the very young son of the absent cheikh—a pale and sickly child in a *djellabah* made of dark cloth—serious dignified individuals with welcoming smiles and gentle manners. They speak of the sultan, of his beneficial reforms, and of the crimes of the Rogui,[3] as if they were reciting a learned lesson . . .

But in the end, they are too intelligent to embrace all these quarrels. They wish to remove themselves from them, in their immutable and closed world, to live like their pious ancestors lived and to direct in silence, in shadow, the affairs of the believers, without worrying or not about the master of the mogh'rib, always so effaced and so far away.

Magnificent black women slaves serve us tea and the diffa made of milk and peppered meat. Under their mlahfa made of dark wool, they have supple and muscular bodies with a perfection of form noticeable at each movement. And they half smile, rolling the white globes of their big eyes with caressing animality.

3. Translator's note: Bou Hamara was also nicknamed "the Rogui" or "the Rougui Bou Hamara."

How far away this zaouïya is from the horrors of the outside world, hidden behind walls and successive enclosures and courtyards and corridors! How immaculate and peaceful it is compared to the putrefaction and howls of Oudjda!

It is with this impression of deep calm, deriving from mystery that I leave.

Under the noon sun, we again cross all the chaos of Oudjda for the last time, and we leave by the same eastern door.

It's the end. The sumptuous green and silver curtain of the olive trees has closed on all these short visions, on this dream of a few hours deriving from drunkenness and nightmare.

And in spite of all of this, with all its contrasts—sordid, starving, and prostituted Oudjda—the city of putrefaction and of death left me with one of my deepest and most-gripping impressions of Africa. I left it without fleeing, almost reluctantly, keeping the nostalgic memory of the rare moments when, as if furtively, she showed herself to me, calm and smiling with the melancholic beauty of a fallen princess plunged into the heart of dread and deep in ruin, in this country where everything is sleeping and where everything is slowly crumbling under the indifferent eyes of men who do not try to fight against annihilation, who do not believe in human force . . .

Note

In the spring of 1904 Eberhardt returned to the Oranese South. *La Dépêche Algérienne* published a short article on May 1 announcing the departure of its reporter, indicating that "she will make an effort to enter Tafilalet, the industrious and rich region until now closed to Europeans."[4]

4. Translator's note: This note follows "Oudjda," but it is not about Oudjda, which is in northeast Morocco, while Tafilalet is down south. "Oudjda" appears to be inserted as a matter of chronology rather than any content link with the pieces on the Oranese South—except that Oudjda was also caught in the political turmoil of the times.

Oranese South,

PART II

I left Aïn-Sefra last year at winter's first breaths. It was bitter cold, and great howling winds swept over it, bending the frail bareness of its trees. Today I see it in a very different manner, having become itself again, in summer's dismal radiance: very Saharan, very sleepy with its tawny-colored ksar at the foot of the golden dune, with its holy koubbas and its bluish gardens.

It is very much the small capital of the Oranese desert landscape, forsaken in its valley of sand between the immense monotony of the High Plateaus and the South's blazing heat.

It had seemed dismal and without charm to me, because the sun's magic did not wrap it in the luminous atmosphere that creates all the splendor of desert cities. And now that I live there in a small temporary dwelling, I am starting to like it. Furthermore, I will no longer leave it for a gloomy return toward the commonplace Tell, and that is enough for me to look at it differently. When I leave, it will only be in order to descend farther, to leave for the great South, where the hamada sleep beneath the eternal sun.

Among the long pathways of poplars with their white trunks, following the dune's first undulations with newly found scents of sap and resin, I have the illusion of losing myself in the forest. It is a very sweet and very pure sensation colored, at moments, by the sensuality of the more distant breath of a bouquet of flowering acacias. How I love the exuberant greenery and the trunks, full of life, wrinkled like an elephant's skin, of these fig trees swollen with bitter milk, around which swarms of golden flies buzz!

In this garden, surprised by its own full dryness, I spent long hours lying on my back, intoxicating myself with immobility beneath the breezes' lukewarm caress, watching the hardly moving branches come and go on the sky's dazzling background, like the tackle of a gently rocking boat.

Beyond the last and already more spindly and shriveled poplars, the path of sand rises and ends abruptly at the foot of the immaculate dune seemingly made of delicate gold powder.

There, the sky's winds play freely with each other, building hills, digging valleys, opening precipices, and creating, with each day's whim, new ephemeral landscapes.

All the way at the top, dangerously perched on a slightly more stable slope with its ridge of black stones, a reddish-colored "blockhouse" watches over the valley; an empty-eyed sentinel who has seen pillaging armies and bands and who now watches the silence and peace of faraway horizons.

The flaming golden-red dune contrasts sharply with the severe blue background of Djebel Mektar. The day ends gently over Aïn-Sefra, drowned in light haze and sweet-smelling smoke. I feel the predeparture sensation of delicious melancholy and a strange rejuvenation. All the worries, the heavy malaise of the last months in fastidious and unnerving Algiers, all of what constituted my blackness, my "blues," have stayed down there.

In Algiers I had to spurn things and people. I don't like to spurn people or things. I would like to understand and excuse everything. Why does one have to defend oneself against stupidity when one has nothing to fight about, when one is not part of it! I just don't know anymore. These things don't interest me: the sun remains for me and the road tempts me. This could just about be an entire philosophy.

Closer to me, I'd had the opportunity to see a pure and strong passion growing in a soul that I believed more emancipated, and I said to my friend, "Be careful, for when one is happy, one no longer understands anything about the suffering of others . . ."

He was headed for happiness—at least he believed so—and I was headed toward my destiny.

Now I have distanced myself, and I feel my soul again becoming healthier, naively open to all joys, to all the delicate sensuality of one's eyes and one's dreams.

In the only Arab street of the village, I find again calm scenes of "being at home," dating from last year's month of Ramadan.

Many a familiar face on benches and mats in front of the *cahoudaji* [*sic*]. Many a friendly greeting to be exchanged.

And with that, the intimate joy of thinking I'm going to leave tomorrow as soon as it's dawn. Though these things please me this evening, I will leave all of them behind.

But who, except for a nomad, a vagabond, could understand this double-edged sword of pleasure?

My heart still moved by all that had taken me and all I had left, I tell myself that love is a state of anxiety and that one must love in order to be able to leave, because beings and things have only transient beauty.

Against the iron bars of the window of a Moorish café, in front of pots of basil, people are slowly gathering.

Someone is playing a pipe and I enter; this monotonous and sad music will lull my daydreams and especially will excuse me from speaking . . .

Musicians from the West

A square room painted pale blue with pink panels. In the corner to the right is the smoke-stained oudjak and the cups, glasses, and trays on wooden shelves. Wooden benches and ordinary tables made of rusted iron clutter the café. A captive bird dozes in a cage.

What a strange little Saharan café patronized by Moroccans and nomads! The audience is packed in. Among the Arabs in grubby burnooses and haïk are a few spahis and mokhazni, the native horsemen.

All are quiet, turned attentively, with elbows on knees, toward the corner of the room where the musicians are lined up on a bench. They are Beni-Guil from the Chott Tigri.

With their reddish-colored rags and their sandals, they bear little resemblance to the singers and musicians from the Algerian High Plateaus, who wear embroidered vests and silk ties in the cords of their turbans in an attempt at Arab coquetry or perhaps to appear learned. These musicians from the West retain the look of their coarse race, and the stiff black beards along the jawline give their faces a deceptively Hindu look.

However, on one of them, the thick veil covering the wide white turban frames a beautiful face with regular features, an aquiline nose with vigorous nostrils, and sorrowful eyes. Another one, the flute player, is blind. He puts all his soul into the moans and whispers of his reed. As if he were speaking to it, he rolls the dull globes of his dead eyes, and his chest marks the beat with rhythmical swaying. The troupe further includes an old dulcimer player and, a little to the side, a strange singer whose eyes are closed and whose head is thrown back as if drunk.

The only luxury of these destitute people consists of two pipes wrapped with leather and polished copper rings, and blue silk braids intertwined with small silver chains and Moroccan coins.

The offbeat muffled rhythm of the tambourine stretches out indefinitely, the beating of its human heart alternately moved and wrathful, weakening, exhausted, and voluptuously dying. The pipes have the barely discernible murmurs of peaceful water or a mild breeze.

The Beni-Guil—clumsy and awkward, people of the desert surprised by benches and tables—invade the room.

However, they smile, proud of their brothers' success among the m'zanat.

Big sols and white coins fall with a clear sound onto a tray on the ground. At each offering, the tambourine player blesses the whole group for the donor's generosity.

However, the Beni-Guil content themselves with encouraging the musicians through their gestures and their approving exclamations. Very rarely does one of them reluctantly drop a sol onto the tray after having dug for a long time in his *zaboula*, a sort of bag made of filali (red leather from Tafilalet).

One of them, a very young man, stands up suddenly and does a rhythmical slow dance, the end of his knotty staff balancing on his chest.

Everyone laughs.

The café owner, with a red and green fouta wrapped around his waist, moves about, serving trays of tea. With each order of tea, the owner identifies the customer and blesses him in the name of the Rewarder.

Muslim Death

The first morning sun comes up on the horizon like a large purple flower. The sand dune, dotted with esparto grass tufts, is set ablaze around the koubba of Sidi-Bou-Djemâa, overlooking the route from Beni-Yaho to Sfissifa. Pink glimmers light up the tops of the black fig trees, and the tall willows cry tears of iridescent silver.

Arabs are awakening around the koubba. They are pilgrims who have come from far away to ask for the great saint's protection. Facing the rising day, they line up and pray for a long time with the Muslim rite's beautiful, serious gestures that make even the most ragged seem to grow in stature.

Behind the small outer wall, women are already chattering around a fire made of dry wood. They are nomads who have come with the men of their tribe. They barely cover their faces.

Under a tree, a crazy man in rags leaning on a staff aimlessly chants the Koran, mixing verses out of order. He is beautiful—with his emaciated face, his black hair pulled back on his forehead by a strip of white cloth, and his large burning anxious eyes fixed on a point in space visible only to himself.

From time to time the crystal clear "you-you" sound of celebration days rises from the group of women.

But a procession appears at the top of the dune. Arabs move forward slowly to the beat of a rhythmical and serious chant.

Behind the first group, four men carry a stretcher covered with a long white sheet on their shoulders; and at the sight of an unknown believer entering eternity on this glorious morning, all the joyful sounds cease.

Then most of the men go down to the cemetery, to the tombs dotting the sand with their anonymous stones whose dates have been worn away. A grave is quickly dug in the moving sand. Then the body is laid down next to it, facing the sun.

And then, standing in a semicircle, the Muslims murmur their prayer for the dead.

Very quickly, above a row of bricks, they fill in the grave, planting three green palms. The mound where the new trees are planted is sheared off immediately by the cool breeze . . . Then everyone leaves.

Next to me, Si Abdelali, a man of letters from Marrakech, begins singing in a hushed voice an ancient lament about the fate of those already gone.

Here it is: I am dead, my soul has left my body.
They cried over me the tears of the last day.
Four men put me on their shoulders,
Attesting their faith to the only God.
They carried me all the way to the cemetery,
They prayed over me the prayer without prostration,
The last of the prayers of this world.
They threw earth on me.
My friends left as if they had never known me,
And I stayed alone in the tomb's darkness,
Where there is neither joy, nor sadness, nor moon, nor sun.

I no longer had any companion other than the blind worm.
The tears dried on the cheeks of my next of kin,
And thorns grew on my earth.
My son said, "May God accord him his mercy!"
Know that he who has gone to the mercy of his Creator
Has left the heart of creatures at the same time.
Know that no one cares about the absent in the abode of the dead.

Oh you who stand before my tomb,
Do not be surprised by my fate:
There once was a time when I was like you,
The time will come when you will be like me.

The melody of this lament is melancholy and soft, the Moroccan taleb's voice harmonious ... And I look at the small mound abandoned there forever in the emptiness of the sandy desert.

We were going to Sfissifa, a small completely Muslim town without a single European, not even a Jew.

More dark boulders of the Oranese South and, in the ksar's interior, a decayed life, crumbling adobe walls, with the veiled faces of mummies. Everything is falling in ruins, but we taste very sweet sleep beneath a large pomegranate tree in the dazzle of the already-high sun ...

Sickly inhabitants of the ksar with a pallid complexion, humble gestures, effeminate clothing; a race degenerated by sedentary life, by the shadow of the narrow ksour, and by the ancient custom of intermarrying. Ksour falling in ruins in the shadow of delicious gardens, invaded little by little, devoured by the desert. A whole people slowly dying from indifference and oblivion.

On our return, the sun had just disappeared, but a great red brightness still bathed the valley.

We again pass by Sidi-Bou-Djemâa.

A deep silence, a tangible silence bordering on anguish, weighs on the koubba and the cemetery where a few saints' tombs rise among the small, anonymous stones—coarse rectangles made of dry earth.

The door is closed, and in front of it sits an old beggar, his staff leaning against the wall. Slowly, from within the shadows of his blindness, he mutters a few words without inflection as if he were telling himself stories.

Up above, two mokhazni in black burnooses have dismounted and are praying all alone in the day's last purple radiance.

A chained dog with small, slanted, blood-red eyes raises his wolflike muzzle toward the sky and emits a long howl, a sort of infinitely sad lamentation.

The desert of sand and esparto grass darkens. In the oued's willows, the owl's melancholy hoo-hoo hurls its alternating responses.

On the Road

After a short moonlit night spent on a mat in front of the Moorish café of the makhzen, I awaken feeling happy, with the delicious sensations that always seize me after I've slept outdoors under the big sky, and when I'm going to take to the road again.

I'm going to sit on the side of the road and wait for Djilali ould Bahti, the mokhazni with whom I must go to Béchar.

To go to Béchar! To finally go beyond this fateful limit of Beni-Ounif in order to enter the real southern Oranese bled—this suffices so that I feel calm and joyful, so that the boredom that was beginning to invade me in Aïn-Sefra finally dissipates.

Time passes, and Djilali is late in coming.

The day rises, a splendid summer day without a cloud, without mist. A cool breeze, blowing since last night, has chased away all the dust and haze. The sky opens up, infinite and deep with the green transparency of a calm ocean.

At the horizon, in all this golden green, a more yellow and more burning glimmer rises, soon going from vivid orange to red. Across the way, in the dark west, the moon descends, pallid as the face of a dying man.

Quite near to us, Sidi Slimane's large white koubba stands out in gold against the sky's still, green-copper color. Orange-colored rays bathe the dark ground, the tombs, and the cracked houses.

Djilali finally arrives, and we leave, turning our horses toward the moon, whose light finally goes out.

This mokhazni is a tall brown-haired boy with the good candid face of a Tarfaoui nomad from Géryville.[1] He is pleasant and "resourceful" and will be a good traveling companion for me.

We make our way in the valley of black stone, between Djebel Grouz, still completely iridescent, and the low burned hills of the Gara.

---

1. Eberhardt's note: *Tarfaoui*, from the Trafi tribe.

Toward the right, Mélias's pretty little palm grove, drowsy with its *séguia* and its clear pools at the entrance of one of Grouz's deep gorges.

Last year the pursued djiouch came to quench their thirst there in the deserted gardens, today so peaceful and smiling.

As we distance ourselves from Beni-Ounif's sterility, the esparto grass appears on the sandy ground. Oued are dug out of the ground and filled with more and more bushy small shrubs. A few large mastic trees—the providential tree of raging solitudes—cast their circular shadows on the red earth throughout the empty hours.

A cloud of dust approaches from the west in the opposite direction of the wind.

It's a company from the Legion, blond and very tanned men covered with dust who are returning from the South singing German or Italian ballads.

The sick are lying down on the train's araba loaded with baggage.

Perched very high, they watch the monotony of the countryside with the mournful indifference of the feverish, calculating silently the probable hour of their arrival in Beni-Ounif, from where tomorrow they will be transported by train to the hospital in Aïn-Sefra.

An hour goes by. We join up again with a small convoy of araba escorted by infantrymen.

The men have gotten rid of their bags and rifles, which they've loaded onto carts; they walk very slowly, inching forward with the mules like people taking a walk.

They go by. We sink back into the road's silence.

From time to time Djilali begins singing a lament, which he then doesn't finish.

There's a bit of a breeze; we turn our backs to the sun, and the heat is not overwhelming. We feel good and have no wish to speak.

It is like this on the deserted southern roads: long hours without sadness, without boredom, vague and restful, when one can live off silence . . . I have never regretted a single of these lost hours.

A Halt in the Desert

Last year, in order to go to Béchar, one went toward the east, behind the mountains via Bou-Yala's small outpost, abandoned since then in order to transfer farther west the border's line of protection. Bou-Ayech is now the first stopping place after Beni-Ounif, thirty-five kilometers away.

It is ten o'clock and the valley is blazing. Reddish-brown vapors tremble at the blurred horizon. The heat becomes scorching. A thin trickle of blood flows from the dried-out nostrils of our mares. An immense languor invades me, and I let myself go on my Arab saddle, which is as comfortable as an armchair.

Ben-Zireg is no more than twenty-eight kilometers away, and we'll have all the time we need to lie down there. But what's the point of hurrying?

One must arrive at the entrance of the Bou-Ayech "village" in order to see it, so much is it the same color as the ground.

About ten huts made of planks, a redoubt made of yellowish earth, and about a hundred formless gourbi made of brushwood, where the Moroccan workers, who work on the railway, live. One hundred meters away, all of that blends in with the esparto grass and the dust, and this corner of the valley seems as deserted as the others.

For the time being, the state railway line stops a few kilometers beyond Bou-Ayech, and the work gives a feeling of commercial vitality to this lost outpost.

Already the country is simultaneously taking on more-Saharan and less-dreary aspects than in Beni-Ounif; under the green-gold coat of esparto grass, the pale sand does not produce the impression—sometimes painful to the point of anguish—of the black hamada of Ounif.

Spaniards drink anisette at a wooden table in one of the "village" huts.

Craggy, shaven, sunburned, and weather-beaten faces; large hats made of black felt; small jackets; espadrilles—a separate type of race, coarse and rough, used to all kinds of solitude, and all deprivations, under the most inclement of suns.

The clerk of Beni-Ounif's free warehouses is distributing supplies to the workers through an opening in the hut wall. I notice that the latter have almost all abandoned their earthy rags for the horrible European getup of the *trabadjar*, which clashes with their large white turbans.

They are almost all Moroccans from the North: bearded energetic faces, many of which have very regular and very beautiful features and narrow wild eyes.

A few are blond Berbers with blue eyes, of the particular type found in Kabylia and which is certainly due to a far-off contribution of Germanic blood.

Among these workers, only the men from Figuig and the fellows from Tafilala keep their Arabic rags. They've only come there temporarily to earn a few coins and then to return to their ksour.

Bou-Ayech was restful for us.

Since we were cooking potatoes in a hole dug in the sand, a bit to the side of the outpost's group of huts and the Moorish café, in the shadow of beautiful mastic trees as big as oaks, men in tunics and gray berets circled around us under the legionnaires' eyes. I recognized in them the army's "excluded," of the lowest category, the military's condemned, employed for public works in far-off outposts. Some of them were naked to the waist. Of another savagery on this savage earth, they displayed extraordinary Parisian tattoos underlined with pessimistic, rebellious, or obscene slogans.

The excluded and the legionnaires come and talk to us out of boredom. At first this amuses me, and it's difficult for me not to laugh as I hear them say among themselves, "The little spahi is so buxom, and his skin is delicate!"

A few mokhazni join us. They're from Beni-Ounif, and I recognize in them friendly faces from last year.

We prepare the coffee with them in a mess tin, and we chat like people of the South chat, in short replies with naive jokes and without offensive words.

Camped above in the full sun, the Douï-Ménia sokhar come and sit next to us. The mokhazni tease them, ridiculing their odd speech. The nomads answer as best they can, apparently without taking offense. But in the end, one can certainly sense the old hatred that divides the people of the Algerian High Plateaus and the Moroccans.

The sokhar finally leave, and the mokhazni begin preparing the *mella*, the Saharan road bread.

One of them kneads the semolina with water from a goatskin on a folded haversack. Djilali digs a hole in the sand with his hands while the others bring armfuls of wood.

A fire is lit in the bottom of the hole, on which large gray pieces of galettes are laid out and then covered with leaves or simply with fine sand. Another fire is lit on top of that, and at the end of a half hour the mella is cooked. It certainly is a bit heavy, but it's hot and it's much better than horrible canned food.

"Mella," declares Djilali, "is for men like esparto grass is for horses: it doesn't fatten you, but it gives you nerve."

In the evening, the noncommissioned officers of the first division of the Legion, who saw me last year on an excursion to Hadjerath-M'Guil, recognized and celebrated me.[1]

I will carry away with me an even better memory of them in that, knowing full well who I am, they strictly respect my disguise.

We lingered on in an insignificant chat for the sole pleasure of talking about the Saharan country, about the bled, the troop movements, the construction works, the future of this corner of lost earth. That evening, after the "cooking," I felt like a soul mate of a soldier from the South. Without constraint, I was interested in the stories of these courageous people, in the way one enjoys stories told during an evening's gathering on a peasant farm, discovered after a long walk in the countryside . . .

In this way I have families, households, and bivouac fires in my memory. During hours of isolation and daydreaming, I find all of that again in the smoke of a cigarette, and it is even more of a tonic than the memory of great enthusiasm, which leaves holes in its wake, and more than great expecta-

1. Extensive segments rewritten by Victor Barrucand are italicized.

tions, founded on the value of beings, which end always, almost always, in disillusions and in failures.

I come to the conclusion that one must never look for happiness. It goes by on the road, but always in the opposite direction . . . I have often recognized it.

Now the night is dozing, all in blue, over the valley's calmness.

At the redoubt, the Legion's bugle slowly sounds out, one by one, the melancholy notes marking the extinguishing of fires.

In these small, isolated outposts, in the middle of silent solitudes, the evening's bugle call has something poignant in it: afterward one feels the desert all around . . .

The last sounds and the last lights go out. I fall asleep with a sense of infinite well-being. Tomorrow I will leave for other countrysides, and who knows if I will ever return to sleep there at the foot of this redoubt in this setting that pleased me? . . .

Ben-Zireg

We leave Bou-Ayech in the delicious predawn freshness. The waning moon swims in a greenish sky, and its weak light slides over the trail's black rocks. Djilali, in a dreamy state, ends up telling me that it is better to wait for daylight before crossing Ben-Zireg's gorges, the old passage of prowlers.

We get off our horses in the wide and not very deep bed of a dry oued; and releasing the horses to graze in the esparto grass, we lie down on the delicate sand for a brief nap.

When we wake up, it is full daylight.

We've slept in a charming site. Wild bushes with thin clusters of violet flowers rise above the very green swell of the esparto grass, where lavender and absinthe create broad silvery swaths. Asters sow their small mauve stars in the shadow of the tall mastic trees: there is the entire unaffected naturalness of a wealth of flowers and plant life in the middle of the hamada.

The terrain rises again and becomes rough. We enter the furrowed, tortured ravines where the road hangs over a deep oued hemmed in by high reddish cliffs. The sun has quickly risen to the horizon, and we enter the Ben-Zireg valley in full light.

What an unforgettable vision upon leaving the gorges! Before us lies the most lugubrious, the most desolate of all the South's arid scenery.

Between the abrupt spur of Djebel Béchar and Antar's high wall, the hills are as sharp as the teeth of a saw, and chains of mountain peaks still hem in the valley's delicate slope toward the oued. And everything, the hills, the pulverized slate, the stones, everything is black, an olive greenish and dull black. At the foot of the slopes, overlooking Djebel Béchar, is the white redoubt, of a pallid whiteness that accentuates the horror of this countryside in mourning.

The "village": a few barely finished hovels containing Moorish cafés and canteens.

On the opposite bank of the oued, a few wooden crosses, the Christian cemetery.

Not a shadow, not a blade of grass, just two or three skinny date palms in the oued.

Horrible country of exile, a depression bled, as the legionnaires so rightly say.

Nothing will ever grow in this cursed small valley. No one would ever consent to living here without being forced to, across from these soot hills, in this charred hollow with no horizon.

I have a strange impression: Ben-Zireg resembles one of those deathly countries seen in bad dreams.

Everything there is dull, black, lit by a pale day that seems false. The heat becomes suffocating. Myriads of flies stick to our eyes.

We got down into the oued to try to nap under the date palms' revolving shadows. Impossible to sleep on the steeply sloped, burning stone ground with the sirocco and the flies. Besides which we have to get up every quarter hour and move: the shadow inexorably follows its course . . . Overwhelmed, brutalized, we await evening, deliverance.

And during the short moments before nightfall, this dark corner of Ben-Zireg seems to be made of water and of supreme gripping beauty.

Then all of a sudden it was over. The hazy night, full of mystery, fell abruptly.

We lie down on a mat in front of a Moorish café. I'll leave before daylight so as to retain of Ben-Zireg the last vision of the evening.

Lying Water

Today, this stage of the journey will be long. We have hours to slowly make our way at the even and slow pace of our mares.

Since we've left the Ben-Zireg corrie, the valley, still the same, has become larger; here and there is a oued with a bit of greenery and some beautiful mastic trees. Then, once again, infinite dust and stones.

Halfway there, in Hassi-en-Nous, we have lunch, and we're going to then have coffee with the mokhazni of the Bel-Haouari outpost, the "Rzaïn" nomads of the Saïda Circle, camped in light shacks.

These good souls who have put back on their earthy Bedouin burnooses in the desert could easily be taken for a djich.

Beyond Bel-Haouari, from the viewpoint of an immensely open, white-hot horizon, we walk alongside an amusing and unique double chain of hills. Because it's a good idea to educate oneself while traveling, I ask my companion the name of this geological architecture.

"Look closely," he says, "and you'll know why the people from here call them the *Bezaz el Kelba* (the Bitch's Teats)."

While going by, he again points with his finger at a black line in the valley that is as open as a plain: the Ouagda palm grove.

Under the flaming sun, shapes are already beginning to distort. It's impossible to judge distances: a sort of dizzy movement dances before our eyes; and still, to the right and left, there are the incredible Bezaz el Kelba.

The slightest variations in the terrain influence the light and are either painful or restful for my eyes.

After the rocky area, there opens up a zone of pure sand. For the first time in the Oranese South, I once again experience the profound impression from long ago, which I felt upon entering other Saharan regions.

I recognize it in all its splendor, with its mournful enchantments and fairy-tale extravaganzas, the earth swooning in an eternal solar caress without any volcanic trembling, without the mountain's immense efforts.

All of a sudden the horizon oscillates, the distance loses its shape, and the red sand disappears. A great sheet of blue water stretches far out, and in it are reflected date palms.

The water, of infinite purity, shimmers under the sun . . . Djilali begins laughing like the big child that he is.

"Si Mahmoud, see how the *srab* (mirage) makes fun of us who are so thirsty! If we had only this cursed lying water to quench our thirst, we could die of thirst or suck the bitch's teats!"

A troop of red horsemen advances at the edge of the imaginary lake. A large scarlet banner floats in the wind above its close-ordered ranks . . . The squadron goes by and disappears. It was mules returning to Ouagda, and it was also the high framework of a Saharan well where the mirage had hooked onto it scraps of purple cloth.

The arrival in Béchar thus revives in me already-distant memories of the Oued-Rir and the salty chott in southern Constantine, another country of fever and mirage.

From far away, we follow the Ouagda palm grove between the small tombs scattered the length of the road. Across the way is a reddish-brown dune with a white spot at the bottom: the "Collomb" redoubt.

Béchar, Taagda, Collomb, all these diverse names are mixed-up. Béchar is in fact the name of the country, as it is that of the mountain closing the horizon.

Taagda is the ksar and the upper palm grove above Ouagda.

A disoriented name, "Collomb" designates the village under construction.

Perfume of the Oasis

The mysterious lake has disappeared. Only a few puddles remain in the distance, azure rags scattered among the tawny dunes. But the palm grove's shadow already tempts our mounts. Finally we arrive under the tight arches of the date palms, and our horses stretch out their bloody nostrils toward real water as they enter the very wide oued, halfway up their legs, in the middle of the bulrushes.

What relief, what completely physical joy is this arrival in shade where the breeze is a bit fresh, where our painful eyes rest on the deep green of the beautiful palm trees, on the pomegranate trees with their blood-colored flowers, and on the clumps of oleander.

After the deceptive water, the taste of truth.

We stretch out on the ground and will not enter Béchar until evening, following the afternoon nap.

Djilali falls asleep, and I look at this new scenery resembling others that I've loved, which have revealed the mysterious charm of oases to me. I also find that light odor of saltpeter so particular to humid palm groves, that odor of cut fruit that spices up all the other perfumes derived from life in the shade.

In the deep tranquility of the isolated clearing, innumerable emerald lizards and chameleons changing color delight in the spots of sun as they stretch out on the rocks.

Not a bird song, not an insect cry. What beautiful silence! Everything is sleeping heavily, and the scattered sunrays slip in between the tall date palm trunks like heads of hair out of a dream . . .

Béchar

At the foot of the dune in Béchar, the valley slopes imperceptibly toward the oued's green belt.

On the bank behind the large cemeteries, where the wind and camel feet are erasing the headstones bit by bit, is the old ksar of Taagda, flanked by square towers, surrounded by high gray walls with no opening, where one enters through low arched doorways; Taagda looks like a fierce citadel.

Inside, on the soft silent earth, we followed small alleyways in ruin, long covered passages that were so dark we had to grope our way in full daylight. Where are Figuig's beautiful lines and full curves? It's a jumble here. The tall houses made of toub, a few of which have two floors, are squeezed one against another and span the streets.

In Béchar, as in all the ksour, everything is sleepy and falling into ruin. The exhausted ksour's activity is slowly disappearing, the energy sources are running dry, and agony's heavy sluggishness weighs on these failed attempts at sedentary and laborious life in the middle of the desert destined for the nomads.

Black Kharatines, for the most part, but Arabic speakers, the people of Béchar are silent and distrustful. They already have a bit of Moroccan haughtiness and feel repulsion for people from the East, the m'zanat; however, they are from the ksour—peaceful gardeners, and not men of gunpowder.

Last year during the occupation of Béchar, Taagda and Ouagda were raided by the makhzen and the infantrymen. This year, somewhat reassured, the ksourians have gotten their courage back and are returning to their gardens.

The center of the town of Collomb is still nothing but a muddle of unfinished buildings, materials, and rubble. The ugly "dugouts" are still there, as in all the Oranese South outposts, whitewashed with pale dirt, tiny rooms built quickly to shelter the eating places, the junk shops, and the Moorish cafés.

The Spanish and Jewish element is dominant here, like everywhere in the new country.

The Kenadsa Jews, dressed in green and red rags, come and put up their ragged tents, and they quickly light their small forges in order to transform the "douros" of the officers and spahis into jewelry.

In Béchar's gardens, I once again discovered sensations formerly felt in the unforgettable heart of the oued of Bou-Saâda, the South's pearl.

Squatting there on the pebbles are women in blue or black mlahfa washing rags by beating them with palm stalks . . . Yes, these are very much the charming memories of the Bou-Saâda oued during the luminous days of summer, but with a more distant, darker note—the Moroccan note—evoked by this scenery of Béchar's sleeping palm groves.

In the gardens, under the bushy pomegranate trees and in the unhealthy shade of the fig trees, inviting niches meet the eye; in addition, the blue-green vault of the date palms offers something of the mystery of true forests. The irrigation séguia whisper in the short grass, and from all over rises the small sad voice of the southern toads, a single note, endlessly echoed as far as the arid dunes on the road to Kenadsa in the last séguia half choked with sand.

Legionnaires and Mokhazni

High up is the redoubt of Béchar with its low adobe walls; its wide eternally guarded doors; and, inside, materials, piles of stones, all the chaos of a city under construction.

To the left, a large courtyard where the French makhzen's hobbled, small, skinny horses lazily chew hard esparto grass. The mokhazni stretch out under the shacks, their heads on the pommels of their saddles, their rifles within reach, their cartridge holders tightened around their dirty gandoura . . . They laugh, joke, sing, waiting without concern for the order to leave, and—who knows?—maybe never to return.

What does it matter? What is written must happen, whatever one does. And they don't even think about it, except to write laments about all the uncertainty of their lives in these far-off outposts where death lies in wait for them at each moment.

The Arab understands masculine honor, and he wants to die as a brave man facing the enemy, but he has absolutely no desire for posthumous glory. Especially these simple men, these crude nomads who voluntarily offer their valor, their beautiful audacity, and their inexhaustible endurance to the service of France.

In addition to the mokhazni, other heedless people erected the Arab Bureau buildings, but they—the legionnaires—were much more complicated. Everywhere, in all the southern Oranese outposts, it is they who put up the first walls and they who, by dint of energy and patience, sowed the first seeds in the small gardens that appeared as if by magic in the most arid locations. They built despite troubled times when they had to defend themselves against pillagers, after nights spent on the lookout in great fear of probable surprises.

There is not a wall, not a dugout made of toub, in Béchar or elsewhere in the country, that is not the work of the Legion, anonymous work, perhaps more arduous and more meritorious than the beautiful acts of courage accomplished every day in that deep and still country.

Reflections in a Courtyard

Among these courageous people I feel no discomfort. I entered their home and sat down in a corner of the courtyard. They didn't even notice me. There is nothing remarkable about me. I can go anywhere unnoticed. An excellent position from which to see well. If women are not fine observers, it's that their dress catches people's attention; they have always been made to be looked at, and they don't yet suffer from it. In the long run, this feeling seems to me too flattering for men.

I have often been reproached for enjoying myself with the common people. But where is life if not among the people? Everywhere else, the world seems narrow to me. In certain milieus, I have the feeling of an artificial atmosphere: I breathe poorly there. I never know what will be "appropriate." In all truth, I don't suffer much from poverty, naivety, not even coarse language. I don't suffer profoundly from them. What seems intolerable to me in the long run is the eternal mediocre shame felt by certain people. And then this lack of braveness that distinguishes them, this prudence, this affectedness in living in a rational and well-calculated way. In fact, I have always seen that by this method one ends up making errors of calculation. I've always been very surprised to note that a stylish hat, a correct bodice, a pair of well-laced ankle boots, a small set of furniture made of cumbersome small pieces of furniture, some silverware and china were enough for many people to calm their thirst for happiness. At a very young age I felt that the world existed, and I wanted to know its far-off places. I was not made to go round in a carousel with silk blinders. I didn't create an ideal for myself: I went in search of discovery. I know full well that this manner of living is dangerous, but the moment of danger is also the moment of hope. Besides, I was obsessed by the idea that one can never fall lower than oneself. When my heart suffered, it began to live. Very often, on the roads of my wandering life, I wondered where I was going; and I ended up understanding, among the common people and with the nomads, that I was returning to life's sources, that I was accomplishing *a voyage into humanity's depths. Contrary to so many subtle psychologists, I didn't discover any new feeling, but I relived strong sensations; all the pettiness of my life's fortunes broadly shaped the desired curve of my existence.*

I will make myself clear with these words—which perhaps do not have enough follow-up coherence, but which I sincerely feel—why I can be interested in many humble things.

Now my eyes are resting on this small courtyard in Béchar's redoubt, they're photographing its aspects, they possess it in its simplicity.

Killing Time

Under a small ragged nomad tent invaded by flies, a white ksour inhabitant from Kenadsa has set up a Moorish café. Makhzen saddles and rifles, pathetic old soldiers' uniforms are piled there in storage.

Mokhazni and spahis come inside the precarious shelter to drink tea and play endless games of Spanish "ronda" or dominoes with the passion that all Arabs bring to the game.

When they play, the sirocco can shake the tent, the sand can whip faces, the flies can blind one's eyes: nothing, except for a mobilization, could detach the eyes of the players from their filthy cards or the little rectangles made of ebony and bone. Yells, laughter, sometimes terrible fights—which without fear of the leaders would result in bloodshed—accompany these games that siphon off most of their earnings. In the courtyard of the Arab Bureau of Béchar, as in Beni-Ounif, as elsewhere in the evening after the prayer, loud free singing wakes up the echoes of the dead plain . . .

The pensive, carefree, and sensuous soul of the nomads rises up from these beautiful wild poignant songs that speak to the heart and the senses, penetrating my soul with a sweet, soothing, infinite melancholy.

Kenadsa

Kaddour or Barki, the head of the Ziania of Béchar khouan, gives me a black slave, Embarek, to serve as my guide. We leave the makhzen douar at the pink-and-green-hued hour of dawn. The weather is clear with no signs of sirocco. Only a light mist covers the palm groves along the floor of the oued.

Like all the Oranese valleys in the South where we make our way, I on horseback and Embarek on foot, the valley we're in stretches between two ranges of hills. On the left, above these low undulations rises the powerful outline of Djebel Béchar.

Golden sand, soft undulations, always the same countryside since we left the Bezaz al Kelba, the same monotonous harmony of great swoops without angles, without bumps, almost smooth.

As we move toward the west, the hills become lower.

To the right we skirt the strange dune, crowned with precariously balanced rocks, that dominates Béchar. This lasts for a long time, while the sun, immediately scorching, rises behind us and lengthens our shadows on the pale ground.

Finally we arrive at the ridge of a rocky slope dotted with flint and pieces of slate, like the desolate Ben Zireg valley.

Kenadsa appears on the horizon, clouded in a pink haze: black spots of scattered trees, the bluish line of a large palm grove, and a broken minaret that appears reddish brown as it towers above the sand in the still-slanting sun . . .

Farther on, we follow a path that is lined with a row of tall date palms for more than a kilometer, all alone in the valley's emptiness.

Under their moving shadow is a clear fresh underground séguia with small inspection holes here and there.

Kenadsa rises in front of a large ksar of dark, warm-colored toub, flanked by beautiful, very green gardens on the left. The ksar falls away sharply in a lovely jumble of stacked terraces, following the gentle slope of a hillock. To the right, the golden dune with its rocky entablatures rises up almost abruptly.

A very white koubba shelters the burial place of a Muslim saint of the very illustrious family of Sidi M'hammed-ben-bou-Ziane, the founder of Kenadsa and the brotherhood of Ziania: Lalla Aïcha.

Around the koubba, innumerable scattered tombs protrude from the sand, which partially covers them.

We pass close to these haphazard cemeteries, moving alongside all the accumulated human dust of centuries, abandoned and forgotten, and following the path around the ksar's dark, walled rampart without crenellations or arrow slits.

On a small square, men are half reclining, mostly Kharatine.

You enter the ksar through large square double doors. Then you must cross the mellah, the neighborhood of the Jews, who lodge in narrow shops along the street.

Here, Jewish women wear the same clothing as in Figuig, but they are not cloistered. They chatter and cook at their doorsteps, or quickly wash their faces.

Yet another bend in the road, and we enter a different street, a narrower and cleaner one ending in a stark contrast of shadow and light beneath the span of its houses.

Entrance to the Zaouïya

Dismounting in order to pass through another door, we find ourselves in the zaouïya.

The Ziania marabouts are no threat to French authorities here. Peace loving and civilized, they welcome those who rule justly. Every day, they demonstrate their deference and respect for the written word.

Kenadsa is situated beyond the border, and it recognizes the rule of the sultan of Fez. Thus we find ourselves in Moroccan territory, twenty-five kilometers from Béchar, French land.

Where is the border in reality? Where does Oran end, where does Morocco begin? No one bothers to find out.

But what use is a skillfully designed border? Today's situation, muddled and unclear, suits the Arab. It harms no one and makes everyone happy . . .

Three or four black slaves receive us. My guide repeats to them what Kaddour or Barka said to him: I am Si Mahmoud ould Ali, a young Tunisian intellectual traveling from zaouïya to zaouïya in order to learn . . .

I am then made to sit down on the ground on a folded bag made of wool while someone alerts the current marabout, Sidi Brahim ould Mohamed, to whom I give a letter of introduction from one of his khouan in Aïn-Sefra.

Lined up against the wall, the slaves wait and are silent. Two of them are Kharatine. Young and beardless, they wear the gray Moroccan djellaba and a white muslin cloth wrapped around their shaved skulls. The third slave, blacker and taller, in white clothing, is Sudanese, and his face bears marks of deep gashes made by red-hot irons. All three are armed with a koumia, a large dagger with a short blade, in a sheath of chiseled copper slung across their shoulder, held by a beautiful sash of brightly colored silk threads.

Finally, after a wait of fully fifteen minutes, a big, strangely ugly black slave with small, lively, round, and inquisitive eyes comes and respectfully kisses the small tassels of my turban.

He takes me into a vast, silent, barren courtyard with a gently sloping floor.

The atmosphere exuded a disquieting calm. The succession of doors that closed on me added to the distance I had just covered.

Yet another small low door, and we enter a large square room resembling the interior of a mosque. The dim light is diffused by a quadrangular opening in a ceiling made of tastefully placed beams.

Rugs are put down; I am at home. This is where I will live . . . God knows for how long.

While the Negroes go fetch me coffee and fresh water, my eyes get used to the half-light, and I examine my lodging—half with an eye toward its security.

A steep, narrow staircase of black stone leads to the terrace. To the left is a deep alcove for preparing tea, fitted with an iron brazier whose smoke escapes through a hole in the ceiling. In the middle of the room is a small square basin, and on the edge of it is an earthenware jug full of water: all the necessities for ablutions. The basin's still water can serve as a mirror. Four columns serve as buttresses. In the corner of the room, a wooden door with a painted panel displays primitive flowers in faded colors.

This guest room must be very old, for the toub of the walls and the ceiling beams has taken on a greenish black. The columns, as tall as a man, gleam from years of hands and clothes rubbing against them . . .

New Life

I finally begin to doze off next to Sidi Brahim, the marabout of Kenadsa. Of stout build, with a necklace of graying beard and smallpox-marked face, he stands before me, his smile gentle and welcoming. There is nothing fierce about him. He wears very simple, very white clothes under a thin wool haïk. He has on a large round turban rolled on a chechiya with no veil covering his face. He looks both like a Moroccan city dweller, with the typical lisping accent, and an inhabitant of a southern ksar.

Si Mohamed Laredj, Sidi Brahim's nephew and right-hand man, accompanies him.

Smaller, almost thin under his snowy-white veils, he too has a gentle face, an almost-timid smile, but intelligent and deep eyes without harshness.

Sidi Brahim welcomes me with great dignity and then discreetly questions me.

That lasts an instant, with intervals of silence and renewed politeness. Soon the marabouts withdraw like shadowy white figures.

Our interview has been short and leaves me feeling that I am safe. I am the guest of these men. I will live in the silence of their house. Already they have brought me all the calmness of their spirit; a shadow of peace has penetrated the innermost recesses of my soul. Days are going to come that will pass over me, long and without needs; and my curiosity will be as gentle as a nightlight in a sickroom. I will retreat deeper into the recesses of my tumultuous conscience. The great conflagrations that set us ablaze with science, hatred, or love will slumber under the ashes; I will be able to live my life with a steady breath. Is this then what I came here looking for? Is all my thirst finally going to be quenched, and for how long?

A thought of good nirvana is already softening my heart. The desert that I've crossed was that of my own desires. When my will awakens, it seems to me that it shall wish for new things and that I will remember nothing more of my past sufferings. I dream of a sleep that would be a death, and from which I would emerge armed, strengthened with a spirit revived by oblivion, reimmersed in unconsciousness.

Embarek goes up to the terrace and throws a mat onto "the eye of the house."

Then, in the darkness, the swarms of flies that were assaulting me scatter. A bit of coolness, a breath of air comes to me from above, with an immense silence that feels eternal.

I lay down on the rug. I am alone, and I slowly pass from a very calm rest to the heavy sleep of midday.

Slaves

To be always surrounded by black faces, to see new ones every day, to hear only the shrill voices of slaves with a drawling accent, this is my first daily impression in Kenadsa—a strange and powerful impression.

Apart from a few uncommon Berber families, all of the ksar's inhabitants are black Kharatine. In the zaouïya, the Sudanese element adds yet another note of an even more distant strangeness.

The fathers of these slaves—sons of captives from Souah and Mossi—came to Kenadsa after long suffering and very complicated peregrinations.

Taken at first by men of their own race in the course of perpetual battles among villages and petty kings, they were sold to Moorish traffickers, then put into the hands of the Touareg or Chaamba, who, in turn, passed them to the Berabers.

Their children did not retain the language of their country of origin; only a few old people still understand it. Everyone speaks Arabic in Kenadsa. Chelha, the Berber idiom so widely used on the Moroccan border, is unknown here.

As long as their blood remains pure, the Sudanese of the zaouïya are robust and often beautiful, of a completely Arab beauty that contrasts strikingly with the ebony-black color of their skin. However, those born from interbreeding with the Kharatine are usually sickly and ugly, with angular faces and lanky, disproportionate limbs.

The worrisome and repulsive impression given me by the Negroes stems from their evasive eyes, which move in unusual facial expressiveness; their features twitch and grimace incessantly. It is an invincible impression of animal rather than human nature, a reaction that I childishly feel at first in the face of my brothers, the blacks.

Among the slaves, Sidi Brahim's turnkey and right-hand man, Ba-Mahmadou, or Salem, is the only one toward whom I feel sympathetic.

He is a big, calm Sudanese man whose face has gashes made with a red-hot iron. He wears pure white clothing under a long black burnoose. In the expression of his face and in his gestures, as in his regular features, there is nothing of the man-monkey, cunning and tricky, with none of the animallike craftiness that serves as intelligence in the blacks.

Ba-Mahmadou stands out from the other Negroes. He finds the secret of serious gestures and respectful attitudes deep inside himself or in his slave culture. This feeling is not that of depressing servitude. There is nobility in his greetings. Negroes don't ordinarily know how to act when greeting someone.

Each time that Ba-Mahmadou appears before white Muslims, he begins by bowing three times in front of them, and only comes forward barefooted, leaving his worn-out old shoes at the door. However, the feeling that he has respect doesn't diminish him.

A very odd study could be written about the slaves living here. To attempt it, you could not have prejudices toward anyone and must write natural history as much as social history. I feel that one would have to be cured of the prejudices of superior races and the superstitions of inferior races.

Almost all these slaves own houses in the ksar, gardens in the palm groves, even small herds. They sell wool, meat, dates for their own profit, but they remain forced to work for their masters.

In order to marry, they must ask for authorization from the head of the zaouïya, but they are their own masters at home, "caïd in their house."

Thus they lead a double existence of virtually free men outside, but slaves inside the zaouïya, where, in addition, the functions are distributed rather unclearly.

Women's Small World

The women here make up a small world of its own with its own hierarchy.

First of all there is Lella (Madame).

Sidi Brahim's mother is in charge of the entire household: expenses, receipts, almsgiving. She is never to be seen, but her power is felt everywhere; feared and venerated by all, this old Muslim queen mother lives here almost cloistered, going out only rarely and completely veiled, in order to go to the tombs of Sidi Ben Bou-Ziane and Sidi Mohammed, who was her husband.

An entire small world of pale women, the marabouts' wives, gravitates around her. Further below is the community of Negresses, virgins, married women, widows, or divorcees.

Among these women of color reigns a great laxness of moral standards. For a few coins, for a piece of cloth, and even for pleasure, they give themselves to anyone, Arab or Negro. They openly make advances to the guests and offer themselves with unconscious brazenness, which is sometimes amusing.

The male slaves still rein in their urges, but all the black femininity abandons itself to instinct, and their quarrels are as futile as their loves. Sometimes piercing fights explode in the courtyards before the women leap naked into the sun for fistfights.

One morning, two Negresses hurl violent abuse at each other in front of my door.

"Mellah Jews' whore!"

"Renegade! Thief! Seed of calamity! Bitter root!"

"May God make you die, Jewess, daughter of a vulture!"

All of a sudden the hissing voice of Kaddour, the steward, comes and puts an end to the scandal.

They separate like vicious dogs with their teeth bared, with insults and biting words as if flesh.

Transformation

It's been more than a week since I've been here, and my life is flowing gently like a lazy séguia. Up until now, I had not left the zaouïya. Here, you may do nothing whatsoever without Sidi Brahim's authorization. One would collide with the slave's silence and inexorably closed doors.

Why didn't they wish me to leave? This was starting to weigh on me and worry me. My cherished solitude was no longer voluntary; my room, so favorable to interior visions, resembled too much a quiet prison...

This morning, finally, I asked to see the marabout, and I told him my wish.

The good marabout smiled.

"Si Mahmoud, my child, don't conceive of any bitter thoughts! If you wish to go out, that's no problem ... But then you'll have to change clothing. You know that the Algerian's clothing you are wearing is looked at askance here. It would not present any real danger to you, but it would surely cause you some problems; you'd be openly treated as a *m'zani.*"

In truth, the Moroccans loathe the Algerians, whom they consider to be renegades.

Perhaps the Moroccans detest the Algerian Muslims even more deeply than the Christians themselves, because they believe that the former forsook Islam whereas the latter merely remained what they were: infidels.

Forgetting Islam's pure principles of tolerance, the Moroccans harbor feelings of irreconcilable hatred for Christians and m'zanat.

... And so, in order to go out this evening, I transformed myself into a Moroccan male, abandoning the heavy gear of Algerian horsemen for the lightweight white djellaba, the yellow worn-out old slippers worn on bare feet, and the small white turban without a veil, rolled into a halo around a chechiya.

It's lighter, fresher, but I think fearfully of the fierce midday sun, and I wonder if, with this almost-transparent head gear, I will not be felled, as if struck by lightning.

I share my worries with Ba-Mahmadou. He smiles but is not worried.

"If you came here with confidence and sincerity, God and Sidi M'hammed-ben-Bou-Ziane will protect you!"

Let's hope that Ba-Mahmadou's reassuring prediction will come true and that this new clothing, which for the time being amuses me, will not prove to be my undoing.

The Barga

The "Barga" is the strange dune overlooking Kenadsa, crowned by blocks of stone with a few rocky outcrops in the form of a pyramid here and there.

I go for a stroll on a cool clear morning.

I cross the cemeteries. Behind the koubba of Lella Aïcha, which is adorned by pink hues like a shadow of modesty, I climb the sand path that sometimes passes under stone entablatures that look as if they are about to roll into space.

The distances recede into infinite transparencies. On the horizon to the east, the very blue Djebel Béchar rises, commanding the whole country from Ben-Zireg to Kenadsa.

The sun slowly rises. It swims in an ocean of crimson sparkles, melting gradually into the zenith's green-gold color.

The golden sand, the cold gray metallic stones, become iridescent. Green reflections, orange-colored or red reflections, a fleeting sheen on the arid hillside.

Behind the Barga, another valley as narrow as a ravine, interspersed with layers of black stone, then another rocky hill . . .

Toward the east, Kenadsa's valley opens up, offering itself to the sun's daily caress. Below, at my feet, the ksar of multicolored toub, giving it a combined hue both warm and dark with elements of deep violet and reddish brown, with a few newer walls where the earth still has hues of dull gold or silvery fawn like the sand of a dune.

Above the chaos of the ksour's dwellings, two or three tall houses whose windows are covered with screens, inhabited by the marabouts.

To the far west of the ksar, in the middle of a sort of square where there are tombs, is the koubba of Lella Keltoum (another female saint from Sidi Ben Bou-Ziane's lineage). It is a very old square of blackish toub, with ornaments in the shape of pointed horns at the corners. In the middle of its terrace rises a small eight-sided cupola. A woman in a faded pink mlahfa, undoubtedly a beggar, is at the window. The white minaret, yellowed by time and sun, juts toward the yellow light above, like a tall stone tree. A few Ouled-Djerir, ragged and armed with rifles, are leaving for the Guir, driving before them about twenty mangy camels laden with long black wool sacks full of wheat.

And like always, surely like long ago, about two hundred years ago, when the blessed cheikh M'hammed professed his humanitarian and mystic teachings here, a great serene calmness reigns over this valley and the ksar.

The Enlightened One

Atop the Barga, within a large cairn of dark rocks, an enlightened one dwells at the bottom of a narrow cell carved out of the rock.

Dressed in blackish rags, tall, his body all skin and bone, with a delicate face that is tanned and emaciated, the anchorite has long gray hair and an unkempt beard. His shining eyes gaze fixedly, and his lips do not cease their unintelligible murmuring of the same mystical invocations that have sustained his constant ecstasy for nearly twenty years.

In his youth, the enlightened one, who had not yet been touched by the gift of unconsciousness, traveled extensively in Morocco, Algeria, the desert, and the Sudan. It must have been of those remarkable treks that, in our day, only the Arabs still know how to undertake, going from one village to the next by foot, asking for shelter and bread on God's path.

Then, weary of the vanity of human knowledge and the monotony of things, the saint returned to his country and withdrew to his gray cell for good; he will no longer leave until he's carried away by believers to his final resting place in the faraway necropolises at the foot of the mountain.

I look at this beautiful Saharan anchorite, and I think that the Christian recluses of the first centuries must have resembled him, in the equally desolate settings of scorching Thebaid and Cyrenaica.

They, too, were searching by other means, ecstasy, for satisfaction of this imperious need of eternity that lies dormant in the heart of all souls.

The Marabout's Indignation

Yesterday during the afternoon rest, Sidi Brahim enters suddenly, a letter in hand, filled with consternation. "Si Mahmoud, I've just received a letter from Oudjda, informing me that Hadj Mohammed ould Abdelkaut, the head of the Kadriya, was assassinated by Bou-Amama's people—may God smite them!

And the marabout lets himself drop to the carpet as he holds out the letter to me.

This letter was brought by a servant delegated by the zaouïya of Oudja. It is written on a very crumpled piece of gray paper.

Bou-Amama welcomed the messenger and lavished him with promises. But upon his return, one of the old bandit's men joined up again with Hadj Mohammed on the plain and led him far away from his companions under the pretext that he had a secret to tell him. At the bottom of the oued, bandits lying in wait then massacred the unfortunate marabout.

Deciphering the illegible scrawl, I envision sad Oudjda falling prey to starving, desperate soldiers, the populace alternately pleading and threatening as it treads the mud of decaying carcasses.

Set in ruins with pink peach trees abloom, Kadriya's white zaouïya is the backdrop to all this horror—normally the calm and meditative refuge of Hadj Mohammed, who provided me a safe home only three months ago, before being assassinated by traitors.

"Si Mahmoud, the Mogh'rib is lost if we begin killing God's defenseless creatures, men of prayer and alms who bear neither swords nor rifles," says Sidi Brahim to me. God must certainly have blinded the Mogh'rib's sons for them to thus abandon his path, for them to betray their sultan, descendant of the Prophet—many prayers and salvation be upon him!—through Mouley Idris, and to follow miserable impostors like Bou-Amama and the Rogui Bou-Hamaral!"

In his soft and slow voice, Sidi Brahim continues lamenting Morocco's fate.

"How can one really give any explanation but madness for the popularity of Bou-Amama, the son of a lowly secondhand goods dealer, a man without lineage or education, troublemaker, dispenser of false miracles and deceptive promises? By God, Bou-Amama's house is built on the unstable foundations of lies and iniquity! But aren't desert nomads made thus; the more nonsense they are preached, the more likely they are to believe it.

"And woe to him who comes to tell the truth: they scorn him, and if they can, they exterminate him . . . And what do you say, you who have read God's word, who have visited many cities and countries, what do you say about the Rogui? How do you explain the incredible adventure of this man whom no one knows, and who, from one day to the next acts as sultan, emir of the believers? He says that he is Moulay M'hammed, the dispossessed brother of Mouley Abdelaziz. But how is it that not a single trustworthy man can be found among those who knew Mouley M'hammed, to say to the believers at large 'in truth, it is he' or instead to expose the imposter? Others claim that Bou-Hamara originates from the Sanhadja of the Djebel Zerhaoun. And how is it that no one among the Sanhadja and the Beni-Zerhaoun knows this man?

"One could suspect that this Bou-Hamara is not a son of Adam, but is really a *djenn*, a spirit whose essence is fiery, a sign of the times, God's curse who descended from the sky or ascended from the earth to punish the depraved and criminal Mogh'rib! . . . You others, sons of the East, you are happy. You peacefully enjoy the good things accorded to you by our Maker. And we, unhappy sons of the Mogh'rib, we live in a country of starving wolves, where the rivers overflow with blood and where iniquity triumphs. At any given hour of day and night, we tremble for our lives and for our possessions . . . You see, Si Mahmoud, we had important revenues in Tafilala, in El-Outtat, in Fez, and especially in the Angad region. Now that the impostors' armies have invaded the country, we no longer receive more than one quarter of our previous income . . . And the poor, the orphans, the unprotected women, the students, and the travelers flock here and ask us for refuge and bread that we must give them according to our master's pure law—may God be satisfied with him!—Ah, Si Mahmoud, let us pray to God to annihilate Bou-Amama, the son of the peddler, the inventor of treachery, and Bou-Hamara, the mysterious man who wants to mount the steps of a thousand-year-old throne astride a she-donkey and claim the heritage bequeathed by Mouley Idris to his followers by the will of the Heir of the Worlds."

And in this way, every day, Sidi Brahim comes and gives me the news from the West, the sad news and the clamor from outside. However, they only arrive diluted in this distant place, these echoes of the torment rumbling across corrupt Morocco . . .

Nothing happens here, and when it finally enters our warm, untouched sanctuary, news from the outside world no longer contains the iciness of tragic reality.

I am losing, little by little, the notion of agitation and unleashed passions in the monotonous life I lead here in Kenadsa. It seems to me that everywhere else, men and things must be as immobile, as drowsy or languid as here . . .

Message

A long day of fever and suffering, heavy hours spent in the little terrace room, lying on a mat with a view of the fiery horizon . . .

In the evening, as the air cools a bit, I feel better, and I drag myself as far as the parapet: one of my favorite sensations—this languidness bordering on voluptuousness—watching the sun set over Kenadsa like this every evening, encircled with a halo of royal purple.

However, the slaves are late in coming today. Night is falling, a lunar night of infinite transparency.

Still nothing, neither tea nor dinner, barely a little water in the bottom of the slowly dripping leather *delloua*.

I call out.

On a neighboring terrace, an old Negress comes out of the shadow: all the slaves have left for a funeral wake in the neighborhood of the mosque.

So I roll out my rug as well as I can on the still-hot terrace, and I fall asleep under the clear pink of the moon descending toward the horizon.

As soon as it's dawn, Ba-Mahmadou comes, looking contrite with salutations even more respectful than usual:

"Sidi Mahmoud, 'Lella' sends me to tell you that she begs of you to pardon her in the name of Sidi ben-Bou-Ziane, to chase all bitterness from your heart. Last night we all went to sit in vigil over the body of a holy woman, Lella Fathima Angadia, who died at the hour of the mogh'rib—may God grant her mercy! This is why 'Lella' forgot to send you tea and the evening meal. She asks that you pardon her for this involuntary offense and invokes God's blessings and those of her ancestors on you."

I will never see her, this all-powerful "Lella," so venerated, and who pushes the cult of hospitality so far as to send to an unknown person a message imbued with such gentle humility, to ask for forgiveness for an inconsequential oversight . . .

What is she like, this great Muslim woman, into whose presence I may not enter because I am Sidi Mahmoud and I continue to be treated as such? Even if there are some suspicions through Béchar's indiscreetness, people will be very careful not to let me notice, for this would be a serious breach of Muslim politeness.

Does she have her son's serious manners? And what thoughts occupy the mind of this woman placed in such a particular situation, cloistered and yet also invested with an authority in the face of which her son himself yields?

A Vision of Women

Rays the color of red copper slip across the tawny toub of the walls in the large courtyard. I sit on a rock and wait for Sidi Brahim. Like every evening, the women came to the fountain, and I watched their slow procession and the splendor of their ragged clothing in the light.

There were young and old, beautiful and ugly, and others who went by with their heads bowed without one knowing anything about them, offering only barely murmured greetings.

Two young women stopped under the low archway of the interior courtyard door. One was a Sudanese Negress with a round face and large reddish-brown eyes as soft as an animal's. Small but heavy silver chains through her earlobes dropped back down onto her shoulders, and silver ribbons joined the two long braids of her very black hair spread out on her bosom.

A lemon-yellow mlahfa wound its soft folds around her tall thin body. Sitting with her elbows on her knees, she spoke, the expressive gestures of her upturned palms setting her bracelets ajingle.

The other, a mulatto woman, remained standing. She was beautiful, and of a strange beauty, with her dark and delicate aquiline profile, her large sad eyes, her voluptuous, curved lips revealing pointed teeth.

A supple red wool mlahfa, the color of pale blood, draped her pure form. One of the panels of her veils fell straight and stiffly from her head to her arched back, passing behind her beautiful naked arm, the color of ancient bronze. She held herself very erect, her large terra cotta amphora placed on the curve of her hip.

The mulatto listened seriously to her companion, without smiling.

A light breeze disturbed their veils, emitting a penetrating aroma of spicy cinnamon and sweaty black flesh. Against the grayish pink backdrop of the wall, in the violet light of falling dusk, the two women stood chatting for a long time under the archway.

The two African women in their brightly colored clothing seemed very beautiful to me against the completely dirty background of the corner of the courtyard.

Friday Prayer

Today, Friday, went out to the mosque for the public prayer.

Shortly after noon, in the torpor and silence of the afternoon rest, a drawling voice reaches me from afar, as if in a dream: it is the *zoual*, the first call.

I get up and try to vanquish some of my heavy sleepiness with a cool bath. In the courtyard's glare, I arrive ahead of Farradji, a silent Sudanese man. We follow narrow alleys; we follow crumbling garden walls in order to avoid the dark corridors that crisscross the ksar. We emerge in the sand valley.

Everything is burning and shimmering, metallic reflections on the Barga's dry stones and on the salty sand of the sebkhas, where oscillating reddish-brown vapors sketch indistinct mirages.

It is the deadly hour of sunstroke and fever, the hour when one feels crushed and pulverized, one's lungs on fire and one's head empty.

We finally arrive. Enter the ksar where there is little shade. When the believers pass by, blind beggars chant their supplication. The mosque door is blocked with a beam, high enough to prevent children and animals from entering. Taking off our worn-out yellow shoes, carrying them instead, we cross the courtyard barefoot at a near run to escape the intolerable heat of the burning sand.

Right at the entrance, a delicious feeling of coolness, of bluish twilight, of infinite peace.

Everything is white and bare in this ancient Saharan refuge; the walls, the heavy square buttresses supporting the ceiling are old beams constructed from carved palm trunks. Filtered diffused light falls from above through slit-shaped "eyes," which leaves the rear of the mosque entirely in shadow. The people of Kenadsa and nomads pray on worn-out mats. To the right, beneath a larger dormer window, bathed in even warmer light, students and professors of the *médersa*, the tolba, chant the Koran. Behind them, the school children repeat the lesson of their elders.

Here and there, squatting next to a pillar, a lone taleb recites the Prophet's litanies out loud.

And all these voices—the men's low voices, a few very pure and very beautiful voices that dominate the others, and the children's clear voices—blend into a great indistinct murmur, a monotonous and melancholy melody ending in long, drawn-out syllables.

The hypnotic chant echoes lingeringly in the air of the nave.

Then, all of a sudden, high up in the minaret, the muezzin shouts out his second call. His voice seems to descend from unknown realms simply because he is very high up and we don't see him.

At the end of the last verse, the tolba's voices die out with a long sigh. With the great clack of small lesson boards being laid down, the children run out.

Now everything becomes quiet; all heads bow attentively.

From the darkness of the *mihrab*, the large recess indicating the direction of Mecca, the *imam's* cracked, quavering voice rises up. He reads the *khotba*, the long prayer, mixed with exhortations, that takes the place of a sermon, and which one listens to seated and in silence.

The imam is not a priest at all—Islam has no regular clergy—he is simply the most educated of the audience. Any literate man can serve as an imam: he must simply recite the prayer.

In Islam, there are no mysteries, no sacraments, nothing that necessitates the priest as go-between.

During the khotba, there are more moments of contemplation, of great sweet calmness.

A man in a white shirt belted with a simple rope, his head uncovered, carries a bucket of fresh water and a clay cup: he is giving the old and the sick a drink. It is an essential good deed that he performs every Friday.

A last call from the muezzin, and the old imam finishes his reading and begins to pray.

Everyone stands and raises their two hands to the height of their faces, then lets them fall again the length of the body, saying with the imam and the chanter, "*Allahou Akbar!*" (God is the greatest!)

Everyone bows down to the floor.

The prayer having finished, I remain with the tolba and the marabouts, still chanting the Prophet's rhymed litanies in verse.

"Prayer and peace be upon you, O! Mohammed, Prophet of God, you who are the best of creatures always and forever, in this world and in the other . . . Prayer and peace be upon you, O! Mohammed the Chosen, Arab Prophet, Torch of the Darkness, Key of the Believers, O! Mohammed the Koreïchite, Master of Mecca and of Medina the Flowered, Lord of Muslim men and women, for always and forever . . ."

The marabouts have beautiful, low voices. They know the ancient melody that carries so nobly the sonorous verses of this litany, which the common people are content to recite very quickly in a nasal and staccato manner.

It's over . . . We get up, we pick up our babouches, which we had folded and placed on the mats.

Timidly, I follow Farradji through the maze of black corridors so low that we have to bend in half for more than a hundred meters. The darkness is impenetrable in this narrow passageway with its uneven ground, with its age-old dampness.

After the quiet of the hour spent in the mosque's blue half-light, this return resembles a nightmare in all this blackness.

Lella Khaddoudja

Ba-Mahmadou daydreams on the steps of the staircase while the tea water sings softly in the kettle. He looks at the bedroom and the primitive paintings on the door at the end of the room.

"Where is the mistress of this dwelling at this hour?" he suddenly asks with a sigh.

Since I question him, the Sudanese man recounts that this house belongs to a certain Lella Khaddoudja, a relative of Sidi Brahim. A widow from a very young age, with two children, a boy and a little girl, the maraboute—who was very pious—got married a second time, to one of her cousins, under the express condition that they would leave immediately for Mecca. The cousin kept his promise, and Lella Khaddoudja left the zaouïya, leaving behind only her son.

"The day she left Kenadsa," said Ba-Mahmadou, "all of us, the servants, accompanied her all the way to the Ain-ech-Cheikh fountain on the Béchar road. Sitting astride her mule, she looked at the ksar one last time, and said to us that she would never return, for she desired to live and die on Hedjaz's sacred ground . . . This winter, it will be two years since she left. She has since written to her brother to let him know that she arrived late for the Djeddah pilgrimage and that she was waiting in Bith-el-Kods (Jerusalem) for the one this year, after which she would settle permanently in one of the two holy cities . . . May God grant her aid and mercy! She was pious and charitable toward us poor slaves!"

Then I begin to dream about this unknown Lella Khaddoudja, who undoubtedly has a somewhat adventurous soul, since she broke with the sleepy routine of her own kind of women, in order to go somewhere else of her own will to begin again with a new existence, under a new sky.

What took place in the heart of this traveling maraboute? Why did she abruptly resolve to leave her native ksar for good? What novel per-haps exists that no one will ever know of . . .

[. . .] In fact, for the illiterate Sudanese man, this Bith-el-Kods, these Syrian and Arabian cities are the farthest vistas . . . For him they must seem like dream cities, almost imaginary . . .

Nomad Lords

Five o'clock in the evening, under the riad's white arches, the tall portico that opens onto the interior garden in Sidi Brahim's house.

Outside in the valley, the sirocco stirs up whirlwinds of dust, but here there is no more than a light puff of wind dissipating the air's heaviness in the last heat of the sun . . .

Sidi Brahim is half reclined on a large rug in beautiful lively colors made by Rabat women, his elbow on a silk pillow embroidered with gold olives. Smaïn lets his ebony prayer beads fall one by one; sitting against a wall, Si Mohammed Laredj pours two bags of Spanish douros—oxidized by the dampness of the silos—onto a square of scarlet silk.

In front of him, three Doui-Ménia leaders of the Oued Guir are crouching in a half circle.

The first one, his face the color of earth, scarred by deep wrinkles, weather-beaten by the sun, with a white beard of tough bristly whiskers, is wrapped in an old haïk made of thin wool, with a koumia that has a copper handle and sheath.

The second man, also old, covered in a worn-out burnoose, hides his weapons under his veils and adopts solemn poses that conform strangely with his angular manners and his raptorial profile and long hook nose above a toothless mouth. He is a representative of the Ziana from the Guir.

The third, the youngest of the three and yet the most important, is maybe thirty-five years old. He is tall, muscular, and wearing white clothing underneath a heavy burnoose made of black camel hair. His damascened koumia with a gold handle is held in place by a thick violet silk cord worn as a chain. Another cord, orange colored, holds a bag made of red filali with golden embroidery from Fez. He is also carrying a magnificent revolver with a chiseled silver grip.

However, his feet are bare; he has left his sandals, his archaic nomad naala, near the door.

Very tanned, his eyes intelligent and evasive, with a delicate expression and an energetic face framed by a thick black beard, the cheikh Embarek would be handsome if his wolflike teeth had not grown so long. They extend beyond his lip, which gives his face a cruel and repugnant appearance as soon as he moves his mouth.

Embarek exercises great influence over the Ouled-Bou-Anane, and he is scheming in order to make himself definitive head of the tribe.

Since the Ouled-Bou-Anane made peace with the French and frequent the southern Oranese markets, Embarek foresees total annexation and is ready to work toward that goal, for he hopes then to be the great leader of all the Douï-Ménia, the one to whom the Christians will give a scarlet burnoose and decorations.

Embarek is an ambitious and crafty man, but he is also a man of gunpowder, a bandit, having only renounced traditional pillaging in hopes of gaining more profit from peace than from skirmishes.

Sidi Brahim wants to put the nomad leaders in charge of important purchases of sheep on the Guir. They are returning, coming from Beni-Ounif, where they provided camels for the Beni-Abbès' convoy, and it is the sheep's price that Si Mohammed Laredj is in the process of counting, with his golden tongue and gentle manners.

With their raptorial eyes, the Douï-Ménia look on covetously at the jingling douros piling up. Involuntarily drawn, they lean toward the money, which must pass through their hands; it is they who will actually sell the sheep, at the highest price, under the guise of a negotiated purchase.

They pretend not to know how to count, and they willfully muddle Si Mohammed's calculations. Then, seeing that it's taking forever, Sidi Brahim requests that I put the calculation in writing.

I scribble on my knee with a reed in numbers known as Indian, but used by the Arabs, so that Embarek, who knows how to read, can check my calculations.

Finally, the nomads face the facts.

The old raptors are already holding out their bony hands toward the money, but Embarek has not made his final offer. He stops them with a gesture:

"Sidi Brahim," he says with his most engaging smile, "the amount is incorrect: six hundred fifty douros are needed to pay for the sheep at the current prices, and the money is here. We are certainly your servants and those of your glorious ancestor, Sidi ben-Bou-Ziane—God grant him his blessings! But we will have to go get the sheep among our brothers who are scattered along the course of the Guir . . . Then we'll have to escort them all the way here, so that the Ouled-Nasr and the Berabers Aït-Khebbach don't steal them. We'll take care of all of that, and in truth, we are happy to serve you. You have nothing to fear—if God so wishes! But we are poor nomads ruined by war, and your generosity will certainly not forget us. Give us a reward . . . for our troubles."

Sidi Brahim smiles. Si Mohammed Laredj lowers his head and adopts an impenetrable demeanor:

"And what reward do you wish?"

"Give us two hundred French francs, and may God return your good deeds."

"Pray over the Prophet," Sidi Brahim then says, "and curse Iblis, the one who interferes among men and sows hate between them, the one who also makes them desire material things over truth and justice! If it is the case, and if your services must be bought for such an immoderate price, I prefer to send my slaves to the Guir."

For a long time still, the Douï-Ménia negotiate, but despite their rapaciousness, the marabout does not give in.

While the nomads get worked up and go so far as to raise their voices, Sidi Brahim and Si Mohammed remain silent. They wait.

Finally, seeing the uselessness of their efforts, Embarek and the old men once again find good words, with forced smiles.

"Sidi Brahim, you are our master, and we dare not gainsay your decisions, for what you are doing is well done. Remain in peace, and pray to God, his Prophet—may prayer and peace be with him!—and Sidi M'hammed-ben-Bou-Ziane for us, for tomorrow, starting at dawn, we will certainly take the road for the Guir . . ."

"Go in peace, my sons, and may God protect you and lead you on the right path."

And then the nomads get up with a clanking of weapons; then they turn around once more to look regretfully at the beautiful douros that Si Mohammed Laredj puts back in the sacks, where they fall with clear jingling sounds.

Messaoud

For a few days I have been served by a young black of the Khartani, Mess-
aoud. He is maybe fourteen years old. Already big for his age and cunning,
he wears white shirts cinched at the waist with a gray wool strap. His brown
face is pleasant and expressive. He has big brown eyes without an iris, which
reflect a particular mischievousness. On his shaved skull, a little tuft of frizzy
hair, a sign of bondage and also prepubescence, remains planted in a very
funny way above his right ear. This strange ornament adds something even
more comically monkey-like to this mobile, cheerful physiognomy without
naïveté. In his ear's pierced lobe, Messaoud, for lack of rings, wears a tiny
roll of blue paper.

Inquisitive, nimble as a cat, a petty thief, a liar, as talkative as all Negroes,
Messaoud is a type of mischievous little slave.

When I send him to buy tobacco from the Jew, Messaoud runs there atten-
tively; but upon his return, he cheats me on the very complicated calculation
of the Moroccan exchange rate. He clearly sees that I understand nothing
about the confusing currency system used in the West, and he cuts profits
from my ignorance.

When I reproach him for his methods, he offers denials, a goodly number
of pledges, and sad little looks. Then he ends up bursting with laughter, as if
my reproaches seem very funny to him.

He would do anything for a cup of mint tea. Other than that, his laziness
is incurable, and he has a way of not hearing orders, which implies a deep
level of complex animal cunning. He has reached the point of openly making
fun of slaves, his elders, and everyone, almost with impunity.

Ba-Mahmadou, the turnkey, looks at Messaoud with horror:

"He is a black pest, a child of sin, a disaster!"

And Ba-Mahmadou rolls his big soft eyes, trying to glare at Messaoud,
who laughs and runs away.

When the black rascal wants to get something, he acts humble and affec-

tionate, with blandishments and a charming simper. He becomes exaggerat-edly thoughtful, often troublesome, which then ceases as long as he is given what he wanted. Voracious and greedy, he licks plates and nibbles on stolen sugar all day long.

Messaoud doesn't like anyone, not even Blal, his old father, a humble ten-ant farmer in Sidi Brahim's gardens. When the old man risks coming all the way into the courtyard, Messaoud brutally chases him away, feigning the scorn of the well-placed domestic for the peasant.

To all my reproaches about this matter—which interests me because I have the vague idea that many children do not naturally love their parents—the good-for-nothing merely answers with jerky faces.

"He's dirty! He smells like dung! He's full of fleas!"

Messaoud is just respectful enough toward the marabouts to avoid getting hit. They scold him, and he sticks his tongue out at them as soon as they turn their backs.

A little animal full of charms and vices, an evil spirit for whom no one has much respect, this rascal demonstrated many things to me about white children.

Saharan Theocracy

The age-old influence of the Arab marabouts has profoundly modified the institutions and customs of Kenadsa's people.

With all the other Berbers, it is the *djemâa*, the assembly of subtribes or of the ksour, that is sovereign. All the political or administrative questions are submitted to the deliberations of the djemâa. If a leader is needed, the djemâa names him. As long as he keeps his nomination, this leader is obeyed, but he always remains responsible to those who chose him.

These Berber assemblies are tumultuous. Passions have free rein; violent, they often end in blood. However, the Berbers always remain protective of their collective rights. They defend themselves against autocracy by suppressing those who dare aspire to it.

In Kenadsa the Arab theocratic spirit has triumphed over the republican and confederative Berber spirit.

The head of the zaouïya is the only hereditary lord of the ksar. It is he who resolves all questions and names the military leaders in case of war. It is he who renders criminal justice, whereas civil affairs are judged by the cadi.

Sidi M'hammed ben-Bou-Ziane, the founder of the brotherhood, tried to make a peaceful and hospitable association of his disciples.

The zaouïya enjoys the right of asylum: any criminal taking refuge there finds himself sheltered from human justice. If it's a thief, the marabout makes him return the stolen goods. If it's an assassin, he must pay the price of blood. Under these conditions, the guilty do not incur any punishment as soon as they've entered the zaouïya's enclosure or even a piece of land belonging to it.

Capital punishment is not enforced by the marabouts. If it happens that a criminal is put to death, it is by the victim's relatives or sometimes by his own kin, never at the marabout's condemnation.

However, Sidi Ben-Bou-Ziane's descendants prove to be very severe toward thieves and troublemakers among the inhabitants of the ksar or the slaves, whom they punish by beating.

It is customary that one of the assistants stands up and asks for mercy for the guilty one during the enforcement of the latter. Sometimes women send a slave or a Negress for this purpose; the marabout always relents.

Misery is unknown in Kenadsa, thanks to the zaouïya. There are no beggars in the streets of the ksar; all the unfortunate take refuge in the zaouïya's friendly shadow, and they live there for as long as they wish. Most of them make themselves useful as servants, workers, or shepherds, but no one is forced to work.

The marabouts' influence on Kenadsa has been so profound that Berbers and Kharatine have forgotten their languages, no longer using anything but Arabic.

Their behavior has softened and become civilized, compared to that of other inhabitants of the ksar.

Disputes, and especially fights, are rare, because the common people are in the habit of bringing all their disagreements before the marabout, who calms them and imposes mutual concessions on them.

Since the marabouts have been on neighborly terms with the French and their friendship has even grown, a gnawing dissatisfaction has invaded the hearts of the lower classes.

No one dares raise his voice and criticize the decisions of the leaders. They yield, they repeat Sidi Brahim's opinions, they praise them; but in the end, were it not for his great moral authority, they would be ready to consider him and his people as m'zanat.

What is Kenadsa's future, and what will remain of this small theocratic state—so distinctive, so closed—in a few years?

Certainly, after the Figuig-type harshness and the somber chaos of Oudjda, finding this peaceful spot at the desert's entrance—which calls itself Moroccan and resembles other parts of Morocco so little—creates a truly remarkable impression!

In the Margin of a Letter

I don't know what day it is any longer. It's the heart of summer. I have a fever with doleful, lucid, and voluptuous respites.

Yesterday, I received a letter completely bathed in a sun other than mine. And what joys, because new ideas have smiled at you, can you become egotistical enough to propose to old friends?

When I return to that Algiers, where my heart leapt, where my desire no longer settled, where the orange-colored sweetness of mornings darkened my grief, what will we talk about, if not about ourselves, and how?

Women cannot understand me; they consider me to be a strange being. I am far too simple for their taste, enamored as they are of the artificial and artifices. They ramble on about an eternal comedy on the same subject. They don't even allow one to change clothing. When woman will become man's comrade, when she will cease to be a toy, she will begin another existence. In the meantime, women have been taught to breathe only in tempo and to a waltz theme.

It appears that another generation is making itself known and that certain young women know how to speak other than with their eyes, without, because of that, falling into lecture-style gossip and workers' demands. I don't believe any of it, and I imagine that it is once again a question of education's dupery, which will not resist the mood of the literary circles.

Besides, what would they be, the husbands of these sincere female friends, since men, especially in the provinces, are still only amateur skirt chasers.

Woman, she will be everything wished for, but it has not been proven to me that men wish to modify her other than within fashion's limits. A slave or an idol, this is what men can love—never an equal.

I jotted down these reflections in the margin of a letter that came to me from so far away, that brought a fresh and cruel breeze of unconcern to me. Immediately after, I once again fell into my feeling of exile, with the taste for plunging myself even further into this hostile South, without any desire for the Paris that I knew and where the verbal feminism of the newspapers was still less kind to me than instinct's coquettishness.

I put nothing in my response that was worth being read . . . What for?

One day, paths separate, destinies are isolated one from the other. It's already a lot to have met friends. When they do us the honor of inviting us to share their foreign joy, let us show them all that the brotherhood of minds can do.

Let us regret nothing, since our mutual happiness will be to let us go one day to mysterious currents that will lead our souls adrift toward impossible shores. Then we will taste the drunkenness of decay and ruin; and wandering on night's immense beaches, we will feel our chests burst under the germination of seeds of pain.

Saint's Afternoon Tea

In order to entertain me, knowing that I am sick, Sidi Brahim sends me an invitation to an outdoor meal in the gardens of the zaouïya. Si Abdel-Ouahab, a man of letters who has come from the East in order to settle in Kenadsa, is charged with this mission.

I admire how the smallest things become opulent and noble. Casualness and lack of bother are European qualities that make life easier. When one is used to the frankness of the masses, it is very difficult to take seriously certain airs feigned by the most vulgar beings, the most incapable of delicacy and feeling, on certain days and under some circumstances. All their politeness sounds false. When they speak, they seem to be putting on their Sunday best. But here, politeness is not a formula, it is a way of being and it is genuine; it has nothing vulgar and nothing affected about it. It is liked.

At first, Sidi Brahim's invitation surprises me.

In Europe or the Algerian Tell, no one would dream of organizing a country meal in such weather. The sky is murky black, pallid clouds are racing low, almost scraping the tops of the dunes. They go by, are torn to pieces, and return, strangely twirling around on themselves like the tatters of a shredded veil. A violent wind chases them, which is not felt on the ground, which doesn't even skim over the tops of the motionless date palms. Heavy, warm raindrops are beginning to fall.

Here in the desert burned by eternal thirst, this light humidity in the air, this sky without heat and dazzle, these are exquisite delights.

The water drops refresh the dried-out skin like a somewhat brutal caress.

I can barely drag myself there after ten days of intense discomfort lying on a mat, laid low by fever. However, I go.

The garden is at the foot of some tall houses facing west. The crops are below, overlooked by the path leading to a terrace where beautiful rugs from Djebel Amour are spread out, their thick, soft wool taking on reflections of dark velvet under the storm's dull light.

Below, the Virginia creepers freely wrap themselves around the slender trunks of the date palms and the fig trees' gray twisted branches. Two captured gazelles play at chasing each other under the foliage and jump over the séguia invaded by golden mint.

Sidi Brahim is leaning on his elbows on a pillow.

Around him, a few relatives, a few intimates. First, Taleb Ahmed, the khodja (secretary) of the zaouïya, tall and robust with a strong inflow of Negro blood under his glowing skin. Very intelligent and very astute, Taleb Ahmed contrasts with the marabout because of his simple, almost-jovial facial expressions.

Si Mohammed, Taleb's predecessor, a true Berber from the ksour, with a wide pale face and a thin almost-red beard, is there too. He seems to be back in favor.

With his soft, almost-shy smile, Sidi Mohammed Laredj remains silent, half reclining on the rug whose arabesques he traces with his finger. His thoughtful and kindly expression accentuates meditations and detachments without anything ascetic: in his eyes there is a kind of artist's pulling back, which sees the world as a show.

Sidi Embarek, Sidi Brahim's maternal uncle, has an entirely different direct expression. On his delicate tanned face and in his eye without depth, one can see passions that do not wait, sudden resolutions, the fierce naïveté of the ceremonial Arab, decorative and made for decorations: a known type in Algiers in office antechambers and on café terraces. He is the strong head of the family. He's had affairs that all resemble one another, a lot...

In the garden, slaves prepare the small low tables and the dishes covered by tall funnels made of straw dyed with bright colors.

Although they are treated very gently, the slaves, even the favorite ones and the children, never mix with the whites; besides, their respect for white men borders on veneration.

The conversation naturally centers on Morocco's affairs, on the Tafilala; and the hated names of the Rogui and Bou-Amama are pronounced.

But today, Sidi Brahim has not received any bad news, and everyone is cheerful. Humorous anecdotes are told with the absolute purity of language observed by Muslims of high birth, in public, and especially among relatives.

In the date palms, stripped of their dust by the rain and turning blue against the dull sky, bustles a whole flock of swallows with small quick piercing cries.

"It's the bird djemâa (assembly) here," says Taleb Ahmed. "They're gathering here to manage their tribe's affairs and make serious decisions. These creatures, hardly larger than flies, make as much of a racket as one hundred Douï-Ménia, all discussing at the same time."

And the marabouts laugh, busy pestering with the end of their cane the familiar gazelles who at first make a skillful mock attack only to then come to an abrupt stop.

After the meal of unleavened bread that smells good and has aniseed grains in it, it's tea, the eternal tea solemnly prepared by Sidi Embarek with hallowed gestures. Making tea here is man's work, and that of a free man.

When the gray day falls, we leave, for the hour of the moghreb prayer is approaching.

With polite salutations, the marabouts scatter in the ksar's shadow.

The garden walls and the terrace ground made of toub were very old, very worn-out. For how many generations have the Kenadsa marabouts been gathering there for their peaceful pleasures, the only ones they permit themselves in public?

There again, I had the impression of the immobility of beings and things that I have felt in all the old cities of Islam, which gives the illusion of their permanence, almost of their eternity.

The Rebel

Today, after the Friday prayer, I find the ksar completely in turmoil: a young white Muslim woman has hung herself.

I mingle with the crowd stationed in front of her house, out of which rises women's mournful wailing.

I gather information, I reconstruct the drama, I try to fathom the reasons . . . I'm told that she didn't get along with her female relatives, that she had no one to complain to; her husband, Hammou Hassine, didn't listen to her. He wanted to control her with his blows. The little shy Bedouin, after some rebellions, had relinquished, at least outwardly; but the feeling of freedom, a strange freedom, had entered her.

Several times she had fled to her brother's home; he returned her to her husband. She was prevented from asking for protection from the cadi or Sidi Brahim. She was a slave, more of a slave than the Negresses, for she suffered from her bondage. In the end, she had calmed down, for she had understood the great secret of moral freedom. One evening when everyone was at the mosque, she had gathered all her forces for the escape; she had stood up on her little feet; she had clung to hope beyond life, with her long silk belt, without confiding in anyone, an isolated woman.

A race in which suicide is still possible is a strong race. Animals never commit suicide, nor do Negroes, unless excited by alcohol. Suicide is also a state of drunkenness, but willed drunkenness.

The passive people have turned away in horror from the woman who forgot her duty to live. However, some men of letters take pity on Embarka and come to pray over her corpse, which the matrons have washed and sewn into Islam's egalitarian white cloth shroud.

The body is laid out on a mat in the middle of the courtyard. It is no longer anything but an indistinct, rigid, and immaculate form.

The women's wailing has ceased. One can only hear the low, rhythmic, and slow murmur of six or seven men chanting the chapter from the Koran entitled "Ya-Sine," which is the prayer for the dead.

Everything has become calm, solemn, and serene in the courtyard from which the noisy women have withdrawn.

The voices rise in a sad soft chant: it's now the *borda*, the funeral elegy.

The body is stretched out on the *naach*, the stretcher made of unfinished wood, and it is covered with a large red veil. Everything is silent, and then four men load the precious little body on their shoulders, and the sad procession leaves for the cemeteries.

The stretcher is placed on the sand, and everyone lines up in a half circle, their faces turned in the direction of Mecca: this is the last prayer for Embarka.

On the burial mound, which the wind is starting already to erode, three palm leaves are planted and will dry out there.

Hammou Hassine, a man of about forty, ugly and distorted, arranges dried figs and unleavened flatbread on a red cotton handkerchief on the ground; this is the *sadaka*, the ritual alms given to the poor in memory of the deceased, and which replaces the useless bouquets of flowers and tinsel crowns.

It's over. We leave in disorderly fashion. The old puritanical men of letters did not accompany the funeral procession of the woman who committed suicide. Only the young students prayed for her.

One of them said to me, "She was unhappy!" He probably didn't know what unhappiness is. When men understand suffering, they become hard. They don't sympathize, they condemn . . . And yet it seems to me that one's heart should open more and more.

There are wise men who have tried to learn until their last day . . . Why is it that what is true in intelligence would be less so in the education of feelings? Since I've lived in this zaouïya, in the shadow of Islam, since I've had a fever and been alone, voluntarily alone, I have come to loathe some of the hours of my turbulent past; my senses have more delicacy. After this refuge, if I return to life going by, I will know how to understand love . . .

Sudanese Festival

It's four o'clock, and finally the sirocco drops abruptly. Little by little, the dust clears, a light breeze blows from the east. People begin to breathe. Doors slam. Inhabitants of the ksar and marabouts go out again into the streets where the wind has stretched out a shroud of fine sand. Gray haze still hangs in the sky, covering the sun's face. The horizon is still red and hazy.

A sound rises in the ksar, a sort of rhythmic and muted pounding that slowly gets closer. The Sudanese drums are approaching. Their unusual noise brings into the Saharan background of Kenadsa a stranger note from a more distant Africa.

Through centuries of Islam, the Sudanese have kept the practices of a forgotten fetish-laden antiquity, a poetry of noise and gesticulations that had its full meaning in the deep forests haunted by monsters. Against the drums' muted leaping, the clear laughter of double copper casta-nets—attached to wrists with leather straps—stands out. A few Negroes dance at the head of the procession. The others sing a half-Arab, half-Sudanese threnody, interrupted by piercing and monotonous refrains.

A hoard of children accompanies the slaves. The comical little black urchins stand out with their tufts of hair gummed onto their little shiny skulls and their grimy shirts. The little whites, budding marabouts wearing brightly colored gandoura, their skin hardly bronzed by the sun, their delicate features, seem vaguely Chinese with a single braid of slippery hair hanging down their back from the top of their shaved head. Everyone roars with laughter and dances around the impassive Sudanese, who vaguely remember that their festival is a sacred ritual of their race.

The musicians stop, take off their sandals, and first come and kiss the marabouts' clothing; then they form a half circle and begin their racket again.

Two of the singers enter the half circle and, one facing the other, begin dancing with monkey leaps and sudden squatting. They tap the ground with their feet, they clap the pink palms of their hands above their heads. All their old Negro blood wakes up and overflows, triumphing over the artificial habits of reserve imposed by slavery. They become themselves once again, both naive and shy, greedy for childish games and barbaric drunkenness, very close to primitive animality.

One of the dancers, an old man with a bony muzzle and long yellow teeth, with ecstatic eyes, becomes excited to the point of madness. He howls out inarticulate sounds that are cries of wild joy.

The Sudanese suddenly collapse, prostrated and overwhelmed. After a moment of ecstatic inertia, they halfway straighten up, crouch painfully, turn toward Sidi Brahim.

A strong wildcat odor rises from their sweat-soaked veils, from their skin streaming with sweat, which seems blacker.

All hands rise above their faces, their palms open like books.

Sidi Brahim recites the *Fatiha*, the Koran's first chapter.

Then he calls for God's and Sidi M'hammed-ben-Bou-Ziane's blessings for all blacks, all the assistants, the inhabitants of the territory of Kenadsa, for all the Ziania, and all Muslim men and women, dead or living.

Afterward, with touching care, the marabout prays, asking God to protect and aid the servant of the Lord and his Prophet, the Algerian si Mahmoud-ould-Ali, at all times and in all places.

With the Students

The evening of that day, the slave Farradji came and got me, very mysteriously, as if it concerned a plot.

He announces to me that Si El-Madani, Si Mohammed Laredj's brother, and a few of his friends, students at the great mosque, have invited me to go have tea with them . . .

I can't help but be reminded of the descriptions of vile orgies in Mouliéras's book, Unknown Morocco, attributed to Moroccan students. Why does Farradji take all these precautions in order to transmit to me the invitation from these young men?

I've met El-Madani several times at prayer. He is a thin, scrawny young man with polite manners. However, I accept the invitation.

We cross empty stables and silent courtyards where hundred-year-old trees twist their fragile trunks. There is no one in the entire neighborhood. Our footsteps resonate on the tiles, as if we were passing under archways.

At the end of a black and humid maze of corridors crowded with stones and debris, we suddenly enter a delicious little courtyard surrounded by faded white archways.

Above the wall, as if leaning on the terrace, a date palm gently rocks its crowns of curved foliage. A creeping vine climbs up the length of a pillar and wraps itself around the slanted trunk of the palm tree, to then fall down again in a rain of leaves and budding clusters.

Si El-Madani and a few other students come out to greet me.

They welcome me with great courtesy. They are the sons of marabouts and of the inhabitants of the ksar, pale and weak as if wilted in the ksar's mournful shadow.

Si Abd-el-Djebbar, a nomad from the Hamian of Méchéria who has come to the zaouïya to study, stands out among all of them. He's a full head taller than these degenerated and sedentary men, this son of the border's warriors; he is robust, muscular, with the male's fierceness in his attitudes, plain and delicate features, a tanned complexion, and the look of his long red eyes, brilliant with a flame that is undoubtedly not that of intelligence.

We enter the tea room through carved double doors that creak on their rusted hinges. A hazy half-light reigns there. The elegance of a few delicate columns with the lacework of a frieze of arabesques carved into the milky stone contributes to the charm of the place. Small dormer windows in a cupola opening on the sky's luminous watery appearance pour pale light onto the Nile-green earthenware decorating the walls, which are the height of a man, and onto the walls of the worn-out area.

A stone step leads to the second half of the vast apartment, slightly raised. There, carpets from Rabat and mattresses made of white wool cover the floor.

Under the ceiling's black beams, interlaced with reeds dyed in green and red, a short inscription runs all around the walls, made of cinnabar letters: "el afia el bakia"—eternal health.

In small recesses, on shelves, on large chests painted with tarnished gold flowers, a jumble of disparate objects is piled up.

Arab books, cooking utensils, clothing and saddlery objects, musical instruments and weapons, everything clashing in a charming disorder. Contrasting with cheap pottery from Béchar, a gracious pitcher from Venice stands out because of its crystal, filled with the emotion of a rare color.

Here are more copper lamps with long spouts, a piece of porcelain historiated with clovers, earthenware of blended colors, and, to perfect the joy of our eyes, under a brilliant piece of silk, with beautiful trays and the tea paraphernalia, little multicolored glasses appearing like wildflowers.

I settle in near the window covered with wire mesh, looking onto a chaos of ruins faded by rain. This building material, once kind to human beings, now crumbles into dust and again becomes dry earth under the sun.

Farradji and his brother Kaddou light dry palm leaves in the courtyard while Si El-Madani explains to me, without my having asked him, the reason for the purposeful mystery with which the Negro surrounded the students' invitation.

"You know, Si Mahmoud, that usage and customs demand that our parents and our elders remain unaware of our pleasures or at least be able to pretend to be unaware. We gather here to spend hours rejoicing our hearts through music and the recitation of the sublime works of ancient poets and through cordial discussions. No one must know what happens here except for God and us . . . without that, however innocent our entertainment is, we would feel great shame about it and we would bring ourselves severe reproaches. That's why I've chosen this apartment, the only one remaining inhabitable in this old casbah left to me by my ancestor Sidi Bou-Médine. No one comes by here; no one comes and gives us advice or is in charge of the freedom of our minds' entertainment."

The meeting passes in conversation. As if to make clear the recreational intimacy, after our presentations one of the Muslim men of intellectuals returns to his sewing and looks for silks for a white gandoura that he is decorating with delicate embroidery. Among the Moroccan students, this sewing and cloth ornamentation work is favored: they are proof of taste, and even engaging in it in public is not demeaning.

El-Madani picks up a three-string guitar and in a nonchalant voice begins to sing an old Andalusian motif that drags and turns around the same note. His cousin Mouley Idris, a sickly adolescent with a bilious-colored complexion, quietly accompanies him on a tambourine. The beautiful Hamiani Abd-el-Djebbar sees in the music only a reason to yawn; stretched out full length on the rug, he stays there like a big sloughi, stretching out his horseman's dry muscles, irritated by inaction.

I listen to the languorous and sad song, and I reflect on the nature of these Muslim students' lives.

For years, scholastic studies in the barren simple setting of ancient mosques, pious exercises, reaching—for the majority of these young men, already affiliated with mystical brotherhoods—daily ecstasy.

Beneath all this forced austerity hides a great naive cheerfulness, raging sensuality that creates the most-complicated and the most-dangerous love affairs, and, it must be said, many hidden vices, especially here in the West. An almost-cloistered life favors this perversion of the senses.

And then some day, the Moroccan student, who is subjected to paternal authority without a whisper of protest, marries without joy. Then his existence changes. Finished are dreaming and studying. He enters society, he no longer exists in his personal vices and his felineness; he takes on the calm and imposing manners of the world with a correct and stiff face.

He will, however, very often miss the voluptuous atmosphere of the care-free bith-es-sohfa, the gathering place, the students' communal room.

Whether they be marabouts or notables, the young men of letters quickly take on an air of importance. A few years, a few months are enough to profoundly modify their personality. They participate in the djemâa's deliberations, and a man who deliberates does not think too much for himself. They go to war, many of them travel through Muslim countries, others go to Mecca . . .

Ancestry takes back all its rights and does not allow the individual to develop at all. He quickly becomes the man of his milieu. He feels pleasure and pride in being that man. When, at the end of a few years, these former students, verse singers, and readers have seen their sons grow, they will pitilessly impose on them the same severe rules about which they complained so often in their own young men's discussions, and the latter will, in their turn, be led to secret pleasures of their own.

For the well-born Muslim, especially from the city, nothing of personal affairs, family life, pleasures, and loves must be shown to the external world.

The public display of pleasures, so dear to the students of Europe, is unknown in Islam. At a very young age the Moroccan intellectuals are prepared to hide their joy. Thus can be explained their passionate but contained nature, their strong internal passions without any appreciable external appearance of such, and their voluptuous intellectuality that so quickly wilts.

The hour passes. My thoughts become more hazy. I abandon myself to the great melancholic and outdated charm of the instruments, without a desire for action in this background of unchangeable resignation where everything is smoothly dying, serenely under Islam's setting sun. The red letters of faith's watchword creeping around the walls stretch out their arabesques in the shadows. My mind is calmed beneath an ivory caress.

The touch of possessed time is like that of a cold pale hand on a burning forehead . . .

Strength and tranquility of things that seem to last indefinitely because they are slowly making their way toward nothingness, without a roar, without revolt, without agitation, not even a shiver toward inevitable death . . .

Evening Reflections

Night, yet another night, falls on the sleepy zaouïya. Processions of draped women, decorated with brilliant colors like glaze on ceramic, arrive at the fountain in the same way that other women have arrived for two centuries. They have the same supple, strong gait from their waist, their bare feet planted fully on the dusty ground. Others have passed through and today are no longer anything but a little ungrateful lost dust under the small stones of Lella Aïcha's cemetery.

The light wind shivers in the hard fronds of a large noble date palm rising behind the wall like a bush made of lances. Of all the trees, the date most resembles the column of a temple. There is war and mysticism, a belief in the Only One, an aspiration, in this branchless tree. Like it, Islam was born from an idea of uprightness and of bursting forth into the light. It was the expression in the divine domain of palm trees and fountains.

I feel an infinite calmness descend into the turmoil of my tired soul. My lightness comes from within me and from the weight of a burning day that has finally lifted and the gentleness of a nascent shadow on my dry eyelids.

It is the charming hour when, in the cities of the Tell, consolatory alcohol elates lazy brains . . . When the sky sings over cities, man needs to place himself in unison, and lacking a dream, he drinks for need of an ideal and enthusiasm.

Happy is he who can get drunk on his thoughts alone and who knows how to etherize all of the universe's rays through his soul's heat!

For a long time, I was incapable of this. I suffered from my weakness and my lukewarmness. Now, far from crowds and carrying unforgettable words of strength in my heart, no drunkenness will equal that poured forth in me by a golden and green sky. Brought by a mysterious force, I have found here what I was looking for, and I taste the feeling of blessed rest in conditions in which others would tremble with boredom.

One day, a young delicate woman, seeing her too-pale blood evaporating under Algiers's sky, said to me, lifeless on the pillows of her chaise lounge, as she listened to the noisy groups descending from the heights of Mustapha one Sunday evening, "Life must be very sad to make people sing so loudly!"

Alas! We all made noise, more or less. It was our student savagery letting off steam.

Love's sufferings should ennoble our destiny. We were fortunate not to drop anchor on a shoal of happiness where our existence would have gone by balanced on the small, soft waves of everyday life. Let's congratulate ourselves for having known the earth and for having known the very small space that the greatest thought could occupy. Here we have touched a corner of the world where the thirst for innovation alters no one. Material life, however, leaves its strong mark.

So what events do fascinate these nomads, representatives of the most ancient past, and these marabouts full of serenity who, disdainful of work, bathe their forehead in a future light?

Their life goes by under my eyes and I am reflected in it . . .

This evening, I again wish to be mirrored in this beautiful water of the South. I wish to drink again the water gotten by the women at the desert's fountain, to feel it flow on my hands heated by fever, to see it fall, drop by drop, like the rosary of the highest wisdom . . .

The Return of the Herd

Next to me on the still-burning terrace, Ba-Mahmadou or Salem softly sings the Prophet's old litanies. The red light from the west oxidizes his dark face with bronze reflections and warms up his white veils again . . .

All of a sudden, in the silence of the already-sleepy ksar, a great noise rises up followed by creaking doors and confused bleating and cries of joy:

"The *harrag* is returning! They're bringing back the harrag!" And in fact, it is the unhoped-for return of the large herd of the marabout and the ksar, recently plundered by Arab and Aït-Khebbach Berber pillagers.

These bandits had led the herd to the west, but the Ziani sherif Mouley Ahmed, having the origin of this booty explained, said to his people that they had committed a great sin by stealing the zaouïya's herd on holy land. "You have stolen," he explained to them, "the fortune of the poor, travelers, orphans . . . If you want God and Sidi M'hammed-ben-Bou-Ziane to grant you their favors, you will not wait to return it."

After some hesitation, the pillagers gave in to Mouley Ahmed's orders, and they designated one of their allies, El-Hassani, from the Aït-Atta Berbers, to bring back the harrag to Kenadsa and to ask, in their name, for Sidi Brahim's pardon.

The slaves ran to announce the happy news to the marabout, who was finishing praying in the cool shade of his large white apartments.

Sidi Brahim comes into the courtyard.

I come downstairs again.

The black goats invade the courtyard, are crammed in, and jump, frightened, one onto another, taking refuge all the way into the long horse's trough. Three men on foot, black slaves from Bou-Dnib, armed to the teeth, push them.

The Berbri, mounted on a skinny gray horse, dismounts in front of the large door.

Sidi Brahim, who is blind, his hand leaning on little Messaoud's shoulder, moves forward slowly, painfully, through the herd's confusion.

"Welcome, my sons! May God recompense you for the good deed that you have just accomplished!"

Then these tough men piously kiss the marabout's veils and hands, and he, very moved, kisses them in turn . . .

VARIATION

Evening at the Kenadsa zaouïya.

The slave Kaddour and I return from a long walk in the palm groves and gardens. In the large courtyard bathed in pink light, the Negresses go by with their water skins and amphorae.

Above the interior courtyard wall, near the fountain, a date palm leans and rustles in the light wind that stirs up small whirlwinds of dust.

I need to set up the large carpet and the wool blanket used for my bed and to hang the cool delloua as far away as possible from the overheated walls that give off an oven's heat.

All of a sudden, in the zaouïya's silence, there is a great noise made of voices, creaking doors, joyful exclamations, and confused bleating. "The harrag is returning! They're bringing back the harrag!"

It's the zaouïya's goat herd recently stolen by nomads. It was Aït-Khebbach Berbers; they had taken the stolen herd toward the west through [. . .].

Mouley Ahmed, the great marabout, master of the country, reproached them for the theft.

"The herd belongs to a holy and venerated zaouïya. It's the property of the poor, orphans, and travelers who all find refuge in Kenadsa. If you want God's forgiveness, you must return this herd."

And so the Aït-Khebbach sent back the herd.

El-Hassani is a young man of medium height, beardless, skinny, and muscular. He wears modest clothes made of very clean white wool. A *tercha*—which is a small round turban—is wrapped around his skull; leather straps passed between his toes attach the nomad's sandals to his feet. His thin pale face stands out as energetic and intelligent, with a mocking smile that often plays on his delicate lips. El-Hassani is thought of as a man of gunpowder.

While the Bou-Dnib Negroes exchange salutations and embraces with their Kenadsa brothers, the Berbri remains sitting near the wall, his Winchester rifle between his knees. He is indifferent and silent.

Sidi Brahim comes and asks me if it would displease me if El-Hassani and Mouley Sahel, one of the Bou-Dnib blacks, were lodged with me.

On the contrary! I accept eagerly. The marabout then talks to me for a long time about the Berabers.

"If you ever wish to go to the West, the Berabers, and especially the Aït-Atta, will be your best guides. When one of them has said to you, 'You are under God's finger and mine, I will answer for you,' you can go with him everywhere he'll want to lead you. You'll return safe and sound, unless both of you die. Berabers never go back on their word."

Then, the marabout adds, laughing, "Now, if you wish to judge the skill of these people, follow closely the movements of El-Hassani, who is still in the courtyard."

From the top of the terrace, I glance down through one of the crenellations into the courtyard crowded with slaves and inhabitants of the ksar coming and going so as to tell apart the goats. El-Hassani, indifferent to all this commotion, is still at his post. He has fulfilled his mission and that is sufficient for him.

Sidi Brahim gets up and calls the Berbri:

"Come and join us, my son, and pass through the terrace."

The Berbri gets up smiling. He throws his rifle onto his shoulder and makes a bundle out of his burnoose, which he then vigorously throws at our feet with a turn of his wrist.

For an instant he inspects the smooth wall made of toub, which is easily six or seven meters tall.

Suddenly, with a monkey's agility, he jumps and hangs, with the nails of his hands and his bare feet, on to bumps that I don't even distinguish. In almost a single bound, he is on the terrace's parapet.

And I remain stupefied. How did he do that?

"Si El-Hassani," I said to him, "in truth, it's better to be your friend than your enemy, for where could one flee to? Walls don't exist for you."

The Berbri smiled and answered with perfectly good grace:

"Mouley Mahmoud, all those who serve Sidi M'hammed-ben-Bou-Ziane are my brothers and my friends."

He speaks Arabic with a light accent, however, unlike the other Bera-bers' speech.

El-Hassani has the calm and easy manner of a man who knows his own worth and who feels sure of himself. Mouley Sahel, his black com-panion, who was content to take the stairs, speaks to him in the Berber language and, laughing, hurries him. In order to answer his companion's wish with more than boasting, El-Hassani then tells us of an adventure from three years before.

"With my brothers, the Aït-Atta, I wanted to get revenge on the inhabitants of a ksar situated on the Tafilala road. First we chased them. As night was approaching, we wanted to occupy a small, isolated, and well-enclosed casbah. I climbed the wall so I could go open the doors. Having arrived at the top, since I wanted to climb down inside, I was assaulted by four or five inhabitants of the ksar hidden in the courtyard. They riddled me with rifle shots and stones. I wanted to set myself up on the top of the wall to easily shoot those dogs, but I got caught on the point of a beam by the folds of my *seroual*. So, suspended in the air, but with my arms free, I began to shoot. I'm sure that I killed two of them, those who had rifles; as for the others, they escaped and jumped the opposite wall so as to flee into the countryside. My companions took care of flattening them in the esparto grass. Inside the casbah there was ground wheat, goatskins full of butter, a cool water tank, and sweet dates: we made a good meal in return for our troubles."

El-Hassani recounts this as an unimportant and humorous incident in his life as a wall climber.

Sidi Brahim leaves us.

The two men from the West stretch out on the rug, tired, their rifles under their folded burnooses, which serve as a cushion. They quickly fall asleep. I remain alone and awake in the diffuse light of the moonlit room.

These travelers will leave tomorrow. They will have passed through my life like supernatural shadows with gestures of a warlike pantomime. I think of other less beautiful jumping jacks operated by less solid strings. I imagine El-Hassani shooting into the void in the middle of a circus of European amateurs who would clap for him, sitting on crimson velvet benches as they bite into delicacies; and I also think of what Sidi Brahim told me: I say to myself that, in truth, it would be so simple to leave some day with men like those, to walk my dream and my thirst for the unknown through the zaouïya of Morocco, in Bou-Dnib, in the Tafilala, toward far-off Tisint, everything down there at the entrance to the great empty desert . . .

Oblivion Seekers

I discovered a kif den in this ksar where there is not even a Moorish café, where the people have no place to gather other than the public square and the earthen benches at the foot of the ramparts on the road to Béchar.

It is a long room lit by a single "eye" in the middle of a ceiling made of twisted and smoky beams, in a sort of house half in ruins behind the mellah. The walls are black and cut across by lighter cracks resembling wounds. On the rarely swept, slightly dusty beaten ground, pomegranate peels and debris of all kinds are lying about.

This strange place serves as a refuge for Moroccan vagabonds, nomads, and all sorts of disreputable people who look unwell. The house seems to belong to no one; as in a shady hotel, one unadvisedly spends a few nights there. It seems made for picturesque theater, and it seems like an antechamber for crime.

In a corner, a clean mat with a few cushions from Fez made of embroidered leather. On the mat is a large Arab trunk historiated with brightly colored paintings; it serves as a table. Here is a rosebush with small pale-pink roses, matching a bouquet of garden herbs soaking in a large earthenware jar from the Tell, decorated with geometric designs and arabesques. Farther on is a copper kettle on a tripod, two or three teapots, and a basket stuffed with dried Indian hemp. That's all the background, all the production for the coterie of kif smokers, people fond of their creature comforts.

I almost forgot, on a perch made of palm stalks, a captive vulture attached by his foot.

Berrania (foreigners), wanderers who haunt this lair, join up with the kif smokers, though the latter form a very closed, small association that is rather difficult to enter. For they too are travelers, transporting their reverie throughout Islam's countries, and these devotees of the hallucinatory smoke who group together in Kenadsa belong to the more elevated class of men of letters.

Hadj Idris, a tall skinny Filali, tanned and with a soft face lit up as if by an internal light, is one of these wanderers without a family, without a fixed occupation, who are so numerous in the Muslim world. For twenty-five years he has been wandering from city to city, working or begging depending on the opportunities.

He plays the *goumbri*, a small Arab guitar with two strings stretched over a tortoise shell and a neck made of carved wood.

Hadj Idris has a low, clear voice, beautiful for singing old Andalusian narratives with melancholy and very tender melodies.

Si Mohammed Behaouri, a Mékinez Moroccan with a pale complexion, caressing eyes, still young, is a poet wandering through Morocco and the Algerian South, seeking Arab legends and literature; to earn his living, he composes and recites verses about love's delights and torments.

Another one comes from Djebel-Zerhaoun. Doctor, sorcerer, small, dry, muscular, his skin weather-beaten by the sun of Sudan, where he traveled for many years, he wandered with caravans, from the Senegalese coast to Timbuktu. He spent his days making medicines and leafing through old Moroccan books of magic spells.

Chance has brought these people together in Kenadsa. Tomorrow they will leave, scattering themselves on roads going different directions, each one going toward the accomplishment of his destiny with a perfect lack of concern.

The community of their tastes has brought them together in this yellow-brown refuge, where they enjoy the slow hours of a life free of worries.

In the evening, a slanted pink ray of light falls from the eye into the room's half-light. The kif smokers gather, their turbans decorated with a fragrant stem of basil. Squatting on their mats, they line up against the wall and smoke their small red clay pipes filled with Indian hemp and dusty Moorish tobacco.

Hadj Idris stuffs and distributes the pipes after having carefully wiped the pipe stem on his cheek, out of politeness. When his pipe is full, he delicately gathers the little ball of embers remaining in the bottom—he doesn't feel the burning—then, with his pipe full, it is this burning cinder that is used by the Filali to rekindle the small hearth, which won't go out for hours. Very intelligent, with a delicate and penetrating mind softened by a continual state of half drunkenness, dreamy [...] slow soft narcotic to which [...] supposed aphrodisiac qualities are attributed in Europe ... The oblivion seekers sing lazily, clapping their hands; their dreamy voices rise up late in the night to the murky light of a lantern made with panes of mica; then their voices are slowly lowered, become slower, more oppressed. Finally, the kif smokers are quiet, their eyes fixed on their flowers, in a state of ecstasy.

They are epicureans, voluptuous beings, maybe even wise men who know how, in the black den of Moroccan vagabonds, to distinguish enchanted horizons and to build marvelous cities full of happiness.

Kenadsa Evenings

After the asr prayer, toward four o'clock, the sun begins to go down on Morocco's rocky hills.

The overheated earth utters the implacable day's great weariness; the bad hours of torpor and exhaustion have gone by. Then I have a feeling of well-being comparable to that left by a danger avoided or a nightmare awoken from. And I go with a slave into the gardens, cut through by walls that we must climb over.

In Kenadsa there are none of the great damp palm groves like in Figuig or Béchar: the gardens extend into full desert and painfully fight against the sand's slow and stubborn invasion, against the deadly dryness of the neighboring hamada. There are families of date palms, five or six originating from the same root, the lighter shade from fruit trees full of velvety fruit falling into the trickle of the séguia running along the small golden fields where the meager barley has already been harvested.

Against walls where the sun is less fiery, in the jumble of vines wrapping around the palm and pomegranate trees, and under the low fig trees, there are, however, corners of shade and delicious coolness.

Here and there, large greenish ponds get the excess water from irrigation brooklets. Innumerable little oasis toads inflect their melodious song.

Tenant farmers, mostly blacks, cultivate the gardens in exchange for their share, a fifth of the harvest. They live slow days there in the middle of the trees, and they are very good at decorating the charming disorder of their plantations. All of them grow *zafour*, so beautifully orange colored that the women use them to dye cloth and as makeup. A few of the farmers add a wild shrub to the long slender clusters of mauve flowers and violet asters growing in the desert's oued. There are also large rosebushes with one hundred leaves, called *Ouard ech-Cham*, rosebushes of Syria.

The hospitable tenant farmers hurry and prepare tea. They carry small golden apricots and almonds in the folds of their soiled burnooses: the zaouïa's guest is welcome among them.

One evening, the most ancient of them—an old Moroccan man from the Sedjaa tribe, completely stooped and with a mummified face—brought a bouquet of pomegranates and a bunch of onions to me as a present.

"You see, the flowers and fruit from my garden are not abundant; I'm a poor old man, and I have nothing else to offer you in welcome. Accept these few vegetables—God dispenses all riches; accept my humble offering and forgive me . . ."

I didn't dare refuse this naive and touching present for fear of offending the old gardener, who gazed at me with pathetic ashamed eyes as if he owed me his garden's produce.

At the edge of the séguias, mint and basil grow in the shade; they are pale and wilted, yet strongly aromatic. Their perfume hangs in the still-warm air with other more tenuous and indefinable plant smells.

I find, once again, the calm and the soft drowsiness of other Saharan gardens in these Kenadsa gardens, without, however, this mysteriously oppressing "something" that is the soul of deep palm groves and forests.

The day goes down. The date trees are bathed in the sky's crimson hue. We leave the gardens where the noxious smells of fever will ascend.

Large violet shadows lengthen on the stones reddening in the sun's last fires.

Eternal daily enchantment of the South's evenings, yet never the same. Sad, almost-agonizing hour! All of a sudden one feels the desert darkening and closing up again, as if to guard forever against intruders.

On the path running along the rampart, women from the ksar come to the fountain of Sidi Embarek. In the setting sun's light, their veils have shades of incredible intensity. The cloth shimmers and, magnified, resembles precious brocades. From afar, one would say the women are dressed in the rarest silks embroidered with gold and precious stones. Conscious of their charms, the women bustle about, their groups mingle, and the violent range of colors endlessly changes like a moving rainbow.

A few of them, especially Sudanese women or nomads, have pure movements, flawless poses; the hollows of their backs and their curved arms lift the heavy full amphorae all the way to their shoulders. There are some whose faces have beautiful features and expressions with both shy sensuality and a wild look; and all of a sudden in the abrupt flash of a smile, the fervor of their senses freely explodes.

A strong odor of damp skin and cinnamon rises from the groups into the balmy air.

Men, Negroes or nomads, Douï-Ménia, Ouled-Djerir, Ouled-Nasser come and water their horses.

While the black slaves laugh and joke with the women whom no one deigns to even hide from them, the desert men look at the latter out of the corners of their eyes with brief flashes in their tawny pupils.

How many love affairs have been started near Aïn Sidi-Embarek while the weary horses were reaching their nostrils into the cool jet of subterranean water!

With subtle gestures and brief glances, nomads and women communicate with each other and make disturbing promises for the favorable hours of the night.

There again I find a little of the poetry of Arab loves and nomad love affairs, which so often finish in bloodshed.

The Jewish women—less watched over and bolder—freely approach the men, winking provocatively with eyes whose lids are reddened by the acrid smoke of dried palm leaves in the black stalls of the *mellah*.

It's the free and cheerful hour, the hour when, far from the weighty authority of men, the women chatter and laugh and play the dangerous game, the eternal game of love.

Desert Gypsy Women

I like taking note of the nature of such diverse indigenous races who know how to remain mostly pure.

Here, for example, are strange women, even here, who arrive to us from an encampment of Douï-Ménia-Ouled-Slimane, settled for a few days at the foot of the Barga to the east of Lella Aïcha.

The Meniaï are taller and leaner than the women of the ksour and also more robust under their dark blue veils. Their difficult elegance consists of what one could call "the art of wearing rags."

That a woman—with bijous, tawdry jewelry, ribbons, complex hairstyles, styled clothing, affectations, strong perfumes, all the science of the dressmaker—could look like a packet of rags is what most of Algiers's Jewish women prove, having renounced their traditional clothing in order to dress in the style of the French. On the contrary, beneath the woolen rags with which they drape themselves, the women of the pillaging nomads have an abruptness in their bearing that reminds one of casual fashion. They are, perhaps, the only women in Africa who know how to walk with a high step. The miserable rags with which they cover their nakedness seem to form one body with their bronze architecture. When the biting wind makes them even thinner and plasters their tunic against the nervous forms of their legs, they stand out like skinny wolves against copper skies and the paleness of dead earth. One would say that they are age-old and that they, too, bring back their part of the war's plunder to the cave . . .

Berber interbreeding has somewhat deformed the appearance of their thin, weather-beaten faces; however, a certain Semitic expression remains, which seems to be inherited from wild Asia. I imagine that the female warriors from Sémiramis must have had these curves devoid of even the most scrawny grace and the same eyes—long and tawny colored like those of black sloughi.

These women have gestures that I have not seen among Arab women, even less so among Moorish women: they walk without shyness and without sway-

ing in front of the men from other tribes. They seem to show no flirtatiousness, and yet the smile on their red lips is stronger than Sudanese sensuality and the complacency of Jewish women's mouths.

For the man from the South, the Jewish woman is impure. Never have the nomads noticed the slightly sickly white beauty of the girls of the mellah. The two races rub shoulders and tolerate each other without ever mixing or even approaching each other. The pastor and the plunderer often need the Jew, and they can fight bitterly with him; but once the moment of their business has passed, no other interest, no other thought brings them together.

The Douï-Ménia women are the desert's gypsies with more of the unexpected. They have a wild beauty that allows itself to be visible through the holes of their earth-colored tunics. Poverty is a natural thing for them and not a sign of degeneration. They think that all riches can be found in the beauty of a horse or in a dagger handle.

In the Mellah

Late after nightfall, the confused noises near the fountain die down bit by bit in the ever-vaster silence of the valley falling asleep.

The violet night has fallen on the finally peaceful earth.

Let us go through the doors of the city walls.

There in the mellah, I often have the impression of a large magic lantern. I come there as if to a performance, in order to see the dancing of flame-lit forms. In front of their doors, the Jewish women have set up improvised hearths; there they cook the evening meal in large witch's cauldrons.

The long flames from dried palm leaves and the dull reddish glow from fires made of camel droppings illuminate the whitewashed facades and the walls made of toub, which then take on a fleeting patina of red gold and burning pink.

White silhouettes bustle about like ghosts, and their shadows dance on the low houses and the sand crisscrossed by bloody-colored reflections.

The men wait, stretched out on the ground or busy with small tasks in the light of smoky candle ends.

Children play, passing by again and again in the light waves like slippery worms. Sometimes a beautiful Jewish woman stands up and stretches in front of the hearth, weary and catlike in the glory of the flames of blood, which completely bathe her in pink light and tint her wilted paleness an artificial crimson . . . [. . .] the burst of her large blue eyes under heavy eyelids.

Fleeting glimmers, metallic clinking of jewelry, white forms resembling dream apparitions . . . Kenadsa's mellah, ugly with poverty and irremediable filth during the day, appears beautiful to me in this first hour of night, like a corner of some enchanted city, a worshipper of devouring and powerful fire.

. . . A Jewish woman sings in a shrill voice in an attempt to lull her screeching baby to sleep. A melancholy donkey brays in a neighboring stable. It's late, and the Jewish women go inside. The fires go out in front of the closed doors.

In the distance, the moueddhen shout out their unfathomably sad call, and the numbing peace of Islam finally obscures the last visions of the transformed mellah.

Note

We note here a break in the narrative: Isabelle Eberhardt becomes ill, most likely from malaria. For the edition of *Dans l'ombre chaude de l'Islam*, Barrucand had added in his own hand, after having thoroughly reworked the chapter: "Shortly afterward, fever overcame me and threw me into strange dreams."

Negresses with slim and supple bodies were dancing, bathed in bluish light. The enamel of their teeth shone in remarkable smiles in their nighttime faces. They draped their gracious forms with a long veil, either red, blue, or sulfur yellow, winding and unwinding to the strange rhythm of their dance and floating in the wind, sometimes becoming as diaphanous as vapor.

Their dark hands shook the iron double castanets used in Sudanese festivals. Sometimes the castanets beat a wild cadence, sometimes they hit one another with scarcely a sound.

. . . But the Negresses slowly detached themselves from the ground and floated into the air.

Their bodies lengthened, writhed, lost their shape, whirled around like desert dust on the evenings of sirocco. Finally, they vanished into the shadows of the ceiling's smoky beams.

My eyes opened painfully and clung to things. I looked for the strange creatures who, only a few seconds before, were dancing in front of me.

I had seen them, I had heard their throaty laughter like muted chuckles, I had felt on my burning forehead the hot breaths lifting up their veils. They had disappeared, leaving me the memory of an inexpressible anguish . . .

Where were they now?

My tired mind strove to escape the limbo it had been floating in for hours or for centuries: I no longer knew.

It seemed that I was returning from a black abyss where beings lived, where things were under the influence of laws different from those governing the world of reality; and my overheated brain painfully forced itself to chase away the ghosts haunting it.

A great silence weighed on the zaouïya overcome by sleep. It was the deadly hour of noon, the hour of mirages and death pangs. The heat spread out on the white-hot terraces and the dunes glimmering in the distance.

I had been placed on a mat in an alcove looking onto a high terrace. The small room opened wide on to the leaden sky and the desert of stone and sand burning under the sun.

From the ceiling's palm tree beams hung a small water vessel made of goatskin, and water dripped slowly from it into a large copper platter placed on the ground.

Each minute the drop fell, ringing on the metal with a clear regular noise, with the monotony of a hospital or prison clock's ticktock. And this noise made me suffer sharply, as if the obstinate drop had fallen on my burning skull.

Squatting next to me, a Sudanese slave, with cheeks marked by deep grooves, silently moved a horsehair fly whisk, dyed with henna like the tail of a parade horse.

I watched the slave. For instants as long as years, I imagined the relief I would feel after he had taken away the platter, on my order, and when the drop of water would finally fall on the beaten earth with a dull sound. But I was unable to speak, and the drop still fell, ringing inexorably on the polished copper.

The ceiling's beams disappeared, a sky caved in before my eyes. Now there were silver-blue palm trees swaying and rustling above my head.

Around tapered date palm trunks and beneath their arched foliage, very green vines wound themselves, and flowering pomegranate trees bled in the shade.

I was lying down in a séguia on long aquatic grasses as soft and enveloping as heads of hair. Fresh water flowed the length of my body, and I voluptuously luxuriated in its humid caress.

Another rivulet sang within reach of my mouth. Sometimes, without moving, I let the icy water flow between my lips; I felt it go down my dry throat and into my chest where, little by little, thirst's intolerable burning was extinguished. Water, beneficial water, blessed water of delicious dreams!

I luxuriated in numerous visions, in slow ecstasies of the Paradise of Waters . . . there were large blue-green ponds under the graceful date palms; there, innumerable clear streams flowed; gentle waterfalls flowed from boulders covered with thick mosses, wells creaked from all sides, spreading around treasures of life and fecundity . . .

Somewhere, very far away, a voice rose, a white voice that yelped in the silence. It came from unknown horizons through greenery and eternal shade.

The voice disturbed my rest. Once again my eyes opened on to the small room of exile.

The voice turned out to be real, and rose again: the man from the mosque was announcing the midday prayer.

Then the slave watching over me raised the black forefinger of his right hand, attesting to God's oneness and Mohammed's prophetic mission; then he got up, draping his large ebony body in his white veils.

He prayed. At each prostration, his koumia—his long Moroccan dagger with a curved blade and a chiseled copper sheath—hit the ground. He said, "God is the greatest." And he bowed low, his forehead in the dust, his eyes turned toward Mecca.

I followed the slave's slow gestures with my eyes.

When he had finished praying, the Sudanese man took his place again next to me and began moving his long orange-colored horsehair whisk.

Reddish vapors rose from cracking terraces. In the still air as heavy as molten metal, not a breeze went by, not a breath. My white clothes were drenched with sweat, and I felt a crushing weight oppressing my chest. A burning thirst, an atrocious thirst that nothing could quench, was devouring me. My limbs were crushed and aching, and my heavy skull rolled around on the bag that served as my pillow.

The slave soaked a muslin rag in a vase full of water and moistened my face and my chest with it. Then he poured a few drops of lukewarm mint tea into my mouth.

I sighed and stretched my arms, which had fallen asleep.

The *mueddhen*'s voice had hushed over the ksar overwhelmed by heat. Once again my mind floated in indistinct regions peopled with strange apparitions where holy waters flowed.

The day of fire went out in pink radiance over the valley and hills. Beyond the sebkha, the date palms lit up like tall black candles.

Once again the mueddhen cried out his melancholy call. I was now completely awake. My eyes with their bruised, heavy eyelids opened eagerly on the evening's splendor.

Suddenly, unending sadness descended into my soul. Childish regrets invaded me.

I was alone, alone in this lost corner of the Moroccan earth, and alone everywhere I had lived, and alone everywhere I'll go, always . . . I had no country, no home, no family . . . I had passed through like a stranger and an intruder, awakening around me only disapproval and estrangement.

At this hour, I was suffering, far from any help, among men impassively attending the ruin of everything around them, men who cross their arms in the face of illness and death, saying, "*Mektoub!*"

In no place on earth was any human being thinking of me and suffering my suffering.

More lucid and calmed, I scorned my weakness and I smiled.

If I now found myself alone, was it not because I had wished for that during conscious hours when my thought rose above cowardly sentimentality of the equally crippled heart and flesh?

To be alone is to be free, and liberty was the only happiness necessary for my nature.

So I said to myself that my solitude was a good thing.

A hot breath rose toward the west, a breath of fever and anguish. My already weary head fell back onto the pillow; my body was annihilated in an almost voluptuous numbing, and my limbs became light, as if weak.

The summer night, dark and starlit, fell onto the desert. My spirit left my body and again flew off toward the enchanted gardens and the large bluish ponds of the Paradise of Waters.

Strong Images

In the great happy weariness into which I have fallen, I no longer have the strength to think carefully. Images join together in my mind in the most fleeting way. They are scumbles, sketches of diaphanous lightness; then suddenly the contours become clear, and forgotten scenes now become engraved etchings before my eyes.

For an entire hour I saw myself again in Aïn-Sefra. I had found notes in a notebook, and I was leafing through them like childish images lying around on a sick person's bed . . .

There was a small dazed soldier in a Moorish café among the picturesque and musky crowd. I see him very clearly . . . He must be slightly tipsy. And now he starts singing. Soon his reedy voice dominates all the others. All of a sudden he stops and lets his forehead drop on his neighbor's chest:

The little soldier is crying. "Look, Abdelkader," he says, "do you see those turtledoves in a cage? Well, I'm crying for them, because they reminded me of my father's house in Frenda. We also had captive turtledoves . . . There, I'm crying because I won't see them again. The old people are dead, and the turtledoves must have died . . ."

The scene changes.

In a deserted street opening onto Tiout's small dunes, the soldiers are leaving in groups under the sirocco's hot breath.

For months and months, their rough hands have clenched the solitary bunk beds on bad nights here. The terrible anguish of the unsatisfied rutting period threw them into the small dead streets of Djenan-ed-Dar for the impossible search of a woman to embrace.

Many of them have succumbed to the appalling loves of the barracks, prisons, and penal colonies.

Now they're off to appease life's tyrannical instinct to perpetuate itself— they are leaving for the sad hovels whipped by the desert's wind . . .

Eight o'clock. The soldiers who have not been able to go in, for lack of space, settle themselves in front of the public house. They yell and knock with their fists and feet on the door, which then cracks under their tremendous pressure.

Finally, a noise of heavy clumping shoes rings out.

A clamor of wild joy rises from the group. I see my small soldier again, the very same one who was crying over the caged turtledoves that afternoon.

In the midst of bursts of laughter, he is already unbuckling his belt.

Music of Words

The fever comes back.

In order to clarify my vacillating ideas, I would have liked to note some of the maxims dropped before me by the marabout of Kenadsa, Sidi Brahim. But the calam is already trembling in my fingers, the letters of my handwriting are getting larger, snaking and crawling up the walls. They are living, threatening inscriptions that, suddenly calmed, sing in an ancient and smooth voice:

"Curse the world and its days, for life is created for pain . . . But oh surprise! Life is man's enemy, and he adores it!"

No, this is not a thought from the cloister, a cold thought; this is delicious music. It penetrates me and lifts me with a deep emotion, as if some spirit were speaking to my spirit in order to say to me, "Forget!"

And now my soul is like a large overflowing goblet, containing these words: "The world is flowing toward the tomb like night is flowing toward dawn!"

But I know even more music, faraway friend, such sweet engaging lullabies that, if you were to sing them to the little beloved one, she would burst out laughing in your face, for your little beloved one has never had a fever. She knows only how to look at herself in a pocket mirror, how to gently blink her eyes and purse her lips.

However, I know that she has thick hair and the prettiest smiles in the world—intelligent smiles. She understands halfheartedly. When her eyes ecstatically roll back in her head and her eyes are rimmed in blue hollows, don't go thinking that she loves you in the least: it's a quiver of the ego.

And why would she love you, you whose love, like mine, is nothing but passionate suffering, whereas hers is light joy? Just as easily, sing for her—in order to see her smile—lullabies composed for other idols resembling her.

This evening, these monotonous love chants, this music for words carried through the zaouïya's silence, reached all the way to my heart . . . In spite of all my efforts to pay attention, I didn't see the lips move on the person singing them.

It was a traveler. He'd said to me, "Listen to this song from Egypt." And then his eyes were speaking to me, yes, nothing but his deadly eyes:

"My glance didn't lower at all in the face of the two-edged Indian sword's threat. Before the burst of my beloved's black eyes, my gaze was disturbed and fell to the ground.

"Like the eagle's eye, my eye was not at all dazzled by the sun. The look of my beloved disturbed my reason and my sight.

"However, as long as she was in my presence, even inaccessible, I felt happy. A mortal cannot reach the stars, and yet his contemplation of their brilliance is sweet.

"And now that she is no longer there, my reason flees and my tears flow from my heart to my eyes and from my eyes to the sand."

I would like to fall asleep to these voices, listening to the one that keeps vigil at my bedside and those voices that sang nearby on horseback as we crossed the luminous hamada in the morning.

"Tell me what happened to my beloved.

"Is she alive or is she dead?

"If she remembers me, and if she is crying, I will die of this. And let her tears wash my body.

"If she has forgotten me, if she is laughing, if she is playing, if she is undoing her hair, I will die from this. And then let her hair serve as a shroud in which to bury me."

Powers of Africa

The fever has left me bit by bit, but I am still weary with no desire for action. It's been a very long time since I received any letters, and I no longer wait for any. I work at noting my impressions of the South, my aberrations, my inventories, that I write merely for the sake of writing, not knowing if they will ever be of interest to anyone.

I tried to possess this country, and this country possessed me. At some hours, I wonder whether the land of the South will not call back to itself all the conquerors who will come with new dreams of power and liberty, because this land distorted all the former conquerors.

Isn't it the land that makes men? . . .

What will the European empire of Africa be in a few centuries when the sun, with the new races' blood, will have accomplished its slow work of African assimilation and adaptation to the deep rhythms of the climate and soil? At what moment will our northern races be able to say they are indigenous like the red-haired Kabyle and the pale-eyed inhabitants of the ksour?

These are questions that often preoccupy me. I'll think about them later. Others will answer for me.

There is one thing that I feel is profoundly true: it is that it is useless to battle against deep and irreducible causes and that a lasting transposition of civilization is not possible.

I breathe African smells during the hot nights like an incense ever rising toward mysterious and cruel divinities. No one will be able to completely deny the existence of these idols; they will still seem monstrous, on nights of fever, to those who will place the nape of their neck on this earth, so as to sleep, their eyes gazing at the cold stars.

Moghreb

What relief, almost voluptuousness, when the sun goes down, when the shadows of the date palms and walls lengthen and climb, putting out the last glimmers on earth!

The mournful indifference that overtakes me with malaise during the hours of the daytime dissipates. And it is once again with an eager and charmed eye that I observe the daily splendor of this already-familiar background of Kenadsa. Its simple beauty with its sober lines and both hot and transparent colors abruptly increases the foreground's monotony, while diaphanous vapors drown out the distance.

Every evening, this renaissance of the soul is very sweet and consoling.

In the gardens, the day's last hot hour flows by softly for me in tranquil contemplations and in lazy conversations interrupted by long silences.

At the hour of the moghreb, when the sun has set, we pray in the hamada at the entrance to the large cemeteries and at blessed Lella Aïcha's nearly iridescent white koubba.

At this charming hour, everything is calm, everything is dreaming, everything smiles.

Women go by, leaving barefoot for Aïn Sidi Embarek. Men who were conversing, reclining on the ground, get up.

A great murmur of prayer rises from this corner of desert overlooked by the ksar and the Barga.

Having finished the prayer, people stay sitting on their laid-out burnooses, their hands telling black beads and red beads . . . lips softly chant the Prophet's litanies.

To be healthy in body, pure from any stain after long baths in cool water, to be simple and to believe, to have never doubted, to have never battled against oneself, to wait for eternity's inevitable hour without fear or impatience . . . This is certainly Muslim peace and happiness—and who knows?—maybe wisdom.

Certainly the hours here flow by with the gentleness and tranquility of a river in a plain, where nothing is reflected except for very hazy thick clouds that go by and don't return.

. . . Little by little, regrets and desires are disappearing in me. I let my mind float in vagueness and my will be dulled.

Dangerous and delicious numbness, leading imperceptibly, but surely, to the threshold of nothingness.

These days, these weeks, when nothing has happened, when no one has done anything, when no one has even made any effort, when no one has suffered, hardly even thought, must we cross them out from existence and lament their emptiness? After the unavoidable awakening, must we, in contrast, yearn for them like the best weeks of our lives?

I no longer know.

Only as the feeling of old immoveable Islam—which here seems to be the very breath of the earth—flows through my blood, as my calm days end, the necessity of work and fighting diminishes more and more. I, who only a short while ago dreamed of even more distant voyages. I, who wished to act, I'm coming to the point of wishing—without yet daring to frankly admit it to myself—that the hour's intoxication and the current sleepiness can last, if not forever, at least for a long time yet.

However, I know well that the wanderlust will take hold of me again, that I will leave; yes, I know that I am still very far from the wisdom of the Muslim fakirs and anchorites.

But what speaks in me—what torments me and what tomorrow will push me again onto life's roads—is not the wisest voice of my soul. It is the spirit of agitation for which the world is too narrow, and which has been unable to find in itself its universe.

To end up in peace and silence in some southern zaouïya, to end up reciting ecstatic prayers—without desires or regrets—facing splendid horizons.

In fact, this would be the wished-for ending when weariness and disenchantment will arrive after many years.

Departure

For the last time, I wake up on the terrace, to the moueddhen's hoarse drawling voice in the night.

It's cool. Everything slumbers.

The Berbri El-Hassani and the Negro Mouley Sahel get up. Like me, they must leave this morning—but in the opposite direction.

I'm going to go back up to Béchar and Beni-Ounif, and then reach Aïn-Sefra to be cared for there for the rest of the summer so that I can then take advantage of autumn's first convoys.

My companions are also preparing to go to Bou-Dnib. They would like to take me with them, and I would like to have the strength to follow them.

"Think carefully, Si Mahmoud," said the Berbri to me. "There is still time. We'll walk for a whole month, we'll cross countries where you'll have many chances to see many things and to learn. We'll go back up the Guir, we'll go all the way to Tafilala or even all the way to Tisint . . . You'll be received everywhere as our brother."

The temptation is very strong . . . But to leave in this way, weak as I am, without authorization, without letting anyone know . . . Wouldn't this trip made for study and out of curiosity be badly interpreted? Very reluctantly I resign myself to taking the Béchar road today . . .

How different this return voyage will be from what it was during the outward journey, when I was walking toward unknown country!

"No, El-Hassani, I cannot. It will be for later, in a while. I'll let you know when I can."

"May God facilitate the accomplishment of your plans!"

Two other Negroes who will leave by foot are also there, seated against the wall, immobile, with their rifles on their knees. They barely understand Arabic, for they were born and grew up on the road to Fez with the Aït-Ischorouschen, the coarsest and the most closed of the Berabers.

One of them stays fiercely silent and gives me a mean look. In his eyes I am obviously nothing more than an outcast, a cursed m'zani.

On a brief order from El-Hassani, the Negroes saddle the horses. My companions from the zaouïya point the way to Guir, where they are going. However, they will not abruptly leave me. They're determined to accompany me for a while, and then they'll retrace their steps.

"We'll go with you," says El-Hassani to me, "all the way to the entrance of the cemeteries."

We leave. My throat is so tight with emotion that I can hardly respond to the words spoken to me. However, I must keep my man's heart all the way to the end.

Among the small sharp flagstones, planted like a field, like slates in the hard clay, marking the length of the tombs with protrusions where accustomed horses rarely stumble, we dismount as is the custom when friends separate, embracing each other three times.

"Go thus in God's peace and security!"

"May you encounter good!"

Back on our horses, we leave in opposite directions: El-Hassani toward the unexplored West, where I would have so ardently wished to follow him, and I toward the disenchantment of known regions.

For a long time, from the top of a hillock, my eyes follow the Bou-Dnib people riding away. They finally disappear amid the maze of dunes, beneath the rising day's pink radiance. With them, the last glimmer of hope disappears for me: for a long time, I will not be able to go deeper into Morocco, maybe never.

While my mare approaches with slow steps, my desolate eyes get lost on the valley, which I had found so beautiful in the summer sun's splendid nativity when I first came here. And because I am going back, because maybe a long exile from the beloved desert starts for me today, I find the countryside very nondescript, almost ugly, bristling with a thousand points where no ray of sun catches. A great charm has disappeared.

Then, squeezing my white mare's flanks, I angrily rush forward in a crazy gallop, and the desert wind dries out my moist eyes . . .

Note

This text, entitled *Sud oranais*, second part, had remained completely unedited at the time of the author's death. We owe its existence to the dogged will of Lyautey, who had the ruins of Isabelle Eberhardt's house searched for days by his soldiers. After the discovery of the manuscripts, he carried them in his own hands to Victor Barrucand, who dedicated to the general the publication titled *Dans l'ombre chaude de l'Islam*.

Taking as a pretext the poor condition of these pages, Barrucand inserted in them passages of his own invention: "The Black Stallion," "The Drama of Hours," "Looking Back," and "Nocturnal Breaths," which we have eliminated from this current edition. On the other hand, Barrucand rewrote some chapters that had become mostly illegible in the manuscripts; we have reproduced them in italics.

The Daily Journals

First Daily Journal

I am alone in the face of the murmuring sea's gray immensity . . . I am *alone* . . . alone, as I have always been everywhere, as I will always be throughout the great engaging and disappointing Universe . . . *alone*, with a whole world of disappointed hopes, of dead illusions, and of more distant memories behind me that have become almost unreal, from day to day.

I am alone and I dream . . .

And, in spite of the profound sadness invading my heart, my dreaming is neither desolate nor despairing. After these last six months—so tormented, so incoherent—I feel my heart is forever strengthened and henceforth invincible, capable of never weakening, even through the worst storms, through all the annihilations and mournings. Through the profound and subtle experience of life and human hearts that I have acquired (at the price of what sufferings, my God!), I clearly foresee yet again the strange and very sad enchantment that these two months spent here will be for me—here where I have ended up by chance, in large part because of my prodigious unconcern for everything in the world, for everything that is not this world of thoughts, of sensations and dreams that represent my real me and that are hermetically sealed to the curious eyes of all, without any exception whatsoever.

For the audience, I wear the borrowed mask of the cynic, the debauched individual, and the devil-may-care type . . . Until this day, nobody has known how to pierce this mask and perceive my *true* soul, this overly sensitive and pure soul that floats so high above the low acts and degradations where I enjoy, out of disdain for conventions and also out of a need to suffer, dragging my physical being . . .

Yes, nobody has been able to understand that in this chest, which seems nourished only by sensuality, a generous heart beats. Long ago this heart overflowed with love and tenderness, and now it is still filled with infinite pity for everything that suffers unfairly, for everything weak and oppressed . . . a proud and inflexible heart that has voluntarily given its whole self to a beloved cause . . . to this Islamic cause for which I would so much like to shed this burning blood that boils in my veins one day.

Nobody has known how to understand all of that and treat me accordingly, and alas, nobody will ever understand!

So I will obstinately remain the drunkard, the debauched person, the dish breaker who drank her crazy and lost head off in the desert's intoxicating immensity and, this autumn, throughout the Tunisian Sahel's olive groves.

Who will give back to me the silent nights, the lazy rides through the salty plains of the Oued Righ', and the white sands of the Oued Souf? . . . Who will give back to me the both sad and happy sensation invading my abandoned heart in my chaotic encampments among my chance friends, the spahis or the nomads, among whom not one suspected me of this hated and disowned personality with which destiny has nicknamed me for my sins?

Who will ever give back to me the wild rides through the mountains and valleys of the Sahel in the autumn wind, intoxicating rides making me lose all notion of reality in a glorious state of drunkenness!

At this instant, moreover like at every hour of my life, I have but one desire: to don as quickly as possible the beloved personality that, in reality, is the real one and to return down there to Africa to take up that life again . . . To sleep in the deep coolness and silence under the breathtaking fall of the stars, with the infinite sky for a roof and the warm earth for a bed . . . to doze off with the sweet and sad sensation of my absolute solitude and the certitude that nowhere in this world does any heart beat for mine, that on no point of the earth does any human being cry for me or wait for me. To know all of that, to be free and unfettered, camped out in life, this grand desert where I will never be anything but a stranger and an intruder . . . Here it is, in all its deep bitterness, the only happiness that Mektoub will ever give to me, to me to whom real happiness—that after which all humanity is running, panting—is forever refused . . .

Far from me, illusions and regrets!

What illusions are there to still keep when the white dove,[1] who was the sweetness and light of my life, has slept there for two years in the earth in the peaceful cemetery of Annaba's Believers!

When Vava, in his turn, has returned to the original dust, and when nothing remains standing from that which seemed so tenaciously durable, when everything has crumbled, is destroyed for time and eternity! . . . And when fate has separated me, strangely and mysteriously, from the only being who approached my real soul near enough, even if only a pale reflection of it—Augustine . . .

And when . . . But no! Let all these recent things forever recede into slumber.

Henceforth, I will let myself be rocked by the inconstant waves of life . . . I will let myself be carried away by all sources of intoxication without being upset if all of them inexorably dry up . . . Finished are the battles and victories and the defeats from which I emerged, my heart wounded and bleeding . . . Finished are all these youthful indiscretions!

I came here to flee the ruins of a long past of three years, which have just caved in, alas, into the mire, and so low, so low . . . I also came here out of friendship for the man met by chance whom Destiny put on my path at the precise moment of a crisis—if it pleases God, the last one—when I didn't give way, but which threatened to go very far . . .

And, strange thing, from what I have noted today and from what caused me endless sadness emerges an absolute change of feeling for . . .

My friendship has been enhanced by it . . . So much the better! But of *illusion*, from the first day, the first hour, none!

I see once more that I am beginning to lose myself in the *inexpressible*, in this world of things that I feel and that I understand so clearly and that I have never known how to express.

However, even though my life has been nothing but a web of pain and sadness, I will never curse this lamentable life and this sad universe

1. Translator's note: The "white dove" is Isabelle's deceased mother.

. . . where Love mixes with Death and where everything is ephemeral and transitory.

For each one has given me drunkenness that is too deep, ecstasies that are too sweet, too many dreams and thoughts.

I regret nothing, and I desire nothing further . . . *I am waiting.*

Thus, a nomad and with no country other than Islam; without a family and without confidants, alone, forever alone in the haughty and gloomily sweet solitude of my soul, I will continue my path through life until the hour of the tomb's great eternal sleep rings . . .

MAHMOUD ESSADI

And the eternal, the mysterious, the anguishing question is asked once again: where will I be, on what earth and under what sky, at the same hour in one year? . . . Undoubtedly, very far away from this small Sardinian town . . . Where? and on that day will I still be among the living? . . .

CAGLIARI, JANUARY 9, 1900,
ABOUT FIVE O'CLOCK IN THE EVENING

Impressions, Public Garden.

A tormented landscape, hills with rough contours, reddish or gray, deep potholes, cavalcades of sea pines and gray mournful Barbary fig trees. Luxuriant greenery almost disconcerting in the middle of winter. Immobile and dead salty lagoons, their surfaces the color of gray lead like the chott of the Desert.

Then, a city's silhouette all the way at the top, scaling the furrowed steep hill . . . Old ramparts, old square crenellated tower, geometric silhouettes of flat roofs, all of it a uniform white, turned brown and outlined against an indigo sky.

Almost completely at the top are more and more greenery and trees with unchanging foliage. Barracks altogether similar to those of Algeria: long, low, covered in red tiles, with peeling and rundown walls, also browned by the sun like everything else.

Walls washed in glowing pink or in blood red or in sky blue like the

Arab houses . . . Dark old churches filled with sculptures and marble mosaics, luxurious in this country of sordid misery. Vaulted passageways where footsteps harshly resonate, awakening sonorous echoes. Small tangled streets climbing then descending, sometimes cut into by gray stone staircases; and because of the absence of haulage in the upper part of the city, the small sharp cobblestones are covered with delicate wilted grasses of a green, almost-yellow color.

Doors opening into large cellars down below, where poverty-stricken families rest in age-old shadows and humidity. Others stay in vaulted vestibules and sit on earthenware steps.

Shops with small displays in loud colors, narrow and smoky oriental stalls, out of which come nasal and drawling voices . . .

Here and there a young man leaning against a wall using gestures to converse with a young woman leaning over her balcony . . .

Peasants with long headbands that drop down their backs, wearing a wrinkled black jacket folded above white plain-woven cotton pants. Bearded tanned faces, deeply sunken eyes beneath thick eyebrows, distrustful wild faces resembling the Greek mountain dwellers and the Kabyle in their odd mix of facial features.

The women with their Arabic beauty, their large, black, languorous, and pensive eyes . . . Resigned and sad expressions of poor fearful beasts.

Whining, obsequious beggars attacking the foreigner, following and harassing him wherever he goes . . . Infinitely sad songs or refrains becoming a sort of strangely agonizing obsession, cantilenas that one cannot distinguish from those down there in Africa. At each step, everything here reminds me of and makes me miss more intensely that Africa.

CAGLIARI, THURSDAY, JANUARY 18, 1900,
FIVE THIRTY IN THE EVENING

Since I've been here in the dulling calmness of this life, which chance— or rather destiny—has suddenly put on my adventurous path, strangely enough, memories of the Villa Neuve are haunting my mind more and more . . . the good as well as the bad . . . I say the good, for one mustn't be unfair—now that everything is certainly over and certainly dead—to the pathetic place . . . I mustn't forget that it sheltered Mama's goodness and gentleness and Vava's good—though never fulfilled—intentions . . . and especially the whole chaotic world of my own dreams. No, no curse for that long-ago life. What blessed hours didn't I know, in spite of all, in spite of the captivity, the problems, and the injustices! Since I left forever that house where everything went out, where everything was dead before falling definitively into ruins, my life has been nothing more than a rapid dazzling dream through disparate countries, under different names, with different appearances.

And I know very well that this calmer winter spent here is only a pause in that existence that must remain mine all the way to the end.

Afterward, in a few days, the true wandering and incoherent life will begin again. Where? How? Only God knows! I can't even dare to make suppositions and hypotheses about that any longer—at the moment when I was resolving to stay months and months more in Paris, I found myself in Cagliari, in this lost corner of the world, which I'd never thought any more about than any other, taken note of by my distracted eye on the map of the inhabited world.

After that, suppositions and hypotheses were over.

There is, however, one thing that makes me rejoice: as I move further away from the past's limbo, my character is forming and establishing itself just as I had wished. What is developing in me is the most unrelenting and invincible energy and honesty of the heart. These are two qualities that I value more than all others and that, alas, are so rare in a woman.

With that and most probably four months of desert life for this spring, I am sure to become someone . . . and also because of this, to sooner or later reach my life's sacred goal: vengeance! Vava always recommended that I never forget the task Mama handed down to him, to Augustine, and to me . . . Vava is dead; Augustine was not born for that at all, and he has forever committed himself to life's beaten paths . . . I'm the only one remaining.

Fortunately, all my past life and all my adolescence have contributed to making me understand that peaceful happiness is not at all made for me. And that, solitary among men, I am destined to fight a determined battle against them, that I am, if you wish, the scapegoat of all the iniquity and misfortunes that hastened these three beings to their end: Mama, Wladimir, and Vava.

And now I have begun my role. I love it better than all egotistical happiness, and I will sacrifice to it everything that is dear to me. That goal will always be my point of direction throughout life.

I have given up on having a corner for myself in this world, a *home*, a hearth, peace, fortune. I have put on the sometimes very heavy livery of the vagabond and the stateless person. I have given up on the happiness of returning home, of finding loved ones, rest, and security.

For the time being, I have the illusion—in this temporary home in Cagliari, where I again find myself with a sweet sensation—of seeing a being whom I truly love and whose presence has imperceptibly become one of the conditions of well-being . . . Only, that dream, too, will be short: afterward, for difficult and perilous peregrinations, it will be necessary to become alone again and to abandon the sleepy tranquility of the couple's life.

But this must be, and it will be. And in the darkness of such a life, there will at least be the consolation of knowing that, if only at my return, I will still perhaps find a friend, a living being who will be happy to see me again . . . or at least content . . . Only, there is this terrible thing: a long enough separation can result in encounters . . . And perhaps I will one day find my place taken. This is even very probable, given his ideas on women and marriage. It would be very odd if he never met the companion who would share these ideas, so much the opposite of mine. Oh, I know well that, while he is a wanderer and in exile, that companion will not be found unless he contents himself with knowing that somewhere in the world, a wife—if she loves him—will tremble for him during times of danger, from far way, herself safe and warm.

As for the one *who*, like me, would be there precisely during the bad hours and whom nothing will stop, he will not find that woman.

But afterward, when that transitory period has gone by, he will be seized by the nostalgia for domestic life and rest, just like Augustine and everyone.

On that day, I will be able to begin again my race through the world with the sad certitude of always finding inexorably empty the hotel room, the gourbi, or the tent that will serve as a temporary refuge in my nomad's existence. ❥ *Mektoub!*[2]

Let us enjoy the passing moment and the intoxication that will soon be dissipated . . . The same flower does not bloom twice, and the same water does not bathe twice the bed of the same stream.

Why not have confidence in this friend? Why judge him before seeing him in action, and why, especially, attribute to him ideas about marriage and domestic rest that he doesn't have?

His life will always be a life of battle for noble ideas among others; in all cases he will always be the soldier of Islam's Holy Cause—he will always be standing like a rock amid the ruins of his compatriots' decadence.

No, he will never marry. Nevertheless, his happiness will be to rest his exile's head on the breast of a true friend.

His happiness will be having a heart that will beat in unison with his and having affection and a tender soul in whom he will confide his pains and his joys. This woman friend, this heart, this soul—he believes he has found them in you. Then why doubt?

"Why does human life not finish as do Africa's autumns, with a clear sky and warm winds, without decay or foreboding?" (Eugène Fromentin, *Une année dans le Sahel*).

Note written in Cagliari, January 1, 1900, during a moment of infinite sadness and without true motives.

CAGLIARI, JANUARY 29, 1900

O wherefore in such haste
For the dread day to break?
. . . .
My hour doth fly away,
My kisses gladly take!

giovanni prati

2. The words and phrases translated from Arabic are preceded by the symbol ❥; and those translated from Russian, by †, according to René-Louis Doyon's edition.

The brief dream of peaceful contemplation—under a softly pensive and clement sky in the old Sardinian city in the heart of this very African countryside—is over.

Tomorrow at the same hour, I will already be far away from Cagliari's boulders, out there on the gray sea that has been rumbling and unfurling for days and days . . .

Tonight Cagliari's echoes were full of the sound of rumbling thunder . . . Today the sea is at its most sinister; it has dull and pale reflections. Everything is over here, and tomorrow I am going to leave to begin again the sinister battle, the determined continuing battle over a tomb that has been closed for eight long months, over an abolished life returned to its original mystery . . .

And this evening as the grayish night falls in our dear desolate hut, devastated and handed over to departure's disorder, I feel the profound sadness that accompanies changes in one's existence, the successive annihilations that lead us, imperceptibly, to the definitive annihilation.

And what will be this new epoch of my life?

The thirtieth, four thirty in the early evening. Mektoub has delayed my departure by a few hours. But the horizon has also darkened.

GENEVA, SUNDAY, MAY 27, 1900,
NINE THIRTY IN THE EVENING

Here, once again, I am dating this sad daily entry in this cursed city where I suffered so much, which almost cost me my life.

I've been here for barely one week, and I feel the morbid oppression of times past. And I wish to leave here forever.

Under the low, cloudy sky, I again saw the unlucky residence—closed, mute, lost in the wild grasses as if plunged into a morose and funereal dream.

I again saw the road, the white road, as white as a river of dull silver, straight as an arrow, leaving for the great melancholy Jura, between the tall velvety trees.

I again saw the two tombs in the incomparable background of this cemetery in the land of exile, so far from the other sacred hill of eternal rest and immutable silence . . .

And I feel absolutely foreign, and forever so, on this land that I will leave tomorrow and where I hope never to return.

This evening, unfathomable, inexpressible sadness and more and more absolute resignation in face of inescapable Destiny . . .

What dreams, what enchantments, and what intoxications does the future still hold for me?

What very problematic joys, and what certain pains?

And when will the hour of deliverance, the hour of definitive rest, finally ring?

PARIS, APRIL 1900

One evening, saw—in the indistinct light of the stars and street lamps— the white silhouettes of the crosses of Montparnasse's cemetery, outlined like ghosts against the tall trees' velvety blackness . . . And thought that the entire powerful breath of Paris, roaring in the vicinity, did not succeed at all in troubling the ineffable sleep of the unknown sleeping there . . .

Second Daily Journal

In the name of God the powerful and merciful!

We have no cause to weep for you.
Although you died on earth, you are reborn above.

TORQUATO TASSO, *Gerussaleme Liberta*

Peace to your ashes, to those lying down over there in
the distant foreign earth, and to you resting on the
sacred hill above the blue Mediterranean's eternal ebb.

EPITAPH written down from a grave in Vernier's
small cemetery, June 4, 1899, during my last
pilgrimage to Vava's grave on the day I left Geneva.

> † *"It is not I who write; my hand is*
> *guided by you who love me, and*
> *each discordant sound would have*
> *tortured you in your state of rest."*
> *And everything was once again*
> *as in days past . . .*

PIERRE LOTI, *Le mariage de Loti*

Returning from the Vernier cemetery. Infinite sadness.

The mind falls asleep as it gets used to travels; one gets used to
everything, to the most remarkable exotic sites, as to the most

extraordinary faces. However, during certain hours when the mind awakens and again finds itself, one is suddenly struck by the strangeness of everything surrounding one.

L O T I, Le mariage de Loti

The funerary hill over there above the great blue gulf of the unforgettable Annaba should sleep today beneath the burning light of summer's ending days in Africa . . . The tombs of white marble or of multicolored earthenware should seem to be so many flowers bursting among the tall black cypresses, the creeping vine, the blood-colored flowers or paling flesh of giant geraniums, and the *keram* of this Barbary Coast country.

And I, during this moment, returned here for a very short time on the land of exile; I was sitting on the short grass of another cemetery . . . Across from the two gray tombstones where spring's wild grasses have grown, I thought of the other, of the white Muslim tombstone where † *the White Spirit* rests . . . And I thought, once again, about the great mystery of annihilated lives in the heart of immutable Nature . . . The innocent and peaceful birds were singing above the countless amounts of human dust accumulated there.

A very remarkable thing: my *Daily Journals*, all the notes I've taken up until now, could be summed up in these few words, so few in number, so simple: "endlessly repeated observations of the unfathomable sadness in the core of my soul, in my life's core; more and more vague allusions, not to encountered beings or to observed facts, but only to always sad and gloomy impressions that these beings and facts produce in me."

A useless and mournful notation of despairing monotony.

The notes of joy, and even of hope, are absolutely lacking.

The only consoling thing that can be discovered there is the growing Islamic *resignation* . . .

In my soul, I'm *finally* noticing the beginning of *indifference* toward things and *indifferent* beings. This is the more powerful affirmation of my ego.

I find the importance too long attributed to miserable things, to useless and insignificant encounters, low and unworthy of myself . . .

Even the finding—completed this evening—of my *radical inaptitude to be part of some coterie, to be comfortable among beings* united not by passing chance but by a common life, even fate's sanction, felt for a long time, and which fatally condemns me to solitude . . . even that which would have made me cruelly suffer before, does not distress me.[1]

Besides, is it really a bad thing? Is it not fate's teaching that, from all points of view, seems to want my soul to grow in solitude and pain?

". . . But adversity is the touchstone of souls, and those who have not suffered are incapable of doing great things."

For the time being, at least my desiderata are clear to me: I would like the one who wrote the few words quoted above, the one who, more directly, said them to me in person during my last days in Paris—the day of my last confession—to understand what I said to him and what I wrote to him . . . and then I would like him to give me, as quickly as possible, the opportunity to act, to do these *great things*, which seem to profoundly and deliciously intoxicate him as they do me . . .

I would like to see that man smile at me as only he knows how to, and to hear him say to me, in that tone of voice used on the day that I almost opened my heart to him, "Go, Mahmoud, accomplish great and beautiful things . . . Be a hero . . ."

The strange thing is that all those lilting words of Faith and Glory do not ring, have never rung, falsely to my trained ear, in this intellectual's mouth—the only one in whom I've never found dissembling hypocrisy or lack of understanding.

Certainly, from among all of those whom I've met on my path, that one whose dear image is before me is the most beautiful: he speaks to the soul and not to the senses, he exalts what is great and spurns what is base and vile . . . Certainly, no one has ever had such a powerful influence on my soul, *for the better*. No one has ever known how to understand and comfort those blessed things that were germinating in me, slowly but surely, since the death of † *the White Spirit*: faith, repentance, the desire for moral improvement, the desire for nobly *deserved* glory,

1. Eberhardt's note, penciled in the margin: "Today, after four years of suffering, still much less. Algiers, April 8, 1904."

selflessness, the shameful voluptuous pleasure of my suffering and my renouncement, and the thirst for great and beautiful actions.

I judge and love him such as I've known him up until now. The future will tell me if I've been clairvoyant, if I've understood him such as he really is, or if, once again, I've made a mistake. I assert nothing, but nothing has, up to the present, created the slightest suspicion. And yet my distrust is terrible and invincible, especially since Samuel. The *naïb* affair could be the touchstone of this soul. I'm sure that what he will do, he will do out of his own thought, without allowing himself to be influenced either by Abd-el-Aziz or by anyone else. Based on what he will do on this occasion, I will probably be able to acquire the so-searched-for *certitude*.

Thus, I am waiting in all conscience for the events, so as to pronounce my judgment on this man . . . If I have not taken the wrong road, I have many chances for *moral* salvation.

On the contrary, if he too is nothing but dissimulation and pretense, it will be impossible, from now on, for me to believe in anyone among the men I will meet in the future.

It will be over—and good riddance, if what I consider pureness itself hides a stain, if what seems to me to be true beauty conceals hideousness so many times encountered. What if the light that I take for that beneficial light of an indicator star or a lighthouse in life's dark maze is nothing but a deceitful game destined to lead the traveler astray, into fatal errors—what will I have to still wait for?

But once again, up until now, nothing, absolutely nothing speaks in favor of this cruel hypothesis . . . What I believe is that it will perhaps cause me great but beautiful sufferings . . . he will perhaps be the one to send me to my death, but he will not bring about the supreme resentment of disillusionment.

GENEVA, JUNE 15, 1900

Stand ye in the ways, and see, and ask for the old paths, where [is] the good way, and walk therein, and ye shall find rest for your souls.

JEREMIAH 6:16 (King James Version)

I am still in the grayness of present time, still a dream, still a new intoxication . . .

How long will it last? When will the toll sound? How will tomorrow be? However, the memory of these few *better* and more *lively* days will remain forever dear to me, for here again are a few moments torn from life's appalling ordinariness, a few hours saved from nothingness.

I will always feel attracted only to souls suffering from the elevated and fruitful suffering called dissatisfaction with oneself, thirst for the Ideal, for the mystic and desirable thing that must set our souls afire, raise them to the sublime spheres of the realm beyond . . . Never will serenity of the goal reached attract me; and for me, the truly superior beings of the world—such as it is these days—are those who suffer the sublime pain of perpetually giving birth to a better self.

I hate the person who is satisfied with himself and his fate, with his spirit and his heart.

I hate the idiotic jabbering of the *deaf, mute, and blind* bourgeois *who will not retrace his steps* . . .

You have to learn to *think*. It is painful, it is long, but without that, nothing can be expected from the point of view of individual happiness, this happiness that, for such beings, cannot come from anywhere but a *special world*, a closed world that should make us live and suffice.

It is impossible to say how much I despise and hate myself for this inept character trait: the need to see people, even indifferent ones, the need to prostitute my heart and soul through loathsome explanations.

Why, instead of looking in myself for the satisfactions needed by my soul, do I go and look for them in others, where I am sure not to find them?

Oh! Will I not be able to react against that, to rid myself of this useless jumble still entangling my life? Except for with very few beings, intellectual communion is impossible. Why then voluntarily look for disillusions?

Of all the beings who are not at all in agreement with me about important matters such as faith, love, etc., etc., there are two whom I am incapable of not loving from the bottom of my heart, toward whom I cannot feel indifferent: my brother and Véra.

And I truly am suffering from what the latter, for example, does not understand about what just happened, from what she doesn't believe I am swearing to her—that the memory of these few days of intimacy with Archavir, days followed, as he said yesterday, by a lifelong friendship, from nearby or afar, will remain among the dearest memories of my life.

IDEAS ABOUT LITERATURE

To begin with, it seems to me that it is urgent to nurture the artistic side, the side of *form* above all. *Rakhil*—a defense in favor of the Koran against the modern Muslim world's prejudices(—will not be of interest). *Rakhil*, a song of eternal love, beautiful in its form, lilting in its phrases, and glistening in its images, will intoxicate many voluptuous souls or simply those enamored by art, which, all in all, comes to the same thing.

A striking image of all that has become of, of all that will probably always be my life—the sign there, *Room For Rent*, at the window of this miserable room where I live between a cot and papers and my few books. It's ironic, and it's sad.[2]

Nothing in my chance lodgings could express more clearly my profound solitude, my absolute abandonment in the middle of the vast universe . . .

What hours of discouragement, of heavy, bleak sadness!

GENEVA, JUNE 16, 1900

Next day, three o'clock in the morning.

After a night of suffering, a strange morning . . .

I see that I cannot write at this moment.

I will note only the situation's word: desire, purely intellectual, to modify my condition for the better, to work only halfheartedly, neither for one nor for the other . . . Grayness.

2. Eberhardt's note in margin: "Prophecy, Algiers, April 8, 1904."

꙰ *Ugh! for life and for days—for it was created for pain;*
Worries are not interrupted for a moment—neither for an earthly king
    nor for a slave.
What a surprise for life and for what is related to it!
Here is a female enemy of men who is loved by them!
I left you, and my heart does not cease being near to you;
And life's sweetness, after your departure, has become bitterness;
And the screen of separation has been placed between me and you,
As the tomb is placed between the living and the dead!

And all of a sudden here is a spahi who—in the middle of all this overflow of rowdy madness—lifts a glass of champagne and makes this unexpected toast: For those who have fallen in Mecké and in Bobdiarah! (Pierre Loti, Roman d'un Spahi). This toast, which the author of this story did not invent, is very strange . . . This toast to health is very unexpected! Tribute to memory or sacrilegious joke addressed to the dead? . . . The spahi who had made this funereal toast was very drunk, and his roaming eye was dark.

The same day.

The day before yesterday, I wrote these words: *in a ksour of the far-off Oued Igharghar.* I suddenly felt bursting forth and strengthened in me, the resolve to leave for Ouargla, whatever the cost. I was determined to try once again to sequester myself in the great silence of the Desert and become accustomed to its slow, dreamy life.[3]

All in all, nothing is against it.

If need be, I'll go without letters of introduction from Abd-el-Aziz. My meager income will allow me anyway to live there as well as can be, as well as it is desirable to live.

---

3. Eberhardt's note in margin: "In memory of that fateful date, June 19, 1900. And here is how unconsciously, by certain inspiration, my fate was decided, how, all of a sudden, bursting forth from the darkness of my soul, there then appeared to me the path to follow, the one that would lead, months later, to the Bir-Azélir garden, to Slimène, to my entry into the khouan, to Behima, and to salvation. Marseille, Tuesday, July 23, 1901, eleven thirty at night."

Strange thing is I haven't at all forgotten everything I suffered there, the incredible deprivations, the illness . . .

And yet it will only be the fault of adverse circumstances. And now that outcome gives me great pleasure.

That harsh life of the Desert, a little less tiring because I will not have to stay up at night, will complete my education as a man of action, this Spartan education that is an indispensable weapon in my position . . .

. . . And what bitter sensual delights: first of all, the adieus here, farewells to Véra, whom I love with all my heart, who is the most humane being one could ever meet, to that strange Archavir, who gives me remarkable hours, simultaneously infinitely bitter and sweet . . .

Then, in Marseille, the solemn scene of embarkment and the farewells to the brother who makes me live in this world . . .

Then, the sad and sweet Annaba pilgrimage . . . the sacred hill where her tomb is . . .

Then, Batna, where so many memories bring on nostalgia . . .

Scorching Biskra, where, long ago, I spent such charming hours in the evening in front of the Moorish cafés . . .

And the difficult and blazing road of the arid Oued Rir' . . .

And sad Touggourt, asleep under its sand shroud, above its dark chott . . .

Then, this unknown Ouargla at the entrance to the mysterious void of the great Sahara, to the valley of the Oued Igharghar with its strange name that used to make us dream long ago . . .

"Friends are like dogs: things always end badly, and the best is not to have any" (Loti, *Aziyadé*).

In memory of the Souk-el-Haljémine and Elassar of Tunis: "To be a boatman dressed in a gilded jacket somewhere in the south of Turkey, there where the sky is always pure and the sun always hot . . . After all, it would be possible, and I would be less unhappy there than elsewhere" (Loti, *Aziyadé*).

GENEVA, MONDAY, JUNE 25, 1900

"June 15—The more we go, the more we can play the world's tiring comedy—out of politeness—which everyone plays so naturally and without any effort, etc." (Edmond de Goncourt and Jules de Goncourt, *Journal des Goncourt*, Tome I, pp. 194–95).

————————————

GENEVA, WEDNESDAY, JUNE 27, 1900

After an interesting discussion with Véra, I feel, once again, but with even more burning intensity, the necessity to work—enormously—the almost-uncultivated, almost-fallow field of my intelligence, much further behind than that of my soul.

It is an overwhelming task to develop this intelligence, especially now. But it seems to me that the fruits of this work would be so surprising that I would be the first to be stupefied. Here is this moment's dream . . . will it ever be carried out?

To go down there to Ouargla, to the Sahara, the threshold of the great ocean of mystery, and to settle myself there, *to set up home, this home that I miss more and more.*[4] A little *tob* house in the shade of date trees. A few crops in the oasis, Ahmed for servant and companion, a few fine people to warm my heart, maybe a horse—a dream, this with time, and some books.

To live a double existence, the often adventurous one of the Desert and the calm sweet one of thought, far from everything that could trouble it.[5]

To sometimes come from down there to be near Augustine, to go to Paris . . . Paris, return to this silent Thebes . . .

To create a soul, a conscience, an intelligence, a will.

There will certainly be accomplished in me a marvelous flowering of this Islamic faith, which I need so much and which is fading here . . .

In principle, an attainable dream . . . will it be attained? *That is the question!*

One day perhaps, this notebook will replace an entire library, an

4. Eberhardt's note in margin: "Another prophecy whose meaning I don't understand. March 28/VIII 1901."

5. Eberhardt's note in margin: "This dream was fulfilled beyond all hope and was crowned seven months later in Behima, March 23/VII 1901."

entire crowd of books now inaccessible to me in my wandering and henceforth sad life.

For the person who will some day, by chance, take the trouble to read it, it would also be a faithful mirror of the more and more rapid process of my development, maybe already almost definitive . . .

The quotations themselves, found here at each step, depict the different moods that I'm going through . . .

What an interesting personality Saadi-Ganéline has, representing the life of the bohemian intellectual worker and vagabond, so often dreamed of . . .

"Eyes that seem like the evening's eyes" (Goncourt and Goncourt, *Journal des Goncourt*, II).

SATURDAY, JUNE 30, 1900

Noted eight o'clock in the evening.

After two days of deadly boredom and physical suffering (yesterday and today), I'm trying to get back to work . . .

I feel more and more disgust for this second self, a morally disorganized lout who makes his appearance from time to time. A curious thing to notice: that character generally appears, if not always (something to be observed later), under the influence of purely physical agents. Thus a state of improved health would produce a noticeable change for the better in my intellectual and moral life . . .

. . . The night before last, a long discussion between Archavir and me, of our eternal topic of sensual pleasure. I uphold my theory: diminish one's needs and thus avoid disillusions as much as possible and also the dulling of sensitivity through disagreeable sensations and the souring of one's character.

In contrast, Archavir upholds the idea that one must develop one's needs, then, with one's last bit of energy, work at assuaging them. In that he sees † *the proof of self-perfection.*

At this moment, the idea came to me to write a dissertation on this subject. It could be published in the *Athénée.*

The day before yesterday, during a conversation with Véra, I found the means of pulling myself out of the imbroglio that made the execution of *Rakhil* almost impossible.

In short, I am again going through a period of intellectual incubation that I believe will be the most fruitful of my life up to this day.

Reading the *Journal des Goncourt* did me the greatest good. I will have to take advantage of my stay in Marseille in order to read and make note of the other volumes.

Up until the present, I've looked for readings that make one dream and feel. From this comes the overdevelopment of my poetic sense to the detriment of pure thought.

The *Journal des Goncourt* is a book that makes one think *deeply*. Look for other similar readings and profit from my stay here to speak and discuss, as long as there is still society around me . . .[6]

Why *is* the very clear consciousness of the absolute *uselessness* of certain acts in my life—how numerous, alas!—of their *ineptitude*, and of the *real danger* they present from the point of view of my future, not powerful enough to react against my will and curb the execution of its acts?

This is a question to study in order to know how to set it right.

"Now, there is nothing more in our life than one great interest: *the emotion of the study of truth*." Without that, boredom and emptiness . . . (Goncourt and Goncourt, *Journal des Goncourt*, II).

Noted the same evening.

A remarkable thing that I feel more and more when writing: the more I develop, the more I finish my subject, the more it *bores me*, and hence these so discouraging doubts about the interest it could present to the reader.

Thus, without exaggerating, I no longer know if *Rakhil* is no more than a loathsome agglomeration of badly written police documents.

From this comes the need to read to someone else, to *objectify* . . . If my book produced the impression on the ensemble of readers that it

6. Eberhardt's note in margin: "Great improvement in that. March 23/VII 1901."

is now producing on me, then certainly no one would read beyond the second page after the prologue: a pure work of art.

... This evening things are peaceful in spite of the idiotic noise of the vulgar boulevard ...

A pale-blue sky, slightly azure, opaline, with light thick gray clouds. Grayness in the sky and grayness over the Salève ... Grayish mists over things in perfect agreement with the soft grayness of my present state of mind: no excessive emotionalism, no enthusiasm at all. Peaceful desire to work, to develop my intelligence.

One mustn't attribute this egoism of the self, bursting forth from each page of this book, to megalomania ... No ... Solitary person's habit, accustomed to looking endlessly into himself, first of all; then, necessity of creating a book that is later able to give me a true image of my soul today; the only means with which to judge my present life and to see, later on, if my individuality is truly progressing or not ...

The same evening, after reading Nadson.

† *Today I feel particularly weary.*
From the morning on, a gnawing irritation grew in me;
From the morning on, I noticed around me with meanness
Everything capable of arousing scorn in my soul.
In others' gaiety I found vulgarity;
In their sadness, hypocrisy; in their composure, faintheartedness,
And in my own heart, the weakening of the best strengths,
An oppressive anguish and childish disgust!

Noted in Geneva, July 3, 1900.

How many days have I not spent like that, these mournful days when all my faculties seem accessible only to disagreeable and painful sensations!

Eleven thirty in the evening.

† *What good are these tears? Is it to pity her*
With an insanely persistent pain?
Oh, if only we could all die this way
With a soul as pure?

If all of us were to say adieu to the earth
With the same serene hope?
Beyond the coffin there waits for us, not at all eternal sleep
But the world of wonderful goodness.

. . . The idea has come to me to write a short story, the counterpart of "La Voie" ("The Route"), but with very different types: Séméonow, Andréyew, Sacha in Paris.

Same night, two o'clock in the morning.

I'm not sleeping. No desire at all to sleep. Downstairs the piercing cries of a Russian woman giving birth ring out . . . a sinister entrance into this world, honestly, on a rainy night, in the midst of the mother's lugubrious cries . . . a sinister entrance and, who knows? maybe *symbolic.*

The first act of life . . . to cry . . . And since our arrival resembles our departure, with the only difference that, all in all, the departure is much less sad than the arrival followed by so much boredom and suffering!

"Weep ye not for the dead, neither bemoan him: but weep sore for him that goeth away: for he shall return no more, nor see his native country" Jeremiah 22:10 (King James Version).

"Seeest thou a wise man in his own conceit? There is more hope of a fool than of him" Proverbs 26:12 (King James Version).

"Boast not thyself of tomorrow; for thou knowest not what a day may bring forth" Proverbs 27:1 (King James Version).

July 4, 1900, midnight.

"... and in our obscure life there is also *its* happiness, and *its* pride ..."
(Ivan Tourguenieff, *The Night Before*).[7] † *Yes, there is some ... Bitter, bitter happiness, and somber. Pride of renouncement; they are not accessible to all, and he who has been forgotten by life's feasts and has not experienced them, must perish.*

JULY 11, 1900

Nine o'clock in the evening.

Written after a few horrible days of worries, quarrels, painful explanations, frights, and disillusion ...

Written in bed, here on this camp bed in front of the open window on an opaline evening reminding me, with an extremely sweet intensity, of nights long ago in Africa.

Oh unforgettable glamour of summer's twilights on the white cities and the dead expanses of Africa.

Soon, if it pleases Allah, I will find all of that again, far from men and their baseness, their cruelty and especially their monstrous egoism.

Until when will my soul finally find peace?

But I know *where* I will find it and at what price!

Two o'clock in the morning.

† *Every day of our lives flees away rapidly like waves.*
Our path to the tomb becomes shorter each hour.
Pour, thus, comrade, the cup of health.
How do we know what remains ahead?
You will die; you will be buried; you will no longer rise for the
  feast of friends.
Give me your hand, comrade; let us drink! (repeat)
Let us drown ourselves in the wine of bitter separation! (repeat)

7. Doyon's note: A page from Tourguenieff's *The Night Before* follows. This sentence is commented on in Russian by Isabelle.

In memory of life in Geneva, June–July 1904, in the company of Chouchinka, Yasbka, Pop, Tchork and Ganta:

⤎ *I left you, and my heart does not cease to be near to you;*
And life's sweetness, after your departure, has become bitterness;
And the screen of separation has been placed between me and you,
As the tomb is placed between the living and the dead!

GENEVA, NIGHT OF JULY 13, 1900

† In love, there is no rest; in science, there is no rest; whatever you undertake, there is no rest. I wish for no one to be as pitiful and unhappy as me. It's because of this that I have a confusedly pleasant feeling when you said to me: My shadow will follow you everywhere . . .

We met each other by accident on life's path; both of us are solitary beings in a populated universe; both of us unhappy and disorganized. We have spent a few marvelous minutes together, far, far from men . . . The end has arrived, and men have separated us for always . . . We have taken a moment from destiny's cruel stepmother . . . And I regret nothing.

DEPARTURE FROM GENEVA, JULY 14, 1900,
SEVEN THIRTY IN THE EVENING

Gray, stormy, somber weather. Infinite sadness at leaving Piatnouchko and Chouchinka. Where am I going? . . . *In Destiny's path!*

And Archavir, Archavir whom I never did see again?

Yesterday at midnight, wandered like a shadow in front of the white house on Arquebuse Street where I must no longer return . . .

JULY 15, 1900,
FIVE O'CLOCK IN THE MORNING

Arrived in Marseille. Glorious sunrise over the plain of Crau.

Impression of Africa. Good arrival.

An idea that comes to me while reading this sentence in the *Journal des Goncourt*: "finished *Manette Salomon* today." No work of literature is ever finished, to the point of no longer being able to continue it or, even more often, to improve it. The finished product is what is satisfying, a bit like the permission to check out of a hospital given to a sick person who has been fixed up enough to be able to start living again as well as can be . . .

In spite of all the disorder, all the discouragement of the last days in Geneva, this month of Russian life—undoubtedly the last of my life—will remain among my most cherished memories.

In any case, I have never lived with someone loved, in such a similar intimacy, as that which existed between me, Véra, Chouchka, and Ga Hahn.

This sad short novel with Archavir also had its great charm. In spite of everything, I am separating from him without a grudge or resentment.

† *In those people, there was no vulgarity.*

That is all of the situation's difficulty.

"Meanness in love, be it physical or moral meanness, is the sign of Societies' end" (Goncourt and Goncourt, *Journal des Goncourt*, III).

The day before yesterday, during an early twilight of a stormy day, beneath a gray and heavy sky, I left Geneva.

Sad, slow, especially intense impressions at the thought of the undoubtedly eternal separation from Véra and Chouchka.

Archavir leaves me a very sweet memory, a bit mysterious as is his strange nature, as was our strange novel.

This man, having escaped from the ridiculous and the vulgar, leaves me a very pure sensation without a stain. Russian life does not vulgarize the Oriental soul, whereas the French influence creates puny runts like Abd-el-Aziz or monsters like Aly, the one plunged in coarse vulgarity, the other in the vulgarity of the so-called chic Westerners, still badly copied.

From the Armenian, Archavir has a dreamy, dark, violent, and poetic nature. From the Russian student, he acquired the indefinable style that I love, that is so agreeable to me, so familiar.

I don't know if I'll do it, but I would like to draw up a reasoned and systematic report on my stay in Geneva.

If the inspiration comes, I'll do it. It would be a very useful and very interesting work.

While on this subject, I don't remember having ever worked other than out of obligation, and especially out of inspiration. I never work in order to flee boredom, for then the work would not succeed. I often read, and then boredom, like the dark anguish of bad nights, almost always passes by.

The present goal always remains the same: intellectual and moral perfecting. From the intellectual point of view, this work is perhaps more overdue, but much easier.

I thought last night and today of going to join Chouchka in Bulgaria.[8]

But no: it would only be in order to perpetuate, to make to live again the epoch that has just ended. And it's time to finally understand that *one cannot make to last that which is finished, nor resuscitate that which is dead. Nothing that has been will ever begin again.*[9]

I returned to Geneva to take up again the life of my first stay. Did I find it again?

Far from it! I buried it. So I will probably go to Ouargla.[10]

Only I'm starting to fear that the crushing heat will overwhelm me, from the point of view of work. Yet here, it appears to be forty degrees today, and I don't feel at all more exhausted than I ordinarily do.[11]

Not only for work, but again as a hygienic measure, it's imperative

8. Eberhardt's note in margin: "God wrote me nothing; he wrote for me: El Oued, Slimène, and to finish: Behima."

9. Eberhardt's note in margin: "Taking note of infinite sadness. March 12/ VII 1901."

10. Eberhardt's note in margin: "Up to this point, God has written nothing."

11. Translator's note: Forty degrees centigrade.

that I react against the involuntary languor produced by this summer Saharan climate.[12]

For the time being, I want to do two things here: continue *El-Mou-kadira* and finish reading the *Journal des Goncourt*.[13]

Yes, I'm starting to finally see the formation of what my whole life will be, even if success comes one day and crowns my literary efforts: somber enchantment, with black paintings, changing with fantastic rapidity, as well as the backgrounds . . . A crazy race in pursuit of the eternal Chimera more inaccessible for me than for any other.[14]

All of my life's dreams will certainly resemble those, more conscious, of these last days.

But, though it must fatally be thus, I would like to try my luck at a semblance of happiness, the only one, I believe, that can happen in my coarse and poor life: to create for myself, independently from everyone, far from everyone, a solitary nest to which I could always return and shroud the successive bereavements that still await me.

I'm going to try to create this nest there, at the heart of the Desert, far from men. For months, isolate myself, isolate *my soul* from all human contact. Especially, henceforth avoid shared lives with whoever it might be, embarrassing unions, and the mixing of my affairs, of my interests, with, of course, the opposing interests of others.[15] At least that will produce a much smaller dose of suffering.

I also must force myself to create an interior world of thoughts, of sensations that console my solitude, my poverty, and the absence of aesthetic pleasures, something that has become too costly in my present situation.[16]

12. Eberhardt's note in margin: "Blindness: no work could ever give me what was simply given to me by my presence in El Oued. March 23/VII 1901."

13. Doyon's note: Isabelle notes (Marseille, July 16, 1900) in German a thought of Nietzsche and a page by Kistemackers taken out of the *Heures suprêmes*: the Hour of Judgment; then in Russian, a long poem by Nadson.

14. Eberhardt's note in margin: "On the contrary, *more accessible to me*. March/VIII 1901."

15. Eberhardt's note in margin: "A few days later, Mektoub tied my entire life to Slimène's."

16. Eberhardt's note in margin: "To start with, faith, then my Art; that's enough, for these two things are fruitful and encompass the whole universe. March 12/VII 1901."

I must, at all costs, put into practice my theory of the possible diminution of needs.

That will hardly be difficult, if my health does not betray me.

Even there, with a sedentary—that is to say, fixed—existence, I'll be able to create an almost entirely hygienic life.

I'll be able to avoid the well-known causes of illness.

Mentally, it is now critical that I force myself to work.

It is not only a chance for me to be able to continue living—my meager means of existence now exhausted—but great protection against suffering.

I also must learn to devote myself to *the present hour*, to not live solely in the future, as I've done until now, which is a natural cause of suffering. To live in the past, in what it has that is good and beautiful, is a sort of seasoning of the present. But the perpetual waiting for "in a little while," "the day after," inevitably produces continual discontent that poisons life.

I must learn to feel *more deeply*, to see *better*, and especially, to *think* again and again.

JULY 17, 1900,
ABOUT THREE O'CLOCK IN THE EVENING

Finished writing *El-Moukadira*.

JULY 18, 1900, NINE O'CLOCK IN THE EVENING

For a man of talent or a genius, showing oneself is tantamount to diminishing oneself . . . The artist can take life levelheadedly; the writer must seize it in flight like a thief . . .

GONCOURT AND GONCOURT, *Journal des Goncourt*, III

So, it seems to be finally decided that I leave Saturday for the Africa that I left only nine months ago. My God, if only I were to find the courage, having arrived in Ouargla, to create this nest that I miss so much, this solitary owl's nest, and to stay there at least six months, and especially *to work* there.[17]

I will read my entire novel, *Rakhil*, this evening. What I am completely lacking in order to judge it is an *overall view*.

Now, for it to be completely finished as a story—not as a work of art—it's missing nothing but the entirely artistic scene of the Jewish women's stroll, a half hour of work.

Before any other thing, I must finish reading and annotating the *Journal des Goncourt*.

Then, note a few salient passages from other authors: some Baudelaire, some Zola, some Loti.

I also must, on the way, carefully note not only the *information*, but the impressions as well. From this crossing of the sea, then of Algeria's Tell, and of the Oued Rir, be able to make an interesting, picturesque voyage—the first thing to write down there.

Then, take note of everything in the oasis; start by visiting everything and making a detailed plan with notes as complete as possible. After, begin a *literary journal* of my stay there.

Along with this, I'll have to make the book *Rakhil* what it truly must be: a work of art.

I'll have to write, in Russian or for Russians, the account of my fall voyage in the Sahel, and a few † *short stories*.

It is a crushing amount of work on which salvation depends. After, when the Villa Neuve has been liquidated, if I have the means, I'll go to Paris, lead an entirely different life there than before, and throw myself into the determined battle to arrive with the baggage that I'll bring.[18]

This is the only reasonable plan that I can now establish.

If we head toward Morocco in the fall, naturally I'll follow the movement as I continue to take minutely detailed notes.

Yesterday, the seventeenth, at four in the afternoon, I went down through the Devilliers Square and on the omnibus to Fraternity Quay. Marseille appeared to me very colorful, in its true character.

17. Eberhardt's note in margin: "Reassuring observation up to a certain point: far from seeming to have gone by very fast, these nine months seem as lengthy as years. The more monotonous and sedentary life is, the more time would seem fleeting? *To be studied.*"

18. Eberhardt's note in margin: "Nothing is reasonable except for that which is written."

Stationed myself in the "Bar Idéal," where I wrote a heartfelt letter to Véra and Chouchinka.

Then, with Augustine, a long walk on foot, first to the Fort Saint Nicolas Bridge. Saw the bridge turned with the strength of men's arms, in order to let through a Greek sailboat, the Elnh. In the bow, a boss with a coarse-looking face, sleeves rolled up, wearing a felt hat, yelling out from moment to moment: *Vira, vira, vira!* to men laboring in the stern in the capstan in order to get the boat in.

Silhouettes of young swimmers in trunks, happy to be naked, wet, and in the sun, and adopting different poses.

Crossed the old port in a ferry beneath the Saint Jean Fort; passed by La Joliette Quay across from boats coming from Africa. Then went to see the coal.

Enormous black piles, black dust, black men in rags, their faces covered in soot, where their eyes are open and seem dirty white and their mouths are like a wound, where each spot of real skin bursts forth like hideous leprosy. A cabaret, also black, where a tanned owner, whose face looks like a pirate's, is arguing with a coal man who is visibly afraid. Return to the jetty. Aquamarine greenish horizon, sea somewhat agitated. Watched a net pulled out between two violently shaken small boats.

Lazaret Quay. A man we'd seen in the coal café who'd asked me for a light and who, already very drunk, was singing and making noise; we find him on the quay, perched on his cart, gesticulating, holding forth, and laughing in the middle of the crowd, under the benevolent smile and eyes of policemen who are probably waiting to arrest him . . . I don't know what for: the drunkard smashed a soldier's leg.

Went home at eight o'clock. Tired, intense headache, heartache. Good night.

MARSEILLE, FRIDAY, JULY 20, 1900,
TEN O'CLOCK IN THE EVENING

Everything is finished, wrapped, tied up . . . There's nothing there other than my camping bed, which will wait for morning.

Tomorrow, at one o'clock in the afternoon, I leave for Algiers.

All in all, I didn't believe very much in this departure for Ouargla. So many circumstances had already hindered me in carrying out my bold project.[19]

I'm leaving well equipped, so I have every chance for success. Emotionally, I feel great sadness every time I leave this house, like I do now, even though I am but a passing stranger.

What causes that?

I know that reading the *Journal des Goncourt* plays a large part in this rather somber sadness that I've felt for two days.

Unfortunately, with all this packing and all these errands, I haven't had the time to finish the reading. The volumes written by only Edmond don't have the same interest as those written by Jules . . . Perhaps attributable to the great blow suffered by Edmond because of his brother's death.

I don't feel in good shape to write about my own sensations. They're mournful.

But hope is reborn in me. I know that this feeling will pass as soon as I'm in Algiers, near my friend Eugène, and subject to new impressions.

In any case, I must work, I must write when I'm down there . . . My God, if I could find the energy to put my back into it and finish at least a part of everything I have to do! My God! If I'm not afflicted with problems, especially here, I'm sure to do something, to succeed.

Strange phenomenon: my stay in Geneva seems already to have moved away from me into a far-off voyage . . . The beloved silhouettes from over there seem to have been spirited away, to have become dream entities . . . Fortunately! And yet it was only one week ago . . .

But I feel forever attached to Véra and Chouchka by a much stronger bond than before.

As for Archavir . . . without understanding the causes of this impression, it seems that we will *find each other* again, as he said to me one evening . . .

Alas! The sad, pale, and incoherent beginning of today in these notes again resembles those of long ago.

19. Eberhardt's note in margin: "Ah! How I would like to leave, now, for far away, to an unknown country, but a country of Islam, of Africa, for a long time, March 12/VII, 1901."

I'm going to reread *Onward to the Blue Horizons*, to which I'll add the fruit of my notes, en route.

I mustn't spend too much time on Algiers . . . too well-known!

Shouldn't I even begin the Algerian trip with Bône and not Algiers? If there are sensations worth noting, transport them in the form of memories to another epoch. It would be a pretext for a few beautiful melancholy pages, genre African sketches.

With this trip, a book, a beautiful book will be quickly written and will maybe appear *before Rakhil*. Nevertheless, I'll have to work on *El-Moukadira*, no matter what, in order to bring it back finished.

Sometimes I become so pessimistic that the future becomes an object of irrational terror for me, as if it could be nothing but bad or threatening, whereas, on the contrary, many dark clouds have moved far away from our life's horizon: Samuel, the birth, etc.

All of that seems to corroborate the fact that, for the *two of us*, destiny is, all in all, inclement only for *small things*, and *temporarily*, if it pleases God! May it be thus in the future!

ALGIERS, JULY 22, 1900,
ELEVEN O'CLOCK IN THE EVENING

Yesterday, on a hot afternoon, I took off on the boat that had already carried me last September, but in such different circumstances![20] I followed Augustine's silhouette with my eyes until it disappeared after the boat had tacked. Then I began contemplating the scenery. The port, with powerful red-and-black silhouettes of transatlantic liners.

Then the city . . . At first, when the boat was in the middle of the harbor, Marseille appeared to me in a range of delicate grayness: the vaguely smoky sky's grayness, the mountains' bluish grayness, the pink grayness of the rooftops, the yellowness of the houses (glimmers) . . . , ocher-colored and burning glimmers of Endoume's boulders, Notre Dame's hill, chalky and blazing . . . the sea's lilac-and-silver grayness . . .

20. Eberhardt's note in margin: "July 21, 1900, one o'clock at night, departed Marseille on the *Eugène-Pereire*. July 22, arrived in Algiers three o'clock in the morning."

The boulders' hardy plants threw greenish-brown spots into all these grays . . . Only the plain trees' greenness, the cathedrals' golden cupolas, and the statue of the Virgin stood out in clear and vivid tones of color.

Then, when the boat had gotten farther away, everything changed; it was a uniformly golden color of unheard-of intensity . . .

Watched the sunset in gray purplish haze over a dark, severe, violet-tinted sea . . . Spent the night peacefully on a bench in the stern of the boat. True sensation of well-being; woke up at about two forty-five in the morning. The sea is a bit rough, and the lighthouses of the Balearic Islands are in view to our right . . . Waning moon.

Strange and indistinct sensation of mystery, but sweet . . .

Sunrise while the sailors set up the awning . . . Lilac-colored pink dawn, at first. The sea takes on a lilac color, silvery on the surface. Then the sun's disk in crimson, without rays, emerges from the middle of a violet-purple mist. Slightly above, delicate lacework of pink clouds edged with pale gold . . .

During the night, well-known feeling of mysterious well-being produced by the view of the ship's lights above my peaceful sleep.

Tomorrow morning I'll continue this account.

Oh blessed Impression of the *return*, felt this evening, to the solemn mosques, in the middle of the Arab *tabadji's* old humdrum routine on Jénina Street!

Oh remarkable intoxication, this evening, in the vast peace and half-light of the djemâa Djedid during the *icha* prayer!

I am once more reborn to life . . . ❧ *Lead us on the straight path, the path that those, to whom you have been generous, must follow!*

ALGIERS, JULY 23, 1900,
TEN THIRTY IN THE MORNING

For a long, long time, one could only see Matifou—plunged into a world of gray haze—from the Algerian coast.

Then Algiers's triangle with the snowy, white cascade of the old city . . . Finally, all the amazing panorama appears in full light.

After a very short stay in my room with Eugène, I went, alone, on a search. But my hat bothered me, cutting me off from Muslim life.

So I came back, and having put on my fez, I went out again with the servant Ahmed, first to the djemâa el-Kebira ... Impression of coolness and peace under the white and lacey arcades inside. Said hello to the *oukil* of the mosque, a venerable old man sitting in a side alcove and writing on his knee.

Nothing surprises him any longer. No displaced curiosity, no indiscretion ... Then went up to the charming, blue-colored zaouïya of Sid-Abd-errahmane with Mohammed, the head porter.

A stay across from the mihrab in its cool shade on thick rugs ... Drank water perfumed with jasmine from an earthenware water jug placed on the windowsill.

The zaouïya is an admirable pearl, and I will return there before leaving Algiers ...

Blue-tinged whiteness, pure in the green of Marengo Garden ...

Crossing the latter, smelled an indefinable fragrance, intoxicating and sweet, from what flowers, I don't know.

Had supper at El-Hadj-Mohammed's place, at the corner of Jénina Street. There, I *intensely* felt the joy of return, the joy of once again being there, on this African land to which I am attached not only by the best memories of my life, but also by this remarkable attraction, felt before I ever saw it, long ago at the monotonous Villa.

I was happy there at the table of that cheap restaurant ... Indefinable sensation not felt anywhere else but in Africa.

How the Arabs resemble each other!

Yesterday at Hadj-Mohammed's, I thought I saw men come in whom I knew long ago—in Bône, in Batna, or in the South—except in Tunisia where the racial type is completely different.

What is the cause of that? The lack of development of individuality or Islam's equalizing influence? No doubt both.

In the evening after dinner, went and prayed the icha in the djemâa Djedid, less beautiful than the two others, but where I felt a wonderful surge of Islam.

Entered the cool half-light hardly dissipated by a few oil lanterns.

Impression of old Islam, mysterious and calm.

Long stay near to the mihrab. Then behind us from far away arose a clear, high, fresh voice, a dream voice, making the response to the old imam standing in the mihrab and reciting the *Fatiha* in his quavering voice.

Then, standing in a line, we prayed, alternating two voices—intoxicating and solemn at the same time—one voice in front of us, broken and antiquated, but rising little by little, becoming strong and powerful; and the other voice bursting forth as if from above, in the mosque's far-off dark corners, in regular intervals like a radiant song of triumph and unwavering faith . . . announcing the coming inevitable victory of God and his Prophet . . . Felt an almost-ecstatic sentiment swelling my chest, bursting toward the celestial spheres from where the second voice seemed to come . . . in an accent of *melancholic, serene, sweet, and convinced happiness.*

Oh! to be lying on the rugs of some silent mosque, far from the stupid noise of the contaminated city, and with my eyes closed, the soul's eyes lifted toward the sky, to listen endlessly to Islam's song of triumph!

I remember, on this topic, the night last year when, after having wandered until the morning, looking for Aly and the poet, I had ended up in the Morkad ruins at the foot of the minaret whose windows were lit up . . . There, in the great dead silence of the Tunisian night, the *mueddine's* voice reached me, mysterious, infinitely serious, singing the calm and rhythmic song that still rings in my ears, the prayer: "Prayer is preferable to sleep."

After the delicious hour of the icha, went out wandering . . .

About ten o'clock, on my return, stop in a narrow street in front of a small shop lit by an oil lamp. A guitar, pipe stems, a cutout paper decoration . . .

In front of the shop, the merchant lying down on an oval-shaped mat, a brown-haired man, rather handsome, indifferent, with infinitely slow movements, as if he were absent . . . Would that be the effects of kif?

Bought a small pipe and some kif . . .

Here is the fairly complete accounting of all of yesterday . . .

Incomparable day of arrival.

I'm not suffering too much from the heat, which is, however, humid and heavy.

Left Algiers July 27, eight in the morning.

Arrived in Méroïer the twenty-ninth at about ten o'clock; afternoon nap, left at five fifteen.[21]

Stopover in El-Ferd at around midnight. Stop in Ourlana at about two o'clock. Stopover in Sid-Auvrau at two thirty. Last stopover at dawn in El-Moggar. Arrived in Touggourt at eight in the morning on the thirty-first. A bit of fever between Mrayer, Ourlana, and Sidi Amram.

Relatively good frame of mind, then spoiled by the presence of Lieutenant Lagrange's mistress, a horrible repugnant creature.

In Sidi Amram, lay down during the stopover near a fire made of dried djerid, near a French soldier who'd come from I don't know where, drank a coffee, weakness, a touch of fever ... The fire's flames lit up the toub wall with a strange red glimmer beneath the falling constellations.

TOUGGOURT, TUESDAY, JULY 31, 1900, NOON

I'm sitting down in the almost-dark dining room, in order to flee the countless flies in my room.

This evening, if the Arab Bureau is not opposed, I'll leave for El Oued, where I'll try to settle down.

All in all, I risk much less down there, from the point of view of my health, than in Ouargla. I'm happy to notice that the desert's crushing heat is not overwhelming me too much. Even then, I'm not completely in my normal state, given the fatigue of the trip and the recent prolonged periods of being awake at night. I can work and think. Besides, it's only today that I'm beginning to regain my self-control. I won't entirely manage that until the day that I'll be settled in El Oued, when calmness will have established itself around me.

I'm also beginning to be careful with money and developing the willpower necessary not to uselessly spend my little bit of remaining money.

I also must not forget that I came to the desert, not in order to indulge

21. Eberhardt's note in margin: "Where is my mournful and prestigious Oued Rir'? And will I ever see it again? March 12/VIII 1901."

in last year's sweet idleness, but certainly to work, and that this voyage can become a dreadful shipwreck of my entire future, or rather a path to material as well as moral salvation, depending on whether I'll know how *to manage* or not.[22]

In Algiers, from the first to especially the last evening, overall I've forever kept a charming memory of it.

On the last evening, I had gone to a tobacco seller on the Saulières Plateau, with Mokhtar and Abdel-Keim Oulid-Aïssa. After a rather animated conversation, we took a melancholy walk along the quays. Ben Elimaur, Mokhtar, and Zarrouk, the medical student, softly sang melancholy cantilenas from Algiers.

In Algiers I had a few moments of intense life, of completely Oriental life.

The long trip in third class, almost alone together with the youthful and kind being that Mokhtar is, also had its charm.

I said adieu, for a long time perhaps, to the great Azure Expanse . . .

Then it was wild Kabylia, its broken-apart boulders. Then, beyond the grayish hills of Portes-de-Fer, the desolation of the high clayey plateaus, indistinctly gilded by fields cut high by the Arabs—long spots of silvery fawn against the fields' red chalk and ocher colors.

In Bordj-bou-Aréridj, the plain offers a spectacle more despairingly and mournfully sad than anywhere else.

Saint Arnaud resembles Batna. It's a big village lost in the middle of the high plateaus of Chéonïya country. However, Saint Arnaud, *Elelma* in Arabic, is verdant. Its gardens remind one of the Randon column in Bône.

The cadi is a noble, calm old man from another age . . .

Alas! In ten or in twenty years, will young Algerians of our days resemble their fathers who are tinged with the solemn serenity of the unwavering Islamic faith? Initially, his son Si Aly seems sluggish and ponderous. He is, however, an intelligent man and not at all indifferent to the nation. Si Ahsenn, of Turkish origin, is a man who charms with his candor.

22. Eberhardt's note in Arabic in margin: "Everything is in what has been written."

On the first evening in Elelma, I had an intense, very sweet impression of old Africa and the Bedouin country: in the distance, the dogs barked all night long and the rooster's cry could be heard. Serenity, sweet melancholy, and lack of concern.

Felt, like long ago, en route from Biskra to Touggourt, the engaging, intoxicating impression of dawn in the desert . . . Yesterday, in Bir Sthil, when the old guardian had us drink coffee, and this morning, in El Moggar, when I was preparing the morning coffee, sitting in front of the fire.

Tonight, at about two o'clock, crossed the gloomy Ourlana oasis: large gardens enclosed by adobe walls, with seguia smelling of saltpeter, humidity, and fever . . .

All the houses made of ocherous tob have fallen into a strange sleep . . .

Then, in Sidi Amram, stretched out on the ground near a fire made of dry djerid, on the warm sand beneath the bedazzlement of uncountable stars . . .[23]

Oh Sahara, threatening Sahara, hiding your beautiful dark soul in your inhospitable and mournful solitudes!

Yes, I love this country of sand and stone, this country of camels and primitive men, country of dangerous chott and sebkha . . .

Last night, between Mraïer and El Berd, saw strange and fetishistic silhouettes of indistinct human forms decorated with red and white rags. A few years ago a Muslim was assassinated there. This sort of primitive monument is set up there in memory of the blood of the man who was buried in Touggourt . . .

BORDJ TERAJEN, AUGUST 1, 1900,
SEVEN O'CLOCK IN THE MORNING

Left yesterday evening at 4:34 on N'Tard-jallah's she-mule with Mohammed El Hadj from Taïbet. Arrived in Mguétla at about nine o'clock.

23. Eberhardt's note in margin: "There was a French soldier who'd come from I don't know where."

Noticed at sunset the fawn-colored dunes becoming an incomparable golden shade of incredible fervor.

In the first quarter of the moonlight, infinite whiteness; side lit by the sun, golden; back side—*dhaar el ereg*—bluish and translucent. Delicate and extraordinarily pure shades of color.

Last night, in spite of a little fatigue, excellent impression of first encampment.

At night, an almost cold wind, the whisper of the sea in the dune. Impression of desolate, infinite, and groundless sadness.

Wonderful dawn. Got up at four o'clock. Pure sky, rather cool strong northeast wind.

Left at five o'clock. Camped and made coffee in the dune. The mail caught up with us. Rode a camel all the way to Terdjen. Arrived at eight o'clock. The guardians and the porter assert that the fine doctor is still in El Oued.

Excellent frame of mind. State of health, idem.

How well I did to leave Europe and to choose, yesterday, El Oued as a residence. If only my health stays under control, I'll have to stay in El Oued for as long as possible.

And especially, may this time be not at all lost, from all points of view, especially from that of my intellectual and moral development, and that of literature. ✹ *If it pleases Allah!*

EL OUED, AUGUST 4, 1900,
SEVEN O'CLOCK IN THE MORNING

After finishing writing down my notes in Terdjen, I sat down on my bed across from the door.

Felt a sensation of inexpressible well-being, of profound joy at being there . . . Afternoon nap interrupted by children and goats.

Left, with the mail, at about two thirty. Intense heat. Malaise. Got back on camel. Arrived in Mouïet-el-Caïd toward the maghreb (six o'clock).

Absolutely white night. At two o'clock, saw a red glimmer, without rays and dull, above the dune.

Then, in dawn's indistinct radiance, passionate Lucifer rises. ⊻ The Arabs say it has gone up to the bordj.

Woke up Habib. Made a fire, prepared coffee at four o'clock, left again for Ourmès. Arrived at about seven thirty. Crossed the largest dune. Found several dead camels, among which, one, lying in a position of extreme abandon, had died recently . . .

Ourmès. Afternoon nap in the gardens. Enchanted spectacle. Poor nap because of the flies and the heat of the inevitable burnooses. Left again at four thirty. Arrived in Koïnine about six o'clock. In El Oued toward the maghreb.

Got down in front of Habib's house in the middle of the street. Thought about my life's strangeness.

A bit of fever before falling asleep. Good night. Got up at four thirty. Went to visit the house of a caïd on the square across from the bordj. Rented. Started living arrangements.

Saw the captain. Noon. Smothering heat. Good afternoon nap.

Evening of the arrival, beautiful mule race with Habib's brother, Abd-er-Rahmen, to Bir Gharby to the *aiguadi*. Transparent night in the white sand. Deep garden asleep in the shade. Coolness and sweetness of things.

Stopped in front of a Moorish café last night. Then raced on foot to the well. Light bout of fever. Weakness. Good night in the courtyard. Got up at four forty-five.

Here I am, finally arrived at this goal that seemed somewhat imaginary as long as it was still only in the planning stages. It's done, and now I must act with all the energy I feel capable of.

As soon as I've received the money from Eugène, I must pay for the housing, pay Habib, and then buy what is necessary.

Today the baggage should arrive. As soon as my living arrangements are a bit less temporary, I'll have to get to work, to do the book about my trip and in which Marseille will be the first chapter.

I'm far from the world, far from civilization and its hypocritical intrigues. I am alone in the desert on Islam's earth, free and in excellent living conditions. Except for my health, and still the results of my undertaking depend thus only on me.

AUGUST 4, 1900,
THREE THIRTY IN THE AFTERNOON

I am starting to feel annoyed that the baggage has not arrived and that I can't definitively set up my house and my life . . .

A gray frame of mind, a bit of irritation, all without cause.

Habib's house. In one of the winding streets, a floor made of fine sand, not from the dune, a square building of tob, not whitewashed.

In a corner, a small brown goat with an amulet around its neck. A bitch with her little ones. Habib's numerous brothers come and go. The old man's wife, tall, thin, dressed in long white veils with an entire mountain on her head: braids of black hair, braids and tassels of red wool, in her ears, heavy iron rings held in place by cords attached to her hair. When she goes out, she throws a blue veil over all of that. Strange, tanned, ageless, thin face with mournful black eyes.

The kif smoker, plunged in a sweet daydream.

Went to see Abd-el-Kader ben Taleb Saïd. Impression of craftiness. El Mohammed El Héchni, impression of darkness. Profoundly hidden man.[24]

Obviously, it's best to leave aside these people and affairs that have already cost me a lot.

They left Mchara for Ouargla. Abd-el-Kader says he'll go to Paris. The naïb is no longer loved. ⌣ *May God's mercy be upon him!*

Soon the coolness will begin. Already a light wind blows from time to time.

To summarize, I have not yet entered the path of my new life. There is still too much that is makeshift.

EL OUED, THURSDAY, AUGUST 9, 1900,
SEVEN THIRTY IN THE EVENING

For the time being, nothing is fixed in my completely Arab existence, which is sluggish, but not dangerously so, for I feel certain that it won't

24. Eberhardt's note in margin: "Blindness."

last. My small household is starting to be set up. But I'm still in need of money.

I must avoid borrowing any from the *bach-adel*, for it's obvious that he is not disinterested. The heat is diminishing bit by bit. No more fever. Excellent state of health.

In a few days I believe I'll completely modify my way of living.

Every evening, a race to Bir R'Arby. Crossing snowy-white, almost-translucent sands in the moonlight. We pass by the mournful and sinister silhouette of the Christian cemetery: high gray walls mounted with a black cross . . .[25] Mournful impression. Then we go up the low dune and into a narrow and deep valley, and the garden appears, resembling all Souafa gardens: a crater widened on one side toward the entrance paths and the wells. The tallest date palms are over there at the foot of the crater's steep inner walls. The smallest ones are toward the wells.

In the moon's blue-green faint light, they're diaphanous, resembling delicate plumes of feathers. Between their beautiful chiseled trunks, verdant cultivations of melons, watermelons, and fragrant basil stretch out.

The water is clear and cool. The well's primitive framework creaks, and the noise has already become familiar to me; the goatskin oumara falls and for a moment gently splashes in the well's darkness, then comes back up dripping with water. Then, throwing my chechiya onto the pure sand, I soak my head in the oumara and greedily drink the rather fresh water with the almost-agonizing sensation of voluptuousness that fresh water causes here. Then we lie down for a moment on the sand.

Great silence reigns in the blue night; and the Souf's eternal wind rustles mysteriously in the date palms' foliage, with an almost-sea-like sound.

Then slowly, painfully comes the return to the sleeping city, toward the white house that is, God knows for how long, my residence . . .

A few days ago, spent the night with Slimène in a large garden owned by the Hacheich caïdat, to the west of El Oued.

An oblong, very deep crater embedded between tremendous white sand walls whose ridges are decorated with small hedges of dried djerid in order to avoid being choked with sand.

25. Eberhardt's note in margin: "Predestined garden."

Not a living soul in the date palms' warm shade. At first we sat down near a well that I had, in vain, drawn from with a torn oumara. We're sad, abysmally sad, maybe felt the same way in both of us, because, overall in me, the idea of possible problems resulting from indiscretions in the neighborhood was a large part of it.

Certainly, in me, in all my sadnesses, there is always an unfathomable and unanalyzable background of sadness without a known cause, which is my soul's very essence . . .

Alas, my soul has aged. It no longer deludes itself, and I can only smile at the dreams of Slimène's very young soul, Slimène who believes, not in eternity, but at least in the indefinite duration of earthly love, and who dreams about what will be in a year, in *seven years*.[26]

Alas, a bit of gray ash at the bottom of two solitary souls, without a doubt very far from one another and separated forever by piles of other foreign ashes, already deformed and indistinct memories . . .

⮿ *But they don't know!*

And what good is it to tell him, to make him sad, to make him suffer. That will happen by itself on the day of the inevitable separation.

But it's true that, for some time, I've acquired a profound experience of life.

Not only on that score does no illusion remain in me, but even more so *no desire at all* to delude myself, nor to make *last* the things that are sweet and good only because they are ephemeral . . .

But there you are, those things are so personal to me, so much *mine*, that it is impossible to explain them clearly, or especially to make them understood and admitted by someone else.

Experience is acquired at the price of life's great sufferings, but it is never *transmitted*.

After an hour spent with tears in our eyes talking about the really terrible possible contingencies, we went to sleep on our burnooses under the date palms, with a roll of sand under our heads.

---

26. Eberhardt's note in margin: "In a year!" One year has flowed by, and my life is . . . more intimately tied to his for always! March 12/VIII 1901."

Slept until about two thirty. Then in the growing predawn coolness, went painfully back up the sand paths and returned through the caïdat of Hacheich. Small tangled streets where a heavy odor of saltpeter reigned, rather like that of the Oued Rir oasis! Crossed the market, where only a few camels were sleeping with their drivers around the great well's immobile framework.

Last night, mounted the bad white horse owned by the *deira* of the Hacheich caïd, Misbah's father. And on the Kouïnine road in El Oued's small outskirts where white and black goats graze on the zeriba roofs of djerid.

The still-pallid dune becomes more and more golden, becomes this burning metallic color from before the maghreb. The shadows lengthen disproportionately.

Then everything becomes a violent red, and the edges of the dunes turn violet blue and green in a variety of unheard-of nuances.

In the West, toward Kouïnine and Touggourt, the sun, a bloody ball, is going down in a fire of gold and purple crimson. The crests of the dunes—as if on fire from within—have colors that darken from moment to moment. Then, when the sun's disk has been swallowed up in the distance, everything sinks into purplish nuances of color . . . Finally, everything becomes white again, with the dull whiteness of the Souf, blinding at noon.

This morning, the day rose dark and cloudy, and it was one of the most unexpected spectacles here in the country of the implacable blue sky, of the immutable and tyrannical sun . . .

Felt a furtive impression of certain autumn awakenings there long ago, in the profound distances of time and space . . .

Sadness, these last days.

Besides, my life is badly employed here for the moment. Afternoon naps play a big role.

In addition, it's this inertia that takes over me every time I establish myself in a new country, especially for a rather long stay. But this will inevitably be over.

Since this morning, a rather violent sirocco. The sand flits about and the weather is heavy. They say there's no more than about twenty days left of big heat.

For the time being my health is excellent; and except for great languidness, I feel sometimes better than ever.

I would like to be able to get down to work. But for that, I have to be able to get up at least when I awake and, after Slimène leaves, not to go back to bed . . . Alas, if I do that, it's only out of boredom and idleness.

I must go out as soon as I awake, go into the gardens, and sometimes take a morning ride on one horse or another depending on the occasion.

Spent a quarter of an hour taking administrative measures against the flies that had invaded my two rooms . . . These small tasks for my so minimally complicated existence will one day be dear memories for me.

But for that I mustn't at all have my mind *elsewhere* all the time, always *on hold*. Yes, to dedicate myself to the present hour such as it is and to try, according to Eugène's advice, to discover the good side of all things, a side that inevitably exists.

Oh! If only present life could last, if Slimène were to stay forever the good comrade, the brother that he is for me at this moment. And if only I were to devote a bit more to local life and, once cool weather has arrived, to work!

Here, when a young woman marries, she is carried to her husband's house on a man's back. The husband must hide for seven nights in order to see his wife, come after the magh'reb and leave before the *sobkh*.

An obvious vestige of abductions from long ago . . .

AUGUST 18, 1900,
THREE THIRTY IN THE AFTERNOON

Last night, alone and on horseback, went in the direction of the Touggourt road into the small cities scattered the length of the trails: Gara, Teksebet, etc. Crossed Teksebet. Small melancholy city, fallen into decay, almost deserted, crumbling ruins at each step.

Took the El Oued path again at sunset. In the grayish dune, looked at the sand flowing forever like the white waves of a silent ocean. Toward the west, the summit of a large pointed dune seemed to smoke like a volcano. Then the sun, at first yellow and surrounded by sulfurous haze, was slowly colored with each evening's rich shades of apotheosis . . .

Yesterday, as I was mounting my horse, I heard nearby the lamentations announcing death among the Arabs . . . Salah the spahi's little girl, little Abd-el-Kader's sister, died. And today, in a market shop, saw Salah playing and smiling with his son.

Last night, at magh'reb, they buried the little one in the hot sand . . . and she was swallowed up forever in the great night of beyond, like one of the rapid meteors that often cross the profound sky here.

MONDAY, SEPTEMBER 3, 1900,
FIVE THIRTY IN THE EVENING

Left by camel for Touggourt. Arrived in Ourmès eight forty-five. Passed through in front of the bordj. Left on the fourth at four in the morning. Arrived in Mouïet-el-Caïd at about ten in the morning. Afternoon nap. Left by donkey at four in the afternoon. Spent the night between M.-el-Caïd and Terdjeun. Afternoon nap. Left again at about four o'clock. Spent the night in Mguétla. Left at two thirty. Arrived in Touggourt on the sixth about eleven o'clock. Day at Talèb-Saïd's home. Spent the night. Left at eight in the evening on the seventh. Slept near Arsa Touggourt. Left again around three o'clock on the eighth. Arrived in Mguétla eight o'clock. Nap. Left again three o'clock in the afternoon. Arrived in Terdjeun about seven thirty in evening. Spent the night near the bordj. Left the ninth at one forty-five in the morning. Arrived in M.-el-Caïd about eight thirty in the morning. Nap.

Noted in El Oued, September 17, 1900, noon.

I don't believe in it (in death); it's a dark passage that each of us meets at a given moment in one's life. A lot of people are alarmed by it, those who are afraid of the dark, especially children.

As for me, the three or four times that I found myself near death, I saw a small light on the other side, I don't really know which one, but obvious, and which completely calmed me. (Fromentin, *Une année dans le Sahel*)

Yes, there is certainly a small light beyond the Great Darkness.[27]

MONDAY, OCTOBER 9, 1900,
NINE O'CLOCK IN THE MORNING

Last night, some short time after the maghreb, went on Souf to the house of Abd-el-Kader, the deïra, to get the saddle for this morning. Went behind the café through the wide, sandy streets between the houses half in ruin.

The red sun had just disappeared behind the dunes of the Touggourt road, and the bordj and the houses stood out in delicate gray silhouettes against the setting sun's incandescence.

Having arrived at the road in front of the deïra, I looked at the incomparable spectacle before my eyes: the dunes, of an infinitely delicate nuance of silvery fawn, standing out against an orangish-and-purple sky, the whole thing bathed in inexpressibly pure lilac light.

A few moments before, when the sun was about to go down, when El Oued was gleaming and drowned in exploding gold, saw, like a halo of apotheosis, two silhouettes of Arabs in white standing on the small dune with the lime ovens. Biblical impression of a return to the ancient ages of a humanity worshipping great celestial lights . . .

And in the evening, on the borders of the city and the desert, once again found an impression of autumn and winter sunsets in the country of exile, when the great snowy Jura seemed to come closer and to melt into gold and bluish tints of color . . .

The mornings have become cold. The light has changed color, and the sky, too. There is no longer the mournful radiance of overwhelming summer days. The sky's blue is intense and has become invigorating and pure.

27. Eberhardt note: "Written in the El Oued hospital, February 5, 1901, after the Behima incident." (Doyon's note: Note added one year later.)

Everything is coming to life again. My soul, too, is being reborn to life . . . But as always, too, I feel an infinite sadness invading my soul, an inexpressible desire for something I can't say, a nostalgia for *elsewhere* that I can't name.

For a few days now, intellectual work has repelled me much less than during this summer, and I believe that I will write again . . . The spring doesn't seem at all dried up to me.

Went through a period of material trouble and problems that have not yet ended. The day after certainly is gray, and I cannot at all even foresee the end of my stay here in sand country . . .

For now, even if I had the means, I feel incapable of going away, of leaving Slimène forever. Besides, why?

I believe that I have finally reached a state of peace in my heart, if not of my mind—I'm very far away from that, alas . . .

Incredible variation of sensations! Just now, as I began these notes, I felt myself in one of these clear and melancholy states of mind felt especially on particular luminous mornings while wandering at a gallop *in the country of tombs* on the Amiche road. At present, while finishing, I feel a kind of unreasonable and unfounded irritation so well-known to me and which makes me brutally rebuff those who speak to me.

Changed lodging the evening of October 14. Brigadier Nemouchi's house.

EL OUED, OCTOBER 27, 1900,
NINE O'CLOCK IN THE EVENING.

The seventeenth, was in Amiche looking for Sid-el-Hussine.

Left at about six o'clock on a cool morning. Arrived very quickly at the zaouïya of the white cheikh, which seemed very empty and very abandoned at the edge of vast sad cemeteries . . . Left with two servants, crossed long successions of houses and gardens scattered in picturesque disorder.

Zaouïya of Sid-el-Imann, solitary and falling into ruin on a ridge of dunes surrounded by ruins and a beautiful verdant garden. Turned left from there through the Chaamba colony. Met Gosenelle and the doctor . . . Then, two Chaamba carrying one of their own on a stretcher, to eternal rest.

Finally found Sid-el-Hussine all the way at the end of Ras-el-Amiche on the Ber-es-Sof road, across from the infinite sands leading to mysterious Rhadamès and faraway Sudan.

Spent the afternoon nap with the cheikh in a narrow crude room without a window, vaulted and sandy, making up the whole interior of a solitary house.[28]

A strange man came, an almost-black man from the South, with eyes like coals, afflicted with a kind of epilepsy that makes him hit whoever touches or frightens him . . . and at the same time eminently kind and marked with extreme sweetness. About three o'clock, left with the cheikh for the Chaamba colony. Left again alone at about three fifteen. Arrived at sunset in the cemeteries situated to the right of Amiche. At the magh'reb, stopped on the dune overhanging the Ouled-Touati.

The completely pink plain, empty and whose boundary is marked at the horizon by purplish dunes, stretched to the left. In the village, a few women in blue rags and a strangely shaped, reddish-brown dromedary. Absolute silence and peace . . . Returned about five fifteen.

Here I am, finally arrived at the state of absolute destitution that had been anticipated for a long time. But also, having brought me to El Oued, Providence seems to have wished to save me from an inevitable loss everywhere else.

Who knows, perhaps these blows dealt by adversity will only serve to modify my character, to wake me from this sort of devil-may-care fatigue that often invades me concerning the future.

May God make it so! Up to this day I have always emerged safe and sound from all the worst and most dangerous situations. Perhaps luck will yet again not abandon me. † *God's paths are impenetrable.*

Today, with Souf, on the very beautiful Debila road, up hill and down dale, among slightly wild gardens and old houses in ruin.

---

28. Eberhardt's note in margin: "Noted December 22, 1900. A few days later, this house, where we took an afternoon nap, was devastated by typhus, which carried off five people, among whom were the two old men."

A few salty lands, small reddish-brown chotts among the whitish grays of the dunes and the dark-green color of the palm trees.

Arrived at the slaughterhouse situated in the middle of an even more extensive chott surrounded by dunes. Looks abandoned and sad.

NOVEMBER 4, 1900

This morning, was on Souf among the dunes and gardens that separate the Touggourt road from that of Debila. Steep paths at the dunes' summit overhanging deep gardens.

It had rained the previous night, and the sand was moist with a yellowish tint and a light salty odor that was fresh and pleasant.[29]

In the distance, on the Djerid road and to the east toward Tréfaoui, the tall dunes seemed tinged with blue like the waves of a tormented sea.

On the monotonous hillsides, a few succulents have grown, sort of spindly pale-green sedums. In the gardens, carrots and bell peppers hurl bright-green carpets beneath the palm trees now rid of their gray dust. Everything is coming alive again, and this African autumn certainly resembles summers from over there in the country of exile, especially in the evening at sunset.

My existence is still the same—monotonous and without noticeable variations. For some time, it has even become very secluded, divided between my house—which I consider to be only a campsite, because we must soon exchange it for another—and Mansour's. Otherwise I go to Abd-el-Kader's, to whom I am becoming sincerely attached. It would be a great consolation to me if I could find a few books at his house.

As for Slimène, nothing has changed except that day by day I become more attached to him, and he is truly becoming a member of my family,

------

29. Eberhardt's note in margin: "Autumn will return down there in the country of pale dunes. Once again, under the purer sky, the sun shining less hotly and the morning's cool wind will dissipate the night's cool fog, and the humid sand will spread its sea odors. And the horizon will turn blue, and the gardens will become green once again . . . But I will not be there wandering and dreaming. Everything will be the same in the beloved Sahara's immutable decor . . . But we will no longer be there seeing and dreaming . . . We'll be far away, far away in the land of exile . . . Batna, April 1, 1900."

or rather *is my family* . . . May this last eternally in this way, even here in the unchangeably gray dunes! . . .[30]

However, sometimes I pause on the slippery slope of the drowsiness invading me more and more, and I cannot help but be amazed at my extraordinary destiny . . .

After so many great dreams, so many trials and tribulations, to end up in a lost oasis in the depths of the desert! . . .

And how will this present situation end? . . .

EL OUED, BEGINNING OF NOVEMBER 1900

Noted November 6, 1900, in El Oued (hospital).

Sin, that is to say *evil*, is man's natural state, as it is that of all animated beings . . .

All the *good* that we do is often but *illusion*. If, by chance, it is a *reality*, then it is nothing but the result of a slow and painful victory that we have won against our natural disposition, which, far from pushing us to do good, endlessly distances us from it . . .

"Upon awakening this morning, he had still felt anguished, as if invaded by a premonition of death, in face of the irreparable act" (Pierre Loti, *Matelot*).

Memory of waking up on board, July 22, 1900 . . .

EL OUED, DECEMBER 1, 1900

Salah ben Taliba's house.

It's raining . . . The weather is gray and dark, and the dune has taken on the appearance of mourning from bad days . . .

The beginning of December strikingly resembles that of the disastrous year of 1897 . . . Same weather, same violent wind furiously whip-

---

30. Eberhardt's notes in margin: "Noted January 28, 1901. Even here in the gray sands! And today, what would I not give to never again leave them, these marvelous sands of the Ouady Souf, and to one day sleep the sleep of eternity!" ". . . And the day after this day, I was so close to staying there forever. March 12/VIII 1901."

ping my face ... But then I had as horizon the gray immensity of the Mediterranean in furor, beating the black rocks of the Lion with a cataclysmic roar ... And in my still very young soul, in spite of the so-recent and so-cruel mourning, the joy *of living*—latent, powerful—still existed.

But since then everything has changed, everything, even my aging soul, ripened by a strange, tremendous, tormented destiny ... Augustine has finally found his port, the "haven of grace," from where, it seems, he is no longer destined to leave ... After so many trials and tribulations, after so many adventures, he has finally calmed down, and in a strange manner.

As for me, I also *believe*, or rather I am *beginning to believe*, that I have also found my port.

I, for whom the peaceful happiness in a city of Europe or the Tell will never suffice, in an hour of inspiration, I have conceived of the daring project, attainable for me, of establishing myself in the desert and looking for both peace and adventures, things that are reconcilable with my strange nature. Domestic happiness has been found and, far from diminishing, seems to strengthen day by day ...

And only politics threatens it ... But alas! *Allah knows the sky's and the earth's hidden things!* And no one can predict the future.

Went and met, only fifteen days ago this evening, the *beloved*, just below Kouïnine, at night.

Went out on Souf in dark grayness, causing me dizziness ...

Got lost several times ... Strange sensations in the plain with the horizon seeming to rise up in the form of dunes and the villages representing djerid hedges ...

Remembered the passage from *Aziyadé* about Stamboul's tombs lit by solitary night lights, and then suddenly found myself in front of the door of the koubba of the Teksebet cemetery.

For several days, spent every afternoon, with Khalifa Tahar or alone, on the Debila road. Gardens just above the sand, melancholy palm groves, enclosures with the Souf's eternal dunes as background.

On a day of solitary walking, had a singular sensation of *recall*, of return to the dead past ...

Going through the chott, stopped my horse beneath the palm trees. My eyes were closed and I was dreaming as I listened to the wind rustling the leaves . . . Recalled the Rhône's great woods and the Saracen park during pensive summer evening hours . . . The illusion was almost absolute.

But suddenly a brusque movement of Souf brought me back to reality . . . I opened my eyes again . . . The dunes stretched out infinitely, gray and flecked with whitecaps, and above my head the rustling foliage was that of the tough djerid . . . A moment of profound melancholy . . .

Another day, I was on this same road with Slimène.

Returned alone through the dunes and the back of the city . . . Marvelous sunset . . . Red clouds in an opal sky turned crimson . . . At the hour of the magh'reb, went by the mosque at the top of the city, where white forms hurried in the radiance of the blaze of glory inundating the earth.

Behind our house, at the foot of the dune next to an enclosure containing three low palm trees, a small very African-looking mosque rises up, built of ocher-colored plaster looking like toub . . .

There is nothing but a small egg-shaped, buttressed koubba. Behind it a beautiful date palm rises and, from our terrace, seems to emerge out of the koubba. Went up there yesterday during the magh'reb . . . In the sunset's blaze, gray silhouettes turned crimson circulated in front of the outpost in the distance . . . And there to my right, as the little red dome seemed to be on fire and the *moueddin*'s drawling voice repeated the evening prayer on all the sky's horizons, in his drawling slow voice, men came down the dune in the glory of the melancholy hour.

These last days, the poignant memories of the end of † *the White Spirit* have come to haunt me . . .

EL OUED, FRIDAY, DECEMBER 14, 1900,
TWO O'CLOCK IN THE EVENING.

After two days of suffering and boredom, I seem to be coming alive again.

It's getting colder and colder. Last night, thick fog reigned, reminding me of the foggy days of the *land of exile*.

It will be rough spending winter here without fire and money . . . And yet I have no desire at all to leave it, this strange country . . .

The other day, sitting with Abd-el-Kader in the courtyard of the zaouïya of Elakbab, I was considering with surprise the strange setting: singular heads half-veiled in gray, of tanned Chaamba . . . almost-black faces, energetic to the point of savagery, from South Troud . . . all of that in the run-down zaouïya's courtyard surrounding the enormous redheaded cheikh with soft blue eyes . . .

A singular destiny day by day, more so than mine!

And yet if I regret anything, it is my dreams of literary work . . . Alas, will they ever be attainable?

Among my memories of the South, the one that will undoubtedly be the most vivid will certainly be that of the memorable day of December 3 when I had the privilege of attending the most beautiful of sights: the return of the great marabout Si Mahmoud Lachmi, the indefinable, fascinating, attractive being who charmed me, in Touggourt, by the strangeness of his personality . . . Man of another age, with thoughts and attitudes from long ago. Si Lachmi is made to exercise a strange influence on adventurous souls . . . What a singular intoxication, on that iridescent and pure winter morning, caused by the gunpowder, the Nefsaoua's wild *bendar* music, the crowd's frenetic cries cheering the descendant of the Prophet and Saint of Bagdad, and furious wild stampedes in the smoke and noise . . .

DECEMBER 24, 1900 (RAMADAN)

In spite of my illness, my weakness, the problems of the past, and those, even more serious, of a material nature, the Ramadan nights and mornings had in store for me calm and pleasant sensations of serenity, almost joy, in a very unexpected way.

It has also been very pleasant for me to note that the friend from old days—good or bad, but especially bad—Augustine, still remembers the brotherhood of spirit that long ago united us, from nearby or from afar, in spite of all the traps and obstacles that life has seemed to wish to place endlessly between us . . .

From day to day I note that, in fact, there is only one way to live—if not entirely happily, because there is illness, misery, and death, but at least calmly—it is to isolate oneself as much as possible from men, except for a few rare chosen ones, and to not at all *depend on them*.

Arab society—disorganized and vitiated by contact with foreigners—doesn't even exist here such as it does in large cities. As for French society... it has lost a lot here, from what I've gathered from the lieutenant of the infantrymen and especially from the doctor.[31] The only thinking and good being here was my old Domercq with whom I could speak about things of the soul and mind.

JANUARY 28, 1901,
EIGHT O'CLOCK IN THE MORNING

Once again, everything is disrupted and broken in my sad existence: the languid, sweet life in the incredible scenery of the moving sands has ended! The delicious tranquility that both of us indulged in has ended!

On the evening of the twenty-third, we learned, by providential chance, of Slimène's relief and the return to Batna . . . Hour of inexpressible anguish, almost of despair . . .

Besides, added to the infinite sadness of the departure, and the harsh life in Batna, farther away from each other, was the anxiety of our material situation, the one hundred–franc debt, a sum of which we had not one cent.

Dismal, sleepless night spent smoking kif and drinking.

A rapid, anguished race to Sidi Lachmi's the next morning. Found myself surrounded by pilgrims who will leave tomorrow for the great ziara of the grand cheikh of Nefta. Spent more than an hour, full of emotion, my mind elsewhere, talking halfheartedly about futile things. Finally, took the cheikh aside and agreed to return after the magh'reb with Slimène. Returned home at a fast trot, exhausted, with my legs stiffened in the stirrups.

Found Slimène half crazy, haggard, almost unaware of what he was doing. In the evening, shortly before the magh'reb, left on Souf. Sent

31. Eberhardt's note in margin: "Blindness of human judgments: shortly afterward I had the chance to appreciate the great goodness and true intelligence of this same doctor. Batna, April 13, 1901."

Aly to the cemetery of the Ouled-Ahmed with Slimène's burnoose. At sunset, arrived at the last scattered tombs on the road. Deep anxiety at not seeing the beloved come. My heart had not been as full of emotion, as on that evening, for a long time. Lugubrious ideas rushed into my feverish head.

Finally, after the *edden* of the magh'reb, Slimène arrives at nightfall on the road of the Ouled-Ahmed mosque. We galloped all the way to the Hama Ayéchi garden, leaving Aly, whom I had sent to the neighborhood.

Sinister route in the indistinct glimmer of the Safar-el-Kheir crescent moon . . . Sharp fear of seeing Slimène fall off the horse, and anxious to know what the cheikh would do for us . . . We finally arrive, and we impatiently answer the repeated salutations of Guezzoun and other servants, and here we are sitting in front of the cheikh in the vast sandy room with low, powerful arches . . . A candle lights the large red carpet that we're sitting on, leaving the corners of the room in indistinct shadow.

There was a great heavy silence. I sense well that my poor Rouh' can't talk; and as for me, it seems that someone is strangling me.

I see that Rouh' is crying, and I too want to burst into tears.

But the cheikh reminds us that we can come, that we mustn't betray ourselves.

For a long time I try, in my troubled state, to explain to him what is happening to us and what our situation is . . . He remains quiet, burdened, as if not there.

Finally, the cheikh and I exchange a look, which I try to put all my soul into, showing him Rouh', who is burning with fever and beginning to completely lose consciousness . . . Then the cheikh gets up and goes into his house . . . His eyes were misty; it was time . . .

A moment later he returns and places 170 francs in front of Rouh', saying, "God will pay the rest."[32]

Then, without saying anything, without even taking the bills, Rouh' looks at them and laughs with a crazy laugh that makes the cheikh and me afraid . . . A silent laugh that was sadder to see than tears.

32. Eberhardt's note in margin: "Carry away beneath you, my Lord!"

I anxiously wondered if he was not going to completely lose his mind. Finally, I went out behind the zaouïya . . . In the distance the gloomy dunes on the Taïbet Guéblia road were sleeping in the unclear lunar light.

Before me in the stony sand, the strange silhouette of the small cemetery of the cheikh's children rose up, where so many innocent beings sleep, hardly born into life and immediately carried away into the mysterious darkness of the world beyond. Little souls whose earthly eyes barely opened on to the great horizon of the barren dunes and then immediately went out . . .

In the sands accumulated by the west wind against the thick buttressed wall, I stop, and in the deep silence I see, close by me, the furtive passage of a fox or small sand fox, who knows? My eyes lifted to the sky, I recite, in a low voice with sincere fervor for God, the *Fatiha*, and I implore the Emir of the Saints whose prayer beads I am wearing and whom I serve . . .

I return . . . Then we leave again, our hearts relieved, but melancholy nonetheless.

We're afraid of getting lost in the immense cemeteries and pale dunes.

In fact, we go home through the village to the east of the Ouled-Touati. While taking the narrow path that overhangs the deep garden of Hama Ayéchi, we look at the strange spectacle: at our feet the palm trees are sleeping in the shadows . . . Between their trunks, a few vaguely pink silvery rays of light filter through.

Very low toward the western horizon, above the immense dunes overlooking the Jewish cemetery, the moon's upside-down crescent is about to go down.

It's near ten o'clock, and no sound comes to trouble the silence of the desolate solitudes where we are. This evening everything seems to take on the particular character of things on the days when our ephemeral destinies are being decided.

Profound mystery reigns around us, and both of us feel it intensely. We become quiet and listen to the soft sound of our horses' hooves on the stirred-up sand of the road.

When we enter the Ouled-Ahmed cemetery, the moon is going down: for a moment, only the crescent's two red horns appear at the crest of the great dune, a strange and disturbing spectacle . . . then it's over, and everything is swallowed up by the night . . .

We have hardly moved forward for fear of tripping and falling: the road is strewn with tombstones. At our departure after the magh'reb, misbah burned in the cemetery in the small gray necropolises, colorless flames in the day's ending light: it was a Friday night.

Now everything has dropped back into shadow, the lights are extinguished and the tombs slumber in darkness. Ah! To leave this country and perhaps never see it again! . . .

The next day, Slimène alerts Embarek and the brigadier Saïd, both of whom have revealed themselves to have fine and honest hearts.

Day before yesterday, about eight o'clock, left with Aly for Guémar. Went past the cemetery and the Sidi Abdallah road. Then turned off toward the west from Teks'ebet and passed under Kanimine, a little to the right of the Touggourt road. Cool morning, a few clouds. Arrived in the dunes, left Aly behind, and rode at a gallop, then trotted.

Desolate aspects of Tarzout's great plain, with, on the northern horizon, the silhouette of the great koubba of Ti Djouya . . . From far away, Tarzout's and Guémar's palm trees merging at the horizon of the gloomy plain, where the immense cemeteries stretch out, gives rather well the illusion of the arrival in Touggourt, seen from the last dunes of the Souf road . . . Same gray plain and black line of palm trees among the whitish houses. Thought, with an intense pang of anguish, that in a few days we'll have to take this road and go back up north, and maybe for the last time, alas!

It is certainly during these days of anguish, incertitude, and sadness that I feel how much I've become attached to this country and that wherever I am henceforth, I will always bitterly miss the country of sand and sun, the deep gardens, and the winds rolling the clouds of sand on the surface of the dunes, capriciously shaping them throughout the ever-same and monotonous centuries.

Contemplated the strange cemeteries, especially the one below and to the right of Tarzout: tombs in the shape of pointed bells, small koubbas shaped like buttressed towers; all the picturesque disorder of the necropolises surrounding the two sister towns: Tarzout and Guémar.

Easily found the run-down zaouïya of Sid-el-Houssine. Sad conversation in the sparse room opening on to the vast courtyard crowded with strangely shaped stones . . .

Finally, out in the exterior courtyard, I saw Rouh's red silhouette taking the road to the market, and I sent Aly running after him . . .

Hearing of our sufferings and seeing Rouh', who looks deathly pale, the good cheikh cries when thinking of our next separation.

Many memories also tie us to him . . . My errands with him to Amiche and Ourmès, our long discussions, and the mystery of joint undertakings . . .

Shortly before the asr, we leave . . . We separate in the Kouïnine dunes. With Aly, I once again take the El Oued road to the west, leaving Kouïnine to the left. A few women veiled in blue cloth are returning, bent under the weight of full guerba . . .

As soon as we've gone past Kouïnine, I leave again alone, at a gallop, hoping to catch up with Slimène.

It's too late, and at nightfall I return home on the deserted road to the Sidi Abdallah cemetery.

JANUARY 29, 1901,
NINE O'CLOCK IN THE MORNING

The day before yesterday, at about four thirty, Aly announced to me that Guezzoun had told him that Sidi Elimam was supposed to leave yesterday (the next day) for Nefta . . . I hesitated for a rather long time; however, it was absolutely necessary to see Sidi Elimam and try with him the procedure that had worked so well with his two brothers.

About a quarter of an hour before the magh'reb, I finally left on Dahmane's horse.

A rapid trip in the sunset's red light.

In the village above the zaouïya of Elbayada, I heard the edden of the magh'reb.

Finally, on the small low hill, I saw rise up the silhouette of the zaouïya of Sidi Abd-el-Kader, with its two cupolas, the first known in the Souf . . .

The village was beginning to fade in bluish, transparent soft shadows. Rather calm and good state of mind.

Found ... (*Interrupted on that day.*)

Left for Behima at about ten thirty, came back the day after, the thirtieth, at about three in the evening.

Went to the hospital January 30 ...

Where are you my unforgettable friend, my true and only friend?
Where are you, king whose voice spoke to us of truth and love?
Where are you, and you, good and simple Chouchka, where are you?

You were able to guess, in the middle of the dust and rot that had then invaded my soul, what was burning again in it, the holy spark of light. Thanks to all of you, dear, charming, and unforgettable ones! Thank you!

At the hour of pain and suffering, in the grip of separation, your dear memories rise in front of me from the shadow of the past. Will fate reunite us again?[33]

FEBRUARY 3, 1901

Is it for a long time—Oh Life—that my destiny is to
    wander the earth?
Where are you, Port where I'll be able to rest?
Where is the look I'll be able to admire?
Where is the chest I'll be able to lean against?
Eternally alone ...

Alas! There was a port here in the middle of the gray tinted desert. There were also the honest eyes of a friend-brother, and the honest chest, but everything has gone!

This morning during a moment of tender, mysterious sadness: in front of the door of the mournful room, on the gray sand, an unusual

---

33. Eberhardt's note: "Marseille, June 23, 1901, nine in the evening. 'I am alone at the house; it's dark and sad here, and the one who lights my path is far away. Where are you, dear ones?'" (Doyon: Note in pencil in Russian.)

small titmouse as gray as the desert sand, rising on long spindly feet with a black ring on its pearly chest, had come to hop and sing, reminding me of the *land of exile* . . .

. . . Had the impression—simultaneously tender, sweet, and agonizing—that it was perhaps † *the White Spirit's* soul coming, in this gracious form, to console my oppressed soul in the mournful city . . .

More than ever, I am losing myself in the inexpressible, dark innermost depths of my soul, and I am struggling in the darkness. The dream is dark . . . What will I awake to, and what will the day after bring?

Pale and luminous impressions of long-ago springtime.

> ❧ *We hold fortune and our parents in trust.*
> *And it is necessary to restore them one day.*

† *Memory of the White Spirit.*
❧ The same day: always the same thought, always the same bursts,

> Toward years gone by, toward perfected love.
> Fall asleep in my chest, Snake of Memory!
> Do not trouble my sad rest!
> From her eyes, which, beneath life's storm,
> Drew for me long ago love's warmth,
> In the humid earth, beneath the stone slab,
> I know: for a long time, there has been no trace!
>   Hazy shadows from the past,
>   Serene tears from the past,
> Oh! Why did you wake up unexpectedly,
> In a pained and moaning heart?
> Leave. Trick no longer, with your charm,
>   My dead soul, weary of living!

. . . Everything feels like spring. Above the archways of the gray house across the way, the sun's dazzling canopy glistens . . . And I, I am in agony, suffering on a pathetic hospital bed, alone and abandoned!

Evil, being a disorder in the functioning of God's laws, cannot fatally follow a regular path toward its own fulfillment. This is why there is a mass of torn stitches and a mass of pitfalls.

By its very essence, evil can only end badly for whoever is its instrument.

A thought that came to me this evening after the extraordinary hour, the indefinable hour of the magh'reb when I felt burst forth in me a whole world of new sensations, a process, a transporting toward a goal that I remain unaware of, that I dare not guess.

Yes, during these hours, the most troubled of my life, my soul is yearning for its birth.

We live in complete mystery, and we both feel the powerful wing of the Unknown lightly touching us among the truly miraculous events favoring us at each step . . .

This evening at about five o'clock, Abdallah Mohammed was transferred to a prison cell.

I saw him coming, and I looked at him while the infantrymen searched him . . . Poignant impression of profound pity for this man, the blind instrument of a destiny whose meaning he does not know . . . And from this gray silhouette standing with head bent forward between blue turcos, I had perhaps the strangest and the most profound impression of *mystery* that I've ever felt.

I search hard, in the depths of my heart, for hatred for this man, and I find none. Even less contempt.

The emotion that I feel for this man is odd: it seems to me, thinking about him, that I am next to an abyss, a mystery whose last word . . . or rather whose first word has not yet been said and would *contain all the meaning of my life.* As long as I don't know the word for this enigma—and will I ever know it! God only knows—I will know neither *who* I am nor what are the *reason* and the *goal* of my destiny, one of the most incredible that exists.

However, it seems to me that I am not destined to completely disappear without having become conscious of all the profound mystery surrounding my life, from its singular beginnings up to this day.

The incredulous in love with ready-made solutions, whom mystery makes impatient, will say "craziness."

No, for the perception of the abysses concealed by life, which three-fourths of men are unaware of and don't even suspect, cannot be treated as craziness in the same way as the disdain of a person born blind for the splendors of a sunset or a starry night described to him by an artist.

It is easy to calm one's fearful soul, frightened by the proximity of the Unknown, by means of an ordinary explanation drawn from the false experience of men and from "common ideas," a pack of formless, disjointed scraps of ideas, from superficial knowledge and hypotheses taken for realities by the immeasurable moral cowardliness of men!

If the strangeness of my life were the result of *snobbism*, of *pretension*, yes, one could say, "She wanted it" . . . But no! Never has a being lived more day to day and more by chance than I, and it is certainly the events themselves, through their inevitable connection, that have led me to where I am and not I who have created them.

Perhaps all the strangeness of my nature can be summed up in this very characteristic trait: to look for, at all costs, new events, to flee inaction and immobility.

FEBRUARY 5, 1901,
TWO THIRTY IN THE MORNING.

And nothing that I could say, for entire pages or volumes, would communicate the nameless melancholy of that impression . . .

PIERRE LOTI, *Fantôme d'Orient*

I dream of El Oued, of the dear house next to the pulverulent dunes . . .[34] I am still there in the unique city, but I no longer have the impression of being there . . . and this morning, when I was looking through the battlements across the street at the café, the street, and the wall of the Messaaba's caïd's house, it seemed to me that I was looking at just any landscape, for example that of no particular one, seen from the bridge

34. Eberhardt's note in margin: "Change of dressing and removal of drains on the fifth, nine thirty in the morning."

of a ship during a short stopover . . . The profound and almost painful link that attached me to it has been brutally severed . . . I am nothing but a stranger there anymore . . .

In all probability I will leave with the convoy on the twenty-second, or in seventeen days . . . And it will be over with, perhaps for eternity.

Nothing will remain for me from this life of six months but its sweet, melancholy, and unfathomably nostalgic memory . . . and the undoubtedly immutable affection of the good and honest being who was by my side at the most cruel hours and who, in spite of all the difficulty of living close by me, belongs to me entirely, forever, without a doubt . . . He is certainly the only one whom I have ever loved, loved as a brother, and in whom I have had the most absolute confidence . . .

Finally, at the foundation of all my misery, I know that—somewhere in the big wide world—there is a being ready to share my life, whatever it might be, who values what is good and who pardons what is bad in me, who tries to help by healing the bleeding wounds of my heart.

Reminiscence: the evening of the day that Abd-el-Kader had received his dismissal, we went to the zaouïya of Elbeyada at about six o'clock, in great mystery.

Preceded by Aly, we walked carefully, having met each other at the Christian cemetery. We took the western road (lower). I was sick . . .

I remember being behind the zaouïya and having the agonizing feeling that I would not be able to get back onto the horse. My head was spinning, an unspeakable heaviness invading my limbs.

Returning about nine o'clock, we arrived at the city's first houses in the deep night under the shimmering vault of the radiant stars. A heavy silence reigned, troubled only by the regular clinking of the Arab bits in the horses' bruised mouths . . .

But soon the Souakria's ferocious dogs, raised in the Souf oued's solitary bordj, discovered us and began their shrill racket. At that moment, a shooting star detached from the sky on the western horizon and slowly descended in the direction of the Allenda road . . . Suddenly, exploding like a silent Roman candle, it grew in size and shot up in an iridescent, wonderful blue blaze that lit up all the pale countryside in an instant . . .

Then everything went out, and the stars resumed their impassive and peaceful sparkling once again.

"It's the torch of the saints . . . Sometimes at night it descends like that toward those who must die."

Abd-el-Kader's voice faded in the silence, and we reached my residence in silence.

Once again I think: where will I be, under what sky and on what earth, one year from now, at a similar epoch?

THURSDAY, FEBRUARY 7, 1901,
EIGHT O'CLOCK IN THE EVENING

*Conclusion of the narrative interrupted January 29
by the departure from Behima.*

As we arrived in the vast courtyard, we found the servants. Sidi Elimam was still counting off his prayer beads after the evening prayer.[35]

While waiting for him, I listened to the tolba recite the Koran rhythmically and slowly in the vast mosque already filled with shadow . . .

I finally saw the cheikh appear . . . Sitting on a mat under the wall, I was waiting impatiently for the many visitors to greet Sidi Elimam. Finally, we retired into the vast sandy room under the first cupola.

Then, while the cheikh had gone in to order dinner and prepare what I had asked of him, I leaned on the mosque wall near one of the open windows.

In the dim light of a candle stuck against one of the walls, grayish groups of the faithful appeared confused. Slowly, rhythmically they repeated Djilani's dikr:

"ﺽ *There is no God other than God!*"

Profound and sweet sadness. Dined alone with the cheikh in one of the zaouïya's vast rooms, served by strange Negresses speaking to each other in the language of faraway Bornou, with its plaintive and melodic accents.

---

35. Eberhardt's note in margin: "Conclusion of the errand in Elakbab. Ended in Batna, April 12, 1901, five o'clock in the evening."

Quickly left again under clear and transparent moonlight. Arrived about ten o'clock.

The last time I went to Elakbab with the *toubib*, returned by going through the Trefaoui road dunes. Took the main road to Elbayada.

Never have the Souf gardens seemed so beautiful to me in the great golden afternoon light. Impression of profound tenderness for this country whose splendor I have perhaps never felt with such intensity.

<hr>

BATNA, APRIL 12, 1901

Reread the melancholy register after a horrible day of heavy boredom and mournful sadness.

The sirocco has been blowing for several days; the heat has become suffocating. I feel overwhelmed and sick . . . Still about 310 days of this intolerable life!

Following some excerpts from Nadson.[36]

In truth, these eleven months of forced reclusive life in Batna will have perhaps been the most difficult of all of my life's trials. What torments me is not poverty—it's misery, that is to say the absence of the most minimally necessary, without which one is the slave of unending material worries, unending agonies for the following day.

A thousand blessings by comparison on the last agonizing days in El Oued, the Behima catastrophe and the first days in the hospital. That was suffering. Here, it's boredom, the mournful boredom of living among beings devoid of intelligence, living in horrible mediocrity and in the midst of the indiscretion of females who cannot be dignified with the name of human beings. Oh! When will the two of us have the desert's blessed solitude and silence, far from humans and their stupidity!

The only being whose presence is not at all a burden to me, outside of Slemane, is Khelifa, the simple and good servant, a link to the past who speaks to me about our Souf and the days that have gone by. The

36. Noted by Doyon.

only hours when I can savor some rest are at night, close to Rouh', in the *calm safety* offered by those hours when nothing comes to separate us. There are hours, too, when—alone with Souf—I dream opposite fields inundated with light, far from the city, one of the most vile and stupid that there is, in the restful silence of grasses and flowers, to the naive songs of birds living happily.

Here, or at Lamri's, anywhere I'm not alone together with Rouh' or completely by myself, I feel irritated; a quiet anger arises in me toward people and things, and an insurmountable feeling of disgust.

This record contains at least a sort of outline of my life, of my thoughts and impressions, during the most strange, the most agitated, and without a doubt, the most decisive period of my life.

Started with quotes on the eve of my departure from Paris, continued in Marseille, Geneva, Algiers, and especially in El Oued, this book reflects well the sadness, the wanderings, and the anguish of that period, so recent, but now dead and buried.

In reality, this period of my life ended in Behima on January 29 . . .

Third Daily Journal

Notes, Thoughts, and Impressions Begun in the
Military Hospital, El Oued, February 1901

In the name of the powerful and merciful God!

ᴗ *"All those on earth are mortal; only your God—venerable and worthy of praise—will live on."*

"Oh! The bitter and irremediable sadness of never ever being able again to exchange with her a single thought!" (Loti, *Fantôme d'Orient*).[1]

FEBRUARY 3, 1901

*Noted in the hospital, in memory of the nights of
January 28, 29, and 31, 1901.*

† Night's long winter drags on interminably without sleep in the dead silence. Here in the narrow and cramped hospital room, it is dark and suffocating. The nightlight, hung on the wall near the window, faintly illuminates the poor and pitiful scene: the damp walls with the yellow baseboards, two white soldiers' cots, a small black table, shelves with books and flasks . . . The window is covered with a military-issue blanket . . . Not a sound in the enormous barracks courtyard . . . From time to time a far-off, prolonged barking reaches my hearing, made keen by illness . . . Then everything becomes silent again. Shhh! One can hear whispering, a soldier's regular and mechanical step. Then a sharp snap of rifle butts, a cold, brief order . . . Then more steps heard leaving to the right in the direction of the infantry barracks. The door guard has

---

1. Doyon's note: Some poems by Nadson follow; then the personal secrets begin again on these pages, written in Russian.

been relieved . . . Once again silence falls . . . And I languish alone. My wounded and shaken head burns . . . My whole body hurts . . . As for my half-ruined arm, I don't know where to put it. It makes me suffer, bothers me, and is horribly heavy. With my intact right arm, I transport it from one place to another with boredom . . . No rest anywhere. Wherever I put it, I hurt; I hurt to the point of nausea . . .

Dark, terrible thoughts slip into my sick, inflamed head. My situation seems even unhappier and more inextricable than it is in reality. Despair takes over my soul. My chest is bound by a cold terror. "Yes, I will not escape from the assassins' hands . . ." And everyone, everyone, even the doctor, is part of the plot. Then suddenly my eyes fall on the rules artistically transcribed on a piece of white paper tacked to the wall . . .

The room is half dark, but I begin—almost despairingly—to read these ordinary lines. The effort hurts my tired eyes, but I force myself to decipher this sergeant's tight rounded writing all the same . . . And the impossibility of deciphering the lines oppresses me, puts me into a state of despair.

Then, all of a sudden I recall the details of the fateful day . . . Here I am, hit on the head—I lift my eyes: in front of me with his arms lifted high stands the assassin . . . I can't tell what he is holding in his hands . . . Then I teeter, moaning, and collapse onto a chest . . . My head is spinning, I'm in agony, and I'm nauseated, my thoughts are going numb . . . Everything has suddenly gone dark; the lights have all gone out . . . I am rolling in a bottomless abyss . . . One single thought goes through my benumbed brain: *Death . . . Neither sadness nor fear . . .* "There is no other God than God and Mohammed is his prophet!" Everything has gone dark . . . Cold sweat covers my forehead. And once again, with despair, I transport my sick arm from one place to another . . . The bone causes me gnawing pain; the muscle that has been cut contracts and makes my fingers contract . . . The deep-stitched wound burns and causes shooting pains. I can't take it any longer! Terrible, inexpressible anguish takes over my soul, and the powerless tears of a child flow down my cheeks . . .

Through the window above the door I look at the pale moonlight above the building across the way where the autopsy chamber is located, with its iron table and containers of disinfectants . . . Maybe I'll be

there soon on that horrible slab! Death itself doesn't frighten me . . .
I'm only afraid of suffering, of long and absurd suffering . . . and still of
something dark, undefined, mysterious, and invisible surrounding me,
yet perceptible only to me . . .

The exploding stars look on impassively with their clear eyes, as if
they were glancing from inaccessible skies into my prison . . . Mystery,
the world's great mystery, forever impenetrable! I lean my head down,
discouraged: I am alone, poor, sick . . . I have no place from which to
receive mercy, help. The meanness of men is incommensurable . . . The
only being who loves me, who is dear to me, has been torn away, separated from me by the Pharisees . . . and the touching brotherly attention of
a pure soul has been pushed away from my bed of suffering. I am alone!

Mamma is dead and her White Spirit has left the earthly world—a
stranger to her—forever. The old philosopher has also disappeared into
the gloom of the grave; the brother-friend is too far away . . . I am alone!
Forever . . .

And if it is written, if my destiny is to die here in the hoary desert, not
one brotherly hand will pass over my dead eyes . . . At the last earthly
moment, not one brotherly mouth will open to console and caress me . . .

And, powerless, I cry, I cry for my abbreviated life, lost prematurely . . .

Slowly, as if with premeditated slowness, the day begins to break . . .

Finally, above the gray cupolas, the western horizon turns gray too
. . . Dismal black-blue clouds are suspended above the earth, and an
unwelcoming and mournful morning penetrates my room . . .

Strange impression here, where the sun is always so ardently clear
and so tirelessly royal!

My soul is even darker, dimmer . . .

The countless roosters of the city call out to each other in the distance . . . According to the sound, my habituated ear recognizes in which
neighborhood they are singing, and in my tired imagination arise the
portraits of my life spent here . . .

But suddenly next door, a hoarse bugle rings out under the low portico of the infantrymen's barracks, then becomes shrill and strong . . .
Immediately, one hears the squeaking of the fortress's heavy doors being
opened for the day. Then in the hospital building itself, sounds that are

already familiar to me can be heard: the nurse in Arabic slippers worn-down at the heel, the two corporals in heavy nailed shoes, the sergeant, all these people begin coming and going. In the barracks the sounds of yelling, hailing, singing, and laughing rise up . . . Far away, toward the east, one hears the spahis' horses neighing as they are taken to water . . . It seems like a stone is falling from my soul.

Once again, the day, the world, noise! The limping nurse, taciturn and gentle, will soon arrive with a coffee pot and a glass . . . And then light steps will echo on the cement sidewalk . . . In the door a bright red tunic will appear, and the wonderful and soft light of brown eyes, his soft and radiant light, will illuminate the whole dismal room . . . A low chesty voice, a bit tremulous, with the singsong accent of the North will be heard . . .

And once again my soul will feel more serene, and once again my heart will be warmer . . .[2]

". . . And the mere name of Senegal made him see again the infinite sands, the listless red evenings when an enormous sun goes down on the desert . . . All of that strangely attracted him, especially the Saharan shore, the Moors' impenetrable shore" (Pierre Loti, *Matelot*).

EL OUED, FEBRUARY 20, 1901,
SEVEN O'CLOCK IN THE MORNING

Yesterday, first outing on horseback, on the Amiche road . . .

These last few days, the gray walls of the neighborhood have weighed on me, have seemed to tighten around me and to strangely oppress me. I felt like a prisoner there . . . But after yesterday's ride, I aspire only to stay confined there until the day that I'll leave the Souf oued—without a doubt forever.

After this brief outing, I felt some of the bitterest sadness of my life!

The dunes are still there, and the gray city, and the recessed gardens . . .

But the great charm of this country, the magic of its horizons and light, has gone . . . and the Souf is empty, irremediably empty.

2. Doyon's note: The text in Russian ends here.

The dunes are desolate, no longer as extraordinary or full of mystery as I once found them to be long ago . . . No, they are dead . . . The gardens are sickly and without charm . . . The horizon is empty and the light is dull and leaden . . .

And I feel more foreign here than anywhere else, more solitary, and I wish to leave, to flee this country that now is nothing but the ghost of what I once loved so much.

And I realize now, no longer able to trick myself henceforth, that all the charm that we attribute to certain regions of the earth are but deception and illusion. As long as aspects of surrounding nature *respond* to the state of our soul, then we believe we have discovered in them splendor, a particular beauty . . . But from the day when our ephemeral soul changes, everything falls into ruin and disappears . . .

And I feel sad, infinitely sad. I would have liked to leave the Souf in the frame of mind in which I found myself before Behima, to leave it behind me with the illusion that it kept its great melancholy charm and that it would jealously guard it for me for the day of the problematic and certainly far-off return . . .

When I arrived here seven months ago, that charm *was not there* . . . From then on, how could I believe in the true existence of every mysterious thing, which I believed I felt in this country and which was nothing other than the reflection of the sad mystery of my soul!

And I am condemned to thus carry in myself all my great sadness, forever unformulated, all this world of thoughts through the countries and cities of the earth, without ever finding the Icarus of my dreams!

What weighs on me especially is to be unable to express all the crushing burden of ideas and sensations that live in the solitary silence of my soul, which often cause me very painful agony.

Is it possible that my soul will thus continue to darken through the months and years, and what deadly gloom must be the result?

Is it possible that what still makes the singular happiness in my life—and which certainly emanates from myself and not from the exterior world—will also dissipate, and that I will remain definitively *alone* in the world, without any possible consolation?

I believe that, in this moment, if I could have the *absolute, reasonable,* and *irrefutable* certitude that I will reach this lugubrious denouement in a short period of time, that the *black*, unfathomable *boredom* that sometimes takes over me and tortures me beyond all measure, could become my normal and *constant* state, I would immediately find the power to avoid this eventuality through a very calm and very coldly envisaged planned death . . . For it is only this closed and personal world living in my soul that keeps me from suicide . . . and the hope to see this world last as long as me and, perhaps, still develop and become larger. Very sincerely, life in *itself* is nothing to me, and death exercises a strange attraction on my imagination . . .

Yesterday, I wanted to try to note all that has made me suffer so much, which seemed so clear, so undisputable to me . . . But, as always, I didn't succeed, and this temptation has had no result other than creating trouble and uncertainty in my mind . . .

I *know nothing, nothing* about myself and about the external world . . . That is perhaps the only truth.

THE NEXT DAY, FEBRUARY 21, 1901

Noon.

Yesterday I went to the home of the good cheikh Sid-el-Hussine with the toubib.

Well no! The Oued Souf is not at all empty, and the Sahara's great sun has not gone out at all . . .

The other day, it was my heart that was empty and dark. It was my soul that had become oblivious to the splendors surrounding it.

Yesterday, a rather quick and unplanned outing under a beautiful pale sun. The wind laid a shroud of gray dust on the palm trees and disturbed the dunes between Kouïnine and Tarzout once again. Blown by winter's great winds, the small sad towns of Gara, Teksebet, and Kouïnine seem more deserted and more desolate than ever.

Under a pale sky, the Souf is wan and the dunes are white . . . Sometimes in the evening, from over by the Messaaba, the enchanted sounds and infinitely sad modulations of a small Bedouin flute reach me . . .

These faraway sounds, which I will not hear again a few days from now, fill me with unfathomable melancholy.

… This morning while the toubib was humming, I felt a sensation of remoteness from my Tunisian life—very dead, however, and very deeply buried under so many gray ashes, like my Saharan life will soon be …

I remembered that September evening two years ago leaning out the small window of the bellowing Jew of La Goulette, with Aly. It was the night before the lugubrious departure, when I felt everything collapsing around me and in me; only death seemed a possible outcome. I was listening, on one side, to the calm sea gently murmuring, and on the other, to the pure and clear voice of Sidi Béyène's little Noucha singing the sad Andalusian cantilena: "॰ *My sanity has fled, my sanity has fled!*"

Aly's warm, passionate, and sonorous voice began the melancholy refrain again, as if in a dream, and I was listening …

I sometimes have sudden reminders of the recent past, the most forgotten of late. Memories of Tunis haunt me especially. Street names, forgotten and indifferent, come back to me unconsciously …

… The white cheikh has returned. I'll see him again tomorrow … What for?

Today I went to the house, and I felt a horrible sensation of emptiness.

While going through the door, I thought, with an intimate shiver, "Rouh' will never again cross this threshold …"

Never again, beneath the white arch of our little room, will we sleep in each other's arms, wrapped tightly around each other as if we had had a dark foreboding that enemy forces were looking for us in the dark in order to separate us … Never again will the drunkenness of our senses unite us under this roof that both of us loved so much.

Yes, everything has ended.

In four days I too will leave and once more take the northern road that I had so much wished to never follow again.

In a last feeling of melancholy childishness, I would like for my tomb to be in the white sand made golden and purple by the great devouring sun, morning and evening …

I must leave … Very far away at the horizon is the honest and good loving being—the goal of this voyage—whom I have chosen to soften my wandering and solitary life . . .

There is this very young soul that belongs to me, whom I jealously love. With all my strength, I am going to try to make him—not in the image of mine, which would be a sacrilege—but such as I would like it, especially as † *the White Spirit* would have liked! Oh, She for whom naive goodness and the pureness of the heart were everything would have certainly loved him with all her soul!

I must leave, and here I am missing, not only the wonderful country where I would have wished to live and die, but even this "hospice," even this neighborhood to which I have accustomed myself, even the familiar faces of the nurses and the infantrymen . . .

I especially miss the exchanges—often acerbic, never hateful or hypocritical—with the good toubib, almost the only thinking and adequately sincere being here.

I believe that this man was able to guess that beneath all the strangeness, beneath all of my life's incoherence, there is a foundation of honesty and true sensitivity, and that the light of intelligence still burns in my mind.

And I begin to feel for him the tenderness—largely stemming from gratitude—that I feel for anyone who doesn't throw any foolish or brazen stones at me and who discerns who I really am despite all the accumulated debris. Who sees what I would have become were I not an abandoned person and had I not suffered so much.

How I love rereading these *Daily Journals*, these books—choppy and incoherent for others—where there is everything . . . *everything that makes my soul live!*

There are hours when I am alone and this reading is restful and salutary.

Their variety in itself is one of their charms . . .

I would like to see all that has charmed me faithfully and intelligently reflected in them . . . .

Departure from El Oued, Monday, February 25, 1901,
at one thirty in the afternoon.

February 25 Went all the way to Tarzout with the doctor. From there, went to the home of Sid-el-Hussine. Spent the night. The twenty-sixth, eight in the morning, departure with Lackhdar; deïra. Rejoined the caravan in the dunes.

Bir-bou-Chama, dark and sad impression.

February 26 Arrived in Bir-bou-Chama toward the magh'reb. Black sky, gray darkness, and violent and icy wind from the north.

Caravan: Bach-hamar Sasi. Deïra: Naser and Lakhdar. One infantry-man, Rezki; Embarek C. Salem; and El Hadj Mohammed—all three from Guémar. Two crazy men accompanied by a young man (from Algiers). Hennia—mother of the spahi Zouaouë—and his son Abdallah.

Sif-el-Ménédi.

February 27 Left on the twenty-seventh at about seven in the morning. Arrived in Sif-el-Ménédi at about five in the evening. Road: trees, plains of mica and talc, scrub; a few chott in the area around the bordj.

Bordj on a very low hillside, horizon of scrub. Very cultivated garden, salty marshes nearby. Very good impression, that of the salty oases of the Oued Rirh. In the evening, Lakhdar's méhari having left, the deïra went to look for him. I was exhausted, had a headache (walked one-third of the route). Sitting on my bed, I thought of the pleasure of living some time in this bordj with the immense city of scrub as the horizon. Children were singing in the garden. Persistent impression of the Oued Rirh.

Noted in Stah-el-Hamraïa, Thursday, February 28, 1901, evening.

February 28 Thursday, left about seven in the morning with Lakhdar via the Chott Bou-Djeloud. The caravan is making a detour. Salty, rocky, gray-yellow, clayey lands. Sparse creeping vegetation. Then a few clayey slopes and knolls in the form of peaks, blue-and-red clay. Chott cut through by rocky slopes. First, brown chott; then saltpeter just above the ground. Toward the left (west) and toward the right, deep, flooded chott. Clear water tinged with blue. Toward the west, toward the great Melriri chott, immense blue-green lakes with stratified archipelagos in the form of small perpendicular walls emerging from the water and reflected in it. Between two islands the infinity of the Melriri chott opens without any appreciable horizon, as if opening on to the pale, slightly hazy azure sky.

Larks rise up from rocky terrain, giving their melancholy and tender cries as they beat their wings, then swoop down into the bushes.

Very difficult crossing of the softened great chott.

At each step, Souf slips. Crossed on foot.

At the entrance to the chott, two pyramids of dried stone indicate a place where two tribes battled thirty years ago.

Terrains with yellow rocks just above the ground cut through by the chott's white, blue, or plum-colored splashes. In certain places, the ground absolutely has the color of iced gingerbread.

The Stah-el-Hamraïa bordj on a rocky slope with the chott very low to the west. A garden above the chott, a big fountain to the north.

Discussion with the bach-hamar. Received permission to sleep in Stah-el-Hamraïa. A bit of a fever. Very nice weather in the morning, a bit of wind and clouds around noon.

How this sonorous and exotic name of Stah-el-Hamraïa—the name of a place I love—makes me dream the most profound and melancholy dream.

――――――――

CHAGGA, FRIDAY, MARCH 1, 1901,
NINE O'CLOCK IN THE EVENING

Spent the night in Stah-el-Hamraïa. Spent the evening in the bordj's room listening to Lakhdar and the camel herders sing.

Went to sleep with Khelifa and the infantryman Rezki. Left at red sunrise with a bloody sky rising slowly above the immense chott cut through by reddish terrain.

El Hamraïa garden: muddy, salty terrain full of marsh grasses. A few palm trees, tamarinds, and fig trees scattered in the marsh to the northwest of the bordj.

Left on horseback. Sometimes salty, sometimes rocky terrain. White-flowering broomweed, Saharan trees, small bushes with blue flowers. A few chott, salty yellow earth and sand. Dismounted near the first guemira. Had lunch beyond the second one behind the last chott . . . barren; broomweed.

A little before this guemira, to the left is a good fresh well in the scrub. Bought some hares from hunters. Left again on foot. Met several caravans. Noticed an engineer captain's tent at the bottom of a slope to the left.

The Chott Melriri appears again, a milky sea without a horizon, dotted with small white islands. Rocky terrain. Arrived at the El-Mguébra bordj with Rezki. Drew water, drank coffee, then left El-Mguébra (on horseback). Bordj up high. The guemira, to the southwest of the bordj, surmounting a construction in ruin. Three wells below, one of which is very brackish. Garden near the well where we drew water to drink using Rezki's belt.

Left again. Passed the caravan a little before the sunset. Met Elhadj Mohammed, one of the crazy men, and their guide. At nightfall, dismounted again, had Elhadj mount. To our right we see one of the crazy men from Chegga.

Arrived at night. Argument with the guardians.

Chegga, March 1.

The gardens are scattered in the white salty terrain.

Khelifa, Rezki, and I are sleeping in the small room to the left. Next to us are Hennia and her son in the large bedroom. In the other are the crazy men, the guide, and the exiles. The deïra are sleeping outside with the camel herders, next to the fountain.

Next door, in the garden flooded with salty water, the toads are singing melancholically in the great desert silence.

This evening, on the road, the birds sang languorously. Torrid heat all day long.

Thought lovingly about this Sahara that has bewitched me for life, and about the joy of returning there. Impression of audacity and boundless energy all day long in the face of destiny . . . especially this evening.

However, another thought comes to haunt me and sleep flees my tired head: down there in Batna different kinds of drunkenness await me, and at this idea alone, I feel voluptuous anguish tightening my heart.

The day after tomorrow, or in two days, I will be able to give free rein to the sensual madness torturing me this evening, and to relive the beautiful mad nights of El Oued . . . hold my master in my two arms, to my heart oppressed by too much unappeased love . . .

This evening I am aware that I am still young, that life is not at all black and discolored, and that hope is not abandoning me in the least . . .

As long as the Sahara's wonderful immensity will be there, I will have a refuge where my sorely tormented soul will have respite from modern life's pettiness.

Take Rouh' far away into the desert, far from men, in order to pursue daring adventures and indescribable dreams interrupted by wild hours . . .

BATNA, MARCH 20, 1901,
ELEVEN O'CLOCK IN THE EVENING

Slept in Chegga March 1.

Went into the garden, left at dawn on March 2.

The red sun was coming up above the massif. The Aurès, to the north, were becoming iridescent with bright-red and pink shades. Garden: seguia and large pool of water at the entrance.

Left by horse and went as far as Djefir. Got ahead of the caravan, arrived trotting. Didn't find the guardian, drew water at the large well. Met a convoy going to Touggourt. Sent a greeting to Si Saïd. Left again. Me on foot, Rezki on the horse. Lunch in sight of Saada. Left again by foot. Met Rouh' a quarter of an hour before Saada. Left again by horse. Stopped beyond the oued.

Arrived in Biskra March 2. Arriving in Biskra at the magh'reb, stopped our horses, did an about-face toward the purplish Sahara in the sunset's fire. Spent the night at Zitouni's.

Spent the day of the third and the night in Biskra. Left for Batna on March 4 at one in the afternoon. Arrived at about five o'clock. Spent the night at Goussou's. Changed lodgings on the fifth.

March 17, five in the evening, left for Constantine, slept. Arrived at nine o'clock. Slept in the Grand-Hôtel restaurant. Eight o'clock in the morning, went to the court-martial. Left again on the eighteenth at 3:35. Arrived in Batna on the eighteenth at eight thirty in the evening.

I wouldn't care for the present real misery and the cloistered life of Arab women . . . The absolute dependence in which I henceforth find myself vis-à-vis Rouh' would be blessed . . . But what tortures me and makes life hardly tolerable is the separation from him and the bitter sadness of being unable to see him but for a few rare furtive moments. What does the rest matter to me when I live again, like yesterday, as I hold him in my arms and I look into his eyes, "face-to-face," as Aziyadé said?

Thus the great love of my life—which I believed must never come— has been born unconsciously, involuntarily!

What torments and what joys, what distresses and what ecstasies!

BATNA, TUESDAY, MARCH 26, 1901,
ONE O'CLOCK IN THE AFTERNOON

Today, went to the foot of the mountain with Souf, let the horse go out to pasture, and stretched out under a pine tree: I dreamed as I looked at the large valley, the blue mountains across from Batna, panic stricken in its slums, the city of exile and misery. Sensation of voluptuous rapture in the great air and the great sun, far from the gray walls of my monotonous prison. Everything is turning green again, the trees are flowering, the sky has the blue of an abyss, and innumerable birds are singing everywhere . . .

Up there on that mountain that intensely reminded me of the Jura or the Salève, the junipers and white cedars perfumed the air.

The cool and vivifying wind rustled softly in the pines against the mountain's sonorous echoes.

Where is the far-off autumn day when, my eyes closed and my heart at peace (oh, deep blindness of human nature!), I listened to the Souf's eternal wind rustling in the tough djerid of the Chott Debila palm trees! Where are our Oued-Souf, its white dunes and its gardens, and Salah ben Teliba's peaceful house bordering on the Sidi-Mestour dunes and the silent necropolis where the Ouled-Ahmed will sleep! Where is the land of the saintly zaouïya and the marabout's tombs, the harsh and radiant earth where faith's flame burns and where we were happy? Where is all of that, and will I ever see it again?

Here, total destitution . . . No food, no money, no heating . . . Nothing!

And yet all of that does not worry me at all.

Today my soul is plunged into limitless, but resigned, calm and sweet sadness.

The days emerge and subside, falling into the past's black nothingness; and each new dawn brings us closer to the day of deliverance, to February 1902, which all in all will be for both of us the *beginning* of true life.

 ꙮ *And would that Allah were to manifest a desire and say, "May it be, it will be!"*

Everything is in God's hands, and nothing is done *but according to his will.*

BATNA, FRIDAY, APRIL 12, 1901,
FIVE O'CLOCK IN THE EVENING

Every morning these days, I leave astride my faithful Souf in order to spend a few peaceful hours along the roads.

After a few wild stampedes on the parade ground and a lesson given to Souf, I take the Lambese road, and I go beyond the fourth kilometer.

There I dismount; and sitting at the edge of the road, at the corner of a field of rapeseed, a vast carpet of bright gold at the foot of the dark Ouled-Abdi, I smoke while dreaming, holding Souf's reins as he greedily eats the green grass sorted out carefully from among the flowers.

Wretched farms stretch out along the road's white ribbon, with intensely green fields.

In the distance toward the north, fields of "sulfur flowers" throw carpets of pale and silvery lilac onto the slopes. The silhouette of the sad city of barracks and official buildings is far behind me. I turn my back to it and look at the flowered countryside where skylarks are singing and rapid swallows flock.

And in this already-familiar place, I find a few moments of true happiness and profound peace.

One of these evenings, lying next to Slimène on Khelifa's mat, I was looking out the window at the blue sky where a few clouds gilded by the setting sun were drifting, at the trees' peaks suddenly turned green, and at the top of a poplar tree: I suddenly felt a yearning for the past, intense to the point of tears . . . These days, in general, in this similar country, memories of Villa Neuve come to haunt me.

The sirocco has been blowing for two days. The sky is clouded over and we feel burdened. Today, a long slow walk on the sad and charmless Biskra road. Then boring errands for Lamri's family.

Returned at about one thirty, exhausted; stayed to read my former *Daily Journals* stretched out on the mat until four thirty. Sadness, nostalgia for the Souf, boredom, and malaise . . .

BATNA, APRIL 26, 1901,
ELEVEN O'CLOCK IN THE EVENING

I've been vaguely sad this evening, and for a few days, in an indefinable manner. The loneliness without Ouïha weighs on me terribly, and boredom is gnawing at me. After yesterday's storm, Batna is flooded, dark, freezing, and full of mud and filthy streams. My poor Souf is very ill, and I am even deprived of my melancholy walks along the roads, or in the desolate cemetery perched up there at the foot of the gray hill, where the vandalized tombs—as frightening as doors slightly opened onto the horrifying void of human dust—are scattered in wild disorder among the fragrant tufts of gray *chih* and red *timgrit*, near the green field where violet flax, white anemones, and scarlet poppies are flowering . . .

The other day, I wandered among Muslims attempting to call forth rain with their flutes and drums, with the flags of Islamic formal occasions. This rain will make the ephemeral and hasty Algerian spring last a bit longer, mixing summer and spring flowers in its haste for renewal, and seeming already prepared to end on days of heavy sirocco.

Yesterday, after six long days, when I saw him only furtively at night for a few short moments by the door of the cursed neighborhood where he is exiled, Rouh' came . . . I held him in my arms; and suddenly after the wild passion of our first almost-savage embraces, tears flowed from our eyes, and our hearts very mysteriously felt pangs of anguish without comprehension and without words.

Then at night after an idiotic race under the torrential rain, submitted to out of pleasure in taunting Tarhat—a hypocrite who all the same had the good taste not to dissemble—and after reading a little, I fell asleep and Vava appeared to me, lavishing Rouh' with tenderness and expressing to me his appreciation of him in a tone from long ago . . . Vaguely, as if it dated from long ago, I remember this dream and its impression as profound and sweet, like a very mysterious confirmation of Augustine's comforting telegram.

Yesterday, I noted the ingenuousness, the goodness, and the beauty of Slimène's lovely soul, which belongs to me, because of the childlike joy I felt from Augustine coming back to me and acknowledging us. In spite of everything that I have had, everything that I have, and everything that I will still have to suffer, I bless God and destiny for having led me to the unforgettable city of sands in order to give me to this being who is my *only consolation*, my only joy in this world where I am the most disinherited of all the disinherited and yet where I feel the richest of all, for I have a priceless treasure.

And sometimes, even often, out of a habit of suffering too much, I wonder with profound anguish whether this happiness won't be taken away from me by jealous destiny, by death.

But after him, because of past experience, I know it's useless to wait and to hope. Even more so: if I even knew that I would find another who would love me as much were he to disappear, I wouldn't want that other, for the sole reason that it would be another and it is Slimène whom I love with absolute love, as deeply sweet and tender as he is passionate.

I've often been harsh and unjust toward him, I've harangued him for no reason, I've been crazy enough to the point of hitting him, feeling ashamed at myself because he didn't defend himself and instead smiled at my blind fury . . . Afterward, the slightest shadow of misconduct toward him causes me real pain and a sincere disgust in myself.

In the evening, went to the house of the policeman whom the enemy has certainly made me responsible for spying on. It doesn't matter what I said to him the other evening, I will repeat it openly, and it's true, because *it is he who first* made the supposition that it was P . . . who had wished for my death and that the assassin would not be punished. If this is the case, it will be my death sentence everywhere I go in the South, the only country where we can live . . .

The Behima crime not punished or lightly punished, it will be a cynical admission and also a clear indication for the Tidjanya: "Kill Si Mahmoud, you have nothing to fear."

However, God has already once stayed the assassin's hand, and Abdallah's sword missed . . . May his will be done! If God wishes for me to die as a martyr as I asked on the night of Elhadj, wherever I am, God's will shall reach me. If not, all the machinations of those who have piled crime upon crime onto their heads will serve nothing except to confuse them.

Death does not frighten me, only I would not like to die obscurely and in vain. I know now, for having seen it very close, for having felt its black and icy wing brush me, that its approach instantly leads to an absolute detachment from, a definitive renouncing of things of this world. I also know that my nerves and my will hold strong in great *personal* trials and that I will never make my enemies joyful due to cowardliness or fear.

There is, however, from the point of view of the future, one thing that frightens me: I am absolutely not hardened against the misfortunes that could happen to Slimène or Augustine. In the face of those, I am horribly weak. There my entire prodigious carefree attitude abandons me, and I become weaker than a child. It is difficult to imagine more profound misery than that where I am struggling: well, it only worries me because our debts can cause a disaster for Slimène.

Otherwise, in spite of the turmoil to my aristocratic nature, caused by the inevitable calculations of every cent—from this point of view—I really don't give a damn about the situation in which I personally find myself, but which very few would tolerate. Fortunately, the enemy believes I'm rich, as I have been able to discern from the policeman's words.

I was right to throw money out the window two years ago, here and in Biskra: the reputation of my wealth is as useful to us from the point of view of our defense as the reality of this wealth would be. Ah! If only those fools knew that I am in black misery and that they could lose me by the smallest humiliations, they would not miss an opportunity to do so!

And what crimes they must have on their conscience after all, what fear of the light, to tremble so before me—I who, first out of nonchalance, and then out of fear of harming Slimène, have not done much all in all, except to make inquiries in El Oued!

Obviously they are scared. Without that, why don't they arrest me, for example, for espionage, and why don't they deport me?

All of that because, as P was saying, "That crazy woman could cause us a lot of trouble."

I was right to attribute to a carefree life and eccentricity the miserable kind of life that I lead here: that way, my misery doesn't show too much.

The fact is that I have reached the point of knowingly going to people's homes *in order to eat*, with the goal of maintaining my health, something that would have seemed as impossible in the past as this other thing that I also did, however: to go find the closed-off and mysterious characters who are the marabouts and to ask them for money.

This constitution of mine is probably one of iron, since it is holding its own against all likelihood: the anguish of the last days in El Oued, the wound, the nervous commotion and the enormous loss of blood in Behima, the hospital, the trip half done on foot, the misery, here, the cold and the bad food of which the most obvious is the bread—all of that has not succeeded in toppling me. How long will this last?

I truly believe that the strength of my lively soul and my carefree personality count for a lot in this, and that all it would take to make me sick would be to begin brooding over my situation.

How the devil can one explain that at home, with excellent clothing, fire, and healthy food, among other things, even with Mamma's idolizing care, the least chill turned into bronchitis, yet now—though I have suffered from El Oued's icy cold, including in the hospital, though I have been exposed to the road's bad weather, though I am freezing here, my feet continually damp, dressed in summer clothes and torn shoes—I don't even have a cold?

The human body is nothing, and the human soul is everything. Besides, a beautiful soul is the only real beauty, since without it physical beauty itself does not exist for a true aesthete . . . Why do I adore Rouh's eyes? It is neither for their shape, nor for their color—it is for the soft and honest radiance that makes them so surprisingly beautiful . . .

For me, the soul's supreme beauty can be translated in practice by fanaticism leading *harmoniously*—that is to say, by a path of absolute sincerity—to martyrdom.

Sidi Mohammed Taïeb is truly dead, and I feel profound sadness thinking about this man whom I can see once again on that evening of my departure last September, his beautiful eagle's head in the blue light of the full moon, on the terrace of Taleb Saïd's crumbling house across from the small gray dunes to the north of Touggourt . . . And I hear his voice say to me, "We will see each other again ᵛ *if it pleases Allah!* Si Mahmoud."

He was unaware, and all were unaware of what was being plotted in the enemy shadows at that moment, against my life and his, and that this goodbye must be the supreme and eternal adieu! And that we must never meet again ᵛ *until the day of resurrection*, in that great beyond where there is undoubtedly reason and justice, now absent from this world, where the just and the martyrs are crushed under the feet of the crowds who run, in their own blood and in the dust of their dead ones, to kiss the footsteps of tyrants, impostors, and bandits!

And what will be the deplorable result of this death for the future of the brotherhood and for our cheikh?

Nine forty-five in the morning.

Learned of new expulsion last night.

❧ *Oh, Toura, you see: Will there be an end to my night. See if there will be support for my love. I spend my night suffering the torments of love. And the ardor of my desires has a stimulant. I hide my love: in my heart, a sign reveals my love. I hide my passion and my desire from Her. And I don't show my heart's love. I will remain patient until the day when my wish will be fulfilled. The reward that crowns patient waiting is worthy of praise!*

The same day, three o'clock in the evening.

Once again, everything is broken, destroyed, ruined. Once again destiny has come to thwart all human expectations and to bend our heads under its cruel breath.

But this world's trials, already too numerous in my life, are only strengthening my soul. I will have the courage to fight against the monstrous iniquity striking me, and I hope to triumph with God's help and that of our master El Djilani.

However, how will I distance myself—God knows for how long—from Rouh', to whom my moral being is attached by such tight bonds, who has ended up becoming a part of me? How can I be deprived of seeing him when the days without him seem unending?

There was no longer but a single and unique joy, only one consolation in my life: to see him. We will sleep in each other's arms two more times ... Two more times I will see his silhouette appear in the door of the poor room that has become dear to us like all the successive lodgings for our love.

And then, nothing more ... The mournful memories of Bône and Marseille, where there is certainly the joy of seeing Augustine again, but what joy would be real without my gentle brother Zizou?

His love and goodness have brightened the darkest hours of this last year ... In his absence everything will be black and grim.

In the midst of the terrible disarray of my life these last few days, darker than any other period that I've lived through, I joyfully note the durability of the sense of beauty, love of art and nature.

I've arrived at the final limit of misery where there are hunger and impoverishment, the continual anxieties of material life. I am like an animal being constantly hunted with the obvious goal of killing it, of annihilating it. I shall be separated from what is most precious to me in the world, from what brightened, in spite of everything, my sad existence, *essentially* sad as it has always been. For years I've known with *certitude* that I would reach this level of misery.

But at the heart of all of this, after all the rifts—and in the face of all the dangers—I feel that I will not weaken, that two things remain intact: my religion and my pride. I am proud to suffer from these not at all common sufferings, to have spilled my blood, and to have been persecuted for a faith.

Life's force has not at all been annihilated in me, prodigious and invincible henceforth; and life—bitter, dark, cruel—is not at all *discolored* and *repugnant.* To brighten it further, from nearby or far away, there is the deep love of Rouh's soul, essentially beautiful and open to all true beauties. There is also the feeling, perhaps more subtle and more sincere even, of art, Beauty and Nature.

It seemed to me, as if to almost everyone, paradoxical in the past (although I already sensed it) that the surrounding misery and vulgarity could not at all impose silence on the sacred meaning of the beautiful, on the love of the good. Well no . . . In me, misery and vulgarity magnify it instead.

There is beauty in all things, and to know how to discern it is the gift of the poet alone: this gift is not at all dead in me, and I glorify myself from it in this manner, for the only *imperishable* treasures are those of *Thought.* A monument's stone, mute for the vulgar, jealously guards—as long as it lasts—the very thought that created its form.

While waiting for the charity that—*perhaps*—will deprive my enemies of a last triumph, leaving aside all human respect, I was able to read and taste today the beauty of a refined book by D'Annunzio . . .

When I was poorer, I was deprived of these subtle joys, and I delighted in the purple and golden reflections of setting suns on the undulating crests of the white dunes of my country of choice . . . I felt the harmony of the undulating curves and the rich spring colors of the hills scattered with flowers and fragrant plants of sad Batna, city of exile and torments.

Poor, poor as the great Eynoub once was, incarnation of human suffering, I felt—and I was—the sovereign master of the marvelous stretches of the beloved desert and the wild mountains of the Aurès.

Sitting like a vagabond on the side of a road, near the faithful and humble unconscious companion who too will be taken from me forever, I looked with the eyes of a feudal lord at the golden fields of flowering rapeseed, at the emerald color of the wheat and barley, and at the opal of the chih with its heady aroma. Only the tomb can take that richness away from me, and not men . . . and who knows, if Mektoub accords me the time to formulate even a few fragments of it, it will survive in the memory of a few people.

Only these superior forms of life are worth being lived, and the greedy and idiotic rich person, if he knew, and the "woman of the world," rich, adulated, believing herself to be beautiful, would envy the miserable old castoff, the lice-ridden lodgings, and the miserly food of someone who has found the source of love (only possible and real when none of the vulgar questions of interest are mixed up with it) and who knows how to proudly make her own the vast Universe and her mysterious soul, to possess it and delight in it entirely more than any autocrat from old delights in his illusory power.

Divine and unique joy of reading, in the mirror of a human eye, the *absoluteness* of earthly love and, in the world's vast horizons, all the way to the breathtakingly far away stars, the indisputable *property title*! "The useless regret of all lost joy, the recalling of all fleeting good, the supreme imploring fleeing full sail on the seas, hiding from all suns behind the mountains, and the implacable desire, and the necessity of death, all these things happened in the solitary song transmuted by art's virtue into sublime essences that the soul could receive without suffering from them" (D'Annunzio, *The Fire*).

Noted in Bône, May 8, six o'clock in the evening.

Left Batna May 6, 1901, four in the morning. Arrived in Bône the same day, three in the morning. Spent the night of sixth in Khoudja house, all day long and night of the seventh, all day long and night of the eighth.

No, life without Slimène is definitely impossible. Everything is discolored, sad; and time is endlessly drawn out. Poor Ouïha Kahla! Poor Zizou! When will I see him again?

MARSEILLE, MAY 22, 1901,
NINE O'CLOCK IN THE EVENING

Wednesday, departure.

Left Bône Thursday, May 9, at six in the evening, aboard the *Berry* of the General Company of Maritime Transportation, fourth-class booking under the name Pierre Mouchet, day laborer. Arrived in Marseille Saturday the twelfth, three in the morning. Disembarked on the jetty. Rode tramway all the way to Oran Street.

Tomorrow, when I've rested somewhat from all the fatigue of the last two days, I'll note in detail my impressions of Bône, of the crossing, and of the first days in Marseille . . . This evening I just want to note the psychological side of this last period, which, having started in tears and anguish, has transformed into a pleasant period, for it is *useful* and has brought happy strokes of luck. For example, the extraordinary meeting with the old friend Abd-el-Aziz-el-Agreby from Sousse, a meeting that will be able to bring great improvement to our situation, to Ouïha and me: maybe he'll obtain something from Algiers; maybe he'll find someone to change places with Slimène in Tunisia? (which would be a dream!) And, in any case, it is very possible that he will start to slowly pay back a part of what he owes me . . .

There is no deportation order for me, and at least that danger, in reality a terrible one, has been avoided. Thus, I'll be able to return to Slimène as soon as I have the means to do so. The war council will furnish most of them to me between now and June 18. Until then, and *starting tomorrow*, I must start working on the Russian project and finish it, for I have the time.

The horizon has cleared a lot everywhere. After the strange encounter yesterday with Abd-el-Aziz, I felt for him *sincere friendship*. A strangely sweet sensation, great joy, and sincere emotion.

Perhaps it is God who for now has put him in my path in order to help me cross this difficult period of my life!

I think of Slimène now, and I think of him *rationally*, for the *first time* perhaps.

Yes, when I will once again be near him, from the first moment, I will have to change my way of being with him, under the threat of compromising the happiness for us as a married couple. Marriage must not be solely based upon love, which—however great and powerful it might be—is not a solid enough foundation. I will have to assume the responsibility of the task, often difficult but indispensable, of devotion. My conduct toward him must be one of constant goodness, a consolation for him in the face of all of life's bitterness. I must develop enough self-control in order to no longer be violent and egotistical toward him, so as not to some day tax his patience, for without that, no common future will be possible . . . I must impose on myself what, given my nature, is the most difficult for me: submission. This of course has its limits and must not go so far as obsequiousness. However, it would make life smoother for both of us. To sum up, I must make a great effort to reform my character and make it more tolerable, which won't be difficult given Slimène's good character and his indulgent sweetness . . .

MARSEILLE, MAY 12, 1901

May 6, left the house on Bugeaud Street at three in the morning. Great calmness, moonlight, profoundly silent streets. Went all the way to the station door with Slimène, Labbadi, and Khelifa . . . Brief rest on a bench in the train station avenue . . . I turned around a last time to see again the almost-indistinct dear red silhouette in the shadow . . .

We separated without too great of a pang of anguish; however, we felt deeply sad: both of us had the sense that we would see each other again very soon . . .

The countryside from Batna to El Guerrah is very poor and sad . . . The sebkha, or lakes, drowned in white haze. From El Guerrah, unheard-of richness of colors and nuances: carpet of poppies thrown like bloody stains onto the dark green of the harvests, snowy anemones, crimson gladiolas, cornflowers spotted with the gold of the rapeseed . . . resembling, alas, my field down there on the Lambèse road, at the fourth kilometer where I came on clear April mornings with my poor faithful Souf . . . Where is Batna, the city of love, of exile and bitterness, which I miss today because the poor friend with the good loving and soft heart remained behind there? . . . Where is Souf, the valiant and faithful horse, quiet companion of my unforgettable races in our country's dunes? Where is Khelifa, where are all those poor things piously brought from El Oued because they were the sacred wreckage of our adored lodging down there? Where is all of that which destiny's wind has dispersed, annihilated?

. . . Arrived in Bône at three o'clock. Intense impression of past days at Khoudja's house in the narrow bluish courtyard where, so many times, I came to dream, still carefree at the enchanted hour of summer's sunsets and where † *the White Spirit* came, she too, to sit down! Impression of a *dream*, of *unreality*, left by this city of which I've seen nothing again, except for the Arab dwelling and the incomparable silhouette at the departure.

Embarked under a pure and luminous sky on May 9 at five in the evening . . .

May 12, these notes were interrupted by a sudden ebb of all the horrible despair caused by the separation with Slimène . . . How can I live without him, God knows for how long, exiled, without lodgings, I who had already gotten used to having my *chez moi*, however poor it was!

Days of boredom and anguish, spent struggling against the anguish of letting Ouïha get lost, against Khoudja's malevolent inertia, and the very dark persistent impression of the unreality of what was surrounding me.

Bône has certainly remained, in its immutable silhouette seen from the sea, the unique, incomparable city that, for two years of nostalgia and suffering, haunted my memory . . . Strange thing, since I came back in 1899, the magic attraction of Annaba seems interrupted; and if the White Spirit's tomb were not there, perhaps I would no longer even aspire to return there!

Feverish, hasty departure. Running, I crossed the hardly glimpsed old town with some porter . . . Watched the once-familiar silhouette of Annaba, henceforth a stranger forever, move into the distance . . . On the *Berry*, under my miserable sailor's outfit and the assumed name of Pierre Mouchet, sat up front, feeling the sadness of an emigrant, of someone exiled, torn violently from his native soil . . . And there, under the surprised eyes of unsmiling passengers, I couldn't hold back the very bitter tears that I had nowhere to go and no means of hiding . . . Watched, with a deep pang of anguish, the multicolored and tumultuous quay and the rust-colored ramparts and Idou and Saint Augustine and the sacred green hill with dark black cypresses . . . Reflected, with sharp pain, that this was Africa's earth, the passionately loved earth of Slimène, that of the Sahara, already very quickly moving far away and being lost to sight in the evening's growing shadows.

This return to Bône resembles a nightmare, so furtive and short, especially agitated and tormented as it was.

Sitting on my bundle of clothes near the winch, thinking about all the deep misery into which I have fallen, about the henceforth absolute destitution where I find myself . . . Thought too about the *background* of the past, about the *prophetic* sailors' outfits worn out of affinity, about the already-distant days of prosperity.

Made my bed in this same rather-warm place and in a true feeling of well-being—the strangely sad and voluptuous well-being of the *Heimatlos*[3]—began to fall asleep with this thought already completely peaceful, out of the habit of suffering: Eden-Purée . . . , as the inscription said, scribbled by the ironic hand of some *Joyeux*[4] on the optical post's door in Kef-ed-Dor . . .

3. Eberhardt's note: *Heimatlos* refers to a "person without a country."

4. Translator's note: The *Joyeux* refers to a soldier/soldiers in a battalion that included recruits who had received a criminal sentence. These battalions were known for their strict discipline and the men were reputed to be daredevils.

Awoken by a violent storm . . . carried my rags under the bridge near to the lamp room . . . Sent away from there, wandered under the torrential rain with my dirty and wet untied bundle.

Finally, thanks to a good sailor, found refuge in front with two half-wild Neapolitans and an old ghost, I believe, from Japan and dressed in a black Arabic *kachébia*.

Went in search of a little water. Drank from the tank! Rather good night, slept on ground. Slept all the following day (May 10) until four o'clock. The rough weather is beginning; the old Neapolitan is sick. Flooding chased me behind the anchor machine. The grumpy cabin boy set me up on a pile of rigging on the starboard side.

Furious storm all night, violent pitching, masses of ocean water each moment into the bow falling back onto the bridge with a sound of thunder. Horrible night: splattered every moment, serious fears of misfortune. The wind screams and moans, the enormous waves roar and howl . . . A great symphony of fear.

From the desperately lucid reasoning of this night of fever and delirium, this is what I remember:

"It is the *voice of Death* that screams like that, and it is she who is raging and working away furiously against the *Berry*, poor little shaken and tortured thing, tossed about like a feather on the evil vastness."

And, a surprising thing is that I look attentively for the words to polish these sentences without an end, as if to write in spite of the physical suffering: rather mild seasickness, stomach cramps due to hunger, pain in my right side, icy cold, fatigue and low back pain, having to always brace myself on the hard and wet riggings . . .

At night, all the passengers on the bridge went down into third class. Stayed alone with the noise of thunder above my head, isolated by the continuous torrents of rolling water falling down again on the bridge, threatening to smash someone who might have tried to pass by . . .

Arrived on a clear and sunny afternoon. Quietly got onto a tram and, after the Magdaleine, continued painfully on foot with my bundles. Fear at not finding news from Slimène. During the night, awoke suddenly with a start, and was so anxious that I almost woke up Augustine.

Morning spent without a moment of rest until the arrival of Slimène's telegram . . . That gives me courage to undergo this new trial, the most difficult of all: separation.

Here, happy, *not for myself*, but to find—if not comfortable living—at least the security of a well-being that is richness compared to my destitution.

Lively impressions from the past have returned, especially those from my stay here in November 1899. Just a while ago I was listening to the ringing of Marseille's old *inversion* bells, and I was reliving the memories of the sunny days when Popowa and I wandered in this city that I love with a strange sort of love but where I dislike living . . . The Château d'If and Saint Victor . . . Clear autumn Provençal days already so far off!

. . . But who will give back to me my eternally sunny Souf and the white zaouïya and the calm dwellings with their gray cupolas and the infinite sand horizon . . . and all that was the background of that last half year of life there in the wondrous desert . . . Who will give Slimène back to me, the brother and the lover who is my whole family in this world? . . . Perhaps God . . . in whom I have faith and confidence, and Abd-el-Kader Djilani . . .[5]

MARSEILLE, TUESDAY, MAY 28, 1901,
TEN THIRTY IN THE EVENING

. . . Thought, this evening, about the misery that is henceforth my lot on this earth.

I was leaning on the kitchen windowsill, alone in the house as usual; and in the peace and lucidity of this clear evening, I finally acquired the absolutely sincere conviction that misery, whatever it might be, cannot react *directly* on the aesthetic sense and that at this moment I felt as much as before, *if not better*, the splendor of things—a consoling conclusion among many others . . .

Boredom and worry, knowing that Slimène is down there alone surrounded by all those loathsome people, Mouloud, Bornia, etc. . . . who are my cowardly and venomous enemies. I think that he will emerge victorious from this trial ∽ *if it pleases Allah!*

5. Eberhardt's note: Text from this entry, "recopied and completed May 25."

For him I am ready for all; face-to-face I can give him absolute sweetness and submission, but *toward him only*; but I don't want a stranglehold on my liberty, on my dignity, from this vile herd that imagines that it has rights over this man—why?—when he alone has a right over me, and I over him, his faithfulness, and his behavior. ❧ *May a curse be on them in all centuries.*

For all these miserable people I feel the same ferociously cold hatred that animated me against an Aly or a ben Osman, not because they robbed me, but because they outraged me and because they are *vulgar,* vile, and insolent.

Baseness and evil vulgarity have always made it even more hateful and more detestable to me, like all *mediocrity* besides.

MARSEILLE, JUNE 3, 1901,
NINE O'CLOCK IN THE EVENING

I feel the need to quickly note the hour's sensations and a few rather correct and important conclusions.

First of all, the dominating note is the desire to leave as *quickly as possible,* to see Slimène again, and to never leave him again, in order to jealously keep him; for I've finally acquired the conviction that I have only him in the world and that life is no longer possible for me far away from him. Augustine has certainly done all he can for me, but his marriage has distanced him from me for good and I cannot count on him anymore as I imagined I could in the past. Besides, there is his wife's forced *unawareness,* a child of the people and of the most *impulsive* people that exists, which makes life together intolerable for me, I who *understand* too much of life and things.

The only being with whom I have reached the point of living in harmony, near whom I have felt secure—how much the reminder of this sensation is sweet in the middle of the current anxieties!—is Slimène.

I currently imagine the hour of our reunification as an hour of deliverance, and I imagine that I will feel at that moment the happy sensation felt by someone who has carried a crushing and threatening weight all his life and then is suddenly rid of it.

I even think—since that would change nothing concerning the matter of the war council—that were I to receive the money from Agreby in Wednesday's mail, I would surely leave for Philippeville on Saturday, in order to hasten by one week the happiness of seeing each other again and the end of the perpetual anguish in the midst of which I've lived since my departure from Batna—that is, for a month.

I will certainly have to try to arrange my life in a way that makes it tolerable there, especially if we must stay in Batna for a more or less long time . . . When I return there after the meeting, we will only have *eight months* of suffering remaining, at the end of which there is the *certitude* of the official marriage and liberty. Until now God has taken pity on us and has never abandoned us during the cruelest hours. I am already accustomed to thinking about him and about Djilani, the mysterious protector, with a feeling of comfort.

I also take note that I have crossed, and am still crossing, one of the incubation periods from which I am beginning to notice some results: I understand men and things better, and my life's horizon is less dark, if still infinitely sad.

Life is not only a perpetual battle against circumstances but rather an incessant battle *against ourselves*. It is a truth as old as the world, but three-quarters of men are unaware of it or don't take it into account at all; from this results unhappy and desperate people, and evildoers.

The soul's power over itself is *colossal*, especially in some individuals, and this power grows through use.

This beneficial faculty is often especially acquired, as in me, through suffering. Suffering is good, for it ennobles . . . undoubtedly prepares one for the unfamiliar paths leading to the beyond, for without the beyond, everything is *ignoble and stupid*. Only suffering engenders the splendor of great courage and great devotion, as it engenders that of great sensations and vast ideas . . .

What enchants me in heroism, notably, is not at all the *raucous* side, which can make the man of the people enthusiastic and make of him an *unconscious* hero: it is the *pure beauty* of the act, the *harmony* of its lines, so to speak, and especially the immediate elevation through the absolute *renunciation* of all deep attachments to our animal nature, to absolute *sincerity, impossible* outside of the supreme culminating hour when, according to the consecrated expression, man finds himself face-to-face with death . . . But for that, he must have the absolute *certainty,* within the measures of the human absolute, of the *imminence* and the *inevitability* of death, without which heroism is often only, especially in the simple man, exaggerated confidence in this vague thing, less consoling, that we call luck.

To die consciously, calmly, attesting to and in order to attest to one's faith, whatever it might be, that is pure splendor. But, I repeat, the act must be *conscious.*

On my account, I am sure that between immediate and indubitable death and *abjuration,* I would choose death for many reasons: for the solemnity of the hour first of all; for pride with regard to myself especially; for the equilibrium of the moral and intellectual world, which is so closed and which makes me live, would be seriously compromised, if not forever troubled; and then, out of instinctive disdain for life itself without that which embellishes it and renders it worthy of being lived and *studied.* Strange thing: in starting these notes, that is to say after having talked in them about my feelings regarding Slimène and present life, I wanted to say something completely other than what I have said and said so *imperfectly.*

There is one thing that I now take note of and that I have never understood and will never understand: Augustine's character and life. Did he become how he is, or rather has he always been that way? I rather tend toward the latter, although upon his return from Corsica and until his departure for the First Foreign Legion, and during the initial period following his return from Tunis, he had really been what I had believed I discerned in him. Now, it's well and truly finished, and he seems to sink further and further into his present life, a life in which the intellect has almost no more role and which more and more repels me and becomes foreign to me.

And in these conditions, what is the future—very dark in my opinion—that awaits this being who very mysteriously resembles me physically and who, I am sure without being able to say why, will have many psychological affinities with me . . . Poor little Hélène in whom I recognize my character traits with a sort of *tenderness* and *anguish*! You will undoubtedly remain unaware of me for always, I who hold so little place in your house where you must grow up and where, henceforth, I will only appear as *rarely* as possible! What will her parents do with her?

And where is the affinity of our two natures, Augustine's and mine, remaining, he who used to affirm it so loudly? Alas, alas, the more I look, the less I see it again!

Oh Slimène, Slimène, remain what you were for me for ten months, do not abandon me, and let me take refuge near to you . . . I still have you, you alone!

MARSEILLE, TUESDAY, JUNE 4, 1901, NOON

Spent a horrible night doubting everything, especially Rouh', which tortured me so much that I thought I was losing my mind. I have rarely suffered so much, physically and morally, as since Sunday. The reason is in large part physiological; a violent disruption of my entire circulation provoked by the idiotic scene of the other day.

What anguish, what black notions!

I blew out the lamp at two o'clock in the morning and, for a long time afterward, dozed, then awoke with a start at three o'clock, feeling anguish without a cause, a prelude to a horrible crisis of despair that lasted until full daylight.

Irritation, anguish, nervousness, acute moral suffering—almost madness—this is what my last stay here brought me to. And, more and more each day, my heart leaps toward Slimène. There, too, there will be suffering, misery, boredom, and the eternal deprivations . . . But there will be the immense consolation of knowing he is there, of seeing him, of hearing him speak to me, of finally having a confidant for all my pains, all my thoughts, someone for whom almost all of me is intelligible and for whom I am what he is himself for me.

To be *tranquil*, sure that in the evening † *we will relieve our souls.*

There is a glimmer of hope concerning the Russian work, which has a good chance of bringing a serious improvement.

Oh! If Atabek were to send me twenty francs and Agreby, thirty, I would be able to leave on Friday, go to Batna, and finally put an end to this intolerable state of things. Reason would even recommend not *starting up again* more such sufferings for a week, and that would avoid the problem of dealing with those rogues from the Bornia family.

All, my God, all in order to see him again, were it even only furtively at the entrance to the neighborhood, just like during the week.

MARSEILLE, FRIDAY, JUNE 7, 1901

On the sixth, publication of my letter concerning Behima in the *Dépêche Algérienne*.

Sent a corrected letter on the seventh.

Text of the Letters

To the Director,

On June 18 the Constantine war council will consider the case of a native named Abdallah ben Si Mohammed ben Lakhdar, from the village of Behima, near El Oued (the Touggourt circle). This man is accused and convicted of murder, or rather of an attempt at premeditated assassination.

It is I who was the victim of this aggression, which almost cost me my life.

I was very surprised to note that no Algerian newspaper whispered a word of this affair, one of the strangest, however, and most mysterious that an Algerian tribunal has ever had to judge. I assume that the press did not have the details of this affair communicated to it. In the interest only of truth and justice, I believe that it would be good to tell the public the details of this trial before it is decided. I thus respectfully request that you publish the present letter under my signature. I assume full and entire responsibility for it.

May I be permitted to first give a few explanations necessary to the understanding of the story that will follow.

During the investigation in the trial of Abdallah ben

Mohammed, the officers responsible for this investigation repeatedly expressed their surprise at hearing me declare that I am a Muslim woman and even initiated into the Kadriya brotherhood, and in seeing me wear Arab clothing, sometimes female, sometimes male, according to the circumstances and the needs of my basically nomadic life.

In order not to be taken for an emulator of Dr. Grenier[6] or for a person donning a costume and attaching a religious label to myself with some self-seeking goal, I am anxious to declare here that I have never been Christian, that I am not baptized, and that although I am a Russian subject, I have been a Muslim for a very long time. My mother, who belonged to the Russian nobility, died in Bône in 1897 after converting to Islam, and she is buried in the Arab cemetery of that city.

Thus, I had no reason to make myself a Muslim, nor any reason to put on an act, something that my Algerian coreligionists understood so well that the cheikh Si Mohammed-el-Houssine, brother of Si Mohammed Taïeb, naïb of the Ouragla brotherhood, consented with no difficulty at all to initiate me, thereby confirming that which I had already received from one of his mokaddem. I was anxious to start by saying all of this for the reasons stated above, and then so that Abdallah's attack is not explained as the result of a fanatic hatred against all that is Christian, for I am not Christian and all the Souafa know that, including Abdallah!

Here now is the story of the aggression that I was a victim of on January 29, at three o'clock in the afternoon, in the house of a certain Si Brahim ben Larbi, property owner in the village of Behima, fourteen kilometers to the north of El Oued, on the Tunisian Djerid road.

Having passed through El Oued at the time of a first excursion into the Constantine Sahara, which I undertook in the summer of 1899, I had kept the memory of the deep impression made on

6. Doyon's note: Former deputy of Doubs who feigned Islamism even in the Chamber of Deputies and in the streets.

me by this country of immaculate dunes, deep gardens, and shady palm groves. Thus I came to settle in El Oued in August 1900 without knowing exactly for how long. This is where I was initiated into the Kadriya brotherhood, whose three zaouïya situated in the area around El Oued I henceforth frequented, having acquired the affection of the three cheikh, son and brothers of Sidi Brahim and the late naïb of Ouargla. On January 29 I accompanied one of them, Si Lachmi, to the village of Behima. The cheikh was going to Nefta (Tunisia) with some khouan for a ziara at the tomb of his father, Sidi Brahim. Personal circumstances preventing me from going as far as Nefta, I accompanied the cheikh all the way to Behima, where the pilgrimage was going to spend the night. I was counting on returning that evening to El Oued, with my servant, a Soufi, who was accompanying me on foot. We entered the house of a man called Si Brahim ben Larbi; and while the marabout was withdrawing to the other room for the afternoon prayer, I stayed in a large room overlooking an antechamber opening onto the public square where a dense crowd was gathered and where my servant was guarding my horse. There were five or six Arab notables from there and the environs, almost all Thamani khouan. I was sitting between two of these people, the owner of the house and a young merchant from Guémar, Ahmed ben Belkassem. The latter requested that I translate three commercial dispatches, one of which, very badly written, was giving me a lot of trouble. My head was lowered and the hood of my burnous was pulled over my turban, which prevented me from seeing in front of myself. Suddenly, I received a violent blow to my head, followed by two others on my left arm. I raised my head and saw before me a badly dressed individual, thus unknown to the gathering, who was brandishing a weapon, which I took for a club, above my head. I quickly got up and rushed to the opposite wall in order to seize Si Lachmi's sword. But the first blow on the top of my head had stunned me. So I fell onto a trunk, feeling a violent pain in my left arm.

The assassin—disarmed by a young mokaddem from the

Kadriya, Si Mohammed ben Bou Bekr, and a servant of Sidi Lachmi called Saad—succeeded in extricating himself. Seeing him come toward me, I got up and again tried to arm myself, but my dizziness and the sharp pain in my arm prevented me from doing so. The man jumped into the crowd, yelling, "I'm going to get a pistol in order to finish her off." Saad then brought me a bloody Arab sword made of iron, and he said to me, "This is what that dog used to wound you!"

The marabout, having rushed toward the noise, and to whom the murderer was immediately named by people who had recognized him, had the independent cheikh of Behima called, belonging, like the assassin, to the Tidjanya brotherhood who are, as is known, the most irreconcilable adversaries of the Kadriya in the desert. This singular local official obstinately resisted the marabout, claiming that the murderer was a sharif, etc., etc. The marabout then publicly threatened to denounce him to the Arab Office as an accomplice, and he forcefully demanded that the assassin be immediately arrested and taken away. The cheikh complied with very bad grace.

The assassin, taken to the room where I had laid down on a mattress, began by simulating craziness; then proven to have lied, by his own fellow citizens who knew him to be a rational, calm, and sober man, he began to say that God had sent him to kill me. Being fully conscious, I noted that the man's face was completely unknown to me, and I began to interrogate him myself. He told me that he did not know me either, that he had never seen me, but that he had come in order to kill me and that if he were released, he would try anew. To my question of why he had something against me, he answered, "I don't hold any grudge against you, you have done nothing to me, I don't know you, but I must kill you." The marabout asked him if he knew that I was a Muslim, and he answered affirmatively. His father declared that they were Tidjanya. The marabout obligated the local cheikh to forewarn the Arab Office and asked an officer to take away the murderer and initiate the investigation for him and to get the army major doctor for me.

At about eleven o'clock, the officer in charge of the investigation, a lieutenant in the Arab Office, and the major arrived. The major decided that the head and left wrist wounds were insignificant; providential luck had saved my life: a laundry cord was stretched just above my head and had softened the first blow of the sword, which, without that, would have killed me without fail. But the joint of my left elbow was opened on the external side, and the muscle and bone were cut open. Due to the enormous loss of blood over a period of six hours, I was in such a state of weakness that I had to be left that evening in Behima.

The next day, I was transported on a stretcher to the military hospital in El Oued, where I stayed until last February 25. In spite of the devoted and intelligent care of Monsieur Dr. Taste, I left the hospital weakened for the rest of my days and incapable of using my left arm for even the most insignificant amount of work.

Even though, at the time of my first trip, I had had some troubles with the Arab Office of Touggourt on which that of El Oued depends (troubles provoked solely by the distrust of this office), the chief of the El Oued annex, the officers of the Arab Office, and those of the garrison, as well as the army major doctor, all showed me the greatest kindness, and I am anxious to publicly attest to my appreciation.

The investigation established that Abdallah had spent five days before his crime trying to locate firearms to purchase but had found none. That the day of our arrival in Behima, he had transferred his family—this wretched man has young children—and his personal property to his father's house, from which he had been living separately for six years. Being well-known Tidjanya, he and his father suddenly withdrew from their brotherhood, and the father declared to me that he was Kadriya and the son affirmed during the investigation that he belonged to the Mouley-Taïeb brotherhood. The judiciary police officer, Monsieur Lieutenant Guillot, convicted Abdallah of lying about this point.

A few days before my departure from El Oued, I heard it rumored in native circles that Abdallah, formerly crippled with debts, had gone to Guémar (center of Tidjany) a few days before his crime and, upon his return, had supposedly paid his debts and even purchased a palm grove. About this time, Abdallah's father went to Sidi Lachmi's zaouïya and told him in the presence of witnesses that his son had been paid to attack me, but not knowing who the instigators were, he would very much like to be authorized to see his son, before whom it may concern, in order to invite him to completely confess. The marabout had advised him to speak with the Arab Office. The old man asked to speak to me through one of my servants and said to me, "This crime does not come from us," and revealed to me also his desire to see his son in order to push him to confess to everything. Here are the facts.

It is obvious first of all that Abdallah did not try to kill me out of hate for Christians, but was pushed by other people, and then that his crime was premeditated. I declared to the investigation that I attributed this attempted criminal act in large part to the hatred of the Tidjanya for the Kadriya and that I assumed that it was Tidjanya kaba or khouan who had agreed to get rid of me, whom they saw as liked by their enemies, which proves the great sorrow of the khouan when they learned of the crime. When I went by, carried on a stretcher through the villages surrounding El Oued, when I was being transferred to the hospital, men and women came out onto the road and shouted and wailed in the way they do at funerals. I hope that the Constantine war council will not be content with the pure and simple condemnation of Abdallah ben Mohammed but that it will try to clarify this dark business.

For me, Abdallah was nothing but an instrument in the hands of others, and his condemnation cannot satisfy me or, additionally, all those who venerate truth and justice.

It is not Abdallah alone whom I would like to see sitting on the bench of the accused, but rather those who instigated the crime, that is to say, the truly guilty ones, whoever they might be.

I hope, Mister Director, that you will not refuse me the publicity of your esteemed newspaper through this communication, which, I dare say, is not devoid of interest. If the Algerian Tell does not differ noticeably from the political point of view, if not the social, from other departments of France, it is not the same in the Sahara, where things happen in an entirely different manner and even in a way not even suspected in France.

ISABELLE EBERHARDT

MARSEILLE, JUNE 7, 1901

To the Director,

I wish to thank you very sincerely for having decided to include my long letter of last May 29: I didn't expect any less from the well-known impartiality of the *Dépêche Algérienne*, which has always shown great moderation in the midst of the violent acts that have unfortunately become rather a rule of conduct for certain Algerian newspapers. However, Mister Director, at a time when the issue of foreigners in Algeria has become a current news item, it seems to me that not only do I have the right, but even the duty, to give a few candid and public explanations to all those who will have taken the trouble to read my first letter.

You have credited me, in an entirely undeserved manner—and I am not anxious to take credit for it—with a certain religious influence on the indigenous locals of Touggourt; now, I have never played nor sought to play any political or religious role, considering myself to have neither any right at all nor the necessary aptitude to become involved in things as serious and as complicated as religious questions in such a country.

In 1899, before leaving for Touggourt, I believed it was my duty to go personally to inform Lieutenant Colonel Fridel—then head of the Biskra circle—of my departure. This officer, who received me very well, asked me with a wholly military candor if I were not English and Methodist, to which I answered, presenting to the head of the circle documents irrefutably establishing that I am Russian and perfectly in order vis-à-vis the imperial authorities with whose authorization I live abroad. Furthermore, I exposed to Mr. Fridel my personal opinions concerning the question of English missions in Algeria, saying to him that I detest all proselytizing and especially the hypocrisy that is the character trait of the English, as little sympathetic to us Russians as it is hateful to all French people.

In Touggourt I found, as head of the Arab Office, in the absence of the commandant Captain Susbielle, a man of a very particular character and, to use a popular expression, not at all easygoing. There again, I had to prove that I was not at all a young lady disguised as an Arab but very much a Russian scribbler. It would seem to me, however, that if there is a country in the world where a Russian should be able to live without being suspected of bad intentions, this country is France!

The head of the El Oued annex, Captain Cauvet, a man of great intellectual value and very devoted to his service, had, for six months, the opportunity to note with his own eyes that I could not be reproached for anything except for great eccentricity, a type of life that is odd for a young woman but very inoffensive . . . he did not judge that my preference for a burnoose instead of a skirt and dunes instead of a domestic household could become a danger to public security in the annex.

I said in my first letter that the Souafa belonging to the Sidi Abd-el-Kader brotherhood, and those in other friendly brotherhoods showed their anguish upon learning that someone had tried to assassinate me. If these fine people felt a certain affection for me, it is because I helped them as best as I could and because, having some minor medical knowledge, I cared for some cases of ophthalmia, conjunctivitis, and other common ailments in these regions. I tried to do a bit of good in the region where I was living. That is the only role that I have ever played in El Oued.

There are very few people in this world who have no passion, no mania at all, if you like. To speak only of my sex, there are women who would do crazy things in order to have shimmering clothes and there are others who grow old and pale over books in order to earn diplomas and go help muzhiks. As for me, I only wish to have a good horse—a faithful and silent companion in a solitary and dreamy life—and a few servants who are hardly more complicated than my mount, and to live in peace as far away as possible from the agitation of the civilized—in my humble opinion, sterile—world, where I feel I am not welcome.

In what way do I cause harm by preferring the undulating and indistinct horizon of the gray dunes to that of the boulevard?

No, Mister Director, I am not a politician, I am not an agent of any party, because, for me, they are all equally wrong to carry on the way they do. I am merely an eccentric, a dreamer who wishes to live far from the civilized world, as a free nomad so as to then try to tell what I have seen and perhaps to communicate to a few the melancholy and charmed shiver that I feel in the face of the Sahara's sad splendors. That's all. Sonia d'Hugues le Roux's intrigues, the betrayals and ruses, are as foreign to me as her character little resembles mine. I am no more Sonia than I am the English Methodist that someone once believed they saw in me. It's true that in the summer of 1899 it was excessively hot in the Sahara and that mirages deform many things and explain many errors!

ISABELLE EBERHARDT

Finally I am almost certain that I will leave next Friday. Thus, I only have seven days left to stay here. I'm sure that Augustine will do his best to procure the necessary money.

Poor Augustine! This man, as completely enigmatic as he can seem to me, is food for me, and nothing in this world will ever destroy the profound and eternal affection that I feel for him. Oh! What a regret that his marriage prevents him from joining Slimène and me for a life that would have been very sweet!

However, it is better for everyone that I leave, and at the end of this week there will be the immense happiness of seeing Slimène again, of holding him in my arms and, ᵛ *if it pleases Allah*, of no longer leaving him.

Yesterday, once again, I spent half the night suffering atrociously—dizziness and horrible headache.

When I am finally in Batna, I'll have to set myself to saving every penny, to getting reimbursed as much money as possible, and especially to working in Russian: that's the only chance I have of beginning to earn money before relatively long. That won't be too difficult if only my terribly weakened health holds up. To work in order to stay with Ouïha, that is my duty. He'll know how to console me about this difficulty.

This evening, I wrote a letter for Ahmed Chérif, and in writing it I remembered autumn 1899.

Where is the adventurous, mysterious life in the Sahel's immense olive groves?

How much these names, formerly so familiar to me, now sound strange to my ears: Monastir, Sousse, Moknine, Esshyada, Ksasr, Ibellal, Sidi N'eidja, Beni-Hassane, Anura, Chrahel, Melloul, Grat-Zuizoura, Hadjedj . . . Where is that country, unique in this world, that African Palestine with its green and soft plains, and small white villages reflected in the blue water of peaceful gulfs?

Where is Sousse, with its white Moorish walls and its revolving lighthouse, and the white shore of Monastir where moaning waves eternally beat on the shoals?

Where is Kasr-Hellal's white minaret and the big solitary palm tree that gives the character of some desert village to this city of the Sahel and that I still see silhouetted against the immense fire of a setting sun on the evening I went with Chérif to Seyada's beach in order to watch the night fall on the ocean drowned in white mists while my beautiful Mellouli, the predecessor of poor Souf, remained impatiently tied to one of the garden's olive trees?

Where is Melloul's garden where, among the pomegranate trees and the hendis, Chérif and I dreamed and spoke at the hour of the magh'reb? And the moonlit road we were following when the revolt of that tribe of brigands exploded, through which I had such difficulty clearing the way, my only weapon a riding crop in my hand, while Chérif spoke to them.

Left Marseille Thursday, June 13, 1901, noon. At sea night of thirteenth and fourteenth.[7] Arrived in Philippeville Friday the first at ten in the

7. Doyon's note: Isabelle returns to Constantine in order to attend her aggressor's sentencing.

evening. Spent the night on board with Ammara, from the Ouled-Aly tribe, a prison convict from Chiavari. Saturday the fifteenth, six o'clock departure for Constantine. Arrived at 9:10. Was at the Café Zouaouï. Left with Hamou the porter in search of Ben Chakar. At about noon, found him. Evening in Sidi Ksouma's café. Sunday the sixteenth, six o'clock train, met Ouïha. Night in Hôtel Métropole, Basse-Damrémont Street. Monday the seventeenth, Sidi Lachmi arrived.

Eighteenth, six o'clock—war council. Left at eleven o'clock. Thursday the twentieth, left at six thirty for Philippeville. *Arrived at 9:35.* Night in the Hôtel Louvre.

"First notebook of the second part of *Life in the Sahara,* which ends at the arrival in El Oued. In the primitive description of the Souf, I spoke of the construction of the Kouïnine gardens; Tekeen and Igarra are described. The work stops at the description of the Amour hills; it finishes thus: "The wood resounds strangely in the middle of the desert's mortal silence above the ensemble of gray cupolas already drowning bit by bit in the evening's bluish mist."[8]

Isabelle Eberhardt's Declaration[9]

As I have already declared, as much to the investigation as in my two letters to the *Dépêche Algérienne,* I am certain, and will always be certain, that Abdallah ben Si Mohamed ben Lakhdar was the instrument of other people who had an interest—real or imaginary—in being rid of me. It is obvious that, even if he declared to his father at the time of his arrest that he was paid in order to kill me, Abdallah could not hope to enjoy the price of his crime, since he attacked me in an inhabited house and in the midst of people favorably disposed toward me. He was sure to be arrested. It is thus clear that Abdallah is an unstable man and a maniac. He has shown remorse and even apologized to me in court. Thus I find

---

8. Note in Russian.

9. Doyon's note: As soon as the judgment was handed down (twenty years of forced labor for her attacker), Isabelle is the object of an expulsion order, which she indicates so dryly in her itinerary. Here is the declaration made by her before her departure.

that today's verdict was excessively severe, and I am anxious to declare to you that I regret this severity. Abdallah has a wife and children. I am a woman and can only feel sorry, with all my heart, for this widow and her orphans. As for Abdallah himself, I feel for him only the deepest pity. I was very painfully surprised to learn upon exiting this morning's meeting that I am the object of an order of deportation taken against me by His Excellency the governor general. This order forbids me to stay in all Algeria without any distinction between civil and military zones. I wonder what motivated this measure taken against me, a Russian who, in all good conscience, has nothing to reproach herself for. I have never participated in, nor had any knowledge at all of any anti-French action, either in the Sahara or in the Tell. On the contrary, I defended with all my power the late naïb of Ouargla, Sidi Mohammed Taïb, who died gloriously beneath the tricolor flag, against the accusations of a few Muslims knowing nothing about Islam—the true, that of the Koran and of the Sounna—who were accusing the naïb of having betrayed Islam by installing the French in In-Salah. I have always and everywhere spoken in favor of France—my adopted country—to the indigenous peoples. Thus, why am I the object of a measure that, profoundly hurtful to my Russian feelings, is furthermore the cause of an immense sadness of another order, since it separates me—for months—from my fiancé, who being a noncomissioned officer in the Batna garrison, cannot follow me. I would perhaps have agreed that, in order to shield me from the revenge of Abdallah's tribe, I be forbidden to stay in territories under command. But I don't plan to return to the South at all. I ask only that I be allowed to live in Batna, to marry the man who has been my companion in misfortune and who is my only moral support in the world. That is all . . .

JULY 4, 1901, NOON

Zuizou's departure on the *Touareg*. Black day of deadly boredom, anguish and despair . . . When will we see each other again?

I put my confidence in Allah and our lord and cheikh Abd-el-Kader El Djilani. Amen!

Once again I am going through a period of oppressive boredom and suffering, all the more difficult to tolerate because of my nature, as it is slower, more muted: no crises, no successive stages. Rouh' left yesterday, I am exiled there, I can't return unless I make an audacious move ... and still not in the province of Constantine. I will probably have to wait fifteen days for Zuizou to return. Half a month of dreary boredom, suffering, malaise, and perpetual anguish at the idea that down there the enemy is keeping vigil and that he will do everything possible to impede us yet again.

But I must be patient, for no one except God can change anything about this situation.

Yesterday, dismal ride by tram to Joliette. Gray sky, furious wind. The boats are dancing at the port.

The passengers boarded the *Touareg* ... During the entire operation, I didn't stop looking at Zuizou, my heart torn apart, my soul in mourning ...

Returned slowly via the Mérentie Boulevard, with neither haste nor the desire to prolong this walk that resembled a return from the cemetery after a burial.

Profound and absolute indifference for the whole world. Returned and lay down, didn't get up until about eight o'clock in the face of Augustine's entreaties.

Spent this half day in a sort of indistinct, formless, and anguishing delirium. When night had fallen, I had a moment of horrible desperation. Now everything here reminds me of Zuizou, and that increases my pain.

A strange thing in my nature is the *fundamental* need for *variation* of settings. Without that, joy is insipid, flavorless, monotonous; and insipid happiness crawls along, and I am overwhelmed by pain. On the contrary, great battles, crises of despair, lift my energy again and calm my nerves . . . Monotony and mediocrity of settings and ambiance, those are the enemy.

This is why the half month will certainly seem more difficult to tolerate than the black hours in El Oued, Behima, and Constantine . . .

. . . There will be a lot to say about my impression of this last period . . .

First, the evening of my arrival in Philippeville on the *Félix-Touache*, I felt the well-being, the *rejuvenation*, that I always feel when I arrive on the blessed coast of the African homeland, which contrasts so strikingly with the darker and darker sensations of arrivals in Marseille . . . Impressions as morose as the others are cheerful!

Philippeville at night: black silhouette of a tall hill, spotted with yellow gas fires.

Errand in town with Si Mahmoud ben Hassen from Bône. Returned on board at midnight. Found the criminal Ammara from the Ouled-Aly tribe, between Sétif and Bordj-bou-Aréridj, suffocating in the steerage.

Went up onto the deserted bridge, settled on the starboard side in the port's nocturnal silence and coolness. At three o'clock, went alone down to steerage: soaking wet matches, impossible to light. Got dressed feeling my way in the dark. Went back up to the bridge, woke up Ammara, folded the cot, made up the bundles, gray morning. A few drops of rain.

Philippeville during the day: European city without character, but charming, in the middle of a tumble of greenery above the blue bay. Flat neighborhood next to the sea, impression of Bizerte's port seen furtively on a summer night in 1899 . . .

Left at six o'clock. Mountains, slopes, and fertile plains all the way to Constantine. Ammara's childish joy upon seeing fields, tents, and herds. In his dark, distorted, and unrepentant soul, the vivacious love of the Bedouin for the Muslim land, for the nomads' homeland . . . Finally, Constantine's extraordinary boulders stand out against the horizon.

We get out at the train station. Si Mahmoud goes with me as far as the first street to the left. We separate there, and I haphazardly take the streets in front of me. Finally I enter the Café Zouaouï, ashamed of my roumi's cap . . . After a rather long stop and a conversation with the owner, an old kif smoker, I leave with the *hamel* Hantou in search of Mohammed ben Chakar. Winding and narrow steep-sloping streets, complicated intersections, shadowy silent corners, immaculate carved porches of some ancient mosques, covered bazaars; all of that makes me feel a well-known intoxication, that which I always feel in old Arab settings. Impressions of Tunis or Algiers, especially of the former . . .

Endless peregrinations and questionings . . . We finally discover the mineral deposit of Ben Chakar: all the way at the top of a small street in the shape of a staircase, a dead end above which is the beam floor of an *ali*, hardly 1.6 meters off the ground, a sort of dark cave where one has to walk bent over for four or five meters. Then a Moorish interior, bluish white, like those in Bône.

Mohamed ben Chakar's brother, a smoker of kif and *chira*, sometimes a porter, at other times a café owner, a fritter merchant, very nice. His wife is also kind, resourceful, and mannish.

As soon as it's afternoon, departure with ben Chakar for the gorges of the Rhummel, tremendous abysses where fragile footbridges are suspended, often in the shade, with subterranean staircases and endless circuitous routes.

Met a few craftsmen from Constantine. In the Jewish baths, fantastic swimming hole for older children. Came back by the road overhanging the abyss, on the bank opposite the city.

Went to Sidi Ksouma's café in the evening with the very clear feeling that *Zuizou was in Constantine* . . . Sitting in a corner in my Arab clothing—which put me at ease—I listened to singing and drumming until it was late. Beldia celebrations, pale and distinguished faces, expressionless, their eyes half closed . . .

Bad night because of worry and *fleas* . . .

SUNDAY, JUNE 16, 1901

Useless trip to the train station. A walk in Bab-el-Oued with little Salah. Met Biskra's bach-adel.

The evening, in desperation, with still no news from Zuizou, went to the train station with Elhadj, at 6:35, when the train from Philippeville arrives. Sitting on a rock, discouraged, we wait. Finally, Elhadj sees Ouïha dressed in indigenous street clothing. Dressed as a Moorish woman, went and ate at ben Chakar's, then went to the Hôtel Métropole in Basse-Damrémont Street, very far away.

A night of joy, tenderness, and peace.

As soon as it was morning, Monday the seventeenth, went to the train station to meet Sidi Lachmi. In front of the station, saw the great statures of the Souafa witnesses: Hama Nine, Mohammed ben bou Bekr, and Brahim b. Larbi.

Strong emotion at finding there *those countries* who speak with the accent from down there and who embrace me with tears in their eyes, especially good old Hama Nine.

Interrupted. Began again the same evening at six o'clock.

... This evening, I feel a very rational sense of great calmness. Hope and a frame of mind as good as it can be far from Ouïha. My physical state is also good. If this feeling could only last for our entire separation—the last one!—❧ *if it pleases Allah!*

And why all this change in my frame of mind? For what very mysterious reasons? I don't know!

Was on the quay, with the group of Souafa, to greet the great beloved cheikh, who smiles at seeing me.

Endlessly running around with Hama Nine in search of a hotel. Hostility and refusal everywhere. Finally a temporary arrangement at the Métropole. Very sweet feeling at finding the cheikh, Béchir, and the others again. Problems at the hotel. Nomad zaouïya transferred to the Hôtel Ben Chimou, at the camel market near the theater.

Spent the night in a Jewish accommodation, 6 Sidi-Lakhdar Street, on the third floor.

On Tuesday the eighteenth at six thirty we arrive at the council. The *chaouch* brings me some coffee in the witness room where I am alone, the object of curiosity for all who go by, officers and women, ever more numerous.

I see Abdallah, his hands bound, between the Zouaves escorting him.

Captain Martin, government commissary, comes with his sister to shake my hand. Finally, at seven o'clock the bailiff comes and gets me. The room is filled. I don't feel too shy, and I go and sit down next to Sidi Lachmi on two chairs, in front of the double witness stand. This witness stand is out of the ordinary: expressive and tanned faces, white or dark clothing with, like a bloody stain, the red burnoose of the traitor Mohammed ben Abderrahmane, the cheikh of Behima. Sidi Lachmi is dressed in green and white.

The court: a group of uniforms, chests bedecked with decorations, stiff and impenetrable attitudes. Arms are presented: the president—timid—opens the session with a weak and stuttering voice. The clerk reads the indictment and counts the witnesses, beginning with me. We are immediately made to leave one by one.

In the witness room, Captain Gabrielli and the young lieutenant, his secretary, come and shake my hand. A rather long discussion follows, and someone comes to get me.

The president begins calling the witnesses. The clerk places me in front of the president, standing. The oath is taken.

Shy and stammering, he questions me according to some notes. It's not long . . . The interpreter calls Abdallah and says to him, "Do you have a response to this woman?"

"No," says Abdallah, very simply and very firmly, in spite of what has been said. "I have only one thing to say to her, which is that I beg of her to forgive me." I sit down again. Sidi Lachmi appears. Calm and simple statement. Then it's the cheikh, then ben Bou Bekr, then Brahim b. Larbi, then the father, in tears as always . . .

Then, after a five-minute break, Captain Martin's summing up (for the prosecution), based on certainly an erroneous thesis, but a warm defense of the Kadriya, the Ouled-Sidi-Brahim, and me. Plea of the lawyer who exasperates me . . . Martin's response, lawyer's response back. Then the council withdraws. Commotion in the room. Angellini tells me that he's available to me. General Labattue approaches me. Fairly pleasant conversation that stirs up general curiosity. I see Taste speaking animatedly in a group.

I'm going through a strange period of physical and moral calm, of intellectual awakening, of hope *without the elation of enthusiasm*; and time is going by fairly quickly, which is the most important thing right now.

I notice, too, since the great Constantine trial, a strong awakening in me of the literary spirit. Currently the aptitude for writing is truly being born in me. In the past, I had to wait, sometimes for months, for a frame of mind that was favorable to writing. Now, I begin writing almost every time I want to. To sum up, I think that I've arrived at the emergence of the incubation that I felt in myself.

From the religious point of view, things are working for the better: my faith has become sincere, I no longer need to make the slightest effort; and every evening, when I'm about to fall asleep, I take a searching look into my conscience, where I find the very sweet peace of the mysterious *certitude* that henceforth will be my strength.

For me, life has acquired a meaning since the day when I knew that our passage here is human perfectibility moving toward another life: from this, inevitably, follows the rational necessity of moral and intellectual perfecting—inept, because it is useless without that.

Right now two things interest me, and I am planning on dedicating myself to them: first, literary perfecting, and through it, intellectual perfecting, which will be very easy if I find a prospect for articles in the style of "Printemps au désert" and "El-Magh'reb," sent to Angellini this evening.

Read certain books in the genre of *Essais de psychologie contemporaine (Essays in Contemporary Psychology)*, by Bourget. As soon as I'm settled, subscribe to a serious library and reread the *Journal des Goncourt*, which had such a beneficial influence on me last year, and other works able to exercise a similar influence on my intellect . . .

But the other question disturbing me, of an entirely different order and which I would certainly not dare formulate, except to Slimène, *who alone will understand* and admit it, is the *question of the marabout*, that which spontaneously took root in my soul the evening of the day when Abdallah was transferred from the civil prison to his cell . . . And, without a doubt through unconscious intuition deriving from the great intimacy of our souls, Slimène suspected as much!

It seems to me that with a lot of will, it will be easy for me to arrive at the very mysterious end that would delight me and open in front of me horizons that no one can foresee . . . ❧ *Lead us in the right path*, and I believe that, for me, the right path is here.

God has sown in my soul a few prolific seeds: a lack of interest, pushed to an extreme point, vis-à-vis all things in this world; faith; undying, pitiful, infinite love of all that is suffering. This pardoning of evil is an unlimited sense of devotion for the Islamic cause, the most beautiful of all, since it is that of Truth . . .

Oh, the long hours of the past spent in woods full of shade and mystery, and the sleepless nights spent contemplating the incredible world of the stars . . . , should all that not be the direct path to religious mysticism!

A choice different from the one I made, of a lifelong companion, would certainly have failed to lead to this necessary way toward a future that is still perhaps far away. But Slimène will follow me where I wish; and of all those I have spent time with, he is the *only* one who is a *true* Muslim, because he *loves* Islam with his heart and not with his words . . .

And to say that, if a learned man, a psychologist or a writer, were to read these lines, he would not fail to cry out: "She is one step removed from insanity!" And yet, if ever the flame of my intelligence has burned, it is certainly now, and I feel too that it is but the *dawn* of a *new life.*

Unconsciously, without knowing what he was saying, and in a completely different meaning, Monsieur de Laffont said a truth that he does not at all suspect, that no one suspects: he said that I should be grateful to Abdallah. Yes, I am grateful toward Abdallah, and furthermore, I *sincerely love him*: in truth, this man is certainly God's envoy whom he declared himself to be.

It is probable that other people, the truly guilty ones, pushed him to do what he did, but that proves nothing. And he personally, *he alone*, was certainly sent by God and by Djilani; for since that fateful day in Behima, I have felt my soul enter a completely new phase of earthly existence. Very mysteriously, Abdallah will without a doubt pay with a whole life of suffering for the redemption of another human life. But I doubt that he is unhappy, for he is a martyr and the *voluntary* martyr—as was Abdallah—is the happiest of men: he is a chosen one. And who knows if his martyrdom will not buy many thousands of other souls and not only mine, which would be a failure!

Abdallah is going away to the other face of the world, to the farthest away of earthly far-off places. But Abdallah's work and the seed that he has sown in me have stayed, and I truly believe that it is already taking seed and that it will burst forth one day or another from the shadow where I am hiding it from all eyes. That is my secret, the one which must not be confided and which I will confide to no one, except to one only, he who guessed it one day and who never desecrates, with a mocking laugh, my soul's sanctuary that I may only sometimes open to him all the way to its inmost depths; which no one else must know, for he, too, is *predestined*.

May all of those, blind but who believe themselves visionaries, shrug their shoulders or smile with a condescension that they would do better to transfer to themselves in the face of our union. It comes from other causes, other feelings, and other goals than do their unions, foully lucrative, ambitious, bestial, or childishly sentimental . . . It cannot be explained to them.

THURSDAY, JULY 11, 1901

Nine o'clock in the evening.

It seems to be tiresome, *for the time being,* to continue the story of the war council's meeting. For the time being, other thoughts and other memories are haunting me.

Last night, like already the night before, boredom, feeling of ill-being. This morning, anguish and very strong physical malaise at not seeing Ouïha's letter arrive.

Went down in the course of the chapter at about nine thirty to take a letter to Zuizou. Boredom, weakness. In the afternoon, began to do the Russian work without enthusiasm. Finally, at about three o'clock, received a good letter. The question of the permutation is settled and *certain,* and Zuizou's return is no longer but a question of days—days that will go by very quickly now that I am *sure* he will come.

It seems to me that he'll be able to be here by the morning of the twenty-third . . . That will certainly be the dawn of the new life. We will certainly still have black days, hours of distress, for without that, life would no longer be life. But it seems to me that the era of separations is going to be finally closed.

My God, with what a sigh of relief we will leave the office of the mayor, who will have finally tied us one to the other and who will have *required* men to recognize our union . . . for God has recognized and blessed it for a long time since he gave us love. Finally, men will no longer have the material right to separate us.

In a few days it will have been one year since the beginning of the great enchantment that was my stay in the Sahara.

Well! I curse nothing about this stay, no episode, except for the exile, and then again, why curse it, all in all? I don't even curse Behima, the tragic and splendid Behima that opened to me so many new horizons, that was like a landmark placed to the side of my life's adventurous path.

How many years have I spent in vain, in sterile and inept recriminations against this sublime and painful life, a noble path toward our future destinies. During those years of blindness it seemed hideous . . . and now, *since Behima*, it seems beautiful.

Who knows? Perhaps, after being so close to death, having been at its mysterious threshold, I have finally glimpsed the truth; I have understood that it has a *meaning*, a logic, and a goal, this poor life that so few know how to appreciate and love! For—and this may seem paradoxical, but it is true—very few men love life not at all bestially, unconsciously, but for its *genuine* and splendid beauty.

Inept pseudophilosophers with their hypochondriacal illnesses, their spleen, always scream insults—which are blasphemies—to the life-giving Demetra-Mater!

Memories of last year, at the same time period, are coming to haunt me . . . Geneva, the anxieties and joys of my dear Russian life there, days of which I will undoubtedly never again live, and the embarking for the beloved and fateful earth, for the Barbary Coast earth from which I am exiled for now. But where I will soon be able to return with my head held high ❧ *if it pleases Allah!* And Algiers, Algiers the White Lady where

I lived a *double* life, extraordinary and intoxicating, among people who valued me, admired me even, all the while knowing nothing about me, not even my sex!

Strange and dizzying races with Mokhtar, kif dens . . . walks with the intelligent and likeable Oulid-Aïssa, especially the refined Si Mustapha . . . and the enchanted villa of Bouzaréah, and Slimène ben Elman Turki's boutique, at night, on the Saulières Plateau . . . and the walk along the quays, singing Algiers's sad cantilenas . . . and the white zaouïya of Sidi Abder-Rahmane ben Koubrine, little dream city, turned gold by the setting sun and toward which the Marengo garden's perfumes rose . . . and the ecstatic hour of the icha prayer in the Hanéfite mosque, *djema Djedida* . . . Then Saint Arnaud again. And Biskra, and the unforgettable Oued Rir with its magic spells and its singular splendors . . . And sleepy Touggourt in its salty desert, reflected in the mournful waters of its chott . . . and later the familiar road marked off by gray and melancholy guemira . . . Then, at the end of this long voyage, the dazzling silhouette of the unique City, of the chosen city, of El Oued the fateful!

As a background to all these tableaus . . . beneath a murky and black winter sky, a pale chaos of smoky dunes . . . A stormy and moaning wind in the gorges and dead valleys . . . A small troop advances slowly to the dull sound of the benadir of Sidi Abd-el-Kader's brotherhood. Then, a long stop on a tall dune, the last one, and from where one discovered a vast gray and desolate plain scattered with abandoned tombs.

And all the way over there on the northern horizon, a silhouette of gray city with small low cupolas—it, too, surrounded by tombs . . . and against the sulfurous glimmers of the setting sun, standing out in black, the solitary and funereal silhouette of a single palm tree, giant disheveled sentinel posted alone in the winds and in the night at the door of Behima.

"Man does not ever escape from the hour of his destiny."

Same evening, quarter of eleven.

Once again I am recaptured, obsessed by the haunting enchantments of far-off lands . . . to leave, to leave and go far away, to wander for a long time! . . . Haunted by Africa, haunted by the Desert . . . My nomad's soul is awakening, and anguish invades me at the thought that I am perhaps immobilized here for a long time . . .

Run! Walk! The cloud only stops
In order to burst,
And the Gypsy only settles down
In order to cry!

MONDAY, JULY 15, 1901,
ELEVEN O'CLOCK IN THE MORNING

Last night, a very particular sensation without a noticeable cause: memory of the arrival in Sousse two years ago . . . and the desire to travel alone to a still completely unknown place in Africa where no one knows me, in the way I arrived in Algiers last year . . . But with sufficient means to carry out this voyage in good conditions.

In general, a desire for *mental isolation*; not for very long, however, for I still always miss Slimène. I would like to have, a month before his return, the necessary money to travel alone, unhurriedly . . . I would be certain to bring back very precious and very profound impressions.

However, I am going through a mentally clear and well-thought-out period, a period of work, especially. Naturally, the hope for a better life, before long, counts for a lot in this state of mind.

Soon it will be six months since the fateful day in Behima. That day, unconsciously, I entered one of those periods of incubation that have marked my entire life up to now, for, incontestably, my intellectual development has been made and continues *haltingly*, so to speak: periods of worry, of discontent, of incertitude, then the birth of a superior form of self. An evolution to be studied, perhaps to be described in a story or novel.

During the six or seven months that we'll spend here, and during which it will be necessary to find a definitive resolution for our future, I will also have to be dedicated to literary work in all its forms.

Since my departure for Bône in 1897—alas already so distant!—I had not occupied my time with the art for which I've always kept an invincible love, however—drawing, painting. Now, I'm starting it again and will try, during my stay here, to take a few useful lessons, to gain some elementary knowledge of portrait and especially genre painting.

Our life, *real* life will not start again until after February 20, 1902, ... what will it be like? It is very difficult to predict, but after Slimène's return we will have to resolve this problem. If, between now and then, the Moscow affair could be settled in the form of an annuity, the best thing would be to go and establish a peaceful refuge in the Tunisian Sahel—near Moknine, for example—and to make of it the dream home that I'll need in order to live. If not, the only reasonable thing would be an interpreter's career somewhere in the South, wherever, for a few years—a few years in the Desert would also be lovely.

Certainly now the big problem of all my life is posed ... Everything that has happened until now was only transitory ... ❧ *And Allah knows the unknown of the skies and the earth.*

TUESDAY, JULY 23, 1901

This evening, great, profound sadness, but resigned and without bitterness, without boredom or disgust.

Here we have come to a point of complete misery, even more threatening since I can do nothing about it, for I could perhaps manage, surrounded by people like myself, with very small sums sufficient for very small needs. But this isn't the case, and they must keep up appearances. However, for the two of us, Slimène and me, the end of suffering and anxieties will be announced soon. But we will still have to bring help here, and that won't be easy. Alone, with what Slimène will earn and my way of managing the household, we could have lived very carefully and calmly without lacking the little that we need ... But what will we have to do?

There will be no way at all to come to a settlement if they don't consent to come and eat at our home. I won't ever have enough money to give them what they need to make a style of living on their own. As soon as Zuizou arrives, we'll have to both agree about this subject, unless the approach that I will be forced to try with Reppmann succeeds: I will leave to them everything that Reppmann will send to me, and they will have at least what they need to manage with for a month or a month and a half if Reppmann agrees to lend me 100 rubles or close to 250 francs. That would save us all, for it would give *us* the possibility of setting up our own small household, buying the few things that I need. Once I'm dressed as a woman, I would certainly find some small job to do while waiting for something better.

For that, during the few days of solitude still remaining to me, I must push as much as possible the literary work, write a few more articles and copy them such that I will have—if I receive satisfactory answers from some place or another—something to present without being forced to write during the initial period of our life here together, nor to abandon the opportunities that could present themselves, especially toward the start of the newspaper and journal literary season.

In a furious wind I carried a letter for Slimène that *maybe* will reach him. Hope is very weak. I went by foot to Arenc and from there returned to the house after passing by the Africa Bar.

Tomorrow I'll see if there will be some way to earn, here and there, a few cents by writing letters in Arabic. However, I feel that I'll not at all lose courage, personally. If I feel fear, it's for Augustine. Provided that he doesn't fall for Volodia's out-of-money plan! As long as I'm in the house, a collective suicide is impossible. But afterward?

Finally, ✌ *if it pleases Allah*, may the era of dark dramas end.

A thought to meditate about, found in *Notebook I*:

Do today as much good as you will be able to do,
For tomorrow, perhaps, you will die.
(Inscription from the roadside cross of Trégastel, country of Trégor, Brittany)

That was a repetition of Epictetus's words: "act as if you must die immediately afterward."

Deep and consoling thought, wonderful sursum corda.

In spite of all the perils, all the disillusionment, all the pain, remain strong like the cliff against the furious breaking waves of the Ocean. Whatever the cost, I must do good and conserve the cult of beauty, the only thing that makes life worth living. It is better to be *great than happy*.

With my old conception about things of this life, my present situation would have been horrifying, *intolerable*. I *believed* that I possessed wisdom. And it is only now that I am beginning to establish my moral life—upon which the other depends entirely—on the immovable rock of Faith.

In order not to weaken, I must say to myself again and again that life down here is but a period, a test—not in order to earn immediate and eternal happiness after death, but rather for outcomes whose splendor and end no one can foresee.

There is no eternal pain. Circumstances from down here finish down here. Further on is the great Unknown, but there is certainly a *Beyond*, a *something else. Sapienti sat!* Here is the force, the invincible force that, based on Eternity, cannot be conquered by ephemeral earthly life.

In my place, very few would resist.

I'm in black misery, perhaps on the verge of hunger. Well! Never, never for a single moment, in all honesty, has the idea come to me to admit the possibility of getting out of this threatening misery through the ordinary path of so many hundreds of thousands of women. There is even *no temptation at all* against which I must fight for that. It's *impossible*, that's all. And it seems to me, from now on, that sometimes—for strong souls are very rare—the excuse of misery is invoked in vain, by those, at least, who have an intellectual and moral culture, who are not *flesh to live on*, quite simply. I am not casting stones at anyone, and I will always keep my large indulgence for human weaknesses, for all of them are the result of such terribly complicated and dense factors that very few can penetrate and elucidate them.

But man's salvation is Faith.

No, not glum formulaic faith, but the living faith that makes for strong souls; not faith that breaks one's will and energy, but that which exalts and magnifies them.

It is not enough to say and even to be convinced that ༚ *God is God and Mohammed is his prophet.* That is not at all sufficient in order to be a Muslim. It is necessary that he who calls himself a Muslim give himself—body and soul, and forever, as far as martyrdom if need be—to Islam, that the latter penetrate the believer's soul, animate each of his acts, each of his words. Without all of that, all the mystical practices serve nothing.

God is Beauty. This word sums it up entirely: Good, Truth, Sincerity, Pity . . . all these words are only made to designate, according to diverse manifestations, Beauty that is God himself . . . With that faith, animated by that spirit, man becomes strong . . . He acquires a force that, in the eyes of the common herd, is supernatural. To use the common word, he becomes a marabout. "Whatever you do, wherever you come from, wherever you enter, say: *Bismillahi Rahnani Rahimi*,"[10] said the wise and inspired cheikh Ecchafi'r, God's prophet. But what he taught was not, when beginning an action, to *say*: in the name of God! He taught us *to do* nothing, unless it is in the name of God, that is to say, to do always and only what is *beautiful*, thus good and true. It is useless, in fact, to say *"Bismillah"* when beginning an ugly action contrary to God! One must attach oneself, in everything that one does, to first finding what is divine: eternal and Divine Immanence. The side of *everything* is worth being considered. Form is nothing if one attaches oneself to it. It is then nothing but an instrument of ruin and unhappiness.

I've reflected enough for years so as to finally succeed, after Behima, in understanding these things, which nonbelievers will surely treat as mysticism in their senseless passion for sentences devoid of meaning, for completed classifications that allow them to speak without thinking. And if, as I hope and *believe I have foreseen*, it is written that I will cross the entire cycle of this blessed evolution, it will be in the path of Pain to which, from here on out, I sing a hymn of gratitude. But in all of that, there is an acquired fact: my soul has finally emerged from the deadly limbo where it wandered for so long and where it risked being swallowed up many times.

THURSDAY, JULY 25, 1901,
ABOUT ELEVEN O'CLOCK IN THE EVENING

More and more, without Rouh', the stay here is becoming painful to me. Neither Augustine nor Helene are, nor will they ever be, capable

---

10 Translator's note: *Bismillahi Rahnani Rahimi* means, "In the name of the almighty merciful God."

of loving me, for *they will never understand me*. Augustine has become deaf and blind to all that enchants me; he understands nothing about the wonderful things that I have finally understood.

Here, I am *alone*, more than anywhere else. But finally the end of the month will be here, and Zuizou can no longer delay showing up and putting an end to my torture.

Today I received the two issues of *Nouvelles*, Algiers, dated July 19 and 20, containing "El-Magh'reb" and "Printemps au désert." This success consoles me and already opens a path for me. Thus, I will have to persevere and have patience all the way to the end. But especially fiercely withdraw into myself and no longer talk about either my affairs or my ideas to these people who don't *understand* them, and who don't *want* to understand them.

In spite of all the appearances of these last two years, it was thus certainly written that *I alone would be morally saved*, among all of those who lived the abnormal life of the Villa Neuve, about which Augustine used to complain so much in the past and whose smallest details he seems to be determined to copy now. I must, at all costs, adopt a system of silence and impenetrability in order to finish this lamentable horrible stay here.

How will it finish under their roof? What are they counting on? What do they think about? I don't know, and that frightens me, for in spite of it all, my heart feels the same for them.

Given the force of things, given Slimène's character as well as mine, their household is going to fall heavily again into our arms as soon as we've settled here. Because of that, if Reppmann doesn't save me, there will be a lot of deprivation and suffering to endure. But in this, as in all and always, we do what we must and what will happen will happen.

I ask very little of God: Slimène's return and our marriage and the end of this state of affairs here—let them figure things out, and may their life not be a new specter for me! May they obtain what they need to live on, *in their manner*, provided their destiny no longer be a subject of constant and horrible sorrow for me, especially in the state of powerlessness that I am in to help people diametrically opposed to everything in me.

FRIDAY, JULY, 26, 1901,

TEN O'CLOCK IN THE EVENING

In order to finish this accounting of the last year of my life, begun in all the melancholy uncertainty of the hospital, I have almost only gray and sad things, even though the moral evolution that I've accomplished remains mine. It is obviously the milieu in which I live, overwhelmed by the preoccupations of an inextricable material situation, that produces the mental depression in me from which I've been suffering for three or four days. My soul is fundamentally calm.

Personally, it is only this indefinite delay in Slimène's return that weighs on me, and patience is now costing me great personal efforts. I need, perhaps more than ever, his dear emotional presence. My heart is overflowing and irresistibly dragging me toward him, as if toward the last refuge remaining to me on this earth. But the days are counted, and now I must hold on to both courage and patience, even more so because I have a lot of work to do, in French as well as again in Russian, according to Madame Paschkoff's letter. Ah! If only this effort were crowned by the same success that rejoiced me yesterday! Finally from the deepest part of my soul that is starting *to know how to dominate itself.*

MARSEILLE, SATURDAY, OCTOBER 29, 1901,

FOUR O'CLOCK IN THE AFTERNOON

Of all the worries of three months ago, the majority have finally been moved away from our horizon.[11]

Since the seventeenth, we are *officially,* thus indissolubly united. Also, the interdiction of staying in Algeria no longer exists, and besides, the exile is probably coming to an end: a month from now we will leave for the beloved overseas earth. God and Djilani have not at all abandoned us. May they finish their work of salutation and redemption!

11. Doyon's note: Having been transferred, Slimène Ehnni is made part of the dragoons stationed in Marseille, where he officially marries Isabelle Eberhardt.

Nine O'Clock in the Evening

I didn't note those thoughts from January 1902 . . . What does it matter? Three years later, in another place of exile, in the middle of equally profound misery and solitude as absolute, I note the profound change that destructive time has accomplished in me since then . . .

Other peregrinations, other dreams, and other sun intoxications in the silence and magic of other deserts, harsher and farther away, have passed over these things from then. On the horizon, in a few days perhaps ❧ *if it pleases Allah*, I will once again leave, and it will be toward the mournful magh'reb of mystery and death that I will go. At the same date in one year, will I still exist and where will I be?

Same evening.

This evening, reading these books from the past, full of dead things, I felt obsessive fear and deep melancholy at finding the same almostforgotten names—the Souf, Bordj-Ferdjeun, Ourmès with its enchanted gardens, El Oued, Behima. So where are they today?

In two years, in five years, the now familiar names of Aïn Sefra, Figuig, Beni-Ounif, and Djebel-Amour will have the same nostalgic sonorities for my ears.

Many other corners of the African earth still charm me . . . Then, my solitary and painful being will itself be erased from the earth where it will have passed in the midst of men and things, always as a spectator, a *stranger*.

12. Doyon's note: The following entry was added by Isabelle seven months before her death.

Fourth Daily Journal

Notes and Impressions Begun in Marseille on July 27, 1901,
Finished in Bou Saada on January 31, 1903

In memory of † *the White Spirit*

In the name of God the powerful and merciful!

MARSEILLE, JULY 27, 1901

After a few days of boredom, mournful sadness, even anguish, I got up once again this morning with energy, patience, a taste for work, and hope.

If the torture of waiting for Slimène were to end, if I at least knew *exactly* what date he'll arrive, I would feel calm and I would go through, mentally, one of the better periods of my life. At the beginning of autumn the misery will probably end, and with it, so many problems, so much powerlessness especially. Ah! To finally receive the money from the unfortunate Villa Neuve and see again the African earth, who knows, maybe even the unforgettable Souf! To be able once again to read, to write, to draw, maybe even paint, to finally make a living from an intellectual life and lay down the foundation of my literary career! Perhaps, instead of going to Algeria, should I go to Paris, reasonably, with a certain number of articles to place?

Finally, it seems ᵛ *if it pleases Allah*, that this autumn must finally mark the end of this long period of suffering, worries, anguish, and misery. *I have put my confidence in Allah and in Djilani.*

Eleven o'clock in the morning.

Yesterday, I received a letter from Slimène, which has once again over-turned everything. He's been in the hospital since the twenty-eighth. After this, it's impossible to ignore the very mysterious warnings that have announced to me, for years, all the phases of my *via dolorosa*!

All my limbs are trembling. And yet I must write; I must recopy *Amira* and send it to Brieux.

The same day, twelve thirty at night.

Slimène, Slimène! Perhaps *surely never* have I loved him as saintly and as deeply as now. And, if God wants to take him back, may his will be done. But afterward, I don't want to try anything more—nothing but one thing, with all my power: go where people are fighting in the South-west and look for death, at any cost, ≽ *testifying that there is only one God and his prophet is Mohammed.* This is the only ending worthy of me and worthy of him whom I have loved. Any attempt to re-create another life would be not only useless but criminal; it would be an *insult.*

Perhaps he will soon go to the one whom he regrets not ever having met, to tell her all that our two hearts—united forever—have suffered down here.

"White Soul" who is up there and you, Vava, undoubtedly you see my tears in the night's silence, and you read the depths of my soul. You see that near to him I have purified my poor soul in suffering and per-secutions, that I have not weakened, and that finally my heart is pure! You see: judge and call on the two of us, whom you left alone in this world of pain, God's forgiveness, this God who made the White Soul sleep among the believers. Call forth, too, God's punishment for those who unjustly burden us.

Why did I not leave, as I wanted to, with Sidi Mohammed Taïeb; why did I not go and die at his side in Timmimoun? Why did destiny take this poor child and, uniting him to my inevitable ruin, pull him from his former peaceful existence for so much suffering and, maybe, a premature and cruel end? Why wouldn't I go alone? But does he regret having loved me? Does he regret having suffered so much for me?

Who will ever guess the infinite bitterness of these hours that I cross, of these nights of solitude? If help arrives, all will be saved. Even sick, cared for by me, near me, he will certainly get well ... But without that, in destitution and misery, his poor health will weaken and hereditary sorrow lies in wait for him ...

<hr/>

AUGUST 2, 1901,
FOUR O'CLOCK IN THE AFTERNOON

Started out the day with a bit of courage and hope, thanks to Augustine's talk with (a friend).

<hr/>

MONDAY, AUGUST 5, 1901

Visit to Colonel Rancongne. State of mind: a bit worried and sad. Night: bad. *General* sorrow about my whole life. Confidence in Djilani for the future.

<hr/>

TUESDAY, AUGUST 6, 1901,
ELEVEN O'CLOCK IN THE MORNING

Rather gray mood. Great fatigue for my current life. No deep interest in anything. Tired of boring and mournful impressions, although violent, of recent days. Release. Only *mental energy* to finish what I must still try, but no drive.

Received a letter from Brieux: I have noted that I have an overwhelming amount of work to do from the literary point of view. Resolve, *because I must, to do it.*

Strange thing: while I was writing these lines, slight *improvement* in my state of mind, due to the idea that I believe I can do the story for *L'Illustration.*

After my daily reading of Dostoyevsky, I suddenly feel tenderness for this little room, so similar to a prison cell, that certainly doesn't resemble the rest of the house.

Each room where one has lived for a long time is imbued, so to speak, with a little of the soul of the one who has lived there and thought there.

MONDAY, AUGUST 12, 1901

Everything that is born is born in a state of waiting and suffering.

Sad, worrisome, indefinable days in which only work and reading save me. From what? I don't know. After resting the first fifteen days of July, my soul has again entered a painful period of incubation.

My present life, as far as *surrounding conditions* and *circumstances* are concerned, is horrible, hateful. The calm and isolation of prison would be much more tolerable and more useful. But mentally, of course, there is yet another trial . . . but alas how painful!

This wait for Slimène and the *incertitude* concerning him are making me positively *ill*. All my nerves, all my faculties are strained to the point of breaking, and without the double distraction in the form of work and reading, that would probably finish badly—God knows how! My vigorous nature seems to no longer resist as well, and the fits of weakness, palpitations, and anguish happening to me are signs of fearsome weakening. How much time can this situation last? I don't know anymore, but it seems to me that I'm coming to the end of my strength . . .

THURSDAY, AUGUST 15, 1901,
EIGHT THIRTY IN THE EVENING

For a few days now, my nostalgia for the desert has been invading me once again and is intense to the point of pain! To just go to Old Biskra's last seguia where Slimène and I stopped on the evening of our return, last March 2 . . . *already six long months ago!* To go there at dawn or at sunset and glance lovingly with our exiles' eyes at the great Sahara . . . one single glance!

Ah, to be free now, both of us, and well-off and leaving for down there, for *our country!* Will I ever see my great splendid desert again?

But something deep in my heart, something like a vague feeling, tells

me that yes, I will return there . . . and even on a not so far-off day and
⭢ *God knows!*

I would give God-knows-what, during these present hours, to leave this cursed earth, this land of exile and suffering, and return there to the land of Africa.

I'm looking at drawings from there on the wall, and the dark horizon where the far-off guemira rise up makes me dream. To go far away, to start a new life in the great, free, and wonderful air! I'm suffocating here between four walls in a city that gives me nothing but the darkest malaise!

To leave, as the free vagabond I once was, even at the cost of whatever new sufferings! To run in haste down the Joliette quay—the only part of this city that I love *because it is the door to Africa*—to embark, humble and unknown, and to flee, finally flee *forever*. This is what I dream about—these are the thoughts haunting and tormenting me!

To see again the solitary bordj and the road of the Oued Rir-salé, then the white Souf, and the guemira, the gray guemira that are the enchanting lighthouses of the beloved ocean.

Run! Walk! The cloud only stops
In order to burst,
And the gypsy only settles down
In order to cry!

I have certainly only come here to cry, to regret, to struggle in darkness and anguish, to suffer, to be a prisoner! When is the radiant departure? When is the return there where I can live, on the unique earth of the land where I am not at all an exile, a stranger?

FRIDAY, AUGUST 16, 1901,
ELEVEN O'CLOCK IN THE MORNING

Oh, yes, leave *for good*, leave all, abandon all, now that I know, to the point of never being mistaken again, that here I am more a stranger than anywhere else, that of all that is dear to me, of all that is sacred to me, of all that is great and beautiful, it is impossible to admit anything in this house of blind people and of *bourgeois* . . . bourgeois all the way to the end of their fingernails, encrusted in the vulgar preoccupations of their rapacious and animal life.

Only, *they're right* to push all of that to the last degree of disgust, for thus, I am entirely detaching *my heart* from it. In the end, I'm no longer suffering from the vulgar and mean scenes here. It doesn't matter to me, and all of that has no other result than to bring me more passionately closer to my dear Ideal, which makes me live, which is my salutation, and also to *Slimène's beautiful soul*, which, I see in his letters, has entered the path of thought, a path that will lead him to the same radiant path where I am advancing, in spite of all. As for the others—*they don't see, and deaf, mute, and blind, they will not retrace their steps*, as the *Book of God* says . . .

All my current suffering derives from this anguished wait for Slimène.

But, too, I must no longer sacrifice all for *here* and finally think of *my* household.

Reppmann and Brieux don't at all suspect, especially the first one, that I took away nothing from his kindness and that I begged for others who show me no gratefulness at all! *My beloved is right; I'm an idiot; we're doing good for people like that!*

Only, in their conscience—one expresses out loud what the other thinks—they don't suspect *how much they are harming* their material interests so dear to them . . . dearer to them than everything in the world, for, when it comes to *other interests*, which make the rest of us live, they don't have any. I will certainly no longer deprive myself for them. Since they always talk about how we'll have to "make arrangements at our own risk." So let them do so, too. It will be the best punishment and the most *salutary*.

In what I'm saying here, there is neither vengeance nor hatred nor meanness—it is only *justice*. They don't want to do anything for us, we are poor and abandoned; we have nothing to do for them.

It's a stupid speculation about my goodness, based on the ignorance of my true personality, for, with me, there is a certain line that one must not cross.

And this line has been crossed.

Why am I obligated to take care of such low and repulsive things and to take such measures?

Finally, a few more days of patience, courage—and all of that will be over *for good*.

———————————

SATURDAY, AUGUST 17, 1901

Admittedly, I understand only too well the *reason* for all this change . . . But it isn't this order of ideas that haunts me today. First of all, there is naturally the continuous worry concerning the leave, the permutation. Then there is something else. He too, down there, seems to be thinking about it, considering his last letter, about this troubling and intoxicating thing that is the love of the senses. Now, the most delicious and the least chaste dreams are visiting me. I would certainly be incapable of telling such a secret . . . except to the brutal and oversensitive confidant that Dr. Taste was. Maybe it's very regrettable, from the intellectual point of view, that it's not with Mauviez, of an even more sickly and curious intelligence, that I found myself in contact during the unforgettable stay in the hospital. It seems to me that he was more refined, more subtle . . . "Doctor Subtle," still not forgotten! However, incontestably, I love Taste . . . the man who, sensually, attracted me the least, at least physically. Admittedly, the sometimes brutal and violent—sometimes refined to the point of neurosis—eroticism of this man didn't displease me. I said things to him that nobody heard . . . D—— is too down to earth, and he has a hint of tolerance that is too broad and too brutal.

Now that all these people are far from me and my life, I consider with surprise Toulat's personality, and I wonder if, there again, there isn't some thousand-year-old atavism: in fact, how is it that in about ten years of Arab life, the *Arab soul* especially, has been able to rub off on this man, this Frenchman from Poitiers? Yes, Toulat is Arabic. He is dark, he loves the wild and harsh life of the desert; of all the French officers I've known, he is the only one who is not bored there. Aren't his violence and his hardness themselves Arabic? In his love, too, there is something wild, not French, not modern, for he certainly loved me.

His love was at its peak the day when he so desperately cried at the time of our arrival in Biskra. He loved me, didn't understand me, and feared me. He believed he'd found salvation in fleeing and abandonment.

How far away all of that is! So much further away that, when I remember them, anger no longer rises in me: the one who thought she loved *them*, those far-off ghosts, is *dead*. And the one who is living is so different from the other that she is no longer responsible for her past erring ways.

All questions of sensuality will certainly always continue to interest me, *intellectually*, and for nothing in the world will I abandon my studies on this subject. But in reality and for my personality, the sexual domain is very clearly limited right now, and the banal phrase—"I no longer belong to myself"—is very true. In the sensual domain, Slimène reigns as the uncontested and unique master. Only he attracts me, only he inspires in me the state of mind necessary to leave the domain of the intellect in order to descend—is it a descent? I strongly suspect so— toward that of the much-vaunted sensual fulfillments.

Generally, in the modern world—false and unbalanced—in marriage, the husband is never the sensual initiator. Vilely and stupidly, the young woman's life is linked to a husband with a ridiculous personality, in the end. The woman's material virginity belongs to him. Then, most often with disgust, she must spend her life near him, submitting to "conjugal duty" until the day when someone else, in darkness, degradation, and lies, teaches her that there is a whole world of sensations, of thoughts and feelings that regenerate one's whole being. And this is just how our marriage differs from so many others—and makes so many bourgeois indignant: for me, Slimène is two things, and he instinctively knows how to be them even though the husband is almost never more for his wife—the lover and the comrade.

What did that strange guy—the Colonel de R——, admittedly captivating and bewitching for many very superior women—mean, when he said, "Have you been the object of unending covetousness in Algeria?" That, up to a certain point, I only know too well, having suffered from it.

For all of those who have known me, for the officers especially, Slimène's personality in my life is naturally *inexplicable*. Domercq ended up facing the facts . . . Taste *pretends* that he understands nothing, but up to a certain point he understands. What must I think of R——? I certainly would like to see this man again and know him better. The impression that he left me with is not at all banal, and he cannot be a vulgar man.

I've noticed that things in life—at least in mine—have a strange tendency to always arrange themselves against *all* likelihood, against the much-vaunted *theory of probabilities.*

And now I'm starting to simply wait without making further hypotheses.

Thus, I no longer know if seeing Slimène again is going to come soon or not. I certainly desire him with all the fibers of my being, but I no longer clutch to *dates,* out of fear of being disillusioned.

I've gone through several days of somber anguish and burdensome dreams. Then it started to clear a bit, but working was impossible and I felt myself pushed toward inaction. To pull myself out of it, I had to make a violent effort of will yesterday . . .

I still know nothing of Brieux's kindly personality, except that he must be very good . . . But is he excessively simple, like his brief letters, simple, frank, and straight, or is he the most complicated of the complicated?

Among the personalities here, there is Mohammed ben Aïssa the courageous one, who must have left for Algiers now and who has a good heart.

Smaïne ben Amma—a vicious being all the way to the end of his fingernails, worn out, *deformed,* and already almost completely shapeless. He'll end up with delirium tremens if he drinks, or with general paralysis.

Unpleasant to the last degree! Zuizou didn't need to warn me against him.

If I had to choose between this "aristocrat" and the porter–kif smoker Slimène, it's certainly the latter whom I would choose.

———————

MARSEILLE, THURSDAY, AUGUST 22, 1901, NOON

Martyrdom continues. And yet, by *reasoning,* instead of letting myself go to dark instinctive sensations, there is an immense improvement in my situation: Zuizou is no longer in that unfortunate Batna; he is on the way and, furthermore, is in Bône, in this city where her tomb is. May She be able to welcome him and inspire him, take him forever under her posthumous protection!

Here, I've finally understood the very complicated mechanism of the intolerable state of things that has been established. † "Women's little business, women's little subterranean work; everything broke anyway."

It's useless to insist. Admittedly, Augustine is only slightly responsible—for his *weakness* only, and not all of that comes from him.

He has committed an irreparable mistake, and for now, nobody can do anything about it. But, reasonably, there is no longer for him but one chance of salvation: *that would be that his enemies die and that he comes back to us,* which would be certain. It would probably be very painful for him, but it would mean moral salvation. Must I wish for that to happen? No, for only God knows the depths of the heart. Leave it to time and Mektoub, namely God, the care for this life on which I can no longer act. Slimène suspected it, and he will understand better than anyone else. *Praise be to God!*

For now, I feel peaceful about this, for I *know* and I *understand.* There's no more incertitude. My state of mind is very complex. Right now, my physical condition is a large part of it, the state of things here also. Slimène's delay, too, but that feeling is childish.

My God! Thank goodness if only Exempliarsky would be willing to loan Augustine a sufficient amount of money, to at least save us from any preoccupation regarding him and also to help us avoid burdensome expenses, maybe even fatal ones!

We have so many personal expenses and so many debts and things to buy that the twenty-five francs from last night would really make us happy. ♥ *May God facilitate!*

I must make a great effort in order to spend this week without letting myself go to despondency, and I should even try to employ my time usefully—which is the most difficult. What is the most curious is that here the *blessed,* calm, resigned, and salutary melancholy never comes to me. If there is a city in the world where these feelings are foreign to me, it is certainly here. This city will never *inspire* me . . . especially as long as I'm under this roof. After, with Zuizou all to myself in another neighborhood, maybe that will pass.

The reading that suits me the best right now is Dostoyevsky—maybe because all his novels correspond the best with the vague, unformed, and painful state of mind in which I've been struggling for a long time.

Last night I reread letters from my friend Eugene. God, what a change in him, too, in these six years of friendship! What an evolution since his first such immature letters and his last arrival from the depths of the desert, from Touat, whose name alone makes me dream! What a darkening of his soul! It seems to me that this love novel in Algiers influenced Eugene a lot in this sense. For that especially, given the nature of this man, that love had to be real and profound. It is, I believe, what happened to him, judging by his so painful letter in which he announced to me his sudden departure, almost his escape into the extreme South?

I too—maybe more than he—have changed immeasurably since then. There is an abyss between the child that I was then and what I am now. It's pointless even to say it: between my *self* in Bône—and yet that was only four years ago—there is a difference such that my memories from then make me smile—very sadly, it is true. It is probable that, without the terrible misfortunes that befell me since Bône, my development would have been much slower. It would have been so even this year, *without Behima*. What I have noted and learned to understand *here* has also had an enormous influence on my character and will have a definite repercussion on the whole course of my life, henceforth.

On my horizon, as the ultimate refuge, as the only *human* hope, there is nothing other than Slimène—*he alone*. The rest has disappeared like barely existing ghosts—having existed only in my sickly imagination. Only he is *real*, is not a trap and a sham.

FRIDAY, AUGUST 23, 1901,
ELEVEN O'CLOCK IN THE MORNING

Had a horrible day yesterday, thanks to a new little jab from . . .

Crisscrossed the city from three to five—drained, exhausted, unsteady on my feet—looking for Smaïn. Didn't find him. Went to Joliette, found

Slimène's porter. Borrowed fifty-five cents, sent telegram to Zuizou. Sli-mane gave fifteen cents for tobacco. Returned to the house. Immense fatigue, malaise, pain in my whole body.

Reflected and prayed during the night. Today—undoubtedly thanks to Djilani—I've somewhat pulled myself together. If there are no idiotic troubles here, I hope to hold out this way for the five days remaining to me until the arrival—*this time certain*—of Zuizou. I think I'll even be able to devote myself to working—up to a certain point, at least. The most important thing is not to let myself reach a state of mental help-lessness. Why, for example, had I let myself imagine that Zuizou's delay hid something deadly or distressing? In large part because my position here is intolerable.

Oh! To need to put on an act, if only just to a certain point! To feel next to oneself an unconscious enemy (conscious not of his hatred, but hateful *without knowing why*—for when it comes to reason, there is none) and to be unable to leave! Why didn't I leave today with Zuizou's money? In order not to break with Augustine, who I believe is very unhappy. But this role that I have to play—in no way out of fear, for such an enemy and his stupid hatred would only *make me smile*, but so as to not finish off the other and in order to not establish a completely impossible state of things—repels and disgusts me.

Finally, it is yet another trial, and I mustn't show myself as less than capable of facing the trials sent by God. Fortunately, the latter will be brief!

SATURDAY, AUGUST 24, 1901,
TEN O'CLOCK IN THE EVENING

God and Djilani have finally heard us! After yesterday's bad news, the colonel came in person to announce that the permutation had been pronounced. In three days, Zuizou will be here, for certain, and now we have the colonel's protection.

Oh impenetrable human destiny! Oh unknown paths by which God leads his creatures!

≈ *I have no coquetry with you, Oh Abou Alam! You watch over me. God forbid I should be afraid.*

They have not abandoned us, for they read hearts, and they know that ours are pure ≈ *if it pleases Allah.* They will complete their work in what remains to be done!

MONDAY, AUGUST 26, 1901,
ELEVEN O'CLOCK IN THE MORNING

Yesterday, after the mild upset of these past few days, I went through a strange crisis . . . Suffering from stomach pain with a backache, I had lain down in the afternoon. At about four o'clock, I was overcome by a more and more violent headache, then an intense fever. I was in the grip of this *conscious delirium* that was so terribly fatiguing. Well! They left me alone in the house, without help, until ten o'clock . . . And when they returned, they couldn't even bother to come in to see what was happening . . . This is a fair portrait of those beings, their harshness, their ferocious selfishness, and their unconsciousness! Finally, thanks to Allah, there are only two days left of this horrible existence, of this atrocious misery.

I'm thinking that I'm now like the privates whose inscriptions illustrate the walls of the bordj, and I say, if I'm not rubbing my hands with glee, but at least with a sigh of relief: *The end is in sight after all! Only two days left to get through!* How time drags when one only has, even if only momentarily, no other goal than to get through the days, to kill time at whatever cost!

Today I am weak, worn-out, broken. I still have stomach pain and a backache. As long as the fever doesn't come back this evening! Little does it matter, in fact, if they're here or not: there is no help to wait for, and as for begging for any, I won't do that today any more than last night. If only I could hold out until Thursday! Then Zuizou will care for me, console me, and everything will be fine.

. . . Another idea (my ideas lack order): I could surely write on the door of this room, in all truth: *Eden-Purée.* Oh no! This room will not leave many good memories. What I wrote above was a pure and short illusion, one evening.

But I've noticed, in fact, that my health has succumbed to distress. I'm sure that if this hell were to last much longer, I would become seriously ill. And who even knows how this current state will finish? I'm sure that I've never gone through anything like it, except at the start of serious illnesses: influenza, jaundice, and measles. Perhaps the best for today is only a momentary triumph of my robust health? But I don't think so. I hope I can hold on at least for these two more days that I have to get through.

If I'm not sick tonight, I'll have to go see the hotel room, for tomorrow I'll have to go find the doorman Slimène and Smaïne.

TUESDAY, AUGUST 27, 1901, NOON

It's been a long time since I've been as calm as today. Strong mistral, gorgeous fall weather. The air is pure and clear. It's cool. The sun is shining, and *tomorrow I will leave this house.*

To sum up everything, I pardon all, and it is for him to judge. I have done and will do, until the end, my human duty, and that for She who is no longer with us. I've been wrong with Her and with Vava. Involuntary wrongs, certainly, but which I must make up for by walking the straight path, by doing good for the good and for them and not for gratitude from those for whom I am doing good. Slimène will certainly understand me and will agree with me. What could be more beautiful than to have a peaceful soul and to feel that one acts generously even toward the blind!

Some calm has finally returned to my life and into my soul. There are still many questions to take care of, notably our marriage, which has been made difficult because of the money issue. But given the colonel's obvious protection, I hope that, again, that will go well . . .

Besides, Djilani has not at all abandoned us, and he will not abandon us in the future, for we will continue to be his just, generous, and faithful servants.

How many clouds have been removed from our horizon! And especially if God does not separate us through death, the era of separations has permanently come to a close.

LEFT AUGUSTINE'S HOUSE, AUGUST 27, 1901, EVENING

Was at Joliette Quay at four o'clock. Zuizou arrived on the *Ville-d'Oran*, August 28, 1901, at eight thirty in the morning, in very beautiful clear weather and strong wind.

OCTOBER 1, 1901, THREE O'CLOCK IN THE AFTERNOON

67 Grignan Street

A month has gone by since I wrote those last lines. Everything has certainly changed. Zuizou is here, near me, and his health has not been impaired as much as I feared. We are alone and *in our home*—what a delicious feeling! Our marriage is no longer more than a question of a few days, and the Villa has been sold.

Poor, dear Villa Neuve, which I will certainly never enter again, which most likely I will never see again!

Since yesterday, the date on which I learned that *the house* had been sold on September 27, I've been haunted by memories from there.

The first of my ideas here is that this time, for good, the story of life there is over! Everything has scattered, finished, been buried. In only a few days, the old furniture itself, the inanimate witnesses of the past, will be sold off by auction, scattered . . . As for us, whose psychological ties are tightened more each day, after the five months of exile remaining, we will go as far away as possible in the South, and this time, *if it pleases Allah, for good.*

God has had pity on me, and he has heard my prayers: he has given me the ideal companion, so much and so ardently desired, without whom my life would always have been incoherent and dismal.

For now, we are going through a period of trials and miseries, but †
only he who will have suffered until the end will be saved.

Only God knows what he intends for us. Thus we must resign our-selves and courageously face adversity with the firm consciousness that our earthly life is but a path toward other unknown destinies.

One year has already gone by since the luminous and melancholy autumn in the Souf... Down there, the date palms are already shedding their dusty shroud, and the sky is bright and clear above the resplendent dune and the brown chotts of Debila...

And we are here in this loathed, repugnant, bleak city where every-thing is gray and gloomy!

MARSEILLE, NOVEMBER 21, 1901,
EIGHT O'CLOCK IN THE EVENING

For a few days, I have been going through—or rather, a remarkable thing—we have been going through a period of deep sadness, not at all mournful but rather unfathomable; and I feel the beginning of the sensation about which someone was recently talking to me: the premo-nition of a departure. ❥ *God knows!*

Memories of the Souf, the undying and deep love, lying dormant in me, for my chosen country, all of this haunts my heart both painfully and deliciously... All I need to hear, by chance, is a bugle call, and that is enough to awaken a whole world of sensations in my soul that seemed drowsy.

There are also my great preoccupations with the world beyond that used to make me dream so much, during long nocturnal hours of silent contemplation, leaning out the window of my room, from where one could see the big sky out there and the often-snowy jagged outline of the Jura and the blurred, black masses of big trees, out of which emerged the giant silhouette of the farm's old poplar tree.

In the lilac groves, full of shadow and soaked with dew, every spring night there were innumerable nightingales whose songs filled my soul with a strange languor... The strange thing is that in my mind, most-ly during my childhood, strange *associations* of ideas, sensations, and memories were formed...

Thus these spring memories of flowering lilacs are always linked in my memory with the remembrance of light and clear evenings *after the rain* . . . followed by warm, balmy nights and the innumerable songs . . .

In today's uncertain and monotonous life, all of that comes back to me now.

Finally, for the first time since the death of my dear old ones, that is to say, since the entrance into conscious life, I am *externalizing* my *self* a little bit; I have a duty to fulfill *outside of myself.* That is enough to ennoble these formless days and this charmless existence, since I have been dragging in this city of exile—where I have no attachments, where everything is foreign and repugnant to me—for five long months . . . How the vulgar person—not only the coarse commoners surrounding us but even he who prides himself in intelligence and development— hates everything that doesn't bend to his demands and stupid and arbitrary laws! How the plebs get irritated when they see a being surge forth—especially a woman—who wants to be *oneself* and not resemble them! How mediocrity flies into a rage when it can't level everything, reduce everything to its stupid and low level!

I've now discovered an ability that I hadn't suspected—that of composing classes, especially about history, with overall views not devoid of breadth.

Madame Paschkoff is not at all a type who enchants and captivates. A remarkable mixture but a lot of unconscious egoism, immense pride, and intellectual superficiality. Russian mobility, especially *worldly.*

My hatred of problems with the masses is innate, and I don their rags in order not to have any problems with them. However, in a conversation, it is, and will probably always be, impossible for me to say, and to say forcefully, what I consider to be true and just.

Worldly and modern indifferentism is not made to rub off on me. And at least the sincerity of my hatred is a chance for moral salvation.

The most terrible misfortune that can overwhelm a human being is to fall into the mournful moral nihilism of a Nicolas Stavroguine or into the egotistical debasement of the intellect as with Augustine. Admittedly, this constant and *real* preoccupation with things that are not at all ourselves, that *materially bring us nothing,* is in fact what ennobles and soothes the soul, what makes it larger than banality and the pervading pettiness.

Now more than ever, I feel that I will never tolerate sedentary life and that the attraction of elsewhere, bathed in sunshine, will always haunt me . . . The only place that I'd accept to finish my life would be El Oued, and I wouldn't even want to return there unless it were in order to stay forever.

NOVEMBER 26, 1910,
ONE O'CLOCK IN THE MORNING

Today, calm sadness, desire to leave, to flee this room, this city, and the people here . . . for the only one among them that we'll miss will certainly be F——.

More and more, it seems to me that we are now certainly going through the *last days* of our exile here . . . May God make it thus, for the Marseille nightmare has lasted long enough!

What rejoices me is that Ouïha is starting, more and more, to penetrate, too, the hidden domain of sensations and thoughts where I am henceforth no longer alone. Obviously, one day he must also see all these very mysterious things that are *beneath* life and are inaccessible to the common herd.

Thus, here is another proof of this fact confirmed by everything: he was the companion always destined for me . . . and what an unfathomable mystery thus envelops our earthly existence: for ten, twenty, twenty-five years our destinies were pursuing each other, far from one another, without either of us even suspecting each other's existence in the world, yet aspiring to find the *essential* companion, without which all earthly happiness is *impossible*, for it is necessary for nature itself . . . Then, afterward, a seemingly completely accidental combination of circumstances, the meeting in El Oued . . .

Certainly, and it is a very strange thing in itself, my destiny began to come out of the shadow, to reveal itself to me in Geneva on June 19, 1900. It was in the dirty, sad room at Mother Pons's house. I was writing some chapter in the story of *Rakhil*, and all of a sudden I saw the idea of *going to Ouargla* surging forth in my mind! That idea was the beginning of everything!

Oh! If only we could foresee, during each hour of our lives, the major importance of certain thoughts, certain acts, and even certain words, which, in appearance, are miniscule and indifferent! And isn't one led by such examples to conclude that, in human life, there are *no indifferent moments at all* that are without a result for the future!

In a very different vein . . . Studying the history of Carthage with Ouïha, I am struck by the resemblance between ancient and harsh Carthage and modern England: rapaciousness, hate, and scorn for the foreigner, implacable, limitless egotism . . . Is this perhaps the fortune of all great *maritime* powers, that is to say those who have *maritime genius* and not those who were powerful and were sea merchants by chance, and for a relatively short period of time, like Spain, for example?

Now, in order to complete my intellectual development and to open broader horizons for myself, I'd have to have the possibility of doing serious historical studies. Alas, the grocer and tailor bills have come and taken the precious time that I would like to dedicate to thought!

Nothing is more depressing and nothing creates disgust and boredom as much as living with the common herd, with beings whose only preoccupations are the trivialities of daily life . . . and for me at least, nothing irritates my superior faculties as much . . .

SATURDAY, NOVEMBER 30, 1901,
THREE O'CLOCK IN THE AFTERNOON

The monotonous, gray days go by in the banal and boring preoccupations caused by the inextricable situation in which we have found ourselves for a year, but which is now getting more serious.

It is intensely cold, and to warm ourselves we only have the wood given to us out of *concerned* charity . . . from M—— ↝ *May Allah's curse fall on the disbelievers and their mentality!* as Slimène says.

What will happen to all this mess that we're immersed in here?

Certainly, if we manage to free ourselves of our main debts and if our friend Eugène sends one hundred francs to me again, we'll leave immediately for Bône, where we'll stay an unlimited amount of time. When will we be able to reach Algiers? Only God knows!

However, in all the trouble, in the midst of all the material and psychological suffering at present, I've observed one thing that really delights me: Zuizou's soul is approaching mine more and more closely.[1] The dreamed-for comrade has finally been found. May he last as long as our earthly existence will last!

We are living in the full haze of uncertainty, in more darkness than ever before. However, there is radiant hope at the horizon: the upcoming and definitive—without a doubt—return to the chosen *country*.

Went through a period of problems and growing irritation due to the state of uncertainty in which we were struggling. Presently, relaxation and great weariness. However, we seem to have been saved, and the return to Africa is no more than a question of a few days.

Before that, there will be a sad, rapid, and furtive return to Geneva.

BÔNE, TUESDAY, JANUARY 21, 1902

Left Marseille January 14, at five in the evening, aboard the *Duc-de-Bragance*. Arrived in Bône at eight in the evening, January 15.

The dream of return from exile has finally come true; here we are, once more, in the great eternally young and luminous sun, on the beloved earth across the great murmuring Azure whose deserted stretches remind one, in the evening, of those of the Sahara—closer now—which is no more than a day from here and which, with help from God and Djilani, we will undoubtedly see in the next year, a year that began in such a consoling way!

May this year be the beginning of a new life, of the so-desired and so-deserved calm!

BÔNE, WEDNESDAY, JANUARY 29, 1902,
ELEVEN O'CLOCK IN THE MORNING

Life in the open air and the simplicity of surrounding things are starting to give me back the strength that I'd finally lost during the long and

1. Eberhardt's note: *Mon frère Yves*: "That evening I understood that he had more of my manners, my ideas, and sensations the same as mine, than I would have thought." (Translator's note: from *Mon frère Yves* [1883], by Pierre Loti, a semiautobiographical novel.)

painful exile in Marseille. Furthermore, my intellect is also awakening, and I think that I'll write here.

Just the idea that the great Mediterranean separates us from the three-times-cursed Gehenna of Marseille where we suffered so much, just that idea gives me a *physical sensation* of well-being, of immense *relief*.

In twenty-one days the servitude, the trouble caused by the attachments that still connect Zuizou to military service and that force him to reckon with intruders, will also end. Afterward, thrown all alone into the vast, wonderful universe—changing, sometimes engaging, sometimes disappointing—we'll have to figure things out . . .

These few years of earthly life are not at all enough to frighten me, except for, however, the possibility of losing my travel companion and remaining all alone. He thinks that he has enough experience in order to advantageously manage—in the sense in which I mean this word—our material affairs.

Mentally, *almost*-absolute resignation and relative calm, in which, I repeat, physical agents count for a large part. For now, no desire at all to be involved in men's lives, to live city life again: the isolation in which I live charms and attracts me.

The other evening, the two of us going alone to meet Ali Bou Traïf on the Casbah bridge, there was a full moon rising on the peaceful sea. Hour full of mystery and unfathomable sadness. Similar impressions to those felt sometimes in the past in the South, in the face of mysterious vistas—in the region of the chott and in the salty Oued Rirh'. We stopped at the curve in the road leading to the cemetery.

Under the blue sky, still slightly lit below, the sea—an indistinct color between silver blue and linen gray—stretched out.

The *mystical bridge* of the Slavic legend, woven for the nymphs of silent nights by lunar rays, trembled slightly, all in gold against the imprecise background of the waters. A cloud like a gray band, interposed between the moon and the waters, shared its shadow with the latter, just like a low dune stretching out in the form of two headlands, separating the sea into two parts: one very vast, very blue, very lit up, the other opening onto the empty space of the horizon, imprecise, dark gray, hazy, and where a fishing boat floated with a lateen sail, with no reflection in the hazy water, with no movement, a sort of ghostly boat that ended up sliding away imperceptibly and disappearing into the world of faraway vapors.

FEBRUARY 14, 1902,
THREE O'CLOCK IN THE AFTERNOON

One month has already gone by since we left the Gehenna of Marseille; and here, everything is already going wrong thanks to the perpetual intrigues of the Moorish women.

Here, as elsewhere, I note the instability of Slimène's personality and the harmful influence exercised on him by the milieus where he lives. Will that change some day? I don't know, and in any case, with such a personality, the life of misery to which we are reduced is even more difficult.

It's better to go begin again a life of hardship and trouble in Algiers—where it will always be less horrible than in Marseille—than to stay here where hospitality is manifested by being continually snubbed and by unending discussions.

The literary spirit is awakening in me, and I will at least try to make a name for myself in the Algerian press, while waiting to be able to do as much in that of Paris, which alone is worth taking care of, and alone makes one a reputation.

For all of that, I have to have some time of absolute calm, almost of reclusion. In Algiers I'd have to find a guy capable of teaching Slimène what he doesn't know, and that would be a lot of work to do—and in this way I could free myself of all these burdensome worries that prevent me from working. ☙ *God will see to it!*

More and more, I'm becoming indifferent to the troubles and the friction of daily life. Essentially, I've become very cold toward everything and toward the world. What I just want to flee from, at any cost, are the disputes and the nagging, for those are *materially* intolerable things.

If we succeed today or tomorrow in fleeing to Karéza, we will not only finish more peacefully, but also more agreeably, the few remaining days here.

Once again I will go and say adieu to the white tomb on the green hill made more so by the intoxicating spring, then we'll go farther in pursuit of our changing and tormented destiny.

In Algiers there will be a few recollections from the past, already dating from two years ago, and which led up to the epic of the Souf. What there will be further along ⨯ *Allah knows!*

Left Algiers on the Messageries du Sud coach,[2] March 12, 1902, at six fifteen in the morning. Beautiful clear weather. State of mind: good, calm. Difficult and long trip up the slopes of the Sahel. Birmandreis, Birkadem, Birtouta, Boufarik, Beni-Mered. Arrived in Blida at twelve thirty, went to the café on the Place d'Armes. Lunch at the stopover, left on Médéah coach. Sidi-Medani, the gorges. Ruisseau des Singes,[3] hotel, beautiful torrent, narrow gorge. Numerous waterfalls running underground along the road. At the sixty-eighth kilometer, junction of the Oued Merdja to the left and the Oued Nador to the right, descending from Djebel-Nador. At the seventieth kilometer, Camps-des-Chênes.[4] Forest house and hamlet. Saw an infantryman having his meal near the well (noticed black Souf). Crossing of road number one with the Takitoun path, commemorative plaque of the army of Africa, dated 1855. At the seventy-fourth, farm. At the seventy-fifth, bridge over the Oued Zebboudj. The valley has become wider since the sixty-seventh kilometer. Masses of flowering laurustine[5] toward the junction of the Nador and the Zebboudj. A lot of ferns everywhere. Ruins of a plaster works at the seventy-sixth kilometer. At the seventy-seventh kilometer, stopping point and rest at Moorish café of Ndila, stop a bit farther in R'eich.

Arrived in Médéah at about eight thirty. Difficult ascent five kilometers long, and long circuit. Stop in Moorish café. Sent a telegram to Ouïha. Stop on the square, on a bench, then in the train station's café-restaurant.

2. Translator's note: Messageries du Sud was a parcel and mail service.
3. Translator's note: Monkeys' Stream.
4. Translator's note: Camps-des-Chênes means "Camp of Oaks."
5. Translator's note: Laurel thyme.

Left again in Boghari coach. Ghardaya at ten thirty. Arrived in Berrouaghia at one forty-five in the morning. Slept in the Hôtel des Voyageurs. Got up at seven o'clock. Was at Moorish café with a deïra. Left on horseback at eight o'clock. At first, a road suitable for vehicles, passing by the civil prison. Then Arab paths entering a countryside of hills separated by deep ravines where streams flow, very heavily wooded with thickets. Stopped in a gorge with warm baths, Moorish café. Direction: northwest. Along the road, marabout Taïeb and farther away Tablat toward the right. Arrived around twelve thirty. Beni-bou-Yacoub, halfway up a hill rising at the foot of the mountain. At the bottom of the gorge, in the oued, caïd's house.

Stayed until two in the morning. Left by mule with two servants riding. Path: elevated hills, gorges, deep ravines, innumerable oueds, soaked paths transformed into torrents. Waded about all night and lost our way several times.

The colorless day comes up in a sad valley. Ragged clouds in the narrow and deep valley between rather high blue mountains.

Walked for some time in order to rest my numbed legs. Arrived at the Moorish café situated in the middle of a rockslide on the side of the hill above a miserable douar. Arrived in Hassen-ben-Ali (Loverdo) at about nine in the morning. Sent the servants back. Spent the day in the Beranis Moorish café. Got up at noon and took a walk. A few European houses made of reddish adobe, looking miserable on a hill above the deep valley in the direction of Beni-bou-Yacoub. Horizon made of elevated mountains. Impression of desolate sadness. Boredom and extreme fatigue. Gray weather, violent wind, and intense cold. At three thirty, went to train station and sent a telegram to Ouïha. Bought ticket. Fine, icy drizzle. Wandered on the only road.

Took five o'clock train. Changed trains in Blida. Fell asleep on a bench. Awoken by a worker. Took the P-L-M train arriving from Maison-Carrée. Arrived in Algiers at 9:35 in the evening, Friday, March 14.

➻ *God does not put the mass of crazies on the right path!*

Today's situation: lacking money. We're counting on Si Mohammed Cherif to save us and assure our existence for the remaining few days. The days are spent working.

Last Thursday, trip to Barrucand's; Villa Bellevue, Mustapha. Pleasant impression. Modern, fine and subtle mind, but subject to the century's ideas. Went to Médée Rampart Street to Madame Luce ben-Aben's workroom. Felt a certain pleasure because of the conversation with intellectuals, a feeling I've forgotten for a long time.

The generous man writes in pencil the harm caused to him and in ink the good done to him.

"Act in this world as if you had to live forever, and act for the end as if you had to die tomorrow!" to compare with Marc-Aurèle's idea (*Pensées*).[6]

APRIL 1, 1902, NINE O'CLOCK IN THE EVENING

We are still at work, disheartening in its quantity, and the small amount of time—how small!—remaining for these out-of-date studies, now burdensome. Now we need to make a very big effort. What is harmful is the variety and multiplicity of the subjects. Finally, ॐ *God will help!*

During these last days, a spontaneous and sincere burst for poor dear faraway Popowa. Only God knows if I'll ever see her again! If ever there was a pure and noble being, going as far as moral austerity in certain things, it was Popowa. She was probably the initiator in me of the movement of psychological recovery dating from my stay in Geneva in 1900, before my departure for El Oued. Oh, to have her here near to us, so strong, so good, so full of life and energy during these hours of suffering, boredom, and incertitude!

However, in looking closely at it, I must note that our current life now, that of poor students without a cent, is the *dreamed-of life*, long ago during the days of ease.

---

6. Translator's note: Eberhardt is comparing this hadith to the writings of Marcus Aurelius in his *Meditations*.

At that time I didn't foresee the torments, the anguish, the painful powerlessness, and I certainly didn't know what slow, long, and even more difficult patience was required of my nature. An effort, almost superhuman, but rapid, in a single burst, is not difficult for me. But this uninterrupted and endless series of small, hardly perceptible efforts, without any apparent worth, without an immediate and appreciable result, this succession of battles against myself, against my tastes, my aspirations, my desires, and my most legitimate needs—with my nature, this is the most harsh and painful test.

In our current situation, I must still have the courage of two of us; I must, in the face of the blackest situations, lift Zuizou's spirits, give him back hope and courage without which we will be infallibly lost. However, I'm beginning to get used to it, to coldly envisage, but with an unchangeable hope, a henceforth strong faith in God and Djilani, the most perilous situations.

The other day, Barrucand was saying to me, "In life there are knots on the threads that we follow, and if we can manage to bypass these knots, we find, for still more time, a smooth and even surface . . . until the final knot, the Gordian knot that Death comes and severs . . ."

It seems impossible to me that the human spirit can *truly, sincerely represent* to itself Death as a *true, absolute* cessation of life. As for me, I believe that I *feel* in myself the *certitude of eternity.*

However—◡ *I ask Allah the Very Great to pardon me*—if Death really meant absolute annihilation, it would not be frightening. In short, doesn't three-fourths of Pain lie in the horror of the *memory* we keep of it, that is to say, in the *consciousness* that we have of it? . . . No more consciousness, no more memory, almost no more Pain . . .

"The issue is not one of living, but of leaving." (Marshal Maurice de Saxe).

17 Soudan Street

By some unlikely chance, there's not too much work this evening. I have a moment of contemplation, and I read Nadson, the old gospel of my younger and happier days, after having translated the Christian woman for the dear good Madame Ben Aben.

And I think that over there, very far away on the banks of the blue Rhône, at the foot of the still-snowy Jura, spring is beginning. Slender, fragrant foliage covers the trees like clouds, and the first flowers are growing in the rock gardens of the Villa Neuve, in the shade of the tall dark pine trees, and on the two tombs in the Vernier cemetery . . .

This year, everything is about the same as those vanished springs from long ago, and immutable nature comes alive again . . . But I'm no longer there to dream and to suffer . . . and Vava and Mamma and Volod have sunk into the great Unknown! Everything is over, razed, annihilated . . .

ALGIERS, MAY 4, 1902,
ABOUT TEN O'CLOCK IN THE EVENING

A visit to a witch today, lodged in a miniscule shop on a high street, reachable by dark stairs from Devil Street. Acquired the certain proof of the *reality* of this incomprehensible and mysterious science of Magic . . . And what horizons, at once vast and dark, this reality opens to my mind, what reassurance, too, demolishing all doubt!

These days, I've found again the calm and melancholy state of mind from long ago. Algiers is certainly one of the cities that inspires me, especially in certain neighborhoods. I like the one in which we live, our lodging, too, after the horrible dump of Navy Street. Here, for certain, without the boring and continual, thankless work, without the problems and anxieties of our current situation, I should have a few days of peace, of contemplation, and of fruitful work.

How can the imbeciles swarming in the "world" and in literature say that there is no longer anything Arab in Algiers? I—who have seen many other cities—feel certain impressions from the most pure Orient!

One of them, very gracious, is that of the maghreb on the port and on the terraces of the upper city with the laughing Algerian women, a whole world frolicking in pink or green against the slightly bluish white of the uneven, incoherent terraces; one can discover all of that from Madame Ben Aben's *moucharabia*.[7]

The bay of Algiers, with that of Bône, is the prettiest, the most deliciously exhilarating corner of the sea that I've ever seen.

How far we are here from ignoble Marseille, with its ugliness, its stupidity, its vulgarity, and its moral and material filth!

In spite of the hoi polloi introduced here by prostituted and prostituting "civilization," Algiers is still a gracious place, and it's very peaceful living here.

However, for many days, the encounter with the cadaver of Zeheïra the Kabyle—who threw herself into a well in the Médée cul-de-sac in order to flee a hateful marriage—carried on a stretcher covered with a thick gray cloth, had thrown a heavy, dark mourning veil onto this luminous Algiers . . . Now, it's over . . . only the surroundings still keep something of that shadow, and I no longer like to go through there . . .

The more I study—badly and too quickly—the history of North Africa, the more I see that my idea was correct: the land of Africa eats and reabsorbs everything that is hostile to it. Perhaps it is the *Predestined Land* from which the light that will one day regenerate the world will burst forth!

An old, peaceful-looking man came to the French camp at the time of Sidi-Ferruch's landing in 1830. He said only this one sentence: ﻉ "*God is God and Mohammed is his prophet!*" Then he left and was never seen again.

This man had come to announce something that nobody understood . . . and it was the durability of Islam, there, in the bewitching land of Africa!

---

7. Translator's note: *Moucharabia* refers to carved wooden grillwork in Arab architecture, allowing one to look out and to remain unseen.

Eleven Thirty in the Evening.

Life continues monotonously with, however, a touch of an *outline of the future* in the great moral disarray in which I find myself.

Once again I am going through a slow and sometimes very painful period of incubation. The kind of life we are living, both monotonous and uncertain, contributes a lot to pushing my soul toward investigations that are often painful.

Of the two people who have helped us here, Barrucand and Madame Ben Aben, both very good and very refined, I'm beginning to understand the character:

Barrucand, a dilettante of thought and especially of feeling, a moral nihilist, is very positive in practical life, *knowing how to live.*

Madame Ben Aben is, after my mother, the second type of woman that I've met who is essentially good, with a great love of the ideal. In real life, how ignorant both of them are! *Even I*, who have the intimate conviction that *I don't know how to live*, know better than they.

Augustine has been erased from my life. For me, the brother so loved long ago is dead. As for the individual in Marseille or elsewhere, the husband of *Jenny the worker*, he doesn't exist and I only think of him rarely. He's the one who did everything to create this situation, and once again the unforgettable Old Man displayed his incredible clairvoyance.

Since the good summer heat has returned very suddenly, since the great, blinding light blazes every day on Algiers, I am once again finding, bit by bit, my impressions of Africa. I will soon find them again completely, especially if the planned trip to Bou-Saada takes place ... Ah, this trip! It will be a brief return, if not to the resplendent Sahara, at least very close, to a land of date palms and sun!

Notes from Algiers.

As long as it was cool, the grayish shadow of the dim streets of the upper city was dark, almost gloomy. Now, because of the opposition of shadow and light—suddenly, violently juxtaposed—it has become African again, or at least *Arab*.

No, the true African landscape is apparent in none of the large cities, especially of the Tell. The African perspective is indistinct, the horizon far away. A lot of space and emptiness under the immense light: that is the classic example of the African landscape! Algiers's architecture doesn't at all follow that pattern. There is a packing together of houses, fearfully huddled at the end of dead ends, in a city accustomed to sieges and sudden attacks. Because of a lack of space, the floors encroach on the street and stretch across it all the time.

And too, the *crowd* dishonors the street of Algiers. In silence and half-light, these streets would have their charm.

With the mixed crowd, the stupidly noisy crowd in which the Arab element is represented almost exclusively by the horrible Kabyles in "roumi costume," these neighborhoods resemble bad places, cutthroat back alleys.

For the uninitiated foreigner, the dirty burnooses worn over ragged European dress, the faded chechiya without a tassel, and the numerous Moorish women are the *local color*. For one who knows, it is exactly that which takes from Algiers its Arab character, because it doesn't conform to Arab customs. Once again the uninitiated finds the maze of Algiers's old streets very *African*. Medieval, Turkish, Moorish, whatever you wish, but neither Arab nor African especially!

In the truly Arab towns like the ksour of the South, the poignant and captivating mystery of the African soil is truly felt. It resides in the large space, in the small, low—very white or even the same tint as the indistinct surrounding space—houses in ruin, in all the light and the mournful sadness of the ensemble.

Its contemptible population spoils Algiers. The contemplative life of the street, that happy, calm, and creative life that I love so much, is impossible there, especially in the neighborhoods where inanimate things, and some beings, are there to see . . .

I ferociously, blindly hate, more and more, the crowd, that born enemy of dream and thought. It is what prevents me from *living* in Algiers as I've lived elsewhere. Oh, dirty, wicked, and idiotic *civilization*! Why has its infection been brought here? Not the civilization of taste, of art, of thought, that of the European elite, but that of the vile swarming from below!

M'SILA, JUNE 29, 1902,
TWO O'CLOCK IN THE MORNING

In cloudy and threatening weather, I left Algiers yesterday, June 28, at 7:50 in the morning . . . The trip, almost without a stop, was as rapid as a dream. The loveliest hour until now was during the voyage yesterday from Bordj Bou-Arreridj to M'sila last night, perched on Bou-Gettar's wagon.

I'm in a tiny hotel room "in order to wait for supper" and the departure for Bou-Saada. The heat is suffocating. From Portes-de-Fer, the sirocco is blowing, and the country resembles a Moorish bath. The sky is covered with the white-hot haze caused by the *ch'ilé*.[8]

Here the city resembles the new Biskra in its vegetation and the old in its construction. We are in the new M'sila, whereas the old, very ancient, rises up with some disheveled date palms that make it look like ksour, behind the rocky oued crossed by an iron bridge. The inhabitants have the looks of the South.

The road from Bou-Arreridj to M'sila crosses sometimes parched, sometimes marshy solitudes, with an occasional sinuous oued along the road, all planted with oleanders studded with flowers. An acrid odor of chott and humidity reigns there.

Here and there are a few uninhabited villages falling into ruin. In the middle of the path, there is a post house that gives a false impression of a Saharan bordj: low construction with square angles and a large double door. Behind is the humid chaos of the oued. On the road, a few houses, even a French café: this is Medjez.

From Medjez to M'sila, slept as well as I could on a crate. Arrived at about three in the morning. Went to the Moorish café. Errand to market with Fredj. Ate in the cool and shady mosque where the flies are relatively less numerous. Then, came here for an afternoon nap.

---

8. Translator's note: *Ch'ilé* is a local word that refers to the hot wind coming from the south.

As always, this voyage, this sudden separation from Ouïha, seems like a dream to me . . . Poor Ouïha without a cent, in the growing daily boredom of Algiers! If only I could at least bring back some relief to him from this voyage!

I'm going to try to fall asleep again so I won't be dead tired tonight.

BOU-SAADA, JULY 1, 1902

After a morning spent on explanations with the Sid-el-Hokkaïn, we spent the afternoon in a garden belonging to the zaouïya.

As a city, Bou-Saada—in a picturesque site—resembles old Biskra.

M'sila, a city made of toub and cut in two by a oued with a deep bed. The gray-brown houses have the decaying look of the ksour. A few date palms complete the illusion. I have kept a sweetly poetic vision of M'sila.

It was during the mogh'reb, and I had gone alone to wait for Si Embarek near the mosque located on the edge of the oued. The sun was going down in a sirocco haze. Across the way, behind the rocky oued full of clear water, the old city, with its strangely shaped marabouts resembling those of the Oued Rir', and its dark gardens, looked completely Saharan. After a short stop in the bottom of the oued, we emerge into the immense plain with the empty, calm, vast horizon. Tahar Djadi's mare is excellent, and I wasn't able to resist the desire to make her run a bit. A feeling of return to the past's better days, of liberty and peace . . . The bordj of the tolbas that we reach at nightfall is a square made of toub, looking wild and dark in the surrounding desert. Had supper, or rather had supper again, outside against the wall. Then went out again into the darkness reigning over the plain, the strange refuge, and the dilapidated houses falling into ruin.

Spent a bad night in the courtyard, eaten alive by fleas. When I saw the pale moon, bathing in the haze, rising in its last quarter, I awoke the taleb and we left. We took Arab shortcuts through Saïda and Baniou. From Saïda, in the predawn darkness, we saw only the black silhouettes of houses made of toub, without a tree, without a garden, looking mournful in the desert.

While the taleb prayed the fedjr, I lay down farther away on the ground of the sebkha forming the western point of the Hodna. After, Si Ali, the taleb, left us mounted on the red mare accompanied by her son, a gracious small bay colt trotting at his mother's side.

We leave alone, Baniou, a bordj up on the heights and a few houses made of toub. Alley of poplars.

Under the shade of some tamarisk trees in the yellow sand, drank coffee full of flies and muddy water.

In the sebkha, before Baniou, exhausted by the gray mare taken back at the bordj of the tolba, and got off to walk barefoot for a long time.

After Baniou, stop in Bir-el-Hadi: abandoned houses built of toub, a well with good water. The heat increases, continued on a mule. En route, drank from a camel herder's guerba.

Bou-Saada appears between bluish mountains with its casba on a rock and a few small very low dunes that seem white from far away.

The arrival in Bou-Saada: the oued goes around a part of the city. On one side, vast gardens walled in by toub. On the banks, oleanders studded with flowers. On the other, higher side, the houses of the city, undulating and picturesque, cut through by verdant ravines and gardens where, in the dark green of fig trees and vines, a few oleanders create vivid pink patches and the flowering pomegranate trees display their intense purple.

The heat, almost burning yesterday because of the sirocco ending in a violent storm this evening, gives this whole countryside particular aspects, well-known and loved. Bou-Saada is surrounded by high, arid, reddish hills blocking the horizon.

We dismounted under the arches of the house of the cheikh, near the justice of the peace. Across the way, a scraggly, enclosed French garden. To the left, a munitions factory and a wild garden where frogs sing at night. The population, subservient toward the *hokkam*, is much more vulgar and brutal than that of the Sahara.

In spite of yesterday's heavy rain, the soil is dried out. There are beautiful Saharan camels with delicate ankles, who come and kneel in front of the cheikh's house.

I am alone on a mat under the arches with little M'hammed, the son of Dellaouï, and he doesn't leave me for a second.

This evening we will leave for El-Hamel . . . When will we return? When will I see Zuizou again? So many questions.

I finally see that I can return peacefully to whichever military post without any particular problems; only, henceforth, I will have to go directly to the hokkam in order to avoid errands like those of this morning . . .

The official plantation plantings are a very green blackberry bush and a sort of acacia flowering with little yellow balls.

Finally, were it only a trip, I would not regret having come to this corner that I still didn't know about and that, all in all, is a corner of the South I love so much. In my current situation, this relatively distant voyage was an unhoped-for opportunity.

The women's clothing is unsightly, especially the enormous flat coiffure. This clothing of the women of the South, if not worn gracefully by a tall, slender woman, is horrible. That of the Souf is more delicate and prettier. Concerning feminine style, nothing to say about it: I haven't seen it. The little girls, overly tattooed, have pale and wild faces.

EL-HAMEL, JULY 2, 1902,
DURING THE AFTERNOON NAP

Last night, after the Moorish bath, we learned that Lella Zeyneb had returned to the zaouïya, but the black night, the wind, and the rain prevented us from leaving. We slept under the arches.

Woke up very early. Dark, sad night. Stayed until dawn talking with Sid Embarek, then left without coffee, he on a mule, I on a pretty, young white horse.

The Arab road to El-Hamel passes between hills and the rather high mountains surrounding the city of Bou-Saada. The oued follows this road from afar and, near to the zaouïya, bathes the gardens where the date palms give off their particular color. The village made of toub is very light and seems whitewashed. It is rather large and situated halfway up the slope, looking out on the gardens and the valley.

The highest point is occupied by the zaouïya, which resembles a fortress with the *dar enneçara* with green shutters . . .[9]

9. Translator's note: *Dar enneçara* means "House of Christians."

Here . . . with disconcerting rapidity, everything has changed again, completely transformed.

Almost yesterday, it seemed that our stay in Algiers must last indefinitely, still just as monotonous, made of a series of morose, slow, boring impressions, and finally producing the effect of a drop of water incessantly falling on the same place, or of a noise, apparently minimal, hardly perceptible, then finishing by becoming an obsession.

Oh! Those periods of my life like that in Marseille or Algiers! How black they are in my memory!

I certainly was not born for the life of everyone, for the frightening life of ordinary large cities.

From this voyage, rapid as a dream, coming back from Bou-Saada, I've returned stronger, cured of the sickly languor that was eating away at me in Algiers . . . my soul, too, has been reborn. Nomad I was already when, as a little girl, I dreamed, watching the road, the alluring white road that left beneath a sun that seemed even brighter, straight toward the captivating unknown . . . nomad I will stay all my life, in love with changing horizons, still-unexplored faraway places; for every voyage, even in the most frequented and best-known countries, is an *exploration*. In fact, never have two beings—does the exception perhaps exist?—seen the same landscape, the country in the same way, under the same day, under the same color. The universe is reflected in the changing mirror of our souls, and with them its image changes indefinitely . . . This idea would lead one to think that the *true* face of the great Universe is forever ungraspable and unknown . . . This *absolute* face would in fact be the *face of God*.

On the morning of July 3, took the road again from Bou-Saada, after a night spent in the large vaulted room in the silence troubled by the roar of the wind and thunder. Returned on horseback to town, visit to the captain. Left at noon in the vehicle from Aumale, a horrible wagon jam-packed with Jews.

At first the road is sandy, drinn and jujubee trees spread across the vast plain where low dunes run to the foot of the hills, all of that looking completely Saharan. The first stops, too—abandoned, crumbling bordj, small houses made of toub, and date palms—give the illusion of a return to the South.

Then, starting in Sidi-Aïssa, the road becomes suitable for vehicles; the landscape becomes mountainous and harsher. Spent the night, in vain, moreover, looking for a tolerable sleeping position.

Aumale, verdant city of the interior. Almost-uninhabited large barracks. Left again at ten thirty in a good vehicle. Road through fertile areas. Took the train in Bordj Bouïra, returned to Algiers July 4, seven thirty in the evening. Spent the fifth doing errands. The sixth, at seven fifteen in the morning, took the train from Orléansville. Took the wagon again at two in the afternoon. Arrived in Ténès at night.

ORLÉANSVILLE, JULY 17, 1902,
NINE FIFTEEN IN THE EVENING

Here I am again on the road . . . for boring Algiers. Fortunately, it's only for a few days for the business of the zaouïya and of Madame Ben Aben. After, I'll return to Ténès—ᵛ *if it pleases Allah!*—for a long time, for Slimène's appointment would be the best thing to happen to us.

I left Ténès by transport at six in the morning in clear weather. I was without energy and sleepy. Found the rural policeman and a good horse upon my arrival in Trois Palmiers. Went up to the home of the caïd Ahmed. The house, overlooking the douar of Baghdoura, is situated on a tall hill, and the view is very beautiful: arid hillsides of the African earth follow one another with their luminous, varied, and pure coloring in the distance. Left again on horseback. Arrived at about six o'clock in Orléansville, which is certainly one of the prettiest cities of the interior, especially in its location. On the northern side, it overlooks the Chéliff from very high up, and it is surrounded by lush gardens.

A violent fever has taken hold of me since my arrival, and I had a few moments of semiconsciousness . . . I'm having difficulty writing. If only I don't become sick in Algiers, far from my poor cherished Zuizou! . . .

This arrival in Orléansville and my state of mind (present) remind me of recollections of other arrivals, long ago, in other places, and I feel the pervading impressions in the same way as long ago, which is very consoling . . .

DOUAR MAÏN (TÉNÈS), AUGUST 25, 1902,
IN THE EVENING

I'm sitting on an arid hill facing the valley and the chaos of the hillsides and the mountains drowned in gray flax-colored haze. The high mountains closing the horizon stand out in gray against the red orange of the setting sun. Great calm in the Bedouin country untroubled by the few diffuse sounds from the douar: barking dogs, yells of complaining men. To the right, beyond the gorges, one can make out an imprecise vista of the sea on the emptiness of the horizon. To the left, at the top of a pointed hill, in a dense thicket of mastic trees, a few hidden blackish stones, a place of pilgrimage: it is the tomb of a marabout. Night falls and the noises die down.

TÉNÈS, THURSDAY, SEPTEMBER 8, 1902,
NINE O'CLOCK IN THE MORNING

Autumn arrives. A great wind often blows, and gray clouds cover the sky. It also rains sometimes. The wind moans, like the north wind did long ago down there. Our monotonous life continues and would be tolerable without the eternal issue of money. However, we at least have the strict necessary minimum here.

If it were not for the rancor of the milieu we must rub shoulders with, and the little vulgar intrigues, we would have been relatively happy for the last two years. What poisons Ténès is the herd of neurotic, orgiastic, empty-of-meaning, bad females. Naturally, here as everywhere else, the hatred of the vulgar commoners targets me. In itself, I am indifferent to all this mud, but it bothers me when it tends to get close to me, to reach all the way to me. Moreover, there is the precious resource of departure, of isolation on the great roads with the tribes, in the grand peace of the blue and pale-gold horizons.

I did a lot of errands in Maïn, Baghdoura, Tarzout, Cape Kalax, and M'gueu . . . As many escapes to the countryside, to the rest of the still very vast Bedouin country.

Psychologically, these last days have been gray; and the strange thing, as almost always now, Ouïha shares my state of mind. His health worries me. Finally, maybe with a regular treatment, he will permanently heal. If he could be named caïd and if we could leave for a douar, far from the stupidity of Ténès, into the great pure air of the mountains, with a lot of rest and well-being, he would certainly be happy. From the literary point of view, these last few days are lost. I fell into a sort of stagnation, which didn't allow me any effort. Today I'm starting to feel better; but this evening, I will undoubtedly leave for the big annual *taam* in Sidi Merouan. I'll be able to make the account of the festival the subject of my next article for the unrewarding *Nouvelles*. The site and the subject lend themselves to this work. Melancholy impressions of autumn. My health, which had gotten better, has weakened these last few days. Has the physical influenced the moral, or vice versa?

MAÏN, SEPTEMBER 21, 1902,
TEN O'CLOCK IN THE EVENING

Once again the boundless stupidity of the Algerian administration has attacked me: the superintendent has received a letter from Algiers. What more could they do than what they've already done? In any case, the little people of Ténès have written a report. ❧ *Cursed by their father: the dog!*

I'm here in a small, clean room. There is only one inconvenience: outside the window a billy goat won't stop bleating and jumping with the goats. Maybe he'll finally fall asleep . . .

I took the road alone under a clear sky and a big wind. The road to Maïn is long and not monotonous, with great blue horizons through the mountains and the oueds.

Among my memories, I brought back a good one from Sidi Merouan.

Strange thing and in contradiction, at least apparently, with all their character: the educated natives easily take a woman like me as a confidant and certainly speak with her in a way they don't speak with any man—witness the talk between me and Si Elbedrani on the night of the *taou* at the edge of the path in the blue predawn clearness . . .

MAÏN, SEPTEMBER 22, 1902,
TWO O'CLOCK IN THE AFTERNOON

I am alone in the small room; as always, suddenly, without a noticeable cause, the heavy boredom of the last few days has disappeared and a fruitful, salutary melancholy has taken its place.

I've just reread my journals from years ago. Present life is certainly happy compared to that of the years gone by, even in Geneva. Compare these days with those in Marseille!

Great seemingly eternal silence reigns here. I would like to come and live here (or in a similar place) for months and to no longer see anything of the ugly European humanity that I hate more and more, that I especially despise.

In Ténès there is only the friend Arnaud with whom I enjoy chatting.[10] Moreover, he too is held in contempt by the band of Philistines who imagine themselves to be someone because they wear tight pants, a ridiculous hat, indeed a kepi trimmed with a braid!

In spite of all their faults and all the darkness in which they live, the most loathsome Bedouins are far superior and especially much more tolerable than the idiotic Europeans who poison the country with their presence.

Where can we flee, where can we go live, far from these wicked, indiscreet, arrogant beings, who imagine that they have the right to level all, to make everything like their own ugly effigy?

I'm going to write to Chalit, to Naplouse, to study the question of a transplantation down there, to Palestine, the day—no doubt soon—when I will have received money from † *the White Spirit.*

To flee Europe, even transplanted, and go to an Arab country undoubtedly similar to the one I love, to live another life . . . Maybe that can still be done! ❧ *God knows hidden things and the sincerity of testimony.*

10. Doyon's note: The writer Robert Randau.

The year is coming to an end, and this record, too. Where will we be in a year, at the same time, at the moment of the first rains, when the countryside will don its veil of pale sadness, for autumn's drowsiness, and when the white asphodels will bloom again along the winding paths? Probably not in Ténès. For both of us, the stay here seems like it won't last. How will our destiny definitively settle, and will it ever settle!

El Oued is the only country where I would accept to live indefinitely, always . . .

It's raining and it's cold. I'm worried about Ouïha's health in this bad weather . . .

The trip to Bou-Saada is nearing . . . Another return to the South, toward the date palms and the sand, toward the gray horizons.

I've been here ten days, far from the peaceful residence in Ténès, far from the sweet, little companion of my life . . . I am sad with the kind of creative sadness that gives birth to thought . . . And the strange thing is that I am starting to see this country better, to savor its distinctive splendor.

The broad gray-blue gulf stretches out, smooth as a mirror. Over there, the other bank is violet with pink houses . . . On Mustapha Hill, great peace reigns.

Yesterday's moonlit night was uniquely splendid. The blue light seemed to come from below, like a dawn rising from below the transparent sea, from below the dark countryside where only the white villas were turning blue . . . Great sadness last night . . . Calm sadness today. Once again I am going through a period of incubation that was very painful at the beginning, and aggravated by illness . . . Now the birth is very close. Fortunately, I can write.

Maybe this winter I'll have to go to France for the very important question of the report on the insurgents of Margueritte. Oh! If only I could say all I know, all of what I think about that, all of the truth! What good work that, continued, would become prolific and, at the same time, would make a name for me! In this, Brieux was right: start my career standing up squarely in defense of my brothers, the Muslims of Algeria.[11]

When will I return there? I don't know. I still must stay at least eight more days here. Then, a lot of work down there. I'll have to make a brochure, probably write one article per week for the *Dépêche*, slowly prepare a volume of short stories for the day when, after the Margueritte trial, my name will be somewhat known in Paris. That way, this winter I will have taken a big step toward salvation and peace, so that we, my Ouïha and I, will be able to more peacefully continue our dream until the predestined hour.

Oh, Mamma! Oh, Vava! See your child, the unique only child who followed you and who, at least after the tomb, honors you! I do not forget you. If the thought of you is not, as years ago, constantly present in my mind, it is because the battle is difficult and harsh, because I have suffered too much. But your dear memory will never leave me. During my worst hours of distress, is it not you whom I have called upon?

ALGIERS, THURSDAY, OCTOBER 30, 1902

Once again illness has come to torture and trouble me . . . But it will be completely gone the day after tomorrow, when I will have left for Ténès . . . Finally . . .

After long days of terrible storms, rain, and wind, while Ouïha was here, the sun has reappeared and spring weather is smiling upon the reanimated countryside . . . In autumn, this Algeria in Algiers has its languorous, melancholy, likeable sweetness. Over there in the mountains of *Chelha* country, it must already be almost winter . . . More-austere and more-rugged landscapes, simpler people, retired and silent life, far

11. Translator's note: The unsympathetic, and more often brutal treatment of the indigenous Algerians—including depriving them of their best lands—by the French colonial administration, led to an insurrection of Arabs who sacked the village of Marguerrite and killed several French, Italian, and Spanish colonists on April 26, 1901.

from the worries here . . . I'm beginning to miss all of that, and especially the good mare Ziza and the long, solitary rides . . .

As long as we can get out of the debts that we've run up this winter, everything will be fine! A lot of work will occupy the monotony of this winter's hours.

But all that remains for us to do is to praise God and Djilani for the absolute improvement in our situation compared to last winter and this spring 1902, here in Algiers.

Soon, Ramadan, with its sweet, melancholy memories of El Oued, will come again . . . We must return to the *farika* through the dikr and prayer. Admirable moral and intellectual hygiene!

November 23, 1902, three in the morning.

TÉNÈS, MONDAY, DECEMBER 1, 1902, TEN O'CLOCK IN THE EVENING

In beautiful, bright, crystal clear weather, I left for the douar of the Herenfa, far away at the border of the department of Oran. All the way to the picturesque market of Bou-Zraya, I had as my companion Elhadj Lakhda ben Ziou, a somber and only slightly interesting individual. The road from Trois-Palmiers to Fromentin passes above the heights of Baghdoura. It is furrowed and crosses torrential oueds. The poorly built bridges are collapsing, and soon there is nothing but an Arab path. At a certain point, it passes by the foot of a hill topped by a sheer cliff, in the form of a sharp angle. The soil of the cliff is tinted a beautiful, warm, brown-red color, and this whole site has a grand appearance. Fromentin appears for a moment in the distance between two mountains or rather two tall hills. It is a recently constructed village planted with eucalyptus, without character, like all these villages constructed on the lands taken away from the poor fellah who now work there under the draconian conditions of the French *khammesat*. The peasant complains but tolerates his fate very patiently. Until when?

We turn off to the right. The caïd of the Beni-Merzoug lives in the gourbi on a low slope overlooked by the Saharan-looking hill called Mekabrat el Mrabtine, from the name of the tribal community of the

Mrabtine, whose women are almost all prostitutes and about whom strange stories of bewitchment are told. Two white koubba, the main body of the very low oblong building, topped by a tall egg-shaped cupola. One of the koubba, at the top of the hill, is new. The other, situated lower, is falling into ruin. The tombs, piles of stones and posts, are crowded around and tumble down toward the colonists' fields.

Having not found the caïd, his son and I return to Fromentin, where they can find me no other guide than an idiot named Djellouli Bou Khalem. We leave and begin wandering aimlessly. He doesn't know the road. We go down a very uneven path toward a very old, large, solitary bordj in ruin, which the caïd is going to rebuild. Farther away is a valley where the *mechta* of the rural police of the Beni-Merzoug is located, with a strange night-bird type of face. Then we endlessly follow the Oued Merzoug. The sun is setting when we reach Herenfa. The oued is wide and rocky at the bottom of a valley closed by clayey, yellowish hills. A few bordj are scattered in the hilly countryside, as in all this region of Ténès. The caïd's gourbi are to the left on the bank of a tributary of the oued. On the horizon, above the great, even, marine-looking plain of Chelif, rises the great pale-blue massif of the Ouarsenis, the peak and its remarkable spur in the shape of an elongated terrace. Above the gourbi, piles of stones from the cemetery, then the twists and turns of the rocky oued. The next afternoon, we went to the tribal community of the Ouled-Belkassem, an hour and a quarter away on the road. This tribal community, a minor bordj and a mechta surrounded by a thorn hedge, is in a splendid location. The entire plain of the Chelif and the Oued Sly stretch out, overlooked by the royal Ouarsenis. To the left, Orléansville appears like an oasis of black greenery. To the right, the first plains of Oran stretch out as far as the eye can see. Closer by are the clayey hills of Herenfa and, to the left, the wooded and more wild ones of the Ouled-Abdallah. What brings us there is sad; and except for the admirable panorama opening from above, I brought back from this part of my short trip a sinister impression: we went there to see a little girl who had been burned alive in unusual circumstances, the secret of which will never be known by anyone.

Great peace reigns over this faraway lost country, far from all European contact. It is still a corner of rest where one can flee civilization's invasive, ugly stupidity . . . Stopped at nightfall in the bordj of a cheikh of the Djilali-Mokhtari tribal community; plaster room resembling, except for the unsquared beams of the ceiling, the residences of the Souf.

Sunday morning departure, at about seven o'clock, via another route at the top of the hills. In certain places, before arriving at the boundary marker of the Beni-Merzoug, the soil is made of delicate, yellowish sand like that of Bou-Saada and planted with bushes of ar'ar on mounds, like all the vegetation of sandy terrains, waterlogged by the rain. The sky is clouding over; and when we arrive at the Beni-Merzoug, it is coming down in buckets with the great, freezing west wind that had shaken our gourbi the night before. I arrive frozen in the gourbi of the *djemaa* where borrowers from the Provident Society are registered. The gourbi is flowing with water. Someone brings me a *kenoun*. Lunch in a corner of the barn next to a big, bright fire. Left alone in torrential rain. From 5:49 in the evening, trotted under the rain and wind. How sad is this long, deserted road, from Fromentin to Cavaignac! Under the black sky, it seemed mournful, winding along indefinitely at the top of the hills . . .

Brought back good memories from this long ride. All of a sudden, once more, I had an inspiration, which I believe to be happy. I was riding along slowly under the sun, on the road from Baghdoura to Fromentin, and having for lunch a delicious, smoky-scented galette from the market and a few dried figs that my chance companion—whose name I don't even know—had given me: to write a novel, the original and melancholy novel of a man—my own kind—living the life of Voudell, but a Muslim sowing everywhere the fruitful seed of good. I would have to find a simple, strong plot . . .

Ramadan began today—this so-special time of the year, so full of strange sensations and, for me, of dear and melancholy memories. It's the third one since the day that our two destinies, Ouïha's and mine, were united . . . And we are happier to be together and to love each other. These three years of accumulated or slow, brutal, or tormenting sufferings, have brought us closer together than ten years of prosperity would have been able to do. For now, our life is calm and without any immediate worries. ❧ *"Praise to God who has delivered us!"*

DECEMBER 11, 1902,
SEVEN FIFTEEN IN THE EVENING

Departure with Mohammed ben Ali

"Another thing is to know that somewhere, very far away, certain men busy themselves torturing others, inflicting on them all varieties of suffering and humiliation, and it is another thing to witness this torture for three months, to see these sufferings and humiliations inflicted on a daily basis"

TOLSTOY, *Resurrection*

ALGIERS, DECEMBER 25, 1902

Twelve thirty, midday.

The past and Christmas anniversaries are far away . . . All of that will perhaps soon no longer move my heart. Now, the nostalgia for the past no longer goes further back in me than the Souf. In the most recent past, the most peculiarly, mysteriously melancholy memory is that of the trip to Dahra, the first night especially, in the silence interrupted at long intervals by the cries of jackals in the mountains.

Here my state of mind is rather gray, and the end of Ramadan—which would have been, without the always, for me, whimsical Mektoub, very sweet in Ténès from which I fled—is dying in profound sadness, almost without charm.

The most difficult thing, perhaps the only difficult thing, is to free oneself and even more so *to live freely*. The even remotely free man is the enemy of the masses, which systematically persecute him and hunt him down in all his refuges. I feel an increasing irritation against life and men who do not want to let exceptions exist and who accept slavery in order to impose it on others. Where is the faraway solitary retreat where people's stupidity would no longer find me and where, too, my senses would no longer trouble me?

Same day, eleven o'clock in the evening.

My boredom and discontent with things and people is increasing more and more . . . discontent with myself, too, for I have not been able to find a modus vivendi, and I'm very afraid that with my nature, one is not at all possible.

There is only one thing that can help me spend the few years of earthly life destined to me: it is literary work, this forced life that has its charm and that has the enormous advantage of leaving our will an almost entirely clear field, of allowing us to express ourselves without suffering from painful contacts with the outside. It is a precious thing, whatever might be the results from the point of view of career or profit; and I hope that with time, acquiring more and more the *sincere* conviction that real life is hostile and inextricable, I will know how to resign myself to living from that life that is so sweet and peaceful. I certainly will make many more forays into the gloomy domain of reality . . . but I know, in advance, that I will never meet the searched-for satisfaction.

Now I will probably go spend five days of Ramadan in Médéah or Bou-Saada. This will be a voyage, a diversion in the surrounding monotony. Then I will go all the way to Biskra, where I will return to the last seguia of the oasis to take a nostalgic look at the Souf road and the incredible Oued Rir', a look at the road from the past . . . gone by and well over, alas, forever!

Once again my soul is going through a period of transition, of incubation. Once again it is in the process of modifying itself and probably of darkening once again and becoming sad . . . If this progression in black continues, to what frightening result must I arrive one day?

However, I believe that there is a remedy, ❤ *but this goes back to the religion of Islam, in all humility and in all sincerity.*

There I will find the final appeasement and joy of the heart. The troubled and mixed atmosphere in which I find myself, so to speak, where I live, is worth nothing to me. My soul is wilting and withdrawing on itself for distressing observations.

Thursday evening, December 11, as it had been decided, I left under Ramadan's moonlight on this voyage to the Dahra.

I went to set my mind at rest, with the conviction of ending up with nothing, for the gift of foresight is asserting itself more and more in me . . . a gift that would be precious if it were given to us to change something in the inescapable course of things . . . but alas, that gift is painful because it is useless, since it does not permit me to modify anything at all in my circumstances, but only to know in advance the despairing uselessness of any attempts that my reason still obliges me to make.

The evening was clear and cool. Great silence reigned in the deserted city, and the horseman Mohammed and I ran off like shadows. This man, so Bedouin and so close to nature, is my favorite companion, because he fits so well with the landscape, the people . . . and my state of mind. Furthermore, unconsciously he has the same preoccupation as I have with dark and troubled things of the senses. He wants what I understand, and he certainly feels it more intensely than I do, exactly because he does not understand it and does not seek to understand it. Stops in the Moorish cafés in Montenotte and Cavaignac. Beyond Cavaignac, we leave the route that is suitable for vehicles, and we enter into the tangled maze of this inextricable country of Ténès. We cross oued, we climb slopes, we tumble down ravines and skirt cemeteries . . .

Then, in a desert of *diss* and *doum*, above a sinister Saharan-looking shallow where the bushes are perched high on mounds, we dismount in order to rest and eat. At each noise we turn around because of how unsafe it is. Then I see an indistinct silhouette, white against one of the bushes in the shallow. The horses move restlessly and snort . . . who is it? It disappears, and when we go by there, the horses show their anxiety.

Then the road follows a narrow valley cut through by numerous oueds. Jackals howl very near by. Farther on, we climb, following the side of the mountain separating this region from the sea, and we arrive at the mechta of Kaddour-bel-Korchi, the caïd of the Talassa.

The caïd isn't there, and we have to go farther along horrible paths. We find—at the beginning of the land of Baach—the caïd in the mechta of a certain Abd-el-Kader ben Aïssa, who is pleasant and hospitable. There we have our second meal, and when the moon has gone down, we leave again for Baach on rocky paths bordered by potholes and full of rolling stones . . . At dawn the bordj of Baach, the most beautiful in the region, appears very high on a pointed hill, very similar to a Saharan bordj.

ALGIERS, DECEMBER 29, 1902, TWO THIRTY IN THE MORNING

What a strange dreamy impression—is it pleasant? I couldn't say!—that the life in Algiers produces in me, a rather nocturnal life with the weariness of the ending Ramadan!

This Ramadan! The first days down there in Ténès had the particular sweetness of this month *as a family*. Ours is a strange family, combined and composed by chance, Slimène and I, and Bel-Hadj from Bou-Saada and Mohammed, half part of the unforgotten Souf and half part of those poetic hillsides of Charir that overlook the bay, tinged with blue, and the road to Mostaganem . . .

DECEMBER 31, 1902, MIDNIGHT

Yet another year that has fled . . . One less year to live . . . And I love life, out of the curiosity of living it and of following its mystery.

Where are the vanished dreams, the dreams tinged with blue, of long ago, there across from the snowy Jura and great oak woods? Where are the dear beings who are no more? Alas, very far away!

Long ago, I contemplated—very early on, and with terror—the time of death of the dear, beloved old ones, Mamma and Vava . . . And it seemed impossible to me that they would die! And now, for five years Mamma has been sleeping, by a chance of which they both carried the secret to the grave, among Muslim burial places, in the land of Islam . . . Shortly it will have been four years that Vava and the unexplained Volodia have been resting in the land of exile, there in Vernier . . . Whereas in Bône, Algerian winter flowers are blooming around Mamma's tomb, over there the two tombs are undoubtedly covered with snow . . .

And all is annihilated. The fatal, unlucky house has passed into other hands . . . Augustine, wiped from the horizon of my life that he occupied for so many years, undoubtedly gone forever . . . All that once was then is cut down, annihilated, done away with forever . . . And for four years, I have been wandering and suffering alone in life, with, as my only companion on the road, him whom I went and looked for down there in the immaculate Souf, in order to ease my solitude, to never leave me again ❧ *if it pleases Allah!*

Profound modifications have occurred in me, even still in recent time, during this marvelous month of Ramadan, finishing yesterday in sweet mystery, in the melancholy impressions of the icha prayer of the Hanefite mosque . . .

Everything goes by, even that which seems eternal . . .

❧ *All those on earth are mortal*, and only the face of your venerable God will last!

What does this year hold for us? What new hopes and what new disillusions? In spite of the changes, it feels good to have for oneself a loving heart, kindly arms where I can rest from the battles that lying civilization has brought to life's combat . . .

What is the companion of my life doing, and what is he thinking of, far from me? There again, even to that question I must answer ❧ *God knows.*

ALGIERS, SUNDAY, JANUARY 9, 1903, MIDNIGHT

It would be good to die in Algiers, there on Mustapha Hill, facing the great both voluptuous and melancholy panorama, facing the great harmonious gulf with its eternal murmur of sighs, facing the faraway jagged outline of the mountains of Kabylia . . . It would feel good to gently, slowly die there during a sunny autumn, watching oneself die while listening to sweet music, breathing perfumes with which our souls, as subtle as they, would finish rising up in slow voluptuous pleasure, in infinitely gentle renunciation, with neither torments nor regrets.

After several days of mournful sadness and dark anguish, I am coming to life again. Everything in my current life is temporary and uncertain . . . Everything is vague, and the strange thing is that this no longer makes me suffer.

Who knows how long this life in Algiers will last; who knows what it will lead to? Who knows where I will be tomorrow? Maybe I'll go to

Médéah and Bou-Saada in a very few days. Another return to the South, toward the sand, toward the blessed earth where the fiery sun walks the blue shadows of the date palms across the sterile earth. Then, undoubtedly, I'll return here for more work and more battle; this last one, made of many small phases, tires me.

Afterward—and it will almost be spring—I will return down there to Ténès. What I would like, in the present circumstances, would be to live a free and peaceful life down in Ténès and to ride from tribe to tribe in pursuit of my dream.

BOU-SAADA, WEDNESDAY, JANUARY 28, 1903,
TWELVE THIRTY AT NIGHT

Left Algiers Monday the twenty-sixth at six o'clock in clear weather. Rain from Bouïra to Beni-Mansour. In Beni-Mansour, caught the Ziar train, going to Mansoura (M'sila). Arrived in Bordj-bou-Arréridj at about three o'clock. Went to Si Brahim Soufi's house, then to the administrator. Left at five o'clock with the M'sila post. Slept en route. Arrived at about three in the morning. Spent the rest of the night in the café in the room of the habou. Left M'sila on the twenty-seventh at eight thirty in the morning on horseback with Si Sakhdar Kadri. A stop in Chellal at about eleven o'clock. In Banjou at about two o'clock. In Bir-Graad at about three o'clock. Arrived in Bou-Saada at seven thirty in the evening, went to the Moorish bath. Thus this second return to the South has been accomplished. More than ever, I vividly feel here the weight of the strange, mysterious, vaguely threatening heaviness that burdens all the territories under command; it is something indefinable but can be felt by someone who knows the hidden sides . . . There are so many ambiguities, so many innuendos, mysteries . . .

In spite of the fatigue of the trip, the lack of sleep and food, I have a good impression, since Beni-Mansour, of this voyage. The Ziar—simple, courageous people—were singing the *medha* of their saint, with the alternating sounds of the *gasba*, the *zorna*, and the bendar. The train thus left in the cheerfulness of the rediscovered sun . . .

I was not able to see M'sila as I should have . . . But the road, the beautiful deserted road, made me relive the vanished days of long ago, the joy of finding again the empty and calm horizon of the great plain. The illusion would be complete in the Hodna, if it were not for the ring of mountains closing the plain. However, toward the east the foothills of the desert range are reflected in the flooded chott; and to the left of the dune a wide, vast door opens onto the infinite turmoil of the water and the sky.

Chellal, a miserable hamlet made of toub, miserable hovels in a flooded depression where an acrid smell of iodine and saltpeter reigns.

The indigenous population is composed of not very friendly Ouled-Madhi and Hachem. The maghreb was wonderful, with the mountains standing out in bluish black against the sky's golden-red color. These mountains of Bou-Saada are very strange with their geometric contours and their sloping terraces.

Today, after morning errands to the Arab Bureau, took a walk at about one o'clock in the *dechra*, the Arab city, and in the oued where the Arab washerwomen radiate blue or especially red colors of incredible lively warm tones. Nothing has become green again on the surrounding hills. They are still as threatening and barren as in the summer.

This afternoon, still gray state of mind that for now is leaving. Unable to see well.

Tomorrow morning I am going to El-Hamel. My trip to Boghari seems certain. It will be made in a very unknown part of the country, Had Sahari, which I like the name of and which is very lost in the middle of Arab country. Once rested, tomorrow night in El-Hamel, I will note my remarks better than this evening. Physical fatigue and the lack of food until this evening have greatly exhausted me. The fair walk from El-Hamel will prepare me for the long trip from Sahari and Boghar . . .

It appears that I am no longer being persecuted: I am told that no one was warned about my arrival, and they have shown themselves to be very amiable, even the commander . . . shadowy and mysterious people!

The most complete chaos seems to reign in El-Hamel, and everything is going to the dogs.

About four in the afternoon.

From Sidi Mohammed Belkassem: In the old times of the Chorfa, of the Ouled Sid Ali, subtribe of the Ouled Bou-Zid, from the Djebel Amour, three brothers returning from Mecca came through this region. One continued his route toward the west, whereas the other two settled on the side of the mountain and founded El-Hamel.

In clear and bright weather, left at about two o'clock for El-Hamel. The boredom of the past few days has somewhat dissipated, almost entirely. I will undoubtedly see Bou-Saada better on my return.

A strange thing that I have noticed for a long time is that I cannot see a country well during the first days of my arrival. I always feel a sort of vague malaise and weariness.

However, during the first days of my wandering life, it was not at all entirely like this. It keeps becoming more pronounced, which is strange since my life is becoming relatively more and more nomadic and the habit should be established.

Leaving Bou-Saada, the road enters rocky and arid terrain where nothing can grow but the desert ar'ar and thorny, gray, creeping bushes that only camels graze on. The ocher-gray hills are furrowed, sometimes stratified from the top to the bottom with white grooves. The scene is harsh and poor. On the road beyond the garden belonging to the Arab Bureau and guarded by an Arab living in a bordj made of toub falling into ruin, two stations of tolba are set apart. One is a solitary bordj perched on a hill overlooking the road. The other, below the latter, is an agglomeration of a few small bordj made of toub in an area off the beaten track overlooking the oued and a date palm garden in an indentation of the deep riverbed. Finally, El-Hamel, divided in two, appears at a bend. It is built on two hills. The first, almost conical, supports the village of the Chorfa, of very Saharan character, made all of dark toub. On the other, higher hill, the zaouïya rises up and resembles a fortress with its covering of very light, almost-white toub.

The same day, six o'clock in the evening.

Great heavy silence reigns here, hardly interrupted sometimes by the noises of the village and of the zaouïya, the far-off barking of the dogs, or the wild, hoarse cries of the camels.

El-Hamel! How well named is this corner of old Islam, so lost in the barren and dark mountain and so veiled with heavy mystery.

Now that the entirely material reason for the heavy malaise in which I have been plunged these last few days has been revealed to me, I am feeling better, and I am hoping for a lot from the return to Bou-Saada and from the faraway trip toward the west still remaining to be accomplished.

I am sitting on my bed near the chimney of the large vaulted room. With the cheerful flames and this bed on the floor, the room has taken on a feeling of cheerfulness and comfort that it did not have earlier this evening.

To finish with the description of this country, seen from the road, El-Hamel is placed right at the foot of a tall massif whose main summit is a pointed cone. To the left, chaotic leprous hills, sometimes with rounded backs, sometimes isolated peaks above the infertile valleys. On the side of the oued nicknamed El-Mogtaa there are vast gardens belonging to the habou and the Chorfa where the scent of now barren, blackish-violet deciduous leaves harmonize strangely with the still-green date palms.

A maze of short walls made of bricks of toub intertwines in the gardens planted haphazardly on the bulges of the hilly terrain. In the village a few smoky shops of the dyers, the *sekakri*, open on to the edge of the road. Here, as in all the ksar, houses differ greatly in shape but are of a monotonous color the same as the earth itself, overlapping each other and forming angles, alleyways, and narrow or vaulted passages. In the bottom of the oued, the road passes beneath two low vaults dug into the reddish and rocky clay. One must bend over in order to go through on horseback. To the right, El-Hamel; to the left, the big cemetery, a true valley of Josephat with innumerable raised stones, then on the heights facing the zaouïya, the bordj, also made of toub, of the caïd El-Haïdech.

About thirty families of the Ouled Mokran live entirely at the expense of the habou . . .

The "hotel," a large square building, has a deep and desolate interior courtyard where bricks and stones have accumulated, which depends on the upper floor divided into two rooms, a small one and a large one entirely vaulted with a full arch like the rich houses in the Souf. One of the windows looks toward the southeast onto the cemeteries; the three others, to the east. There are three French-style beds, an oval table, chairs, all on a thick carpet . . . With a bit more truly Arab taste, this locale would look very impressive. I would like to be able to arrange it as it deserves and as I please. Next door, toward the west, are the tall buildings made of toub that enclose the apartments of the maraboute. To the north, the new mosque with its large round cupola surrounded by other smaller ones and, in the interior, the tomb of Sidi Mohammed Belkassem.

Nothing more difficult than defining with one correct word the deceptive color of these mountains surrounding Bou-Saada and the Djelfa road. It is lilac brown with whitish-gray stripes and spots. In the distance, the mountains in the foreground have a very transparent hue, crimson or pale wine colored, whereas those of the range behind are intense blue. The terrain seems rocky, furrowed, of frightening sterility; and certainly nothing in this poor and ossified décor would anticipate the large agglomeration of El-Hamel.

I'm going to go to bed and rest, for tomorrow I'll have to get up early to see the maraboute. Undoubtedly, I will return tomorrow night to Bou-Saada, and I will try to arrive at the maghreb. Afterward, I will have eight days ahead of me to really see Bou-Saada, and I must not waste my time. Who knows? In my life it would seem that I only go *twice* to each place: Tunis, the Sahel, Geneva, Paris, the Souf . . . Who knows if this is not my last trip to Bou-Saada?

One week from today I will leave with some Arabs for Had-Sahari. I will need three days to arrive in Boghar, one to go to Berrouaghia. I will also perhaps go all the way to the zaouïya of the Aïssaouas in the area near Loverdo: let's count two days, and one for the return to Algiers, which would make seven days, and fifteen days total to be back in Algiers, where I will definitely have to stay five days. That puts my return to Ténès in twenty days, which is February 18.

Thus my separation from my poor darling Ouïha will have lasted two long months, for I was forgetting the probable visit to the cadi of Médéah Abd-el-Moumen.

Far away, the dogs are barking in the silence, and one can sometimes hear the hoarse voice of a nearby camel...

BOU-SAADA, SATURDAY, JANUARY 31, 1902,
ONE O'CLOCK IN THE MORNING

Yesterday, Ben Ali and I returned from El-Hamel at about three in the morning. Every time I see Lella Zeyneb I feel a sort of rejuvenation, of joy without visible cause, and of relief. Yesterday I saw her twice during the morning. She was very good and gentle with me and showed her joy at seeing me again.

Visit to the tomb of Sidi Mohammed Belkassem, very small and very simple in the great mosque that, when finished, will be very beautiful. Then, prayed on the hillside across from the tomb of the founding pilgrims of El-Hamel.

With Si Bel-Abbès, wild galloping on the road under the bland eye of Si Ahmed Mokrani. There were women from the brothel returning from El-Hamel. Adorned and made up, rather pretty, they came to smoke a cigarette nearby us. In their honor we did a fantasia all along the road. Laughed a lot...

Toward the southwest, El-Hamel closes and commands long, wide, very hilly gorges, in the middle of which rises a high kef and which, on the horizon, closes an absolutely conical mountain resembling a guémira. Behind this opens a mysterious and immense bluish plain... The houses of the Chorfa close to the zaouïya have high walls surfaced with smooth toub halfway up, and the rest of the walls show the grid pattern of the bricks made of toub. These houses look like Babylonian fortresses with their juxtaposed squares and their flat terraces overlooking the geometric courtyards. The towering almond trees have not yet flowered.

The legend of the El-Hamel pilgrims makes me dream. It is certainly one of the most biblical of Algeria . . .

This journal, begun over there in the hated land of exile, during one of the blackest times, the most painfully uncertain, and the most fertile in sufferings in my life, finishes today.

Everything—including me—has radically changed . . .

For a year, I have once again been on the blessed African earth that I would like to never leave again. In spite of my poverty, I've been able to travel again, to see unknown regions of the adoptive land . . . My Ouïha lives, and we are relatively happy in material terms . . .

This journal, begun a year and a half ago in that loathed Marseille, finishes today in transparently gray, gentle, and as-if-pensive weather in Bou-Saada, which is still a corner of the South so missed!

This small room in the Moorish bath—which resembles me and my type of life well—is becoming familiar to me. I will live here a few more days before leaving on the trip for Boghar, for regions that I still don't know: a badly whitewashed rectangle, a small window looking on to the street and the mountain, two mats on the floor, a rope to hang my clothes on, a small torn mattress that I sit on in order to write. Baskets in the corner; the corner fireplace on the other side; my scattered papers . . . That's all. That suffices for me.

Of all that has happened during these eighteen months, there is but a very weak reflection in these pages haphazardly written during hours when I needed to *put something into words* . . . For a foreign reader, these pages would almost always even be incomprehensible. For me, it is what remains of the former cult of the past. One day perhaps, the day will come when I stop noting in this way some thoughts, some impressions, so as to perpetuate them for a while. For now, I sometimes feel great sweetness in rereading these *Journals* from bygone hours.

Great silence, the silence of the South, reigns over Bou-Saada. In this city still so far removed from the stupid movement of the Tell, one certainly feels strongly the characteristic torpor of the South. May God keep Bou-Saada intact for a long time yet!

I'm going to start a new journal. What will I have to write down, and where will I be on the still-far-off day when, like today, I will finish this still-white volume at this hour of the vague book of my vague existence? "God knows hidden things and the sincerity of testimonies!"

Note

In 1913 Madame Chloë Bulliod, the wife of a doctor from Bône (Annaba), had had the opportunity to purchase some of Isabelle Eberhardt's manuscripts from a member of Slimène Ehnni's family. She entrusted them to René-Louis Doyon, an editor and lecturer often present in Algeria.

Doyon used the main part of these papers to put together *Mes journaliers* (*My Journals*), which he prefaced with a long text entitled "La vie tragique de la bonne nomade" ("The Tragic Life of the Good Nomad"). Here is what he indicated in his foreword to the 1923 edition: "The journals are made up of a small canvas-bound notebook faded by the mud and silt of the flood and of three hardback notebooks . . . The 'White Spirit' is the term used to designate Isabelle's mother; Vava, that used to designate her father [*sic*]; Ouïha and Zouizou, equivalent to 'darling,' designate her husband . . ."

Les journaliers, probably incomplete, have a particular status in Isabelle Eberhardt's work: more literary journals than personal, perhaps written with a view to being published.

Rather than dividing them up so as to include them in the chronological order of the texts, it seemed preferable to us to publish them, in their continuity, at the end of the volume.

We have not been able to find a trace of the manuscripts published by René-Louis Doyon in 1923 in *La Connaissance*. Therefore, we must trust him when he claims "not to have changed a single comma."

Appendices

Things from the Oranese South

In Figuig I was able to see a few natives familiar with the affairs of the West, probably in connection with the emissaries of the nomads.

According to them, discord reigns among the different hostile tribes: Berabers, Ouled Djerir, Beni Ghil, and dissident Douï Ménia.

Since the Taghit attack, when they had agreed to elect Mouley as their head, the nomads were forming a sort of association or naturally chaotic and anarchic confederation.

Currently, undoubtedly influenced by the extreme misery to which they have been reduced and the defeats they have suffered, the nomads have scattered, and serious quarrels are exploding among the different groups.

It is certain that all these hostile subtribes view our settling in Bechar and the creation of the Taagda post unfavorably.

Recently, it was rumored in native circles that threats had been addressed by the nomads to the Commander Pierron, head of the Béchar unit. The nomads are reported to have threatened to attack the unit if it does not withdraw. These rumors seem unfounded, for such threats would certainly have provoked fierce repression.

On the other hand, it is claimed that the Beni Ghil have reunited with Bou-Amama in hopes of satisfying their hate of the Hamyan and of taking revenge for the last harka of the latter, which cost them a certain number of tents.

The occupation of the posts of the Oranese Southwest is today a fait accompli.

This act of our African policy has given rise to many controversies, to arguments in the press, and to recriminations. Many have contested the timeliness and the wisdom of this policy.

Whatever our opinion may be on this question, it is no less evident that the extension of our Oranese territory has created an extremely serious situation. In fact, not only do we find ourselves in continual contact with the Moroccan state in complete disorganization and in perpetual civil war, but, furthermore, we are in contact with numerous unruly nomad tribes who have never recognized any sovereignty, no more that of Morocco than ours, and up until now have been resistant to any organization.

What particularly complicates the situation is that the majority of these tribes have, as traditional routes, territories that are supposedly Moroccan and others that have been acquired by us. Consequently, we must take care of these tribes and organize them so that they do not perpetually remain a cause of bloody violence.

Thus, we are trying to study the means by which to obtain, as quickly and in the least costly way possible in human lives and in money, the pacification and the organization of the Oranese Southwest, after this reporter's return from a fairly long stay in Figuig, which is, for the time being, the center of contact with our neighbors.

In order to approach this question and clearly show the stages of a solution, let us say a few words about this region and its inhabitants.

Starting in Aïn Sefra, the country clearly takes on the appearance and the characteristics of the desert: largely unproductive lands, except in certain places where one encounters Saharan pastures favorable to raising camels and sheep. *Alfa*, drinn, and a few creeping, shriveled bushes can almost always be used as food for the camels. As for the sheep, their existence is entirely dependent on the winter rains that produce a more tender and more nutritious herbaceous vegetation.

Watering places are more and more spaced out as one descends farther into the South. Many of them, the most important ones, are inhabited. Sedentary Berber tribes have constructed small ksour and have engaged in farming: date palms, vegetables, fruit, and sometimes a few cereals, principally barley.

Figuig and its neighbor Béni-Ounif, having become French, and Tagit, Igli, Béni-Abbès, etc., are very important water supply points. The water table is not very deep, which has greatly facilitated the settlement and development of the ksour, by permitting the fellah more extensive cultivation, if not more varied.

The desert territories, except for the hamada—rocky and arid regions—provide the ksourians with precious construction materials: toub, which is dirt mixed with manure. Depending on the soil used, toub is sometimes very solid and allows one to inexpensively build houses with floors, which can be resistant to bad weather and often not without elegance. The date trees provide beams strong enough to build roofing and terraces.

Let us now deal particularly with Figuig, from where one can today write a fairly exact account of the general situation in the Southwest.

Figuig is an agglomeration of seven ksour: Zenaga, Oudar'ir, Ksar el-Abib, El Maïz, Ouled Slimane, Hammam Foukani, Hammam Tahkoui.

These ksour occupy the two levels of a splendid valley: Zenaga below toward the southwest and the *hammamine* on the western slope of the upper terrace, while the other ksour occupy the upper terrace.

A powerful ring of mountains protects the valley from all sides: the Grouz toward the northwest, the Béni-Smir range toward the northeast, the Djebel Ta'la toward the southeast, the Djebel Mélias toward the west.

Wide and deep passes give access to Figuig's valley: to the east the Tal'a Pass, to the south the Zenaga Pass, to the southeast the Juive Pass, and to the west the Moudjahdine Pass. The ksour are close to each other, except for Zenaga, which is isolated at the foot of the cliff (*djorf*) that ends the upper terrace toward the south.

A magnificent palm grove surrounds the ksour to the southwest, south, and east.

The water table is at almost no depth. A remarkably ingenious system irrigates the palm groves. In addition to large rectangular ponds lined with toub, there exists a whole network of subterranean canalizations—negotiable passages where channels have been built and where precious springs have been tapped. The water is excellent.

The palm groves are cultivated with extreme care. There are a few fruit trees growing in their shade: fig trees, pomegranate trees, and vegetables consumed by the natives: peppers, cucurbitaceous plants, onions, turnips, etc. The inhabitants of Figuig cultivate a bit of barley in irrigated fields worked with a shovel, as straight as a die and most beautiful. The gardens of Zenaga and those of the place called Baghdad, above the ksar of the Ouled Slimane, are the most beautiful.

The valley of Figuig is fertile, rare in desert country, and only an age-old lack of security has prevented the fellah from extending their cultivation far beyond today's actual limits.

Since Morocco has never had but a purely nominal authority in its Saharan part, Figuig has remained autonomous, keeping a rudimentary republican and confederative organization with, in each ksar, a meeting of notables—the djemaa—it alone deciding all business. Justice is in the hands of *kadi,* and the djemaa represents the executive power. Currently, as a result of troubles in the region, there is total anarchy.

It has pleased our sense of diplomacy to complicate even more the imbroglio of Figuig by installing there, in the ksar of Oudar'ir, an amel, or Moroccan governor, who, in reality, has no authority and who, consequently, has not been and will never be able to be of any use in the pacifying and organizing work that France must accomplish there. This innovation, while indisposing the people of Figuig, who do not like Morocco, has had no other result than to give—in the eyes of Europe and the makhzen itself—a semblance of reality to the Moroccan domination in Figuig . . .

We will thus have to act—as we have done until now anyway—outside of the amel.

It is also absolutely useless to think of pacifying the region by means of the supposed influence of the Pretender (the Rogui Bou-Hamara): as much as the sultan, his competitor is powerless to organize the vast regions of the Moroccan hinterland.

As for Bou-Amama, his political influence is hardly felt. He seems aged and weary, and an alliance with him would not assure us peace.

We are currently required to do everything ourselves with our own strength.

We have before us two absolutely distinct populations whose interests are opposed most of the time. The sedentary inhabitants of the ksour are attached to the earth that they cultivate and own and are thus directly interested in the pacification of their country and of the nomads. It is an error to believe that the famine alone is the cause of the nomadic incursions: traditionally and since the origin of the world, the nomads have always been quarrelsome and pillagers, which can be explained by their type of life itself.

It is the nomads who are the cause of all the violence, of all the bloodshed devastating the region we are concerned with.

Only rapid organization of the acquired territories, leading to a new era of prosperity, can legitimize, in the view of reason and fairness, our march forward into the desert regions.

Thus, peace and security are the first conditions of all progress.

Must we continue the costly and bellicose system of expeditions against one or another tribe, whom we will almost never reach and who will return again tomorrow?

Must we perpetuate that of simple defense, that is to say fight almost continuously?

Or must we, as some have dared to propose, especially in Algeria, engage in systematic extermination of dissident nomads?

All these systems are equally bad.

There is another much more economic and more humane one: limiting to the utmost the strictest armed intervention, made—unfortunately—necessary because of the continual incursions of armed and pillaging hordes.

General Lyautey, who directs the subdivision of Aïn Sefra, breaking with old military routines, had the fortunate inspiration of recently putting this system to the test for Figuig, and it is beginning to give excellent results there.

We mean to speak of the *isolation* and the *surveillance* of *Saharan markets*.

In fact, in order to live, the nomads—animal breeders, caravanners, conveyors, and pillagers—need the Saharan markets where they get supplies, where they sell their herds, where they serve as intermediaries between the inhabitants of the ksour and the Moroccan Tell, especially Ouezzan.

Without the markets, the nomads, reduced to famine, would find it absolutely impossible to exist. On the other hand, their routes, sometimes very vast, are limited; and a given nomad tribe is attached to a given ksar or market by all its traditions.

Consequently, it is easy to understand that once the markets are under surveillance and off-limits to any dissident tribe or subtribe, very soon the latter are required to submit, being unable to survive.

Thus, in the place of numerous complicated, colossally expensive—in terms of men and money—military operations, there would only be a few police measures to take, rapidly and only relatively costly.

Figuig has been placed under the surveillance of the French commissariat headquartered in Béni-Ounif. In the north, it has been isolated by the creation of the El Ardja post. Because of these measures, the market in Figuig has been isolated from all contacts with the dissidents, and after a few months the latter are beginning to obey and to frequent the market openly. Notably, the Beni Ghil have recently started negotiating with the French authorities of Béni-Ounif.

But Figuig, pacified and having become an instrument of pacification, is not enough.

This is where the greatest of all the difficulties created by our presence there appears. One measure is required, without which we will never obtain a lasting peace: the pacification of Tafilalet, the center around which all the nomad tribes gravitate.

The train is being continued in the direction of Béchar, where the Taagda post has just been established. This train will begin the Tafilalet road. Afterward, the remaining work will be to clear this road and to isolate Tafilalet, which will lead to the rapid submission of the nomads: Ouled Djérir, Douï Ménia, even Berabers.

It is up to our diplomats to explain to the sultan that it is not at all a question of conquest and that we are not considering removing his nominal suzerainty of the hinterland but instead wish to eliminate the old hideout that has always served as a sanctuary to all the pillagers who constantly make forays into our land.

Tafilalet pacified and thus prosperous, commerce reestablished and powerfully developed by the vicinity of the railroad, all these improvements will profit the sultan as much as us.

In order to completely convince our readers of the fact that the pacification of Tafilalet is indispensable, that without it we would be perpetually in a state of war without any profit, let us remember that the year-long food shortage in Tafilalet, which is starving the nomads who are deprived of resources from Figuig, is the only cause of their apparent and current appeasement.

But if the year is good in Tafilalet, then the supplied nomads will begin again their *razzia*, which only absolute necessity can make them give up.

It is thus very urgent to assure the protection of Tafilalet against all relationships with the dissidents and the pillagers. Weakened by famine, exhausted by nearly a year of constant battles, the nomads will only put up relatively weak resistance this year. As for the inhabitants of the ksour, those of Tafilalet and Figuig, today they will quickly understand that they have all interest in the reestablishment of commerce and the establishment of a lasting peace. Practical and hardworking people, the inhabitants of the ksour will become a precious instrument of pacification and economic penetration.

It goes without saying that the rapid construction of the railroad is the necessary guarantee of the upcoming organization of the Southwest.

The inhabitants of Figuig are beginning to supply themselves through us. They go to the Béni-Ounif market, and they bring an average of six wagons of merchandise each week.

The train station from Taagda to Béchar would become, if the pacification of Tafilalet were accomplished, a very important commercial stop.

It will be necessary to pursue the construction of the Saharan railway all the way to the far-off posts of the Southwest, as far as Aïn-Beni-Abbès, via Taghit and Igli, which will noticeably diminish the great expense of getting fresh supplies via convoys and which will assure security on the Southwest road.

To sum up, in order to justify our presence in the Oranese Southwest, France has the most pressing duty to impose a beneficial peace and to use all economic means to improve the fate of this country and to bring normal economic development.

Without this, the conquest, whose timeliness has already been so contested, would remain an undertaking without any usefulness and that any sensible mind would not hesitate to severely condemn.

BÉNI-OUNIF, FEBRUARY 1904

La Dépêche Coloniale has published a letter from one of its correspondents returning from a tour in the Oranese Southwest. The assessments of our colleague are the most absolute optimism. For him all is going as well as possible there, and he affirms that in six months there will be no more djiouch . . . He even announces that in the same period of time the *moral conquest* of the Berabers will be a fait accompli.

Our colleague must have traveled very quickly through the region, for otherwise he would have perceived that the situation there is much more complex and delicate than it seems to him.

After a stay of two months in Béni-Ounif, very frequent and *unpretentious* trips to Figuig, successive conversations with all the local elements—European military and civilians, natives—here is the current situation based on what I believe to have understood.

We find ourselves there in the presence of two absolutely distinct races in terms of morals, character, and consequently of very different even opposed *interests*: the inhabitants of the ksour, farmers, artisans, all possessing some property, thus essentially sedentary and peaceful; and the nomads, the dissident Ouled Djérir, Douï Ménia, Beni Ghil, Amour, etc.

These people—with no attachment to the earth, shepherds, mobile, turbulent, hard to discipline, up until now almost elusive even—are traditionally accustomed to the bloody *nefra* between tribes, between subtribes, even between families. They are equally used to the harka, razzia practiced out of vengeance and also interest, on neighboring tribes or on inhabitants of the ksour, whom the nomads despise.

In relation to us, the nomads simply continue their accustomed way of life, nothing more nor less.

The people of the very indistinct border do not at all claim to be in a state of *holy war* against us. It is even more indisputable, for without that, how could one explain that the nondissident subtribes of the same pillaging tribes serve us without any repugnance and in a dignified way, according to all the officers, who give them the highest praise?

The people of the Moroccan Southeast, no more than those of Figuig and Tafilala, do not consider themselves subjects of the Cherifien makhzen. They have always lived independently; thus in fighting against us in the same way they have been fighting among themselves for centuries, they believe they are only serving themselves and not the sultan of Fez or the Rogui.

It is known that even in Algeria there exists a certain hostility between the Tellians and the Saharans. This hostility exists in an acute state in Morocco, where it held sway in Algeria before the conquest.

Basically, there are two very distinct questions, although linked by form: the Moroccan question and that of the Oranese South or rather of the Southeast of the Bled Saïba.

Today, it is useless and pointless to lose precious time in vain recriminations or to wonder if we should have gone to Tidikelt, Touat, Béni-Abbès, or Figuig . . .

Have we not gone so far as to pronounce the stupefying word *evacuation*! Others have pushed the level of naïveté as far as proposing to combat the *djicheurs by means of good bread* . . . Still others have affirmed that we must exterminate them, "bump them off,"[1] according to the fashionable term.

It is useless to stop at such daydreams. Currently, there is a situation, a reality, that must be taken account of. We are in the presence of vast territories where there are a few agglomerations of ksour; thus we must, as quickly as possible and with the least expense, put ourselves in a position to take advantage of this situation, as Mr. Jonnard has already pointed out in one of his parliamentary speeches.[2]

---

1. Translator's note: The verb used by Eberhardt is *zigouiller*.
2. Editor's note: Governor-general of Algeria.

The agglomerations of ksour, like Figuig, were at the mercy of the nomads serving them as sources of supplies and outlets for their products, sometimes from Moroccan commerce, especially from the Ouezzanis,[3] sometimes simply plunder reaped in the course of harka.

The existence and the free practice of large markets of the ksour are the condition sine qua non of the current existence of the nomads. Without these markets, they cannot continue their anarchical and age-old banditry.

It is not a question of—instead of considering the question from the practical point of view—dreaming of aged, exhausted Bou-Amama, in addition having close to him the rather Francophile influence of his son Si Taïeb. Nor should we indulge in untimely flirtatiousness with the Rogui. Neither one nor the other will give us, any more than the sultan, what we need the most: peace.

There is a complex, delicate, but not impossible task to accomplish.

In this order of ideas, we could not be better inspired by confiding this mission to General Lyautey, who is young and incomparably active and energetic and who has known how to, in so few months, get a very clear idea of the situation and make a plan of action. We have also shown great wisdom by giving the general the liberty and independence that he needed, above all, to carry out a task requiring a perfect unity of direction, constant surveillance, a personal vision of things, and especially a well-timed mind constantly on the alert.

We can also hope to soon see accomplished, thanks to the activity of the general and his collaborators, who are as devoted as they are intelligent, not as our colleague from *La Dépêche Coloniale* says, the "moral conquest of the Berabers," but instead the pacification and the conquest of the region.

The *miad* (delegation) of Beni Ghil—very ornamental and truly beautiful looking—which today came and closed five long days of negotiations with General Lyautey . . . Five *chioukh* and the great caïd Abderrhamane announced this evening that they were accepting the conditions asked of them and gave the kiss of peace to their enemies of yesterday, the caïd Hamyan from the circle of Méchéria.

These men in long djellaba made of fine cloth, turbaned in white, have beautiful bronze faces, very closed and very energetic, with a harsh accentuation of traits and the fiery look of long tawny-colored eyes.

3. Translator's note: The Ouezzanis are from the oasis of Ouezan. "Wazzan" is the English transliteration.

The severity of their dark clothing of the moghrib adds a particular style to their physiognomy which is so different from that of the Hamyan leaders in long crimson burnooses bedecked with French decorations.

They have come from their western refuges in order to finally announce a new era of peace for this country that so needs it, after months of bloody quarrels, of djiouch, of harka, of skirmishes, a whole strange and old-fashioned epic that the Bedouin improvisers, camel herders, or illiterate mokhazni, are beginning to sing about in innocent laments.

After lilting and solemn words, after embraces that, however, conserve a very recent aftertaste of blood, now it remains for us to wait for acts.

The Beni Ghil have accepted the conditions demanded of them, of which the major ones are to first reintegrate their former travel territory, common with that of the Hamyan, which they had abandoned since quarrels had exploded between the two tribes; to devote themselves as best they can to bringing back to us their still-dissident fellow creatures; and finally to truly and sincerely abandon Bou-Amama, around whom their mass exodus had pushed them.

If these conditions are carried out, brought closer to our hosts, surrounded by Hamyan, who have long been faithful and directed by men of valor—the superior command of the circle of Méchéria and the agha El Hadj Habib—consequently subject to constant and firm surveillance, they will with great difficulty become once again elements of political turmoil and internecine battles in the region.

Besides, it won't be long before the Beni Ghil themselves feel the benefits of peace, and their example will benefit the other dissident tribes.

This sort of declaration of peace made by the Beni Ghil is, it seems to me, the direct result of the ingenious as well as firm political stance that General Lyautey takes so well toward the nomads: reduce them to powerlessness by cutting off their *supplies,* that is to say by depriving them of the Saharan markets where they were getting their supplies and where they were selling merchandise—pillaged or bought—brought by caravan and their herds, and all of this as long as they remain in a state of *dissidence.* Clearly accept, if prudently, their peaceful offers when they offer guarantees of truthfulness and when they are made in acceptable conditions. As long as the nomads carry out their commitments, treat them with benevolence in such a way as to prove to them how much they have an interest in living on good terms with us. As soon as they show any bad faith in their acts, show them with an energetic attitude that we will not allow them to betray their word. Never compromise our dignity, no more through acts of brutality or any other provocation than through weakness. Rigorously respect our commitments toward them in order to have the right to demand in return the same respect and the same faithfulness.

Unfortunately, behind the Beni Ghil, there is the old and still-venerated agitator, Bou-Amama, whose influence is still hostile.

Even admitting, which is nothing less than certain, that the Beni Ghil represented by the miad are today sincere, especially hounded by need, isn't it very possible that they change sides tomorrow, with their usual capriciousness and inconsistency, and this either because the abundant rains will have brought back some prosperity to their herds or because of the influence of Bou-Amama?

That the latter (influence) is clearly hostile to any agreement between us and the Beni Ghil is even more understandable since, for now, the Beni Ghil form the majority of Bou-Amama's people.

In order to convince oneself of these feelings, all one has to do is go to Figuig, like we just did, and talk with the Zoua, servants of Bou-Amama and his brother-in-law living in Hammam Foukani, Si Ahmed ben Menouar. The Zoua engage in the most bitter mockery of the miad; they treat the chioukh and the caïd Abderrhamane as imposters unjustly claiming themselves to be the representatives of the majority of the Beni Ghil. Concerning this, one of the most important Zoua said to us, "I bet anything that Abderrhamane's Beni Ghil tried to deceive the French by promising everything demanded of them in order to lay in supplies, to make up for losses, and to return to a state of dissidence at the least favorable opportunity."

Although this opinion of an *amaoui* was generated by hate and anger, it is perhaps true.[4]

What seems to indicate that the Beni Ghil are still rather far from the promised appeasement is that another miad, led by Bou-Amama's son Si Taïeb, left about twenty days ago for the camp of the Pretender. According to the last news that has reached Figuig, an agreement has been reached between the Pretender and Bou-Amama, through the intermediary Si Taïeb. Bou-Amama is supposed to help the Pretender . . . , via the former's

4. Translator's note: An *amaoui* is a member of a tribe.

influence and men, to get rid of Mouley Abdelaziz, the sultan of Morocco. In exchange, the Pretender would give him a sort of proconsulate over all the South of Morocco.

Si Taïeb's first action on this path should be to concentrate on Oudjda in order to fight the makhzen of the sultan.

What is true in this news? It is still the case that there is nothing improbable reported.

If this alliance between the Pretender and Bou-Amama is truly carried out, then won't the Beni Ghil—at the sign of the least success—abandon us in order to follow their kind, who have remained faithful to Bou-Amama?

We see how complex and delicate the situation is.

While recommending, in relations with tribes such as the Beni Ghil, not only the greatest prudence but even constant distrust, we do not hesitate, however, to say that it would be very impolitic to turn away the miad who come to us. It would be much better to try to gain an advantage from them so as to be able to say to the nomads, "Every time you have come with acceptable proposals, we have received you, and we have always respected our commitments."

To come back to the Beni Ghil, it is curious to observe the contrast between the pessimism of the inhabitants of Figuig, whoever they are (except, naturally, the people of the amel), on the subject of the Beni Ghil and the optimism of the Hamyan and the Amour of Aïn Sefra. However, this contrast is quite natural: beneath the pessimism of the inhabitants of Figuig, there is fidelity to Bou-Amama. Beneath the optimism of the Hamyan, there is flattered pride about what they consider to be the humiliation of their enemies. As for the Amour, they are under the influence of the agha Sidi Mouley of Tiout, who played an important role in the negotiations with the Beni Ghil.

After many conversations with the most diverse elements, we think that the current period should only be considered as a waiting period during which we must stay on guard and keep the most actively possible watch over the Beni Ghil, while at the same time requiring the Hamyan—almost as turbulent as the Beni Ghil—to respect our commitments while not engaging in any act of violence.

We will especially need to profit from a few months of calm, which, in any case, will be the result of the agreement with the Beni Ghil. This will be necessary in order to improve and reinforce our guard posts in a way that will show the Beni Ghil that we will be capable of punishing them if they try to betray us.

It would also be necessary, as much as possible, to *morally* influence the Beni Ghil, thus counterbalancing Bou-Amama's influence by demonstrating to them all the interests they have in remaining faithful to us.

In my next letter, I will speak to you about the other tribes and the situation in general.

Note

Special correspondent for *La Dépêche Algérienne* in the Oranese South in 1903 and 1904, Isabelle Eberhardt wrote a series of articles, for the Algerian daily, about the troubles at the Algeria-Morocco border. These texts are a remarkable contrast to the accounts and the stories that she ordinarily published in the Algiers press. Eberhardt justifies the French penetration of the oases of the western Sahara.

As a journalist officially recognized by the general government of Algeria, thanks to Victor Barrucand's connections, Isabelle Eberhardt benefited from the friendship and esteem of General Lyautey. He facilitated her daily life and, in particular, her movements. Under the influence of the officer, undoubtedly, she does not hesitate to defend the "politics of the markets," the foundation of the theory of the protectorate advocated by Lyautey. The latter, an admitted visionary, prefers it to the classic colonization, which he categorically disapproved of at that time.

Did Isabelle Eberhardt believe in the sincerity of this military man? Undoubtedly, she must have thought that his proposed solution represented a lesser evil after she had noted the misery and the suffering of the southern Oranese populations, and those of Oudjda.

Back in France, this political policy defended by the radical government would soon harden and return to a more classic colonial position.

After February 1904 Isabelle Eberhardt's opinion certainly evolved: shortly before the catastrophe in Aïn Sefra, she invited a member of the anarchist community of Tarzout (near Ténès) to the region of the Southwest in order to show him the ravages and "atrocities of colonialism."

One could think that it is because of this series of articles republished in *Akhbar* in 1914 (at the beginning of World War I, Victor Barrucand was undoubtedly very keen to evoke the patriotic sentiments of his former colleague) that a rumor spread in Algeria and persists today, according to which Isabelle Eberhardt was a spy in the pay of Lyautey.

During an era when national sentiment and the notion of borders are almost totally absent in this region of the Sahara, Isabelle Eberhardt does not seem to see other solutions except for the French military penetration into the South, on condition that it be about establishing "peace and prosperity." However, two years earlier she had denounced the humiliations suffered by the populations placed under the authority of the French military.

In the final analysis, Isabelle Eberhardt is persuaded that "the land of Africa absorbs all civilizations foreign to it . . ."

In any case, it is easy to contrast these texts, and their somewhat heavy journalistic style (but they have the value of historical documents), with the notes she had written at the time of her travels in the Tunisian Sahel: "In Tunisia, notably, the protectorate is nothing but a euphemism concealing total annexation . . ."

Works Dedicated to Isabelle Eberhardt

Blanch, Lesley. *Les rives sauvages de l'amour*. Paris: Plon, 1956. Four portraits: Isabelle Eberhardt, Aimée Dubucq de Rivery, Isabel Burton, and Jane Digby el Mazrab.

Bowles, Paul. *The Oblivion Seekers*. San Francisco: City Lights, 1972.

Brahimi, Denise. *L'oued et la zaouïa*. Algiers: Office des publications universitaires, 1983. Also published as *Requiem pour Isabelle*, Paris: Publisud, 1983.

Charles-Roux, Edmonde. *Un desir d'Orient*. Paris: Grasset, 1988.

D'Eaubonne, Françoise. *La couronne de sable, vie d'Isabelle Eberhardt*. Paris: Flammarion, 1967.

Déjeux, Jean. *Femmes d'Algérie: Légendes, traditions, histoire, littérature*. Paris: la Boîte â documents, 1987.

Delacour, Marie-Odile and Jean-René Huleu. *Sables: Le roman de la vie d'Isabelle Eberhardt*. Paris: Liana Levi, 1986.

Errera, Eglal. *Sept années dans la vie d'une femme: Isabelle Eberhardt, lettres et journaliers*. Arles: Actes Sud, 1987.

Kobak, Annette. *Isabelle: The Life of Isabelle Eberhardt*. London: Chatto and Windus, 1988.

Mackworth, Cecily. *The Destiny of Isabelle Eberhardt*. London: Routledge and Kegan Paul, 1951; New York: Ecco Press, 1975; London: Quartet Books, 1977. Work translated into French as *Le destin d'Isabelle Eberhardt*, trans. André Lebois (Oran: Fouque, 1953).

Noël, Jean. *Isabelle Eberhardt: L'aventureuse du Sahara*. Algiers: Baconnier, 1961.

Nouel, Elise. *Carré d'as aux femmes*. Paris: Guy Le Prat, 1977. Four portraits of women: Lady Stanhope, Isabelle Eberhardt, Marga d'Andurain, and Aurélie Picard.

Randau, Robert. *Isabelle Eberhardt: Notes et souvenirs*. Algiers: Charlot, 1945.

Rezoug, Simone. *Isabelle Eberhardt*. Classiques Maghrebins. Algiers: Office des publications universitaires, 1985.

Robert, Claude Maurice. *L'Amazone des sables.* N.p.: Soubiran, 1934.

Stephan, Raoul. *Isabelle Eberhardt, ou La révélation du Sahara.* With a preface by Victor Margueritte. Paris: Flammarion, 1930.

Tournier, Michel. "Isabelle Eberhardt, ou La métamorphose accomplie." In *Le vol du vampire: Notes de lecture.* Paris: Mercure de France, 1981.

Works by Isabelle Eberhardt

Dans l'ombre chaude de l'Islam. Paris: Fasquelle, 1906. Edition prepared, annotated, and cosigned by Victor Barrucand. Comprised of the second part of *Sud oranais*, and completed by *Choses du Sahara, Heures de Tunis*, and by "Notes sur Isabelle Eberhardt" by Victor Barrucand.

Notes de route. Paris: Fasquelle, 1908. Edition prepared and preface by Victor Barrucand. Comprised of the first part of *Sud oranais* and by *Sahel tunisien.*

Au pays des sables. Bône: Em. Thomas, 1914. Small volume prepared by Chloë Bulliod.

Pages d'Islam. Paris: Fasquelle, 1920. Collection of stories with preface by Victor Barrucand.

Trimardeur. Paris: Fasquelle, 1922. Novel, with preface and finished by Victor Barrucand.

Mes journaliers. N.p.: La Connaissance, 1923. Personal notebooks collected, prefaced, and annotated by René-Louis Doyon (republished by Introuvables [Paris, 1985]).

Amara le forçat, l'anarchiste. Les Amis d'Edouard. Abbeville: Frédéric Paillart, 1923. Collection of stories prefaced by Réne-Louis Doyon.

Contes et paysages. N.p.: La Connaissance, 1925. Deluxe edition of 138 copies. Stories selected by René-Louis Doyon: "Yasmina," "Au pays des sables," "Doctorat," "Pays oublié," "Amara le forçat, l'Anarchiste," "Le major."

Au pays des sables. Paris: Sorlot, 1944. Collection of stories prefaced by René-Louis Doyon, using texts published in 1925.

Yasmina, et autres nouvelles algériennes. Paris: Liana Levi, 1986. Stories chosen, annotated, and prefaced by Marie-Odile Delacour and Jean-René Huleu.

Lettres inédites. Internationale de l'Imaginaire 9 (Winter 1987–88).

Glossary of Arabic Words

French editors' note: *Throughout her texts, Isabelle Eberhardt uses quite varied spellings. Because of this, we have endeavored to standardize these spellings in this glossary, and to correctly transliterate each word.*

Translator's note: *This glossary contains Arabic words, in French transliteration, used throughout the text. I am keeping the French spellings in order to preserve some of the flavor of the original text. I also give, in parentheses, the Arabic words transliterated into English if the spelling is different. Sometimes there is more than one spelling, because of the lack of standardization, and sometimes the word is the same. For greater clarity, I have also added to the original French glossary several more terms that appear throughout the text.*

abeya: overall cover or dress for both men and women.
'acha: evening meal.
'adel: judge, religious notary.
'adjedj: dusty wind, windstorm.
agha: a leader ranking above a kaid, in Algeria.
aghalik: notable placed above the kaid.
aiguadi: water source.
alfa: from the Arabic *halfa*, a kind of North African grass.
aman: confidence, security, protection.
'amel: governor.
'araba: cart, harness.
'ar'ar: aromatic plant for smoking.
'asr: midafternoon prayer.
'assas: guard, supervisor, (night) watchman.
bachagha: high-ranking indigenous civil servant.
bach-hammar or *bach-hamar:* caravan or convoy guide (the one in command).
bahri: humid sea wind.
baraka: divine blessing, beneficial influence, produced by a living or dead saint or by a sacred object.

baroud: "powder"; by extension gun powder or war, battle.

bendir or *bendar* or *benadir* (plural: *banadir*): nomad drum.

Berbri or *Beraber:* Berber.

berdha or *berd'a:* pack saddle for a mule.

berrania (*barrani*) (masculine: *berrani*): female foreigner.

beylik: Ottoman title of nobility; lord; by extension, power.

bith ech char or *bet ech-cha'ar:* literally "house of animal hair"; Bedouin tent made of camel hair.

bled: country, countryside, village.

bled el 'atteuch: the country of thirst.

bled-es-siba: country of disorder.

bordj (*burj*): fortified place, bastion, citadel, tower.

btom: terebinth, sumac.

burnous (*burnus, burnoose*): large hooded wool cape or cloak worn by men.

cadi or *quadi:* Muslim judge.

cahouadji or *quahouadji:* café owner.

caïd or *qaid* (*kaid*): leader, commander; during French colonization, local civil servant representing France at the head of a tribe.

calam: see kalam.

Chaabane (Shaaban): the eighth month of the Muslim calendar.

chaouch: orderly, sergeant, guardian, attendant, porter.

cheche: turban made of a long veil.

chechia or *chechiya:* skullcap, headdress.

chehili: the sirocco, desert wind.

cheikh (plural: *chioukh*)(English: *sheik, shaykh*): head of a fraction (tribal subdivision) named by the governor, subordinate to the kaid, and controlling several moqqademin (muqaddum); old man, spiritual director, head of a brotherhood.

Chelha: Berber dialect.

chih: mountain herb used to make tea.

chira: grass; barley.

chorba: soup.

chott (*shatt*): dried-out salty lake, closed depression in arid regions, whose bottom is filled by a sebkha.

ciradjou: shoe shiner.

dar: house.

dar ed-diaf: local community house reserved for travelers and guests.

dar el ghannyat: a house for female singers.

dar enneçara: house of the Christians.

dechra: village.

deira: municipal guard, patrol, rounds.

delloua: a bucket made of wood or leather for drawing water from a well.

derbouka or *darboucca:* musical instrument formed from a piece of animal skin stretched over pottery.

derouich (feminine: *derouicha*): a member of a Muslim brotherhood; by extension, a man or woman living his or her passion for God in extreme poverty; sometimes considered insane.

diffa: a meal given in honor of one or several traveling guests.

dikr (*dhikr*): invocation, repetition of the name of God, ritual and sacred formula pronounced by the members of the same religious brotherhood.

diss: dry grass, bulrush.

djebel: mountain.

djellaba (*jellaba*): long robe, piece of clothing with a hood.

djemaa or *djemâa:* local assembly of the inhabitants of a douar; mosque.

djerid: palm leaf, or leaf of a palm tree.

djich (plural: *djiouch*): literally, army; by extension, armed tribes that loot.

djinn: evil spirit.

djorf: cliff.

djouad: noble, generous, showing proof of liberality.

djouak: reed flute.

douar: a group of dwellings most often bringing together families claiming to be descendants of a common ancestor; group of tents, village.

Doul' kada or *Dou'l Qa'da:* eleventh month of the Hejira.

doum: miniature palm tree.

drinn: desert grass.

eddhen: call to prayer.

erg: a region of dunes in the desert.

farenghi: frank, free; by extension, foreign.

farika: traditional Arab dish.

Fatiha: the first sura of the Koran (opening).

feggaguir (singular: *faggara*): subterranean canal for irrigation, deriving from springs.

fellah (*fallah*): peasant, farmer.

ferrach: carpet, mat, straw mattress, mattress.

ferrachia: woman's veil.

filali: carved leather from the region of Tafilalet (Morocco).

fondouck (*fondouk*): inn, shelter for travelers.

forka or *forqa:* subtribal group.

fouta: towel that one takes to the hammam; sometimes worn as a skirt.

gandoura: sleeveless tunic made of wool, silk, or cotton, worn under a burnous.

gasba or *qasba:* flute made of a sharpened reed.

ghaïta (*rhaïta*): sort of clarinet or reed instrument.

goual or *qawwal:* poet-composer-singer, a sort of troubador.

goum: military contingent composed of nomads directed by their kaid.

goumbri or *guembri:* two-string mandolin whose case is made of tortoise shell.

goumiers: the soldiers of a goum.

gourbi: earthen hut.

guebbla or *qibbla:* in the direction of Mecca.

guellal: musical instrument.

guemira or *g'mira:* boundary stone or landmark indicating property limit, or the course or end of a trail.

guennour: turban-shaped man's headgear.

guerba: goatskin for storing water.

habou: property allocated to a religious foundation.

haïk: large square white veil; woman's veil.

hakem (plural: *hokkam*): administrator.

hamada or *hammada:* stony desert.

hamel: porter.

hammam: Moorish bath.

haram: religious prohibition.

harara (plural: *haraïr*) or *gharara* (plural: *gharaïr*): long bags made of black or gray wool connected to camel packsaddles.

harka: armed band, expedition.

harrag: herd.

Hartani (plural: *Harratine*): descendant of black slaves from the territories of the South.

hassi: well.

hendi: cactus.

hottara: in the Souf (Suf), frame of a well made from the trunk of a date palm.

'icha: evening prayer.

ihram: pilgrimage clothing.

imam: person who conducts the prayer at the mosque (who is in front).

kachabia or *kachébia:* man's shin-length wool winter overgarment with long sleeves and a hood with a tassel.

kacidés or *qacida:* recited or sung poetry.

kaftan (*caftan*): ankle-length robe, often richly decorated.

kaid: see caïd.

kalam or *qalam* (*calam*): a reed sharpened for writing.

kanoun: a burner fed with hot coals.

kaoued(a): go-between, mediator.

kasbah (*casbah*): originally, citadel or neighborhood surrounding the palace; by extension old Arabic city.

kef: rock, rocky hill.

kefenn: a shroud.

kéfer (*kafir*): renegade, nonbeliever.

kenoun: coal brazier.

keram: fig tree.

khalifa (*caliph*): vice-governor of the caidats of the bey of Tunis, local civil servant, adjunct to the kaid or the pasha.

khalkhal: ankle bracelet.

khammes: farmer receiving one-fifth of the harvest; tenant farmer, share-cropper.

khamsin: sand wind.

Khartani: see Hartani.

khodja: secretary, interpreter.

khol or *kehol:* makeup for the eyes, antimony powder.

khouan: brother, member of a religious brotherhood.

kif: hashish.

Koreïchite: a member of the Quraysh (or the Kuraish) tribe.

koubba or *qoubba* (*qubba*): light ornamental structure raised on the tomb of a marabout.

koumia: long curved dagger.

ksar (plural: *ksour*): Saharan village.

lithoua or *litham:* face veil.

maghreb or *moghreb* (*maghrib*): the fifth daily Muslim prayer, the place where the sun sets, the hour the sun sets; also Morocco.

mahakma: local court.

mahalla or *mahall* or *m'hall:* house, household.

makam or *maqam:* saint's tomb, a holy place.

makhzen (*makhzan*): backup corps of the police force or of the army, made up of indigenous troops, to keep order; also designates the Moroccan police force.

marabout (*murabit*): an important holy person, object of popular veneration; burial or holy place; used in *Trimardeur* in the sense of tent.

matara: goatskin for conserving water.

mechta: hamlet, farm.

meddah (*medha*): Arabic rhapsode; originally a panegyric sung by a camel driver.

medersa: Quranic school, school of religious instruction.

mehara: camel race.

mehari: racing camel.

meïda: small, low table.

Mektoub: what is written in the Quran, inevitable, unavoidable, destiny, God's will.

melahfa or *mlahfa:* women's dress from the South, complete veil.

mella: galette, cooked in the heat of ashes.

mellah: Jewish neighborhood (originally means salting tub).

mezouïd: goatskin for storing travel food (semolina, dates, etc.).

miad: delegation

mihrab: recess in a mosque indicating the direction of Mecca.

misbah: oil lamp, lantern.

mlehya or *melaya:* large sheet made of netting worn by women in the countryside.

mokhazni (plural: *makhzenia*): makhzen cavalryman.

mokkadem: director of a zawiya named by the sheik.

mouddarés: teacher.

moueddhen, muezzin, or *mueddine:* person who calls the faithful to prayer.

mouharram: first month of the Hegira (Muslim calendar).

mourabet: see marabout.

m'tourni: convert (from Sabir, a language composed of Spanish, French, and Italian, spoken in Algiers and other parts of North Africa; also, the Franco-Jewish dialect of Algiers).

mufti: religious jurist who pronounces legal opinions.

mzana't: renegade.

naach: wooden stretcher for transporting a corpse.

naala: sandal.

naïb (*naib*): representative, vicar, dignitary.

na'na (*nana*): mint.

narba: quarrel, or to try to pick a quarrel with somebody.

nefra: difference of opinion, discord.

nouba: originally a vocal or instrumental composition; during French colonization, designated the music of North African soldiers.

oudjak: stove, furnace in a Moorish café, often decorated with tilework.

oued (*wadi*): watercourse, stream, riverbed, valley.

oukil or *wakil:* managing agent, administrator in charge of financial affairs.

oumara: leather water skin.

ouzara (singular: *wazir*): minister, vizier.

qadri or *kadri* (plural: *qadriya* or *kadriya*): brotherhood founded in the twelfth century by Abd el-Kader Djilani of Baghdad.

Ramadan: religious fast during the month of Ramadan (ninth month of the Hegira).

redir or *ghedir:* pond, pool, dead branch of a river.

Redjeb: seventh month of the Hegira.

rezzou (plural: *razzia*): pillaging expedition against a tribe.

rhaïta: see ghaïta.

Rogui: a member of the Rouga tribe.

roumi: term originally used to designate Christians; by extension, designates French or Europeans.

sebkha (*sabkha*): salty marsh filling the bottom of a depression.

sefseri (*safsari*): Tunisian burnoose.

seguia: open-air irrigation canal.

serroual: Arab pants.

sidi: mister, sir.

sloughi (*saluki*): desert breed of dog.

smalah: tribe or family, used by Eberhardt to mean "family retinue"; an invocation of Allah to keep away the evil eye.

sob(k)h: sunrise, morning.

sokhar: camel escort.

Souafa (Suwafa): inhabitants of the region of the Souf (Suf) (Grand Erg Oriental).

Soufia: woman from the Souf.

souk or *souq (suq):* Arab market, rural market.

sourdi(s) (plural: *swared*): sou coin.

tâam: food, couscous.

tabadji: tobacco seller.

taleb (plural: *tolba*): student, literate Muslim, or wise man.

tarbouch(a): Turkish headdress, fez.

tellis: bag.

timzrith or *timgrit:* thyme.

toub: dried clay.

toubib: doctor.

turco: colloquial name given to Algerian soldiers since the Crimea campaign (1854).

zafour: saffron.

zaouïya or *zeouïya (zawiya):* religious establishment, school, seat of a brotherhood run by the descendants of a local saint.

zebboudj: wild olive tree.

Zenatia: Berber dialect.

zeriba: hut made of dried palm leaves.

ziar: pilgrim, visitor.

ziara (ziyara): visit, pilgrimage to the tomb of a marabout.

zorna: wind instrument in North Africa similar to an oboe; also called a *rhaita, ghaita,* or *rajta.*

zoual: call to the noon prayer.

www.ingramcontent.com/pod-product-compliance
Lightning Source LLC
Chambersburg PA
CBHW020643110726
47901CB00001B/33